Arnold Readers in History

TITLES IN THE
ARNOLD READERS IN HISTORY SERIES

THE TUDOR MONARCHY

Edited by JOHN GUY

Vice-Principal and Provost, and Professor of Modern History,
University of St Andrews

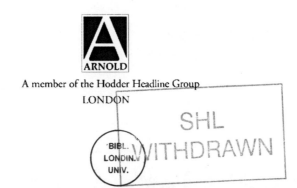

A member of the Hodder Headline Group
LONDON

First published in Great Britain in 1997 by
Arnold, a member of the Hodder Headline Group
338 Euston Road, London NW1 3BH
175 Fifth Avenue, New York, NY10010

Co-published in the United States of America by
Oxford University Press Inc.,
198 Madison Avenue, New York, NY 10016

British Library Cataloguing in Publication Data
A catalogue entry for this book is available from the British Library

Library of Congress Cataloguing-in-Publication Data
A catalog entry for this book is available from
the Library of Congress

ISBN 0 340 65218 7

Typeset by Saxon Graphics Ltd, Derby

Contents

SECTION III POLITY AND GOVERNMENT

Preface

The purpose of this book is to make available a selection of the best recent work on the Tudor monarchy for the use of A-level and undergraduate students, the emphasis being on seminal essays published since 1975 that have become historiographical benchmarks. My selection has been influenced by several concerns. One is practical: I have given some preference to articles first published in places that are relatively inaccessible to students. Beyond this, I have tried to convey a sense of the issues that have preoccupied historians and of the ways in which the traditional horizons of politics and power have been enlarged over the past two decades by growing attention to less conventional facets of the subject: to the wider agenda of, for example, Renaissance political culture and the history of ideas, the phenomenon of minority or female rule, the interdependence of Court and localities, and the significance of frontiers and borderlands in the shaping of the early modern state. Each of the selected articles is compelling in several respects, not merely presenting fresh evidence or challenging old interpretations, but also illuminating the conceptual framework of politics and the state. In particular, I have attempted in an original essay to rediscover some of the conceptual issues raised by the subject of the Tudor monarchy, and to show that there was a genuine debate on kingship and 'counsel' in the sixteenth century. The debates that continue to fascinate students and their teachers are well represented, but the impact of these articles derives from the fact that, collectively, they shift the focus away from the older tradition of 'constitutional' history towards a newer and more genuinely *political* history. This 'new' political history is characterized partly by its desire to define contexts that include ideas and sociocultural networks as well as personalities and institutions, and partly by its fascination with the interpenetration of 'private' and 'public' spheres in ways that were fundamentally political. There can, of course, be no pretence at comprehensiveness in a reader of this type. In an effort to offset this, I have contributed brief introductions to each section that attempt to place the selected articles in context. I have also written a General Introduction, which summarizes the current state of Tudor political history from a historiographical viewpoint.

In refining my ideas and schematic approach to Tudor and Stuart politics and political culture, I have been greatly stimulated by innumerable conversations with the outstanding group of research students it has been my privilege to supervise at the University of St Andrews since 1992: Stephen Alford (who himself contributes an original essay on William Cecil in the 1560s), Alan Bryson, John Cramsie, Lisa Ford, Jamie Hampson, Natalie Mears, and Mark Taviner. While I was distracted by a myriad of tasks as, successively, Head of the School of History and International Relations, Provost, and latterly Vice-Principal and Provost, my students helped to keep my priorities focused on historical activities and research and so enabled me to maintain the momentum of my work in parallel with their own. This book is dedicated to them with gratitude and affection. I also express my thanks to the sixth-form Historians of Channing School, Highgate, London, who allowed me to try out in embryo the arguments advanced in my essay on 'Tudor Monarchy and its Critiques' and offered invaluable feedback prior to publication.

The proposal that I should compile a reader on this subject came from Christopher Wheeler, Director of Humanities Publishing and commissioning editor at Edward Arnold. He persuaded me that the project was worthwhile and viable from a publisher's point of view. I wish to thank him for his advice and support, and in particular for his patience and cooperation in offering all contributors the opportunity to update or make additions or amendments to their previously published articles. I gladly acknowledge the assistance of James Boon, a research student in the School of Physics and Astronomy, who optically scanned the text of those articles reprinted here. Last but not least, I am most grateful for the technical support I have received from Richard Guy, and from my two executive assistants, Elaine Cartwright and Shona Hood. In particular, Elaine and Shona assisted with word processing and correspondence, helped me to escape at critical moments to the History Department or the University Library, and did not demur when asked to print out the contents of this reader more than once.

John Guy
St Andrews
February 1997

Acknowledgements

The editor and publishers would like to thank the following for permission to use copyright material.

The author and Oxford University Press for 'Favourites and factions at the Elizabethan Court' by Simon Adams, from R. G. Asch and A. M. Birke (eds), *Princes, Patronage and the Nobility* (Oxford University Press, 1991); the author and B. T. Batsford Ltd for 'Image-making: The means and the limitations' by Sydney Anglo from *Images of Tudor Kingship* (Seaby, 1992); the author and the John Rylands Library for 'The monarchical republic of Queen Elizabeth I' by Patrick Collinson, from *Bulletin of the John Rylands Library of Manchester*, 69 (1987); the author for 'Ruling élites in the reign of Henry VII' by Margaret Condon, from C. Ross (ed.), *Patronage, Pedigree and Power* (Alan Sutton Publishing Ltd, 1979); the author and History Today Ltd for 'A crisis of the aristocracy? Frontiers and noble power in the early Tudor state' by Steven Ellis, from *History Today*, 45/4 (April 1995); the Royal Historical Society and Cambridge University Press for 'Tudor government: The points of contact: Parliament' by G. R. Elton, from *Studies in Tudor and Stuart Politics and Government* (Cambridge University Press, 1983); the author and Addison Wesley Longman Ltd for 'The courtiers of Henry VII' by Steven Gunn, from *English Historical Review*, 108 (1993); the author and Blackwell Publishers Ltd for 'Thomas Cromwell and the intellectual origins of the Henrician revolution' by John Guy, from Alistair Fox and John Guy, *Reassessing the Henrician Age: Humanism, Politics and Reform* (Blackwell, 1986); the author and Cambridge University Press for 'Wolsey and the Tudor polity' by John Guy, from S. Gunn and P. Lindley (eds), *Cardinal Wolsey: Church, State and Art* (Cambridge University Press, 1991); the author and Cambridge University Press for 'The countervailing of benefits: Monopoly, liberty, and benevolence in Elizabethan England' by David Harris Sacks, from D. Hoak (ed.), *Tudor Political Culture* (Cambridge University Press, 1995); the author and Harcourt Brace and Co Ltd for 'Representation through intimacy: A study in the symbolism of monarchy and Court office in early-modern England' by David Starkey from I. Lewis (ed.), *Symbols and Sentiments: Cross-Cultural Studies in Symbolism* (Harcourt Brace, 1977); the author and Oxford University Press for 'Court and government' by David Starkey, from C. Coleman and David R. Starkey (eds), *Revolution Reassessed: Revisions in the History of Tudor Government and Administration* (Oxford University Press, 1986); and the author and the John Rylands Library for 'Court and polity under Elizabeth I' by Penry Williams, from *Bulletin of the John Rylands Library of Manchester*, 65 (1983).

Every effort has been made to obtain permission to reproduce copyright material. If any proper acknowledgement has not been made, copyright holders are invited to contact the publishers.

Abbreviations

BL	British Library
BM	British Museum
CCR	*Calendar of Close Rolls*
CFR	*Calendar of Fine Rolls*
CPR	*Calendar of Patent Rolls*
HMC	Historical Manuscripts Commission
HMSO	Her Majesty's Stationery Office
HO	*Household Ordinances*
LP	*Letters and Papers, Foreign and Domestic, of the Reign of Henry VIII*, ed. J. S. Brewer, J. Gairdner, R. H. Brodie, *et al.* (21 vols in 32 parts, and Addenda; London, 1862–1932)
OED	*Oxford English Dictionary*
PC	Privy Council
PRO	Public Record Office
SP	State Papers
STC	*A Short-Title Catalogue of Books Printed in England*, ed. A. W. Pollard and G. R. Redgrave (2 vols, London, 1969); 2nd edn, ed. W. A. Jackson, F. S. Ferguson, and K. F. Pantzer (3 vols, London, 1986–94)
Townshend	Heywood Townshend, *Historical Collections: An Exact Account of the Last Four Parliaments of Elizabeth* (London, 1680)
WAM	Westminster Abbey Monuments

General introduction

The purpose of this reader is to make available a selection of the best recent work on the Tudor monarchy for the use of sixth-form and undergraduate students, and in the process to explore the horizons of politics and the exercise of public power in late-fifteenth- and sixteenth-century England. The articles I have selected have been grouped into sections under the headings: 'Renaissance Monarchy', 'Personality and Politics', and 'Polity and Government'. Each of these sections will be preceded by a brief introduction, which sets the scene. The aim of the present General Introduction is to provide a concise summary of the current state of Tudor political history from a historiographical viewpoint, examining some of the approaches that have been attempted since 1960, and discussing their relative advantages and limitations as an agenda for the future debate of the subject.

A transformation has occurred in approaches to Tudor political history in recent years. When the first edition of Sir Geoffrey Elton's *The Tudor Constitution* appeared in 1960, the orthodoxy was that a definitive or authentic account of the 'constitution' could be derived from a meticulous investigation of the legal and institutional structures of the embryonic English 'state': the Crown, the Privy Council, Parliament, the common law courts, the conciliar courts, the local courts, and so on.[1] Despite some rumblings of dissatisfaction with this method, nothing was significantly changed in the second edition of the work in 1982;[2] in some quarters, indeed, Elton's view is still apparently prevalent. As Dr Christine Carpenter, whose *Locality and Polity* is the most important contribution to late-fifteenth-century history since the death of K. B. McFarlane, puts the point: 'all societies have a constitution, even if, as at this period, it consists only of the largely unspoken assumptions of the politically aware about what may or may not be done'.[3] On closer examination, however, Carpenter's definition of 'the constitution' is fundamentally different from Elton's. Whereas Elton's is linked to the functions of central administrative and legal institutions, Carpenter's, like McFarlane's, is socially derived from the unceasing process of accommodation between kings and nobles, royal officials and landowners, centre and localities: there was a 'constitution', but it turns out to be one where 'leverage comes from the centre, in the shape of the king's power to grant money and offices to his nobility, while they in turn raise the gentry's support in the same way'.[4] Furthermore, 'the only way we should ever begin to understand the nature of the constitution of this time was by thinking ourselves imaginatively into the minds of the people who were its constituent parts, and so learn how they saw their relationships with each other and the king'.[5]

A Tudor historian might go considerably further. There was a crisis in late-fifteenth-century England. The Wars of the Roses and Henry VI's deposition sprang directly from monarchical failure and incapacity; McFarlane called this 'undermighty' kingship. Yet, fifteenth-century landowners were far from divided culturally. Their conceptualizations of monarchy and good government were shared. They spoke the same political language. If internal Court politics were vicious, they were not ideological. Nobles and gentry 'had a vested interest in the perpetuating of internal peace ... the dual chain of command, formal and informal, from king to locality could work effectively only if every link in it had confidence in the others'.[6]

In the sixteenth century, politics and political language were transformed by the proliferation of ideas and ideologies.[7] By mid-century the writings of virtually all of the known classical and Renaissance authors had been printed (initially at Paris, Basle, or Venice and elsewhere) and disseminated in their original languages or in translation.[8] Not only did printing serve to publicize a wide variety of ideals concerning monarchy and (civic) republicanism, commonwealth and *respublica*, conciliarism and resistance theory, government and political action, but it also encouraged the composition and circulation of handbooks of political advice or manuals on the art of rhetoric and political persuasion.[9] Machiavelli's *The Prince* (1513–*c*.1515, published 1532) and More's *Utopia* (1516) are only two of a myriad of such treatises. They triggered a surge in the repertoire and sophistication of political debate and vocabulary, and an irreversible shift towards the laïcization and politicization of society.

Next, the pamphlet and propaganda wars of the Reformation opened the floodgates: the critical events for England were Henry VIII's break with Rome, the vernacular Bible, the Prayer Books of 1549 and 1552, the Council of Trent, the Elizabethan Settlement, the French Wars of Religion, the Dutch revolt, and the battle between Archbishop Whitgift and the presbyterians in the reign of Elizabeth I for the soul of the Church of England. Christopher Haigh has stressed that the Reformation created a 'deeply divided' England: the final chapter of his *English Reformations* is entitled 'Reformations and the Division of England'.[10] During the long Elizabethan war with Spain and her ally, the French Catholic League, divisions were indexed against enemies 'without' and 'within' the realm.[11] By the 1580s xenophobia linked to anti-Catholicism and overseas commercial rivalries was endemic in England, but religious divisions within the British Isles were reinforced by the persistence of distinctive regional or marcher identities that Tudor governments tried systematically to smother or subordinate to the values of southern (lowland) England. Within the borderlands of England, Wales, and (largely unsuccessfully) Ireland, repeated attempts were made to fuse Protestantism with 'English civility': a process of cultural colonization involving the manipulation of history, language, law, ethnography, and topography (see below, Ellis, Chapter 13).[12]

Unlike that of the fifteenth century, then, sixteenth-century society was extensively politicized, distinguished by what Maurizio Viroli has called 'the revolution of politics' (even if his use of the word 'revolution' is somewhat melodramatic).[13] 'Not only did the meaning and the range of application of the concept of "politics" change, but also the ranking of political science, the role of political education and the value of political liberty.'[14] No longer was there a shared political language; if anything, a cacophony of voices competed for an audience on the public stage. Conceptualizations of monarchy and polity differed, spectacularly on occasion between Henry VIII or Elizabeth I and their political and conciliar élites (see below, Alford, Chapter 9; Collinson, Chapter 4; Guy, Chapter 3).[15] While this evolution was as potentially unwelcome to the Tudor monarchy as to those of France or Spain, the process could not be reversed. One might, in any case, lay much of the blame, where England is concerned, at the door of Henry VIII, whose divorce campaign propaganda had been crammed with civil theses and humanist-classical and scriptural analogies and whose choice of regal prototypes gave considerable prominence to the history of the later Roman empire.[16] When Elizabeth I sent Sir John Hayward to the Tower in 1599, protesting that his book *The first part of the life and raigne of king Henrie the IIII* was treasonable – the work considered Bolinbroke's deposition of Richard II and was dedicated to the second Earl of Essex – Francis Bacon could retort only that Hayward might well be tried for felony, but scarcely for treason, since most of the offending passages had been stolen from Tacitus, the Roman imperial historian, fashionable in Essex's circle and elsewhere, whose *Annals* covered the period from AD 14 (just before the death of Augustus) to the death of Nero in AD 68!

Bacon's riposte is ironic and iconic. During the sixteenth century, Tudor political culture became distinctively Renaissance in its inspiration and idioms, and therefore (by definition) humanist-classical. This is fundamental, and a basic conclusion follows. It has all too often been the case that Tudor historians have *first* reconstructed the politics of the period, and *only then* attempted to relate their accounts, if at all, to the contemporary literature and other sources. Almost certainly, this is the wrong way round. Or, at any rate, the two stages should be attempted in parallel. As Dale Hoak has put the point, 'the difference between politics and political culture is essentially the difference between political action and the codes of conduct, formal and informal, governing those actions'.[17] The classical, rhetorical, and iconographical traditions that underpinned the practice of politics hold up a mirror to the beliefs, metaphors, and mindsets of those who engaged in politics (see below, Alford, Chapter 9; Anglo, Chapter 1; Guy, Chapter 3). Furthermore, as Viroli has maintained, the language of politics is in itself an integral element of statecraft.

Of course, the historiography is more complex still. As Dr John Watts, author of a superb study of fifteenth-century kingship, has remarked,[18] it is not simply that monochromatic views of the 'constitution' need to be challenged in the light of the work of historians of political thought. An interpretation must be contrived which reflects the true nature of *politics*, and in particular the convergence of 'public' and 'private', 'formal' and 'informal', roles in the exercise of statecraft and authority. This is now being widely attempted (see below, Condon, Chapter 11; Gunn, Chapter 6; Guy, Chapter 12; Starkey, Chapter 2; Williams, Chapter 15). Until 1977, however, a fundamental assumption of Sir Geoffrey Elton and his research students[19] – with the notable exception of Dr David Starkey[20] – was that public affairs and policy-making (and therefore also politics) were confined essentially to the arena of public (or 'national') institutions. And since, by Elton's preferred definition, the royal Court was not a 'public' institution, it followed that *The Tudor Constitution* covered the King's Council, Parliament, the Exchequer, Star Chamber, etc., in depth, but virtually ignored the Court and the Royal Household.[21] Two arguments justified this approach. One was that

> there is a fundamental difference between administration moved from within the royal Household, subject to the personal vagaries of the monarch and capable of producing from the Household by prerogative action further administrative organs to rival the national machinery, and one in which the role of the Household has atrophied to the occasional participation of individuals, while the government is really and truly in the hands of established departments often resting on statute.

The other was that Thomas Cromwell's administration 'witnessed a self-conscious attempt to reorganize the government on the principle of public as against royal administration'.[22]

The first of Elton's statements is *mal à propos*, since it is predicated on a bipolar distinction between 'household' and 'bureaucratic' (or 'national') government, which, when applied to the sixteenth century, is false and misleading. The second statement is unsupported by the evidence, and therefore unpersuasive.[23] But the debate over the 'Tudor revolution in government' is old hat. What is at issue here is Elton's view of *politics*, which centred to a large extent on a belief that the institutions of government and administration were the true venue for the struggle between those 'prerogative' and 'constitutionalist' forces which A. F. Pollard, Sir John Neale, and earlier generations of Tudor historians had located in Parliament.[24] This is, of course, a minimalist, and possibly unfair description.[25] Elton subsequently delivered three lectures to the Royal Historical Society which sought to relate, in turn, Parliament, the Council, and the Court – the so-called 'realities' of government – to the power structures of the governed in order to define the 'points of contact' between rulers and ruled.[26] However, on closer examination, it is only in the lecture on Parliament that anything approaching a socially based interpretation of politics was attempted (see below, Chapter 14), and his final lecture took so narrow a view of Court politics as 'the power politics of an élite' that even the Pilgrimage of Grace – the most dangerous and broadly supported regional revolt of the period, one that had Henry VIII's regime fighting for its survival – was summarily dismissed as essentially a Court conspiracy.[27]

On the opposite side of this argument, a number of historians – of whom Dr Simon Adams (see below, Chapter 10),[28] Dr G. W. Bernard,[29] Dr C. S. L Davies,[30] Dr Steven Gunn (see below, Chapter 6),[31] Professor Eric Ives,[32] Professor Wallace MacCaffrey,[33] Dr Starkey (see below, Chapter 7),[34] and Dr Penry Williams (see below, Chapter 15)[35] were in the vanguard – have pursued alternative approaches to the reconstruction of Tudor politics: focused either on the Court and the Royal Household, or on issues of patronage, factionalism, and the web of socio-political transactions whereby courtiers and councillors built up landed affinities or clienteles in the localities.[36] Yet the striking fact is that, until 1988, when a set-piece debate in the *Historical Journal* between Elton and Starkey resolved the point in Starkey's favour,[37] it was possible for Elton to corral the findings of such scholars into his own model of politics by manipulating the language of the debate. Elton's classic 'move' – which can be seen at its most effective in *Reform and Reformation* (1977) – was to interpret the Court politics of the reign of Henry VIII as, essentially, the factional 'inner politics' that informed the King's mind (often by a process of insinuation) and underpinned his desires.[38] Once the King's mind had been declared or his mood established, his ministers and councillors set about implementing his wishes, and these councillors, in turn, invoked (and, where necessary, remodelled) the machinery of government to achieve the necessary results. In other words, by defining Court politics narrowly, in terms of 'inner politics' and faction, rather than as an integral (if 'informal') component of a matrix of 'counsel', Elton continued to be able to posit a distinction between the roles of 'courtiers' and of 'privy councillors' – even though these were often the very same people operating in the same environment and even in the very same rooms! – and thus to maintain the bipolar distinction between 'household' and 'bureaucratic' government, 'private' and 'public' functions, that had lain all along at the heart of his view of the 'constitution'. In short, 'counsel', like Prometheus, was to be bound in chains: confined to the institutional Privy Council – the 'public', 'official', or 'bureaucratic' institution of government; this in spite of the fact that the literature of the period makes extensive play of the fact that Henry VIII took counsel both formally and informally: at formal meetings of the Council, but also in the Royal Household, in the Chamber or the Privy Chamber, or even (as Sir Thomas Elyot feared) on the pillow!

Attacking a mantra almost identical to Elton's in the historiography of the late fifteenth century, Dr Watts notes that, not only does it create the false impression that 'government' is 'an essentially uncontroversial and bureaucratic exercise, carried out to a large extent by professional administrators under the king's general command', it also confers a wholly anachronistic importance on 'formal' political structures at the expense of 'informal' ones. A belief is created that ' "unofficial" conduits of power were antithetical, or at least extrinsic, to royal ones; that they were not part of the enterprise of government', which in turn reinforces the divorce between the 'personal' or 'private', on the one hand, and the 'public' and 'constitutional', on the other.[39] For Tudor historians, there can be no better illustration of this intrinsic bias than those innumerable, dreary, textbook surveys of Court, Council, and policy-making which presume that the 'proper' forum for policy and political debate was the Privy Council, ignoring the fact that the monarch attended meetings rarely; that debates on 'policy' (as opposed to administration) in the Privy Council were the exception rather than the rule; and that the informal conversations between the monarch and his nobles, friends, intimate body servants, or other members of his affinity were likely to have been far more significant politically than anything done through the supposedly 'official' channels. Until this issue is comprehensively addressed, our understanding of Tudor politics and policy-making will continue to be impoverished and abridged.[40]

The crux is the legacy of Victorian historiography, where any notion that 'political' history might comprise much more than 'constitutional' history was incomprehensible and redundant. As late as the 1970s, historians could still apply these descriptions interchangeably, and, when Patrick Collinson delivered his inaugural lecture at Cambridge as Elton's successor in the Regius Chair of Modern History in November 1989, he took as his title *De republica anglorum*: or, History with the Politics Put Back'.[41] Collinson's lecture was a landmark. It was also a rhetorical masterpiece: subtle, layered, and (at least superficially) unstinting in its *encomium* to Elton, but the compliments were counterpointed by thinly veiled criticisms of Elton's regime and of the 'kind of intolerant hegemony once exercised by political and constitutional history' within its narrowly circumscribed boundaries.

Collinson's lecture became a manifesto for a New Political History: one 'which is social [and cultural] history with the politics put back in, or an account of political processes which is also social'.[42] As the contributions to the present volume show, he was pushing at an open door. Exactly what should comprise the agenda for the New Tudor Political History is an issue which it would be inappropriate to consider at further length here. What may confidently be said is that fresh advances will occur in at least two areas. One is the history of ideas, stimulated by the work of quintessentially Renaissance historians such as Quentin Skinner. The other derives from the work of those scholars who have established that the most compelling issues affecting the exercise of public power and authority occurred at the points where 'public' and 'private' and 'central' and 'local' functions overlapped, and where 'formal' and 'informal' transactions intersected. Beyond this, the future trajectory of the subject remains uncertain, and lies very much in the hands of its current practitioners. I will, nevertheless, conclude with an agenda of my own, which summarizes some of the points I have tried to set out in this Introduction.

1. Tudor 'political' historians should seek to undertake genuinely *political* investigations, i.e. they should adopt holistic and socially derived approaches which attend to the cultural as well as the institutional structures of politics.
2. The focus of a New Political History should be the interrelationships of, and interactions between, people, institutions, and ideas. Historians should seek to contextualize and interpret actions, structures, and concepts in mutually informing ways, envisioning politics as (in Collinson's phrase) the 'active expression of a social organism'.[43]
3. The history of politics and the history of ideas are interrelated and mutually informing: contextualization and cross-reference between them are obligatory. A given statement may be a platitude or a revelation depending on its historical context; a given event may be contingent or dynamic depending on its cultural significance.
4. A New Political History will continue to be primarily archival in its methodology, but should not be narrowly positivist or empirical. It must respond to contemporary fictive and imaginative literature and to iconographical evidence as well as to traditional manuscript and printed sources.
5. Historians must pay the closest attention to the classical and Renaissance traditions which underpinned Tudor political culture, and in these contexts be prepared to reconstruct and explore the intersections between private beliefs and public duty.
6. Tudor history should not be narrowly or unthinkingly 'English' (or lowland English). In particular, further attention will need to be paid to the theory and practice of kingship and government in borderland and Irish contexts.
7. Considerable attention will need to be paid to issues of 'counsel' and policy-making, Court and conciliar politics, and the processes of political advice and persuasion (including and especially the bilateral relationships between the centre and the localities).
8. Tudor historians should be sensitive to the use of language in their sources: this does not imply a surrender to Foucault or Derrida; the use and choice of language can be investigated historically as a form of imprint broadly comparable to a watermark. In this respect, language must be set firmly in the context of the rhetorical and classical traditions that underpinned Tudor educational and political practice.
9. Between 1500 and 1600, politics, for Renaissance councillors and 'men of business', became the state of their art and the art of the state.

Historians need to investigate this process and to illuminate not only
the convolutions of policy-making, but the expansion of the horizons of
politics and statecraft which occurred in the sixteenth century. To
conceptualize what was specifically *Renaissance* about Tudor politics and
government lies at the heart of this challenge.

Notes

1 G. R. Elton, *The Tudor Constitution: Documents and Commentary* (1st edn,
   Cambridge, 1960; 2nd edn, 1982).
2 For the burgeoning dissent, see C. Coleman and D. R. Starkey (eds), *Revolution
   Reassessed: Revisions in the History of Tudor Government and Administration*
   (Oxford, 1986); Alistair Fox and John Guy, *Reassessing the Henrician Age:
   Humanism, Politics, and Reform* (Oxford, 1986).
3 C. Carpenter, *Locality and Polity: A Study of Warwickshire Landed Society,
   1401–1499* (Cambridge, 1992), p. 5.
4 Carpenter, *Locality and Polity*, pp. 5–6.
5 Carpenter, *Locality and Polity*, p. 7.
6 Carpenter, *Locality and Polity*, pp. 9–10, 628.
7 See esp. M. Viroli, *From Politics to Reason of State: The Acquisition and
   Transformation of the Language of Politics, 1250–1600* (Cambridge, 1992).
8 English printing was inferior to the best examples of the Continent, but this positively
   encouraged imports. Classical, Renaissance, and patristic texts, in particular the writings of Plato, Aristotle, Cicero, Seneca, Aquinas, Petrarch, Valla, and Erasmus, were
   prized. Cicero's *De officiis* was first printed at Subiaco and Mainz (1465); Caxton had
   produced translations of *De amicitia* and *De senectute* by 1481; and a Latin–English
   parallel text version of *De officiis*, edited by Robert Whittington of Magdalen College,
   Oxford, was printed in 1534. Aristotle's *Ethics* was obtainable at Oxford as early as
   1479, and his *Politics* at Paris after 1506. Plato's works were printed at Venice in Greek
   type by 1513, and in Latin translation within four years. Justinian's *Code* and the *Digest*
   were available in innumerable editions after 1505–9. Editions of Seneca were published
   at Paris, of Virgil at Venice, and of Tacitus at Rome. Of the four great Latin fathers of
   the church, Augustine was printed in 1505, Ambrose in 1506, Jerome in 1516, and
   Gregory the Great by 1518. The *Summa theologiae* and *De regimine principum* of
   Aquinas were in print by 1508–9. Petrarch's Latin writings were printed at Venice and
   Basle after 1501, and Valla's works began to appear in 1509. Lastly, an edition of
   Marsiglio of Padua's *Defensor pacis* appeared at Basle in 1522, and the text of Jacques
   Merlin's *Tomus primus quatuor conciliorum generalium. Secundus tomus quadraginta
   septem conciliorum provincialium* was completed by 1530.
9 The benchmark is Quentin Skinner, *Reason and Rhetoric in the Philosophy of
   Hobbes* (Cambridge, 1996), part I, 'Classical Eloquence in Renaissance England',
   pp. 19–211.
10 C. Haigh, *English Reformations: Religion, Politics and Society under the Tudors*
   (Oxford, 1993); see also Haigh (ed.), *The English Reformation Revised* (Cambridge,
   1987).
11 John Guy (ed.), *The Reign of Elizabeth I: Court and Culture in the Last Decade*
   (Cambridge, 1995).
12 Richard Helgerson, *Forms of Nationhood: The Elizabethan Writing of England*
   (Chicago, 1992); S. G. Ellis, *Tudor Frontiers and Noble Power: The Making of the
   British State* (Oxford, 1995); B. Bradshaw and J. Morrill (eds), *The British Problem
   c.1534–1707* (London, 1996); S. G. Ellis and S. Barber, *Conquest and Union:
   Fashioning a British State, 1485–1725* (London, 1995); Ellis, 'England in the Tudor
   State', *Historical Journal*, 26 (1983), pp. 201–12; Ellis, *Tudor Ireland: Crown,
   Community and the Conflict of Cultures, 1470–1603* (London, 1985).

13 Viroli, *From Politics to Reason of State*, pp. 1–10.

14 Viroli, *From Politics to Reason of State*, p. 1.

15 See also Guy, 'The 1590s: The Second Reign of Elizabeth I?', in Guy (ed.), *Reign of Elizabeth I: Court and Culture in the Last Decade*, pp. 1–19.

16 Virginia Murphy, 'The Literature and Propaganda of Henry VIII's First Divorce', in D. MacCulloch (ed.), *The Reign of Henry VIII: Politics, Policy and Piety* (London, 1995), pp. 135–58; G. D. Nicholson, 'The Act of Appeals and the English Reformation', in C. Cross, D. Loades, and J. J. Scarisbrick (eds), *Law and Government under the Tudors* (Cambridge, 1988), pp. 19–30; Nicholson, 'The Nature and Function of Historical Argument in the Henrician Reformation', unpublished Cambridge Ph.D. dissertation (1977); M. Aston, *The King's Bedpost: Reformation and Iconography in a Tudor Portrait Group* (Cambridge, 1993).

17 D. Hoak (ed.), *Tudor Political Culture* (Cambridge, 1995), p. 1.

18 John Watts, *Henry VI and the Politics of Kingship* (Cambridge, 1996), pp. 1–101.

19 G. R. Elton, *Reform and Reformation: England, 1509–1558* (London, 1977).

20 In addition to the works included in this reader, see also D. R. Starkey, 'The King's Privy Chamber, 1485–1547', unpublished Cambridge Ph.D. dissertation (1973); Starkey (ed.), *The English Court from the Wars of the Roses to the Civil War* (London, 1987); Starkey, *The Reign of Henry VIII: Personalities and Politics* (London, 1985).

21 See Elton, *Tudor Constitution*, pp. 46, 90, 99, 122–4, 129–32, 195. The Court does not even make the index! The Royal Household – which Elton consistently defined as the 'medieval' element in the constitution – is briefly considered (see esp. pp. 129–32), but only in the narrow context of financial administration.

22 Elton, *The Tudor Constitution*, p. 132, n. 11.

23 John Guy, *Tudor England* (Oxford, 1988), pp. 154–77; Guy, 'The Privy Council: Revolution or Evolution?', in Coleman and Starkey (eds), *Revolution Reassessed*, pp. 59–8; Guy, 'Thomas Wolsey, Thomas Cromwell, and the Reform of Henrician Government', in MacCulloch (ed.), *The Reign of Henry VIII*, pp. 35–57, 227–8, 232–5, 253–9; D. R. Starkey, 'A Reply: Tudor Government: the Facts?', *Historical Journal*, 31 (1988), pp. 921–31; Starkey, 'Privy Secrets: Henry VIII and the Lords of the Council', *History Today*, 37 (Aug. 1987), pp. 23–31; Starkey, 'Court, Council and Nobility in Tudor England', in R. G. Asch and A. M. Birke (eds), *Princes, Patronage and the Nobility* (London, 1991), pp. 175–203; Starkey below, Chapters 2 and 7.

24 See esp. A. F. Pollard, *The Evolution of Parliament* (London, 1920); J. E. Neale, *Elizabeth I and her Parliaments* (2 vols, London, repr. 1969); Neale, *The Elizabethan House of Commons* (rev. edn, London, 1963); G. R. Elton, *The Tudor Revolution in Government* (Cambridge, 1953); Elton, *The Parliament of England, 1559–1581* (Cambridge, 1986); Elton, 'Tudor Government', *Historical Journal*, 31 (1988), pp. 425–35.

25 For example, in *Political History: Principles and Practice* (New York, 1970), Elton discussed the categories and definitions of political history in ways that admitted the socially derived nature of politics, and a similar outlook pervaded his *F. W. Maitland* (London, 1985), although such discussions tended to be liberally peppered with attacks on avant-garde social and intellectual historians who regarded political history as old-fashioned and a spent force.

26 These lectures are reprinted in G. R. Elton, *Studies in Tudor and Stuart Politics and Government* (4 vols, Cambridge, 1974–92), III, pp. 3–57.

27 Elton, *Studies in Tudor and Stuart Politics and Government*, III, pp. 42, 50; see also Elton, 'Politics and the Pilgrimage of Grace', *Studies in Tudor and Stuart Politics and Government*, III, pp. 183–215.

28 See also S. L. Adams, 'Eliza Enthroned? The Court and its Politics', in C. Haigh (ed.), *The Reign of Elizabeth I* (London, 1984), pp. 55–77; Adams, 'Faction, Clientage and Party: English Politics, 1550–1603', *History Today*, 32 (Dec. 1982), pp. 33–9; Adams, 'The Dudley Clientele, 1553–1563', in G. W. Bernard (ed.), *The Tudor Nobility* (Manchester, 1992), pp. 241–65; Adams, 'The Dudley Clientele in the House of Commons, 1559–1586', *Parliamentary History*, 8 (1989), pp. 217–39;

Adams, ' "Because I am of that Country & Mynde to Plant Myself There": Robert Dudley, Earl of Leicester and the West Midlands', *Midland History*, 20 (1995), pp. 21–74.

29 G. W. Bernard, *The Power of the Early Tudor Nobility: A Study of the Fourth and Fifth Earls of Shrewsbury* (Brighton, 1985); Bernard (ed.), *The Tudor Nobility*; Bernard, *War, Taxation and Rebellion in Early Tudor England: Henry VIII, Wolsey and the Amicable Grant of 1525* (Brighton, 1986); Bernard, 'The Fall of Anne Boleyn', *English Historical Review*, 106 (1991), pp. 584–610; Bernard, 'The Fall of Anne Boleyn: a Rejoinder', *English Historical Review*, 107 (1992), pp. 665–74.

30 C. S. L. Davies, *Peace, Print and Protestantism, 1450–1558* (London, 1976); Davies, 'Popular Religion and the Pilgrimage of Grace', in A. Fletcher and J. Stevenson, *Order and Disorder in Early Modern England* (Cambridge, 1985), pp. 58–91; Davies, 'The Pilgrimage of Grace Reconsidered', *Past and Present*, 41 (1968), pp. 54–76.

31 See also S. J. Gunn, *Charles Brandon, Duke of Suffolk, 1484–1545* (Oxford, 1988).

32 E. W. Ives, 'Faction at the Court of Henry VIII: The Fall of Anne Boleyn', *History*, 57 (1972), pp. 169–88; Ives, *Faction in Tudor England* (2nd edn; Historical Assoc., London, 1986); Ives, 'The Fall of Wolsey', in S. J. Gunn and P. Lindley (eds), *Cardinal Wolsey: Church, State and Art* (Cambridge, 1991), pp. 286–315; Ives, *Anne Boleyn* (Oxford, 1986); Ives, 'The Fall of Anne Boleyn Reconsidered', *English Historical Review*, 107 (1992), pp. 651–64.

33 Wallace T. MacCaffrey, 'Place and Patronage in Elizabethan Politics', in S. T. Bindoff, J. Hurstfield, and C. H. Williams (eds), *Elizabethan Government and Society: Essays Presented to Sir John Neale* (London, 1961), pp. 95–126.

34 See also D. R. Starkey (ed.), *The English Court from the Wars of the Roses to the Civil War* (London, 1987); Coleman and Starkey (eds), *Revolution Reassessed*; Starkey, *The Reign of Henry VIII: Personalities and Politics* (London, 1985); Starkey, 'From Feud to Faction: English Politics c.1450–1550', *History Today*, 32 (Nov. 1982), pp. 16–22.

35 See also Penry Williams, *The Later Tudors: England, 1547–1603* (Oxford, 1995); Williams, *The Tudor Regime* (Oxford, 1979).

36 See also R. C. Braddock, 'The Rewards of Office-Holding in Tudor England', *Journal of British Studies*, 14 (1975), pp. 29–47; G. W. Bernard, 'The Fall of Wolsey Reconsidered', *Journal of British Studies*, 35 (1996), pp. 277–310.

37 G. R. Elton, 'Tudor Government', *Historical Journal*, 31 (1988), pp. 425–35; D. R. Starkey, 'A Reply: Tudor Government: The Facts?', *Historical Journal*, 31 (1988), pp. 921–31.

38 See esp. Elton, *Reform and Reformation*.

39 Watts, *Henry VI and the Politics of Kingship*, pp. 81–2.

40 For recent attempts to correct the balance, see Guy, *Tudor England*, pp. 156–77, 309–30, 455–8; Starkey, 'Court, Council and Nobility in Tudor England', in Asch and Birke (eds), *Princes, Patronage and the Nobility*, pp. 175–203; S. J. Gunn, 'The Structures of Politics in Early Tudor England', *Transactions of the Royal Historical Society*, 6th ser., 5 (1995), pp. 59–90. Specifically on 'counsel' and 'council', see Guy, 'The Rhetoric of Counsel in Early Modern England', in Hoak (ed.), *Tudor Political Culture*, pp. 292–310; Guy, 'The King's Council and Political Participation', in Fox and Guy, *Reassessing the Henrician Age*, pp. 121–47; Guy, 'The French King's Council, 1483–1526', in R. A. Griffiths and J. W. Sherborne (eds), *Kings and Nobles in the Middle Ages: A Tribute to Charles Ross* (Gloucester, 1986), pp. 274–94.

41 A version with a retrospective note is reprinted in P. Collinson, *Elizabethan Essays* (London, 1994), pp. 1–29.

42 Collinson, *Elizabethan Essays*, pp. 10–11.

43 Collinson, *Elizabethan Essays*, p. 8.

RENAISSANCE MONARCHY

Introduction

This section groups together five articles which consider the Tudor monarchy primarily from the viewpoint of the Renaissance and its political ideas. I have already argued
in the General Introduction that the history of politics and the history of ideas are
interrelated and mutually informing. Historians must also pay attention to the literary
and iconographical traditions which underpinned Tudor political culture if the events
of the period are to be properly contextualized and understood.

The most spectacular assets of Renaissance monarchy were the person and image
of the ruler. The printing press was still in its infancy at the beginning of the sixteenth
century. In an age of widespread illiteracy, the political significance of magnificent royal
buildings, ceremonies and public spectacles, and heraldic iconography – the symbols
and signs of monarchy – outweighed that of written instruments in disseminating the
'presence' and authority of the monarch throughout the realm. In particular, the coronation ceremony was regarded as the 'eighth' sacrament of the Church. It empowered the ruler as a charismatic priest–king: even after the Reformation, the
monarchy retained this quasi-sacerdotal element, which included 'touching' for the
'king's evil' and the consecration of cramp rings – i.e. it was believed that the monarch
could cure scrofula by the laying-on of hands, and that his touch provided rings of gold
and silver with a protective power against epilepsy or muscular diseases (see below,
Starkey, Chapter 2). Professor Sydney Anglo's article (see below, Chapter 1) examines the processes of image-making, investigating the iconographical ensemble that
was available to the Tudors. He debates the topic, not from a general standpoint, but
in relation to the impact and effectiveness of these techniques. He seeks to clarify
what could be done at a practical level to promote the authority of the Tudor dynasty
specifically, as opposed to the power of monarchy in general. In this way, he is able
to maintain a robust scepticism concerning the limitations of imagery. It goes almost
without saying that magnificence and display were obligatory in the Renaissance: they
commanded deference, and affirmed the abstract authority and permanence of
monarchy. But to what extent could relatively nuanced, less abstract, messages be
transmitted? This leads on to a series of further questions. What constituted effective
symbolism or propaganda? For whom was this material really intended? Did those
who saw it receive the messages they were supposed to see?

David Starkey's 'Representation through Intimacy: A Study in the Symbolism of
Monarchy and Court Office in Early Modern England' continues and expands upon this
discussion in the context of the early modern period as a whole (see below, Chapter
2). For Dr Starkey, the issue of sacred monarchy is a vastly more fertile and complex
topic than it is for those historians who connect it simply with propaganda and the
manipulation of opinion. Applying a number of techniques borrowed from anthropol-
ogy and sociology as well as history, he takes the issue into the Court and Royal
Household (and especially into the king's private apartments or 'Privy Chamber') in an
illuminating, indeed transformative, study of the ways in which monarchy and Court
office incorporated both 'public' and 'private', 'formal' and 'informal' functions in the

early modern period. This article is a historiographical landmark. In particular, it was the first study of its type to identify the charismatic symbolism associated with the 'master-image' of the king's body, and to draw out for historians of politics and government the implications of the fact that the ruler's intimate body servants were the fullest and most perfect form of 'representation' of their master. For historians of the Tudor and Stuart monarchy, the key conclusion is not simply that kingship remained theocratic during this period, but that the king's semi-divinity 'underpinned some of his most important everyday political functions'.

John Guy's article on 'Tudor Monarchy and its Critiques' attempts to rediscover some of the most important conceptual issues raised by the subject of the Tudor monarchy, and to show that there was a genuine debate on kingship and 'counsel' in the sixteenth century, and not simply passive acceptance. He argues that one of the effects of the reign of Henry VIII, and in particular of the theory which underpinned the King's first divorce campaign and break with Rome, was to create a latent ambiguity, or binary opposition, within the theory of monarchy. On the one hand, 'official' pronouncements maintained that the king was endowed with secular and ecclesiastical *imperium*. On the other, the 'unofficial' exponents of conciliarism and common-law doctrine stressed the role of councils, counsellors, and representative institutions if 'limited' or 'constitutional' government were to be preserved. Again, in the controversial and exceptional circumstances of royal minority and female rule between Henry VIII's death and the accession of James VI and I, the binary opposition which was latent in the theory of Tudor monarchy was played out politically: notably the tension in the reign of Elizabeth I between the Queen's view of her 'imperial' monarchy – the idea that sovereignty was vested in her alone – and the conviction of William Cecil and the Privy Council that sovereignty lay in the 'queen-in-Parliament' if the Protestant state were to be preserved, and most especially when the (female) ruler declined to be counselled on urgent and fundamentally political topics. In this way, it can be argued that the most powerful and subversive critique of the Tudor monarchy did not derive from the opponents of Henry VIII in the 1530s, from the Marian exiles in the 1550s, or even from presbyterianism in the 1570s or 1580s; it emanated from the very heart of the Elizabethan conciliar regime.

Next in this section, the patterns of ideas that constituted the defining political culture of the reign of Elizabeth I are examined in two outstanding articles, one by Professor Patrick Collinson and the other by Professor David Harris Sacks. Collinson's essay 'The Monarchical Republic of Queen Elizabeth I' (see below, Chapter 4) is another historiographical landmark. It posits the conceit that Elizabethan England was a republic which happened also to be a monarchy, and vice versa. And invoking both literary and historical evidence, it goes on to tease out the layered implications with authority and subtlety. In particular, it considers the 'acephalous' attributes of Elizabeth's monarchy: the rule of a woman who declined to be counselled on the matters of state that were most important to her Protestant (male) privy councillors. The article is a fresh contribution to the history of politics as well as to the history of ideas. As well as casting a searchlight on the Queen's relationship with William Cecil, it achieves some palpable hits on the nature of the Elizabethan policy-making process, the role of Parliament in the sixteenth century, and the nature of so-called 'resistance' theory. Above all, it conveys a genuine sense of the fear, isolation, and bewilderment felt by the members of the Elizabethan Protestant élite – a mood more often resembling that of a Kafka novel than conventional approaches to political history have allowed. Collinson's wider contribution to Tudor political history has also been noted in the General Introduction.

Lastly, David Harris Sacks (see below, Chapter 5) offers a richly documented insight into the rhetorical conventions of the Renaissance. The conceptual vocabulary of Tudor politics was largely humanist-classical, and an important element was the language of benefits. The most cherished text in this respect was Seneca's *De beneficiis*, which underpinned the conventions of the Tudor and early Stuart patronage culture, and which stressed that the objective was the securing of mutual benefits. It was this language of benefits and the exchange of human affections which provided the key to the resolution of the tense issue of monopolies during the parliamentary clashes of 1601. It enabled Elizabeth in her 'Golden Speech' to discuss the proper duties of her councillors and the differences between public duty and private gain without appearing to cast the blame on specific individuals. In particular, it enabled the unity of the realm to be depicted as depending upon positive acts by which the monarch and her subjects knitted their hearts one to another. This is described by Professor Sacks as the 'composing' of a realm. Yet the effects were far more than merely rhetorical, for, within this single rhetorical envelope, it became possible for two competing world pictures to coexist: one a vision of 'imperial' (or sovereign) authority, the other a vision of a free community of citizens. This conclusion further reinforces the point made in the General Introduction and in Chapter 3 that a mastery of rhetoric and a willingness to endorse the values of the Renaissance were considered integral aspects of statecraft in the sixteenth century.

1

Image-making: The means and the limitations

SYDNEY ANGLO

Immediately after his triumph at the Battle of Bosworth, Henry Tudor began to make his way across the country to London. He proceeded 'like a triumphing general', wrote Polydore Vergil, and everywhere he was greeted with the greatest joy.

> Far and wide the people hastened to assemble by the roadside, saluting him as king and filling the length of his journey with laden tables and overflowing goblets, so that the weary victors might refresh themselves. But when he approached the capital, the chief magistrate (whom they call the 'mayor') and all the citizens came forth to meet him and accompanied him ceremoniously as he entered the city: trumpeters went in front with the spoils of the enemy, thundering forth martial sounds. (Vergil 1950: 2–5)

The whole progress and entry is made to sound like a Roman triumph: but this is probably more the effect of Polydore's Italian humanist vision than of any conscious classical imitation by Henry and his followers. At any event, this was the first public appearance of the Tudor dynasty. It was also, for the great majority of ordinary folk who made up the cheering roadside throng on the way to the capital, probably the last time that they ever saw their monarch in the flesh. And this is the nub of the problem.

Opportunities for the ceremonial exposition of kingship in Renaissance England, as elsewhere in Europe, were varied. The symbols and signs of monarchy were displayed on great state occasions, during progresses and processions, and at solemn entries and Court festivals. Emblems were circulated on coinage and on seals; they decorated palaces, chapels, pavilions, and tombs; and they adorned paintings, tapestries, jewels, and other works of art. The imagery of kingship could be proclaimed from the pulpit, and it could be set forth in books, both in words and in pictures. The means *seem* comprehensive enough: yet a moment's reflection reveals their limitations and transience. A distant view of Henry VIII or Elizabeth I in a procession may have been an exciting, even awe-inspiring, experience. Possession of an image of the sovereign may have been a comfort, especially if it were graven upon a coin. The sheer size of a palace and the opulence of its decoration may have been an impressive evocation of monarchical power. But not one of these things was likely to help a lay observer understand the significance of Constantine and Henrician caesaropapism or to resolve the mysteries of the sieve, serpent, or ermine.

Coronations and funerals

The public appearances of the English monarchy were not designed to purvey such ephemeral and concocted political theories or emblematic conceits to the nation. Their primary symbolic function was to affirm the abstract permanence of kingship, although this – accompanied as it was by the magnificently apparelled figure of the ruler, either alive or in effigy, and by heraldic and genealogical display – inevitably served also to affirm dynastic legitimacy.

The extent to which the major ceremonies were concerned with eternal political verities (or at least those so deemed by contemporaries) is made clear by the continuity of coronation ritual despite the Reformation and despite the unprecedented demands made on the organizers of state occasions by the accession of queens regnant as opposed to queens consort. There was, it is true, an oil change – when Mary, worried that the holy chrism had been contaminated at the sacring of her Reformist brother, Edward, requested a fresh supply from her uncle, the Emperor Charles V – but little else of significance was altered.[1] Even more revealing, especially of the way in which these ceremonies soared above transient dynastic concerns, are the records relating to the coronation of Henry Tudor. One of these, *A little devise of the coronacion of the most high and mightie christian Prince Henrie the vij*[th] – a detailed formulary of the ceremonial – was not only closely modelled on the fourteenth-century *Liber regalis* and the fifteenth-century *Forma et modus* but was, in fact, so hastily adapted from a document originally prepared for the coronation of Richard III that many of the nobles who served on that earlier occasion still figure as participants. Indeed, the *Little devise* assumes that the King will be crowned together with a queen – as was the case with Richard III – and at various points in the proceedings Richard's name has simply been struck through and replaced by Henry's.

The traditional character of the ceremony itself, with its rigidly prescribed order of service, anointing, and presentation of the regalia, is confirmed by the contemporary narrative of the occasion, which omits all details 'because thei be sufficiently recorded at Westminster'. The only personal aspects of the sequence of events which made up the coronation celebrations were heraldic. During the creation of the knights of the Bath on the evening prior to the coronation, Henry instituted a new pursuivant called *Rougedragon* – in allusion to his British descent; in the procession from the Tower to Westminster Hall the horses of the royal henchmen were trapped with 'divers arms and badges of the King'; and, when the King's Champion delivered his customary challenge at the coronation banquet, his horse was covered with a 'riche trapper of Cadewaladras armes' (Anglo 1960).

The coronation, for all its splendour and symbolic significance, was not normally the first great public spectacle of any reign. Paradoxically, this position was occupied by the final exit of the previous monarch, when it was customary for the heir to be proclaimed after the royal corpse had been laid to rest. The heralds would then remove their tabards; hang them on the rail of the hearse; solemnly proclaim that the deceased was indeed dead; and, having resumed their coats, appeal for long life to be granted to the new monarch. This was the procedure for all the Tudor kings and queens apart from the founder of the dynasty himself, who had not inherited the crown from anybody. Moreover, the last rites of his immediate predecessors had been singularly unpropitious. Edward IV, it is true, had been decently interred (Wall 1891: 343–51); but his son and heir, Edward V, had been murdered and secretly buried. So, too, had the last Lancastrian, Henry VI; while Richard III travelled on his cortège, bloodstained and naked, slung across the back of a horse, and his conqueror was obliged to have himself proclaimed on the field of battle. Henry VII's will makes provision for his own funeral, asking that his executors should have a special respect to the laud of God, the well-being of his soul, and 'somewhat to our dignitie Roial', avoiding, however, 'dampnable pompe and oteragious superfluities' (Wall 1891: 365). In the event, Henry's obsequies set a prodigious standard of magnificence and confirmed – even if they did not actually establish – the dynastic display deemed appropriate for such occasions.

He died on 21 April 1509 at Richmond Palace, where his body remained for over two weeks while masses and dirges were performed. Then on 9 May the embalmed, lead-encased, and encoffined corpse was placed on a chariot covered with black cloth of gold. On the coffin rested a life-size 'Picture' – that is an effigy – of the late King,

> crowned and richly apparreled in his Parliament Roobe, bearing in his Right Hand a Scepter, and in his Left Hand a Ball of golde, over whome ther was hanginge a riche Cloth of golde pitched upon Fowre Staves, which were sett at the Fowre Corners of the said Charett, wich Charett was drawen with Seaven great Coursers, trapped in Black Velvett with the Armes of England on everie Courser set on both Sydes.   (Leland 1770: IV, pp.304)

On either side of each courser walked a knight carrying a banner; and at the corners of the chariot walked four barons each carrying a banner of the 'Kyngs *Avowries*' or patrons – the Trinity, Our Lady, St George, and Mary Magdalene. Unfortunately, the banners borne by the knights are not specified in the contemporary records, but Edward Hall later reported that Henry VII's chariot was 'garnished with banners and Pencelles of tharmes of his dominions, titles and genealogies' (Hall, 1809: 506): and this heraldic and genealogical mode is corroborated by the evidence of many other obsequies. Among the funeral expenses for Prince Arthur, for example, in 1502 there was payment for 12 bannerols of 'divers armes devised by garter', including not only the prince's own arms and those of Wales, Cornwall, and Chester, but also those of Cadwalader and Brutus; at the funeral of Henry VIII there were 'twelve banners of descents'; for Anne of Cleves there were 'bannerols of her armes and dyscentes'; and for Queen Mary there were 'great Banners of Damaske of the Quenes Desents'.[2] Early in the seventeenth century, Nicholas Charles, Lancaster Herald, sketched the 'Standards and Banners of Kinge Henry the Eight' which still survived at St George's Chapel, Windsor – where Henry VIII had been buried – and he showed three standards (dragon, greyhound, and lion), three banners (St George, a crowned figure of Henry VIII with sceptre and orb, and another figure of the Virgin Mary and child), and two banners showing the arms of his grandparents (Edward IV with Elizabeth Woodville), and his parents (Henry VII with Elizabeth of York) (BL MS Lansdowne 874, fo. 49).[3]

The chariot bearing Henry VII's mortal remains and robed effigy set out for St Paul's accompanied by a great throng of prelates singing the office for the dead, household officers and servants and other mourners totalling more than 1400 persons, together with nearly 700 torchbearers. When they reached St George's Fields, near Southwark, they were met by another enormous group of London civic dignitaries and religious fraternities, so that, in the end, the cortège included all the Lords, temporal and spiritual, all the judges and councillors, representatives of Florence, Venice, Portugal, Spain, France, and the 'Esterlings' and virtually everybody of political, religious, and juridical significance in the kingdom. The coffin and effigy were placed under a hearse of wax in the choir of St Paul's, and a solemn requiem was sung. The following day, after mass, John Fisher, Bishop of Rochester, preached a sermon which was subsequently printed by Wynkyn de Worde – a unique example of royal funerary publication in sixteenth-century England.[4] After the sermon, the coffin and effigy were removed in similar state to Westminster, where they were set beneath another wax hearse – the most 'costly and curious Light possibly to be made by Mans Hands, which was of xiii principal Stonderds, richly decked with Banners'. The next day witnessed the final ceremonies, when there were three masses; and it was at the last of these – the requiem sung by the Archbishop of Canterbury – that the obsequies reached their climax, which was more heraldic than liturgical.

> First there came Twoe Herauds in their Cotearmours unto the Duke of Buckingham, beinge Chiefe Mourner, kneelinge at the West End of the Herse, goinge before him, from the Herse unto the Place where the Archebishop stoode to take the Offeringe; where he, representinge the Kyngs Person, offered a Testamente of Golde: Which done the said Herauds conveyed him againe to the Place he came frome. Then the

said Herauds came in like Manner unto the Earle of Arondell and unto the Earle of Northumberland, and conveyed them unto a Knight which stoode beside the Herse, holdinge the Kyngs Cotearmoure. Of whom the said Herauds received the said Cotearmour, and delivered it to the said Twoe Earles; which solempnly bearinge the said Cotearmour betwene them offered it up unto the said Archebishop with great Reverence; the which he received and delivered unto a Bishop, which delivered it over unto an Heraud standinge even by them on the South Side of the Churche; which done the said Herauds conveyed the Twoe Earles againe unto theire Places. (Leland 1770: IV, pp. 306–7)

And so the process of heraldic offerings continued: the coat armour followed, one after the other, by the late King's shield, sword, helmet, and then his 'goodlie Courser, trapped in Black velvet, with the Armes of England embrothered upon the same'. After this, again under the supervision of the heralds, the nobles laid palls of cloth of gold across the royal corpse, 'as thick as they might lie', before the last offering of the King's great banner and standard. The Bishop of London preached a noble sermon, the palls were removed, the effigy was taken to St Edward's Shrine, the coffin was revealed and lowered into the vault, the great officers of state cast in their batons, and, at last, the heralds proclaimed 'Le noble Roy, Henri le Septieme est mort' and, immediately thereafter, 'Vive le noble Roy Henri le Huitiesme'.

Again, as was the case with Tudor coronations, there was little fundamental change in the pattern of the royal funeral. There was no need for it. Naturally, at the funeral of Edward VI the four great banners of the King's *Avowries* were abandoned in favour of banners displaying the Order of the Garter, the Red Cross, and the arms of Edward's mother and of the Queen Dowager. And, just as naturally, the religious banners were restored for Mary's funeral before disappearing once again at Elizabeth's cortège. All the rest – the immense procession (that for Henry VIII was estimated as four miles in length), the heraldic and genealogical display, and the huge chariot with the coffin and effigy – remained largely intact. This we can see from the records of that last Tudor funeral at Westminster on 28 April 1603 when the cortège included standards of the dragon, greyhound, and lion; banners of Chester, Cornwall, Wales, Ireland, and England; and 'The Chariott drawne by foure Horses upon which charret stood the Coffyn covered with purple velvett and upon that the representation. The Canopy borne by six Knights.' On either side of the chariot were six nobles carrying twelve bannerols displaying the arms of the Queen's royal ancestors impaling the arms of their wives: Henry II and Eleanor of Aquitaine, John and Isabel of Angoulesme, Henry III and Eleanor of Aragon, Edward I and Eleanor of Castile, Edward II and Isabel of France, Edward III and Philippa of Hainault, Edmond of Langley, Duke of York, and Isabel of Castile,

Richard, Earl of Cambridge and Anne Mortimer, Richard, Duke of York and Cicely Neville, Edward IV and Elizabeth Woodville, Henry VII and Elizabeth of York, Henry VIII and Anne Boleyn (Nichols 1788–1805: II). These genealogical bannerols, clustered around Elizabeth's funeral chariot, constituted the final and most emphatic statement upon the enduring frailty of Henry VII's claim to the throne. Beyond her grandfather, the royal lineage of Elizabeth Tudor was wholly Yorkist.

Royal funerals were immensely lavish and dramatic and, though scarcely more personalized than the coronations, their ceremonial was rather more familiar – not because rulers died more frequently than they were crowned, but because queens consort and princes and princesses were also interred with great pomp, even when the deceased was still in his first year, as was the case with Henry VII's third son Edmund in 1500, or had lasted only 51 days, as had Henry VIII's first-born, Henry, in 1511. Moreover, in addition to the family funerals of the Tudors themselves, the citizens of London would have had many opportunities to witness heraldic obsequies: of foreign potentates such as the Emperor, and the kings and queens of France, Spain, and Denmark; of great lords both temporal and spiritual: of lesser gentry and of important city dignitaries. However much the funerary rites differed in scale – with the number of 'morners of estate', for example, strictly allocated according to rank and ranging from 16 for a king down to two for a merchant – there was little significant variation either in ritual, the offering of weapons and coat armour, or in the overwhelmingly heraldic nature of the imagery.[5]

The most interesting feature of royal funerals was the lifesize image of the deceased, modelled from the death mask and used as a practical solution to the problem of protracted display of the cadaver. One poet, Henry Petowe, lamenting the death of Elizabeth, dwelt on the evocative power and verisimilitude of her funeral effigy.

> Oh, yee spectators, which did view that sight!
> Say, if you truelie say, could you refraine,
> To shed a sea of teares in deathes despight,
> That rest her hence, whome Art brought backe againe?
> He that knew her, and had Eliza seene,
> Would sweare that figure were faire England's Queene.

Indeed, Petowe adds, a man of judgement – not knowing that she were dead, and seeing her lying thus in her rich robes, crowned with sceptre in hand – would have sworn, 'To Parliament rides this sweet slumbring Maide' (Petowe 1603).

The theoretical position, as viewed from a modern standpoint, has been succinctly stated by Ernst Kantorowicz.

> Enclosed in the coffin of lead, which itself was encased in a casket of wood, there rested the corpse of the king, his mortal and normally

visible – though now invisible – body natural; whereas his normally invisible body politic was on this occasion visibly displayed by the effigy in its pompous regalia: a *persona ficta* – the effigy – impersonating a *persona ficta* – the *'Dignitas'*.   (Kantorowicz 1957: 421)

The custom was exported from England to France, where its theoretical implications were gradually elaborated and made explicit. However, in England the whole business remained characteristically vague and inconsistent. Perhaps the most suggestive example of the use of the funeral effigy was at the reburial of Richard, Duke of York, at Fotheringay Castle in 1476. The Duke had been slain at the battle of Wakefield 16 years previously, and his head had been impaled on the gates of York with a crown of paper in an ugly mockery of his regal pretensions. When, at the instigation of his widow, Cicely, his bones were ceremoniously reinterred, the coffin containing his remains was surmounted by 'an Image like to the Prince lieng uppright in a Surcott and a Mantle of blewe velvete furred with Ermyns'. On the effigy's head was 'a Cappe of Meyntenance with an Aungell standing in white holding a Crowne over his hed in Token that hee was kinge of right'.[6]

The notion of regal continuity was here strained to the utmost. The Duke could hardly be regarded as still theoretically alive and participating in his own funeral until the moment that his son might be proclaimed king by the heralds. The Yorkist position was simply that Richard, as king 'of right', *deserved* to have a proper funeral complete with a crowned effigy. Yet he had never been crowned, had never been anointed, and had never reigned. The basis for honouring him with an effigy was no more than the need to make a political statement, coupled with a generalized sense of what was fitting. There is no evidence that anybody felt that regal rituals ought to be congruent and, in England, this vagueness persisted throughout the history of the heraldic funeral from the fifteenth to the late seventeenth century. If it is assumed, for example, that contemporaries seriously regarded such effigies as symbolic expressions of the immortality of the royal *Dignitas*, then why were queens consort such as Elizabeth of York and Jane Seymour represented at their funerals by similar effigies? Why had it been customary, in fifteenth-century England, to parade an effigy of a defunct bishop, clad in full pontificals and with all the insignia of his office, at his funeral? And, although this custom was allegedly outmoded in the following century – 'the figure is not nowe used' wrote one authority about the year 1560 – why was Bishop Stephen Gardiner's coffin surmounted by an effigy at his funeral in February 1556?[7] Contemporaries did not feel obliged to resolve such questions. The practice seems to have been a ritualistic gesture whose force was emotional and intuitive rather than ideologically precise; and it is just this kind of imprecision which makes solemn theoretical pronouncements on Tudor symbolism and ceremonial so suspect.

Progresses and other public spectacles

Coronations and funerals were the most imposing and most symbolically potent of all ceremonies of state. Not only were the lords temporal and spiritual physically present, but the Commons, too – at least in London and the Home Counties – were actively involved either in the customary pre-coronation procession from the Tower to Westminster, or as spectators when the mighty funeral cortèges made their way from Richmond (Henry VII and Elizabeth I), Greenwich (Edward VI), or St James (Mary) to Westminster, or from Whitehall to Windsor via Syon, as was the case with Henry VIII. No other public spectacles could compare, either emotionally or ritualistically, with these. Processions to Parliament certainly involved the three estates, but they evoked little enthusiasm; and it is very striking that the ceremonies on these occasions were scarcely considered worthy of mention even by a London chronicler such as Edward Hall, who was himself a Member of Parliament. Royal weddings and births were also events of dynastic importance which could afford opportunities for celebration at Court and throughout the land. But Henry VIII's nuptials decreased in splendour as they increased in number; the last Tudor marriage was Mary's to Philip of Spain in 1554; and there was no Tudor birth after 1536.

When else did royalty display itself to the people? The Tudor progress, when the monarch and Court left London and undertook gentle journeys through the countryside – sometimes staying at the royal palaces and sometimes being entertained by one loyal subject after another – is commonly described as an instrument of policy. This is undoubtedly true as far as it goes. The trouble is that the royal progress normally did not go very far. Henry VII, Henry VIII, and Elizabeth I all travelled about a good deal; and it is true that there was often some correlation between the places they visited and the relative stability of the realm. This was especially marked, for example, in the case of Henry VII's first provincial tour, when he set out for York 'in order to keep in obedience the folk of the North, savage and more eager than others for upheavals' (Vergil 1950: 11), and when similar considerations induced Henry VIII to undertake a similar journey in 1541. However, the assertion that the progresses of Elizabeth I were 'the means by which the cult of the imperial virgin was systematically promoted' (Strong 1984: 77) is open to question.

The highpoint of Elizabethan eulogy – the fifteen years after the defeat of the Armada – coincides precisely with a marked decline in the geographical area covered by the progresses. In any case, the principal purpose of these royal peregrinations had always been recreational or prophylactic – riding, hunting, and avoiding the London plague season – not political; and they were largely confined to the Home Counties, within comfortable travelling distance from London, and never too far from what was clearly recognized as the essential power base of the dynasty. The Tudor monarchy on the move may well have been a stirring spectacle, but only a tiny minority of English people ever saw it.[8]

Even more severe limitations may be noted elsewhere. The solemn entries of Renaissance rulers into their cities were occasions when *tableaux vivants*, speeches, triumphal arches or other architectural devices, paintings and inscriptions could carry a rich symbolism deriving from history, the Scriptures, and classical mythology, all made more or less relevant to the visiting monarchs, their dynasty, and current affairs. Tudor civic spectacle differed from its Continental counterparts only in its comparative infrequency, poverty, and the rarity of its classical imagery; and, like all such pageantry, its contemporary allusions conveyed more of the hopes, aspirations, and fears of the citizenry than of the visiting monarch's political aims. These shows had, as their principal object, *laudando praecipere* – to teach by praising – but the princes, willing enough to make various *ad hoc* concessions and gestures of goodwill, were so eager to lap up the *laudando* that they generally paid little attention to the *praecipere* on which the citizens built their hopes for better government in the future.[9]

Nor is there anything to suggest that central authority in Tudor England ever dictated a programme for such pageantry or imposed rigorous supervision over its execution. The best illustration of this lack of control is the entry of Queen Mary and Philip of Spain into London on 18 August 1554 – without doubt the most politically sensitive and difficult of all Tudor pageant series. Six months earlier Wyatt's rebellion had ended in disaster for all those implicated, and the Queen had expressed her hope that exemplary punishment of the guilty would purify the kingdom. Retribution was quick and copious. New gallows were set up at every gate and key point in London, and all were liberally festooned with the bodies of the executed – some hanged, some quartered, and some decapitated. The Catholic reaction was under way and the Counter-Reformation in England was soon sealed by the Anglo-Spanish marriage. It is remarkable, therefore, that when the Court of Aldermen met on 22 May to appoint a committee to plan 'such pageauntes and other open demonstrations of joye as they shoulde think meate to be made and sett furthe within the Cytie at the comminge of the prynce of Spayne', they decided to include Thomas Berthelet, who had been King's Printer under Henry VIII, and Richard Grafton, who had held the same position under Edward VI. Berthelet had been responsible for printing, amongst much else, all the Henrician propagandist tracts by Richard Moryson and the anti-clerical works of Christopher St German; while Grafton, who had printed the Great Bible in 1539, had also printed the proclamation for Queen Jane in 1553, and had been deprived of his post as royal Printer by Queen Mary. Even as the aldermen met, the London streets were still disfigured by the gallows and rotting remains of the last display of Protestant defiance. Yet none of this deterred the city dignitaries from appointing men of noted reformist sympathies. And nobody interfered.

More startling still was the result of the committee's deliberations when their second pageant, set up at the conduit in Gracechurch Street, depicted the Nine Worthies augmented by Henry VIII and Edward VI, all armed with maces, swords, or poleaxes, 'saving Henry the eight, which was paynted having in one hand a cepter and in the other hande a booke, whereon was wrytten *Verbum Dei*'. Again, nobody interfered. It was not until King Philip had witnessed the scene and passed on his way that Stephen Gardiner, Bishop of Winchester, having noted the Bible in the pageant-king's hand, summoned the painter, berated him with 'ville wourdes calling him tray-tour', and made him paint out the offending book. The poor artist hastily replaced it with a new pair of gloves, but was so fearful of leaving some part of the book and its reformist title in King Henry's hand that 'he wiped away a piece of his fingers withal'. The point of the story, both for the chronicler who reports it and for John Foxe who elaborates upon it, is Gardiner's hatred for true religion and especially of the Bible. The point of the story for us is that – given the general hostility to the Spanish marriage, the recent insurrection, the bloody public retribution, and the violence of the doc-trinal context – the City of London could still appoint men such as Berthelet and Grafton to plan a pageant series for their Catholic monarchs; that they could produce a pageant showing Henry VIII with the Word of God; and that it was not until *after* Philip had passed this scene that Gardiner noticed anything amiss and tried to do something about it (Anglo 1969: 324–30). This curious episode has been interpreted as though it establishes govern-mental censorship in relation to civic pageantry (King 1989: 101–2), where-as it suggests precisely the opposite. Clearly, until after the event, there had been no supervision or censorship whatever.

English civic pageantry was not the effective means of mass communica-tion that its modern students (myself included, I regret to say) have some-times deemed it to be. The cause of dynastic image-building was not well served when civic pageantry strayed beyond obvious political allusions and a straightforward exhibition of the customary repertoire of heraldic arms and badges. Esoteric and complex ideas were likely to lose the audience. In 1501, for example, there was, amongst much astronomical and cosmolog-ical imagery, a representation of Prince Arthur within the 'Sphere of the Sun' – a cosmic mechanism hinting at a solar apotheosis. The Prince himself was identified both as Christ the Redeemer and Christ the Sun of Justice, while, in the following scene, Henry VII was depicted as God the Father. This seems heady and exciting stuff. Yet not one of the three surviving eye-witness observers (all of them otherwise competent and circumstantial) even hints at having an inkling as to what it was all about (Anglo 1963: 72–81). It is, moreover, a poor instrument of propaganda and communication which is experienced only once or twice in an entire reign. This 1501 entry was the solitary Tudor pageant series in London prior to the visit of the Emperor Charles V in 1522. The citizens of Lincoln, for their part, never saw Tudor pageantry or Henry Tudor himself after his visit in 1486; and those of Worcester only glimpsed him on one day thereafter. York had to wait until 1541 for its first and only view of Henry VIII; and Elizabeth's loyal Londoners would have had to cling to their memories of her entry in 1559 for the rest of the century, because there was no repeat performance.

On the other hand, it is true that the monarch and the Court could be seen in full splendour at tournaments – frequently in the early years of Henry VIII's reign, occasionally in the reigns of his father, son, and elder daughter, and once or twice a year in the reign of Elizabeth. Recently it has been asserted that these spectacular shows constituted events of 'high political seriousness'; that the 'microcosm of the realm provided by a crowded tiltyard on a tournament day was in itself a potent instrument of royal propaganda'; that the costly preparations 'were all part of a serious and far-reaching purpose'; and that 'national unity was perhaps nowhere better in evidence than in the provision of viewing stands for thousands of spectators, arranged so as to express the accepted social hierarchy' (Young 1987: 7, 74, 122). More specifically, the Accession Day tilts for Elizabeth I have inspired one distinguished historian to exclaim, 'what incredible spectacles they must have been, and what an impact they must have made at the time!'; such an impact, indeed, that the tilts became an 'integral part of the aesthetic milieu of the eighties and nineties'; 'everyone knew about them, everyone had seen them' (Strong 1977: 146, 151). Everyone who was a somebody, perhaps: but not everyone who was a nobody. In such exaggerated statements the intentional fallacy has been allowed to run riot. By stepping beyond the bounds of the courtly milieu to make more general assertions about national policy, they stretch, distort, and ultimately destroy the fabric of their argument. That Henry VIII loved to disport himself within the lists is certain. That Elizabeth I enjoyed being celebrated as the Lady of the Tournament is likely. That all this was a deliberate plan to reproduce the social hierarchy in a Court festival and thus somehow influence the nation is a misinterpretation arising from a conflation of three diverse elements: high-flown sixteenth-century theories concerning the 'effects' of the later Valois Court entertainments, especially as enunciated by Balthazar de Beaujoyeulx;[10] a tacit and unwarranted assumption that these notions were shared by the Elizabethan intelligentsia; and an anachronistic belief in the power of mass manipulation by the media. Some historians write as though Renaissance Neoplatonic magic actually worked; or they give the impression that, all over England, Elizabethan fans were following the tournaments as if glued to television sets, sitting enthralled while expert commentators described the lists, interpreted the sexual and political significance of the Queen's apparel, analysed the courtly *imprese*, and assessed the prowess of the tilters. Yet how could the great mass of the Queen's subjects share in the spectacle, devices, and verses which would have been largely incomprehensible and inaudible even to those actually present? Some of the citizens of London may have enjoyed these emasculated neochivalric spectacles, but, apart from the fact that Elizabeth's Accession Day had become a national holiday, it is difficult to see how the rest of England would have been affected.

Much the same may be said of the annual ceremonies of the Order of the Garter. All the Tudors were concerned with these – from Henry VII, who followed the example of Edward IV in resuscitating the Order, Henry VIII, and Edward VI, who carefully revised the statutes, Mary, who re-revised them, and Elizabeth, who, with typical ambiguity, enhanced the ceremonial while leaving it essentially unaltered. The Garter festival was a splendid courtly occasion and, in the latter half of Elizabeth's reign, even became something of a public spectacle. Breuning von Buchenbach, envoy of Duke Frederick of Württemberg, described the ceremonies of 1595, mentioning that 'there was a great crush in the chapel, as many of the common people had thronged thither'; and he also reports that the Queen, with her knights 'marched round the yard three times so that everyone could have a good view of them' (Klarwill 1928: 378). The questions remain: what was the population of England in 1595, and what proportion managed to squeeze into the chapel and courtyard of Whitehall?

State portraiture

The chances of ordinary Tudor citizens pondering the inner meaning of works of art were even more remote, and, had they enjoyed such opportunities, the imagery was more likely to relate to some local dignitary than to the sovereign. Who actually saw the architectural embellishments, illuminated manuscripts, gems, and paintings that are constantly before *our* eyes as evidence of Tudor iconography? None of these things was intended for the uncouth gaze of the multitude. Indeed, it is not always clear just whose gaze they were intended for or whose vanity they were supposed to flatter. There were, for example, a whole series of historical paintings at Cowdray House representing important occasions in the reign of Henry VIII: but they were probably acquired or commissioned by the owner of the house, Sir William FitzWilliam, because he had participated *with the King* in the various events thus celebrated, and not simply because Henry VIII figured therein (Anglo 1966: 304–7). Or consider the famous and oft-reproduced 'Procession' picture of Elizabeth I. Surrounded by courtiers, and covered by a canopy held by her nobles, the seated figure of the Queen appears to float in mid-air – though there can be no doubt that the ill-executed painting is intended to suggest some means of locomotion. According to Sir Roy Strong, she is seated on some sort of wheeled vehicle pushed by one of the grooms of her Chamber, though this is not at all apparent to the untrained eye. All of this, we are told, is *Eliza triumphans*: for the canopy links her procession thematically with that of Alphonso the Great at Naples in 1443, as depicted on the triumphal gateway of his castle; while, beyond that, links are further suggested with the ancient Roman emperors themselves. The picture, in this interpretation, becomes an icon of imperial monarchy and a central source for establishing that there was a 'cult' of Queen Elizabeth I (Strong 1977: 17–55).

However, although, in terms of rank, the Queen is certainly the most important figure in the picture, she is not the person being flattered here. Prominent in the foreground, and basking in the glory reflected on him by his proximity to the monarch, is the Master of the Horse, Edward Somerset, Earl of Worcester, and it is more reasonable to assume that the painting was executed to enhance the courtier's self-esteem rather than to distort it into an arcane allusion to the Queen's imperial destiny.

Moreover, the dialectical leap from mid-fifteenth-century Naples to late-sixteenth-century England is implausible, and it is doubtful that the canopy was regarded as having a specifically imperial significance. It was, rather, a practical convenience – originally intended to protect distinguished personages from the sun or rain – which had developed into a ceremonial stage property. It can be seen depicted at Persepolis as a glorified umbrella protecting an Achaemenian monarch as early as about 521 BC (Roaf 1989: 35), and was still being used in similar fashion by the medieval popes and Venetian doges. Elaborated into a portable canopy, it was used in religious and state processions throughout Europe and was held over kings on solemn occasions such as coronations, entries, and funerals. It was carried over English queens at least from the reign of Richard II, as we know from the *Liber regalis* of the late fourteenth century (Legg 1901: 100, 108, 122, 129); and it came in for special mention in 1509 when Katharine of Aragon, just passing a tavern called the *Cardinal's Hat*, on her way to be crowned with Henry VIII, was caught in so sudden and heavy a shower that the canopy borne over her was not 'sufficient to deffend hyr from wetyng of hir mantell' (Thomas and Thornley 1938: 340). Eventually, the canopy became so commonplace that it functioned simply as an indicator of high rank. Whether alive or dead, the person beneath it was easily recognized as the focal point of the ceremony. Canopies are mentioned in numerous narratives of state occasions and may be seen in many European illustrations of religious processions, royal entries, and funerals, and even in a non-royal funeral such as that of Cardinal Wolsey.[11] Most pertinent are the thumbnail, contemporary pen-and-ink sketches of Elizabeth I herself *en route* to her coronation in 1559. She rides on a horse-drawn litter, protected by the canopy; and proceeds in a manner more dignified than that depicted in the 'procession' painting – especially if this really does show her being trundled along on an invisible wheelbarrow, like a bejewelled sack of vegetables.

Portraiture has been a particularly tempting field for scholars who, possibly influenced by the richly documented decorative programmes for the palaces of Continental princes, have sought to establish the existence of a coherent Tudor artistic policy. An instructive example of this, in relation to Henry VII, concerns the great hall of Richmond Palace, which was described in the only surviving contemporary account as follows.

> In the wallys and siddys of this halle, betwene the wyndowes, bethe pictures of the noble kinges of this realme, in their harnes and robes of goold; as brute, engist, king William Rufus, king Arthur, king Henry and many othir of that name; king Richard, king Edward, and of thoes names, many noble waryours, and kinges of this riall realme, with ther fachons and swordes in theire handes, visagid, and apperyng like bold and valiaunt knightes; and so their dedis and actes in the chroniclis right evydently bethe shewen and declared. Emonge thes nombre of famous kinges, in the higher parte, uppon the left hond, is the semely pictur and personage of our moost excellent and heyghe suffrayn now reignyng uppon us, his liege people, Kyng Henry the vij[th], as worthy that rumme and place with thoes glorious princes, as eny king that ever reigned in this lond.   (College of Arms MS 1st M.13, fol. 62[v])

On the basis of this description it has been suggested that the 'pictures' were designed, probably by the King's painter, Maynard, 'according to the familiar three-quarter bust formula developed by Rogier van der Weyden'; that an observer's eye, travelling along the two lines of wall portraits, 'inevitably rests at the hall's focal point at the higher end where the King's throne stands'; that there, high above the throne, is the picture of Henry VII himself, 'illuminated by light from all the windows and receiving the homage of all the other portraits of past kings'; and that the entire arrangement and composition of these 'portraits' thus constituted the 'first recorded attempt to portray the Tudor monarchy as a font of magnificence, the chief of the Burgundian virtues' (Kipling 1977).

Nor is this all. The contemporary account went on to mention that the walls of the hall were 'hongid with riche clothes of Arres their werkys representyng many noble batalles and seages, as of Ierusalem, troy, albe, and many other'. This is interpreted as a deliberate attempt to establish a chivalric Burgundian context, and it is asserted that 'while the rows of portraits converge on the image of Henry that dominates one end of the great hall, so the tapestries focus upon the throne beneath that portrait' (Kipling 1977: 60–1). A glance at the Tudor text itself, however, shows how far a preconception – that the decoration must be an expression of princely policy – has stimulated the historian's imagination. There is nothing to suggest that the representations of kings at Richmond employed the 'three-quarter bust formula'; nothing to suggest that the likeness of Henry VII was actually the focal point of two lines of wall portraits all paying him 'homage'; nothing to suggest that the whole design culminated in a royal throne; and nothing to suggest that such a throne was itself the focal point for a display of tapestries. In any case, since the parliamentary surveys tell us that the hall was 'adorned with eleven statues, in the sides thereof' (Colvin 1963–82: IV, p. 227), and since the word 'picture' was commonly used by contemporaries to indicate sculpted or moulded royal effigies, there is a strong likelihood that the 'pictures' were not painted portraits at all. None of this renders wholly nugatory the suggestion that the arrangement of the hall carried some political message. But, as far as we can tell, contemporary intentions were less precise and far less self-conscious than the modern reconstruction implies.[12]

Royal portraiture in the reign of Elizabeth I poses very different problems. Here there can be no doubt about the interest of the Queen herself and of her advisers in the style and quality of the portraits; no doubt about the existence of some kind of industry involved in their production and multiplication; and no doubt about the complexity of the imagery employed in some, at least, of these pictures.[13] What remain obscure are the underlying purposes of such images, their distribution, and the attitudes of those who gazed upon them. At the very beginning of Elizabeth's reign there is a curious item of expenditure relating to the furnishing of the new customs house at Pembroke by Thomas Phaer, collector of tonnage and poundage in the port of Milford, who purchased four portraits – one of Henry VIII, one of Edward VI, one of Mary, and one of Elizabeth. We do not know whether this was a personal whim of Phaer's, or whether such royal portraits were regarded as a standard adornment for customs houses, but they can hardly have been masterpieces, since he bought all four for one shilling (Lewis 1927: 330).[14] Perhaps it was the circulation of such pictures that led to the well-known draft proclamation of December 1563. This document, corrected by William Cecil himself, begins by stating that there is a natural desire on the part of all subjects 'both noble and mean' to procure a portrait of the Queen; that this desire has prompted all manner of artists to meet the demand 'in painting, graving, and printing'; but that the portraits thus far produced are so unfaithful that 'daily are heard complaints amongst her loving subjects'. These complaints are such that the Queen has been 'instantly and importunately sued unto by the body of the council and others of her nobility' not only that some special artist might be permitted to 'take the natural representation of her majesty', but also that it should be prohibited to 'draw, paint, grave or portray her majesty's personage or visage for a time until, by some perfect patron and example, the same may be by others followed'. The draft continues that the Queen, though reluctant to sit for her portrait, had been convinced by the 'continual requests of so many of her nobility and subjects' and had agreed to the appointment of 'some cunning person' whose work, when completed, would serve as a pattern to be followed by other well-reputed artists, 'hired by the head officers of the places where they shall dwell' (Hughes and Larkin 1964–9: II, pp. 240–1).

This scheme was never officially promulgated, although something along these lines must have been developed in order to produce the number of portraits of Elizabeth which yet survive and to produce them according to distinguishable patterns. Moreover, the very existence of the draft proclamation suggests that somebody in high places was giving serious thought to the dissemination of copies of the royal likeness; and, since it is unlikely that quantities of 'mean' subjects really did complain daily about inferior portraiture, it becomes all the more interesting that the Council should have insisted that they were. The draft's initial assumption, that to possess a portrait of the Queen was a natural desire, is also interesting. Why was such a desire natural, and what purpose was to be served by satisfying it? Amongst various anti-papal papers collected by Cecil, there is a discourse by Clement Urmeston incorporating typical remarks on the significance of the royal head seal (BL MS Lansdowne 97, fos. 148 ff.). But there is nothing in the draft proclamation, or in any other source, to suggest that there was ever any intention to resuscitate Urmeston's talismanic plan for every householder to have a seal with the royal image.[15]

The most likely reason for owning a royal portrait was as an expression, at an elementary level, of loyalty and enthusiasm: and Sir Roy Strong's suggestion – that the existence of medals showing Elizabeth I's head, cast in base metal and with a ring for suspension, testifies to 'an almost universal cult' of the Queen – is doubtful (Strong 1963: 31–2). We have no evidence concerning the number of such medals issued or the extent to which they were carried, and no way of knowing whether their owners ever pondered the nature of talismanic power and divine kingship. *Amulet* is a word much favoured by culture historians, and it has a much grander sound than *good-luck-charm*: but the latter is surely closer to the spirit in which such medals might have been regarded by ordinary folk if they did, indeed, carry them. In general, surviving medals do not convey an impression that Tudor England was receptive to the more lofty claims of Renaissance numismatists. Rather they suggest much the same sort of *ad hoc* randomness encountered elsewhere in Tudor image-making. Nothing survives for Henry Tudor, and very little for his son, though there is a portrait medal of about 1524 showing on the reverse a Tudor rose and the inscription 'ODOR EIUS VT LIBANI', likening the odour to that of the cedars of Lebanon. There is also a portrait medal of Anne Boleyn and one of Thomas Cromwell, commemorating his election to the Order of the Garter, and, in the latter case, an earl's coronet is attached to the rim to enable the medal to be worn by suspension. Similarly, in the reign of Elizabeth – in addition to a number of medals celebrating triumphs such as the defeat of the Armada, and joyous events such as Elizabeth's recovery from smallpox in 1572 – various of the Queen's subjects employed noted artists to commemorate their own achievements in portrait medals, and at least one of these medals (for William Herbert, Earl of Pembroke, in 1562) was provided with a ring for suspension. Cromwell

later became a Protestant hero and Herbert was a distinguished public figure: but no one has suggested that either of them inspired a cult. The medal
in Tudor England was no mere commonplace token. Nor was it a royal prerogative, a talisman, or an icon.[16]

The coinage, on the other hand, *was* a royal prerogative. Control of its
design, minting, and distribution was always jealously guarded and was the
subject of repeated statutes, proclamations, and grants of privilege throughout the Tudor period. Henry VII gave these matters close personal attention, and it is noteworthy that his measures to reform the coinage in 1504
constitute the only administrative matter to receive a chapter all to itself,
'Justa monetae reformatio', in Bernardus Andreas's *Annales* (Gairdner
1858: 81–2). The coinage was, beyond comparison, the most far-reaching
medium for the display of royal portraiture, dynastic badges, and political
epigraphy; and it remains the most striking evidence of their limited efficacy. There is no reason to suppose that sixteenth-century folk contemplated the coins in their purses more assiduously than we do. The handling of
coins has always been an everyday occurrence: yet how many people are
able – or would have been able – accurately to record from memory their
portraits, badges, and inscriptions? In any case, such descriptive power
would depend on superficial keenness of observation. At what level of cultivated intelligence would an understanding of the meaning of the iconography and epigraphy have commenced? A test case in this respect is the
design and issue of Henry VII's sovereign in 1489. This was a heavy gold
coin based on the model of several Continental issues and notably the *real
d'or* used by Maximilian in the Low Countries from 1487.

The similarity between the design of the sovereign and the *real*, each with
an enthroned figure of a monarch on the obverse and a shield of arms on
the reverse, together with their identical weight, has been interpreted by
numismatists as a deliberate attempt by Henry VII to align English and
Continental practice. It was, in the words of C. E. Challis, in his authoritative study of the Tudor coinage, 'a small yet brilliant addition to the trappings of the new dynasty' (Challis 1978: 47–51). Furthermore, on this coin,
Henry abandoned the traditional open crown of the English kings and
adopted the arched, imperial crown closed over the head and surmounted
with a cross – a form also used on the second issue of his groat and half-
groat. This, it has been argued, may have had implications for English claims
to imperial dominion which were later, in the reign of Henry VIII, associated with the wearing of the appropriate crown (Grierson 1964: 118–34).
My point is not whether this notion is historically correct – something
which, unless fresh evidence is forthcoming, cannot be proved – but
whether those rare contemporaries of Henry VII wealthy enough to handle
sovereigns, and those many folk who regularly handled the groat or half-
groat, ever noticed the shape of the crown, let alone understood its momen-
tous message as reconstructed by modern scholarship. Such contemporary

attitudes are also beyond proof, but they are not beyond the exercise of common sense and reasonable conjecture.

The impact of printing

The role of printing in Tudor image-making is another issue where modern preconceptions are a hindrance rather than a help. The potential power of the press, both in terms of providing sophisticated visual propaganda and disseminating it, seems so obvious to us that we readily assume that it was consistently and effectively utilized in Tudor England to enhance people's perception of the dynasty. Certainly, control of printing, by licensing, censorship, and prosecution, was vigorously if fitfully maintained from the time of Thomas Cromwell; writers were commissioned to advance arguments favourable to royal policies and other authors offered apologetics spontaneously and without official encouragement. Nevertheless, compared with the range and volume of political pamphleteering issuing from the Continental presses throughout the sixteenth century, English production remained insignificant, especially with regard to prints, woodcuts, and engravings.

The extent of England's backwardness is especially striking in the literature relating to royal spectacle and ceremony. Of all the Tudor coronations, funerals, civic entries, and Court festivals, only a tiny proportion were commemorated by printed editions, and those few were primitive, clumsy brochures, devoid of style and quality. In France, by contrast, almost every royal occasion from the late fifteenth century onward was marked by printed accounts of the ceremonies and spectacle – births, deaths, marriages, coronations, entries, funerals, tournaments, festivals – sometimes several for each event, and often illustrated with high-quality woodcuts. It may be asked, of course, where did all this get the Valois monarchy? What good did it do them? But the significance of such commemorative literature is not whether it really achieved anything as propaganda but rather that it demonstrates the extent of royal interest and taste. The positive political value of publicity via the printing press in the sixteenth century may have been very limited. What is noteworthy is that, for a dynasty allegedly concerned with image-making, with winning the support and admiration of its subjects, and with creating a cult of monarchy, none of the Tudors – not even Elizabeth – seems to have tried very hard.[17]

In the wider fields of sixteenth-century controversy, the production of the English presses is no more able to bear comparison with, for example, the great polemical outpourings of the German Reformation or the French Wars of Religion. However, wonders of ingenuity are possible even with limited material and John Foxe's *Actes and Monuments* – Tudor England's only significant combination of polemical text and illustrations – has afforded ample scope. Foxe's theories of universal history, his numerological *schema*, and his apocalypticism have been the delight of the learned from his own to the present day; but since 1970 scholarship – its appetite for exegesis unappeased by the three million (or more) words heaped up in the *Actes and Monuments* – has sought further nutriment from the woodcuts. It has been cogently maintained that the historical outline of Foxe's thesis can be traced through some of these illustrations and that, because it was governmental policy to make the volume available in most churches, those illustrations would have become familiar to the Elizabethan public. Far less convincing is the assertion that the 'climax of the whole book' comes in the historiated letter C of the dedication, showing Queen Elizabeth seated on her throne, which crushes the pope. And should we regret that the fascination of Foxe's accounts of the martyrs' sufferings has drawn attention away from 'the fact that the politico-religious position which he propounds derives its sanction from the traditions, Christianized it is true, of the worldly empire of Rome' (Yates 1975: 43–4)?

An approach of this kind, however much light it may throw on Renaissance erudition for a modern audience, fails to acknowledge the immense distance between what a writer or artist may have intended, and what an ordinary reader or viewer might have understood. We may readily accept that the illustration depicts Elizabeth as a second Constantine, and that it reverses a familiar pictorial tradition of the Papacy triumphing over the Empire. It is more difficult to visualize Tudor citizens clustered around their local copy of Foxe's work, scrutinizing the initial letter C of the dedication, and earnestly debating its historical and iconological message. And it is impossible to believe that these citizens felt that the letter C constituted the climax of their reading.

Another instance of this interpretative stumbling-block is encountered in John Norman King's recent (1989) examination of Tudor iconography, where he provides a learned exposition of the antecedents and significance of the non-martyrological illustrations in Foxe's work, and especially of the sequence of 12 anti-papal woodcuts, *The Proud Primacy of the Popes*, inserted by the printer, John Day, at the end of the 1570 edition. Again it cannot be denied that Foxe held very decided views on the history of the Christian Church, on the relative position occupied within that history by the Papacy and the English monarchy, and on the ways in which these ideas might be conveyed in images. But it is necessary for the modern reader of a sixteenth-century book to retain a sense of proportion, especially when – as in the historico-political illustrations in Foxe – much of the meaning is not immediately obvious and where scholarly exegesis may help to recover an original intention. For, paradoxically, the real difficulty is posed less by such intellectual conundrums than by areas where the appeal of a text is so obvious that the scholar scarcely pauses over them. Thus John King acknowledges only *en passant* that 'most of the woodcuts portray martyrdoms of Protestant saints' and that 'in the popular imagination' Foxe's book is remembered for the 'lurid images of the "roasting" of Sir John Oldcastle' and other violent scenes (King 1989: 134–5).

The inevitable impression given by such cursory acknowledgement is that the heart of the matter lies elsewhere – in the historical and iconological analogues which require elucidation – and the problem of giving due weight to the crude, the commonplace, and the uncomplicated has been skirted. Of the potential Tudor audience, that tiny minority who might have possessed the skill, perseverance, and time to master the bewildering mixture of typefaces and layout and actually read the *Actes and Monuments* would have found the strength of Foxe's polemic in the circumstantial detail and mighty documentation of his atrocity stories. For the illiterate majority, excitement and indignation would have been generated by the evocative woodcuts demonstrating the cruelties from which England had only recently been delivered. Such readers might sometimes have been disconcerted by encountering representations of one and the same gentleman being combusted under different names and at different dates – as was the case, for example, with James Bainham and Adam Wallace; Walter Mille and Kerby; Richard Bayfield, Thomas Benet and Peke; and, in one especially powerful woodcut, John Bent and William Hunter. But, even allowing for such duplication, the pictures of executions still outnumber other illustrations in the text by about 10 to one.

Erudition, courtiership, and conceitful thought

Common assumptions concerning both the migration and the impact of symbols should be questioned very seriously. The context provided for us by academic detective work, however indispensable it may be, is necessarily highly selective and based upon a painstakingly accumulated repertoire of historical antecedents, literary analogues, and iconological parallels; and such specialized knowledge would have been as far beyond the ken of ordinary people in the sixteenth century as it is in the twentieth. Many of the poets who stuffed their eulogies of Elizabeth I with 'lillies / and the dayntie Daffadillies / With Roses damask, White and red, and fairest flower delice, / With Cowslips of Jerusalem, and cloves of Paradice', were not so much ingenious and allusive as iconologically lazy. While to imagine that readers confronted with a phoenix or sieve unhesitatingly fancied imperial renewal or chastity is rather like imagining that ordinary folk have microscopes for eyeballs and perceive in a simple glass of water a reservoir teeming with strange organisms, or in a humble biscuit encounter a mountain of cavorting particles. There are people who do study life under a microscope, just as there were people equipped to decipher symbols. But it is unlikely that such iconographical skill was widespread in Tudor England; and, whatever justification there may be for teasing out hidden and obscure meanings, there is none for habitually conveying an impression that these were more important than the straightforward. When, for example, the English fleet and the weather combined to destroy the Spanish Armada in 1588, the designer of a medal struck at Middelburg simply decorated the obverse with a view of the rival fleets in action (Grueber 1904–11: plate X, no. 16). Ships similarly appear in the background to the so–called 'Armada' portraits (Strong 1963: 74, nos 64, 65). And forty years later, the ships – on shield or banner – have become emblematic of Elizabeth I on the title-pages of books devoted to the defenders of Church and State in England.[18]

On the other hand, it is obvious that artistic and intellectual ingenuity *was* deployed in the closed circuit of clambering courtiership; and this raises another important issue. Granted that our own conception of 'propaganda', with its populist implications, is an anachronism for Tudor England: is it none the less possible that the techniques of political persuasion – and more particularly the manipulation of imagery – did function in the higher reaches of society where some degree of artistic and literary sophistication might reasonably be expected? If so, it would mean that the audience for such material coincided with the politically powerful minority clustered about the Court; and this, in turn, would preserve the notion of 'propaganda' in a limited but more effective area. The notion is tempting: but again there remain the uncomfortable demands of common sense.

There certainly existed a cluster of Latin poeticules around the Court of Henry VII, who scribbled eulogies, in the manner of Virgil's fourth *Eclogue*, concerning the return of the Golden Age; just as there existed cartloads of emblematic flowers, an energetic reworking of all the threadbare conventions of courtly love, adaptations of classical myth, and ingenious manipulation of Christian imagery, in ceaseless adulation of Elizabeth I. The material ranges from puerile and sycophantic doggerel to those massive obscurities of Spenser's *Faerie Queene* which now fuel an industry of numerologists, allegorists, emblematologists, feminists, and hermeneutists. But if all this were 'propaganda', who was supposed to be the manipulator and who the manipulated? Or, to beg an even more fashionable question, if this did amount to a 'Queen cult' what was it supposed to achieve? Could this kind of exaggerated praise ever win over a disaffected suitor?; could it stop any noble from harbouring critical thoughts about governmental decisions?; or could it convince some aristocrat that he should support an issue on which he had hitherto been uncommitted or which was against his interests? The whole panoply of panegyric was aimed upward to please the monarch, not downward to persuade doubting courtiers of the rectitude of the regime. The highly coloured imagery was the currency of aspiring authors, poets, artists, and courtiers to buy attention. The Crown, on the other hand, dealt principally in favours and coercion.

We have, I believe, become both too sophisticated and too gullible. We treat the web-spinning subtleties of sixteenth-century scholars and the intricate flattery of courtiers alike with too much respect – indeed, nowadays it is scarcely permitted to regard even the most arrant toadyism as *mere flattery*

– and it is inevitable that the quest for hidden connotations sometimes results in a species of erudite buffoonery. Scholars may debate the connotations of a flower as though it were some weighty matter of state; bury an innocent and conventional metaphor in the sepulchre of a portentous explication; or simply lose all sense of proportion. It has, for example, been argued that roses were associated with the Blessed Virgin and that this was especially true of the *rosa sine spina*. Lacking the thorns of original sin, this flower grew only in the garden of Eden, and that is why, in lyrics celebrating the virgin, it was also known as the *flower of paradise*, 'signifying the prelapsarian ideal of sinless desire and immaculacy of conception that was made flesh only in the Virgin Mary (the second Eve)'. It was in this guise, it is alleged, that Spenser alludes to the flower of paradise, celebrating England's own 'Eternal Virgin' (McClure and Wells 1990: 54–5). All of this may be iconologically verifiable: but it must be pointed out that the crowned double rose, accompanied by the legend RVTILANS ROSA SINE SPINA, appeared on the crown and half-crown of Henry VIII's second issue of coinage in 1526, and that he was celebrated as the rose without thorn on several coins of his later issues (Hocking 1906: I, nos 823–4, 832–4, 838–9, 852–5, 860, 865, 871). Scholarly ingenuity can accomplish much; but to identify Henry VIII with prelapsarian ideals of sinless desire, or with the Virgin Mary, presents formidable difficulties.

Elizabeth's purity was less equivocal. Her chastity was a boon to poets, mythographers, and modern exegetes. In particular, much has been written about the five-petalled white rose or eglantine which was not only an emblem of her virginity but could be combined with the union rose, or even replace it, to bring the Tudor mission neatly up to date. This is how the flower was used in the decoration of the manuscript *Hymne* presented to the Queen by Georges de la Mothe, by William Rogers in his engraving of Elizabeth as *Rosa Electa*, and by Henry Lyte in the frontispiece to his *Light of Britayne* (Strong 1977: 68–71). Doubts creep in, however, with the most specific of all references to Elizabeth as the eglantine. It occurs in the final stanza of *Eglantyne of Meryfleur* by Sir Arthur Gorges, a versifying gentleman pensioner whom modern scholarship has misguidedly rescued from oblivion.

> Then hyr hye lynage he rynges
> deryved from the Dardane kynges
> discendinge to the Conqueringe lyne
> wheare stately stryff he doothe recyte
> between the redd rose and the whyte
> appeasde in thys brave Eglantyne.
> (Gorges 1953: 125)

Both the Tudor and Elizabethan significance of the imagery are obvious. Yet the fact remains that Gorges had originally drafted the poem for his wife, and only later twisted it into a tribute to the Queen; and, while this does not alter the meaning of the literary figure, it does suggest a certain courtly opportunism on Gorges's part. If compliments addressed to the Queen were largely matters of form, venal, or part of a courtly game, then the term *cult* – which implies worship, devotion, and sincerity – is too highly coloured and tendentious.

The great disparity between outward show and inner meaning is laid bare in the courtly career of Robert Devereux, Earl of Essex. The languid, rose-entwined gentleman of Hilliard's miniature, the enigmatic jouster in the Accession Day tilts, the mediocre sonneteer, eulogist, and courtly lover of Elizabeth – Essex was at the centre of the 'Queen cult' (Strong 1977: 56–83). But what did it all add up to beyond heartless self-seeking and, eventually, petulance and treason when his ambitions were thwarted? That the pretence was politically purposive is obvious. All the more reason, then, to be suspicious of it and to be wary of any assumption that Essex's contemporaries were disposed to treat his courtly utterances with credulity. This noble lover, even at the nadir of his fortunes, was still penning sycophantic epistles to the withered object of his affections, while privately snarling that 'she being now an old woman, is no less crooked in mind than in body' (Camden 1635: 536).

Erudition and conceitful thought merit study. What they do not merit is our confidence that they were sincere, that they were politically effective, and that they were necessarily taken seriously by contemporaries. Even before the Armada opened the floodgates of eulogy, one egregious rhymer and alliterator, Maurice Kyffin – in his wildly enthusiastic celebration of Elizabeth's 'Holyday', *The Blessednes of Brytaine* (1587) – contrived an effective sneer at his fellow flatterers.

> What should I Nymphs, or Goddeses Recount?
> Or AEgypt Queenes, or Romane Ladies name?
> Sith as Supreme, our Sov'raigne dooth surmount,
> In choice of Good, the cheefe of all those same?
> For to compare the great, with simple small.
> Is thereby, not to praise the Best at all.

Kyffin's marginal gloss on his own classical abstinence is devastating and should be better known. 'Besides that such manner of Reciting strange and Hethenish names were here altogether inconvenient,' he declares, 'the author doth also of very purpose, somewhat shun that beaten high way, to fil paper with pestring Names of fained Gods, Goddesses, Nymphs, Persians, Grecians, Romans, &c. Being a thing of some sometimes used, too too much, and to litle effect' (Hazlitt 1875: I, item xxix).

Images which require pages of exegesis before they yield up their meaning do not make for successful propaganda. Easily recognized badges, memorable slogans, and simple messages are what people respond to, and in this respect the sixteenth century scarcely differed from the twentieth. This is why, when we think of Tudor dynastic imagery, it is not abstruse imperial symbolism and arcane emblematics which come most readily to mind but rather the heraldic badges adopted by Henry VII at the very outset of his reign – dragons, greyhounds, portcullises, and roses – and consistently used by all his successors in a pragmatic and thoroughly traditional manner. There is little evidence to support the view that the English monarchy employed a propaganda machine other than sporadically, and the notion that there was a carefully-thought-out systematic sales promotion of recondite imagery to the nation at large is a wholly modern, academic invention.

Notes

1 On English coronations, see Planché (1838); Legg (1901); Jones (1902); Murray (1936); Schramm (1937).
2 For the reference to Prince Arthur, see PRO LC 2/1, fo. l7; to Henry VIII, see Wall (1891: 386); to Anne of Cleves, see Bentley (1833: 304); and for Mary, see Leland (1770: V, p. 315).
3 I am grateful to my friend Peter Begent for drawing my attention to Nicholas Charles's manuscript.
4 *This sermon folowynge was compyled and sayd in the Cathedrall chyrche of saynt Poule the body beynge present of the moost famouse Kynge Henry the vii the x daye of May, mcccccix.* This has been reprinted in Mayor (1876).
5 On English royal funerals and cognate material, see Machyn (1848); Wall (1891); Hope (1906–7); Fritz (1981); Llewellyn (1990). Manuscript sources are rich – but especially noteworthy for Tudor funerals are BL MSS Egerton 2642, Add. MSS 35,324 and 45,131; PRO LC 2/1.
6 On the funeral effigy of Richard, Duke of York, see BL MS Egerton 2642, fo. 191. There is another version of Richard's funeral in BL MS Harleian 48, fos. 78–91. See also Armstrong (1983: 139).
7 The comment on the outmoded nature of the Bishop's funeral effigy is in BL MS Egerton 2642, fo. 195. On Gardiner's funeral, see Machyn (1848: 101).
8 An itinerary of Henry VII is given in Temperley (1917: 411–19). The peregrinations of Henry VIII have to be excavated from LP. The most convenient outline of Elizabeth's movements is Chambers (1923: IV, pp. 75–116).
9 On Tudor pageantry in general, see Withington (1918: I, pp. 157–221); Anglo (1969); Bergeron (1970); McGee and Meagher (1981).
10 For an account of such theories and their intellectual background, see Yates (1947).
11 For examples of the canopy, see Guénee and Lehoux (1968: 13–21); Bryant (1986: 101–4); Legg (1901: 100, 108, 122, 129); Leland (1770: IV, p. 221).
12 Gordon Kipling has corrected his earlier misconstruction of the word 'pictures' as paintings; but he has not revised the interpretation which was based upon it (Kipling 1990: 160).
13 The fullest, and by far the most influential, studies of Elizabethan portraiture are Strong (1963, 1977).
14 I must thank my friend Rhys Robinson for this reference. On Phayre, see Robinson (1972).
15 On Urmeston's theories, see Anglo (1992: 24–8).
16 Tudor medals are most conveniently studied in Hawkins (1885), and Grueber (1904–11).
17 To point the difference, both in quality and density of publication, between sixteenth-century England and France in these matters, it is sufficient to compare de Worde (1533) and Tottel (1559) with the printed accounts of the entries of Henry II into Lyons (1548), Paris (1549), and Rouen (1550). For a still useful list of contemporary published accounts of French royal entries, see Kernodle (1944); and for full

bibliographical information on the official publications relating to French tournaments, coronations, and funerals, see Saffroy (1968–79).
18 For examples, see Carleton (1624); Lever (1627).

References

Anglo, S. (1960), 'The Foundation of the Tudor Dynasty: The Coronation and Marriage of Henry VII', *The Guildhall Miscellany*, 2/1, pp. 1–9.
—— (1963), 'The London Pageants for the Reception of Katharine of Aragon: November 1501', *Journal of the Warburg and Courtauld Institutes*, 26, pp. 53–89.
—— (1966), 'The Hampton Court Painting of the Field of Cloth of Gold', *The Antiquaries Journal*, 46, pp. 287–307.
—— (1969), *Spectacle, Pageantry and Early Tudor Policy* (Oxford).
—— (1992), *Images of Tudor Kingship* (London).
Armstrong, C. A. J. (1983), *England, France and Burgundy in the Fifteenth Century* (Oxford).
Bentley, S. (1833), *Excerpta Historica* (London).
Bergeron, D. M. (1970), *English Civil Pageantry, 1558–1642* (London).
Bryant, L. M. (1986) *The King and the City in the Parisian Royal Entry Ceremony: Politics, Ritual and Art in the Renaissance* (Geneva).
Camden, W. (1635), *Annals, or, the Historie of the Most Renowned and Victorious Princesse Elizabeth, Late Queen of England* (3rd edn, London).
Carleton, G. (1624), *A Thankful Remembrance of Gods Mercie* (London).
Challis, C. E. (1978), *The Tudor Coinage* (Manchester).
Chambers, E. K. (1923), *The Elizabethan Stage* (Oxford).
Colvin, H. M. (1963–82), *History of the King's Works* (London).
de Worde, Wynkyn (1533), *The noble tryumphaunt coronacyon of queene Anne wyfe unto the moost noble Kynge Henry the viij* (London).
Fritz, P. S. (1981), 'From "Public" to "Private": The Royal Funerals in England, 1500–1830', in J. Whaley (ed.), *Mirrors of Mortality: Studies in the Social History of Death* (London).
Gairdner, J. (1858) (ed.), *Memorials of King Henry VII* (London).
Gorges, A. (1953), *The Poems of Sir Arthur Gorges*, ed. H. E. Sandison (Oxford).
Grierson, P. (1964), 'The Origins of the English Sovereign and the Symbolism of the Closed Crown', *British Numismatic Journal*, 33, pp. 118–34.
Grueber, H. A. (1904–11), *Medallic Illustrations of the History of Great Britain and Ireland* (London; repr. 1979).
Guenée, B. and Lehoux, F. (1968), *Les entrées royales françaises de 1328 à 1515* (Paris).
Hall, E. (1809), *The Union of the Two Noble and Illustre Families of Lancastre and Yorke*, ed. H. Ellis (London).
Hawkins, E. (1885), *Medallic Illustrations of the History of Great Britain and Ireland to the Death of George II* (London).

Hazlitt, W. C. (1875) (ed.), *Fugitive Tracts Written in Verse* (London).

Hocking, W. J. (1906), *Catalogue of the Coins, Tokens, Medals, Dies and Seals in the Museum of the Royal Mint* (London).

Hope, W. H. St J. (1906–7), 'On the Funeral Effigies of the Kings and Queens of England', *Archaeologia*, 60, pp. 517–70.

Hughes, P. L., and Larkin, J. F. (1964–9) (eds), *Tudor Royal Proclamations* (New Haven, Conn.).

Jones, W. (1902), *Crowns and Coronations: A History of Regalia* (London).

Kantorowicz, E. H. (1957), *The King's Two Bodies: A Study in Medieval Political Theology* (London; repr. 1981).

Kernodle, G. (1944), *From Art to Theatre* (Chicago).

King, J. N. (1989), *Tudor Royal Iconography: Literature and Art in an Age of Religious Crisis* (Princeton).

Kipling, G. (1977), *The Triumph of Honour: Burgundian Origins of the Elizabethan Renaissance* (Leiden).

—— (1990) (ed.), *The Receyt of the Ladie Kateryne* (Oxford).

Klarwill, V. von. (1928), *Queen Elizabeth and Some Foreigners* (London).

Kyffin, M. (1587), *The Blessednes of Brytaine* (London; repr. in Hazlitt (1875)).

Legg, L. G. W. (1901) (ed.), *English Coronation Records* (Westminster).

Leland, J. (1770), *De rebus britannicis collectanea*, ed. T. Hearne (London).

Letters and Papers, Foreign and Domestic, of the Reign of Henry VIII (1862–1932), ed. J. S. Brewer, J. Gairdner, R. H. Brodie, *et al.* (21 vols in 32 parts, and Addenda; London).

Lever, C. (1627), *The Historie of the Defendors of the Catholique Faith* (London).

Lewis, E. A. (1927), *The Welsh Port Books (1550–1603)* (London).

Llewellyn, N. (1990), 'The Royal Body: Monuments to the Dead, for the Living', in L. Gent and N. Llewellyn (eds), *Renaissance Bodies: The Human Figure in English Culture c.1540–1660* (London), pp.218–40, 275–82.

Machyn, H. (1848), *The Diary*, ed. J. G. Nicholas (London).

Mayor, J. E. B. (1876) (ed.), *The English Works of John Fisher* (London).

McClure, P., and Wells, R. H. (1990), 'Elizabeth I as a Second Virgin Mary', *Renaissance Studies*, 4, pp. 38–70.

McGee, C. E., and Meagher, J. C. (1981) 'Preliminary Checklist of Tudor and Stuart Entertainments: 1558–1603', *Research Opportunities in Renaissance Drama*, 24, pp.51–155.

Murray, R. H. (1936), *The King's Crowning* (London).

Nichols, J. (1788–1805) (ed.), *The Progresses, and Public Processions, of Queen Elizabeth* (3 vols, London).

Petowe, H. (1603), *Elizabetha quasi vivens: Eliza's Funerall* (London; repr. in Hazlitt (1875)).

Planché, J. R. (1838), *Regal Records: or a Chronicle of the Coronations of the Queens Regnant of England* (London).

Roaf, M. (1989), 'The Art of the Achaemenians', in R. W. Ferrier (ed.), *The Arts of Persia* (London).

Robinson, W. R. B. (1972), 'Dr Thomas Phaer's Report on the Harbours and Customs Administration of Wales under Edward VI', *Bulletin of the Board of Celtic Studies*, 24, pp. 485–503.

Saffroy, G. (1968–79) *Bibliographie généalogique, héraldique et nobiliaire de la France* (Paris).

Schramm, P. E. (1937), *A History of the English Coronation* (Oxford).

Strong, R. C. (1963), *Portraits of Queen Elizabeth I* (Oxford).

—— (1977), *The Cult of Elizabeth: Elizabethan Portraiture and Pageantry* (London).

—— (1984), *Art and Power: Renaissance Festivals 1450–1650* (Woodbridge).

Temperley, G. (1917), *Henry VII* (London).

Thomas, A. H. and Thornley, I. D. (1938) (eds), *The Great Chronicle of London* (London).

Tottel, Richard (1559), *The Queens maiesties passage through the citie of London to Westminster the daye before her coronacion* (London).

Vergil, P. (1950), *The Anglica Historia of Polydore Vergil AD 1485–1537*, ed. and trans. Denys Hay (Camden Society, 3rd ser. 74; London).

Wall, J. C. (1891), *The Tombs of the Kings of England* (London).

Withington, R. (1918), *English Pageantry: An Historical Outline* (Cambridge, Mass.).

Yates, F. A. (1947), *The French Academies of the Sixteenth Century* (London).

—— (1975), *Astraea: The Imperial Theme in the Sixteenth Century* (London).

Young, A. (1987), *Tudor and Jacobean Tournaments* (London).

2

Representation through intimacy: A study in the symbolism of monarchy and Court office in early modern England

DAVID STARKEY

The appearance of Keith Thomas's *Religion and the Decline of Magic* marked an epoch in the study of early modern English history. It shows, irrefutably, that the men of that time – from the most educated and sophisticated to the least – were soaked in the occult and the irrational: they believed in astrology, witchcraft, and the direct intervention of providence in everyday life. No more will it be possible to push these aspects of the period into the margin;

rather, they must figure largely in any general explanations. This applies just as much to political history as to religious history or to the history of ideas. From one point of view this has already been understood: thus Thomas himself stresses the propaganda value of the king's powers as a miraculous healer (Thomas 1973: 231–2). But there is more to it than the manipulation of opinion: as this paper will try to show, the actual instruments of government at the command of a miracle-working king are different from those available to a lounge-suited prime minister. The aim, then, is to explore some of the governmental consequences of divine kingship; the method will be a study of monarchical symbolism, since, as religious history shows, symbolism is a particularly direct pointer to the deepest layers of belief.

Symbols were of course a highly familiar mode of expression to a fifteenth- or sixteenth-century Englishman. Jousts and revels signified their meaning through a fanciful and elaborate symbolism (Hall 1809: 520, 568, 597, 688, etc.); a man's political allegiance was announced by the badge he wore in his cap or hung about his neck on a chain (cf. Tudor-Craig 1973: 151, illustrations 45–51); while on the esoteric emblems of heraldry could depend the life of the Duke of Norfolk and his son (*LP* XXI, ii, 555/2/14/17). With the Reformation, it is true, some images – those of saints and martyrs – were deliberately devalued, but others, and especially our particular concern – the symbols of monarchy – underwent a corresponding reinforcement.

Broadly, royal symbolism fell into two main categories: the material accoutrements of monarchy, and the king's own person. The former – the crown, the sceptre, the orb, and so on – are the subject of an extensive and varied literature (Legg 1901; Schramm 1937, etc.); the latter, on which this paper will concentrate, has experienced a comparative neglect. There is only one monograph on the topic, and even that approaches it from a very narrow point of view. In his book, *The King's Two Bodies*, Ernst Kantorowicz shows at length how corporeal symbolism was used to define the king's constitutional position – especially in England. The equation of kingship with the king's body was accepted; then two separate meanings of the symbol were distinguished. On the one hand, the ordinary sense of the word – that is, the king's mortal, fleshly body – stood for the personal, transitory aspects of monarchy; on the other, the king's body considered as the fictive entity of a 'corporation sole' – that is, an undying legal 'body', of which the particular sovereign was simply the temporary representative – expressed the eternal nature of the office. Clearly, since Kantorowicz is concerned with political theory, the distinction between the two bodies is of the essence. But in practice, as contemporaries usually stressed, both bodies fused in the actual person of the king 'for the time being' (Plowden 1816: 455a). The recognition of this fact leads to a quite different emphasis from Kantorowicz's. Only in legal discourse did the king's physical person symbolize merely the private aspects of kingship; ordinarily it was infinitely more resonant. Firm evidence is available on this point: when Stephen

Gardiner was discussing the likely secular consequences (as he saw them) of ecclesiastical iconoclasm, he noted as the worst that:

> If this opinion [i.e. iconoclasm] should proceed, when the King's Majesty hereafter should show his person, his lively image, the honour due by God's law among such might continue; but as for the King's standards, his banners, his arms, [they] should hardly continue in their due reverence.   (Muller 1933: 274–5)

The king's body, 'his lively image', is thus seen as the master symbol, qualitatively different from and hence less vulnerable than the derivative symbols of the royal standard, arms, and so on.

As the master symbol of the office, the royal body was an essential instrument of political management. This meant that, whatever his personal taste, a king with any sense spent much effort on decking out his person as a suitably magnificent emblem of royalty. And if a monarch did not, he generally paid a severe penalty. All this is well brought out by the contrast between Henry VI and Edward IV. Henry (who certainly had very little sense) incurred universal contempt by riding through London in the crucial days of 1471, clad only in an old blue gown (Myers 1959: 5); on the other hand, his successful rival, Edward, was deeply concerned with the projection of his persona. He, of course, dressed magnificently (Nicolas 1830: 115–70); but he also went much further and (like a modern film star or pop idol) manipulated his body as an instrument of publicity:

> He was easy of access to his friends and to others, even the least notable. Frequently he called to his side complete strangers, when he thought that they had come with the intention of addressing or beholding him more closely. He was wont to show himself to those who wished to watch him, and he seized any opportunity that the occasion offered of revealing his fine stature more protractedly and more evidently to on-lookers ... (cited in Lander 1965: 226)[1]

No Tudor could have done better!

But, of course, the symbolic role of the king's person did not stop with his own physical body. Instead, his person was multiplied by various means, of which the most obvious is artistic representation. From the earliest times royal portraits – those symbols of a symbol – had an important part to play. This is shown clearly enough by the iconography of the great seal. The seal itself took the same basic form from the Conquest to the end of the Middle Ages (and, indeed, to the present day). On the one side, there was an image of the king enthroned in majesty, full-face, and equipped with the emblems of royalty; on the other, an image of the king armed and on horseback. The first showed the king as judge; the second, as warrior–defender of his people. The whole was therefore an illustration of the versicle: 'Lo! to fight and to judge are the office of a king.' In other words, it was a double portrayal of the king's person that was used as the symbol of monarchy on its most solemn formal instrument. But the images were entirely unindividualized: only the king's name in the inscription of the seal marked it as his, rather than that of any other king (Piper 1973: 29–31). Fundamentally, then, it would be wrong to oppose such mediaeval representations of the king's person to the material symbolism of the office. Rather, perhaps, we should see these 'portraits' as simple lay figures on which to hang the symbols of crown, sceptre, and orb. Only, in fact, with the new technical resources of Renaissance art does the balance alter, and personality displace symbolism, or better, become a symbol in its own right.

As far as the great seal itself was concerned, the change did not occur until 1542 (Piper 1973: 29–31), but in other areas the shift was considerably earlier. Among the most notable of these was the coinage, which experienced extensive remodelling under Henry VII (1485–1509). His testoons (one shilling pieces) and groats (four-penny pieces) bear a recognizable profile, which is closely akin to the one presented by Pietro Torrigiano's polychromatic bust. The impression – like that made by the strictly comparable Roman imperial coinage – is of a slightly heightened version of reality (Chrimes 1972: 334–5; Mackie 1952: 604; Grant 1960: 238–41). There exists also one realistic oil painting of Henry (probably by Michael Sittow), but, in comparison with the coinage bust, it is a modest, even understated, affair. Things (as might be expected) went much further under Henry VIII (1509–47): in part, because of the flamboyance of the King's character; and in part because Henry found an image-maker of genius in Holbein. The most grandiose and most official of his portraits of Henry was the dynastic mural in the Privy Chamber at Whitehall. In it, the King appeared with none of the formal insignia of royalty; instead, the painter took the essentials of Henry the man – huge, broad-shouldered, and thrusting – and turned them into a supremely powerful and effective image, that, even in the inferior copies which are all that survive of the complete painting, browbeats the spectator as ruthlessly as the King's fleshly presence must have done. The details of colour and texture were of course masterly, but what mattered was the overall shape: the massive trapezium of the King's body set on the splayed columns of legs (cf. Strong 1967). Like similar representations of Marx, or Lenin, or Mao, this brilliantly simplified version of Henry's physical traits has become an independent symbol – in his case, of the whole Tudor monarchy.

The symbolic (rather than merely representational) nature of all portraits of the sovereign is driven home by the way in which they were treated. While they were never worshipped like the images of the ancient Roman emperors,[2] they were nevertheless accorded a profound respect. This fact, of course, played into the hands of the Roman Catholic apologists who sought to defend the use of images in Christian worship; consequently, they gave it much prominence. As early as 1538, the conservative Vicar of Ticehurst in Kent held up a 'King Harry groat'; pointed to the King's image on it, and said: 'How darest thou spit upon this face? Thou darest not do it. But thou wilt spit upon the image [in Church] ... then thou spittest upon God' (cited in Elton 1972: 22). Some thirty years later, the same argument was employed against the iconoclasts by Nicholas Sanders in his *Treatise of the Images of Christ and his Saints*: 'Break if you dare [he challenged his opponents] the image of the Queen's Majesty, or the Arms of the Realm ...' (cited in Strong 1963: 38).[3]

At the other end of the political spectrum, the government itself was fully alive to the importance of the images of royalty. Under Elizabeth, indeed, it actually made some attempt to ensure that the portraits of the Queen which poured out of artists' studios 'expressed the natural representation of her majesty's person, favour, [and] grace' (Hughes and Larkin, 1964–9: II, no. 56, and cf. Strong 1963: 4ff.). However, despite all the reverence and concern for the royal portraits, such representations had a fairly narrow range of functions. The images used in formal contexts (i.e. on the great seal, coins, etc.) served both as symbols of authenticity and instruments of propaganda; in straightforward royal portraits, on the other hand, propaganda ruled supreme. A few lesser purposes should perhaps be added – for example, labelling. This is seen at its clearest in Trinity College Cambridge which is stamped as Henry VIII's foundation by the appearance of his statue over the great gate (Royal Commission on the Historical Monuments of England 1959: II, pl. 255). Lastly, there were special meanings that depended on the highly particular context in which the symbol appeared: here, the obvious example is the use of an image of the late sovereign in his own funeral ceremonies (Kantorowicz 1957: 411–12, etc.). But that exhausts the list of symbolic significances.

So far, then, even the symbolism of the royal body has yielded few instruments of government, as opposed to means for influencing opinion. But the king's person could also be represented in a quite different fashion from any that has yet been mentioned. In his discussion of the profound difference (as he claimed) between the respect paid to royal as opposed to sacred images, the reformer Thomas Bilson made the following comment:

> The reverence given to the officers, arms, or images, which Princes send to be set up, unto themselves, is accepted as rendered to their own persons when they cannot otherwise be present in the place to receive it but by a substitute or sign that shall represent their state. (Bilson 1545: 561)

Thus, as the indifferent listing of animate and inanimate – 'officers, arms, or images' – shows, the human representative of the sovereign could be seen as just as much a symbol of his master as a royal portrait. But, despite his symbolic role, such a representative retained his inherent capacity for independent action. That is, he could be both royal agent and royal symbol, with the former role being given unique strength and resonance by the latter. The remainder of this paper will be devoted to an analysis of this hybrid agent-symbol. The analysis will fall into three principal sections: first, the political functions of the royal person itself (conceived symbolically) will be discussed; second, the major group of personal representatives of the sovereign will be isolated, and their own political role analysed; and, third, the machinery – itself symbolic – by which these men were able to represent the king will be examined from the peak of its importance under the Tudors to its decline and disintegration under the Hanoverians.

I

We begin by looking more closely at the nature and function of the prime symbol, the king himself. The subject is embarrassingly rich, but for the present purpose a fairly simple scheme of classification can be used. On the one hand stand the king's actual powers – formal and informal – that are the subject matter of the political and constitutional historian. These will concern us only obliquely. On the other hand lies our particular province: the semi-mystical aspects of kingship. From the very beginning the institution had been sacred, and its English branch was no exception. The king's other-worldly status was firmly enunciated by his coronation: he was anointed with oil and chrism 'with the which Thou [i.e. God] anointest priests, kings and prophets' (Rymer *et al.* 1816–89: II, p. 35); he made an offering of the sacred elements – bread and wine – 'after the example of Melchisedech' (Rymer *et al.* 1816–89: II, p. 35), who was, simultaneously, 'king of Salem ... and priest of the most high God' (Gen. 15: 18); and, finally, each portion of the regalia – the crown, the sword, the rod, etc. – was blessed, and each was invested with a particular mystic significance (Rymer, 1816–89: II, pp. 34–5). Moreover, the sacrosanctity thus ratified through coronation coloured, and coloured deeply, the whole character of the monarchy. Two points stand out. First, like any other holy man, the king could work miracles – or rather, two particular miracles. In common with his brother the king of France, he 'touched for the king's evil'. That is, he cured (as was supposed) scrofula by the laying on of hands (cf. Bloch 1924). And, as well, his touch endowed rings of gold and silver – called cramp rings – with a protective power against epilepsy and other muscular spasms (Crawfurd 1917: 165ff; Thomas 1973: 235–6). Second, again like any other sacred figure, the king was possessed of an aura or 'mana'. This sounds highly metaphysical, but there is explicit contemporary evidence on the point. Somewhere about 1540, John Hales wrote an unprinted treatise called an *Oration in Commendation of the Laws* ... (BL, Harleian MS 4990). In the dedication he set out the problems which many men (clearly including the author) had in bringing themselves face-to-face with Henry VIII:

> Albeit the King's majesty [he began] be a Prince of so fatherly love
> toward his subjects that he forbiddeth none of them to come to his
> presence at time and place meet ... yet there ought to be in men a cer-
> tain reverence mixt with gentle fear to pull them back again, remem-
> bering that they have not to do with man but with a more excellent
> and divine estate.   (BL Harleian MS 4990, fo. I)

However, this reserve was not merely a matter of courtesy: it was often reinforced by an involuntary reaction:

> Certes, in some men nature hath wrought ... that although they have
> before prepared themselves both earnestly and reverently to speak to
> their ruler and head; yet they have been, when they should have most
> drawn courage to them, so astonished and abashed, so trembling and
> quaking, utterly in a manner muet [i.e. dumb], as if they had been
> taken with the palsy, such is the majesty of a prince.   (BL Harleian
> MS 4990, fos. I–IV)

There is, of course, a measure of courtly exaggeration about all this, but,
once that is discarded, a core of solid truth remains. Hales is describing the
psychological effects of confrontation with the numinous power which
clung to the 'excellent and divine estate' of monarchy like a tangible and terrifying cloak. Some 130 years later, the same phenomenon was analysed
with noble eloquence by Robert South in his sermon on 'the peculiar care
and concern of providence for the protection and defence of kings':

> God saves and delivers sovereign princes by imprinting a certain awe
> and dread of their persons and authority upon the minds of their sub-
> jects ... And this is that property which in kings we call majesty, and
> which, no doubt, is a kind of shadow or portraiture of the divine
> authority drawn upon the looks and persons of princes which makes
> them commanders of men's fears, and thereby capable of governing
> them in all their concerns. *Non fero fulgur oculorum tuorum* [I cannot
> bear the lightning of your eyes] is the language of every subject's heart,
> struck with the aweful aspect of a resolute and magnanimous prince.
> There is a majesty in his countenance that puts lightning into his looks
> and thunder into his words ...   (South 1843: II, pp. 554)

English kingship, therefore, like other sacred monarchies, had a double face:
the beneficent (the king as healer), and the terrifying (fear of the royal presence). Or, in Frazer's own words: the king's 'magical virtue is in the strictest
sense of the word contagious: his divinity is a fire, which, under proper
restraints, confers endless blessings, but, if rashly touched or allowed to
break bounds, burns and destroys what it touches' (Frazer 1963: p. 267).
But we need hardly turn to a twentieth-century anthropologist: a seventeenth-century divine, Richard Burney, hailed Charles II's Restoration with
a series of ecstatic sermons in which he spelled out much the same idea:

God has also seated the latitude of the power of kings, or the highest style of their prerogative in a *maledicere* [power of cursing] and a *benedicere* [power of blessing] ... His Majesty as it were enters into God's mightiness, in as much that the King like unto God, *solus rex inter mortales possit maledicere* [only the king among mortals should curse] ... This *maledicere* in a king is no pravity of nature, but equal, like God's justice, to a benediction, in that it preserves the sincere from that which is corrupt. His Majesty's wrath is potent like the lightning to melt the sword in the scabbard, causes the spirit of the ill-affected to vacillate, till he falls cursed from the tree; every man partakes of His Majesty's *benedicere* that keeps his soul from having any cursing thoughts of the King.   (Burney 1660: pp. 7–9)

Numinous powers on such a scale had necessarily far-reaching consequences. First (as we have already mentioned) they were much used in royal propaganda. In the Middle Ages, for example, their supernatural attributes – as epitomised by touching for the king's evil – had provided the kings of England and France with a crucial weapon in their battle with the overweening pretentions of the papacy (Bloch 1924). By the later Middle Ages that particular battle had been won, but the charismatic aspects of kingship lost none of their importance. Revolutions or intended revolutions sought legitimacy by association with the divine: Henry IV's shaky title was reinforced by anointing him with an opportunely re-discovered vial of oil that had been given by the Virgin to St Thomas of Canterbury (Murray 1954: 179–80); Henry VII (another dubious usurper) elaborated both the ceremony of touching for the king's evil and that of the hallowing of cramp rings (Crawfurd 1917); during the royalist reaction of Charles II's reign the king's powers of healing were made more freely available than ever before; while James II, on the eve of absolutism, seems to have thought of reviving the blessing of cramp rings which had been abandoned at Elizabeth I's accession (Thomas 1973: 228, 231, 236). But there is (as we have also insisted) much more to the sacred aspects of monarchy than the shaping of public opinion: indeed, as far as the king himself was concerned, his semi-divinity underpinned some of his most important everyday political functions.

The reasons for this lay partly in the nature of the royal administration. England had had for some two or three centuries a small, though well-organized, bureaucracy. There were departments of state – the Chancery, the Exchequer, the common law courts – with defined areas of responsibility, salaried personnel, and clear ladders of promotion. But that did not make England a bureaucratic state; the bureaucracy alone could not rule. For one thing, it was too small – numbering a few hundred at most (cf. Aylmer 1961: 470ff.); for another, it was a purely central bureaucracy: there were scarcely any full-time salaried appointments at local level, save for the special case of the customs administration. Instead, county government was in the hands of amateurs, of the country gentlemen who sat on the various royal commissions – of the peace, of sewers, etc. – through which the shires were run. Though it is easy to exaggerate the truculence of these men, they did stand in a quite different relationship with the Crown from feed servants. Their cooperation and even acquiescence could never be taken for granted; rather, they had to be won by conciliation, management, and patronage. On purely institutional grounds, therefore, the formal instruments of administration were inadequate.

But the government of England was also bedevilled by another, more fundamental, issue: the fact that the fifteenth and even the sixteenth centuries had a very undeveloped concept of delegation. The common attitude was summarized by Hugh Latimer in his *Fourth Sermon on the Lord's Prayer*: 'there be some men that say "When the King's majesty himself commandeth me to do so-and-so; then I will do it, not afore"' (cited in Loades 1970: 68–9). The preacher's reply was devastating: such an assertion was 'wicked ... and damnable; for we may not be so excused. Scripture is plain in it, and sheweth that we ought to obey his officers, having authority from the King, as well as the King himself' (cited in Loades 1970: 68–9). In the long term, the sustained Tudor propaganda campaign on obedience (of which Latimer's sermon is a distinguished product) went far towards a solution of the problem of delegated authority. But in the short term (which is what matters in day-to-day politics) the difficulty remained: too many would have joined with the men of Hoddesdon in Hertfordshire, who (in 1534) boasted after their riotous attack on a party of courtiers that

> the Marquis of Exeter was put to the worse in this town; yea, and if the best man within this realm, under the King, being the King's servant or other, do any displeasure to any of this town, he shall be set fast by the feet. (PRO SP 2/Q, no. 15 (*LP* VII, 1120))

Almost all, then, would obey the king in person; but many would obey no other.

Fifteenth- and sixteenth-century government thus faced two essential problems: first, the feed officers on whose service it could depend were insufficient for their manifold tasks, both numerically and in their geographical distribution; and, second, the measure of obedience that would be given to any royal official or to any written royal command was dangerously unpredictable. Neither problem was insoluble: indeed, both tended to yield readily enough to a direct application of the royal presence. Thus 1464 saw an extensive breakdown in public order, which neither the local administration nor royal letters could contain – let alone suppress. Edward IV's reaction was swift: between January and May he rode from Coventry to Worcester, from Worcester to Gloucester, then across country to Cambridge, and finally south to Maidstone in Kent, sitting himself as Chief

Justice in all these places (Lander 1969: 102). Again, three years later, Edward travelled to the north Midlands to settle in person a series of violent disputes between Lord Grey of Codnor and the Vernons (Lander 1969: 102). Nothing shows more clearly than these examples (which could easily be multiplied) the continued dependence of English government on the immediate exercise of the king's authority, on the peculiar royal *numen* that made his command substantively different from any other.

But in a sense the use of the royal presence was no solution at all. Problems happen simultaneously – not sequentially – and no king, however fast he rides, can be in two places at once. What was needed was some device for delegating the special kingly power. One obvious method was through blood relationship. Members of the royal family were thought to share to some extent in the monarch's semi-sacred authority (cf. Bush 1970: 37ff.). So Edward IV made his brother, Richard of Gloucester, virtual viceroy of the north; while in the late 1520s, the administration of the Welsh Marches was devolved onto the Council of the Princess Mary, and that of the north onto the Council of the Duke of Richmond, Henry VIII's bastard son. But the elevation of Princes of the Blood was not without risk. They were too powerful, too near in succession to the throne, for any king to chance too full a confidence in them. Moreover (setting that point aside), the royal family was simply too small: there were not enough of them to cope with the multiple problems of government. So other, more flexible instruments of delegation had to be found. It is possible that a whole range of methods was employed. If so most have left no trace in the record. Instead this is dominated by one class of royal symbol-agents: the servants of the king's Privy Chamber.

II

The Privy Chamber was one of the departments of the Royal Household. It was, in fact, of very recent institution. The mid-fifteenth-century household had been divided into two main departments, each with its own head officer. The hall and the offices (the kitchens, etc.), together with the financial machinery of the household, formed one department, usually called the Household (proper), under the Lord Steward; while the staff of the Chamber (the collective name for the royal apartments) formed the other under the Lord Chamberlain. The latter had a double responsibility: he was in charge of both public ceremonial and the king's private service. However, in the 1490s a new development occurred. The most private of the king's apartments – the Privy or Secret Chamber – began to acquire a staff of its own, under its own head officer, the Groom of the Stool. By 1520 the Privy Chamber's organization was fully developed, and it had secured an almost total independence from the Chamber. In effect, therefore, the household now consisted of three, not two, departments. The change was recognized and ratified by the Eltham Ordinances of 1526, which fall into three sections – Household, Chamber, and Privy Chamber – corresponding to the three departments of the reformed and reconstituted household. The functions of the Household proper remained unaltered, but the Chamber retained only public ceremonial. Its other former responsibility of the king's private service had been transferred definitively to the Privy Chamber (Starkey 1973: 13–273).

Such, in brief outline, was the institutional position of the men whose activities we are about to study.

The Privy Chamber's ability to represent the king's person took many different forms. At the simplest, its members could embody, on one particular issue, that absolute royal will that would not brook nay. Thus, in the autumn of 1532, Anne Boleyn, not Queen Catherine of Aragon, was going to accompany Henry VIII on his state visit to France as virtual royal consort. To underscore the fact, Henry asked Catherine to lend Anne her jewels. The Queen refused pointblank, unless 'le roi le lui envoyait expressement demander'. This the King did, and secured compliance, 'par un de sa chambre' (PRO PRO 31/18/2/1 (*LP*, V, 1377)).[4] Other examples can easily be given. Ordinarily, the Court of Augmentations was itself responsible for the proper disposal of the ex-monastic lands (Elton 1960: 141). However, its usual processes could be short-circuited by direct royal command, which on several occasions was transmitted by the Privy Chamber. For instance, in March 1540 Richard Browne, a Page of the King's Chamber, was granted a lease of the site of Sallam Monastery in Norfolk, free of any fine, by the king's commandment, as related by William Sherington, Page of the Wardrobe of the Robes and messenger of Anthony Denny, Chief Gentleman of the Privy Chamber (*LP* XV, 436/40); in July of that year Benedict Killegrew got a lease without fine or increment, for which the king's command was carried by Denny in person (*LP* XV, 942/121); and, finally, in January 1546 a major gift to Sir Thomas Moyle was countersigned by the Chancellor of Augmentations 'upon the report of your Majesty's pleasure declared to him by Sir William Herbert', Gentleman of the Privy Chamber (*LP* XXI, i, 148/24). The striking thing is, of course, that in all these cases the mere word of a Gentleman of the Privy Chamber was sufficient evidence in itself for the king's will, without any other form of authentication whatever.

So much for simple messages. On the other hand, the Privy Chamber's representation of the king could be far less specific. Rather than transmitting a straightforward command, the Gentlemen of the Privy Chamber would carry instead the indefinable charisma of monarchy. The point emerges most clearly in their military role. However, before that can be discussed, the king's own position as war leader must be sketched in. This is well expressed by a speech put into Henry VIII's mouth by Polydore Vergil. The occasion was a debate between the King and the Council about the advisability of Henry's taking personal command of the expedition to France of 1513. The Council was opposed to the idea, pointing out both the danger to the royal person and the need for the king's presence within the realm. But Henry overrode them, recalling grandly

> the many triumphs over their enemies won by his ancestors when they were leading their armies in person, and, on the contrary, the losses sustained many times by the English state when battles had been fought without the King's presence. (Vergil 1950: 197)

Henry (or better, Polydore) was not necessarily making great claims for the quality of royal generalship;[5] rather he was talking of the psychological effect of the king's presence on the troops.

But, in fact, Henry led his forces in person comparatively infrequently – certainly far less often than either Francis I or Charles V. He had, therefore, to delegate the command of his armies. In this there was a clear division of function. The supreme command in the modern sense tended to fall on a prominent nobleman – usually the Duke of Norfolk or the Duke of Suffolk. The former was a good general; the latter was probably even less competent than Henry himself. At the top level, then, the Privy Chamber had no part to play; instead, the essential contribution of its members came at the second rank of commanders. Their activities as such are best displayed in the Scottish campaign of 1523.

The armies moved forward in the late spring. The general in command was Thomas Howard, then Earl of Surrey, but soon to become third Duke of Norfolk. Under him were the Marquis of Dorset, Sir William Compton, and Sir William Kingston. The status of Compton and Kingston is clear: the first was Groom of the Stool and head of the Privy Chamber (Starkey 1973: 69, 73–5), the second was Knight of the Body in the Privy Chamber[6] (Starkey 1973: 112–14). Dorset's position, though, is more interesting. He was at that date the only marquis in England, and was also closely tied to the royal family as the son of Edward IV's stepson. These would seem qualifications enough for his post of deputy-commander, but Henry VIII appears to have felt that more was needed. Soon after his arrival in the north, Dorset wrote to the King in somewhat extravagant terms:

> Specially and most humbly thanking your Highness for that it liked the same at my departing from your Grace to admit me as one of your Privy Chamber, which was more to my comfort than if your Grace had given me either fee, land, gold, or silver. (B.L. Cotton MS, Caligula BVI, fo. 325 (*LP* III, ii, 2955))

The exact reasons for Dorset's promotion to the Privy Chamber are not stated, but the timing suggests very strongly that his impending military duties and his household appointment were closely linked – perhaps, indeed, that the latter was considered a necessary, or at the least, very desirable qualification for the former.

Thus all the original deputy-commanders of the Scottish expedition were members of the Privy Chamber. While they were on active service we know nothing of their effect, but their departure brought a swift and revealing reaction. Compton spent only a short time in the north: according to Polydore, he was summoned back to court only 'a few days' after setting out (Vergil 1950: 197). This would seem to be an exaggeration, but certainly he was home by late July (*LP* III, ii, 3209). Dorset and Kingston must have returned about the same time, and Surrey was left to battle on alone. Thereafter his letters become increasingly depressed: on 24 September he sent a letter to Wolsey regretting that he no longer had the company of Dorset, Compton, Kingston, etc. (*LP* III, ii, 3360); on 1 October he wrote a formal plea for his discharge – he felt himself decayed in body as well as worn out in purse by the last four years in which he had been continually in the wars (*LP* III, ii, 3384); then, eight days later, there came the full out-burst, which culminated in the following passage:

> Most humbly beseeching your Grace [i.e. Wolsey] to help that some noblemen and gentlemen of the King's house and the south parts may be sent hither though they bring no great numbers with them. God knoweth, if the poorest gentleman in the King's house were here, and I at London and were advertised of these news, I would not fail to kneel upon my knees before the King's Grace to have licence to come hither in post to be at the day of battle.   (Ellis 1824–46: I, pp. 223–7 (*LP* III, ii, 3405))

Thus loneliness and a sense of desertion had wrung from Surrey an explicit statement of the role of the royal body servants (i.e. the 'noblemen and gen-tlemen of the King's house') in the English army. First, the fact that their position was symbolic (rather than military in a simple sense) is made clear by the earl's plea that they should be sent even 'though they bring no great numbers with them'. And, second, one of their functions as a symbol – their effect on recruitment – is illustrated vividly by Howard's description of his hypothetical reaction to their appearance at the front had he been in London. However, clear though it is, Surrey's account has its limitations: the special role of the Privy Chamber (in comparison with the other servants of the Royal Household) is not spelled out; nor is the nature of the Gentlemen's symbolic status, or anything like the full range of their symbolic functions. The first omission is, of course, covered by events: as we have seen, Surrey's original deputy-commanders were all Gentlemen of the Privy Chamber, while, of the contingent sent in prompt response to his letter of 8 October, the three most prominent – the Marquis of Dorset, Sir Nicholas Carew, and Sir Francis Bryan – were again members of the Privy Chamber (*LP* III, ii, 3434). But the broader questions of symbolism can, unfortunately, only be answered inferentially. Nevertheless, the issue hardly seems in doubt: the Privy Chamber obviously acted as symbolic representations of the king himself, and its members' military role, like his, was charismatic: their very presence raised the morale of the troops, and, as Surrey's depression at their absence shows, that of their commanders as well.

So far, we have discussed only partial representations of the king: either the absolute sovereign command, or the charismatic presence. However, the Privy Chamber could also combine the two and stand, in certain circumstances, as a full royal *alter ego*. This is shown most clearly in the one aspect of the Gentlemen's symbolic role that had standing at law. Arrest without warrant or commission had been declared illegal in 37 Henry VI (1458–9), except in the king's own presence and by command of his own mouth (Pickthorn 1934: I, p. 51 n. 1). But when the Earl of Northumberland and Walter Walsh, Groom of the Privy Chamber, were sent to arrest Cardinal Wolsey in November 1530, they were given (for some reason) strict orders not to show their commission. Northumberland tried to arrest Wolsey, but the Cardinal refused to submit until he had seen the Earl's warrant. An altercation began and continued for some little time; then Wolsey caught sight of Walsh and his attitude changed completely. He turned to him and said:

> I am content to yield unto you ... [because] you are a sufficient commission yourself ... in as much as ye be one of the King's Privy Chamber, for the worst person there is a sufficient warrant to arrest the greatest peer of this realm, by the King's only commandment without any commission.   (Sylvester and Harding 1962: 160)

The only explanation for Wolsey's reaction is that he felt that Walsh's presence fulfilled – albeit vicariously – the conditions which the fifteenth-century judges had laid down for arrest without warrant. In other words, that, as one of the Privy Chamber, Walsh was able to represent the very person of the king in both presence and command.

This full representation of monarchy also manifested itself in the diplomacy of the early sixteenth century. At this time, the machinery of foreign relations was undergoing profound change. Much of the revolution has been well studied (cf. Mattingly 1955), but one important aspect stands in conspicuous neglect. This is the set of conventions that I have labelled 'chamber diplomacy'. Its nature can best be understood by an examination of the instructions given to Sir Richard Wingfield, the senior of the four Knights of the Body in the Privy Chamber, when he was sent as resident ambassador to the court of Francis I in February 1520. In his first audience with the French king, Wingfield was ordered to explain that, although Henry

> hath been oftentimes plentiously advertized [of Francis I's good and prosperous state etc.], as well by the French King's ambassador and others his familiar gentlemen for the time being making their abode

within the King's realm, as also by Sir Thomas Boleyn [the previous English ambassador to France] ... yet as well for his further consolation as for to nourish and firmly entertain the said mutual amity, love, and intelligence ... [Henry had sent one] of his right trusty and near familiars, not only to salute and visit him for the said purpose, but also to notify and declare unto him the King's entire love and affection towards him, to thintent that by renovelling of ambassadors new testimonies may be found ... of the perseverance of fraternal love on both parts.   (PRO SP 1/19, fo. 200 (*LP* III, i, 629))

Two assumptions underlie all this: first, that the kingdom was absorbed by the king – that is, that amicable relations between England and France (say) depended only on Henry VIII's being on good terms with his 'good brother' Francis I; and, second, that the best way for the two kings to preserve their friendship was to meet and embrace each other frequently. But of course that was rarely possible. The instructions, then, are grappling with the problem of providing a substitute for these personal meetings. And the one they put forward is the exchange of the kings' 'trusty and near familiars' as ambassadors. Such ambassadors were negotiators only in part; much more, they were symbols of the fact that, circumstances permitting, their kings would themselves have come in their stead. However, the instructions are unclear about the precise status of the 'familiars'. But the point is not really in doubt. To prescribe that ambassadors should be the king's 'right trusty and near familiars' was virtually the same as saying that they should be of the Privy Chamber. And so events proved. For example, between 1520 and 1526 the following were ambassadors to France: Sir Richard Wingfield, Knight of the Body in the Privy Chamber, Sir Richard Jerningham, also Knight of the Body in the Privy Chamber, William Fitzwilliam, who did not belong to the department, Sir Nicholas Carew, Gentleman of the Privy Chamber, and Sir Thomas Cheyney, Gentleman of the Privy Chamber. Thus four out of five ambassadors were of the Privy Chamber, while the one exception – Fitzwilliam – found himself almost forcibly assimilated to the rank by Francis I (BL Cottonian MS Caligula D, VIII, fos. 21–4 (*LP* III, i, 1202)). But there is no need to rely on the weight of numbers alone: explicit evidence of the importance attached to Privy Chamber office as an ambassadorial qualification is also available. It is supplied by the corrected draft of the instructions given to Jerningham when he was sent to Francis I in August 1520. The first version was worded thus: the ambassador was to thank the French king for having sent

as well by letter of his own hand as by sundry of his noblemen and other his familiar servitors to visit him [i.e. Henry VIII] with comfortable words and pleasant messages ... and for a *reciproque* ... his Highness ... hath sent [him], Sir Richard Jerningham ... to be resident [ambassador in France].

The following alterations were then made: 'his noblemen and other' was crossed out, and the phrase made to run 'by sundry of his familiar servitors of his Privy Chamber'; while after Jerningham's name was inserted the following description: 'being of his Secret and Privy Chamber'. The whole now read like this: that Francis was to be thanked for having sent

> as well by letters of his own hand as by sundry of his familiar servitors of his Privy Chamber to visit him [i.e. Henry] with comfortable words and pleasant messages, and for a *reciproque* ... his Highness ... hath sent [him] Sir Richard Jerningham, being of his Secret and Privy Chamber ... (PRO SP 1/21, fos. 20–7 (*LP* III, i, 936))

Thus the vagueness of the first draft was replaced by a tight institutional precision that highlights the significance of the French *chambre* (the equivalent of the Privy Chamber) and the English Privy Chamber itself: whoever the king willed could act as ambassador, but only the personnel of these two departments could represent the royal person, as it were, by definition.

This account of the representative functions of the Privy Chamber could be extended to cover almost all aspects of sixteenth-century government – especially the crucial area of local government. However, there would be problems. In these other fields there is plenty of evidence of what the Privy Chamber did, but very little of how contemporaries reacted to it. In other words, the symbolic nature of the Gentlemen's role, which can be firmly established for their activities in the army, etc., has to be inferred; it cannot be proved. This being so, there seems very little point in continuing a study that must inevitably lose all analytical quality and degenerate instead into a mere census of offices held and missions accomplished. It would be better, in fact, to turn straight away to the mechanics of Privy Chamber symbolism: that is, to a discussion of the circumstances which enabled its members to represent the king.

III

Clearly, everything depended on the Privy Chamber's place within the Royal Household. This has already been sketched in broad outline; it must now be described more carefully.

The Eltham Ordinances of 1526 gave the Privy Chamber the following personnel: six Gentlemen, two Gentlemen Ushers, four Grooms, a Barber, and a Page. As honorific head of the department stood a Nobleman, but its actual working chief remained the Groom of the Stool, who was also counted as one of the six Gentlemen. After 1526 there was very little structural change, apart from the fact that all ranks in the department showed a fairly steady tendency to increase in numbers: in 1526 the total establishment stood at 15; by 1532 it had risen to 24, and by 1539 to 28. But at that latter figure it stabilized (Starkey 1973: 155, 182–3).

The various offices had appeared at different times, *pari passu* with the department's changing social composition. Originally, under Henry VII, the department had been staffed only by the Groom of the Stool and a handful of other grooms and pages. All were drawn from the middle to lower gentry (Starkey 1973: 24–55). However, in September 1518 the office of Gentleman was created specifically to accommodate men of the best families. Its first occupants were drawn from the highest reaches of the gentry, from the point at which that class merged almost imperceptibly into the nobility (Starkey 1973: 80–111). And to underscore the social elevation of the department, within the year the Earl of Devon (the first noble of the blood royal) was appointed to the Privy Chamber as well (Starkey 1973: 129–31). Such a standard could hardly be maintained consistently, but only a very few of the future recruits to the post of Gentleman were of less than decent gentry status.

Before the creation of the office of Gentleman (soon to be followed by that of Gentleman Usher (Starkey, 1973: 116–17)) there could have been relatively little differentiation of function within the department – apart, of course, from the peculiar duties of the Groom of the Stool which will be discussed shortly. But after 1518–19 the increasingly elaborate hierarchy of office allowed for full specialization. Overall, there was a broad functional division between the Gentlemen and the rest (which, of course, corresponded to a social distinction as well). The rest consisted of the Barber, who was simply the king's barber; the Page, who was a page in the modern sense of the word – i.e. a favoured young boy; the Grooms, who were (formally at least) the menial servants of the departments; and the Gentlemen Ushers, who were both masters of ceremonies, and in immediate command of the other lesser servants. It was, that is, in the hands of the upper servants of the department that the king's body service in the narrow sense was concentrated. The Gentlemen dressed and undressed the king; waited on him at table; brought him food or drink or anything else he required between meals; arranged the king's bedtime drink; and, finally, took turns to guard over their master's slumbers by sleeping on a pallet mattress on the floor of the Privy Chamber (Starkey 1973: 168–70). As well as these formal duties, the Gentlemen also served as the king's usual companions in his sports and pastimes: with them he jousted and masked, hunted and hawked, played tennis or cards or even shuffleboard. Henry also found among them many who could share his more cultivated tastes: some were poets and musicians, some builders and gardeners. In one or two cases, the similarity between the King and his Gentlemen went as far as close physical resemblance. The Gentlemen were, in short, more than the king's servants: they were the nearest thing he had to friends (Starkey 1969: ch. II).

The Groom of the Stool, in his capacity as one of the Gentlemen, shared in all their duties and avocations, but, in addition, he had many important responsibilities that were his alone. These fell into two distinct categories. The first consisted of his original tasks. Their nature is implicit in his title. The earliest clear reference to the office appears in a signet warrant to the Great Wardrobe of 15 November 1497. This ordered the Keeper of the Wardrobe to supply to 'Hugh Denys, Groom of our Stool ... first a stool of timber covered with black velvet and fringed with silk. Item a cushion with two pewter basins and four broad yards of tawny cloth' (PRO E 101/413/II, fo. 37). Now though the purpose of these articles is not stated, they can only have been intended for the construction of a close-stool or commode. The Groom was therefore, beyond doubt, Groom of the royal close-stool. As such, he was responsible for the manufacture, maintenance, and transport of the stool (Starkey 1973: 251–2); and, above all, for attendance on the king when he made use of it. For example, in 1528 Thomas Heneage, who was acting as assistant to Henry Norris, the Groom proper, wrote to Wolsey to apologize for not having come to see him, but (he explained) 'there is none here but Master Norris and I to give attendance upon the King's Highness when he goeth to make water in his bed chamber' (PRO SP 1/47, fos. 56–7 (*LP* IV, ii, 4005)). Again, in 1539, Heneage (by this time Groom himself) reported to Cromwell that Henry had felt the beginnings of a cold; his physicians had given him a pill and a glyster (i.e. an enema), and the King had gone to bed early. He then (so Heneage continued) 'slept unto two of the clock in the morning and then his Grace rose to go to the stool, which, by working of the pills and glyster that his Highness had taken before, had a very fair siege' (PRO SP 1/153, fo. 117 (*LP*, XIV, ii, 153)).

The Groom's intimate connection with the close-stool received official recognition at Henry VIII's death: in the inventory of the late king's goods, his numerous and lavish collection of close-stools (many covered in embroidered velvet, stuffed with swan's down, and studded with gilt nails) were bracketed together with the marginal annotation that

> all which parcels the said accountant (i.e. Sir Anthony Denny) claimeth to have by virtue of his said office of the Groomship of the Stool at the death of the late King.
> which parcels we the said commissioners do allow to the said Sir Anthony as pertaining to his said office.   (PRO E 101/427/2)

The charge of the close-stool and attendance on the king when he used it were, no doubt, the sum total of the duties of the pre-Tudor Groom of the Stool. However, with the development of the Privy Chamber and his acquisition of the leading role in it,[7] the Groom had been saddled with his second and correspondingly more varied class of functions. First, the Groom was the sole servant of the royal bedchamber and the other most private rooms: this again is made absolutely clear by the Eltham

Ordinances of 1526, which provided that Henry Norris should occupy the place of Sir William Compton 'not only giving his attendance as Groom of the King's Stool but also in his bedchamber and other privy places as shall stand with his pleasure.' Into the bedchamber and other such rooms, none of the other servants of the Privy Chamber were 'to presume to enter or follow his Grace', save by the king's specific command. At night, the Groom slept on a pallet mattress at the foot of the king's bed (Starkey 1973: 130, 264–5).

Second – and by natural extension of the first – the Groom was the king's invariable attendant wherever he went: at the beginning of the reign, when Henry rode *incognito* in a joust, his only companion was the Groom, Sir William Compton (Hall 1809: 513); and at the end, in 1540, in one order of procession drawn up for the reception of Anne of Cleves, Heneage is shown completely out of precedence, riding immediately before the King himself (*LP* XV, 10).

Third, the Groom was the king's supremely confidential messenger: above all, he handled communications between the king and queen. Thus, after Katherine Howard's arrest, Cranmer reported that about 6 p.m. she fell into another pang of grief, exclaiming that at that hour the King used to send to know how she did by Mr Heneage (PRO SP 1/167, fos. 134–40 (*LP* XVI, 1325)). As well, the Groom seems to have acted as intermediary between Henry and his mistresses: early in the reign, Compton was suspected of carrying on an intrigue on his master's behalf with the Duke of Buckingham's sister (*LP* I, i, 474); while many years later, Mrs Amadas, the wife of the Master of the Jewels, alleged that Norris was bawd between the king and Ann Boleyn (*LP* VI, 923).

Fourth, the Groom regulated access to the king: in 1530 a delegation from Oxford, headed by the vice-chancellor, arrived at Court to sue for the continuance of Cardinal College. But, 'by reason of the great business that the King had and scarcity of friends', the academics were kept kicking their heels about the palace for eleven days; then Norris took pity on them, and they were with the king in a few hours (PRO SP 1/57, fos. 300–1 (*LP* IV, iii, 6539)). Conversely, the Groom could deny the presence if he wished (e.g. PRO SP 3/6, fo. 71 (*LP* VI, 1352)).

Fifth, all the preceding meant that the Groom had to be permanently near the king: consequently his lodgings at court were directly under the Privy Chamber, to which they were linked by a private staircase (Starkey 1973: 265–7).

Sixth, and finally, the Groom had become a major administrative officer: he was in charge of such of the king's jewels and plate as were in daily use; of his linen, and of the furnishings and equipment of the private apartments in general. Above all, he was *ex officio* Keeper of the Privy Purse, and had, as well, important secretarial functions (Starkey 1973: 254–62, 309–56, 357–413).

The Groom's duties thus ranged from the most intimate physical attendance on the person of the sovereign to the management of the large and elaborate administrative machine on which depended the comfort of the king's daily life. Almost necessarily, therefore, the Groom occupied a special place in the royal regard. True, paucity of evidence means that we know nothing of Henry VII's relationship with his Groom, Hugh Denys, but all Henry VIII's Grooms (with the possible exception of Thomas Heneage) were prime favourites. First came Compton: in 1510 the Spanish ambassador described him as the *privado* or favourite (*LP* I, i, 474), and a year later, in 1511, the French ambassador insisted that he enjoyed more 'crédict' with Henry than anyone else (PRO PRO 31/3/1 (*LP* I, i, 734)). Compton's successor, Henry Norris, was 'du roy le mieulx aimé' (Crapelet 1835: 184); while of Anthony Denny, the last Groom of the reign, Leland wrote that the whole Court bore testimony to his 'gratia flagrans' (Leland 1770: V, pp. 151–2).

It would now probably be as well to pick out the main threads in this account of the Privy Chamber. It consisted of a smallish group of men who had many features in common: generally, they came from good families; were similar in tastes and disposition to the king, and stood high in his regard; above all, however, they enjoyed an institutionally defined and exclusive intimacy with their sovereign as his body servants. All this applies equally to the Groom of the Stool, the head of the Privy Chamber, save that both his favour and his intimacy with Henry were correspondingly greater than the other Gentlemen's. Obviously, each one of these points played a part in the representative capacity of the Privy Chamber. The fact that they were in frequent and friendly contact with the king made it likely that he would employ them in his business; while the fact that they were of good family made such employment acceptable to the subject. But other members of the Court shared in these sorts of qualities: what was peculiar to the Privy Chamber, what was theirs alone, was physical intimacy with the king. Only they were his body servants. On this the Eltham Ordinances are unequivocal. They ordered absolutely that 'no person of what estate, degree, or condition so ever he be' who was not of the staff of the Privy Chamber should 'from henceforth presume ... to come or repair into the King's Privy Chamber', except by the king's specific command (Bodl., Laudian MS Miscellaneous 597, fo. 24 (*HO* 154)). And if none but the Privy Chamber was even allowed into the apartment, much less could any wait on the king's person. Similarly, as we have seen, the supremely intimate personal services of the bedchamber were the exclusive prerogative of the Groom of the Stool, as distinct from the other Gentlemen. The essential point can thus be expressed as a formal syllogism. Privy Chamber office is defined (through the limitation of the *entrée* to the private apartments) in terms of the right to give intimate attendance on the king; but the ability to represent the king's person in its fulness is limited to the Privy Chamber; so representation itself must depend on intimacy. Intimacy, that is, is the vehicle through which the Privy Chamber symbolizes the king.

But the vehicle was itself a symbol, with two distinct sets of meanings: one sacred, the other profane. The first can best be understood by a glance at the practices of the late medieval Church. These were dominated by a profound literalism, which stressed the need for a material channel or intermediary for the transfer of divine virtue: thus the apostolic succession was a long chain of the laying-on of hands, going back to Christ himself; while every relic had acquired its powers, either by being part of the body of a saint or martyr, or by having been in contact with such a body. And, of course, the concept of a channel of grace was an awkward one: in practice it was much easier to assume that the object or action itself possessed magical properties (cf. Thomas 1973: 27–57). Naturally, the king's healing powers operated within this context: he cured scrofula, as we have seen, by actual touch – by the laying-on of hands; while, in the case of the second royal miracle, the position is set out fully in the Marian ritual. This described the moment of the consecration of the cramp rings as follows:

> the king's highness rubbeth the rings between his hands, saying: 'Sanctify, O Lord, these rings ... and consecrate them by the rubbing of our hands, which thou hast been pleased according to our ministry to sanctify by an external effusion of holy oil upon them.'   (Crawfurd 1917: 186)

The literalism is transparent: the king's hands had been anointed at his coronation and hence were holy; they then rubbed off their benediction onto the metal. Thus, though there is no formal contemporary evidence on the point, there can be little doubt that in the intimate physical contact of body service the royal charisma was felt to rub off onto the servant, who thereby became himself endowed with part of the royal virtue.

The secular symbolism of intimacy is more directly vouched for. In Sir John Harrington's *Metamorphoses of Ajax* (a 'jakes' = a privy), which was published in 1596 as a puff for its author's invention of a primitive water closet, there appears the following comment:

> it is a token of special kindness, to this day among the best men in France, to reduce a syllogism in Bocardo together. Insomuch as I have heard it seriously told, that a great magnifico of Venice, being ambassador in France, and hearing a noble person was come to speak with him, made him stay till he had untied his points [the equivalent of braces], and when he was new set on his stool sent for the nobleman to come to him at that time – as a very special favour.   (Harrington 1962: 91)

In other words, so Harrington claimed, 'reducing a syllogism in Bocardo together' was a well-understood social symbol or convention for the expression of mutual regard and confidence. True, the custom is described as French, and, by implication, as unknown and even ludicrous in England. But this last point needs careful qualification. The kind of contact that would appear to have become unthinkable between equals (for that is the situation Harrington posits) still remained possible between master and servant. Indeed, involvement in the business of evacuation was a usual feature of late-medieval body service. Thus John Russell in his *Book of Nurture* (*c*.1452) includes the following instructions in his account of 'the office of a chamberlain' (i.e. a bedchamber servant):

> See the privy-house for easement be fair, soot,[8] and clean;
> And that the boards thereupon be covered with cloth fair and green;
> And the hole himself, look there no board be seen;
> Thereon a fair cushion, the ordure no man to teen.[9]
> Look there be blanket, cotton, or linen to wipe the nether end,
> And ever he clepith,[10] wait rady and entende,[11]
> Basin and ewer, and on your shoulder a towel ...
>
> (Furnivall 1868 179)

Even this passage, however, suggests that the master relieved himself alone, only calling in the 'chamberlain' when he required to wash his hands. But royal etiquette was different. As we have seen, the early Tudor Groom of the Stool regularly attended the king when he made use of the stool, while as late as 1689 the groom (William III's great favourite, the Earl of Portland) was still charged with the duty. This is shown clearly by the Bedchamber Ordinances issued in that year, which stipulate that 'none of our Bed-Chamber whatsoever are to follow us into our secret or privy room, when we go to ease ourself, but only our Groom of the Stool' (BL Stowe MS 563, fos. 14[v]–15). Thus, *pace* Harrington, the intimacy of the privy survived in the English Court and was therefore as available for symbolic use as it was in France.

And it was indeed so used. The earliest instance I have found is in Sir Thomas More's *History of King Richard III*, which was written in about 1513, though not fully printed until 1557. The passage in question is the famous one in which Sir James Tyrell is suggested to the king as one likely to rid him of the Princes in the Tower. Richard had already ordered the lieutenant of the Tower to kill the boys, but the lieutenant had refused. News of his refusal was brought to the King, who was alone at the time, save for 'a secret page'. Richard mused angrily on the lieutenant's betrayal of his confidence, asking aloud, 'Who shall a man trust?' The page spotted his opportunity. He had long noticed that Tyrell was an ambitious man who had been deliberately kept back by the King's two principal confidants. So, taking Richard's rhetorical question as a real one, he said: 'Sir ... there lieth one on your pallet without that I dare well say to do your Grace pleasure the thing were right hard that he would refuse' – meaning by this Sir James Tyrell (More 1963: 83). Now there are, as has been pointed out (cf. Kendall 1968: 398–406, etc.), many inconsistencies and even impossibilities in this story, but its truth or falsehood is not an issue here. All that matters is the setting:

More makes the conversation between Richard and his page take place while the King was 'sitting at the draught'. As symbolism, this is brilliant, if a little too complex for our purpose. By one deft stroke, More underlines the confidentiality of the page, the confidentiality of the conversation, and the foulness of the deed that was plotted in so foul a place. All that is missing is a direct link between the symbolism and the Privy Chamber, but that is (of course) inevitable, as in Richard III's reign the department did not yet exist.

The second example was written nearly a century after the *History of King Richard III*. It comes from John Marston's comedy, *The Parasitaster or the Fawn*, of 1606. In it, one of the characters says: 'Thou art private with the duke; thou belongest to his close-stool' (cited in Chambers 1923: I, p. 53 n. 1). This then is straightforward: connection with the close-stool of a princely personage – close-stool clearly having, as in the English Royal Household, both a physical and an institutional sense – is used explicitly as a symbol of confidentiality.

Two examples seem very few. Others may exist, but I have been unable to find them. In any case, however, the two we have are really sufficient. More uses the privy symbolism quite casually, with no special apology or explanation. But – and this is decisive – in the second instance, the whole reference begins and ends in a dozen words that come in the middle of a quick-fire dialogue. The allusion must therefore have been instantaneously comprehensible, which in turn must mean that the symbol was either a commonplace figure of speech, or at least a fairly normal usage.

All this applies directly only to the Groom of the Stool. However, body service in general clearly carried the same overall sense as attendance at the close-stool – though naturally to a lesser degree. Thus membership of the Privy Chamber *in itself* symbolized confidentiality. This emerges quite plainly from Henry VIII's instructions to Ralph Sadler when he was sent as ambassador to Scotland in 1537. The instructions directed that Sadler:

> shall, as of himself, affirm to the King of Scots, that being he of his uncle's [i.e. Henry VIII's] Privy Chamber, and of long season acquainted with his proceedings, he knoweth the King his master's true meaning, upright dealing, and proceedings to be of such reason, truth and innocency, as he wisheth all the world might know the ground and very secrecies thereof.   (*LP* XIII, I, 1313)

Of course (and the instructions exploited the fact with complete cynicism) such confidentiality greatly reinforced the credibility and hence the effectiveness of the messenger.

The double operation of intimacy is now clear. On the one hand, through their bodily contact with the king, the intimates of the Privy Chamber became the direct symbols or representations of the charismatic aspects of royalty. This was the mystical basis of their personification of the king. On the other hand, their intimate attendance on Henry served as a symbol of the high place that they held in his confidence, as men with whom he shared his inmost thoughts. This confidentiality was in turn what we could call the rational basis of their role as royal *alter ego*. But – and the fact cannot be too much emphasized – symbolism is equally significant in both the mystical and the rational forms of representation.

Such, therefore, was the machinery of Privy Chamber symbolism. But so far we have discussed the machinery without the motor. At the heart of the pattern of symbolism lay a particular attitude to the royal body service. Under Henry VIII, there is no contemporary comment – autobiographical or otherwise – on the Gentlemen's duties; instead, we must argue back from their known public standing. This is unequivocal: they were not mere powers behind the curtain or an early kitchen cabinet; on the contrary, they enjoyed the highest general esteem. Indeed, by the middle of Henry's reign the Privy Chamber was usually paired with the Privy Council itself as the second element in the constellation of power. Thus, in Cromwell's list of 'certain persons to be had at this time in the King's most benign remembrance', which dates from the beginning of 1538, the Privy Council is listed first, followed immediately by 'the Privy Chamber' (BL Cottonian MS Titus B I, fo. 497 (*LP* XIII, i, I)). Again, two years later in 1540, the King and Queen went on a short winter progress, accompanied by only four members of the Privy Council and 'the Ladies, Gentlemen, and Gentlewomen of their Privy Chambers' (Nicolas 1834–7: VII, 89 (*LP* XVI, 325)); and finally, as the King's life ebbed away in December 1546, the Court was closed to all 'but his councillors and three or four Gentlemen of his [Privy] Chamber' (Bergenroth *et al.* 1862–1954: VIII, 370 (*LP* XXI, ii, 605)). All this is striking enough, but the decisive argument comes (as ever) with the extreme case. The Groom of the Stool had (to our eyes) the most menial tasks; his standing, though, was the highest: by Act of Parliament of 1541 he was recognized as an officer of state of the second rank (Luders *et al.* 1810–28: III, 867); and by early 1547 he was *ex officio* a Privy Councillor (*LP* XXI, ii, 634/i). Clearly, then, the royal body service must have been seen as entirely honourable, without a trace of the demeaning or the humiliating.

This position was formalized by the Barons of the Exchequer in June–July 1573 when they gave judgment in Sir Thomas Wroth's case. They declared that the officers of the Privy Chamber gave service 'not merely to the body natural' of the Prince (like the king's physician, or surgeon, or music-master) but 'to the Majesty of the body politic ... which includes the body natural' (Plowden 1816: 455*a*). That is, the Privy Chamber's private service had an acknowledged public dimension, which meant of course that it was honourable – indeed, that it demanded men of the highest station: 'for the royal Majesty requires officers of honour, who understand the honourable service that is due to Majesty, and such ought to be men not only of accomplished carriage and deportment, but also of great skill, understanding, and experience' (Plowden 1816: 455*a*).

But, of course, fetching and carrying, dressing and undressing, were not the ordinary occupations of noblemen and gentlemen. Usually, such things were considered as unworthy, as we should think them to be. The point was that the members of the Privy Chamber did them for the king, and he (as we have seen) was 'not ... a man but ... a more excellent and divine estate'. The effect this had is succinctly stated in George Herbert's lines, which deal with the service of an even greater monarch than Henry Tudor:

> Teach me, my God and King,
> In all things thee to see,
> And what I do in any thing,
> To do it as for thee ...
>
> All may of thee partake:
> Nothing can be so mean,
> Which with this tincture (for thy sake)
> Will not grow bright and clean.
>
> A servant with this clause
> Makes drudgery divine:
> Who sweeps a room, as for thy laws,
> Makes that and th'action fine.
>   (Herbert 1953: 184–5)

The title of the section of *The Temple* from which these verses are taken is *The Elixir*. In it, the name of God is seen as an agent of transformation, through which the vile becomes honourable. Similarly, the numinous powers of a king – that god upon earth – transmuted the humblest act of personal attendance into something worthy of the best blood in the kingdom. Indeed, we can go further. With the king, the ordinary social conventions were actually inverted, and the more minutely personal the attendance, the more honourable it was. This is shown clearly enough by the status of the Groom of the Stool; but the point is driven home harder by the Eltham Ordinances. These stipulate that only the Gentlemen of the Privy Chamber shall dress the king: 'and that none of the said Grooms or Ushers do approach or presume ... to lay hands upon his royal person' (Bodl., Laudian MS Miscellaneous 597, fo. 26 (*HO* 156)). Thus the king's body is seen, consciously and deliberately, as sacred flesh which only those of high rank are fit to touch.

And so the argument comes full circle. Intimacy – to which we have attached so much importance – could do nothing of itself: it could function as a publicly acknowledged symbol only so long as the divine attributes of monarchy purged the royal body service of anything which savoured of the menial or servile.

This proposition has been derived from our analysis of the Privy Chamber at the height of its importance; it can be further tested by a discussion of the history of the Privy Chamber and its successor department in the 200 years following Henry VIII's death.

Until the late seventeenth century, the early Tudor position remained essentially in force. Despite rebellion and revolution the reverence for monarchy continued (at least formally), while the structure of the Royal Household indeed experienced a change of name (the Bedchamber replaced the Privy Chamber under James I), but little change of substance. The fundamental continuity emerges clearly from William III's Bedchamber Ordinances of 1689 (BL Stowe MS 563). These have a double importance. On the one hand, they show that the Groomship of the Stool was still very much an office of personal body service: as we have already seen, the Groom was to attend the king when he relieved himself (BL Stowe MS 503, fos 14^v–15); as well, he was to put on the shirt which the king wore next to his skin; he alone (apart from the king) held the key of the private apartments; and finally, he might lodge in the King's Bedchamber, if he so wished (BL Stowe MS 503, fos 5, 7^v, 10). Conversely, the Ordinances established the Groomship of the Stool at the peak of its public dignity. It now stood out as the third great office of the Royal Household (after the Lord Stewardship and the Lord Chamberlainship), complete (like the two senior posts) with a fully developed official symbolism of its own. The symbol chosen was a 'gold key on a blue ribbon', which, as the Ordinances provided, 'our Groom of the Stool may wear ... as a badge of his office' (BL Stowe MS 503, fo. 7^v). Like the other major symbols of office – the white staves of the Lord Treasurer, the Lord Steward, or the Lord Chamberlain, or the seals of the Lord Chancellor, the Lord Privy Seal, or the Secretaries of States – the key functioned in three principal ways. First, appointment to the office was symbolized by handing over the key. This point is made explicitly by the Ordinances of 1689 which state that, when 'we first constitute [the Groom of the Stool] in the said office, it shall be by Our delivery to him of a gold key ... which shall be a sufficient warrant to our Lord Chamberlain or Lord Steward to swear him in the said place' (BL Stowe MS 503, fo. 7^v). Second, the fact that one held the post was signalled by wearing the key. This, as we have seen, figured in the Ordinances as well. And, third, dismissal or resignation was represented by the surrendering of the key back into the king's hands. This is not touched on by the 1689 Ordinances, but it emerges clearly enough from innumerable incidents throughout the eighteenth century. For instance, in 1734 Lord Chesterfield recommended a household reshuffle, for which the way should be cleared 'by taking the gold key from that cypher, Lord Godolphin' (Croker 1824: II, pp. 82–3).[12]

The symbol chosen was dignified: it was also singularly appropriate. As we have seen at length, the Groom was both in frequent and intimate attendance on the sovereign, and as well was an important agent in procuring access to the king for others. These attributes were so well expressed by the ideas associated with a key that the name of the symbol effectively replaced the name of the office in ordinary parlance (cf. Cowper 1864: 147, 155, 157, 164, 166). This usage led to many comments whose meaning vibrates interestingly between the literal (i.e. key as object and symbol) and the metaphorical (i.e. key as means of access to someone, as in 'keys of my heart'). One of the most explicit of these references comes at the beginning of George I's reign, when Peter Wentworth thought that the Duke of Argyll was 'very wise in accepting the Key to the Prince for it will give him frequenter access to court than the junto men care for' (cited in Beattie 1967: 3).

The use of a key as the symbol of an office of intimate attendance is a general one, to be found at widely scattered times and places. For instance, until the reign of Pope Paul VI, the papal chamberlains had a large key embroidered on their backs, while Henry III of France, in order to increase the status of his *gentilshommes de chambre*, directed 'qu'ils portassent la clef d'or pour marque de leur dignite' (Loyseau 1701: 229; cf. also Firth 1973).

Thus in these Ordinances of 1689 the developments we have been studying reached their apotheosis: private body service and great public power and position were fused, and, simultaneously, the fusion was expressed in the vivid symbolism of the key. But the apotheosis was short-lived. In fact, its very existence depended on the customary time-lag between the occurrence of events and the full realization of their implications. The Revolution of 1688 had shattered for ever the concept of a divine-right monarchy in England: henceforth, the king was simply first servant of the state. By the early eighteenth century this fact was beginning to sink in. The consequences for the royal Bedchamber were immediate and striking. Two essential points stand out. First, the actual service of the royal person was abandoned by the noble Lords and Ladies of the Bedchamber[13] and transferred instead to the department's humbler servants. This fact is (it seems to me) obscured in the standard account of the early Hanoverian court (Beattie 1967); nevertheless, it emerges clearly enough from contemporary documents. Most precise of all is the account dictated to Dr Arbuthnot by Mrs Masham, sometime Bedchamber Woman and later Groom of the Stool to Queen Anne:

> The bedchamber-*woman* came into waiting before the queen's prayers, which was before her majesty was dressed. The queen often shifted in the morning: if her majesty shifted at noon, the bedchamber-*lady* being by, the bedchamber-*woman* gave the shift to the lady without any ceremony, and the *lady* put it on. Sometimes, likewise, the bedchamber-*woman* gave the fan to the *lady* in the same manner; and this was all that the bedchamber-*lady* did about the queen at her dressing.
>
> When the queen washed her hands, the page of the back-stairs brought and set down upon a side-table the basin and ewer, then the bedchamber-woman set it before the queen, and knelt on the other side of the table over-against the queen, the bedchamber-lady only

looking on. The bedchamber-woman poured the water out of the ewer upon the queen's hands.   (Croker 1824: I, pp. 292–3)

Thus, there was a clear distinction between the actual body service of the Bedchamber Woman and the largely honorific attendance of the Lady of the Bedchamber. In the case of the Groom of the Stool – the Chief Lady of the Bedchamber – the tendency was carried still further. For example, when the Countess of Pembroke, Lady of the Bedchamber to Queen Caroline, was angling for the Groomship of the Stool, she explained that 'the uncertainty of my health, and being obliged to be, on my brother's account, so much in the country, would make it excessively convenient to me' (Thomas 1847: II, p. 248). The impression that gives of a post with the lightest of responsibilities is confirmed by Lady Suffolk's account of her first week as Groom of the Stool in 1734:

Seven nights quiet sleep, and seven easy days have almost worked a miracle upon me ... I shall now often visit Marble Hill: my time is become very much my own ... I have at this time a great deal of business upon my hands, but not from my court employment.   (Croker 1824: II, pp. 1–3)

In short we find a hierarchy of non-functioning, with the Women (or Grooms) doing much; the Ladies (or Gentlemen) doing a little; and the Groom of the Stool doing almost nothing at all.

But the development of the highest Bedchamber offices into near sinecures was only the first change. There was, secondly, a clear alteration in the attitude towards the royal body service. Lady Suffolk again provides the test case. As plain Mrs Howard she was Principal Bedchamber Woman to Queen Caroline; then, in 1731, on her husband's succeeding to the Earldom of Suffolk, she became Groom of the Stool. Relations between Mrs Howard and the Queen were always delicate as the former was the King's mistress; tension, however, came to a head when the Queen asked her new Groom of the Stool to hold the basin in the ceremony of the royal dressing. According to Caroline herself (as reported by Lord Hervey) Lady Suffolk told her 'with her little fierce eyes and cheeks as red as your coat, that positively she would not do it' (Hervey, 1848: II, p. 16). The background to the incident is filled in by Horace Walpole's comment in his *Reminiscences* that 'from the Queen Mrs Howard tasted many positive vexations. Till she became Lady Suffolk she constantly dressed the Queen's head, who delighted in subjecting her to such servile offices, though always apologizing to "her good Howard"' (cited in Hervey 1848: II, p. 16 n. 11). Obviously, then, as both Lady Suffolk's anger and Walpole's use of the phrase 'servile offices' shows, the monarch's body service had lost all special quality and become a merely menial task, as humiliating and unworthy as personal attendance on anyone else.[14]

Thus, the attitude to royal body service provides a precise index to the general attitude to kingship. Under the Tudors, Lady Suffolk's indignant reaction would have been unthinkable, because the king was simply not on the same plane as even the greatest of his subjects. Rather, he was different in substance. Under the Hanoverians, on the other hand, the monarch was still head of the social pyramid, but he differed from his peers in degree, not in kind.

The abandonment of the royal body service and the concomitant disdain for it brought its own revenge. Now that they had ceased to be the king or queen's domestic servants, the Gentlemen and Ladies of the Bedchamber found their relations with their sovereign becoming progressively less intimate. Already, in April 1716, the Duchess of St Alban's, Groom of the Stool to the Princess of Wales, 'huffed [her mistress] about her not being always with her' as formal etiquette demanded (Cowper 1864: 109). Twenty years later, things had gone much further: as Queen Caroline was dying (in 1737) she was attended by three Women of the Bedchamber, while 'none of her Ladies of her Bed-Chamber were admitted at all' (Hervey 1848: II, p. 496).

Thus the first half of the eighteenth century saw a transformation in both the functions of Bedchamber office and what, for want of a better word, can be called its ideology. From being posts of great intrinsic weight, Bedchamber lordships became mere indices of status won in other ways and for other reasons; they were important in themselves only because they conferred the right of access to the sovereign. The consequent tension between past duties and present situation was common to all the upper reaches of the Bedchamber, but it was particularly acute in the case of the Groom of the Stool. Moreover, the peculiar title of the post (which cried aloud for explanation) permitted the tension to come to the surface. The Groom's abandonment of personal attendance of the king of course meant that the name became an anachronism. But anachronism can be lived with. The real problem was the new attitude towards body service. This made the proper meaning of 'stool' appear as an impossible vulgarism, wholly inappropriate to the dignity of the great nobleman by whom the office was always held. And so the search for a euphemism began. The earliest attempt seems to have been made by Edward Chamberlayne in his *Angliae Notitiae*, the first edition of which was published in 1669. Without a shred of justification from even the highly variable Tudor orthography, he spelled 'stool' as 'stole'; then, on the basis of this mis-spelling, he erected an elegant fantasy. The First Gentleman of the Bedchamber (he tells us) was called

> Groom of the Stole, that is (according to the signification of the word in Greek, from whence first the Latins, and thence the Italian and French derive it) Groom or servant of the Robe or Vestment: he having the office and honour to present and put on his Majesty's first garment or shirt every morning, and to order the things of the Bedchamber. (Chamberlayne 1669: 249–50)

Thus, the idea that personal attendance on the sovereign was honourable was still alive, but only just. In order to conform to the new sense of propriety, the publicly acknowledged content of body service had had to be changed. The lavatorial reality of the office – still clearly apparent in the Bedchamber Ordinances of twenty years later – was suppressed, and instead attention was concentrated on the one disinfected gesture of putting on the royal shirt.

The *Angliae Notitiae*, which soon became a periodical publication (like an early *Who's Who*), enjoyed an immense success and had a corresponding influence. Accordingly, it laid down the whole pattern of interpretation of the Groomship for the next hundred years or more. But by the early nineteenth century a shift is noticeable. Dod's *Manual of Dignities* (first published in 1842) informed its readers that the office of

> 'Groom of the Stole' is usually combined with the duties of the Mistress of the Robes when a female sovereign is on the throne ... The Stole is a narrow vest, lined with crimson sarcenet, and was formerly embroidered with roses, fleurs-de-lis, and crowns; but the office of Groom is a sinecure. (Dod 1842: 138)

And of course, though Dod does not mention the point explicitly, the stole in question was part of the coronation regalia. This explanation of the Groomship is manifest nonsense: the Groom never had any connection with the coronation regalia (whether the stole or anything else); and indeed, in only one coronation (that of Edward VI) did he have any official part to play at all (Leland 1770: IV, p. 326). Thus, while Dod's ideas about the Groom clearly derive from Chamberlayne's, they are on a different level of unreality altogether. The reason is suggested by the last line of the extract from the *Manual*, with its assertion that 'the office of Groom is a sinecure'. In the late seventeenth century, the fact that the Groom still had a role in body service – that he still put on the royal shirt – had given Chamberlayne's mythical etymology a solid anchorage. By the last Hanoverians, however, the Groom had long abandoned even this limited degree of personal attendance: so, in default of any discernible official functions, fantasy was given – indeed, was obliged to assume – the reins.

As a complete, inexplicable, and very well-paid sinecure, the Groomship was peculiarly vulnerable in the early nineteenth century. Popular contempt for the Court (probably best exemplified in John Wade's *Extraordinary Black Book*[15]) was combining with the official pursuit of economy to press for a pruning of the luxuriant royal household. In 1831 a Select Committee of the House of Commons recommended that the salaries of the leading household officers (including, of course, the Groom of the Stool) should be cut by between a third and a quarter – that is, in the case of the Groom, from £2,163 to £1,500. Nothing was done at the time (*British Parliamentary Papers* (1801–52), XXIII, pp. 27ff.), but with the accession of Victoria six years later full effect was given to the recommendations. Indeed, things went further, and, as a new Select Committee reported, 'it is not proposed to fill up the office of Groom of the Stole, or to create any analogous office in the

Household of her Majesty' (*British Parliament Papers* (1801–52), XXIII, pp. 27ff.). The decision was conveyed to the House by the Chancellor of the Exchequer, Thomas Rice, who drew a favourable comparison between the present economy, and the extravagance of the provision for Sarah, Duchess of Marlborough, under Anne. As he read out the list of offices held by the duchess – Keeper of the Privy Purse, Groom of the Stole, and First Lady of the Bedchamber – the mention of the Groomship was followed by 'a laugh' (*The Times* 1837). Since *The Times*'s leader on Rice's speech made no mention of the abolition of the post, that anonymous laugh must stand as the last recorded comment on the Groomship of the Stool.

The story of the Bedchamber in decline is therefore the mirror image of the Privy Chamber at the peak of its importance. The key to both is intimacy. As the Gentlemen, etc., of the Bedchamber ceased to be the king's body servants, so their importance in all spheres declined – with the decline, in the case of the Groomship of the Stool, going as far as the abolition of the office. But the servants of the Chamber or Privy Chamber had suffered similar declines in the past. What was new was the monarch's loss of numinous powers: the last English sovereign to touch for the king's evil was Anne (1702–14) (Thomas 1973: 228), and by the later eighteenth century even Boswell, inveterate monarchist that he was, could comment thus slightingly on that 'superstitious notion which, it is wonderful to think, prevailed so long in this country, as to the virtue of the royal touch' (Boswell 1953: 32). This loss of royal divinity[16] meant that the role of intimacy itself was devalued. It could no longer serve as a road to public greatness. Thus the Women and Grooms of the Bedchamber (who, save under George I, were now the monarch's real body servants) never acquired any formally acknowledged power – however great the influence that some of them (for example, Mrs Clayton, Woman of the Bedchamber to Queen Caroline (Thomas 1847)) might exercise behind the scenes. This failure of the lower servants of the Bedchamber to secure promotion was decisive. It ensured that no successor department to the Bedchamber emerged as, in similar circumstances, the Bedchamber had displaced the Privy Chamber, and, earlier still, the Privy Chamber itself had displaced the Chamber. With the ending of this process of institutional shelling-off, the household's whole existing line of development came to an end as well. There was a brief moment of marking time at the beginning of the nineteenth century; then a violent change of direction. From about 1837 the household's establishment was drastically reduced and its departmental structure simplified until, by the end of Victoria's reign, it had become the comparatively modest and essentially private entourage that exists today.

It is now time to summarize our argument. Clearly, what we have been studying is a coherent and developed system of symbolism, centred on the human body: the king's person was the most expressive symbol of his office; the persons of his body servants were the fullest representations of their master; and, finally, the mechanism by which this latter representation was achieved – the symbolism of intimate attendance – was a type of body symbolism as well. Indeed, in its 'rational' aspect, it is a particularly straightforward and well-documented case of Mary Douglas's 'purity rule', whereby 'social distance tends to be expressed in distance from physiological origins and vice versa' (Douglas 1973: 12). But though these bodily symbols are natural in their origin, their meanings are in no sense natural or inherent. Rather, as we have insisted, the functions of all these symbols – above all, the most 'natural' of body service – depended on their operating within the context of a semi-divine and intensely personal monarchy. Once that context disappeared, the symbols lost their meaning. Or better, their meaning changed, for the symbols connected with the monarch's person and domestic service are still very much alive. The veil of silence which blankets the everyday life of royalty; the impenetrable secrecy of the royal palaces (so different from the promiscuous crowds of Tudor Whitehall or Hampton Court); the extraordinary anonymity of the servants of the Royal Household – all symbolize, vividly and precisely, the absolute separation between the sovereign as an individual and the sovereign as a public figure that is the keystone of the monarchy's constitutional position in modern England. However, the point is made most strikingly by the most intimate bodily function of all – evacuation. In the sixteenth century, the Groom of the Stool's highly personal job as the royal lavatory attendant was the foundation for his rise to public power and influence. Now, on the other hand, the monarch's relieving of him or herself is so awesomely private that one of the usual preparations for a royal visit (so it is rumoured) is the construction of a special WC, dedicated to the king or queen's sole use. Thus the symbol (the close-stool or the modern lavatory) is the same, but its meaning in the twentieth century is not merely different from its meaning in the sixteenth century, but, in fact, is its opposite.

The study of royal symbolism has thus proved a useful exercise. First (and the point can almost be made in passing) it has enabled us to reintegrate the early modern English monarchy into the world-picture offered by Keith Thomas. This needed doing, since the accepted historical opinion on sixteenth- or seventeenth-century kingship has tended to rationalize it. Thus Professor Elton asserts that:

> Tudor divine right, and even up to a point the Bourbon monarchy of the seventeenth century, contained far less of that magic or mystic element that distinguished the newly Christianized barbarian kings. Mysticism there was, but attenuated; religion formed the ceremonial dress rather than the passionate essence of post-mediaeval kings by divine right.   (Elton 1974–92: II, p. 202)

But such a position is tenable only so long as attention concentrates on the material symbols of monarchy; if the focus shifts, the picture changes radically.

Crown and sceptre may have degenerated into mere signs ('I wear a crown and carry a sceptre; therefore I am to be reverenced as King'); however, far from waning, the imputed magical (and hence symbolic) properties of the royal body survived in full and may actually have strengthened. This means that Tudor and Stuart kingship remained theocratic: the only difference was that its symbols centred round the sanctity of the royal body (an essentially pagan notion), rather than around the heavily Christian ceremony of the coronation. Second and more immediate to our purpose, symbolic analysis has shown that the implications for government of divine monarchy were both surprising and exotic. So much so indeed that their absolute importance can easily be exaggerated. Sixteenth- and seventeenth-century English kings had civil servants of a recognizably modern type: in fact, the bulk of the work of government passed through their hands. But the Privy Chamber and so on remained as instruments of last resort, to fill up the interstices in ordinary government. These agent-symbols were, that is, the characteristic (though not the most frequent) agents of the early modern thaumaturgical king; they were also the one specific contribution that that type of monarchy made to the art of government.

Notes

1 For other similar comments, see Jacob (1961: 545–6).
2 But cf. Strong (1963: 31).
3 For the explicitly symbolic nature of the images on the great seal, see Stephen Gardiner's comments in Muller (1933: 274, 289).
4 At this time, the French word chambre, when it refers to the English Court, must be translated by 'Privy Chamber'.
5 For a very cool assessment of Henry VIII's own contribution to the campaign of 1513, see Cruickshank (1969: passim, and esp. pp. 206–7).
6 A short-lived post, created ad hoc in 1519.
7 Here, as elsewhere, I am deliberately simplifying a complex process: under Henry VII, the Groom had been unquestionably the head officer of the Privy Chamber. However, in 1518–19 (as we have seen), for the first time men of really high social rank were put into the Privy Chamber. This meant that the Groom was now at most a first among equals. His position was not fully resolved until the early 1530s, when the office of Chief Gentleman of the Privy Chamber, which carried with it the unquestioned headship of the department, was borrowed from the French Court and given to the Groom. Henceforth the two offices, though formally distinct, were invariable invested in the same person (Starkey 1973: 231–47).
8 =sweet (OED).
9 =vex or annoy (OED).
10 =calls (OED).
11 =prompt(?).
12 See also Cowper (1864: 157).
13 The Queen's Bedchamber (staffed by Ladies, etc.) paralleled the King's, and, as it happens, is much the better documented in the first half of the eighteenth century; accordingly, most of my examples will be drawn from it.
14 See also below, note 15.
15 His comments on the Groomship are as follows: 'Here is another of those courtly offices, which ought to be abolished, augmenting unnecessarily the expenditure of the

civil list. It is not sufficient to say these costly appendages are essential to support the royal dignity. The dignity of the crown is a senseless sound, unless tending to increase the respect and veneration of the people; but mere pageantry, in an enlightened age, can have no such effect: it only revolts the mind from an institution, obviously maintained in useless state, by a sacrifice of the general welfare ... To what public purport, or private gratification of the king, are the offices of groom of the stole, master of the hawks, master of the buck-hounds, master of the horse, or grooms and lords of the bedchamber? These are menial offices, and unbecoming the dignity of a nobleman, if endowed with the genuine feelings of nobility' (Wade 1832: 497).

16 Of course, as Thomas points out (1973: 230), belief in the thaumaturgical powers of monarchy persisted – fragmentarily – until far into the nineteenth century. But it persisted among the lower classes, and the attitude of the upper classes (which alone concerns us) changed, as the text insists and Thomas (1973: 239–40) confirms, in the eighteenth century.

References

MANUSCRIPTS

The Bodleian, Oxford
Laudian MS Miscellaneous 597

The British Library, London
Cottonian MSS Caligula B VI, D VIII; Titus B I
Harleian MS 4990
Stowe MS 563

The Public Record Office, London
E101 (Exchequer, King's Remembrancer, Various Accounts)
PRO 31/3 (Transcripts, Paris Archives, Baschet's Transcript)
PRO 31/18 (Transcripts, Vienna Archives)
SP 1 (State Papers, Henry VIII)
SP 2 (the same, Folio Volumes)
SP 3 (the same, Lisle Papers)

PRINTED BOOKS

Aylmer, G. E. (1961), *The King's Servants* (London).
Beattie, J. M. (1967), *The English Court in the Reign of George I* (Cambridge).
Bergenroth, G. A. *et al.* (1862–1954) (eds), *Calendar of State Papers, Spanish* (13 vols and 2 supplements, London).
Bilson, T. (1545), *The True Difference between Christian Subjection and Unchristian Rebellion* (Oxford).
Bloch, M. (1924), *Les Rois thaumaturges* (Strasbourg).
Boswell, J. (1953), *Life of Johnson* ed. R. W. Chapman (Oxford).
British Parliamentary Papers (1801–52), XXIII (London).

Burney, R. (1660), *Kerdiston Doron* (printed by J. Redmayne, for the Author) (London).

Bush, M. L. (1970), The Tudors and the Royal Race, *History*, 55, 37 ff.

Chamberlayne, E. (1669), *Angliae notitiae, or the Present State of England* (London).

Chambers, E. K. (1923), *The Elizabethan Stage* (2 vols, Oxford).

Chrimes, S. B. (1972), *Henry VII* (London).

Cowper, C. S. (1864) (ed.), *The Diary of Mary, Countess Cowper, Lady of the Bedchamber to the Princess of Wales, 1714–20* (London).

Crapelet, G.-A. (1835) (ed.), *Lettres de Henry VIII à Anne Boleyn* (Paris).

Crawfurd, R. (1917), 'The Blessing of Cramp-Rings', in C. Singer (ed.), *Studies in the History and Method of Science* (Oxford) I, pp. 165 ff.

Croker, J. W. (1824) (ed.), *Letters to and from Henrietta, Countess of Suffolk, and her Second Husband, the Hon. George Berkeley, from 1712 to 1767* (2 vols, London).

Cruickshank, C. G. (1969), *Army Royal* (Oxford).

Dod, C. (1842), *A Manual of Dignities* (London).

Douglas, M. (1973), *Natural Symbols* (Harmondsworth).

Ellis, H. (1824–46) (ed.), *Original Letters Illustrative of English History* (11 vols, London).

Elton, G. R. (1960), *The Tudor Constitution: Documents and Commentary* (Cambridge; 2nd edn, 1982).

—— (1972), *Policy and Police* (Cambridge).

—— (1974–92), *Studies in Tudor and Stuart Politics and Government* (4 vols, Cambridge).

Firth, R. (1973), *Symbols Public and Private* (London).

Frazer, J. G. (1963), *The Golden Bough* (abridged edn, London).

Furnivall, F. J. (1868) (ed.), *Manners and Meals in Olden Time* (Early English Text Society, 32, London).

Grant M. (1960), *The World of Rome* (London).

Hall, E. (1809), *The Union of the Two Noble and Illustrious Families of York and Lancaster* [*The Chronicle*] (London).

Harrington, Sir John (1962), *A New Discourse of a Stale Subject, called the Metamorphoses of Ajax*, ed. E. S. Donno (London).

Herbert, G. (1953), *Works*, ed. F. E. Hutchinson (Oxford).

Hervey, J. (Baron Hervey) (1848), *Memoirs of the Reign of George the Second*, ed. J. W. Croker (2 vols, London).

Hughes, P. L. and Larkin, J. F. (1964–9) (eds), *Tudor Royal Proclamations* (2 vols, New Haven).

Jacob, E. F. (1961). *The Fifteenth Century* (Oxford).

Kantorowicz, E. H. (1957), *The King's Two Bodies* (Princeton).

Kendall, P. M. (1968), *Richard the Third* (London).

Lander, J. R. (1965), *The Wars of the Roses* (London).

—— (1969), *Conflict and Stability in Fifteenth-Century England* (London).

Legg, L. G. W. (1901) (ed.), *English Coronation Records* (Westminster).

Leland, J. (1770), *De rebus britannicis collectanea* (6 vols, London).

Letters and Papers, Foreign and Domestic, of the Reign of Henry VIII (1862–1932), ed. J. S. Brewer, J. Gairdner, R. H. Brodie, *et al.* (21 vols in 32 parts, and addenda; London).

Loades, D. M. (1970), *The Oxford Martyrs* (London).

Loyseau, C. (1701), *Oeuvres* (Lyons).

Luders, A., *et al.* (1810–28) (eds), *Statutes of the Realm* (11 vols, London).

Mackie, J. D. (1952), *The Earlier Tudors, 1485–1558* (Oxford).

Mattingly, G. (1955), *Renaissance Diplomacy* (London).

More, Sir Thomas (1963), *The History of King Richard III*, ed. R. S. Sylvester (New Haven and London).

Muller, J. A. (1933) (ed.), *Letters of Stephen Gardiner* (Cambridge).

Murray, M. A. (1954), *The Divine King in England* (London).

Myers, A. P. (1959), *The Household of Edward IV* (Manchester).

Nicolas, N. H. (1830) (ed.), *The Privy Purse Expenses of Elizabeth of York* (London).

—— (1834–7) (ed.), *Proceedings and Ordinances of the Privy Council of England, 1386–1542* (7 vols, London).

Pickthorn, K. W. M. (1934), *Early Tudor Government* (2 vols, Cambridge).

Piper, D. (1973), *Personality and the Portrait* (London).

Plowden, E. (1816), *Commentaries or Reports* (2 vols, London).

Royal Commission on the Historical Monuments of England (1959), *An Inventory of the Historical Monuments in the City of Cambridge* (2 parts and plans, London).

Rymer, T., *et al.* (1816–89) (eds), *Foedera, conventiones, litterae* (4 vols, London).

Schramm, P. E. (1937), *A History of the English Coronation*, trans. L. G. W. Legg (Oxford).

Society of Antiquaries (1790), *A Collection of Ordinances and Regulations for the Government of the Royal Household* (London).

South, R. (1843), *Sermons Preached upon Several Occasions* (4 vols, London).

Starkey, D. R. (1969), The Gentlemen of the Privy Chamber, 1485–1547 (unpublished fellowship dissertation: Cambridge).

—— (1973), The King's Privy Chamber, 1485–1547 (unpublished Ph.D. dissertation: Cambridge).

Strong, R. (1963), *Portraits of Queen Elizabeth I* (Oxford).

—— (1967), *Henry VIII and Holbein* (London).

Sylvester, R. S. and Harding, D. P. (1962) (eds), *Two Early Tudor Lives* (New Haven and London).

Thomas, A. T. (1847) (ed.), *Memoirs of Viscountess Sundon, Mistress of the Robes to Queen Caroline* ... (2 vols, London).

Thomas, K. (1973), *Religion and the Decline of Magic* (Harmondsworth).

The Times (1837), 24 Nov, p. 3 col. 2.

Tudor-Craig, P. (1973), *Richard III* [catalogue of National Portrait Gallery exhibition, 27 June–7 Oct. 1973] (London).

Vergil, P. (1950), *The Anglica Historia of Polydore Vergil AD 1485–1537*, ed. and trans. Denys Hay (Camden Society, 3rd ser., 74; London).

Wade, J. (1832), *The Extraordinary Black Book* (Effingham).

3

Tudor monarchy and its critiques

JOHN GUY

From the Wars of the Roses to the death of Henry VIII

The most spectacular assets of the monarchy were the person and image of the ruler (see also Anglo, Chapter 1). The king was at the centre of the polity. Power was concentrated around him. As Bishop Russell declared in a parliamentary speech of 1483, 'What is the belly or where is the womb of this great public body of England but that and there where the king is himself, his court and his counsel?'[1] Furthermore, the king's power was 'whole' and 'entire'. (The term 'sovereignty' is found by the 1530s, and was used colloquially by the 1560s.) It was by royal authority that laws were enacted and repealed, and by which taxation was sought, though not granted, since, by 1400, it was received wisdom that taxation was granted by the Commons in Parliament alone, the Lords merely 'assenting' to what they had agreed. Henry VII was the most obvious exemplar of this style of kingship (see also Condon, Chapter 11; Gunn, Chapter 6). Probably the last ruler to do so, he thought nothing of interrupting lawsuits by writ of privy seal, or of ordering on his 'mere mocion' that individuals should make contributions to his war chest or that an error on the engrossed text of a statute be summarily corrected on the rolls of Parliament.

It was universally held that monarchy was instituted by God. The king ruled 'by the grace of God', but did so for the benefit of the community. Justice, in its broadest sense, was the purpose of his government. The king governed for the common good, providing the single will necessary for the formulation of common policy. His duties were threefold: to keep the peace and defend the realm; to maintain the law and administer justice impartially; and to uphold the Church, especially against heresy. These obligations were enshrined in the coronation oath. The rhetoric was that of virtue and good government; the king was a living embodiment of the cardinal virtues of prudence, justice, temperance, and fortitude. He was the fountain of honour and justice. He was valiant in war, the champion of the tiltyard, and was also the protector – Henry VIII by 1531 said the 'sole protector' – of the English Church and clergy.

Late-medieval regality was discussed in language borrowed from Roman law: the king's prerogative was 'ordinary' and 'absolute'.[2] By his 'ordinary' prerogative he enforced juridically the privileges and 'pre-eminences' which he enjoyed as a superior feudal lord. He might also issue pardons or mitigate the effect of statutes for the benefit of individuals. These powers were integral to the common law. They helped to define what the king was king and lord over, and it was in this mode that lawyers spoke of the king's prerogative 'by the order of the common law'.[3]

The king's 'absolute' prerogative was his emergency power. In time of war or revolt he could suspend the law, billet troops on householders, and levy taxation without parliamentary consent. In case of fire he might override the statutes which protected freehold property in order to demolish burning buildings. Furthermore, he was the sole judge of cases of necessity. The judges held in 1292 that 'for the common utility [the king] is in many cases by his prerogative above the laws and customs usually recognized in his realm'.[4] And rulers from Henry IV to James VI and I asserted the obligation of the Commons to grant taxation in cases of 'evident and urgent necessity'.[5] Sir John Fortescue, the most 'constitutionalist' of all late-fifteenth-century theorists of monarchy, himself conceded that the dominion of the King of England was *regale* as well as *politicum*. In his 'politic' role the king might not tax his subjects nor change the laws 'without the grant or assent of his whole realm expressed in Parliament', but when confronted by war or emergency he was untrammelled by such restrictions.[6] By the time of the debates on the Petition of Right (1628), stereotyped versions of Fortescue's theory had been annexed by common lawyers and parliamentarians to justify a thesis of limited or 'constitutional' monarchy. But Fortescue's writings did *not* establish such a paradigm. What Fortescue in fact erected was the model of a self-limiting, self-regulating king who chose by way of concession, or as a matter of honour and duty, not to exceed the bounds of reason or to act contrary to the public good. The dissonance between this interpretation and the model of 'imperial' kingship as propounded by Henry VIII in the Acts of Appeals and Supremacy is less strident than is conventionally imagined.

The king's 'natural' counsellors were the nobility (defined broadly as the temporal and spiritual lords and other leading landowners and officials): their attendance at Court had symbolic and practical importance. Symbolic, because the king's authority was most visible when he wore his crown or purple robes, or took part in processions or solemn religious festivals, or sat enthroned in majesty on days of 'estate' (see also Anglo, Chapter 1; Starkey, Chapter 2). Practical, because no temporal jurisdiction

exceeded that of the king counselled.[7] This protocol was crucial. As Dr
Watts explains, 'The personal will of the king was an essential prescription
for public acts of judgement and so, by analogy, for all legitimate acts of
government.'[8] This did not mean that the king could act irresponsibly,
since the king's power was circumscribed by law and counsel. St Thomas
Aquinas, the doyen of scholastic political theorists, had defined a tyrant as
a ruler who ruled his realm for his own profit rather than for the good of
the community. Or, as the English ambassadors to France were instructed
to put the point in 1439, 'God made not his people ... for the princes, but
he made the princes for his service and for the wele [i.e. welfare] ...of his
people, that is to say to rule them in tranquillity namely by the means of
due [ad]ministration of justice.'[9] Less conventionally, Sir Thomas More, in
The History of King Richard III, compiled between the years 1513 and
1519, described a tyrant as a ruler who subverted the law, subverted the
Church, and pursued a policy of excessive taxation.

Whether expressed in Court, Council, or Parliament, it was counsel that
made the exercise of royal power legitimate. Renaissance theorists continually
emphasized this point. In the humanist-classical tradition, counsel was linked
directly to virtue, since it was the dictates of virtue that impelled the king to act
according to the common good. In *The Book Named the Governor*, dedicated
to Henry VIII in 1531, Sir Thomas Elyot concluded: 'The end of all doctrine
and study is good counsel ... wherein virtue may be found, being (as it were)
his proper mansion or palace, where her power only appeareth concerning
governance.'[10] The pith was that rulers should be suitably advised. Since

> one mortal man cannot have knowledge of all things done in a realm or
> large dominion, and at one time discuss all controversies, reform all
> transgressions, and exploit all consultations ... it is expedient and also
> needful that under the capital governor be sundry mean authorities, as
> it were aiding him in the distribution of justice in sundry parts of a
> huge multitude.[11]

Just as it was obligatory in the Roman world for a magistrate to take legal
counsel before pronouncing judgment, and for a landowner to seek the
advice of his neighbours before manumitting a slave, so the King of England
had a duty to 'govern with the better advice, and consequently with a more
perfect governance'.

A loophole in the theory of counsel was, of course, the issue of whether
rulers must actually act upon their counsellors' advice. In this respect, it was
but a short step from conciliar theory to a full-fledged theory of resistance.
For this reason, 'counselling' was usually held to be a duty and not a right.[12]
As Henry VIII reminded the leaders of the Pilgrimage of Grace in 1536, the
king was free to choose his own councillors and could not be bound by their
advice. Yet, in the Renaissance tradition, it was incumbent on him to listen
affably because the spirit of 'good counsel' was that of *amicitia* or 'friend-

ship'. Closely linked in humanist-classical literature to constancy, mutual loyalty, and a concern for justice, *amicitia* in practice covered everything from genuine friendships to courtesies between rivals, but the crux was that it warranted 'liberty of speech'. The counsellor tendered his honest opinion, which the ruler received in a spirit of 'likeness and equality'. For Elyot, as for almost every other humanist, the golden source was Aristotle's *Politics*, which held that the king's intimates

> must be friends of the monarch and of his government; if not his friends, they will not do what he wants; but friendship implies likeness and equality; and, therefore, if he thinks that his friends ought to rule, he must think that those who are equal to himself and like himself ought to rule equally with him.[13]

Elyot (still addressing Henry VIII!) highlighted the case of Alexander the Great, who 'fell into a hateful grudge among his own people' when he eschewed affability and 'waxed to be terrible in manners', forbidding 'his friends and discreet servants to use their accustomed liberty in speech'. (Plain speaking was Elyot's speciality! A later dialogue contained a thinly veiled comparison between Henry VIII and the tyrant Dionysius II of Syracuse, 'a man of quick and subtle wit', who 'was wonderful sensual, unstable, and wandering in sundry affections'. He delighted in 'voluptuous pleasures' and 'gathering of great treasure', and often 'resolved into a beastly rage and vengeable cruelty'.[14]) Elyot cherished Aristotle, because the latter had crafted Book III of the *Politics* to subvert the legitimacy of monarchy based solely on the sovereign's will. In Elyot's opinion, the defect of monarchy could be averted if government were to be undertaken by the king's 'friends': a body of persons who are both good men and good citizens.[15] Aristotle had concluded that kings are maintained and secured by their 'friends'. The reverse was true of tyranny, where the tyrant relied on the principle, 'All men want my overthrow, but my friends have most power to effect it.' The 'friends' of the ruler were his 'eyes and ears and hands and feet'. They helped him to rule, but they also secured his power. Elyot exploited this conceit to the full, and it reappears in the Rainbow portrait of Elizabeth I at Hatfield House, where the ears and eyes that adorn the queen's gown represent her privy councillors and servants who watch and listen, but do not pronounce. They are her 'friends', but in an explicit allusion to Aristotle they are also her 'colleagues' if not her equals and peers. They support, but also limit, her power. At one level, the Rainbow portrait depicts Elizabeth in royal majesty, but at another it is an icon of limited monarchy.[16]

Inscribed in humanist-classical literature and iconography was a strand which directly linked 'good counsel' (ultimately) to republicanism, or at least to a preference for constitutional or 'limited' monarchy. The intellectual avant-garde of Tudor England were the king's subjects, but inside every humanist was a citizen struggling to get out. The image of citizenship which they advocated centred on the *bonus civis* or *vir civilis*: the 'active citizen' of the Roman republic who was the political equivalent of the 'virtuous man'; one who 'knows how to plead in the law courts for justice and to deliberate in the councils and public assemblies of the *res publica* in such a way as to promote policies at once advantageous and honourable'.[17] Such a man was the hero of Cicero's *De officiis* and the model for the fictional 'Morus' in Book I of *Utopia*. In the monarchies of the Renaissance, of course, a republican model required adaptation, hence it became the mission of the humanists to remould the 'active citizen' to match the models of service, benefits, and the *cursus honorum* prevailing at the royal Court. The 'active citizen' was to be redefined and represented as a 'counsellor' of the ruler.

Considered comparatively, the aims of the Renaissance monarchies were remarkably consistent.[18] They centred on dynastic security, territorial centralization, increased revenues to finance the costs of warfare and building projects, the subordination of the nobility and higher clergy to the Crown, control of local 'franchises' and feudal privileges, and the augmentation of regal power. In particular, rulers proclaimed their territorial 'sovereignty'. They adumbrated this principle by invoking the language of 'empire'. Since the beginning of the fourteenth century, the civil lawyers in France had maintained that the king was 'emperor' in his realm (*rex in regno suo est imperator*), that he recognized no superior save God in 'temporal' matters, that the clergy's jurisdiction was confined to purely 'spiritual' affairs, and that the king might tax his clergy. The pope had no authority to legislate for the kingdom, because the prerequisite for legislation was dominion, and the pope had no dominion over the king's subjects.[19] From there it was but a short step to the thesis that rulers possessed secular and ecclesiastical *imperium* (literally, 'command'). Both Francis I and Henry VIII, though in admittedly different ways, arrived at this position. Their power was likened to that exercised by the Old Testament kings of Israel: David, Solomon, or (in the case of Henry VIII) Hezekiah; or that wielded by Constantine and Justinian in the later Roman empire. Biblical and historical prototypes provided the necessary conceptual models (see also Guy, Chapter 8). Commercial printers, notably in France, England, and Scotland, had already discovered an almost insatiable market for vernacular histories: the rediscovery of the 'ancient histories and chronicles' and 'laws' and 'constitutions' of the kingdom was followed by a plethora of publishing projects whereby the precedents and examples of 'imperial' kingship in action could be illustrated and disseminated.

The crux is Henry VIII's break with Rome and the comprehensive theory of monarchy that was announced by the Acts of Appeals and Supremacy (see also Guy, Chapter 8). The catalyst was the King's first divorce campaign of 1527–33, when Henry VIII annexed the language of 'imperial' kingship in order to break with Rome and declare his supremacy over the English

Church. Henry's political theology was proclaimed in the preamble to the Act of Appeals (1533):

> Where by divers sundry old authentic histories and chronicles it is manifestly declared and expressed that this realm of England is an empire, and so hath been accepted in the world, governed by one supreme head and king having the dignity and royal estate of the imperial crown of the same, unto whom a body politic, compact of all sorts and degrees of people divided in terms and by names of spiritual[i]ty and temporal[i]ty, be bounden and owe to bear next to God a natural and humble obedience; [the king] being also institute and furnished by the goodness and sufferance of Almighty God with plenary, whole and entire power, preeminence, authority, prerogative and jurisdiction....

Henry VIII defined his prerogative in terms of his *imperium*. He argued, first, that the kings of England from the second century AD had enjoyed secular *imperium* and spiritual supremacy over their kingdom and national Church; and, second, that the English Church was an autonomous province of the Catholic Church independent from Rome and the Papacy. The Act of Supremacy proclaimed the king's new style in 1534. However, the role of Parliament should not be misinterpreted. In the mind of Henry VIII the royal supremacy was never equivalent to a doctrine of parliamentary sovereignty. It was modelled on the prototypes of ancient Israel and the later (Christian) Roman empire: the Crown assumed full responsibility for the doctrine and ordering of the Church. Henry's favourite kings were David and Solomon, and he could quote *verbatim* from the Old Testament and the *Code* and *Institutes* of Justinian. The annotations in his personal psalter suggest that, by the 1540s, Henry actually perceived himself as David, and that he increasingly read the Psalms as a commentary on his own divine mission and regality.[20] Nor was Elizabeth I's position significantly different. Despite the purposeful ambiguity of the settlement of 1559, Elizabeth consistently held her royal supremacy to be magisterial. She might delegate the exercise of her authority to royal or statutory commissioners, but *imperium* was vested in the monarch alone. For Elizabeth, as much as for Henry VIII or indeed the early Stuarts, the supreme governor was 'authorized' immediately by God; disobedience to the monarch was ultimately disobedience to God.[21]

In a striking sense, Henry VIII had reinvented the theocratic model of kingship. His *imperium* was ordained by God and embraced both 'temporal' and 'spiritual' government. The kings of England were invested with an 'imperial' sovereignty, part of which had been 'lent' to the priesthood by previous English monarchs. Moreover, royal *imperium* was antecedent to the jurisdiction of the clergy and was inalienable. Despite its partial 'loan' to the clergy, it could be resumed by the king at will. By exercising his *imperium*, the king could redefine the duties of 'his' clergy, summon Church councils within his dominions, revise canon law, dissolve the monasteries, and even expound the articles of faith. In particular, he could require Convocation to rule on his matrimonial affairs, and then invite Parliament to reinforce their (favourable!) verdict by statute and common law.

The neatest defence of royal *imperium* was culled from the *leges Anglorum*, an interpolation of the 'Laws of Edward the Confessor'. The crucial extract concerned Lucius I, the mythical ruler of Britain who was converted to Christianity in AD 187 and wrote to Pope Eleutherius asking him to transmit the Roman law. In reply Eleutherius explained that Lucius did not need the Roman law, because he already had the Old and New Testaments from which he might himself 'take a law' for his kingdom. In a passage which became a Tudor battle-cry, Eleutherius recognized Lucius to be 'vicar of God' in his kingdom; he was the superior legislator who 'gave' the law and exercised *imperium* over Church and State (see also Guy, Chapter 8).

From here it was a short step to Ulpian's thesis that the king was above the law as the prerogative of his *imperium*. His 'absolute' prerogative was no longer to be confined to war or emergency, as Fortescue's theory had required. This line of argument reached its apogee under the early Stuarts, when James VI and I maintained that, *salus populi* (i.e. to promote the public good), he might at his discretion invoke the absolute prerogative for reasons of state. The gist can be found in the notes of Henry VIII's advisers upon the most important legal treatise of the Middle Ages, Bracton's *On the Laws and Customs of England*. Whereas Bracton had stated that the King of England was 'under God and the law, because the law makes the king', Henry VIII claimed that the king was 'under God but not the law, because the king makes the law'.[22] The question thereafter became: What was the extent of the mystical 'absolute' power enjoyed by the Tudor monarchy in Church and State? Could the ruler's *imperium* be circumscribed by custom and the common law?

As to ecclesiastical affairs, the royal supremacy was essentially caesaro-papist: Archbishop Cranmer and Bishop Gardiner, from their very different perspectives, concurred that the king had the final authority over rites and ceremonies.[23] Henry VIII, meanwhile, affirmed his right to define the articles of faith. He even (briefly) claimed the 'cure of souls' until rebuffed by an outraged episcopate.[24] If I may cite iconographical evidence again, by far the most compelling image of the Henrician royal supremacy is Holbein's watercolour (*c.*1535) depicting Solomon's reception of the Queen of Sheba.[25] The figure of Solomon is a portrait of Henry VIII. The Queen of Sheba was a traditional emblem of the Church, and the ensemble illustrates Henry VIII as supreme head receiving the homage of the Church of England. Furthermore, the backcloth behind the throne bears an inscription based on verses from the Old Testament (1 Kgs. 10: 9; 2 Chr. 9: 7–8), intimating that Henry VIII is appointed directly by, and is accountable only to, God. (To cement this point, in a place where the text of Holbein's inscription differed from the text of the Vulgate edition of the Bible as it was traditionally cited before the Council of Trent, a word has been bracketed in order to remove any ambiguity that might imply that Henry VIII had been 'elected' or 'acclaimed' king by popular consent.[26])

The thesis of 'imperial' kingship was 'rediscovered' between 1529 and 1531 by a research team that included Cranmer, Edward Foxe, and Nicholas de Burgo (see also Guy, Chapter 8). It was a quintessentially humanist project, but it sparked off a volley of critiques. These were the issues: Was the king's *imperium* the harbinger of tyranny? To what extent had there been a failure or narrowing of counsel? Had the king's regal power been augmented by the Act of Supremacy? Through what machinery should the king's government of the ecclesiastical polity be exercised?

Elyot composed *The Book Named the Governor* synchronously with the Pardon of the Clergy (1531) and the first insinuation of the thesis of the royal supremacy. He feared the rise at Court of an exclusive cabinet council which spoke only for the anticlerical, anti-papal caucus planning Henry VIII's first divorce.[27] He was the earliest commentator to observe the shift towards a select Privy Council in the 1530s, and he sought to mitigate this development by annexing its intellectual context. This led him to reinterpret the role of the king's 'friends', whom he cast not as the instruments of private tyranny but as the agents of a strong state. His historical grasp was assured: he knew that in the Roman imperial world the emperor's 'friends' (or *amici principis*) had chiefly been drawn from the governors who had served the emperor in the localities, and who numbered among his counsellors when they were resident at Court.[28] He also believed – with Thomas Starkey and (later) Sir Philip Sidney – that a monarchy limited by a strong nobility would insure the state against tyranny. Hence Elyot conceptualized the *amici* in terms of the hereditary nobility and landed élites, who served the Crown at Court, in Parliament, and in the localities. While this contrasted sharply with the ideas of Richard Moryson, whose emphasis on 'true nobility' was tantamount to a defence of meritocracy, Elyot's reading is immediately explicable. His motive was to recreate the mechanism of 'good counsel' whereby the exclusivity of the break with Rome might be averted and traditional links be restored between the Crown and its grass roots. What ultimately underpinned *The Book Named the Governor* was the axiom that rulers should promote the 'best' and most 'experienced' counsellors and that no 'good' (in this sense 'noble') counsellor should 'be omitted or passed over'.[29] For Elyot, the problem of government itself was reducible to one of 'good counsel', because it was 'counselling' and conciliar institutions which effectively guided the ruler and bridled his inclinations to cruelty and vice.[30]

Conciliarism, in short, lay at the core of Elyot's political creed. And the same is true of Starkey, whose eclectic masterpiece, *A Dialogue between Reginald Pole and Thomas Lupset*,[31] was begun about 1529 and completed between 1532 and *c.*1535. In this remarkable critique, Starkey invoked at once (Venetian) secular and ecclesiastical conciliarism and the English baronial tradition against the thesis of 'imperial' kingship. He had studied at Oxford and Padua, and served as Reginald Pole's secretary in the 1520s. He had seen at first hand Florentine refugees and Venetian patricians blending their traditions of civic humanism into a 'myth of Venice', and was attracted to their viewpoint because it retained the princely office of *doge* but relied on the *Consiglio maggiore* as the guarantor of liberty and equality and of government by the *ottimati*.[32] Starkey was particularly enamoured of the Venetian Council of Ten – essentially the republic's inner executive committee – which (in fact) comprised 17: 10 elected councillors, plus the doge and six of his 'privy' councillors.

In his *Dialogue* Starkey stressed the limits of monarchy more strongly than any of his contemporaries. More than any other writer, he fused the idioms of civic humanism and aristocratic republicanism with those of the baronial tradition in order to construct a thesis of 'limited' monarchy.[33] His points of departure were Ciceronian civic duty, and public authority as enshrined in Parliament. Since, however, Parliament was an intermittent institution, Starkey endowed a Venetian-style Council of Fourteen with the 'authority of the whole parliament' when Parliament was not in session. The function of this Council was to 'represent the whole body of the people ... to see unto the liberty of the whole body of the rea[l]m, and to resist all tyranny which by any manner may grow upon the whole commonalty'.[34] Its membership was to comprise four of the 'greatest and ancient lords of the temporalty', two bishops, four judges, and 'four of the most wise citizens of London', and it would ensure that the king and his own (Privy) Council did 'nothing again the ordinance of his laws and good policy'. It should have power 'to call the great parliament whensoever to them it should seem necessary for the reformation of the whole state of the commonalty' and should also 'pass all acts of leagues, confederation, peace and war'. The Fourteen were even to 'elect and choose' the Privy Council, since 'this may in no case be committed to the arbitrament of the prince – to choose his own counsel – for that were all one and to commit all to his affects, liberty and rule'.[35] By imposing such severe restraints of 'counsel' on the king's exercise of *imperium*, Starkey effectively remodelled the English constitution in the image of that of Venice.[36]

Starkey's *Dialogue* was unpublished; indeed the politics of the 1530s made publication in England unthinkable. In comparison, the humanist whose criticism Henry VIII truly feared, Thomas More, virtually courted publicity. While it is conventionally held that More kept silent on political subjects after his resignation as Lord Chancellor, in fact he adopted rhetorical strategies of dissimulation that enabled him not only to continue publishing on 'hot topics', but also to voice his opinions, if obliquely.[37] More delighted in irony. Like Machiavelli and Guicciardini, he was conversant with the writings of Tacitus, the most sceptical and disenchanted of the Roman historians.[38] Machiavelli had cited Tacitus with genuine approval.

Again, Castiglione's *Il libro del cortegiano* had not excluded a talent for dissimulation from its image of the courtly ideal. Within limits that was conventional, and Tacitus was neither a model for Castiglione nor even Machiavelli. Until the 1560s the humanists used Tacitus chiefly as a quarry for Roman imperial history.[39] But, when, in 1533, More openly suggested that Henry VIII and Tiberius were not unlike, his analogy was fraught with implications.[40] Furthermore, in his account of the reign of Nero, Tacitus had described how the Emperor had divorced Octavia in order to marry Poppaea: the circumstances, if not identical, resembled those surrounding the divorce of Catherine of Aragon.[41] There can be no doubt that, when More finally mounted the scaffold, he believed Henry VIII to be a tyrant. There is a moving echo here with one of More's Latin *Epigrams*, written around the year 1515 and published in 1518, one of a sequence that discussed monarchy, tyranny, and republicanism: '*sola mors tyrannicida est*'; death alone is the remedy for tyranny; but *whose* death? – the tyrant's or the victim's? On that issue, More did indeed remain silent.[42]

We have a record of More's analogy concerning monarchy and the royal supremacy to Richard Rich in the Tower in June 1535: 'A king may be made by Parliament and a king deprived by Parliament, to which act any [of his] subjects being of the Parliament may give his consent ... but to the case [in question (i.e the royal supremacy)] a subject cannot be bound because he cannot give his consent ... [in] Parliament, saying further that although the king were accepted [as supreme head] in England, yet most Utter [i.e. foreign] parts do not affirm the same' (see also Guy, Chapter 8). When finally indicted under the Acts of Supremacy and Treason, More denied that Parliament had the power to legislate for the ecclesiastical polity. In the last resort, he died as much to protect the Catholic Church from Parliament as from the king. The reason was that the most influential critique of the break with Rome had come from the pen of the common lawyer, Christopher St German, who went into print to argue that it was not the 'vicar of God' but the 'king-in-Parliament' which was the 'high sovereign over the people'.[43] In a reading proleptic of book VIII of Richard Hooker's *Of the Laws of Ecclesiastical Polity*, St German argued that all law, whether secular or ecclesiastical, was properly made by king, Lords, and Commons in Parliament assembled, 'for the Parliament so gathered together representeth the estate of all the people within this realm, that is to say of the whole catholic church thereof'.[44] St German conceded that both Church and State were directly subject to the king's authority. But, to counter Henry VIII's theocratic claims, he invoked Fortescue's concept of *dominium politicum et regale* in order to argue that the King of England should govern both State *and* Church in a parliamentary way. According to St German, the legitimacy of government rested upon the consent of the governed. Henry VIII was to exercise his 'imperial' authority in Parliament. In particular, St German withheld from the ruler the prerogative to interpret the canonical texts of scripture as Supreme Head of the Church and thus to expound divine law. He argued that Parliament should itself perform this fundamental task since 'the whole catholic church' came together in Parliament.[45]

St German's counter-thesis was anchored in his unshakeable conviction that sovereignty lay in the 'king-in-Parliament', and not the king alone. And, since his *Doctor and Student* together with *A Little Treatise called the New Additions* became set texts at the inns of court, his interpretation of the 'king-in-Parliament' set a benchmark for lawyers and constitutional theorists for several centuries. His political creed mirrored that of Thomas Cromwell, at least as Cromwell's position has been described by Sir Geoffrey Elton in a classic article.[46] A difference, however, is that St German was more 'populist' in outlook than Cromwell; he was, in fact, another conciliarist. In a programme of 1531 for religious and constitutional renewal, St German advocated a strictly parliamentary version of the sort of council which was also to be favoured by Starkey. Called the 'great standing council', its members were to be chosen by Henry VIII but 'authorized' by Parliament, and its functions were to advise the king and to implement a series of sweeping reforms from the time the current Parliament was dissolved until the conclusion of the ensuing one.[47] The relationship between the 'great standing council' and the king's Privy Council was not expressly defined in this draft. In a number of specified matters the 'great standing council' was to 'make ordinance' as seemed to it 'expedient', but in general its agenda was to be defined by statute, so that it might diagnose and redress grievances upon lines laid down in Parliament.

Such idealistic critiques as those of Elyot, Starkey, and St German were not likely to become reality. True, the Acts of Appeals and Supremacy raised issues of immense significance. Of these, the quasi-sacerdotal nature of the royal supremacy was perhaps the most important. The fact is, however, that these issues were smothered or sidestepped in the 1530s, eclipsed by the pace of change and by the preoccupation of the political élite with the Dissolution of the Monasteries and the Pilgrimage of Grace. The touchstone was the issue of obedience: only a few were prepared to cross the line into outright resistance.[48] In fact, a majority of the élite in Church and State had all along been papal minimalists, while conservative bishops such as Stephen Gardiner positively (if reluctantly at first) endorsed the royal supremacy until Henry VIII's death on the grounds that the king was more likely to be a successful bulwark against Protestantism than the pope.[49]

The effect of the reign of Henry VIII was thus to create a latent ambiguity, or binary opposition, within the theory of monarchy. On the one hand, 'official' pronouncements maintained that the king was endowed with secular and ecclesiastical *imperium*. On the other, the 'unofficial' exponents of conciliarism and common-law doctrine stressed the role of councils, counsellors, and representative institutions if 'limited' or 'constitutional' government were to be preserved. The extent of this contradiction should not be exaggerated. The most accomplished Henrician defence of 'imperial' kingship, Gardiner's *De vera obedientia* (1535), successfully incorporated both positions. Gardiner argued that the royal supremacy was ordained by God, but the people had consented to it by their free votes in Parliament.[50] This may be compared to someone who fits two locks, each by a different manufacturer, to his front door. The locks have incompatible mechanisms and different keys, but when used in combination they double the level of security! Apologists from Gardiner to Lord Chancellor Hatton, addressing Parliament in 1589, took this prudent line. Yet the Acts of Appeals and Supremacy created tensions in the body politic. While the novelty of Henry VIII's theory of kingship can be overstated, the doctrine of the royal supremacy was far more controversial. Furthermore, the Dissolution heightened this tension, for the *original* purpose of the Dissolution was to provide a permanent landed endowment for the 'imperial' Crown. Hence theocratic kingship was to be underpinned by what Fortescue had called a 'refoundation of the Crown', so that the king would live perpetually of his own, and parliamentary taxation would only be required in case of war. Henry VIII's war expenditure finally emasculated this plan, but the antithesis remained. 'Imperial' kingship, of which the royal supremacy was a fundamental and intrinsic dimension, could hereafter be cast in opposition to humanist ideals of classical and civic republicanism, and to the common law.

Minority and female monarchy, 1547–1603

In the history of the Tudor monarchy, the death of Henry VIII was a watershed. Looking back on the previous half century from the perspective of the reign of James I, Francis Bacon commented on the 'strangest variety' of reigns: that of 'a child; the offer of an usurpation ... the reign of a lady married to a foreign Prince; and the reign of a lady solitary and unmarried'.[51] Until recently, the acephalous nature of (especially) Elizabeth's rule was scarcely observed (see also Collinson, Chapter 4), but since 1990 there has been a spate of works on the topic.[52] As Carol Levin puts the point,

> if a queen were confidently to demonstrate the attributes of power, she would not be acting in a womanly manner; yet womanly behaviour will ill-fit a queen for the rigours of rule.... Everyone expected she would marry and solve the problem of being a woman ruler by turning the governance over to her husband.[53]

James I well understood the resonances. When he was absent from London and Queen Anne of Denmark attended the Privy Council on his behalf, he jibed at Robert Cecil: 'Ye and your fellows there are so proud now, that you have got the guiding again of a feminine court in the old fashion that I know not how to deal with ye.'[54] He was probably alluding to the other principal aberration of the Elizabethan Court: the fact that ritual courtship and pretended affection were the prerequisites to preferment. As Bacon also recalled, Elizabeth 'allowed herself to be wooed and courted, and even to have love made to her', observing that these 'dalliances detracted but little from her fame and nothing at all from her majesty'. In this remark he put his finger on the essence of Elizabethan politics: first, that to succeed at Court politicians had to pretend to be in love with the Queen; second, that the conduct of the 'game' of courtship was Elizabeth's most effective tool of policy.[55] The dithering, prevarication, and generally dismissive behaviour which was understood to be archetypical of the conventional 'mistress' provided Elizabeth with her weapons of political manipulation and manoeuvre. In order to beat her male courtiers at their own game, she changed the rules and capitalized on the power granted to her by virtue of her gender.

The rule of women or minors was a subject that provoked extreme reactions of fascination, adoration, or loathing in the sixteenth century. The rule of a (male) minor was the easier topic to handle. There the precedents were comparatively straightforward: government would be exercised by a Council of Regency until the king was declared 'of age': in addition, a Protector of the Realm or a Governor of the King's Person might be named to pronounce (or perform administratively) the king's will in consultation with the Regency Council. Such a framework automatically elevated the role of the Council in politics, and tended to stimulate factionalism at Court as leading councillors competed to assume the offices of Protector or Governor (the two might be combined or held independently). Of course, the precedents of conciliar rule during the incapacity of Henry VI were not auspicious: in 1455–6, for example, the Duke of York's efforts to assert himself and his policies irrespective of the costs to the Crown threatened both the conventions of the monarchy and the interests of his fellow nobles and councillors.[56] In the case of the Duke of Somerset's protectorate (1547–9), the key was not only that the Duke arrogated the style of Protector to himself in defiance of Henry VIII's last will and testament, but in addition he pursued an ill-conceived and financially catastrophic policy in Scotland, where he attempted to conquer and (effectively) subordinate that kingdom to the authority of the English Crown by an enforced dynastic marriage between Edward VI and the infant Mary, the future Queen of Scots. More than any Tudor politician except Elizabeth's last favourite, the second Earl of Essex, Somerset equated his ambition with the public good.[57] His overthrow by the Duke of Northumberland, following a Court *putsch* begun in October 1549, was highly reminiscent of the events of 1455–6.

Northumberland's *coup* illustrated precisely how personal Tudor monarchy remained at the death of Henry VIII. In order to capture Edward VI's government, Northumberland had virtually to make the boy-king a hostage: by controlling all access to the prince, he was thereby able to manipulate such tools of administration as the signet and dry stamp, and was able to order almost any action in Edward's name. Politics became a struggle waged at Court for possession of the king's body, 'with both sides scrambling to position themselves and their clients in the royal apartments, next to the king's bedchamber, as close as possible to the king himself'.[58] Maintaining control of the King required a monopoly of access to the Privy Chamber (see also Starkey, Chapter 2). In view of Elyot's opinion that the defect of monarchy could be averted if government were to be undertaken by the king's 'friends', it is a supreme irony that Professor Hoak discovered, when reconstructing these events, that Northumberland achieved his purpose at the crucial moment by procuring, as an eyewitness later put it, 'great frendes abowte the king'.[59]

Debate on the monarchy in the 1550s was further underpinned by the issue of religion. In Edward VI's reign the royal supremacy became a Trojan Horse for Protestantism. Since, however, the King was only 9 years old at his accession, a new regal prototype was required – David and Solomon were also less suitable in the new doctrinal context – and the model select-ed was that of Josiah, one of the kings of Judah whom the Continental reformers especially revered for his attacks on idolatry. Josiah had succeed-ed to the throne at the age of 8, after his father, who had 'walked not in the way of the Lord', had been assassinated. He had purged Judah and Jerusalem from the 'carved images, and the molten images. And they brake down the altars of Baal in his presence' (2 Kgs. 22–3).[60] Again, it had been in Josiah's reign that 'the book of the law' had been rediscovered by the high priest of the temple at Jerusalem, which presented a model for the Edwardian regime's championing of the vernacular Bible and Prayer Book.[61] In the context of Somerset's usurpation of the Protectorate in 1547 and Northumberland's subsequent *coup*, the image of King Josiah made it relat-ively straightforward for the King's councillors to justify a programme of 'fast reformation from above' while maintaining intact the legal authority of the 'imperial' royal supremacy.[62]

Again, the polemical debate of Mary's monarchy had less to do with the controversy concerning the pace of change in the parishes and local com-munities than with gender politics and the Calvinist theory of resistance.[63] It is now better understood that, beyond the circles of the evangelical avant-garde and the relatively narrow confines of London, the south-east, East Anglia, and the Midlands across to Gloucestershire, it was scarcely Mary's traditional Catholic devotion or even her campaign of persecution that stimu-lated intransigence and revolt.[64] It was, rather, her Spanish marriage, her steadfast commitment to the Papacy, and (especially) her resolve to restore to the Church, if and when possible, the ex-religious and chantry lands sold by the Crown to the laity under Henry VIII and Edward VI.

Mary longed to preside over a 'consensus' government – one from which radical Protestants and Northumberland's close adherents alone were excluded – but the reality is that she had to dictate to her Privy Council each of the three major policies of the reign: her marriage to King Philip, the reunion with Rome, and the declaration of war with France. It is true that accounts of conciliar factions in Mary's reign have been exaggerated. The débâcle of April 1554, for example, was the result of an artless attempt by Lord Chancellor Gardiner to 'bounce' the Council into supporting the reunion with Rome and the re-enactment of the heresy laws when it had previously resolved that no contentious religious measures should be laid before Parliament in that session.[65] Yet, despite her marriage, which was celebrated in July 1554, and Parliament's endorsement of the reunion with Rome the following November, Mary was assailed by objections to her rule on the grounds of religion and gender. In particular, a number of radical Protestant exiles who had fallen under Calvin's influence invoked resistance theory against Mary, whom they identified with Jezebel, the wife of Ahab, King of Israel, who had fostered the worship of Baal and tried to destroy the prophets of Israel (1 Kgs. 18: 4–13). She had been killed by Jehu (2 Kgs. 9: 29–37) and her carcass was consumed by dogs.[66]

Christopher Goodman's *How Superior Powers O[u]ght to be Obey[e]d of their Subjects* was archetypical of the genre. Predicated on the principle that 'we must obey God rather than men' – precisely the slogan that Henry VIII had unleashed against the pope in his first divorce campaign! – the book based its attack on Mary's alleged tyranny. Goodman derived all political power from God, regarded the obedience of a subject to temporal power as dependent on an obligation to honour divine law (interpreted in a Protestant way), and argued that a ruler could be deposed by her subjects (and he did not distinguish here between ordinary private persons and magistrates) if she violated either divine or positive law. Mary was unfit to rule: she was a woman and 'a bastard by birth' (and thus barred by the laws of inheritance from rule), and a 'traytor to God'. She had abolished

> that religion which was preached under kinge Edwarde ... so that now both by Gods Lawe and mans, she oght to be punished with death, as an open idolatres in the sight of God, and a cruel murtherer of his saints before men, and merciles traytoresse to her owne native countrie.[67]

Again, John Ponet held that monarchy was subordinate to law. In *A short Treatise of Politike Power* he, too, remodelled arguments directly borrowed from those used by Henry VIII against the pope. Anything done contrary to scripture (and thus divine law) was not lawful, but rather the product of 'cruel tyranny'. Men 'ought to have more respect to their country than to their prince: to the commonwealth than to any one person'. As he continued: commonwealths are antecedent to rulers; commonwealths and realms may live when the head is cut off, and 'may put on a new head'. In a chapter entitled, 'Whether it be Lawful to Depose an Evil Governor, and Kill a Tyrant', Ponet justified tyrannicide and the deposition of rulers at length. As much by historical and biblical allusion as by outright assertion, he upheld the opinion that 'every tree which bringeth not forth good fruit shall be cut down and cast into the fire: much more the evil tree that bringeth forth evil fruit'. He stopped short of direct action by private persons: 'Forasmuch as all things in every christian commonwealth ought to be done decently and according to order and charity, I think it cannot be maintained by God's word that any private man may kill.' But this may have been a rhetorical device, since the crucial exception was in cases where the magistracy had failed: 'where execution of just punishment upon tyrants, idolaters, and traiterous governors is either by the whole state utterly neglected, or the prince with the nobility and council conspire the subversion or alteration of their country and people'. It is highly likely that this exception, from Ponet's vivid description, was applicable to the Marian polity.[68]

It was left to the atavistic John Knox to construct a critique that was the classic of misogyny.[69] Knox's *First Blast of the Trumpet against the Monstrous Regiment of Women* was a sensational diatribe that castigated women's rule.

> To promote a woman to bear rule, superiority, dominion or empire above any realm, nation or city is repugnant to nature, contumely to God, a thing most contrarious to His revealed will and approved order, and finally it is the subversion of good order, of all equity and justice.[70]

And again, 'How abominable before God is the empire or rule of a wicked woman, yea, of a traiteresse and bastard.' Knox openly incited the subjects of women rulers to acts of resistance: to 'repress her inordinate pride and tyranny to the uttermost of their power'. Furthermore, the 'nobility and estates by whose blindness a woman is promoted' had a duty to 'retreat that which unadvisedly and by ignorance they have pronounced'. 'Without further delay', they should 'remove from authority all such persons as by usurpation, violence or tyranny do possess the same'. A woman ruler was a 'monster in nature'! If any man feared to violate an oath which he had taken to her, he should be persuaded that oaths rooted in 'ignorance' were a sin; 'so is the obstinate purpose to keep the same nothing but plain rebellion against God'.[71] Knox's polemic was published in 1559: its intended targets were the Catholic regimes of Mary Tudor in England and Mary of Guise in Scotland. It is hardly surprising that Elizabeth I was incensed when the work appeared without any modification or retraction shortly after her accession. But Knox was unmoved: he merely shelved his proposed sequel, which was to have been entitled *The Second Blast of the Trumpet*!

Stereotypes of gender were indeed so deeply etched into the collective psychology of early modern society that Mary's death and the coronation of a (seemingly!) English Deborah[72] served only to refocus the anxiety that female monarchy instilled, especially once it was appreciated that Elizabeth had resolved to 'live and die a virgin'. John Aylmer's *An harborowe for faith-full and trewe subiectes* was written and published in 1559. Intended as a riposte to Knox, the tract was, to all intents and purposes, an apology for Elizabeth's fitness to rule. In this respect, the scale of the 'public-relations' problem that the Elizabethan Privy Council inherited should not be under-estimated. In 1559 England had a monarch who (in the eyes of the Catholic powers) was a bastard, a heretic, a woman, unmarried, and challenged as to her title and right of succession to the English throne by Mary, Queen of Scotland and Dowager Queen of France.[73]

As a former Marian exile, Aylmer was the ideal author to confute Knox. He had been a tutor to Lady Jane Grey and had sat out Mary's reign in Strasbourg and Zurich. As he maintained,

> it is not in England so dangerous a matter to have a woman ruler as men take it to be. For first it is not she that ruleth but the laws, the executors whereof be her judges, appointed by her, her justices of the peace and such other officers.

He continued: 'she maketh no statutes or laws but [in] the honourable court of Parliament ... What may she do alone wherein is peril?'[74] Or, as Professor Collinson puts the point: Aylmer argued very much 'along the lines that the government of a woman was tolerable because in England it would not be so much her government as government in her name and on her behalf ... One might as well justify the government of Mrs Thatcher on the grounds that her cabinet can be trusted to keep her in order' (see below, Chapter 4).

The analogy is superb. For 'the cabinet' in the Elizabethan context was the Privy Council. It was certain that, under a woman ruler, and especially an unmarried one, the Privy Council would assert its authority as the élite executive board because the inherent social assumption was that the busi-ness of government was properly conducted by men. Under Elizabeth, the Privy Council effectively ran the country. It assumed corporate responsibil-ity for the management of finance, something that Henry VII and Henry VIII had handled personally. It enforced the religious settlement of 1559. It managed national defence and fortifications. And it enforced law and order and regulated trade and the economy. For example, it issued proclamations, regulated the poor laws, fixed prices and wages in London, and advised just-ices of the peace on wages elsewhere; it regulated internal trade; and it con-trolled vagrancy and organized 'watches' for Jesuits and seminary priests. There were 19 privy councillors in 1559; 19 in 1586; 11 in 1597; and 13 in 1601. They worked harder as the reign progressed: in the 1560s they met three or four times per week, but by the 1590s they were assembling almost every day, sometimes in both mornings and afternoons.[75]

Yet politics was a different matter. The crucial political issues of Eliza-beth's reign were her marriage, the succession to the throne, foreign policy (especially in Scotland, France, and the Netherlands), and the alteration of the religious settlement of 1559. Whenever these topics were ventilated, Elizabeth attempted to forbid or limit discussion or declined to take her privy councillors' advice when it was offered. She even redefined these topics as 'matters of state'; they became *arcana imperii* – the Tacitean phrase for the 'secrets' or 'mysteries of state': the issues which, if discussed without the sanction of the ruler, pierced the veil of 'imperial' sovereignty. They were the issues that Elizabeth consistently reserved for her own decision – or more often indecision – by invoking 'humanist-classical' idioms to argue that she needed to be further 'advised' on matters touching her Crown and state, thereby turning recognition of the need for 'counsel' into the excuse for rejecting her councillors' advice.[76] The ensuing process of 'consultation' could last for months, years, or (in the case of the decision to intervene in the Netherlands) decades!

This behaviour created considerable frustration in the Privy Council. 'Our part is to counsel,' Cecil reminded his fellow councillor, Sir Ralph Sadler, on the eve of the Northern Rising; but, except in routine administrative affairs, the Privy Council's advice usually went unheeded.[77] Lobbying the Queen on the Council's behalf in favour of intervention in Scotland in support of the Lords of the Congregation in December 1559, Cecil remarked:

> and as our duties be to give you our advice and counsel, which although we [ac]knowledge ourselves to be unable so well to do as it in such a great case is requisite, yet for the discharge of our duty and upon our sure hope that your Majesty will accept in good part our good wills and endeavours, meaning herein to discharge our consciences as we be bound both by oath and otherwise ...[78]

This was a polite statement of frustration. A less tactful version was that of Sir Francis Knollys, who told Elizabeth ten years later that it was not possible for the Queen's 'most faithful counsellors' to govern her state well unless she could find it in herself 'resolutely [to] follow their opinions in weighty affairs'. As Knollys pressed the point: 'A general in the field seeing an enterprise to be taken' could select some of his captains to consider the feasibility of the plan. What was the point if the general then acted 'contrary to their opinions'![79] And by 1578 the Earl of Leicester was complaining that 'our conference with her Majesty about affairs is both seldom and slender' (see also Collinson, Chapter 4).

The most dramatic clashes between Elizabeth and her Privy Council occurred over the decision to intervene in Scotland in support of the Protestant Lords of the Congregation in 1559–60; over the Queen's marriage and the succession in 1563 and 1566 (see also Alford, Chapter 9); over Mary, Queen of Scots and the succession in 1572, 1584–5 and 1586–7 (see also Collinson, Chapter 4); and over the intervention in the Netherlands in 1585. Particularly in relation to the (linked) issues of the marriage, the succession, and the fate of Mary, Queen of Scots, these clashes centred on disputes between the Queen and her Privy Council that the Council believed it might win if its campaign were transferred into the wider forum of Parliament. This tactic, in reality, achieved little, although the Council managed to get the death sentence on the fourth Duke of Norfolk put into effect in 1572 in the wake of the Ridolfi plot. Still, this was the Privy Council's strategy: there is no better insight into it than Cecil's letter to Walsingham after the Babington plot, when Elizabeth was refusing to sign the death warrant for the Queen of Scots: 'We stick upon Parliament, which her Majesty mislikes to have, but we all persist, to make the burden better borne and the world abroad better satisfied.'[80] Finally persuaded to summon Parliament, Elizabeth was petitioned to execute Mary, but her response was delphic: 'If I should say, I would not do what you request, it might peradventure be more than I thought; and to say I would do it, might perhaps breed peril of that you labour to preserve.'[81] She herself called this an 'answer answerless'.

In respect of these clashes, the existence of differences between Elizabeth and Cecil has always been recognized. But they have usually been explained away as disagreements over timing or as clashes over the choice of prospective husbands for either Elizabeth or Mary Stuart, rather than as fundamental differences of political conviction. Again, there has been a major investment by historians since the 1980s in the argument pioneered by Professor Michael Graves and Sir Geoffrey Elton, which has linked the parliamentary clashes of the reign to 'orchestrated debates', especially in the 1560s.[82] According to this view, Cecil and other privy councillors arranged for 'planted' speeches to be delivered in the House of Commons by 'men of business' or ordinary members in favour of their position, especially on the Queen's marriage and the succession. On this basis, these clashes have been explained away as tactical attempts to 'bounce' the Queen into decisions she refused to take: their political significance has been minimized as a result. If these clashes were purely tactical exercises, they marked points of tension in the Elizabethan political system, but did not necessarily represent clashes of ideology or belief in the way that Sir John Neale had argued in *Elizabeth I and her Parliaments*.[83]

It is not clear how much longer this interpretation will survive. Although Neale's thesis of 'government' versus 'opposition' and the 'puritan choir' in the parliamentary history of the reign has been discredited, it is likely that the new and more sophisticated understanding of the Elizabethan Parliaments that has emerged from the research of Graves and Elton, and that of Dr Alford on the conciliar politics of the 1560s and the Parliaments of 1563 and 1566,[84] will, if anything, make the history of the Elizabethan Parliaments more, rather than less, political (see also Collinson, Chapter 4); for it is increasingly being argued that Elizabeth and Cecil possessed divergent political creeds, and that the resulting tension created a fissure at the very heart of the Elizabethan establishment.[85]

In the first place, Cecil repeatedly wished to intervene in Scotland between 1559 and 1566 in the interests of a Protestant British settlement, and he did finally persuade Elizabeth to intervene in March 1560. Cecil clearly wished to remove the threat of Mary, Queen of Scots, by contriving her deposition, even during her personal rule in Scotland. Cecil's correspondence with his agents and with Mary's opponents shows that he sought not only to establish responsible conciliar government in Scotland, but also that he could happily brook regicide if this was the only way to defeat the forces of international Catholic conspiracy (as he saw them) which sought to use Mary as an instrument for the removal of the Protestant Elizabeth. This contrasts with Elizabeth's own view that monarchy, in Scotland as elsewhere, was a divine institution, and that 'absolute princes ought not to be accountable for their actions to any other than to God alone'.[86]

Second, the work of Dr Alford has established that in 1563, and especially 1566, there is no convincing evidence that speeches were 'planted' in Parliament by Cecil and the Privy Council.[87] On the contrary, this argument was constructed by Graves and Elton largely on the basis of reasoned conjecture in order to explain away what otherwise could only be explained (at the time) in terms of the ideological opposition of a 'choir' comprised of members who wished to force the Queen to settle the succession or to modify the religious settlement of 1559 on Calvinist lines. (Elizabeth refused to do both these things.) What we have in 1563 and 1566 is evidence of spontaneous speeches by those who were within and outside of Cecil's conciliar orbit; but, far more significantly, there is evidence of Cecil himself ignoring the Queen's express instructions, delivered verbally and in writing, to refrain from pursuing the issue of her marriage and the succession in Parliament. Cecil was instructed that he was not on any account to allow the grant of taxation imminent in 1566 to be linked to the issue of the succession or to Elizabeth's promise of 1563 to marry. He was to stop abusing (as Elizabeth saw it) her 'private answers to the realm'. Yet Cecil ignored the Queen's commands, and indeed covered reams of paper with *pro* and *contra* arguments and with drafts and redrafts of civil theses in defence of his case for political action.

What we discover in these and related documents is the evidence of Cecil's internal debate or 'self-fashioning' on the limits of his duty as a councillor and minister. Was he to be the personal servant of the ruler, as Wolsey and Cromwell had been in the reign of Henry VIII, in which case it seemed likely that nothing would ever be done to settle the issue of the succession or to deal with the threat of Mary? Or did he have wider responsibilities as the 'public servant of the state', defined in a humanist-classical, or quasi-republican sense, in which case his defiance of Elizabeth might be justified? (Probably this line of argument could only have been attempted under a female ruler.)

Cecil's private and public agenda was the 'preservation of the state of this Realm', by which he meant, of course, the preservation of the *Protestant* state of the realm. If the Queen refused to act, then the Privy Council would have to 'protect' and 'preserve' the Protestant state at the expense of the Queen's instructions. Or more specifically: if the heir presumptive to the English throne was to be the Catholic, Mary, Queen of Scots, then Cecil and the Privy Council intended to infringe the Crown's sovereignty and to subvert the rules of succession if the worst happened. Faced with Catholic conspiracy and Mary's claim to the throne, the élite of the Privy Council sought to limit the powers of the monarchy should Elizabeth die or be assassinated. Not only were their initiatives predicated on a view of England as a 'mixed polity' not dissimilar from that expressed by Ponet in *A short Treatise of Politike Power*; Cecil's contingency plans, up to and including those of 1584–5, also provided that, in the event of Elizabeth's death, the Privy Council and Parliament should not fail to act despite the lapse of their authority. His contingency (or 'interregnum') drafts for the succession envisaged a 'Council of State', 'Great Council', or 'Grand Council' which would form a provisional government in the absence of a ruler and which would adjudicate the claims of candidates for the succession in conjunction with Parliament (see also Collinson, Chapter 4).[88] Not only was this aristocratic republicanism *par excellence*; one wonders how, if at all, the Privy Council's schemes differ from the initial stages of the Revolution of 1688 when a committee of peers and privy councillors formed themselves into a provisional government in the absence of the king.[89] These plans only became redundant after Mary's execution at Fotheringhay Castle in 1587, when the succession of her son became (at least theoretically) assured.

Until the execution of Mary or thereabouts, the Privy Council's political creed may broadly be summarized thus: (1) sovereignty lay in the 'queen-in-Parliament' in the terms that had been defined by St German in the reign of Henry VIII;[90] (2) the prerogative of the ruler was limited by the advice of the Privy Council; and (3) the assent of the whole realm in Parliament was required to effect significant political or religious change and in particular to resolve the issue of the succession to the throne.

If, however, this was Cecil's political creed until 1587,[91] it is important that we recognize the corollary, which is that for almost 30 years he and Elizabeth subscribed to discordant political philosophies despite their enduring political relationship. As Professor Collinson has remarked, historians have conventionally treated Elizabeth and Cecil 'as if they were the front and rear legs of a pantomime horse' (see below, Chapter 4). The reality is likely to have been entirely different. The dichotomy centres on the issue of 'counsel'. Was the 'sovereignty' of the ruler to be limited by the advice of the Privy Council? Like Henry VIII, Elizabeth believed that her *imperium* was ordained by God alone, her prerogative unlimited by her counsellors' advice. She saw herself as the head of the body politic, but had no sense of the duties of the head to the body when the body tried to counsel it.

The full implications of this dissonance did not become apparent until the spectacular collision between Elizabeth and the Privy Council over the dispatch of the warrant for the execution of the Queen of Scots. The warrant's delivery was authorized by the Privy Council, who acted out of a sense of utter frustration at Elizabeth's reluctance to put the death sentence pronounced against Mary into effect. The letter that the Council attached to the execution warrant justified its action as taken 'for [the Queen's] special service tending to the safety of her royal person and universal quietness of her whole Realm'.[92] But, in this matter, the Council acted not only clandestinely, but in defiance of Elizabeth's most recently expressed instructions, a blatant act of republicanism for which she sought to hang her secretary, William Davison, by royal prerogative (i.e. summarily and without trial) for allowing the warrant to leave his possession. For three months, Cecil feared that her wrath would usurp the rule of law, and relations between the Queen and Council took four months to return to anything approaching normality.

It has also been suggested (albeit at present tentatively) that this same dissonance had been alive, if submerged beneath the waters, since the enactment of the religious settlement of 1559. Professor Collinson has urged that a 'distinct possibility' should not be overlooked that the Queen who (notionally) made the settlement 'was manipulated and constrained, if not inside the Parliament [as Neale had erroneously supposed] then outside it, in her own court and household'.[93] I have myself independently argued that the inexperienced Elizabeth *was* probably outmanoeuvred in 1559, when Cecil seized the opportunity to move further down the Protestant road than the Queen had intended or preferred. The argument rests on work in progress, but, if such an interpretation of the 1559 settlement can be sustained, it would, in turn, become possible to argue that the Elizabethan regime had, all along, been established on false premises from the Queen's point of view.[94]

This is surely the crux. In what Professor Collinson has called the 'acephalous' conditions of Elizabeth's reign, the binary opposition which was latent in the theory of monarchy since the reign of Henry VIII (see below, Chapter 4) was played out: the tension between Elizabeth's view of her 'imperial' monarchy – the idea that sovereignty was vested in her alone – and the conviction of Cecil and the Privy Council that sovereignty lay in the 'queen-in-Parliament' if the Protestant state was to be preserved, and most especially when the ruler declined to be counselled. It has already been noted that it was intrinsic to the tradition of the English monarchy that the supreme authority in the body politic was not the king alone, but *the king counselled*. As the author of *Fleta*, a standard legal and constitutional treatise of the late thirteenth century, had written of Parliament and legislation: 'In his parliaments the king in council holds his court.'[95]

Again, the ideas of the sovereignty of the 'queen-in-Parliament' and the 'mixed polity' were commonly linked in and after Mary's reign. They also made for strange bedfellows. As part of his defence of Elizabeth's rule in 1559, Aylmer had set the notion of 'mixed polity' in a parliamentary context. 'The regiment of England', he observed, is not a mere monarchie, as some for lacke of consideration thinke, nor a meere oligarchie, nor democracie, but a rule mixte of all these ... thimage whereof, and not the image but the thinge in deede, is to be sene in the parliament house, wherin you shall find these three estates

(see also Collinson, Chapter 4). This was almost identical to the line taken by the presbyterian leader, Thomas Cartwright, whom Aylmer, as Bishop of London, later imprisoned. In the course of the Admonition Controversy, Cartwright claimed that the Elizabethan (secular) polity was a 'mixed estate': it was a state in which monarchy, aristocracy, and democracy were admixed and conjoined in the forms of Queen, Privy Council, and Parliament.[96] The Queen, according to Cartwright, was not 'imperial' in the sense understood by Henry VIII. She shared her sovereignty with the Privy Council and Parliament. This, of course, was as much political heresy in Elizabeth's eyes as presbyterianism was doctrinal heresy. The irony is that, until 1587, it was a heresy which Cecil too embraced. In this respect, the most powerful and subversive critique of the monarchy of Elizabeth I – at least until the execution of the Queen of Scots – did not derive from puritanism or the literature of political exclusion: it emanated from the very heart of the regime!

All this changed in 1587. In terms of practical politics, Mary Stuart's execution was a watershed as significant as the death of Henry VIII. James VI of Scotland became the heir (presumptive) to the English throne: he was male, Protestant, and available. No longer was it necessary for the Privy Council to embrace quasi-republican ideas. As a result, there was a swing to the right. The atmosphere became claustrophobic and authoritarian: it has even been argued that the period between 1587 and 1603 was so fundamentally different from what had gone before that it should be called Elizabeth's 'second' reign.[97] This drift to authoritarianism was underpinned partly by the anxiety engendered by the war with Spain and the rebellion in Ireland, partly by irrational fears of religious nonconformity and recusancy, and partly by the economic turmoil that was the result of a succession of bad harvests, rising prices, and outbreaks of plague and influenza. In the 1590s, privy councillors and magistrates became obsessed with issues of state security, the subversiveness of religious nonconformity, and the threat of 'popularity' and social revolt. Moreover, the changed emphasis was mirrored at Court, where the deaths of several of the 'first' generation of Elizabethan privy councillors – including Leicester, Walsingham, and Mildmay – and the ambition of the Earl of Essex, fused with the poverty of the Crown and the competition for patronage to usher in a phase of unusually intense factionalism, self-interest, and instability which – in 1601 – sparked Essex's attempted *coup*.

It was in this mood of *fin de siècle* that the thesis of divine-right monarchy was finally reasserted. As in Mary's reign, the pace was forced by religion. When Cartwright had propounded his ideal of a 'mixed estate', he had touched a nerve which the conformist establishment could not ignore. Even if the Elizabethan regime *was* to all intents and purposes a 'mixed polity' until 1587, the link with religious 'popularity', once Cartwright had made the connection, made it *lèse-majesté* to declare this fact in print or to claim that there were things the Queen could not do without Parliament. In a very real sense, it was the threat of presbyterianism in the 1570s and 1580s which caused the regime belatedly to recognize the true implications of the undercurrents that swirled beneath the (superficially) calmer waters of Elizabethan political thought.

In reply to Cartwright, John (later Archbishop) Whitgift countered that the 'government of this kingdom is a right and true monarchy', and in that monarchy the Queen's authority over Church and State was derived directly from God.[98] This set the tone for subsequent refutations of presbyterianism, which took the line that the rule of a godly prince, accountable only to God, was the model for human government. In both England and Scotland, in fact, it was the deployment of this argument against the threat of 'popularity' in religion which paved the way for the rehabilitation of the thesis of 'imperial' kingship. In Scotland, James VI personally took the lead. In England, the circle of Richard Bancroft, Richard Cosin, John Bridges, and Thomas Bilson formed the vanguard. Moreover, these publicists increasingly aimed at a double target, since the view that England was a 'mixed polity' was also propagated by Catholics eager to frustrate James's succession to the English throne. The Jesuit, Robert Parsons, held that the ruler's prerogative was strictly limited by law and, following Bellarmine, that, whereas the pope derived his powers directly from God, kings drew theirs from the people.[99]

The climax was reached in Cawdrey's Case (1591), a *cause célèbre* concerning Elizabeth's right to delegate the exercise of her ecclesiastical supremacy to commissioners appointed by letters patent.[100] Cawdrey's Case was the *Roe* v. *Wade* of Elizabethan constitutional law. The question was: could the queen legally empower the commissioners? The questions behind the question were: what was the extent of the queen's 'imperial' prerogative by the common law of England? And in particular: could the queen's 'imperial' prerogative override statute and common law?[101] The common-law judges ruled that 'by the ancient laws of this realm this kingdom of England is an absolute empire and monarchy'. And again,

> the kingly head of this politic body is instituted and furnished with plenary and entire power, prerogative, and jurisdiction to render justice and right to every part and member of this body, of what estate, degree, or calling soever, in all causes ecclesiastical or temporal, otherwise he should not be a head of the whole body.[102]

This was the language of Henry VIII's Act of Appeals: at a stroke the judges had reaffirmed and revitalized the theory of 'imperial' monarchy. Their decision meant that they had judged Elizabeth's *imperium* to be theocratic.

They acknowledged that Parliament had enacted the legislation whereby the settlement of 1559 had been erected, but held that Parliament was merely the instrument whereby the ruler's prerogative was set forth. Even if Parliament had never met, Elizabeth was imbued with an 'imperial' sovereignty which she could exercise in person in the Church or delegate to whomsoever she chose.

Driven by envy and frustrated ambition when his bid to dominate Elizabeth's counsels failed, the second Earl of Essex dared to challenge this exalted view of monarchy. At exactly the moment when Essex's feud with Robert Cecil had reached its climax and Essex was excluded from Elizabeth's presence, he was advised that obedience to the sovereign was 'a duty not imposed upon you by nature and policy only, but by religious and sacred bonds: wherein the divine majesty of Almighty God hath by the rule of Christianity obliged you'.[103] To this Essex replied that obedience could not be demanded beyond the bounds of honour. He repudiated unconditional religious obligation with the almost Shakespearian line: 'What, cannot princes err? Cannot subjects receive wrong? Is an earthly power infinite?'[104] By such words Essex handed a sword to his enemies, since they could be made to appear that he had denied the divine authority of kingship and the quasi-sacerdotal role of Elizabeth as supreme Governor of the Church, which became the basis of a charge of atheism.[105]

This shift in tone is reflected in the literature of the 1590s, when writers became fascinated by the themes of kingship, authority, and the acquisition and retention of power, particularly in relation to humanist-classical definitions of 'virtue' in both civic and military aspects. (Shakespeare's *Richard II* and *Coriolanus* are but two compelling examples.) The role of 'counsel' and 'counselling' in monarchies and republics, and the endemic problems of corruption and dissimulation, were put under the microscope in an effort to explain how 'vice', 'flattery', and 'ambition' had come to supersede the traditional values of 'wisdom', 'service', and *respublica*. Political commentary acquired thickly Tacitean overtones which stressed how the Roman emperors and their counsellors had corrupted one another.[106] No longer was Tacitus read simply as a source of Roman imperial history. He became the model for those writers who thought the past too complex and recalcitrant to be reduced to straightforward moral lessons. Tacitus had given the 'secrets' or 'mysteries of state' a distinctive edge by arguing that Tiberius' greatest attribute was his ability to dissimulate. In the hands of Tacitean authors, the idealistic bias that had characterized the writings of such humanists as Elyot and Thomas Starkey in the reign of Henry VIII was dethroned in favour of a cynical and sceptical outlook which intimated that rulers and counsellors attained their ends by the autonomous exercise of politic will, and did so with morally ambiguous results.

Yet the Tacitean slant of late-Elizabethan political literature is only one of many elements which contributed to what has been called the 'classicization' of politics in the late sixteenth and early seventeenth centuries: the process, begun by the humanists, and reinforced by Henry VIII's choice of prototypes of 'imperial' kingship, whereby politics and government were conceptualized in language and images borrowed from classical antiquity. In turn, this process underpinned the incorporation into English political thought of the classical prototype of the 'state': the notion that in England there was a 'state' and 'government' as well as a queen.[107] The 'state' in this sense became a supreme and impersonal form of political authority within a 'body politic' empowered to act in defence of the public good.[108] This notion, which was partly indebted to Bodin, as well as to the translations of Continental republican treatises that began to be printed in England in the 1590s,[109] went considerably further than Starkey's *Dialogue between Pole and Lupset* with its view of 'limited' monarchy. It became possible to say that rulers *themselves* had a duty to consider 'the weal and advancement of the state which they serve'. It became possible to conceptualize the 'state', the 'interests of the state', and (especially under the influence of Italian and French political thought) 'reason of state' in contexts which (certainly in the eyes of conviction-Protestants) meant more than the person or 'private interests' of the ruler. Opinions diverged on the issue of whether sovereignty could be shared. But, following Bodin, it became possible to distinguish the 'state' from its citizens and to envisage the 'state' as a locus of political power which remains distinct from, and superior to, both its citizens and their magistrates.[110]

Ambiguity is never the best note upon which to conclude an argument. But deep ambiguity was the overriding legacy of the Tudors to the early Stuarts in 1603. One element was the thesis of 'imperial' kingship which had underpinned the claims of Henry VIII and Elizabeth I to secular and ecclesiastical *imperium*. By the time of Cawdrey's Case, this view of the monarchy and royal supremacy had been rehabilitated, and in the hands of the Lambeth circle of conformist apologists formed the basis of a revitalized and exalted 'divine-right' interpretation of monarchy and (increasingly after 1589) episcopacy. The competing element was St German's counter-thesis of the 'king-in-Parliament'. This was commonly linked in and after Mary's reign to the idea of the 'mixed polity', forming an amalgam that acquired strong conciliar (and republican) overtones in the 'acephalous' conditions of the reign of Elizabeth I. Yet, if these overtones became audible, they were quickly smothered after 1587 once the succession to the throne was assured. Again, this element, when set into the humanist contexts of classical antiquity and the debate on the nature of sovereignty, provided the eventual rationale for a thesis of the 'state' in something recognizably approaching the modern sense.

Of course, no single Tudor text or document could fully encapsulate all these strands. A comprehensive work of synthesis was improbable for two reasons. First, such a work, if it were to have been written, would have had to acknowledge the potential that existed for ideological conflict between the sovereign acts of an 'imperial' monarchy and the welfare of the community, the 'state', or the 'public'. Professor Sacks has convincingly argued that, while two such differing world pictures *did* exist by the 1590s, conflict between them was averted by resort to humanist-classical rituals of accommodation as long as Elizabeth I was alive (see below, Chapter 5). Second, a gap in the literature may not have been so apparent to contemporaries, since copies of the French and Latin editions of Bodin's *Six livres de la république* streamed into England, as did copies of his earlier treatise of 1566, the *Methodus*, or *Method for the Easy Comprehension of History*. It was said at Cambridge in 1579 that 'you cannot step into a scholar's study but (ten to one) you shall lightly find open either Bodin *De Republica* ... or some other like French or Italian politic discourses'.[111] It is a marvellous glimpse into the hidden world of reading in the Elizabethan period, one which, if true, reinforces my belief that Tudor political culture was also a distinctively Renaissance and humanist-classical culture which can only be properly comprehended and contextualized on such terms. But at that point we have returned to methodology, and the wheel has turned full circle.

Notes

1 S. B. Chrimes, *English Constitutional Ideas in the Fifteenth Century* (Cambridge, 1936), p. 174. I am indebted *inter alia* to G. L. Harris, 'The King and his Subjects', in R. Horrox (ed.), *Fifteenth Century Attitudes* (Cambridge, 1994), pp. 13–28; John Watts, *Henry VI and the Politics of Kingship* (Cambridge, 1996), pp. 16–80; and M. Viroli, *From Politics to Reason of State: The Acquisition and Transformation of the Language of Politics, 1250–1600* (Cambridge, 1992), pp. 11–70.
2 The terms 'ordinaria', 'ordinatia', and 'regula' were variously used to signify the exercise of authority by kings and popes according to rules of positive law. But the theocratic ruler was also above the law as the prerogative of his imperium. In this sphere he ruled *dei gratia* and was *legibus solutus*. W. Ullmann, *Principles of Government and Politics in the Middle Ages* (2nd edn, London, 1966); F. Oakley, 'Jacobean Political Theology: The Absolute and Ordinary Powers of the King', *Journal of the History of Ideas*, 29 (1968), pp. 323–46; Janelle R. Greenberg, *Tudor and Stuart Theories of Kingship: The Dispensing Power and the Royal Discretionary Authority in Sixteenth and Seventeenth Century England* (University Microfilms, Ann Arbor: University of Michigan Ph.D., 1970), pp. 37–42.
3 W. Staunford, *An exposicion of the kinges prerogative collected out of the great abridgement of justice Fitzherbert and other olde writers of the lawes of Englande* (London, 1567).
4 Ullmann, *Principles of Government and Politics*, p. 184 n. 2.
5 For relevant discussion, see G. O. Sayles, *The Functions of the Medieval Parliament of England* (London, 1988); Sayles, *The King's Parliament of England* (New York, 1974); H. G. Richardson and G. O. Sayles, *The English Parliament in the Middle Ages* (London, 1981); E. B. Fryde and E. Miller (eds), *Historical Studies of the English Parliament* (2 vols, Cambridge, 1970); G. L. Harris, *King, Parliament and Public Finance in Medieval England to 1369* (Oxford, 1975); J. D. Alsop, 'The Theory and Practice of Tudor Taxation', *English Historical Review*, 97 (1982), pp. 1–30; Alsop, 'Innovation in Tudor Taxation', *English Historical Review*, 99 (1984), pp. 83–93; M. J. Braddick, *The Nerves of State: Taxation and the Financing of the English State, 1558–1714* (Manchester, 1996).

6 *De laudibus legum anglie*, ed. S. B. Chrimes (Cambridge, 1949), *passim*.

7 As Bacon's essay, *Of Counsel*, later put the point: ancient history 'set forth in figure both the incorporation and inseparable conjunction of counsel with kings ... whereby they intend that Sovereignty is married to Counsel'. (A married woman shared in the administration of her husband's household and mitigated his authority just as equity tempered the rigour of the common law.) *Francis Bacon: A Critical Edition of the Major Works*, ed. B. Vickers (Oxford, 1996), p. 380.

8 Watts, *Henry VI and the Politics of Kingship*, pp. 16–17. See also John Guy, 'The Rhetoric of Counsel in Early-Modern England', in D. Hoak (ed.), *Tudor Political Culture* (Cambridge, 1995), pp. 293–4.

9 Harris, 'The King and his Subjects', p. 13.

10 Thomas Elyot, *The Book Named the Governor*, ed. S. E. Lehmberg (London, 1962, repr. 1975), p. 238.

11 Elyot, *The Book Named the Governor*, p. 13.

12 Watts, *Henry VI and the Politics of Kingship*, p. 27; Guy, 'The Rhetoric of Counsel in Early-Modern England', pp. 293–310, where these complex issues are explored at greater length.

13 Aristotle, *The Politics*, ed. S. Everson (Cambridge, 1988), esp. pp. 51–81, 133–40.

14 Elyot, *Of the knowledeg [sic] whiche maketh a wise man* (London, 1533).

15 For a more detailed survey of Elyot, see F. W. Conrad, 'The Problem of Counsel Reconsidered: The Case of Sir Thomas Elyot', in P. A. Fideler and T. F. Mayer (eds), *Political Thought and the Tudor Commonwealth* (London, 1992), pp. 75–107.

16 See also T. E. Hartley (ed.), *Proceedings in the Parliaments of Elizabeth I, I, 1558–1581* (Leicester, 1981), pp. 129–30.

17 Quentin Skinner, *Reason and Rhetoric in the Philosophy of Hobbes* (Cambridge, 1996), pp. 66–74.

18 Roy Porter and M. Teich, *The Renaissance in National Context* (Cambridge, 1992); Roger Doucet, *Les Institutions de la France au XVIᵉ siècle* (2 vols, Paris, 1948); Doucet, *Étude sur le gouvernement de François Ier dans ses rapports avec le Parlement de Paris* (2 vols, Paris, 1921–6); R. J. Knecht, *Renaissance Warrior and Patron: The Reign of Francis I* (Cambridge, 1994); Knecht, 'The Court of Francis I', *European Studies Review*, 8 (1978), pp. 1–22; G. Jacqueton, 'Le Trésor de l'Épargne sous François I, 1523–47', *Revue Historique*, 55 (1894), pp. 1–43, and 56 (1894), pp. 1–38; J. Russell Major, 'The Crown and the Aristocracy in Renaissance France', *American Historical Review*, 69 (1964), pp. 631–45; Russell Major, *Representative Institutions in Renaissance France, 1421–1559* (Madison, 1960), pp. 126–47; Russell Major, *Representative Government in Early Modern France* (New Haven, 1980), pp. 1–204; John Headley, *The Emperor and his Chancellor: A Study of the Imperial Chancellery of Gattinara* (Cambridge, 1983); F. A. Yates, *Astraea: The Imperial Theme in the Sixteenth Century* (London, 1975).

19 John Guy, 'The Henrician Age', in J. G. A. Pocock (ed.), *The Varieties of British Political Thought, 1500–1800* (Cambridge, 1993), pp. 22–38.

20 D. MacCulloch (ed.), *The Reign of Henry VIII: Politics, Policy and Piety* (London, 1995), p. 180.

21 See, for example, James E. Hampson, 'Richard Cosin and the Revitalization of the Clerical Estate in Late Elizabethan England', unpublished St Andrews Ph.D. dissertation (1997).

22 BL, Cotton MS Cleopatra E.VI, fo. 28ᵛ.

23 *Memorials of Thomas Cranmer*, ed. J. Strype (2 vols, Oxford, 1840), I, p. 43; P. Janelle (ed.), *Obedience in Church and State* (Cambridge, 1930), pp. lxi–lxii, 116–18, 130–2; D. MacCulloch, *Thomas Cranmer* (London, 1996); G. Redworth, *In Defence of the Church Catholic* (Oxford, 1990).

24 J. J. Scarisbrick, 'The Pardon of the Clergy, 1531', *Cambridge Historical Journal*, 12 (1956), pp. 22–39; John Guy, 'Henry VIII and the *Praemunire* Manoeuvres of 1530–31', *English Historical Review*, 97 (1982), pp. 481–503.

25 The watercolour is in the Royal Collection.

26 *Holbein and the Court of Henry VIII* (Queen's Gallery; London, 1978), pp. 129–30.

27 Alistair Fox and John Guy, *Reassessing the Henrician Age: Humanism, Politics and Reform* (Oxford, 1986), pp. 138–40; Guy, *Tudor England* (Oxford 1988), pp. 116–64. I have drawn here and elsewhere on some material from my essay on 'The Henrician Age' in Pocock (ed.), *The Varieties of British Political Thought*.

28 J. A. Crook, *Consilium Principis: Imperial Councils and Counsellors from Augustus to Diocletian* (Cambridge, 1955), pp. 21–30.

29 Elyot, *Book Named The Governor*, pp. 236–41, esp. 238.

30 For discussion of counselling as a 'bridle' upon royal power in Valois France, see John Guy, 'The French King's Council, 1483–1526', in R. A. Griffiths and J. W. Sherborne (eds), *Kings and Nobles in the Later Middle Ages: A Tribute to Charles Ross* (Gloucester, 1986), pp. 274–94.

31 Thomas Starkey, *A Dialogue between Reginald Pole and Thomas Lupset*, ed. K. Burton (London, 1948); Starkey, *A Dialogue between Pole and Lupset*, ed. T. F. Mayer (Camden Society, 4th ser., 37; London, 1989).

32 T. F. Mayer, *Thomas Starkey and the Commonweal: Humanist Politics and Religion in the Reign of Henry VIII* (Cambridge, 1989), pp. 44–5, 132–3.

33 For resonant echoes, see Fox and Guy, *Reassessing the Henrician Age*, pp. 121–47; Guy, 'The Politics of Counsel in Early Modern England', in Hoak (ed.), *Tudor Political Culture*, pp. 297–9.

34 Starkey, *Dialogue between Pole and Lupset*, ed. Burton, pp. 155–6, 164–7.

35 Starkey, *Dialogue between Pole and Lupset*, ed. Burton, pp. 155–6, 164–7.

36 See also Mayer, *Thomas Starkey and the Commonweal*, p. 132.

37 John Guy, Ralph Keen, Clarence H. Miller, and R. McGugan (eds), *The Complete Works of St Thomas More, X, The Debellation of Salem and Bizance* (New Haven, 1987 [1988]), introduction, pp. xvii–xciv; Fox and Guy, *Reassessing the Henrician Age*, pp. 95–120.

38 R. S. Sylvester (ed.), *The Complete Works of St Thomas More, II, The History of King Richard III* (New Haven, 1963; repr. 1974), pp. lxxxiii–xcviii.

39 J. H. M. Salmon, *Renaissance and Revolt: Essays in the Intellectual and Social History of Early Modern France* (Cambridge, 1987), pp. 27–53.

40 Sylvester (ed.), *Complete Works of St Thomas More, II, The History of King Richard III*, p. lxxxix. More also used Suetonius as a source for the history of the Roman empire.

41 A complete Latin edition of the relevant books of Tacitus was published in 1533, and copies were circulating in London and Cambridge: B. Rhenanus (ed.), *Annalium, siue Historiae Augustae, libri sedecim* (Basle, 1533).

42 Clarence H. Miller, L. Bradner, C. A. Lynch, and R. P. Oliver (eds), *The Complete Works of St Thomas More, III, ii, Latin Poems* (New Haven, 1984), pp. 144–5.

43 There is now a large, and important, literature on this topic. See especially *St German's Doctor and Student*, ed. T. F. T. Plucknett and J. L. Barton (Selden Society; London, 1974), pp. 317–40; John Guy, *Christopher St German on Chancery and Statute* (Selden Society, Supplementary Series, 6; London, 1985); Fox and Guy, *Reassessing the Henrician Age*, pp. 95–120, 179–98; Guy, Keen, Miller, and McGugan (eds), *Complete Works of St Thomas More, X, The Debellation of Salem and Bizance*, pp. xxix–xlvi, 395–417; G. R. Elton, '*Lex terrae victrix*: The Triumph of Parliamentary Law in the Sixteenth Century', in D. M. Dean and N. L. Jones (eds), *The Parliaments of Elizabethan England* (Oxford, 1990), pp. 15–36.

44 St German, *An Answer to a Letter* (London, 1535), sigs. G5ᵛ–G6ᵛ; Fox and Guy, *Reassessing the Henrician Age*, pp. 199–220.

45 *An Answer to a Letter*, sigs. G3–G6ᵛ.

46 G. R. Elton, *Studies in Tudor and Stuart Politics and Government* (4 vols, Cambridge, 1974–92), II, pp. 215–35.

47 Guy, *Christopher St German on Chancery and Statute*, pp. 127–35.

48 For a recent discussion of (especially) the theological implications of the Henrician crisis of obedience, see Richard Rex, 'The Crisis of Obedience: God's Word and Henry's Reformation', *Historical Journal*, 39 (1996), pp. 863–94.

49 Glyn Redworth, 'Whatever Happened to the English Reformation?', *History Today*, 37 (Oct. 1987), pp. 29–36.

50 Janelle (ed.), *Obedience in Church and State*, pp. 68–92.
51 J. Spedding *et al.* (eds), *The Life and Letters of Francis Bacon* (7 vols, London, 1861–74), III, p. 250.
52 See especially Carol Levin, *The Heart and Stomach of a King: Elizabeth I and the Politics of Sex and Power* (Philadelphia, 1994); Helen Hackett, *Virgin Mother, Maiden Queen: Elizabeth I and the Cult of the Virgin Mary* (London, 1995); Susan Frye, *Elizabeth I: The Competition of Representation* (New York, 1993); Susan Doran, *Monarchy and Matrimony: The Courtships of Elizabeth I* (London, 1996); Susan Bassnett, *Elizabeth I: A Feminist Perspective* (New York, 1988).
53 Levin, *Heart and Stomach of a King*, p. 3.
54 N. Cuddy, 'The King's Chambers: The Bedchamber of James I in Administration and Politics, 1603–1625', unpublished Oxford D.Phil. dissertation (1987), p. 196. I am grateful to my research student John Cramsie for tracking down this and the previous reference.
55 Catherine Bates, *The Rhetoric of Courtship in Elizabethan Language and Literature* (Cambridge, 1992), p. 45.
56 Watts, *Henry VI and the Politics of Kingship*, pp. 321–3.
57 Guy, *Tudor England*, pp. 199–226.
58 D. E. Hoak, 'The King's Privy Chamber, 1547–1553', in D. J. Guth and J. W. McKenna (eds), *Tudor Rule and Revolution* (Cambridge, 1982), pp. 87–108; Hoak, 'Rehabilitating the Duke of Northumberland', in J. Loach and R. Tittler (eds), *The Mid-Tudor Polity, c. 1540–1560* (London, 1980), pp. 29–51.
59 Hoak, 'The King's Privy Chamber, 1547–1553', p. 87.
60 M. Aston, *The King's Bedpost: Reformation and Iconography in a Tudor Portrait Group* (Cambridge, 1993), pp. 26–7.
61 It was also useful, as John Hooper noted in a book published in Zurich in 1547, that Josiah's grandfather, King Manasseh, had died at the age of 55 – the same age as Henry VIII at his death – 'before he could conveniently restore the book of the law and the true word of God unto the people'. See Aston, *The King's Bedpost*, p. 31.
62 For the speed at which the Edwardian reforms were implemented locally, see Ronald Hutton, 'The Local Impact of the Tudor Reformations', in C. Haigh (ed.), *The English Reformation Revised* (Cambridge, 1987), pp. 114–38.
63 Robert M. Kingdon, 'Calvinism and Resistance Theory, 1550–1580', in J. H. Burns and M. Goldie (eds), *The Cambridge History of Political Thought, 1450–1700* (Cambridge, 1991), pp. 193–218; D. M. Loades, *The Reign of Mary Tudor* (2nd edn, London, 1991), pp. 262–303; J. Loach, 'Pamphlets and Politics, 1553–8', *Bulletin of the Institute of Historical Research*, 48 (1975), pp. 31–44; Loach, 'The Marian Establishment and the Printing Press, *English Historical Review*, 100 (1986), pp. 138–51.
64 E. Duffy, *The Stripping of the Altars* (London, 1992); C. Haigh, *English Reformations* (Oxford, 1993); Haigh (ed.), *The English Reformation Revised*; MacCulloch, *Thomas Cranmer*; R. H. Pogson, 'Reginald Pole and the Priorities of Government in Mary Tudor's Church', *Historical Journal*, 18 (1975), pp. 3–20; Pogson, 'Revival and Reform in Mary Tudor's Church: A Question of Money', *Journal of Ecclesiastical History*, 25 (1974), pp. 249–65; J. Loach, *Parliament and the Crown in the Reign of Mary Tudor* (Oxford, 1986); Loach and Tittler (eds), *The Mid-Tudor Polity, c.1540–1560*.
65 Loach, *Parliament and the Crown in the Reign of Mary Tudor*, p. 93.
66 Constance Jordan, 'Women's Rule in Sixteenth-Century British Political Thought', *Renaissance Quarterly*, 40 (1987), pp. 421–51.
67 Jordan, 'Women's Rule in Sixteenth-Century British Political Thought'.
68 *A short Treatise of Politike Power, and of the true Obedience which subiectes owe to kynges and other civile Gouernours, with an Exhortacion to all true naturall Englishe men* (Strasbourg, 1556). For a slightly different emphasis, see Kingdon, 'Calvinism and Resistance Theory, 1550–1580', pp. 194–6.
69 Jordan, 'Women's Rule in Sixteenth-Century British Political Thought'.
70 John Knox, *On Rebellion*, ed. R. Mason (Cambridge, 1994), p. 8.
71 Knox, *On Rebellion*, pp. 43–4.

72 Deborah was a prophetess and the 'judge and restorer' of Israel who defeated the Canaanites and delivered the people of Israel (Judg. 4–5). The coronation pageants of Elizabeth I hailed the Queen as Deborah, and urged her to reconstitute concord and the 'true [Protestant] faith' (A. F. Pollard (ed.), *Tudor Tracts, 1532–1588* (London, 1903), pp. 367–92).

73 W. T. MacCaffrey, *The Shaping of the Elizabethan Regime: Elizabethan Politics, 1558–72* (London, 1969); Stephen Alford, 'William Cecil and the British Succession Crisis of the 1560s', unpublished St Andrews Ph.D. dissertation (1996).

74 G. R. Elton, *The Tudor Constitution: Documents and Commentary* (1st edn, Cambridge, 1960; 2nd edn, 1982), p. 16.

75 Guy, *Tudor England*, pp. 309–19.

76 See the interesting, if not entirely satisfactory, article by Mary T. Crane, '"Video et taceo": Elizabeth I and the Rhetoric of Counsel', *Studies in English Literature*, 28 (1988), pp. 1–15.

77 Guy, *Tudor England*, p. 309.

78 PRO SP 12/7, fo. 185^{r-v}. I owe this reference and the succeeding one to Dr Stephen Alford.

79 PRO SP 12/49, fo. 57^v.

80 J. E. Neale, *Elizabeth I and her Parliaments* (2 vols, London, 1953–7; repr. 1969), II, p. 104.

81 J. E. Neale, *Elizabeth I and her Parliaments*, II, p. 104.

82 M. A. R. Graves, 'The Management of the Elizabethan House of Commons: The Council's "Men of Business" ', *Parliamentary History*, 2 (1983), pp. 11–38; Graves, 'Thomas Norton the Parliament Man: An Elizabethan MP, 1559–1581', *Historical Journal*, 23 (1980), pp. 17–35; Graves, *Elizabethan Parliaments, 1559–1601* (London, 1987); Graves, *The Tudor Parliaments: Crown, Lords and Commons, 1485–1603* (London, 1985); Graves, *Thomas Norton: The Parliament Man* (Oxford, 1994); G. R. Elton, *The Parliament of England, 1559–1581* (Cambridge, 1986).

83 Neale, *Elizabeth I and her Parliaments*.

84 Stephen Alford, 'William Cecil and the British Succession Crisis of the 1560s', unpublished St Andrews Ph.D. dissertation (1996).

85 For the initial statement of this argument, see John Guy, 'The 1590s: The Second Reign of Elizabeth I?', in Guy (ed.), *The Reign of Elizabeth I: Court and Culture in the Last Decade* (Cambridge, 1995), pp. 1–19. I have incorporated some rewritten passages from this introduction in the remainder of the present essay.

86 Folger Shakespeare Library, MS V.b.142, fo. 26.

87 Alford, 'William Cecil and the British Succession Crisis of the 1560s'.

88 See especially PRO SP 12/28/20, fos. 68–9; SP 12/176/22, SP 12/176/28, SP 12/176/29, SP 12/176/30; Henry E. Huntington Library, Ellesmere MS 1192, annotated and corrected by Cecil. See also P. Collinson, 'The Elizabethan Exclusion Crisis', *Proceedings of the British Academy*, 84 (1995), pp. 51–92.

89 R. Beddard, *A Kingdom without a King: The Journal of the Provisional Government in the Revolution of 1688* (Oxford, 1988).

90 See also Sir Thomas Smith, *De republica anglorum*, ed. M. Dewar (Cambridge, 1982), pp. 78–9; Hartley (ed.), *Proceedings*, I, pp. 129–39; Aylmer on the Queen and Parliament in Elton, *Tudor Constitution* (2nd edn), p. 16.

91 For Cecil's views after 1587, see Guy, 'The 1590s: The Second Reign of Elizabeth I?'.

92 Sotheby's sale of 16 Dec. 1996, lot 40 (purchased by Lambeth Palace Library).

93 P. Collinson, *Elizabethan Essays* (London, 1994), p. 109.

94 John Guy, 'The Religious Settlement of 1559 and the First Elizabethan Polity' (forthcoming), a revised version of a plenary lecture to the International Colloquium on Reformation History, University of St Andrews, 1 Apr. 1996.

95 H. G. Richardson and G. O. Sayles, *The English Parliament in the Middle Ages* (London, 1981), no. 26, pp. 1–49.

96 See Cartwright's controversy with Whitgift in J. Ayre (ed.), *The Works of John Whitgift* (3 vols, Cambridge, 1851–3), I, p. 390; III, pp. 196–7; Peter Lake, *Anglicans and Puritans? Presbyterianism and English Conformist Thought from Whitgift to Hooker* (London, 1988), pp. 55–6.

97 See Guy, 'The 1590s: The Second Reign of Elizabeth I?'.
98 Ayre (ed.), *Works of John Whitgift*, I, 393, 467; III, 196–7; Lake, *Anglicans and Puritans?*, pp. 62–4.
99 J. H. M. Salmon, 'Catholic Resistance Theory, Ultramontanism, and the Royalist Response, 1580–1620', in Burns and Goldie (eds), *Cambridge History of Political Thought, 1450–1700*, pp. 219–53.
100 Guy, 'The Elizabethan Establishment and the Ecclesiastical Polity', in Guy (ed.), *The Reign of Elizabeth I: Court and Culture in the Last Decade*, pp. 126–49; Hampson, 'Richard Cosin and the Revitalization of the Clerical Estate in Late Elizabethan England'.
101 Guy, 'The Elizabethan Establishment and the Ecclesiastical Polity'.
102 Elton, *The Tudor Constitution* (2nd edn), pp. 221–32; J. R. Tanner, *Tudor Constitutional Documents* (Cambridge, 1940), pp. 361–2, 372–3.
103 Folger Shakespeare Library, MS V.a.321, fos. 1–2.
104 M. E. James, *Society, Politics and Culture: Studies in Early Modern England* (Cambridge, 1986), pp. 445–6.
105 Guy, *Tudor England*, pp. 437–52; P. E. J. Hammer, 'Patronage and Court, Faction and the Earl of Essex', in Guy (ed.), *The Reign of Elizabeth I: Court and Culture in the Last Decade*, pp. 65–86.
106 J. H. M. Salmon, 'Seneca and Tacitus in Jacobean England', in Linda Levy Peck (ed.), *The Mental World of the Jacobean Court* (Cambridge, 1991), pp. 169–88; Salmon, *Renaissance and Revolt*, pp. 27–53; Fritz Levy, 'Hayward, Daniel, and the Beginnings of Politic History in England', *Huntington Library Quarterly*, 50 (1987), pp. 1–34.
107 Whereas the term 'state' possessed little political meaning in 1500 beyond the 'state or condition' of the prince or the kingdom, by the 1590s it was used to signify the 'state' in something recognizably closer to the modern sense. In the reigns of Henry VII and Henry VIII, contemporaries had spoken of 'country', 'people', 'commonwealth', 'polity', 'kingdom', and 'realm'. By the 1590s, they spoke of the 'queen and state', 'her Majesty and the state', 'our English state and government', 'arguments of state', 'pillars of the state', the 'profit of the state', the 'public interest', and so on. See John Nichols (ed.), *The Progresses, and Public Processions, of Queen Elizabeth* (3 vols, London, 1788–1805); database search of the *Complete Works of Shakespeare, s.v.* 'state'. The term the 'public interest' was first used by Richard Cosin; see Hampson, 'Richard Cosin and the Revitalization of the Clerical Estate in Late Elizabethan England'.
108 Quentin Skinner, *The Foundations of Modern Political Thought* (2 vols, Cambridge, 1978), II, pp. 349–58.
109 M. Peltonen, *Classical Humanism and Republicanism in English Political Thought, 1570–1640* (Cambridge, 1995), pp. 102–18.
110 Skinner, *The Foundations of Modern Political Thought*, II, p. 356.
111 Citation from the letterbook of Gabriel Harvey, see P. L. Ward (ed.), *William Lambarde's Notes* (London, 1977), pp. 19–20.

4

The monarchical republic of Queen Elizabeth I*

PATRICK COLLINSON

I first met Professor Neale (as he was always content to be known) on a Monday evening in early October 1952, in the England Room of the Institute of Historical Research. I had just come down from Cambridge and Neale seemed pleased with this rare recruit from one of the ancient universities, although most of the new 'Tudorbethans' of that cohort had received a superior education at his own University College. After the regular Monday evening seminar we arranged to meet to discuss a topic. 'Hurstfield!' he said to the late Joel Hurstfield who was standing nearby, 'tell him where my room is. You know where my room is.' One recollects such trivial circumstances in vivid detail, even if one's name is not Richard Cobb. Going down the stairs, an American woman said: 'Don't let him give you something *aw*ful.' This was helpful, for I was in the foolish position of the acolyte researcher who does not know what he wants to research. I only knew that I wanted to work under Neale, and that was because someone had suggested it. But the outcome could not have been happier. Although Dr A. L. Rowse is not unique in regarding the Puritans as a truly awful subject (my wife shares his view), they have kept me out of mischief ever since. And but for Jimmy Neale, as everyone called him,[1] it would not have happened. 'Collinson,' he said, after a while, 'I like to think of you spending the rest of your life on this subject!' And although I laughed 'within myself', like Abraham's wife Sarah when the angel announced her pregnancy (Gen. 18:12), Neale, like the angel, was right. Incidentally, the highest praise Neale could confer on anyone was that he wrote 'like an angel'. He liked my style but did not find it angelic.

My topic was not the only thing I owed to Neale. He was not an intrusive supervisor and to a considerable extent one was left to one's own devices. The thesis, when at last it came together, was emphatically all one's own work, not ghosted by the supervisor. But what Neale *did* impart and in generous manner, pressed down and running over, was enthusiasm and

---

* This is a slightly extended version of a J. E. Neale Memorial Lecture delivered in the John Rylands University Library of Manchester on 8 May 1986, and which grew out of my Inaugural Lecture as Professor of Modern History in the University of Sheffield, given on 16 Oct. 1985. Some of the preparative work was undertaken in the Henry E. Huntington Library, San Marino, California, where in 1984 I was privileged to hold an Andrew C. Mellon fellowship.

encouragement. You were made to feel that perhaps tomorrow you would make that notable discovery which had eluded all earlier historians of the subject: perhaps another minute book of a clandestine presbyterian classis, to match the Dedham Minutes which first brought me to Manchester (Rylands English MS. 874). Nowadays, what might be called the 'dark-continent' approach to history – pushing into the interior in the hope of discovering some hitherto unsuspected tribe, or species, or waterfall – is denigrated for its conceptual and methodological naïvety, and suspect for its complacent practice of the bourgeois ethic of possessive individualism. It must be said, with due deference to the late Sir John Neale, that in many respects it was (and is) a magnificent and fruitful tradition, kept alive and in good heart by some of Neale's severer critics.

I

The Monarchical Republic of Queen Elizabeth I is a phrase with which Neale would not have been altogether happy. To explain it, it will be helpful to travel to Swallowfield, a place equidistant from Reading and Wokingham, physically within Berkshire but by an odd anomaly politically part of Wiltshire, which meant that the village was almost outside the scope of normal local government. That was the occasion for a town meeting held on 4 December 1596, when Swallowfield constituted itself, in effect, a self-governing republic of the 'chief inhabitants'.[2] Further and regular assemblies were planned, at which those present were to speak in order of rank and without fear of interruption: for 'none of us is ruler of himself, but the whole company or the most part is the ruler of us all'. Procedures were adopted for dealing with a variety of common offences and abuses: strife between neighbours, bastardy, alehouse disorders, marriage between young people 'before they have a convenient house to live in', and 'malapert' insubordination on the part of the unruly poor. If all else failed, offenders in these and other respects were to be reported to the justices. But in the normal course of events, Swallowfield hoped to govern itself. For 'we will be esteemed to be men of discretion, good credit, honest minds, and christianlike behaviour, one towards another'.

'Self-government at the king's command' was what a great historian taught us to call that kind of thing, whether at the level of Swallowfield or of the gentry republics which comprised the regime in so many Elizabethan counties.[3] It has become a weary cliché, and yet we are far from having exhausted its implications. Swallowfield's ringing affirmation, the voice of all village Hampdens, 'we will be esteemed to be men of discretion', anticipated the voice of the Clubmen who a generation or two later rose in the agony of the Civil War to defend their homes against the marauding armies of both sides. In Dorset the Clubmen resolved to be represented in every parish by 'three or more of the ablest men for wisdom, valour and estate, inhabitants of the same'.[4]

Swallowfield and the Dorset Clubmen demonstrate the vitality in early modern England of traditions of localized self-government, involving men of very humble status. This was a salient feature of its political culture.[5] It could no doubt be demonstrated that in this society more considerable sums of money were collected and disbursed for public purposes locally than ever found their way to the Exchequer in the form of national taxation. When the sea broke through the flood banks at Terrington in Norfolk in 1600, the cost of repairs was put at £2 000, a sum equivalent to almost three-quarters of 1 per cent of the annual ordinary revenue of the Crown at that time. The Norfolk bench subsequently reported that the damage could be made good for a mere £700, 'which some, wee are credibly informed, maie be easily borne by the land occupiers of the said towne'.[6] If the little community of Terrington could 'easily' find £700 (and in the end it was obliged to spend £500 on inadequate stopgap repairs), it is not clear why the 9 000 or 10 000 Terringtons which made up Elizabethan England could not between them have provided the Queen with an annual income of 5 million or 6 million pounds, 50 times what it in fact was. But Elizabethan England was not that kind of polity. In 1621 James I, who had put a price tag on the coming war with Spain of as much as a million pounds in one year, was told that all England did not contain so much money.[7] Nowadays, central government claims the power through rate-capping to curb expenditure by local government. In the sixteenth century, it was the locality which habitually starved the centre of resources, and had the capacity, through tax strikes, to bring national governments to their knees.

II

When Picasso came to Sheffield to attend a peace rally, he sat on the platform making sketches and dropping them on the floor. Nobody picked them up. These preliminary sketches – Swallowfield and Terrington – can lie where they have fallen. Our subject is neither local government nor village republics but the political culture of England at its centre and summit, in the age of Elizabeth I. Swallowfield has been invoked because its situation was that of all England in miniature, at this critical moment.

As an enclave of Wiltshire isolated in Berkshire, the town was practically without magistrates and had to make arrangements for its own government: and this it did by means of a town meeting of the kind later set up in the vastly greater isolation of New England. And yet it was doubtless the case that a thousand other villages with a similar social structure, lacking a resident magistrate or gentleman, had the capacity to do something similar, in effect to constitute themselves republics, and a good many did, if with less formality. But the whole commonwealth – or republic – of Elizabethan England was potentially in a situation where the chief magistrate might be not merely 'far off' but totally absent, non-existent. This would have been the state of affairs (which many Elizabethans for much of their lifespan thought more likely than otherwise) if the Queen had died suddenly and violently, leaving the vacuum of an uncertain succession behind her.

The sketches with which I shall end have to do with that scenario and with the political responses to it. They will not have the spontaneous originality of Picasso's idle scribblings on a Sheffield platform. We all know that Elizabeth I was a woman and that she died unmarried and without issue, the last of her immediate family line, dynastic ambitions unfulfilled because she had none. But the consequences of her singular endgame for the perceived political future of her people are not always squarely faced. The reason is not far to seek. Elizabeth's subjects professed to be so dazzled by their queen's regal splendour as to be incapable of looking beyond her or of contemplating any feature of their political culture other than her radiant presence. Peter Wentworth dared to say in the House of Commons that 'none is without fault, no not our noble queen', but he was not suffered to continue with his speech.[8] The lawyer and Parliament man Thomas Norton, languishing under house arrest, reflected: 'Lord! how I wonder at my self that I shold offend my Queen Elizabeth! and therefore no marvel though all the world wonder at me, that wonder at my self.' Lawrence Humphrey had written in the opening moments of the reign: 'We advaunce not your might, not your arme, not your wisdom, but wonder at your weaknes and infirmity.'[9] Later he knew better. When we read John Aylmer's apology for Elizabeth's fitness to rule, composed in 1559, along the lines that the government of a woman was tolerable because in England it would not be so much her government as government in her name and on her behalf,[10] we feel sorry for the poor man, who in spite of having served as a tutor to royal and semi-royal personages had to wait another 18 years for his bishopric. One might as well justify the government of Mrs Thatcher on the grounds that her cabinet can be trusted to keep her in order.

Historians for the most part share in the general bedazzlement, and Neale, it must be said, was more uncritical than most. 'This woman', he wrote on one occasion, 'was as vital as Winston Churchill.'[11] Like the older, Victorian, historians J. A. Froude and Bishop Creighton, I am sometimes tempted to exclaim about 'this' or 'that woman' – and to leave it at that. Lest I offend, I hasten to explain that I have no motive to reduce Elizabeth in stature, or to diminish her vitality, if such a thing were possible. I know that her power to overawe, having first won the devotion of those personally and politically closest to her, has rarely been equalled.

Whether this power was predominantly personal, what Max Weber called 'charismatic', or was encased in the office itself and so more traditional, we cannot say. Sir Thomas Smith observed that the prince (in principle, any prince) 'is the life, the head and the authoritie of all thinges that be doone in the realme of England'. The kings of England were 'farre more absolute then either the dukedome of Venice is, or the kingdome of the Lacedemonians was'.[12] Constitutionally speaking, this was faultless. Everything which was done, publicly and by due legal authority, was in a sense done by the monarch. The legislation of Henry VIII admitted of no rival, no alternative government. If there had been doubt on that score in 1533, it was gone by 1536. But although personal monarchy under the Tudors was often literally personal, Smith was giving expression to what Kantorowicz called 'an abstract physiological fiction',[13] and it is a naïve mistake to convert that fiction into a statement of simply literal fact, as if the Queen really did attend personally to everything of any consequence which was done in her name. The Jesuit Philip Caraman published an anthology illustrating the experience of the Elizabethan Catholics under the title *The Other Face* (1960). My concern is with the 'other face' of Elizabethan public life, the Elizabethans without Elizabeth. For if Smith described the Queen as 'the life, the head and the authoritie of all thinges that be doone in the realme of England', he also defined England, politically, as 'a society or common doing of a multitude of free men collected together and united by common accord and covenauntes among themselves for the conservation of themselves as well in peace as in warre'.[14]

That sounds like a good description of a republic, and both statements appeared in a book to which Smith gave the title *De republica anglorum*. To be sure, *republica* in sixteenth-century parlance did not mean, as it has meant since the late eighteenth century, a type of constitution incompatible with monarchy. It was simply the common term for what we call the state. Smith's book was entitled in its English version *Of the Commonwealth of England* and that was a perfectly neutral term, albeit one which the Henrician Thomas Elyot in *The boke named the governour* (1531) found dangerously plebeian in its implications, preferring 'public weal'.[15] Nevertheless, that staunch republican Machiavelli – equally no democrat – would have recognized in Elizabethan England a species of republic, what the Englishman Thomas Starkey called 'living together in good and politic order',[16] not a kind of tyranny or despotism: a state which enjoyed that measure of self-direction which for him was the essence of liberty, but with a constitution which also provided for the rule of a single person by hereditary right. This needs to be said, since historians used to talk about a 'Tudor despotism', and an attempt was made a few years ago to revive this unpromising and unhelpful phrase.[17] It is a striking circumstance, recently underlined in a study of Charles I's *Answer to the xix propositions,* that in sixteenth- and seventeenth-century England it was possible to use the language of classical republicanism in order to deny that England was a republic.[18]

The very fact that 'republic' was an acceptable term for a variety of political systems in itself implies an important historical–etymological assumption about the origins of government, as well as the perseverance of the doctrine, to be found in Plato, that monarchy, aristocracy, and democracy in their pure forms are all less desirable than a judicious blend of all three. So the Elizabethan Bishop Aylmer asserts that

> the regiment of England is not a mere monarchie, as some for lacke of consideration thinke, nor a meere oligarchie, nor democracie, but a rule mixte of all these ... thimage whereof, and not the image but the thinge in deede, is to be sene in the parliament house, wherin you shall find these three estates.[19]

None of this impresses John Pocock in his account of the origins of republicanism among the English-speaking peoples called *The Machiavellian Moment*. Pocock is satisfied that in sixteenth-century English thought the theory of corporate rationality served merely as an ideal and historical account of how political society had begun, and of how the single ruler emerged whose government subsequently excluded the intelligent participation of the subjects. In no way was Tudor England a *polis* or its inhabitants citizens.[20] Nor, according to Pocock, did conciliar government ever imply an acephalous republic. Every privy councillor took a separate oath to the monarch and gave counsel severally, each sitting in his place. To strengthen Pocock's point it may be noted that the death of the monarch, who in life had an absolute discretion and power to summon and dissolve Parliament, led to an immediate dissolution of any parliament which might have been in session at that moment, which happened on 17 November 1558. Only a new monarch could renew and revive governmental and political activity, by appointing a new Council and (only if he or she chose) summoning Parliament. The implication is that the commonwealth of England had no existence, apart from its head. If so, then the origins of 'civic consciousness' must be sought outside the political economy of the sixteenth century, in exceptional modes of thought, mostly religious, which is where Pocock looked for them. *Coriolanus* was written for an audience familiar with the notion of a balanced republic but not itself republican, nor experiencing republicanism. Nevertheless, we must take care not to underestimate both the political sophistication and the political capacity of high Elizabethan society, a society which had cut its political teeth in the acephalous conditions of Edward VI's minority. We should also not forget about Swallowfield.

III

At this point, and before returning to the sketch pad, I shall offer a kind of manifesto on the subject of Elizabethan history and historiography, consisting of five points.

(1) In the phrase 'the queen and her ministers', the copulative usually serves to weld the two elements indissolubly together, as if it scarcely matters how they interacted. Thus the Elizabethan Religious Settlement is attributed to 'the queen and her advisers', or to 'the queen and Cecil', as if they were the front and rear legs of a pantomime horse. Neale departed from this tradition when he attributed the shaping of the settlement (which, since it made England a Protestant state, is no trivial circumstance) to an independent political initiative taken against the Queen by a strongly Protestant House of Commons.[21] Now that brilliant reconstruction of poorly documented transactions in the first Elizabethan Parliament (which Neale never represented as anything more than a plausible hypothesis) has been demolished. The religious settlement looks like government policy after all.[22] But the question who, in the inner counsels of government, whether at Court or Council board, determined that policy remains not only unanswered (and probably it cannot be answered) but so far unasked.

(2) Sir Geoffrey Elton, addressing himself to the Elizabethan Parliaments in general, describes the more active elements in the Commons as cooperating and interacting with the Privy Council, or with particular councillors and courtiers. In the helpful perception of Elton and his pupils this means that they cease to be figures of opposition and become 'men of business'.[23] But it is not clear why that should make the true history of the Elizabethan Parliaments any less political, and Elton has declared it to be a history which was not political at all.[24] Surely our new and more sophisticated understanding of these Parliaments makes them more, not less political?: although the politics is now seen to have been one of differences and contentions within a regime, not of 'government' versus 'opposition'.

(3) 'Regime' has proved a helpful expression, particularly as employed by Professor Wallace MacCaffrey in his book *The Shaping of the Elizabethan Regime,* which describes the coming together and settling-down together of a group of politicians to form a collective, quasi-organic, and, for some considerable time, stable governing group. A similar approach to Elizabethan public life, owing something to Washingtonian studies of the making and unmaking of presidencies, is adopted by Professor Winthrop Hudson in his book on the religious settlement. But these are (significantly) the insights of American scholarship. English historians use 'regime' in a different sense, as in Dr Penry Williams's admirable study *The Tudor Regime,*[25] in which a chapter called 'The Servants of the Crown' discusses the acquisition and enjoyment of office by individuals and the performance of functions by individual office-holders, but not the workings of a regime in MacCaffrey's sense.

(4) The currently fashionable topic of Court faction, the tendency of the regime, of perhaps any regime, to divide against itself, is also helpful and

has been ever since Neale delivered his famous Raleigh Lecture on 'The Elizabethan Political Scene'.[26] But too much attention has been paid to factional in-fighting as the main principle of politics, too little to the practical cooperation of leading members of the regime, its centripetal rather than centrifugal tendencies.[27] In particular, Lord Burghley and the Earl of Leicester are supposed to have been mortal enemies and leaders of mutually exclusive rival factions, anticipating the deadly struggle of Elizabeth's declining years between Burghley's son Robert Cecil and Leicester's stepson and legatee, Essex. Conyers Read believed that in the 1570s the Privy Council was effectively polarized.[28] Yet Leicester could write to Burghley as he did in July 1584, apologizing for an impromptu descent made by himself and his countess on the Lord Treasurer's house at Theobalds, at 3 o'clock in the afternoon, 'without any jote of warning in the world': 'I have byn bold to make some of your stagges afrayd but kylled none. Yf I had your lordship should have been presentyd with our good fortune.'[29] These are not the words of implacable enmity.

It should also be said that altogether too much deference is paid to the report of the Jacobean Sir Robert Naunton, made a quarter of a century after Elizabeth's death, that factions were devices by which the Queen strengthened her own rule, making and unmaking them 'as her own great judgment advised'.[30]

(5) The subject of my fifth and final affirmation is policy. It is often said that Elizabethan policy was the Queen's policy, in the sense that she alone determined what was to be done, or, as often as not, not done.[31] No doubt. But this directs attention away from policy discussion and policy-making, and it buries in oblivion the interesting matter of policies which were constructed but never implemented. In 1577 the English ambassador in the Low Countries received welcome news that Robert Dudley, Earl of Leicester, was to cross the North Sea with an expeditionary force. 'This is his full determination, but yet unknown unto her Highness, neither shall she be acquainted with it until she be fully resolved to send ...'[32] And of course Elizabeth was *not* at that time 'fully resolved' to send a single soldier to the Netherlands. A few months later rumours still persisted that Leicester was about to embark with 10 000 men. But a ranking government official who gave currency to the report added: 'I would this were a true prognostication.'[33]

Another not untypical episode occurred in April 1580, when Sir Francis Walsingham wrote to the Queen's viceroys in the north to advise them that the Privy Council had thought fit to dispatch 1 000 troops to the borders to shore up a crumbling Scottish policy. But 'when ytt came to hyr Majesties consent she wolde none of ytt' and proceeded to cut the force by half, to 500 men. Later the same day she thought better of this – and decided to send no troops at all. Before news of this second decision had reached

Walsingham, and when he still expected to have some force at his disposal, he had signed and sealed a letter which said this:

> I see that Scotland is clene lost and a great gate opened whereby for the losse of Ireland. My lords here have carefully and faithfully discharged their dueties in sekinge to staye this dangerous course, but God hath thought good to dispose other wyse of thinges, in whose handes the heartes of all princes are.[34]

On another occasion Walsingham wrote: 'I am sorrye to thincke of the dayngerouse inconveniences lykely to issue by thes straynge courses: but I see no hope of redresse. God dyrect her Majesties harte to take an other waye of counsell ...'[35]

'God open her Majesty's eyes' is consequently a recurring refrain in the State Papers of the period, and it built up in the Victorian historian Froude a strong prejudice against the Queen and an indignant sympathy for her ministers.

> Vain as she was of her own sagacity, she never modified a course recommended to her by Burghley without injury both to the realm and to herself. She never chose an opposite course without plunging into embarrassments from which his and Walsingham's [skills] were barely able to extricate her. The great results of her reign were the fruits of a policy which was not her own, and which she starved and mutilated when energy and completeness were most needed.[36]

That was unfair in its exaggeration, but anyone who has read the State Papers knows why and how Froude arrived at such a verdict.

My manifesto concludes with two comments. If Leicester could complain, as he did in 1578, that 'our conference with her Majesty about affairs is both seldom and slender',[37] that implies a high-handed autocracy which councillors found unacceptable and which limited their capacity to be useful. Elizabethan government was often government without counsel, or with unorthodox or irregular counsel. But it also suggests that the Privy Council, with whatever futile consequences on some occasions, was in a position to contemplate the world and its affairs with some independent detachment, by means of its own collective wisdom and with the Queen absent: headless conciliar government. Second, one does not have to share Froude's low estimation of the Queen's effectiveness and decisiveness (and what we now know of the conduct of the Spanish War in the 1590s makes it impossible to agree with Froude unreservedly[38]) to perceive that at times there were two governments uneasily coexisting in Elizabethan England: the Queen and her Council, the copulative now serving to distance rather than unite two somewhat distinct poles of authority, as it were the magnetic pole and the true pole. This is not to say that for much and perhaps most of the time the Queen and her sworn advisers did not participate harmoniously and constructively in the conduct of public business.

IV

Elizabethan England was a republic which happened also to be a monarchy: or vice versa. The dichotomy is suggested by one of several 'devices' or memoranda proposing administrative reforms, drawn up at the start of the reign but apparently dating from the acephalous conditions of Edward's time. In this 'Ordre for Redresse of the State of the Realme',[39] one senses a political society taking stock and ordering itself with an attempt at efficiency and rationality. Totally new connections are proposed between Court and Council, and between both Council and Court and the Country, thus on paper solving some of the most vexing problems of Tudor and Stuart government. But our concern is not so much with the details of this green paper, important though they are, but with the fact that it seems to have been an afterthought that the whole scheme would require royal approval if it were to take effect. For another hand has written in the margin: 'It would do well if it might please the prince to ...', and so the memorandum is made to flow on from that essential precondition.

We return to the sketch pad and to two images of the other, non-adulatory face of Elizabethan politics, two moments in the sense that political scientists speak of convulsive episodes in history: 1572 and 1584. Students of Elizabethan history have been here before and the furniture and decorations are familiar: the Queen's safety, the succession crisis, Mary, Queen of Scots. Yet what has sometimes been omitted from the story is the readiness of the political nation, including its leading statesman, William Cecil, Lord Burghley, to contemplate its own immediate political future, a future not only without Queen Elizabeth but without monarchy, at least for a season. This was the Elizabethan Exclusion Crisis.

To take the measure of our two moments something must first be said about what is vulgarly called 'resistance theory' but which is better described as the polemical critique of monarchy. No such critique is supposed to have survived the scorching sun of Elizabeth's benign rule except among certain marginalized Catholic elements.[40] The Protestant resistance theses of Knox, Goodman, and Ponet were now as redundant as the Communist Manifesto at a Conservative Party Conference. By all her true Protestant subjects, Elizabeth was adored with unwavering devotion. Even if their queen had not been a paragon of all conceivable virtue, resistance, criticism almost, would have been unthinkable. Churchgoers were taught by the Homily of Obedience that rebellion was worse than the worst government of the worst prince.[41] This was the outward face of Elizabethan political ideology. But there was another face, an anti-monarchical virus which was part of the legacy of early sixteenth-century humanism. Had not Erasmus preferred the 'lofty-minded beetle' to both eagle and lion, making the meaning of his imagery quite clear in a frankly mordant attack on 'people-devouring kings'? 'They must be called gods who are scarcely men ... magnificent when they are midgets, most serene when they shake the world with the tumults of war and senseless political struggles.'[42]

Elizabeth was not actively resisted by her Protestant subjects, but it does not follow that there was no ideological capacity for resistance, just as it would be a serious mistake to infer from the second Elizabethan peace that this country had no nuclear capability between 1951 and the 1980s. In fact, important weapons of resistance theory were still serviceable, like so many threatening missiles hidden in their silos. These included the conviction that monarchy is a ministry exercised under God and on his behalf; that it is no more and no less than a public office; that as a public officer the monarch is accountable, certainly to God and perhaps to others exercising, under God, other public offices of magistracy or respecting an overriding and transcendent duty to God himself; and that there is a difference between monarchy and tyranny. Sir Francis Hastings noted these points of doctrine delivered at a Leicestershire sermon:

> The Magistrate is the minister of God and must submit him selfe to his worde as a rule to directe him in all his government ... The Magistrate must commande in the Lorde. The subiecte must obey in the Lorde ... Obedience, what it is: it is due unto the Lorde only.[43]

When the lawyer and parliamentarian Thomas Norton advised his son (writing under house arrest in December 1581): 'I have no dealing with the queen but as with the image of God'; and when he wrote to another correspondent 'it is the onely religion of God that knitteth true subiectes unto her',[44] his words would not have pleased Elizabeth entirely, if she had pondered their implications. In translating Calvin's *Institutes* the same Norton chose to speak of 'the outraging licentiousness of kings' as that fault which parliamentary estates existed to correct. Peter Martyr's *Commentary on Romans* (in English translation in 1568) spoke of inferior magistrates 'putting down' and 'constraining to do their duty' princes who transgressed 'the endes and limits of the power which they have received'.[45]

Quentin Skinner writes of 'a few wisps' of resistance theory lingering on in the marginalia of the most popular Elizabethan version of the Bible, the Geneva Bible. That is too dismissive. Geneva Bible readers were taught from sundry Old Testament examples that God takes vengeance on tyrants, even in this life. Queen Jezebel's example of 'monstrous cruelty' was delivered to us by the Holy Ghost that we should abhor all tyranny and (a telling point) especially in a woman. Her terrible death was a spectacle and example to all tyrants. When David refused to kill Saul on the grounds that he was the Lord's anointed, the Geneva Bible turned the apparent moral upside down.

It would have been wrong for David to have slain the King in his own private cause, but as a public act it would have been lawful: 'for Jehu slew two kings at God's appointment' (2 Kgs 9: 24).[46] It would be wrong to label, still less to dismiss, such sentiments as 'puritan' and therefore peripheral. The note on David's sparing of Saul was repeated without alteration in the Bishops' Bible, the official version, as was a highly acerbic comment on King Asa who spared the life of his own wicked and usurping mother (2 Chr. 15:16). The note reads: 'Herein he shewed that he lacked zeale: for she ought to have dyed both by the covenant and by the lawe of God, but he gave place to foolish pity.' This was the passage in the Geneva Bible which so offended James I, and for the most understandable of reasons. For was not his mother in the eyes of many a wicked usurper, and had he not consented unto her death? But James could have found the same comment in the Bishops' Bible and it survived without alteration in the Authorized (or King James) version of 1611.[47] According to Dr Bowler, its author was none other than Edwin Sandys, who ended his days as Archbishop of York, no longer a radical in reputation or spirit but as an old Marian exile, unreconstructed in his opinions.

This serves to usher us into the debates of the 1572 Parliament when the issue was whether Mary Stuart should be executed or simply excluded from the succession: 'an axe or an act?' as one MP tersely put the question.[48] The mind of the political nation had been well prepared for this crucial debate by 10 years of anxious indecision on the subject of the succession. The arrival in England of the deposed Scottish queen, with her pretensions to the English throne, had fanned the political temperature to white heat, especially after the exposure of the Ridolfi plot, in which Mary was apparently implicated together with England's premier peer, the Duke of Norfolk, already judicially condemned for his part in the affair. In the parliamentary oratory of the summer of 1572 both Queen Jezebel and King Asa's mother were never far from the speakers' thoughts. When one MP proposed that Mary's head should be cut off 'and make no more ado about her' (another version of the speech has him say 'her head cut off and noe more harme done to her'), this was an echo of a frequent comment on Jehu's execution of Jezebel 'without any ado made', that is, by lynch law. But it was not so much the Commons as the bench of bishops who advanced these chilling precedents, MPs adding little to the episcopal argument beyond the violence of the language with which they referred to what one speaker called 'the monstrous and huge dragon and mass of the earth'.

In the lengthy episcopal indictment of the Scottish queen we find a kind of double-distilled resistance theory. The act of deposition which had removed Mary from her throne was enthusiastically endorsed. For the bishops she was 'the late queen of Scots'. But if the Queen of England were to fail in her manifest duty to put the deposed Scottish queen to death, she herself would have cause to fear for her throne. Here the most telling precedent was that of King

Saul, who allowed his enemy Agag to live. As the bishops put it, 'because Saul spared Agag, although he were a king, God took from the same his good Spirit and transferred the kingdom of Israel from him and from his heirs for ever'. The moral was spelt out in the New Testament in Romans 13, a passage of scripture normally cited in support of total obedience and non-resistance, for, according to St Paul in that place, the magistrate is the minister of God and the avenger of wrath towards him that hath done evil. But 'yf the magistrate do not this, God threateneth heavie punishment ... Her Majesty must needs offend in conscience before God if she do not punish [the Scottish queen] to the measure of her offence in the highest degree.' The only other Reformation preacher known to me who turned Romans 13 on its head in this fashion was Thomas Muntzer, the arch-Bolshevik of the age.[49]

For our purpose, the most telling implication of the memorials and debates of 1572 is that monarchy is taken to be not an indelible and sacred anointing but a public and localized office, like any other form of magistracy. Even if Mary had not been deposed, as Queen of Scotland she had never been a queen in England, the lawyer Christopher Yelverton asserting 'but for certaine she is to be tryed as a subiect of another nation'.[50] Only two MPs took her part, the part of a queen of Scotland. Francis Alford insisted on the sacrosanctity of anointed kingship. Arthur Hall of Grantham thought that Mary's indelible regality would eventually embarrass her enemies: 'Yow will hasten the execucion of such whose feet hereafter yow would be glad to have againe to kisse.' It is no accident that Hall was openly and scandalously contemptuous of the pretensions of the House of Commons, in effect a complete absolutist.[51] The Queen herself shared Hall's view, but it was the view of an isolated minority. Moreover, the threatening implication of the debate was that Elizabeth was herself little more than the temporary custodian of her kingdom. The bishops insisted that 'being ... a publicke person', the prince ought to have a greater care of her own safety than a private person, 'if not for her selfe sake yet at the leaste for the furtherance of Gode's cause and stay of her countrye ...'.[52] As one speaker put it in the Commons: 'Since the Queene in respect of her owne safety is not to bee induced hereunto, let us make petition shee will doe it in respect of our safety.' And then he added, perhaps with sarcasm: 'I have heard shee delighteth to bee called our mother.' In a paper urging the execution of the Duke of Norfolk, Thomas Digges (of whom more anon) observed that the Queen's safety was 'not her private case', while Thomas Dannet warned that if she were to continue unmindful of 'our safetie' 'after her death', 'her true and faithfull subiectes despairing of safetie by her meanes shalbe forced to seke protection ellsewhere, to the end they be not altogether destitute of defense'. Dr Bowler rightly calls the implications of these remarks, which Elizabeth in all probability never saw, 'staggering'.[53]

In the event, MPs and bishops alike, privy councillors no less, were bitterly disappointed. At first they were told to expect an act rather than an axe. That was disturbing enough, if only because an Act of Parliament to remove Mary's title to the succession (and what would such an act be worth in the future?) suggested that Mary had a title of which she could be deprived. 'This disabling shalbe an enabling.' Robert Snagge said that the bill 'were not to doe nothing but to doe starke nought ... He trusteth we were not called hyther for nought.'[54] And yet even this unsatisfactory second best was withdrawn by the Queen's veto of the disabling bill at the close of the session.

V

Twelve years later 'the late Scottish queen' was still bearing her head on her shoulders and breathing the bracing air of Sheffield. But in the Netherlands William of Orange was very dead and with the State Papers as full of plots as today's newspapers are of terrorism and of fourth and fifth men the never-ending Elizabethan political crisis seemed more desperate than ever: sufficiently menacing to call for the extraordinary measure known as the Bond of Association.[55] This document engaged those who were sworn to its terms and who had applied to it their signatures and seals to pursue 'to the uttermost extermination' anybody attempting by any act, counsel, or consent to bring harm to the Queen's royal person, their comforters, aiders, and abettors: and to resist the succession of any individual on whose behalf such acts might be attempted or committed. This was to hang a sword over Mary's head, to threaten this modern Jezebel with lynch law in the event of an assassination attempt against Elizabeth, successful or not; and in such circumstances to disable not only Mary but her son, James VI.

To examine surviving copies of the Bond in the Public Record Office (they are huge parchments and a special table has to be cleared for the purpose) is to be given a vivid insight into both the autonomous political capacity of the Elizabethan republic and its extent and social depth, a carpet, as it were, with a generous pile. Not only the Privy Council was at Hampton Court on 19 October 1584 to sign and seal its own copy but much of the seniority of the clergy of the southern province. Bishops, archdeacons, deans, and heads of houses had made their way to the Court for this purpose, gathering in a kind of informal convocation. The Cornish bond bears 115 names, that for Hertfordshire 106. The Dorset bond was signed by the mayors of Blandford, Lyme, Weymouth, and Melcombe, representing their fellow burgesses. More than 200 inhabitants of the town of Cardigan took the oath, signed or marked and applied their seals. The Earl of Huntingdon forwarded to the Council the names of 140 principal freeholders and farmers of Richmondshire who had committed themselves to the 'Instrument of Association'.[56] Some 60 residents of Lincoln's Inn, headed by Thomas Egerton, the future Lord Ellesmere, subscribed the Bond.[57] The circumstances in which the Bond was subscribed respected hierarchy. The gentlemen of Lancashire came to Wigan church to witness the Earl of Derby taking the oath first of all, bare-headed and on his knees before the Bishop of Chester, who in his turn administered it to the bishop, followed by the gentry, six at a time.[58]

Later it would be said that the Bond spoke for 'the moost parte of us, your lovinge subiectes'.[59] But 'the moost parte' consisted of Protestants, or of those who would gladly be mistaken for Protestants. In Kent it was thought inappropriate that any known Catholic recusant should be admitted into 'this loyall societie'.[60] Thomas Digges later proposed that all office holders should be obliged to take the oath of association 'for the defence and perpetuation of religion now publiquelie professed within the realme'.[61] Dr Diarmaid MacCulloch has demonstrated that in Suffolk the county government by this time (the critical date was 1578) had transferred into the hands of a group, not to say clique, of gentry whose outstanding quality was their reliability as Protestants, 'Godds flocke', to the exclusion of the East Anglian Catholics, many of whom might in other circumstances have ranked among the 'natural' leaders of their communities. This had happened not by accident but by a careful design in which the Privy Council played the leading part and the Queen probably none, beyond allowing this provincial *coup d'état* to happen, under her very nose and in the course of a summer's stately progress.[62]

Now the Protestant state (for that is what it was, and in a partisan and prejudicial rather than consensual sense) was to be reinforced by the creation of what Burghley called a 'fellowship and societie'.[63] The Bond bore some resemblance to the Catholic leagues springing up in France at this same time, but with this difference: that, whereas the League was a device to oppose the Crown in the name of a higher religious loyalty, the English bond was the handiwork of the regime itself. However, the government found it politic to disguise its interventionist role with the appearance of spontaneity. Sir Francis Walsingham inserted these words into a form of letter which his colleague Burghley had drafted for circulation, probably to lords lieutenant in the counties:

> Your lordship shall not need to take knowledge that you receyved the coppye from me, but rather from some other frende of yours in thes parts; for that her Majesty would have the matter carryed in such sorte as this course held for her [safety] may seeme to [come more] from the pertyculer care of her well affected subiects then to growe from any publycke directyon.[64]

This revealing piece of evidence might seem to tell against the 'republican' argument of this essay. But I think that we can substitute for 'her Majesty would' 'we would'.[65]

In content, the Bond was paradoxical. Its ostensible purpose was to defend the life of the Queen, which was said to be almost the only concern and function of her people. One is reminded of Edith Sitwell's metaphor of the bees and the hive. (So potent and persuasive was this implausible convention that it comes as rather a shock to find Lord Keeper Bacon frankly arguing in 1570 that if Elizabeth were to remain unmarried she would progressively forfeit the loyal duty of her subjects, whose first instinct was always, as we say today, to look out for number one: 'for that the naturall care in the moste parte of them that have possessions and families' was 'to see to the preservacion of them selves, their children and posteritie that must folowe her life'.[66]) Yet the Bond was also a quasi-republican statement. The circumstance it envisaged was the extinction of the Queen, and it provided for the sequel to that terrible event without reference to any laws or rights of succession. The inescapable consequence of its silence on this matter was to imply that the act of vengeance it provided for would be enforced by no other authority than that residing in the body politic. In form it was a covenant, constituted by the oaths and subscriptions of all those bound by it, and its sanctions were those of collective responsibility, investing none of its signatories with greater power or responsibility than any other, and not attributing any defined role to office-holders, as public men. In this respect its republicanism was more advanced than that of Christopher Goodman or John Ponet. According to Goodman, it was only if and when magistrates and other officers failed in their duties that the people were 'as it were without officers' and obliged to take the law – and the sword – into their own hands.[67] But the Bond of Association knew no officers, no magistrates.

Consequently a critic of the enterprise, probably the mathematician, engineer and MP Thomas Digges, pointed out its 'perils':

> Breefly me thought I did behowld a confuesed company of all partes of the Realme of all degrees and estates then risinge in Armes at such a tyme as there is no cowncell of estate in Lyfe, no Lawfull generall ... no presidente, no Judges, no sheriffes, no justices, breefly no officers ...[68]

Yet the devisers and promoters of this putative exercise in total anarchy were not members of the sectarian political fringe but Lord Burghley and Sir Francis Walsingham, in effect the Prime Minister and Foreign Secretary of the day.

The extreme irregularity of the Bond was soon remedied in a parliamentary Act for the Surety of the Queen's Most Royal Person,[69] which imposed by law a general obligation on loyal subjects to revenge the Queen's violent death and by statute excluded from the succession those complicit in procuring her death; and further made the proceedings it envisaged conformable to due legal process. This was the process which duly took effect after the Babington plot, when Mary was tried, sentenced, and, in February 1587 and another Parliament, executed. However, the 1584 Act was as silent as the Bond itself on the delicate subject of who, or what, in the scenario envisaged, would wield the sovereignty by which the tribunals allowed for were to sit and armed force be raised and deployed. Although the statute explicitly excluded and disabled any person pretending a title to the Crown who might by armed force resist the implementation of the Act, it did not presume to say who *should* succeed. Legally, sovereignty and all power to act, all offices and courts, would have lapsed with the Queen, to be at once transferred to her lawful successor – whoever that was. But on that matter the Act was as silent as the Bond, so appearing to condone an irregular, acephalous, quasi-republican state of emergency.

If this was to happen in any case, why not make it legal, or as legal as an English parliament could make anything? Why not a regularized interregnum? This, as a series of documents written or emended in his hand proves,[70] was Burghley's preferred course of action. Burghley was the political veteran of Edward VI's minority and had lived through more than one irregular and potentially violent change of regime, first in 1549 and then in 1553.[71] It was understandable that he should take a very personal interest in the most rational means of handling the emergency in which he, of all people, would be exposed to the greatest risk. Besides, behind the deeply unoriginal mind of William Cecil, Lord Burghley, there often lurked a more inventive intelligence, in this case that of the instinctive analyst, Thomas Digges.[72]

Digges was an able, confident, not to say arrogant man, one of those middling political and administrative animals, 'men of business', and brokers for the regime, whose importance Elizabethan historians are belatedly beginning to recognize.[73] Others were Thomas Norton 'the Parliament man', William Fleetwood, recorder of the city of London, and the exceedingly perspicacious diplomat and clerk of the Privy Council, Robert Beale. Digges was at this time centrally and controversially involved in the Elizabethan equivalent of the Channel Tunnel project: the works to extend and improve the facilities of Dover Harbour, the details of which occupy whole volumes of State Papers Domestic. His reports to his masters of his 'proceedings' at Dover reverberate with such claims as 'I was the first that discovered the grosse errors ...' or, 'I affirmed the contrary'.[74] The notion of a legalized interregnum was not new in 1584, but Digges made a new and original attack on the problem in a so-called 'Brief Discourse',[75] which saw the device as a tolerable compromise between the nomination of an heir apparent, which Digges conceded was not practical, and the no less dangerous vacuum of inactivity.

The root idea of several versions of the interregnum plan was that the Privy Council, or the Parliament, or both, together with all officers and all courts for the administration of justice, institutions which would normally cease to exist or to have any power to act at the moment of the monarch's death, should on the contrary continue in being. Digges proposed that either the Parliament then sitting (the 1584 Parliament) should remain undissolved during the natural life of the Queen (that would have been a 'long parliament' indeed – it would have sat for twenty years!) – or that upon its dissolution some other parliament should be immediately summoned: 'so that some parliament by your Majesty's summons may be in esse at your highness's decease.' Within 30 days such a parliament should hear and determine all challenges to the throne, having a special regard to candidates whom the late Queen would by then be known to have preferred. That is to say, the parliament would, among other evidences, contemplate the late Queen's last will and testament, without, apparently, being bound by it. Pending this process, all officers of Church and State were to remain at their posts and the helm of the ship of state was to be handled by five or seven magnates, temporal and spiritual.

Digges anticipated various objections to this scenario, amongst them the mere fact that it entailed an innovation, without precedent. He met head-on the point that innovations were a bad thing, and added that anyone who had been in Rome at the time of a papal conclave (had this happened to Digges?) would have some sense of 'the monstrous nature of an Interregnum': 'Hell it selfe, every man by force defending his owne, all kind of owtrage, ryot and villanye.' In England it would be worse, since there was, after all, no equivalent to the College of Cardinals. But Digges seemed to think that the alternatives would be worse still. And if there were no precedents for filling the throne, Polish style, virtually by election, so much the more honour would accrue to the Queen for inventing (in effect) a new constitution. That was truly radical, and not how most sixteenth-century political intelligences worked.

But that very unradical mind which belonged to Lord Burghley differed only in matters of detail, and in Burghley's single-minded Reagan-like concentration on ensuring the successful pursuit, prosecution, and execution of those guilty of terrorism. It was to achieve this end, primarily, that an interregnum would be necessary. Burghley's thinking is contained in a number of documents: two pages of notes in his own inimitable hand;[76] a draft of a bill in the solicitor-general Popham's hand, extensively corrected by Burghley (this residing among the Ellesmere MSS in the Huntington Library in California);[77] and, third, what appears to be the most advanced version of these devices: a parliamentary bill endorsed by Burghley 'January 1584[5]. A bill for the queen's safety', and otherwise described as 'to be added to the bill for the queen's safety' – thus indicating that what was in hand was an extension of the 1584 Act 'for Provision to be Made for the Surety of the Queen's Most Royal Person'.[78]

The commanding idea running through these drafts is that, in the event of the Queen's untimely death, 'there remayn an ordinary power, to remedy all violence committed agaynst her.' 'The government of the realme shall still contynew in all respectes.' 'This', says Burghley in his rough notes, 'cannot be without an Interreyn'. 'Ther shall be decreed an Interreyn for some resonable tyme.' Government was to reside in a Great Council or Grand Council, acting 'in the name of the Imperiall Crown of England'. At first

Burghley seems to have thought of a body consisting of the Privy Council with the addition of all the major offices of state. But in the Ellesmere document he (or Popham) conceives that this body should come into being by the Privy Council recruiting from the House of Lords (or as much of it as could be assembled within ten days) to make up a Grand Council of 30 persons, plus the four senior judges. Within 30 days (corrected by Burghley to 20 days) of the Queen's assassination, the Great Council should recall the last Parliament back to Westminster. Thereafter, the Great Council having actively promoted the apprehension and due punishment of all offenders against the Queen's life, 'of what estate so ever they be', Parliament would give sentence against them. Anyone attempting during this period of time to lay claim to the throne by force would be *ipso facto* disabled from succeeding and would be actively resisted by the Great Council. The style to be employed in respect of this body in all writs, warrants, patents, and the like would be thus, in Latin: *Magnum Consilium Coronae Angliae,* a phrase inserted in the documents in Burghley's own hand. One wonders whether such a device would have succeeded in defeating the *coup de théâtre* which brought that other Mary to the throne, against all the odds, in 1553.[79]

The Ellesmere document proposes that the Great Council 'with the said Parliament' shall continue 'above one year, but shall then cease', and sooner if due execution had by then been passed on the public enemy. But it is as uninformative as all previous papers of this kind, white, green, or rainbow-coloured, on how the interregnum is to be terminated and England to find itself once again with a monarch in whose name writs would run. On this the parliamentary bill of January 1585 is more helpful. No one was to acknowledge any claimant as king or queen or affirm any one person to have more right than another. But the act of the Great Council in summoning a parliament – in composition the last parliament to have sat – was now seen as necessary 'because it is likely and very probable that the state of both the Realms [*sc.* England and Ireland] cannot long endure without a person that by justice ought to be the successor of the Crown shall be known'. 'Ought to be' referred to the law of succession. Accordingly, Parliament would in peaceable manner consider and hear any pretensions to the throne and finally (in Burghley's inserted words 'in the name of God and as it were in his presence')

> accept and receive such a person to the Crown of the Realm as shall to them upon their peaceable deliberations *and trials had of them* [Burghley's interpolation] appear to have best right to the same in blood by the royal lawes of the Realm and such a person *so by the said Parliament allowed* [Burghley's hand again] they shall by a Proclamation warranted with the Great Seal of England in form of an Act of Parliament published to the people of the Realm to have the most right to the Crown.

In Burghley's telling interpolations, Poland was not far away.

It was known to Neale and therefore to us that Burghley's own ever-active pen inserted into this parliamentary draft the words 'uppon sure hope of the assent of our Soverayn Lady'. That is to say, Burghley expressed a hopeful presumption of the bill's successful passage and of the royal assent. It is equally well known that not only did the idea of an interregnum not commend itself to Elizabeth but that (so far as we know) there was, after Christmas 1584, no discussion of it on the floor of either house. Burghley had proposed. Elizabeth disposed. And that was that. What would have followed a successful attempt on the life of Elizabeth I we do not know, and Protestants may prefer to avert their imaginations: an interregnum possibly, but not one enjoying the legality, however constitutionally dubious, afforded by an Act of Parliament.

There had been no attempt on this occasion to suggest that that was not how the business of politics proceeded, so long as this remarkable woman lived. Two years later, in 1586, the political nation was back where it had been in 1572, beseeching the Queen to carry out the sentence of death now passed against the Scottish Queen. And it is remarkable that their petition, the petition of both Houses of Parliament, was buttressed with threats, the same biblical threats. And it is more striking still that this document too is extensively corrected and interpolated in Burghley's hand, in the copy which survives in San Marino, California.[80] We may note in particular this passage:

> The neglecting wherof [*sc.* the carrying-out of the sentence] maye procure the heavy displeasure and punyshment of Almightie God as by sundry severe examples of his great Justice in that behalfe lefte us in the Sacred Scriptures doeth appere.

The drift of this essay has not been in the least 'whiggish', to employ the historical cant term. I have not argued for the incipience in Elizabethan England of a kind of constitutional monarchy, still less of a headless republic or even of a continuous, coherent republican movement. When Thomas Digges proposed that Parliament should be always 'in esse', he was not writing in favour of parliamentary sovereignty. I do not see 1649 foreshadowed proleptically in 1572 or 1584. It is Neale, not I, who remarks of Burghley's interregnum plan: 'more congenial to the Commonwealth period of the next century than to the Tudor constitution'.[81] Nor have I set out to argue that late-sixteenth-century England could, still less that it should, have been ruled more or less permanently by a rational regime composed of a team of political equals, experiencing effective collegiality. Early modern European history suggests that few such regimes ever existed, or were likely to survive for very long. The rule of a single person under the Crown, a Richelieu or an Olivares or a Buckingham, was to be almost the norm in the seventeenth century. And perhaps we have found something like that in these documents.

The notion of a *regnum Cecilianum* was a canard invented by the enemies of the Cecils but it was not a total falsification of political realities. Cynics might find in the sketch pad of papers examined in this article, so many of them annotated or corrected in the spidery Cecilian italic hand, reflections not of the republican machiavellianism of the *Discourses* but of the individualistic *virtù* of *The Prince*: Burghley perpetuating his own kingdom, which he ruled in Elizabeth's name, using the likes of Thomas Digges as cat's-paws.

My argument has been less speculative, less ambitious. I suggest no more than that Burghley and his colleagues (and Cecil *did* have colleagues), like Swallowfield, were responding resourcefully and intelligently to a most unusual situation. The strangeness of the Elizabethan scenario, which so captivated Sir John Neale, was commented on soon after its passing by a more jaundiced observer, Francis Bacon. For Bacon, the whole episode of the later Tudors, contained within half a century, had been unique and bizarre: 'The strangest variety that in a like number of successions of any hereditary monarchy hath ever been known: the reign of a child, the offer of a usurpation, the reign of a lady married to a foreign prince, and the reign of a lady solitary and unmarried.'[82] Surely this was not what the inventor of the English monarchy had intended. For Bacon the Tudors were 'these barren princes', and, by contrast, he welcomed the advent of Scottish James and his fruitful progeny as a dynasty likely to endure 'for ever'. Bacon was not to know that the violent death of the second of these perpetual Stuarts would be followed by an interregnum – *the* Interregnum – and a short-lived English Republic. And nor, I think, do Elizabethan historians need to know that.

Appendix

On 30 July 1582 Sir Francis Walsingham sent the following advice to the Earl of Shrewsbury, who had Mary, Queen of Scots in his custody:

> For aunswer wherunto her Majestie doth thinke it meete that you shold lett her [*sc.* the Scottish Queen] understand that, first, shee doth find it straunge that shee shold directe her lettres unto her Counsell, as unto principall members of this Crowne (for so doth shee in her said letters terme them, a cowrse that hertofor hath not bene held), wherof her Majestie cannot otherwise conceave but that there shee doth not repute her to be so absolut as that without thassent of such whom she termeth 'principall members of the Crowne' she cannot direct her pollicie; or els, that uppon this charge given by her of delay used in satisfying of her requests, shee wer by them to be called to an accompt. Of which misconceipt of the said Queen and misunderstanding of the absolutenes of her Majesties government, shee thinketh meet shee

shold by yor Lordship be better enfourmed: For althoughe her Highnes doth carry as great regard unto her Counsell as any of her progenitors have done, and hath just cause so to do in respecte of their wisdome and fidelity, yet is shee to be let understand that they are Councellors by choyce, and not by birth, whose services are no longer to be used in that publike function then it shall please her Majestie to dispose of the same; and therefore her Highnes cannot conceave to what ende a complainte shold be made unto them, unlesse ether shee repute her to be in her minoritye, or els doth meane to use her Counsell as witnesses against her.

(Edmund Lodge, *Illustrations of British History* (1791), II, pp. 276–7)

Notes

1   I believe that the nickname derived from certain early concert party performances which became linked with the character of Sunny Jim as depicted on packets containing the breakfast cereal Force. Not long after the conferment of his knighthood, John Ernest Neale was referred to in print as 'Sir James Neale' (H. J. Habakkuk, 'The Market for Monastic Property, 1539–1603', *Economic History Review*, 2nd ser., 10 (1958), p. 363).
2   Huntington Library, MS EL 6162, fos. 34a–36a.
3   See Diarmaid MacCulloch, *Suffolk and the Tudors: Politics and Religion in an English County, 1500–1600* (Oxford, 1986); and, on the successful 1553 revolution of this 'local ruling establishment' against Westminster, Dr MacCulloch's edition of 'The *Vita Mariae Angliae Reginae* of Robert Wingfield of Brantham', *Camden Miscellany xxviii* Camden 4th ser., 29; 1984), pp. 181–301. Dr MacCulloch's account of a gentry republic which worked pretty well may be contrasted with Professor A. H. Smith's study of neighbouring Norfolk, which indulged more recklessly and openly in factional struggle (*County and Court: Government and Politics in Norfolk, 1558–1603* (Oxford, 1974)). On parliamentary aspects of gentry republicanism, see Mark A. Kishlansky, *Parliamentary Selection: Social and Political Choice in Early Modern England* (Cambridge, 1986).
4   John Morrill, *The Revolt of the Provinces: Conservatives and Radicals in the English Civil War, 1630–1650* (London, 1976), p. 199. Compare Diarmaid MacCulloch's account of 'Alternative Patterns of Politics', chapter 11 of his *Suffolk and the Tudors*.
5   Keith Thomas, 'The Levellers and the Franchise', in Gerald Aylmer (ed.), *The Interregnum* (London, 1972), pp. 57–78.
6   Smith, *County and Court*, pp. 98–9.
7   Conrad Russell, *Parliaments and English Politics, 1621–1629* (Oxford, 1979), p. 189.
8   J. E. Neale, *Elizabeth I and her Parliaments, 1559–1581* (London, 1953), pp. 318–26.
9   Thomas Norton to William Fleetwood, 8 Jan. 1582, BL Add. MS 48023, fo.49^r; Laurence Humphrey, *The nobles, or of nobilitye* (London, 1563), sig. Aii^v.
10 John Aylmer, *An harborowe for faithfull and trewe subiectes* ('at Strasborowe' but *recte* London, 1559), sigs. H3–4^r.
11 J. E. Neale, *Essays in Elizabethan History* (London, 1958), p. 124.
12 *De republica anglorum by Sir Thomas Smith*, ed. Mary Dewar (Cambridge, 1982), pp. 88, 85.
13 Ernst H. Kantorowicz, *The King's Two Bodies: A Study in Medieval Political Theology* (Princeton, 1957), p. 4.
14 *De republica anglorum*, p. 57.

15 Michael Mendle, *Dangerous Positions: Mixed Government, the Estates of the Realm, and the Making of the Answer to the xix Propositions* (University, Alabama, 1985), p. 43.

16 Quoted in Quentin Skinner, *The Foundations of Modern Political Thought* (Cambridge, 1978), I, p. 229.

17 Joel Hurstfield, 'Was There a Tudor Despotism After All?', in *Freedom, Corruption and Government in Elizabethan England* (London, 1973), pp. 23–49.

18 Mendle, *Dangerous Positions*, p. 15.

19 Aylmer, *An harborowe*, sig. H3ʳ.

20 J. G. A. Pocock, *The Machiavellian Moment: Florentine Political Thought and the Atlantic Republican Tradition* (Princeton, 1975). But see A. B. Ferguson, *The Articulate Citizen and the English Renaissance* (Durham, NC, 1965), esp. pp. 42–69.

21 J. E. Neale, 'The Elizabethan Acts of Supremacy and Uniformity', *English Historical Review*, 65 (1950), pp. 304–32; *Elizabeth I and her Parliaments, 1559–1581*, pp. 51–84.

22 Norman L. Jones, *Faith by Statue: Parliament and the Settlement of Religion, 1559* (London, 1982); Winthrop S. Hudson, *The Cambridge Connection and the Elizabethan Settlement of 1559* (Durham, NC, 1980).

23 M. A. R. Graves, 'The Management of the Elizabethan House of Commons: the Council's "Men-of-Business" ', *Parliamentary History*, 2 (1983), pp. 11–38; Graves, 'Thomas Norton the Parliament Man: An Elizabethan M.P., 1559–1581', *Historical Journal*, 23 (1980), pp. 17–35. Cf. G. R. Elton, *The Parliament of England 1559–1581* (Cambridge, 1986).

24 G. R. Elton, 'Parliament in the Sixteenth Century: Functions and Fortunes', *Studies in Tudor and Stuart Politics and Government*, III (Cambridge, 1983), pp. 156–82.

25 W. T. MacCaffrey, *The Shaping of the Elizabethan Regime* (Princeton, 1968); Hudson, *The Cambridge Connection*; Penry Williams, *The Tudor Regime* (Oxford, 1979).

26 J. E. Neale, 'The Elizabethan Political Scene', in *Essays in Elizabethan History*, pp. 59–84.

27 S. L. Adams, 'Faction, Clientage and Party: English Politics 1550–1603', *History Today*, 32 (1982), pp. 33–9: Adams, 'Eliza Enthroned? The Court and its Politics', in C. Haigh (ed.), *The Reign of Elizabeth I* (London, 1984), pp. 55–77.

28 Conyers Read, 'Walsingham and Burghley in Queen Elizabeth's Privy Council', *English Historical Review*, 28 (1913), pp. 34–58.

29 PRO SP 12/172/37.

30 Sir Robert Naunton, *Fragmenta Regalia*, ed. E. Arber (English Reprints; London, 1870), pp. 16–17.

31 W. T. MacCaffrey, *Queen Elizabeth and the Making of Policy, 1572–1588* (Princeton, 1981).

32 PRO SP 15/25/35.

33 PRO SP 15/25/74.

34 Lord Hunsdon to the Earl of Huntingdon, 14 Apr. 1581, Sir Francis Walsingham to Huntingdon, 5 Apr. 1581 (Huntington Library, MSS HA 1214, HA 13067).

35 PRO SP 12/175/35.

36 J. A. Froude, *History of England from the Fall of Wolsey to the Defeat of the Spanish Armada* (London, n.d.), XII, p. 508.

37 Quoted in Williams, *Tudor Regime*, p. 32.

38 R. B. Wernham, *After the Armada: Elizabethan England and the Struggle for Western Europe, 1588–1595* (Oxford, 1984).

39 Huntington Library, MS EL 2625. Another version of this paper, diverging substantially from it, bears the endorsement 'the xvith of Maii 1559. Toching the redresse of the comyn welth' (Huntington Library, MS EL 2580). I have benefited from discussing these documents with Dr Peter Roberts and Dr David Starkey.

40 But see Gerald Bowler, 'English Protestant and Resistance Writings 1553–1603', unpublished London Ph.D. thesis (1981), and his article ' "An Axe or An Acte": The Parliament of 1572 and Resistance Theory in Early Elizabethan England', *Canadian Journal of History*, 19 (1984), pp. 349–59.

41 *Sermons or Homilies, Appointed to be Read in Churches* (1811 edn), pp. 124–38.

42 The references are to the adage 'Scarabeus aquilam quaerit' (Margaret Mann Phillips, *Erasmus on his Times: a Shortened Version of the 'Adages' of Erasmus* (Cambridge, 1967), pp. 47–72). To read this adage in connection with the allegorical passage in Spenser's *Shepheardes Calender* in which the downfall of Archbishop Grindal is approximated to the classical legend of the eagle dropping a shellfish (or tortoise) on the bald head of Aeschylus in mistake for a stone is to appreciate Spenser's barely suppressed republicanism. Erasmus uses this tale to demonstrate that the eagle, cruelly rapacious rather than truly courageous, is also myopic rather than 'eagle-eyed'. 'Anyone who considers all this will almost declare that the eagle is unworthy of being taken as an example of kingly rule.' (On Grindal and Spenser, see Patrick Collinson, *Archbishop Grindal 1519–1583: The Struggle for a Reformed Church* (1979), pp. 275–6; Paul E. McLane, *Spenser's Shepheardes Calender: A Study in Elizabethan Allegory* (Notre Dame, 1961), pp. 140–57.)

43 Huntington Library, MS HA Religious Box 1 (9).

44 BL Add. MS 48023, fo. 33.

45 Bowler, 'English Protestant and Resistance Writings', pp. 305–7.

46 Skinner, *Foundations of Modern Political Thought*, II, p. 221–2; Geneva Bible annotations to 1 Kgs. 21: 15, 2 Kgs. 9: 33, 1 Sam. 26: 9. By contrast, the second part of the Homily of Obedience taught that David was absolutely inhibited from harming Saul. 'But holy David did know that he might in no wise withstand, hurt or kill his sovereign lord and king ... Therefore, though he were never so much provoked, yet he refused utterly to hurt the Lord's anointed' (*Sermons or Homilies*, pp. 131–2).

47 Bowler, 'English Protestant and Resistance Writings', pp. 291–9. See also Richard L. Greaves, 'Traditionalism and the Seeds of Revolution in the Social Principles of the Geneva Bible', *Sixteenth-Century Journal*, 7 (1976), pp. 94–109; Dan G. Danner, 'The Contribution of the Geneva Bible of 1560 to the English Protestant Tradition', *Sixteenth-Century Journal*, 12 (1981), pp. 5–18.

48 T. E. Hartley (ed.), *Proceedings in the Parliaments of Elizabeth I*, I, 1558–1581, (Leicester, 1981), pp. 259–418. Particular references are to pp. 376, 324, 325, 312. The bishops' 'certeine argumentes collected out of the Scriptures ... againste the Queen of Scottes' are on pp. 274–90. I am much indebted to Dr Bowler's article ' "An Axe or An Acte" '.

49 Muntzer's sermon is in G. H. Williams (ed.), *Spiritual and Anabaptist Writers*, (Library of Christian Classics, 25; London, 1957), pp. 47–70. See also E. G. Rupp, *Patterns of Reformation* (London, 1969), pp. 201–2.

50 Hartley (ed.), *Proceedings*, p. 391.

51 Hartley (ed.), *Proceedings*, pp. 315–16, 328, 334–5, 273, 365–6. On Hall, see Neale, *Elizabeth I and her Parliaments, 1559–1581*, pp. 333–45; G. R. Elton, 'Arthur Hall, Lord Burghley and the Antiquity of Parliament', *Studies*, III, pp. 254–73.

52 Hartley (ed.), *Proceedings*, p. 281.

53 Hartley (ed.), *Proceedings*, pp. 376, 294–8; Bowler, ' "An Axe or An Acte" '.

54 Hartley (ed.), *Proceedings*, pp. 374–5.

55 Examples of the Bond are in PRO SP 12/174; earlier drafts are in SP 12/173/81–4. The most recent discussion of the Bond is in David Cressy, 'Binding the Nation: The Bonds of Association, 1584 and 1696', in Delloyd J. Guth and John W. McKenna (eds), *Tudor Rule and Revolution: Essays for G. R. Elton from his American Friends* (Cambridge, 1982), pp. 271–34.

56 PRO SP 12/174/1, 2, 3, 5, 8, 7, 14, 13.

57 Huntington Library, MS EL 1193; printed in *The Egerton Papers*, ed. J. Payne Collier (Camden Society; London, 1840), pp. 108–11.

58 Earl of Derby to the Earl of Leicester, 7 Nov. 1584 (PRO SP 12/175/4).

59 Huntington Library, MS EL 1191.

60 Thomas Scott and Edward Boys to Sir Francis Walsingham, 20 Nov. 1584 (PRO SP 12/176/9).

61 Thomas Digges, *Humble motives for association to maintaine religion established* (London, 1601), p. 6. I have compared this printed text with the MS in the Folger Shakespeare Library, MS V.b.214.

62 Diarmaid MacCulloch, 'Catholic and Puritan in Elizabethan Suffolk: A County Community Polarises', *Archiv für Reformationsgeschichte*, 72 (1981), pp. 232–89. See also MacCulloch, *Suffolk and the Tudors*.

63 PRO SP 12/173/87. My remark about partisan rather than consensual Protestantism is intended to conflict with Sir John Neale's suggestion that, with the accession of Elizabeth, 'the English Reformation ceases to be a partisan story: it became a national one' (*Essays in Elizabethan History*, p. 24).

64 PRO SP 12/173/88.

65 See the exchange of letters between Burghley and Walsingham about tactical matters connected with the Bond, 19, 20 Oct. 1584 (PRO SP 12/173/85, 86).

66 Huntington Library, MS EL 1187.

67 Christopher Goodman, *How superior powers ought to be obeyed of their subjects* (Geneva, 1558). See Skinner, *Foundations of Modern Political Thought*, II, pp. 221–4.

68 PRO SP 12/176/26; further copies in Folger Shakespeare Library MS V.b. 303, fos. 95–9, BL Lansdowne MS 98, fos. 14–18, Add. MS 38823, fos. 14 ff. See J. E. Neale, *Elizabeth I and her Parliaments, 1584–1601* (London, 1957), p. 45.

69 Neale, *Elizabeth I and her Parliaments, 1584–1601*, pp. 50–3.

70 PRO SP 12/176/11, 22, 23, 25, 28, 30; Huntington Library, MS EL 1192.

71 On the events of 1553, see 'The *Vita Mariae Angliae Reginae*'.

72 For Digges, see *DNB*; P. W. Hasler (ed.), *The History of Parliament: The House of Commons 1558–1601* (1981), II, pp. 37–9; and PRO SP 12/171/13, 13 I, 175/18.

73 Graves, 'The Management of the Elizabethan House of Commons'.

74 PRO SP 12/171/13, 13 I–V, 30, 301, SP 12/175/18.

75 PRO SP 12/176/32.

76 PRO SP 12/176/28, 29.

77 Huntington Library, MS EL 1192.

78 PRO SP 12/176/11, 22, 23, 30.

79 'The *Vita Mariae Angliae Reginae*'.

80 Huntington Library, MS EL 1191; partly printed in Neale, *Elizabeth I and her Parliaments, 1584–1601*, pp. 113–14.

81 Neale, *Elizabeth I and her Parliaments, 1584–1601*, p. 45.

82 Francis Bacon, 'A Letter to the Lord Chancellor, Touching the History of Britain' (1605), *Works of Francis Bacon*, ed. J. Spedding, R. L. Ellis and D. D. Heath, X (1868), pp. 249–50.

5

*The countervailing of benefits: Monopoly, liberty, and benevolence in Elizabethan England**

DAVID HARRIS SACKS

By the standards of the age, Elizabeth I's last Parliament was a happy one. Laws were enacted, taxes were granted, and grievances were redressed.[1] At its close, the Queen and her people were seen to be in affectionate harmony with one another. But it was not a parliament without conflict or acrimony. If consent to taxation had proceeded relatively smoothly, redress of grievances had not. At the heart of the controversy were the royal patents of monopoly granted for the exclusive production and trade of specified manufactures. These patents raised the most fundamental questions affecting the polity and its law. They were the fruits of the royal prerogative, with which no subject could meddle without the monarch's leave, but they touched the common weal, with whose preservation and advancement the Members of Parliament were especially charged.[2] They arguably encroached on the liberties of the subject, which protected freeborn Englishmen in their property and persons, but they exemplified the role of political authority in the regulation of the economy, without which those liberties might become quite valueless. When Parliament assembled in 1601, monopolies had been the target of widespread complaints for some time.[3]

A confounding of benevolence

From the mid-sixteenth century, when they were first introduced into England, patents of monopoly for manufactures were used by English

* Earlier versions of this chapter were presented in whole or in part to the Center for the History of British Political Thought at the Folger Shakespeare Library, the Center for Seventeenth and Eighteenth Century Studies at UCLA, the Early Modern British History Seminar at Harvard University, the British History Colloquium at the Huntington Library, the Department of English at the University of Maryland, College Park, the Department of History at the Johns Hopkins University, and at annual meetings of the American Historical Association and the Renaissance Society of America. The author wishes to thank the following scholars for their helpful comments and criticisms: J. D. Alsop, Bernard Bailyn, John Brewer, Harold J. Cook, Stephen Diamond, Stephen Greenblatt, John Guy, Donna Hamilton, Donald Kelley, Mark Kishlansky, Karen Ordahl Kupperman, Wallace MacCaffrey, John Morrill, John Murrin, J. G. A. Pocock, Paul Seaver, Lois Schwoerer, Gordon Schochet, A. J. Slavin, Susan Staves, Lawrence Stone, and Perez Zagorin.

monarchs not only to protect new industrial processes and new products but to favour their subjects with royal bounty. They quickly took their place alongside the monies, titles, rent charges, lands, offices, and the like which regularly flowed from the prince to loyal courtiers and their clients. By the 1580s the original promoters of the monopolies – the projectors seeking exclusive rights for their schemes and inventions – typically enjoyed their patents only second hand as the substitutes of the royal favourites who were the actual grantees.[4]

At the same time, the patent system became subject to serious abuse. Patentees, more interested in the income they could derive from their new rights than in the development of their new inventions, simply licensed craftsmen to continue employing older techniques in competition with the patent – in effect introducing an excise tax on their production. The Crown also began using the patents as sources of revenue, reserving to itself a percentage of the patentees' profits, ostensibly in compensation for the income lost to the customs because the manufactures produced under the grants had displaced imports. It also used them to compensate royal creditors among the nobility and gentry or to reward Crown officials for their service. Once these powerful interests became engaged in the system, a more vigorous and systematic enforcement of monopoly rights was instituted. The powers of the Privy Council and the prerogatives of the Crown were used to intercede on behalf of the patentees, coercing compliance and blocking litigation in the law courts. Informers also appeared in the picture, seeking reward from the beneficiaries of the grants or bribes from those who had violated them.[5]

However, even before 1580, when the monopolies entered what Joan Thirsk has identified as their first 'scandalous phase', they were already a source of complaint. They may have been one of the causes of grievance behind Robert Bell's attack on 'lycenses' in 1571.[6] In 1572 the mere thought that any public action might result in the creation of a monopoly was widely condemned as an evil, even by Sir Francis Knollys, Treasurer of the Queen's Household and a leading privy councillor.[7] By the 1590s the royal patents themselves had become a genuine canker on the body politic.[8] In 1597 a serious attempt to legislate on the matter was forestalled by the promise of remedy made on behalf of the Queen by her councillors in the Commons, yet nothing was accomplished – save that some of the loudest complainers seem to have felt the wrath of the Queen for their presumption.[9] In 1599 some of the basic legal issues involved in the monopolies had been aired in the case of *Davenant* v. *Hurdis* concerning certain by-laws of the Company of Merchant Tailors of London issued under its royal charter. In that case, the judges had found that any economic regulation that deprived a man of the free exercise of his craft without his consent to be against common right and in violation of chapter 29 of Magna Carta.[10] But this decision did not touch the royal patents, whatever the judges might have intended. The Crown continued to issue or renew its monopoly grants without stint.

When Parliament convened again in 1601, a number of members, especially the common lawyers, appear to have come armed with a determination – possibly even a plan – to remedy the matter on their own. Looking at the lists of suspect patents that circulated among the MPs, the petitions that arrived at the Privy Council from aggrieved craftsmen, the crowds in the streets near the parliament house and at the doors of committee meetings, and at Sir Robert Cecil's enraged outburst complaining of these facts, it is hard to escape this sense that something a bit out of the ordinary was afoot. On 4 November, only a few days after the session had begun, Robert Johnson made a vigorous speech against the 'vile Practices' of the patentees. Their 'abuses' were denounced again on 18 November, when the lawyer Anthony Dyott sought to introduce 'An Act against Patents'. The next day, Lawrence Hyde, another lawyer, introduced his own bill, entitled simply 'An Act of Explanation of the Common Law in Certain Cases of Letters Patents', which then became the focus of the debate.[11] Most probably this bill sought to limit the scope of the patents in the light of the principles laid down in *Davenant*. Even Francis Moore, the lawyer who had represented Davenant in his losing effort to enforce the Merchant Tailors' ordinances, came prepared to restrain the patents. He was one of the most articulate critics to speak against them in this session, as he had been in 1597.[12]

The central arguments against the monopoly patents, as it was articulated in 1601 and in the pleadings in *Darcy* v. *Allen* the following year, was that by granting exclusive manufacturing and trading rights to a few private individuals, monopolies deprived free men of their livelihoods, hence of the liberties they were assured by chapter 29 of Magna Carta. The central idea is that every free man had a godly obligation (not just a right) to earn his bread, a duty which could not be abridged without his consent. Therefore, a monopolist was understood – actually said – to be a *vir sanguinis*, a man of blood who in preventing competitors from exercising their crafts threatened their very existence as free men.[13] As the lawyer Francis Moore put it, monopoly 'bringeth the General Profit into a Private Hand; and the End of All is Beggery and Bondage to the Subject'.[14] Monopolists, therefore, were 'Bloodsuckers of the Commonwealth', as said Richard Martin, another lawyer. They sucked 'up the best and principallest Commodities, which the Earth ... hath given Us ... the Commodities of our own Labour, which with the Sweat of our Brows (even up to the Knees in Mire and Dirt) we have labour'd for'.[15] They thereby turned free subjects into bondmen or villeins – deprived them of their ability to use their labour as they chose.

Since human beings were understood not merely to be free to labour but called by God to do so, the opponents of the monopolies believed that they interfered with men's voluntary performance of their spiritual as well as their worldly commitments. They prevented men from pursuing the callings which they were bound in conscience to practise, thereby depriving them of the public and social freedoms necessary if they were to conform themselves to Christian liberty, which required nothing less than absolute obedience to God's commands. This theory, articulated especially by Nicholas Fuller in defending Thomas Allen against Edward Darcy in the case of the playing-card monopoly, saw the liberties of the subject as securing Englishmen in the performance of their duties, that is in meeting their responsibilities to themselves, their families, and the commonwealth.[16]

Although much else was said in condemnation of the monopolies – for example, that they drove up prices and that they resulted in the production and sale of poor quality goods[17] – it was their threat to working men's vocations that had the greatest weight. This threat provided the fulcrum on which turned a theory of what liberties a subject enjoyed by virtue of being a freeborn Englishman and not a villein or bondman. From the start, a link was seen between those liberties protected by Magna Carta, especially in chapter 29, and the requirement that consent be obtained for any act that would touch the possessions of the subject, whether material or intangible. Liberty and consent were inextricably interconnected as 'property' is to 'propriety', as what is possessed is tied to the right to possess it.[18]

Understood in this way, the dangers to the liberties of the subject entailed by the monopolies were dangers to the commonwealth at large. They undermined order by threatening the bonds that held society together. In part this was because the number and economic significance of the grants had grown so great by the end of Elizabeth's reign that they risked touching public necessity. When in 1601 Sir Robert Wroth read out a long list of patents issued since the previous Parliament – a list that contained iron, glass, vinegar, sea-coal, steel, salt, saltpetre, train oil, and many other items – William Hakewill 'stood up and asked ... Is not Bread there? Bread quoth another? ... No quoth Mr *Hakewill,* but if order be not taken for these Bread will be there, before the next Parliament.'[19] Hakewill's point was that, in offering patents of monopoly as royal bounty to her courtiers, the Queen put at risk her duty to provide for the well-being of all her subjects. It is not surprising, therefore, that many members of the House of Commons saw the monopolies as a danger not only to the realm but to the Queen's rule as well. 'There is no Act of Hers', said Francis Moore, 'that hath been, or is more Derogatory to her *Majesty,* or more Odious to the Subject, or more Dangerous to the Common-Wealth, than the Granting of these *Monopolies.*'[20]

By breaking down the web of favour and good will that knit the body politic into unity, the monopolies had generated a threat to benevolence, as Sir George More warned:

There be Three Persons; Her *Majesty,* the *Patentee,* and the *Subject*: Her *Majesty* the Head, the *Patentee* the Hand, and the *Subject* the Foot. Now here is our Case; the *Head* gives Power to the *Hand,* the *Hand* Oppresseth the *Foot,* and the *Foot* Riseth against the *Head.*[21]

In More's view the monopolies risked spreading a disease in the common-wealth, an overturning of proportion and order, a derangement in which the limbs and organs of the social body fell into opposition to one another.

The 'Golden Speech'

The debates over the monopolies continued in the House of Commons for more than a week, but the Queen put an end to them with a proclamation which voided a number of the most hated grants – those for salt, starch, train oil, vinegar, *aqua vitae*, and several other commodities – permitting the rest to be tested at the common law, and in the meantime removing the support of the Privy Council from the patentees. On the day the proclamation appeared, the Commons discussed sending a delegation to thank the Queen. But in their joy, they could reach no decision on whom to send, and, as Heywood Townshend tells us, 'At the last, at the Lower-End of the House, they cryed, All, All, All.' And so it came that 140 members of the Commons, led by their Speaker, assembled on 30 November to give thanks to their queen and to hear her response to them.[22]

Elizabeth's speech – her 'Golden Speech' as it later came to be known – survives in four versions: Heywood Townshend's, recorded by him in his diary of the Parliament;[23] an edition of 1601 said to have been taken down by one 'A. B.' and printed by Robert Barker, the royal printer;[24] an edition of 1628, which was subsequently reprinted in 1642;[25] and a manuscript version in a collection of papers belonging to William Dell, apparently found on his desk while he was secretary to Archbishop Laud.[26] In what follows we shall rely primarily on Townshend's version, since as a member of the Commons in 1601 he followed the debates on monopolies very closely. But the other versions also will help throw light on the meaning of the Queen's words.

The speech as we have it from Townshend falls into three parts: an introduction in which Elizabeth talks about her duty and about her love for her subjects and theirs for her, a middle section in which she shifts to discuss the monopolies issue itself, and a conclusion in which she returns with new force to some of the themes of the introduction and speaks especially of her service to God.[27] It would be easy to think of her words as a conventional, though eloquent, statement of the divine sanction for her power, since a good deal of what the Queen said concerns her relation to God. But in fact it is not primarily a speech about power, divine or otherwise. What holds the speech together, rather, is the idea of duty, especially the monarch's duty.

To unravel the Queen's message, we need to start in the section where Elizabeth explains what went amiss with the monopolies.

> Since I was Queen [she said], yet, did I never put my Pen unto any Grant, but that, upon Pretext and Semblance made unto Me, it was

both Good and Beneficial to the Subject in general; though a private
Profit to some of My Antient Servants, who had deserved well at My
Hands.

In treating the functions of her servants, however, the Queen acknowledged
that something had gone very wrong.

Shall they think to escape unpunished [she asked], that have thus
Oppressed you, and have been respectless of their Duty, and regard-
less of Our Honour? ... I perceive they dealt with Me like Physitians,
who Administering a Drug, or when they give Pills, do Gild them ali
over.[28]

Note the image of the physician. Elizabeth seems to say some of her advisers supported the patents by colouring their harmfulness – presenting them
as beneficial to the subject though a private profit to her servants – as some
physicians obscure the true nature of their noxious potions. What kind of
physicians are these?

According to the Hippocratic Oath the first duty of the physician is to do
no harm and to treat every patient honestly, equally, and fairly. Those who
violate this oath by placing their own advantage over the good of the patient
are false physicians, and so are those who through ignorance or ill-will bring
suffering to whom they treat.[29] The classic example of such a false doctor
was the empirick, that hobgoblin of the professional physicians of the early
modern period. An empirick was an ignorant practitioner who 'fetcheth all
his skill from bare and naked experience' and had no learning. According to
the professional physicians who condemned them, many 'clothed' their
ignorance 'with the outward garments of knowledge', especially by magni-
fying their skills and extolling their strange cures. To conceal the true nature
of 'their vile and contemptible medicines ... from those that know all vsuall
medicines by their colour, smell or taste ... they mingle something with them
onely to alter these qualities' and 'by this tricke, that sauoreth of cousenage'
they enhance their fame 'and increase their wealth'.[30] Queen Elizabeth's
complaint was that her advisers had acted like 'subtill and deceptfull
Empiricks', pretending that established trades were new inventions and that
the monopolists' bitter pills were sweet and beneficial cures. Her councillors
had permitted self-seeking to substitute for the common good.

What, then, was the proper duty of royal councillors? The model of the
physician again helps us understand what Elizabeth had in mind. Starting in
the later sixteenth century, as the Queen and her privy councillors had good
reason to know, the professional physicians, acting through the College of
Physicians, began a concerted effort to establish themselves as the sole practitioners of medicine in London and its environs.[31] They wished to distinguish themselves not only from surgeons and apothecaries, who sometimes
prescribed physic as a by-employment, but also – as Thomas Gale said in

introducing his translation of Galen in 1586 – from those 'honest Artists, as Tailers, Shoomakers, Weavers or anie other handie occupations, that ... should Leave their arte wherein they are perfect, and fall to this art of Medicine'.[32] Thus the physicians acted on the adage, proclaimed in the mid-century by one of their learned colleagues: 'Let no man medle with another mannes corne, but with his owne. Lette the shoemaker medle with his shoes.'[33] To put it crudely, but accurately, the physicians wanted a monopoly of practice in their art.

The writers on the medical profession in the sixteenth century, and the great classical writers on physic upon whom they relied, all stressed the necessity of tempering experience with reason. Without a universal standard against which to measure experience, there could be no true knowledge and therefore no certainty of judgement.[34] As with the physician, so with the political councillor. He too faced a world of variable conditions and continually changing circumstance, and thus he too needed to temper his own experience with knowledge of a wider range of occurrences and of the underlying nature of things. Hence in drawing the analogy between the false physicians and those of her advisers who had promoted the monopolies, Elizabeth implied that a true councillor would be professional in the same way as a true physician. He would exercise judgement for the well-being of his charges, based on a firm foundation of learning as well as experience. Like the physician, his role would be as much diagnostic as instrumental. It would be for him to foresee potential problems and prescribe a preventative, as well as to discern the nature of present discontents and recommend a cure.

Conceiving of the governors of the realm as physicians indicated that they had charge of the welfare of a body politic, with everything organized proportionally and in its proper place. The vision is very much one of a hierarchical division of labour, in which head and members each performed vital functions for the rest. If the realm should fall into 'distemper' or become 'distracted' – words which grew out of the metaphor of the body – the head, the monarch and his councillors, were to restore it to health by re-establishing the proper arrangement of organs and limbs. This understanding was summarized in the concept of *salus populi*, the doctrine that the rulers of the realm were to provide for its social health – its commonweal. *Salus populi* assumes a collective health in which head and body together participate. The monarch is at one and the same time at the head and in the service of the body. As the principal physician of the realm, it is his duty to act disinterestedly in the performance of his function.

Elizabeth recognized this implication in her speech to the Commons. 'Of My Selfe', she reminded them,

> I was never any greedy scraping Grasper, nor a straight, fast-holding Prince; nor yet a Waster. My Heart was never set on Worldly Goods, but only for my Subjects Good. What you bestow on Me, I will not

hoard it up, but Receive it to bestow on You again: Yea, My own Proprieties I count Yours, and to be Expended for your Good; and your Eyes shall see the Bestowing of All, for your Good.[35]

Unlike the monopolists, pursuing private gain, she gathered wealth in only to put it out again for common purposes and public good. From these considerations came a theory of monarchical duty.

Generally speaking, duties arise in three quite distinct ways. They can come from abstract and universal principles of practical wisdom or right action applied to particular circumstances. They can spring from the exchange of words and deeds in the form of a gift or of a contract – that is, from some performance by which we accept an obligation or create one. Or they can derive from our positions, our callings, as is true for ministers, teachers, lawyers, and, of course, physicians. The doctor's duty was to do everything to save his patient and restore him to health, but the duty was to the ideals of medicine, not to the individual. The Queen appears to have conceived of her own duty in a similar way. It arose, she implied, because 'God hath raised Me high' and 'made me his Instrument to maintain his Truth and Glory'.[36] He had put her in the position to rule for her subjects' benefit, and she could do naught but obey this calling. She had a general duty to God, of course, but this duty was the same owed by every Christian, as King James said in *Basilikon Doron*.[37] Her special duties, for which she particularly 'set the last Judgement-Day before [her] Eyes', came from her position, just as the duties of her councillors and as the duties of everyone else in the social order came from theirs. And just as God had put her in this place, so too He gave blessing to her conduct of it, a point she stressed 'to give God the Praise, as Testimony before you, and not to Attribute any thing to My Self'.[38]

In thus stressing her God-given duty, Elizabeth also conceded that she was compelled to act for 'Conscience-sake' against those 'Varlets and lewd persons' who had put her subjects to the 'Errours, Troubles, Vexations and Oppressions' created by her patents.[39] Hence, the Queen expressed her gratitude to the critics of the monopolies because they kept her from the 'Lapse of an Errour', discharging her of guilt for the faults of her advisers and 'Substitutes'.[40]

From these considerations came a theory of the subjects' duty, which properly fell into a coordinated relation with the monarch's. In general, it could be summed up in the 'Loves and Loyalty' they gave her, in part by means of their 'intended Helps' – the grant of subsidies – and in part by their respect for her sovereign rule.[41] Rule belonged to the queen; and with it subjects were not to meddle, any more than shoemakers were to meddle in surgery. It was her responsibility alone to provide for government. But the first requirement of just rule, as Cicero said, was that it do no harm.[42] If faults occurred, she was obligated to correct them or to bear herself the burden of the 'crime'.[43] This meant that, whenever royal authority erred, her subjects had a duty to her as well as to the commonwealth at large to air them in the public forum. The Queen especially praised those members of the Commons who, she said,

> spake out of Zeal for their Countries, and not out of Spleen, or Malevolent Affection, as being Parties grieved. And I take it exceeding Gratefully from them; because it gives Us to know that no Respects or Interests had moved them other than the minds they bear to suffer no diminution of our Honour, and our subjects Loves unto us.[44]

If every person in the realm held to his proper place in this way, each contributing to the common good as God had called him, the Queen would be 'that Person, that still (yet under God) hath Deliver'd you; so I trust, (by the Almighty Power of God) that I still shall be his Instrument to Preserve you from every Peril, Dishonour, Shame, Tyranny and Oppression'.[45]

What then of liberty, which had so much dominated the debates in the Commons? For the Queen and her officials, who had recently experienced the Earl of Essex's abortive rebellion and who were still fighting an international war with the greatest power in Europe, the freedom of Englishmen depended critically on the capacity of the state to maintain stability at home and protect itself from foreign dangers. For them, peril and dishonour as well as tyranny and oppression could come as easily from within as from outside the realm, especially because a state torn by internal strife was vulnerable to foreign conquest. A conquered state was a slave state, since the conquest wiped away existing law and subjected its people absolutely to the conqueror.[46] Hence it was essential that the Queen have the necessary authority and means to serve the realm. Only then could she conserve her subjects in safety and be, in the words of a 1628 printing of her speech, 'the Instrument to deliuer [them] from out of seruitude, and from slauerie vnder our Enemies, and cruell tyranny, and vilde oppression intended against Vs'.[47] For those who thought in this vein, there could be no more certain recipe for the loss of freedom than the collapse of authority at home and of power abroad. The Queen dwelt very heavily on this theme throughout her remarks, explicitly linking her ability to protect the realm from insurrection and invasion with the monies her people had bestowed upon her.[48]

Elizabeth's defence of royal duties, therefore, was also an apology for the supremacy of her monarchical power. If liberty was in danger, it was the ruler's calling to preserve it. Like the physicians, she claimed a monopoly over the health of the body with whose care she was charged.

Rituals of accommodation

The Elizabethan monopolies point to the existence in the late sixteenth century of rival outlooks about the nature of the English polity. Those who created them saw the grant of exclusive trading rights in manufactures and other commodities as a fitting means to order the economy and promote the common good through the due exercise of royal authority. To their advocates, these new-found enterprises fit neatly into the hierarchical ranking of offices and callings which made up the commonwealth. If properly administered, each contributed in its distinct way to the larger good.[49] As Queen Elizabeth herself argued, there was nothing wrong in granting 'a private Profit to some of my Ancient Servants' through her patents, so long as what she did was 'Good and Beneficial to the Subject in general'.[50] Hence, she wished only to prevent the abuse of patents by those she called, according to the 1601 printed version of her speech, 'the thrallers of our people, the wringers of the poore'.[51]

Those who opposed the monopolies in principle, however, saw something inherently contradictory in the granting of public goods into private hands. It was not only that a private man necessarily pursued his own interests, centred his actions on his own advantage, not the public good. The monopolies also corrupted the body politic. First and most obviously, by taking the profits of their skills from certain artisans and craftsmen, which were as land was to a gentleman,[52] they hurt them in their inheritances. Only Parliament, it was argued, could ever impose charges of this kind upon the subjects, for this institution alone had the capacity to grant the requisite consent. Moreover, the grant of monopolies undermined the monarch's obligation to provide equal justice to all freemen in the kingdom. Monopolies turned what properly belonged to everyone into exclusive private possessions, thereby defeating each man's obligations to perform his duties to God and neighbour.[53] In this formulation, what was private could never be simultaneously public.

Such differences could not readily be accommodated to each other. How, then, did England manage to escape for so long the consequences of such ideological division? How, in particular, did the pro- and anti-monopolists in 1601 achieve resolution of their dispute without turning the Parliament into a shambles? To arrive at answers, we must return again to Queen Elizabeth's 'Golden Speech', this time focusing on it as a ritualized acting-out of the principles of social harmony against the threat of disorder and opposition.

The hierarchical image of political society offered by the Queen rested on an ideal of reciprocity in which, as Sir Robert Cecil said, 'the Qualities of the Prince, and the Subject' were seen as inseparably 'good for the one and the other'.[54] But, as Elizabeth depicted it, this reciprocity amounted to more than a mere harmonizing of material interests. It created a moral community whose watchword was 'love'. 'I do assure you', she told the assembled Parliament men,

> There is no Prince that loveth his Subjects better, or whose Love can countervail Our Love. There is no Jewel, be it never so Rich a Price, which I set before this Jewel; I mean, your Love: For I do more Esteem

of It, than of any Treasure or Riches; for That we know how to prize, but Love and Thanks I Count Unvaluable. And though God hath raised Me high; yet This I count the Glory of my Crown, That I have Reigned with your Loves. This makes me that I do not so much rejoyce, That God hath made Me to be a Queen, as, To be a Queen over so Thankful a People.[55]

In return for their love, the Queen herself bestowed love upon her subjects. 'There will never Queen sit in my Seat', she proclaimed,

with more Zeal to my Country, Care for my Subjects, and that sooner with willingness will venture her Life for your Good and Safety, than My Self. For it is not my desire to Live nor Reign longer, than my Life and Reign shall be for your Good. And though you have had, and may have many Princes, more Mighty and Wise, sitting in this State; yet you never had, or shall have any that will be more Careful and Loving.[56]

In this way, she argued, mutual love knit the people's hearts to the queen and became the guarantee of stability and order in the realm.[57]

The love spoken of here was akin to the Greek ideal of *philia*, friendship, for which, according to Aristotle, human beings 'choose to live'. 'Even rich men and those in possession of office and of dominating power,' he said, 'are thought to need friends ... for what is the use of such prosperity without the opportunity of beneficence?.'[58] This theme of beneficence lay at the heart of the monopolies affair. The patents originated in the monarch's general obligation to be bountiful in granting favour and reward to those who had shown loyalty and done service to her. They arose, that is, within the economy of favour and gratitude that characterized all patron–client relations in this period.[59]

This connection is apparent in every version of Elizabeth's speech, but we can see it most clearly in the copy preserved among William Dell's papers. There the Queen tells her listeners that she granted her patents by her 'Prerogative royall' to her servants as a 'priuate benefitt' to them 'by way of recompence for theyr good Seruice done'.[60] The word 'benefitt' is crucial in this connection. It links the Queen's actions to the analysis and advice given in Seneca's essay, *De beneficiis*, which to a very large degree provided the vocabulary and grammar for patronage and favour in this period.[61] According to Seneca, the giving and receiving of benefits provide the 'thing that most of al other knitteth men togither in felowship'. A benefit 'is a frendly goode deede'. It is something immaterial, something in our hearts or minds. According to Seneca, the money or offices given by a patron to his client are only the 'badges of benefites'.

Therefore neither Gold nor Siluer, nor any of the thinges wee receiue of our neighbours is a benefit ... These thinges which we handle and

looke vppon, and which our greedinesse is so fast tyed vntoo are trans-
itorie. Both misfortune and force may take them from vs. But a good
turne endureth still, yea euen when the thyng that was given is gone.

The receiving of benefits also calls forth a need for recompense, initially
acquitted by our gratitude when we accept a gift 'thankfully, by powrying
out our affections' and witnessing them everywhere. 'He that hath taken a
good turne thankfully,' Seneca says, 'hath payd the first paiment of it.'
Through this exchange the giving of benefits forms the bonds of human
society. 'For in what other thing haue wee so muche safetie', Seneca argues,

> as in helping one another with mutuall freendlynes? ... Put eueryman
> too himself alone, and what are wee? A pray for beasts, a slaughter for
> Sacrifice, and very eazie to haue our blud shedde ... Take away this fel-
> lowship, and yee rend asunder the vnitie of Mankynd, whereby our
> lyfe is maynteined.

What was essential was the exchange of human affections, not just the giving and receiving of material things.[62]

This Senecan way of framing the issues, and some of the same language
permeate the rituals of accommodation in 1601. The speech of thanks given
by John Crooke, Speaker of the Commons, set the tone for the exchange.
He was there, he said, 'to present all humble & dutiful thankes' of the
Commons for her Majesty's recent proclamation

> for which they confess they are not able to yeild your Majesty either
> answerable guifts or comparable treasure, but true hearts they bringe,
> with promise of respect & duty befitting true & dutifull Subjects euen
> to the spending of the uttermost droppe of blood in theyr bodyes, for
> the preseruacon of Religion, your Sacred person, & the Realme.[63]

They would make their recompense according to their best abilities, as
Seneca had advised. The exchange was not of material things, but of good
will, exemplified in loyal and loving service. They were especially 'thank-
full', Crooke went on, 'not for Benefitts receyued, which were sued for, &
soe obtayned, but for gracious favours bestowed of your gracious mere
mocon'. Although they knew her

> Sacred Ears are allmost bowed done & open to theyr Suites &
> Complaints, yet now yo^{ur} Ma[jes]^{ty} had ouercome them by your most
> Royall bounty, & as it were presented them by your magnificent &
> princely liberality.[64]

Elizabeth picked up on the theme of benefits right away. She 'well understood', Dell's version reports her as saying, that the Speaker and other members had 'come to giue us thankes for Benefitts receyued'. She wanted them
to know that she returned them 'all the thankes that can possibly be con-
ceyued in a kingly heart, for accepting my message in soe kinde manner'. She

especially thanked the Speaker for delivering it. But, she went on, 'I must tell you, I doubt & cannot be resolued, whether I haue more cause to thank them, or they me. Howsoeuer I am more then glad to see Sympathy between them & me.' She was, moreover, especially grateful 'ffor the money you haue soe freely & willingly bestowed upon me', promising, as we have seen, to bestow it back to them for their good 'for the defence of the Kingdome, & theyr owne Eyes shall see it, and a just Accompt shall be made of all'.[65] The effect of these words was to cast the speech as part of the ritualized exchange of gratitude given for gratitude received which lies at the heart of the Senecan ethic, binding queen and subject, as she says, in 'sympathy'.

This view spoke expressly to the granting of supply, which was still in process when the Queen spoke. The discussion had begun on 3 November, with Sir Robert Cecil's speech on the Queen's necessity and the appointment of a large committee to consider the 'greatest matters', including the provision of new taxes. On the following day, Robert Johnson introduced the grievance of monopoly. The main negotiations on the terms of the subsidy were settled by 9 November, yet the finished bill was not voted until 5 December.[66] There was an explicit sense, as Robert Wingfield put it on 9 November, that, with the terms of the subsidy effectively settled, 'it would please her Majesty not to dissolve the Parliament till some Acts were passed'. Robert Cecil made it clear that she would. The subsidy may have been 'the *Alpha* and *Omega*' of the Parliament, Cecil conceded, but not the entire alphabet.[67] Between the beginning and the end a number of bills indeed were considered and passed, but it was the monopolies that received the most attention. In fact, work on the subsidy proceeded in counterpoint with discussion of the grievances they had stirred. The first reading of the actual bill for four subsidies and eight fifteenths and tenths came only on 26 November, the day following the Speaker's report to the House of the Queen's promise to issue a proclamation to remedy the grievance. The second reading came only on the morning of 30 November itself, two days after the issue of the proclamation and just before members went to Whitehall to thank the Queen for her beneficence and to listen to her response.[68] The two matters – redress and supply – proceeded in tandem, the one requiting the other, not formally as a *quid pro quo* but as one benefit answers another in mutual exchange. In Heywood Townshend's account, the first reading is shown to have occurred only after Sir Robert Cecil reported the Queen's response to the Commons' expression of gratitude for her promised remedy for their grievance. 'You can give Me no more thanks for that which I have promised You', he quotes her as saying, 'Than I can and will give You Thanks for that which You have already Performed'. Townshend adds that she was referring here to the Commons' agreement in principle on taxation.[69]

In the Parliament of 1621, Sir George More suggested that redress of grievances and supply should be thought of 'as twins, as Jacob and Esau' going 'hand in hand' through the Commons, with grievances proceeding first but the blessing falling on subsidies at the end.[70] More was an active member of the Parliament of 1601, who early in the session had moved for the creation of the committee to consider the subsidy and who was very involved in the monopolies matter.[71] He may well have been thinking of the successful matching of redress and supply at that time. In this understanding, Parliament, which brought all the elements of the realm together representatively, was conceived as more than a mere institution for the making of authoritative decisions in the realm. The requesting and granting of consent to statutes or taxes was less the striking of a bargain between competing parties or interests than the ritual recognition that a social and political bond held the governors and the governed together for common profit. As regards taxes, there was no general right of refusal once a case for their necessity had been made. Parliamentary debate was confined merely to determining their size, terms, and conditions, sometimes but not inevitably accompanied by demands for redress of grievances. Completion of the negotiation, as in 1601, signified the renewal of the ties that made the realm a healthy body politic, while failure of monarch and subject to reach concord, as they would frequently do in the early seventeenth century, indicated nothing less than the presence of disease in that same social body.[72]

This sense of the ritualized renewal of the bonds of society was manifested in many of the ceremonies of parliamentary life – for example, in the formalities that opened the session and that accompanied the final presentation of the subsidy and general pardon at its close. Note, for example, the speech of Speaker Puckering at the conclusion of the 1585 Parliament when he presented the subsidy bill as an outward token of the subjects' love and gratitude for the beneficial rule they had received from the Queen. Note, too, the thanks he gave on his knees for her grant of the general pardon. The Queen responded on this occasion, as she would in 1601, by returning her own thanks to the Commons for their care in safekeeping her life, confessing herself fast bound to them through 'the link of your good will' which made her 'heart and head ... seek forever all your best'.[73] The regime of sympathy evoked in this setting was distinctly hierarchical in character – a regime of deference.

This same kind of reciprocity, hierarchical and deferential, was played out in the council chamber at Whitehall in 1601. When the members of the Commons assembled there, they found the Queen sitting in 'her Seat royall ... under the Cloth of State at the upper end ... attended with most of the Priuy Councell & Nobles', whose presence itself honoured her and demonstrated her position.[74] The Speaker began and ended his eloquent address of thanks with 'three low reverences', while the rest of the members of the Commons were on their knees, 'prostrate at her sacred feet', as the Speaker says. At the end of her own speech, moreover, she told her privy councillors 'That before these *Gentlemen* depart into their Countries, you bring them All to Kis My Hand'. It is perhaps no surprise, therefore, that among the gifts for which the Speaker thanked the Queen, one was that it had pleased her 'soe freely & willingly to graunt them this access unto your sacred person'.[75]

But there was something more at work here, something more than the reproduction of hierarchy. For, along with asserting her own authority, the Queen was simultaneously giving her listeners their due. Her speech began with the members of the Commons on their knees, a position in which they remained during its first third while the Queen graciously accepted the thanks she had been offered and spoke of her duty to God and the mutual love between her and her subjects. But at this point she stopped and asked the Speaker and the rest of the members of the Commons to rise and draw closer, because, she said, 'I shall yet trouble you with longer Speech.'[76] Here the matter and tone changed as she took these men, all of them prominent local leaders and officials, into her confidence, explained to them how and why the monopolies had gone so wrong, and thanked them for so disinter-estedly bringing the subjects' grievances to her attentions and keeping her from falling into error by having the uncorrected wrongs committed by her servants attributed to her. In this way, she recognized them as participants with her in the ordering of society, men who not only deserved confidence but who could be trusted to aid her in the performance of her duties. Only after doing so did she turn again to the themes of godly duty and love with which she had opened and offer her hand to all those who had attended. The whole speech was accompanied by what Dell's version calls

> her Majestes gestures of Honor & princely demeanour used by her, As when the Speaker spake any effectuall or mouing speech from the Comons to her Majesty, she rose up & bowed her selfe, As alsoe in her owne Speech, when the Comons apprehending any extraordinary words of favour from her did any Reuerance to her Ma[jes]ty she like-wise rose up & bowed her selfe, etc.[77]

That, 'etc.' speaks worlds, as Sir John Neale noted in commenting on this same passage.[78]

The political culture of benefits

In making her speech, Elizabeth was not only salving a wound but compos-ing a realm. She was bringing the representatives of her people – and through them her people themselves – into an ordered relationship to her. By her words and gestures, just as by her governmental actions, she was dis-ciplining society into a proportional, that is to say, a hierarchical, arrange-ment of parts. But the resulting unity was not automatic; it could not be achieved without this effort just because it was a unity of parts, each of which had its own existence. Here the language of benefits was especially useful, since it allowed those who employed it to refer simultaneously to a world of social and political hierarchy, in which those of differing rank formed a harmony of favour and respect, and a world of independent souls, in which individual acts of good will draw together every man in a unity of thought and feeling. What was important to the theory of benefits was not the material gifts which were its medium, but the mutual and voluntary exchange of beneficence and gratitude which was its spirit. The latter points to every man's capacity to answer voluntarily the gifts he has received with proper gratitude and appropriate actions according to his abilities, even if he has received those gifts from a monarch.

Hence the language of benefits, called up by John Crooke in 1601 and so skilfully used by Elizabeth in response, carried with it two coordinated but distinguishable visions of the commonwealth. According to Sir Thomas Smith, a commonwealth is a 'society or common doing of a multitude of free men ... united by common accord' for their 'conservation ... in peace as in warre'.[79] Its very essence depends on their voluntary coming-together for mutual well-being. It is 'nothing more than a commencement or continual suppedition of benefits mutually received and done among men', as Sir Arthur Chichester said in 1612.[80] This understanding pointed to the inevitability of difference – the inevitability that some would be greater in wealth and power than others. It endorsed the idea that the present social order was the image of Reason in the world, ordained by God, and that political action involved no more than what has been identified as rituals of 'affirmation and celebration'.[81]

This same theory of benefits also saw the unity of the realm as depending upon positive acts by which ruler and subject knitted their hearts one unto another.[82] No subject could legitimately deny his service to monarch and commonweal once the case for it had been duly laid before him. But the subject had to be asked for his aid in due form, with proper deference to his honour and his rights.[83] In the face of demonstrated need, he was morally bound to consent, but he had to consent voluntarily. Yielding to such an obligation was just the opposite of being coerced. It involved an inward judgement on the rectitude of the demand and an inward agreement to answer it as best one may. Only such voluntary acts were worthy of moral praise. Their performance turned the brute realities of a hierarchically ordered society into a genuine moral community, thereby assuring a place for freedom and consent in making England a commonwealth.[84]

The language of benefits allowed two world pictures to coexist, one a vision of sovereign authority, the other of free community. It resolved the possible conflict between these views through the principle of reciprocity by which good will was exchanged. Accommodation would become difficult, if not impossible, should either side press its claims to the extreme – should either side, that is, insist on the absolute nature of its rights.

Notes

1 On the nature of Parliament, see G. R. Elton, *The Parliament of England, 1559–1581* (Cambridge, 1986), ch. 2; Elton, 'Tudor Government: The Points of Contact, I. Parliament', in Elton, *Studies in Tudor and Stuart Politics and Government* (3 vols, Cambridge, 1974–83), III, pp. 3–21; Conrad Russell, 'The Nature of a Parliament in Early Stuart England', in Howard Tomlinson (ed.), *Before the English Civil War: Essays on Early Stuart Politics and Government* (New York, 1984), pp. 123–50; Conrad Russell, *Parliaments and English Politics, 1621–1629* (Oxford, 1979), pp. 35–64.

2 For this distinction, see the remarks of the Lord Keeper in 1571 reporting Elizabeth I's views on freedom of speech in the House of Commons: 'they should doe well to meddle in noe matters of state but such as should be propounded unto them, and to occupy themselves concerninge the commen wealth' (quoted in T. E. Hartley (ed), *Proceedings in the Parliament of Elizabeth I, I, 1558–1581* (Leicester, 1981), p. 199).

3 For a general account of the Parliament of 1601 and the role of the monopolies in it, see J. E. Neale, *Elizabeth I and her Parliaments, 1584–1601* (London, 1957), pp. 369–423, esp. pp. 376–93.

4 See, e.g., Townshend, p. 250. This paragraph and the following are derived from William Hyde Price, *The English Patents of Monopoly* (Boston, Mass., 1906), ch. 1; E. Wyndam Hulme, 'The History of the Patent System under the Prerogative and at Common Law', *Law Quarterly Review*, 12 (1896), pp. 141–54 and 'The History of the Patent System under the Prerogative and at Common Law: A Sequel', *Law Quarterly Review*, 16 (1900), pp. 44–56; Joan Thirsk, *Economic Policy and Projects: The Development of a Consumer Society* (Oxford, 1978), chs 1–3. See also David Harris Sacks, 'Private Profit and Public Good: The Problem of the State in Elizabethan Theory and Practice', in Gordon Schochet (ed.), *Law Literature and the Settlement of Regimes* (Washington, 1990), pp. 123–6; Sacks, 'Parliament, Liberty, and the Commonweal', in J. H. Hexter (ed.), *Parliament and Liberty from Elizabeth I to the English Civil War* (Stanford, Calif., 1992), pp. 95–6.

5 See Price, *English Patents*, ch. 1; Thirsk, *Economic Policy*, pp. 57 ff.; Linda Levy Peck, *Court Patronage and Corruption in Early Modern England* (Boston, Mass., 1990), pp. 135 ff.

6 Hartley (ed.), *Proceedings*, pp. 202, 245 (and see also pp. 207, 224, 238, 436); J. E. Neale, *Elizabeth I and her Parliaments, 1559–1581* (London, 1953), pp. 218–19, 221–2; Neale, *Elizabeth I and her Parliaments, 1584–1601*, p. 352. The prospect of monopoly was also angrily complained against in this Parliament with regard to the privileges of Bristol's Society of Merchant Venturers: see Hartley (ed.), *Proceedings*, pp. 210–11; David Harris Sacks, *The Widening Gate: Bristol and the Atlantic Economy, 1450–1700* (Berkeley and Los Angeles, Calif., 1991), pp. 196–201.

7 Hartley (ed.), *Proceedings*, p. 372 (and see also pp. 264, 384).

8 For this paragraph and those following, see Sacks, 'Parliament, Liberty, and the Commonweal', pp. 93–101; Sacks, 'Private Profit and Public Good', pp. 121–33.

9 Townshend, pp. 103, 234; Simons D'Ewes, *A Compleat Journal of the Votes, Speeches and Debates, both of the House of Lords and the House of Commons Throughout the whole Reign of Queen Elizabeth of Glorious Memory* (London, 1682), pp. 554–5, 558, 570, 573; Neale, *Elizabeth I and her Parliaments, 1584–1601*, pp. 352–6, 365.

10 *Davenant* v. *Hurdis*, Moore 576–91, 672, in *The English Reports*, ed. Max A. Robertson and Geoffrey Ellis (repr., 176 vols, 1900–30), vol. 72, pp. 769–78, 830; Edward Coke, *The Third Part of the Institutes of the Laws of England* (London, 1644), p. 182; see also *Darcy* v. *Allen*, 11 Co. Rep. 86b, in *English Reports*, vol. 77, p. 1263.

11 Townshend, pp. 188, 224–5, 229–37; D'Ewes, *A Compleat Journal*, pp. 644–7. Townshend reports Hyde as attempting to introduce his bill on 18 November, only to have it blocked by the Speaker, apparently at Sir Robert Cecil's behest. But according

to Townshend's account, the bill seems to have been introduced successfully on 19 November, and to have received its second reading and formal commitment on 20 November, after a commotion in the House to have it read and a long debate on whether to commit or engross it. D'Ewes first mentions the bill only in his account of debate on 20 November, but his treatment of the discussion follows Townshend's as regards commitment. Since D'Ewes makes no mention of two readings on this day, it appears likely that the bill was first read on 19 November and received its second reading and commitment on the following day.

12 Townshend, p. 233.
13 *Darcy v. Allen*, 11 Co. Rep. 84b–88b in *English Reports*, vol. 77, pp. 1260–6; Noy, 173–85 in *English Reports*, vol. 74, pp. 1131–41; Moore, 671–5 in *English Reports*, vol. 72, pp. 830–2; PRO SP 12/286/47; BL Add. MS 25203, fos. 543ᵛ. ff.; Edward Coke, *The Second Part of the Institutes of the Laws of England* (London, 1641), pp. 46–7; Coke, *The Third Part of the Institutes*, pp. 181–2.
14 Townshend, p. 233.
15 Townshend, p. 234.
16 Sacks, 'Parliament, Liberty, and the Commonweal', pp. 93 ff.
17 See Townshend, pp. 224–5, 230–6, 238–53; Neale, *Elizabeth I and her Parliaments, 1584–1601*, pp. 377–88.
18 See *Darcy v. Allen* (1602), Noy, 173–85 in *English Reports*, vol. 74, pp. 1131–41, especially Noy, 179–80, in vol. 74, pp. 1136–7.
19 Townshend, p. 239.
20 Townshend, p. 233.
21 Townshend, p. 234.
22 Townshend, p. 259.
23 Townshend, pp. 263–6; the original manuscript version is found in BL Stowe MS 362, fos. 169–72.
24 *Her Majesties most Princelie answere deliuered by her selfe at the Court at Whitehall on the last day of November 1601 ... The same being taken verbatim in writing by A. B. as neere as he could possibly set it downe* (1601). (This is STC 7578 and will be referred to hereafter by that number.) A printed copy is in PRO SP 12/282/67; manuscript versions survive in PRO SP 12/282/65, 66; BL Lansdowne MS 94, fo. 123. If 'A. B.' was a member of the House of Commons, he could only have been Anthony Blagrave, who sat in the Parliament of 1601 for Reading in Berkshire and who was closely associated with the Cecils.
25 *Qveene Elizabeths Speech to Her Last Parliament*. (This is STC 7579 and will be referred to by this number hereafter.) There is no indication on the title page of the place and date of publication but the second edition of the *STC* identifies this version as being printed possibly before 12 July 1628. This version of the speech was subsequently republished in different formats four times in the seventeenth century, viz. 1648, 1659, 1679, and 1698.
26 BL Harleian MS 787, fos. 127ᵛ–128ᵛ. It is unknown whose notes of the Queen's speech are recorded here.
27 This same schema is followed in STC 7579 and in BL Harleian MS 787, but not in STC 7578, which concerns itself more than the other versions with accounting for the wrongs done by the patentees and with thanking the Commons for saving her from culpability for their errors.
28 Townshend, pp. 264, 265. BL Harleian MS 787, fo. 128ʳ, uses a similar figure in relation to the patents. In STC 7578, pp. 3–4, and STC 7579, sig. A3c, the same figure refers to the way in which the outward lustre of a kingly title as it appears to observers covers the cares and burdens of the office borne by its holder.
29 Hippocrates, 'The Oath', in *Hippocrates*, Loeb edition, trans. W. H. S. Jones (4 vols, 1923–43), I, pp. 298–301. On the nature of the medical marketplace in this period, see, Harold J. Cook, *The Decline of the Old Medical Regime in Stuart England* (Ithaca, NY, and London, 1986), ch. 1. I am grateful for Professor Cook's advice and guidance in what follows.
30 E[leazar] D[unke], *The Copy of A Letter written by E. D. Doctour of Physick* (London, 1606), pp. 21, 40.

31 George N. Clark, *A History of the Royal College of Physicians* (2 vols, Oxford, 1964–66), I, pp. 160–1; Cook, *The Decline of the Old Medical Regime*, p. 97.

32 Claudius Galen, *Certaine Workes of Galen called Methodvs Medendi*, trans. Thomas Gale (London, 1586), sig. Aiiib.

33 John Securis, *A detection and querimonie of the daily enormities and abuses comitted in physick* (London, 1566), sig. Biia. The ultimate source for this idea is, of course, Plato's *Republic* 370a–c (Plato, *Republic*, trans. G. M. A. Grube, rev. by C. D. C. Reeve (Indianapolis, 1992), pp. 44–5). But the commonplaces referred to by Securis arise from later sources which are conveniently summarized and commented upon by Erasmus in his collection of *Adages* (*Collected Works of Erasmus*, vol. XXXI, trans. Margaret Man Phillips (Toronto, 1982), pp. 351–2, 411–12; vol. XXXII, trans. R. A. B. Mynors (Toronto, 1989), p. 14).

34 John Cotta, *A Short Discoverie of the vnobserved dangers of seuerall sorts of ignorant and vnconsiderate Practitioners of Physicke in England* (London, 1612), pp. 11–12.

35 Townshend, p. 264.

36 Townshend, pp. 263, 266.

37 James I, *Basilikon Doron, Or His Majesties Instrvctions to his Dearest Sonne, Henry the Prince*, in *The Political Works of James I*, ed. Charles McIlwain (Cambridge, Mass., 1918), pp. 12 ff.

38 Townshend, pp. 265, 266.

39 Townshend, p. 265; see also STC 7578, pp. 5–6; STC 7579, sig. A3c; BL Harleian MS 787, fo. 128^v.

40 Townshend, p. 264; STC 7578, p. 5; see also Townshend, p. 2; STC 7579, sig. A2b; BL Harleian MS 787, fo. 128^r.

41 Townshend, pp. 263, 264–5; see also STC 7579, sig. A2b; BL Harleian MS 787, fo. 127^v.

42 Marcus Tullius Cicero, *Marcus Tullius Ciceroes thre bokes of duties*, trans. Nicholas Grimalde (1556), ed. Gerald O'Gorman (Washington, 1990), p. 63 (and see also p. 59).

43 STC 7578, p. 5; see also Townshend, p. 266; STC 7579, sig. A3b; BL Harleian MS 787, fo. 128^r.

44 Townshend, pp. 264–5; see also BL Harleian MS 787, fo. 128^r; STC 7578, p. 3; STC 7579, sig. A3a.

45 Townshend, p. 263 (and see also p. 266); STC 7579, sigs. A2b, A3b; BL Harleian MS 787, fos. 127^v, 128^r.

46 J. P. Sommerville, *Politics and Ideology in England, 1603–1640* (London and New York, 1986), pp. 66–9; see also J. G. A. Pocock, *The Ancient Constitution and the Feudal Law: A Study of English Historical Thought in the Seventeenth Century; A Reissue with a Retrospect* (Cambridge, 1987), pp. 282–7, 299, 301–2.

47 STC 7579, sig. A2b.

48 This emphasis is especially clear in BL Harleian MS 787, fo. 127^v; see also Townshend, p. 263; STC 7579, sig. A2b.

49 See the remarks of Thomas Fleming, then the Solicitor-General, on behalf of Sir Edward Darcy; in *Darcy v. Allen* (1602), PRO SP 12/286/47.

50 Townshend, p. 264; see also, BL Harleian MS 787, fos. 127^v, 128^r; STC 7578, p. 3; STC 7579, sigs. A2b–A3a.

51 STC 7578, pp. 2–3.

52 *Darcy v. Allen* (1602), BL Add. MS 25203, fo. 574^v.

53 See Coke's report of *Darcy v. Allen*, 11 Co. Rep. 84b–88b in *English Reports*, 77, pp. 1260–6.

54 Townshend, p. 253.

55 Townshend, p. 263; see also STC 7579, sigs. A2a–b; BL Harleian MS 787, fo. 127^v.

56 Townshend, p. 266; see also STC 7579, sig. A3c.

57 See Townshend, p. 265.

58 Aristotle, *The Nicomachean Ethics*, 1155a 7–10, trans. W. D. Ross, rev. J. L. Ackrill and J. O. Urmston (Oxford, 1980), p. 192. The earliest English version of the *Nicomachean Ethics*, by John Wilkinson, is based on Brunetto Latini's Italian summary and dates from 1547; Aristotle, *The Ethiques of Aristotle, that is to saye, precepts of good behauioure and perfighte honestie now newly translated into English*,

trans. John Wyklinson (London, 1547) (*STC* 774); the passage in question is at sig. Hiii͏ʳ. See also Irving Singer, *The Nature of Love* (3 vols, Chicago, Ill., 1984), I, pp. 88–110, 198–232.

59 On this theme, see J. E. Neale, 'The Elizabethan Political Scene', in J. E. Neale, *Essays in Elizabethan History* (London, 1958), pp. 59–84; Wallace T. MacCaffrey, 'Place and Patronage in Elizabethan Politics', in S. T. Bindoff, J. Hurstfield, and C. H. Williams (eds), *Elizabethan Government and Society* (London, 1961), pp. 95–126; Joel Hurstfield, 'Political Corruption in Modern England: The Historian's Problem', in Hurstfield, *Freedom, Corruption and Government in Elizabethan England* (London, 1973), pp. 137–62; G. R. Elton, 'Tudor Government: The Points of Contact. III. The Court', in Elton, *Studies in Tudor and Stuart Politics and Government*, III (Cambridge, 1983), pp. 38–57; Penry Williams, 'Court and Polity under Elizabeth I', *Bulletin of the John Rylands University Libraries*, 65 (1983), pp. 259–86; Peck, Court Patronage, chs 1–3; Linda Levy Peck, 'Court Patronage and Governmental Policy: The Jacobean Dilemma', in Guy Fitch Lytle and Stephen Orgel (eds), *Patronage in the Renaissance* (Princeton, NJ, 1981), pp. 27–46; Linda Levy Peck, ' "For a King not to be Bountiful were a Fault": Perspective in Court Patronage in Early Stuart England', *Journal of British Studies*, 25 (1986), pp. 31–61.

60 BL Harleian MS 787, fo. 127ᵛ; see also Townshend, p. 264; *STC* 7578, p. 3; *STC* 7579, sig. A3a.

61 See John M. Wallace, 'Timon of Athens and the Three Graces: Shakespeare's Senecan Study', *Modern Philology*, 83 (1985–86), 350 ff; Peck, *Court Patronage*, ch. 1.

62 Lucius Annaeus Seneca, *The woorke of the excellent Philosopher Lucius Annaeus Seneca concerning Benefyting, that is too say the dooing, receyuing and requyting of good Turnes*, trans. Arthur Golding (1578), fos. 4ᵛ, 5ᵛ, 22ʳ, 55ʳ; Cicero also treats the theme of benefits in similar terms in his *De officiis*: see Cicero, *Ciceroes thre bookes of duties*, trans. Grimalde, pp. 131 ff.

63 BL Harleian MS 787, fo. 127ʳ; see also Townshend, pp. 263, 264; *STC* 7578, pp. 1–2; *STC* 7579, sigs. A2a, A2b.

64 BL Harleian MS 787, fo. 127ʳ; see also Townshend, p. 262.

65 BL Harleian MS 787, fo. 127ᵛ; see also Townshend, pp. 263, 264; *STC* 7578, pp. 1–2; *STC* 7579, sigs. A2a, A2b.

66 Townshend, pp. 183–5, 188, 197–200, 204–5, 286–7; see also D'Ewes, *A Compleat Journal*, pp. 623–4, 626, 629–32, 668; Neale, *Parliaments, 1584–1601*, pp. 411–16.

67 Townshend, p. 204.

68 D'Ewes, *A Compleat Journal*, pp. 654, 658.

69 Townshend, p. 253. The second reading came only after the Commons, anxious to express their good will to the Queen, were assured that she would 'welcome' all who would come to give her thanks 'without Restraint or Limit' of number, a matter touching their honour which had been in some doubt until then: Townshend, p. 261.

70 *Commons Debates*, 1621, eds Wallace Notestein, Frances H. Relf, and Hartley Simpson (7 vols, New Haven, Conn., 1935), II, p. 21. Attention has recently been called to this passage in an important article: Thomas Cogswell, 'A Low Road to Extinction? Supply and Redress of Grievances in the Parliaments of the 1620s', *Historical Journal*, 33 (1990), p. 283.

71 Townshend, pp. 185, 234.

72 For guidance on this theme, see G. L. Harriss, 'Medieval Doctrines in the Debates on Supply, 1610–1629', in Kevin Sharpe (ed.), *Faction and Parliament* (London and New York, 1978), pp. 73–104; G. L. Harriss, *King, Parliament and Public Finance in Medieval England to 1369* (Oxford, 1979). See also David Harris Sacks, 'The Paradox of Taxation: Fiscal Crises, Parliament, and Liberty in Early Modern England, 1450–1640', in Philip T. Hoffman and Kathryn Norberg (eds), *Fiscal Crises, Representative Institutions, and Liberty in Early Modern Europe* (Stanford, Calif., 1994), pp. 7–66; J. D. Alsop, 'Parliament and Taxation', in D. M. Dean and N. L. Jones, *The Parliaments of Elizabethan England* (Oxford, 1990), pp. 91–116; J. D. Alsop, 'The Politics of Parliamentary Taxation, 1558–1603' (unpublished paper). I am grateful to Dr Alsop for sharing his unpublished work with me.

73 D'Ewes, *A Compleat Journal*, pp. 327–29; Neale, *Elizabeth I and her Parliaments, 1584–1601*, pp. 95–101.

74 See William Harrison, *The Description of England*, ed. Georges Edelen (Ithaca, NY, 1968), pp. 227–32.
75 Townshend, pp. 262, 263, 266; see also BL Harleian MS 787, fos. 127ʳ, 128ᵛ; *STC* 7579, sig. A2a.
76 Townshend, p. 264; see also BL Harleian MS 787, fo. 127ᵛ; *STC* 7579, sig. A2b.
77 BL Harleian MS 787, fo. 128ᵛ.
78 Neale, *Elizabeth I and her Parliaments, 1584–1601*, p. 393.
79 Sir Thomas Smith, *De republica anglorum: A Discourse on the Commonwealth of England*, ed. L. Alston (Cambridge, 1906), p. 20.
80 Sir Arthur Chichester to the Archbishop of Canterbury, 23 Oct. 1612, 'Letterbook of Sir Arthur Chicester, 1612–1614', *Analecta Hibernaca*, no. 8, p. 56, as cited in Peck, *Court Patronage*, p. 13.
81 Mark A. Kishlansky, *Parliamentary Selection: Social and Political Choice in Early Modern England* (Cambridge, 1986), p. 10.
82 Townshend, p. 265.
83 See David Harris Sacks, 'Searching for "Culture" in the English Renaissance', *Shakespeare Quarterly*, 39 (1988), pp. 486 ff.
84 See Sacks, 'Parliament, Liberty, and the Commonweal', pp. 85–121.

SECTION

II

PERSONALITY AND POLITICS

Introduction

This section comprises five articles grouped together to illustrate the impact of personalities on Tudor politics and government. I have already noted that there has been a shift away from an older tradition of 'constitutional' history towards a newer and more genuinely political history. This New Political History is concerned with the interrelationships of, and interactions between, personalities, institutions, and ideas, and with the interpenetration of 'public' and 'private', 'formal' and 'informal', spheres of authority in ways that were fundamentally political.

In the General Introduction, I cited Dr Christine Carpenter's comment that the political élite during the Wars of the Roses 'had a vested interest in the perpetuating of internal peace ... the dual chain of command, formal and informal, from king to locality could work effectively only if every link in it had confidence in the others'. If each element in the complex mixture of 'public' and 'private' authority did its job properly, the interests of the political nation as a whole could be protected. But, as Dr Carpenter goes on to argue, if this system was going to work, 'it is evident that the king had to be the nodal point of both the public and private threads'. In the fifteenth century, the system worked under Edward IV, but manifestly not under Henry VI. That this was so owed a lot to the personalities of these rulers. His own subjects had called Henry VI 'a sheep', a 'natural fool', and a 'lunatic'; J. R. Lander's epithet, 'saintly muff' captures the general drift. By contrast, Edward IV was 'very princely to behold, of heart courageous, politic in counsel, in adversity nothing abashed'. He was scarcely a model of virtue, but Thomas More praised him and remarked that he left England in 'quiet and prosperous estate'. His success was especially due to the fact that, unlike Henry VI, he made his Court and Household the dynamic focus of his regime.

Dr Steven Gunn starts from these assumptions in his article on 'The Courtiers of Henry VII' (see below, Chapter 6). Everyone knows that Henry VII was successful because he exercised close personal oversight of every aspect of government. Again, no one would doubt that the hub of government was the King's Chamber, which, between 1492 and 1503, established an administrative nexus that penetrated to the most distant parts of the land, recording receipts, issues, bonds, obligations, and debts, and dealing largely in cash. What is novel is Dr Gunn's account of Henry's vision of 'magnificent monarchy' centred on the Court. It became important to 'play the courtier' if advancement was to be secured, and proximity to the king became important by virtue of Henry's style of government. In short, the role of the Court as the crucible of politics and the importance of access to the monarch that had characterized Edward IV's regime were reinforced under Henry VII. Counsellors and courtiers were the same people: there was no hard and fast division of roles. A key place in the spectrum of service was held by the nobility and leading landowners, and the bilateral nature of the bonds between centre and localities which had been archetypical of Edward IV's style of government was maintained. Contrary to the image created for him by Francis Bacon, Henry VII knew how to enjoy himself: when he was not hunting, he gambled and played tennis, prompting a boom in tennis-court construction in the first decade of his reign. It was important to know this and to participate; it may even have been important to know how to make Henry VII laugh.

The role of Court personalities in government and the interpenetration of 'public' and 'private', 'formal' and 'informal' spheres in the reigns of Henry VII and Henry VIII are the subject of David Starkey's article on 'Court and Government' (see below, Chapter 7). In the history of the Court, the rise of the Privy Chamber and the separation of its personnel from the formal and ceremonial functions of the Chamber were a crucial change, since it affected who had access to the monarch and was therefore highly political. The power of the Privy Chamber, and in particular that of the Groom of the Stool, grew by accretion (see also, Starkey, Chapter 2). In the reign of Henry VII, the Privy Chamber was essentially the king's own private room. In the reign of Henry VIII, it expanded and increasingly became the hothouse of politics. And in the process, its personnel usurped a wide range of administrative functions that had previously been performed in the Chamber and elsewhere. The role of its staff in the administration of Crown patronage and finance became especially significant after the Dissolution of the Monasteries.

Henry VIII's ministers had a fluid, often uneasy, relationship with the King's Court intimates. The brutal pragmatism with which Wolsey attempted to purge the Privy Chamber testifies to his conviction that those close to the King could undo him. Cromwell, too, sought to stifle the Privy Chamber's influence until he learned to pack and control it. Under the smokescreen of reform, Wolsey twice evicted rivals, replacing them with his own men while attempting to make the Groom of the Stool file monthly financial accounts. Cromwell's role in the fall of Anne Boleyn in May 1536 is now hotly contested. Whether his destruction of the Boleyn faction, and then the rival Carewe–Exeter faction, was the product of a Court struggle or whether it was primarily the implementation of Henry VIII's will, remains unproven. Either way, Cromwell's response to the rise of conservative opponents in the Privy Council by 1539 was to assume the titular headship of the Privy Chamber, placing his own clients there in a desperate attempt to win out. And at the twilight of the reign, it was through Sir Anthony Denny, Groom of the Stool from October 1546, that the Earl of Hertford gained control of the 'dry stamp' used to provide the royal assent for the Duke of Norfolk's attainder and to sign the King's last will and testament.

The role of Henry VIII's ministers has often been debated. Wolsey enjoyed greater latitude than his successor, Cromwell, but this was because the young Henry intervened less in politics before 1527 (possibly 1525) than afterwards. The turning point was the King's first divorce campaign, which began in earnest in the summer of 1527 when Henry personally seized the initiative from an absent Wolsey in soliciting support and orchestrating the debate. Wolsey's main appointments were those of Lord Chancellor, Cardinal-Archbishop of York, and Papal Legate *a latere*. Cromwell was successively Master of the Jewels, Lord Privy Seal, Vicegerent in Spirituals (that is, Henry VIII's lay deputy as Supreme Head of the Church), and finally Lord Great Chamberlain.

Cromwell rose to power in incremental stages. He reached the summit of his career only after Anne Boleyn's fall (May 1536). Between Wolsey's fall and Thomas

More's resignation as Lord Chancellor (May 1532), he acted mainly as Henry VIII's parliamentary manager. As John Guy argues in 'Thomas Cromwell and the Intellectual Origins of the Henrician Revolution' (see below, Chapter 8), it was the circle of advisers led by Edward Foxe and Thomas Cranmer that worked on the thesis of Henry VIII's 'imperial' kingship. Between 1529 and 1534, Cromwell subverted the jurisdiction of the clergy and church courts. He argued that England, Wales, and Ireland formed a unitary state under the 'king-in-Parliament', and he attacked clerical and feudal 'privileges' which conflicted with 'imperial' kingship and common law. He presided over the enforcement of the break with Rome, and planned the Dissolution of the Monasteries. Above all, he steered the Reformation statutes through Parliament. But his role was that of Henry VIII's 'executive agent'. Cromwell was the man who got things done by converting an abstract political theory into practical measures which were enforced. He was not himself the author of the thesis of 'imperial' kingship, as Professor Elton had previously argued. His *personal* political creed was different from that defined in the Act of Appeals; his understanding of the principles of kingship and 'reformed' religion diverged in several important respects from that of Henry VIII. Cromwell was an instinctive politician whose influence should not be underestimated. His biography remains unwritten, and there is much about him that remains obscure.

The Privy Chamber under Henry VIII had tended to be a potential breeding-ground for factionalism. In this respect, the minority of Edward VI was the institution's Indian summer, since, in order for the Duke of Northumberland to seize control of the machinery of government in November 1549, it was first necessary to capture the person of the boy-king. Once the King was surrounded by 'great frendes' (i.e. Northumberland's supporters), the Duke won the power virtually to be king himself! For when he governed access to the prince and controlled his signet and 'dry stamp', he was able to order almost any action in Edward's name. That snapshot confirms just how dependent government remained on the king's person in the mid-sixteenth century.

It was in these conditions that William Cecil served his political apprenticeship. When he assisted Elizabeth I in establishing her regime in 1558–9, he laboured to ensure that the staff of the Privy Chamber were no longer permitted to attempt independent political initiatives. His task was made relatively straightforward by the fact of Tudor gender stereotyping. Since Elizabeth was a female ruler, she necessarily required female bedchamber attendants, yet the stereotype was that government and politics were most properly conducted by men! As a result, the political influence of the Privy Chamber waned after 1559. If the Queen's gentlewomen and bedchamber servants controlled access to her presence, they barely influenced patronage, and policy not at all. Admittedly Catherine Ashley, Elizabeth's former governess and her closest confidante, was punished for forwarding the marriage suit of Eric XIV of Sweden in 1561–2, but the episode is unique.

Cecil himself has conventionally been dismissed as an uninspired or second-rate Elizabethan bureaucrat: loyal, solid, and dependable, perhaps, but essentially dull and two-dimensional. Stephen Alford's article, specially commissioned for this volume (see below, Chapter 9), corrects this impression. Dr Alford shows that Cecil's mental world was underpinned in the 1560s by the classical and rhetorical traditions in which he had been trained at Cambridge, by his vision of a 'British' (or, more accurately, Anglo-Scottish) approach to the political and ideological problems posed by the Reformation in the British Isles, and by a keen sense of (Protestant) providence. He believed that the forces of darkness, in particular the Papacy, Spain, and the Guise, were mobilizing against England and that they intended to use Mary, Queen of Scots, as their instrument. For this reason he believed that the Protestant Reformation had to be disseminated by every available means, even if he took a cautious position (as compared to Leicester and Walsingham) on the issue of military intervention in the Netherlands.

One of the keys to Cecil's mind was his fear that failure in the matter of the 'British' (i.e. English and Scottish) Reformations would incur God's wrath, and for this reason he was increasingly impelled into political action. This has also been discussed in Chapter 3. Yet in the 1560s, as Dr Alford argues, it was still Cecil's concern for effective and responsible government and his sense of frustration with a queen who refused counsel, rather than ideology, that lay at the root of his attempts to drive Elizabeth forward on the issues of her marriage and the succession.

Dr Alford's strong emphasis on Cecil's commitment to the Protestant cause is consistent with the scepticism that historians are increasingly showing on the issue of Elizabethan Court factionalism. Between them, Conyers Read and Sir John Neale established factionalism as the central phenomenon of Elizabethan Court politics, yet the rationales for their factions – policy or patronage – were different and their arguments were in any case relatively weak. Dr Adams explores this issue in his article, 'Favourites and Factions at the Elizabethan Court' (see below, Chapter 10), in order to pave the way for a fundamental re-evaluation of the Elizabethan political system.

The comments of two contemporary, or near-contemporary, observers have created the bulk of the confusion. In the 1630s Sir Robert Naunton organized his vignette of the Elizabethan Court almost entirely around the topic of 'factions' and 'favourites.' He said of Elizabeth, 'She ruled much by factions and parties, which she herself both made, upheld and weakened, as her own great judgement advised.' This oracular proposition has been accepted at face value for generations, but it is, essentially, a travesty of Elizabethan politics. Again, the scurrilous tract, *Leicester's Commonwealth*, wove a web of lies and misleading assertions in order to accuse the Earl of Leicester, the Queen's first favourite and Cecil's supposed political rival, of creating a 'puritan faction' to control the realm. Dr Adams has consistently downplayed or rejected these arguments, and his approach has become the basis of the standard interpretation of the reign. This is not to deny that factionalism *was* introduced into the Court by the second Earl of Essex in the mid-1590s (see also Guy, Chapter 3). But that is a quite different phase, and a quite different argument. Nor was Essex's rise to power factional, as Sir John Neale and others had assumed. As Dr Adams rightly concludes, once the Cecil–Leicester hostility is queried, then the role of the favourite becomes transparent: 'the favourites, like the other central figures of the Court, were there ultimately at the queen's choice'.

6
*The courtiers of Henry VII**
STEVEN GUNN

By 1622, when he completed his *History of the Reign of King Henry VII*, Francis Bacon had had quite enough of courtiers. First he had vested his hopes of a career in government office in the patronage of Queen Elizabeth's dazzling young favourite, the Earl of Essex; but Essex failed to win Bacon promotion, ignored his advice, and ran headlong into disgrace, doomed rebellion, and ignominious death.[1] Apparently undaunted, Bacon attached himself to James I's favourite George Villiers, the future Duke of Buckingham. This alliance won him a seat on the Privy Council and the Lord Keepership of the Great Seal, but in the shifting world of court politics Bacon had to struggle to retain Buckingham's friendship, and in 1621 he found himself thrown to the mercy of a House of Commons hungry to denounce corruption in high places, in a manoeuvre designed to save Buckingham's skin and the King's reputation.[2] It was little wonder that Bacon sought to depict Henry VII, in the model of kingship he offered to James I's son Prince Charles, as a ruler with little time for courtiers and their follies, a monarch who kept his distance from all his subjects and chose for his ministers able, earnest, sober men with more than a passing resemblance to Francis Bacon himself.[3]

It is less the case now than it was in 1858 that 'our notions of the reign of Henry the Seventh are mainly derived from Lord Bacon', as James Gairdner complained in that year.[4] But Bacon's dismissal of Henry's courtiers remains influential. We recognize that the King expended considerable money and effort on the creation of a splendid and fashionable Court, aiming to impress his own subjects with his power and majesty, and the ruling houses of Europe with the permanence and diplomatic weight of his dynasty. Yet we focus only on Henry as the director of this courtly drama, and on his stagehands, Bernard André the poet, Maynard the painter, and William Cornish the pageant-master, not on the courtiers who caught the limelight in contemporary eyes.[5] When William Makefyrr watched Henry and his entourage welcome Philip of Burgundy to Windsor in 1506, he was concerned to note the identity of 'the lords that bare the bruyt': Lord Henry Stafford, with his hat full of diamonds

* I am grateful to Miss M. M. Condon and Dr C. S. L. Davies for their comments on this paper and to the University of Newcastle upon Tyne for the research fellowship which enabled me to write it. In quotations, punctuation and capitalization have been modernized, as has the use of i, j, u and v; and other languages have been translated into English.

and rubies; Thomas, Marquis of Dorset, with a white feather on the crupper of his horse; and Richard, Earl of Kent, with his coat of cloth of gold and crimson velvet.[6] Was Makefyrr wasting his words, and were the lords wasting their money, or was there some point in being counted among the courtiers of Henry VII?

In part the answer must depend on our image of Henry himself. There is no doubt that he exercised close personal oversight of every aspect of government, more so than most English kings before or since; but that did not make him a royal bureaucrat, toiling for long lonely hours at mountains of paperwork. His famous habit of signing account books was, as K. B. McFarlane pointed out, no more than 'the ordinary practice of his magnates', and as the developing Chamber administration required him to sign more often, he simplified his monogram to make the job less trouble.[7] By 1504 his sight was failing and he found writing difficult; he gave up signing each entry in the Chamber receipt accounts and signed only once on each page.[8] The surviving paperwork from the King's hand, and even that generated by his discussions with his ministers and entered in the memoranda sections of the Treasurer of the Chamber's accounts (which never covered more than two folios a month), certainly does not substantiate Pedro de Ayala's claim that Henry spent 'all the time he is not in public, or in his council, in writing the accounts of his expenses with his own hand'.[9] Of course, material has been lost, though even Bacon qualified as no more than a 'merry tale' his story of the destruction by Henry's pet monkey of a notebook full of the King's private reckonings.[10] Henry must also have given time to diplomatic correspondence, as he did to discussions with ambassadors, but such business was highly intermittent: in July 1498 he devoted four hours to the dissection of his latest letters from Ferdinand and Isabella with their ambassador, but then he had not heard anything from the prospective parents-in-law of his son and heir for a year and eleven days.[11]

Henry managed to hold in balance the need to conduct government with what one ambassador called 'gravity and deliberation', and the urge, detected by another foreign envoy, to spend his time on 'nothing but amusements'; in order to understand him we must do the same.[12] In September 1507 he went out hunting and hawking every day, apparently unhindered by his deteriorating eyesight, though in July of that year he shot a farmyard cock by mistake with his crossbow.[13] His Chamber staff included a crossbow-maker and five or more falconers, the senior of whom was salaried at the very generous rate of £36 a year, and his frequent orders for the upkeep of royal parks stressed his personal concern for the state of the game they contained.[14] This declaration of the importance of the royal hunt, by a king who put his money where his heart was, formed a clear signal to those of his subjects who wished to court his favour: they presented him not with accessories for the royal desk but, in 1498 alone, with at least twenty hawks, a dog, and a greyhound (and since these did not suffice for his needs that year, Henry bought at least seven more hawks, a hobby, a sparrowhawk, and two gyrfalcons).[15] When he was not hunting, Henry gambled and played tennis, prompting a boom in tennis-court construction in the first decade of his reign, both at his own residences such as Kenilworth Castle and at those of his councillors such as the Earl of Oxford's Castle Hedingham.[16] Such entertainment for himself and for others was central to Henry's vision of magnificent monarchy, enshrined at his great new palace of Richmond with its 'pleas[a]unt dauncyng chambers ... housis of pleasure to disporte inn, at chesse, tables, dise, cardes, bylys; bowlyng aleys, butts for archers, and goodly tenes plays', provided 'as well to use the seid plays and disports as to behold them so disportyng'.[17]

The way Henry spent his time might not matter if he did not care in whose company he spent it, just as his deployment of richly dressed courtiers in diplomatic display might have made Stafford, Dorset, Kent, and the rest no more than the mannekins in the shop window of Tudor monarchy. There were doubtless times when it was more the quantity than the individual quality of Henry's entourage that mattered, as when he sent out letters to 157 assorted 'lordes ladyes & gentilmen' summoning them to the marriage of Prince Arthur, or when he entertained the Venetian ambassador to dinner with 600 or 700 others present.[18] There were also signs that participation in the King's pastimes was not the solution to every courtier's problems. Thomas, Marquis of Dorset, shot at the butts with Henry in 1495, but he never escaped entirely from the King's suspicion of his loyalty or from the constraints placed upon him as a result.[19] Certainly he never recovered the influence at Court which he had enjoyed under Edward IV.[20] But, as we shall see, others did benefit substantially from their proximity to Henry, and they did so because the King valued their presence. Warrants ordering the prompt payment of annuities to his attendant esquires of the body were justified with their need to prepare themselves 'to attende upon us in this our next progresse', while an annuity unpaid to an esquire of the body whose 'great diseases' had prevented his daily attendance on the King was commanded to be paid notwithstanding his absence, on account of 'his long contynued s[er]vice doon unto us to our singler good pleas[ou]r'.[21] The continuity of service among Henry's closest courtiers and the intensity of their attendance on the King lend substance to the claim of another warrant that he had 'singler regard unto the daily contynuell attenda[u]nce of our trusty s[er]v[au]nt[es]'.[22]

Proximity to Henry was rendered potentially more valuable to the courtier by the King's style of government. A monarch who wrote letters directly to deter those whom he understood to be planning riots, and who intervened readily in legal processes and local quarrels, was an especially useful king to know; while, on the other hand, the ability to mollify in particular instances the King's rapacity towards his tenants-in-chief and all his subjects became increasingly advantageous as the reign wore on and Henry's depredations intensified.[23] As Sir Robert Plumpton found, a direct appeal to the King was the only way to circumvent the hostile influence of a powerful minister such as Sir Richard Empson. Such appeals may not have been unwelcome to Henry, who tried to keep Empson and others under close control, but faced in employing them the problem common to his greater subjects, that those subordinates most talented and zealous in the pursuit of their master's interests were also best able to abuse his power to their own ends.[24] In this respect Henry's courtiers provided a useful means of contact between the King and the world beyond his council chamber.

The particular circumstances which lent significance to Henry's Court were matched by the universal importance of the Court and the courtier in contemporary European government, and by the traditions of the Yorkist court which Henry inherited through his wife's Woodville relations, through the circle of Edward IV's household men who led the revolt of 1483 and then helped Henry to the throne, and through the less influential but numerous Yorkist courtiers who entered Henry's household without the rigours of rebellion and exile.[25] Both the Court's political importance and the clarity of its identity had been increasing fast during Edward's second reign, and Henry did nothing to reverse the trend.[26] In 1489 the Pastons were still listening eagerly to what their 'brodyr Wyllyam heryth sey in [th]e corte', and under Henry anyone who could make his son a courtier still did so, be he Sir William Hussey, Chief Justice of the King's Bench, or Sir William Capel, mayor of London.[27] Contemporaries saw Henry's courtiers not as unusually colourless or powerless, but as courtiers much like those of any other king. John Skelton, who had experience of Henry's Court as chaplain and tutor to the King's second son Henry, Duke of York, confirmed the fact by depicting Henry's courtiers, in his poem *The Bowge of Courte* of 1499, as the personification of all the vices conventionally ascribed to courtiers in medieval satire.[28]

Skelton's characters competed for favour in the attempt to win the 'ryche and fortunate' merchandise aboard the ship named *The Bowge of Courte*. In Henry's England there were greater prizes to be won at the council table than in the Court alone, as Reynold Bray and Edmund Dudley showed, but we must not neglect the fact that a number of the King's leading councillors were also courtiers, men whose power rested as much on their physical and emotional proximity to the ruler as on their professional skills and administrative positions.[29] Despite his legal training, Thomas Lovell began his career in Henry's service as a feed esquire of the body, quite possibly helping the King to dress and undress, and ended it as an enthusiastic Knight of the Garter with an impeccably chivalrous funeral.[30] His discussions of matters of finance and high policy with the King were enlivened by wagers, one in 1502 for the very large sum – for the cautious Henry – of £10.[31] Sir Richard Guildford, Controller of the Household, and Sir John Risley seem similarly to have combined the roles of councillor and courtier, responding effectively to Henry's tendency to canvass informal advice while hunting or in his Chamber.[32] In one sense, perhaps, every councillor was a courtier, but there does seem to have been a real distinction between Lovell, Guildford, and Risley, and others such as Empson, the Chancellor of the Duchy of Lancaster, and Hobart, the Attorney-General, whose careers rested almost entirely on their legal skills, who showed little interest in the chivalrous culture of the Court, and whose work may have tied them to London and Westminster while others were freer to travel with the King.[33] There was no hard-and-fast division of roles – Empson could be found at Court three times in 1508, paying out rewards for the King just like any courtier – but there were various positions in the spectrum of the King's servants.[34] Contemporaries recognized the importance of each element in that spectrum, and among the evil counsellors denounced by Perkin Warbeck in 1497 were not only bishops such as Fox and King, senior councillors such as Bray and Lovell, lawyers such as Empson and Hobart, and financial administrators such as Litton and Cutte, but also such courtiers as Sir Charles Somerset, the Captain of the Guard, Sir David Owen, the Chief Carver, Sir John Turberville, the Marshal of the Household, Sir William Tyler, and Sir Richard Cholmley.[35]

A key place in the spectrum of service was held by those noblemen who combined the King's confidence with great office at Court, a position of regional authority which rested in part on the tenure of local offices in the King's gift, and senior diplomatic and military responsibilities. Such men were central to the process of late medieval state-building and Henry VII had his Giles, Lord Daubeny, Robert, Lord Willoughby de Broke, and Charles Somerset, Lord Herbert, where Louis XI had his Georges de la Trémoille, Charles the Bold his Guy de Brimeu, Edward IV his William, Lord Hastings, Richard III his Francis, Viscount Lovell, and Henry VIII his Charles Brandon, Duke of Suffolk, and John, Lord Russell.[36] Daubeny was very much a power in the Court, where his office of Lord Chamberlain gave him a commanding role, and where contemporaries noted his pervasive influence over appointments: 'Loke hoo stronge he is in the kyngis courte of his houshold servauntis,' commented one, 'for the more partie of his [the king's] garde be of thoos that were my lord chamberlayn servauntis tofore.'[37] Like Hastings, he combined the chamberlainship with the lieu-tenancy of Calais, where he wielded further patronage.[38] Crown steward-ships and constableships built up his power in Somerset, Hampshire, and Dorset, and his military role must have reinforced his leadership among the King's household men, who dominated the vanguard he was to lead into Scotland in 1497.[39]

Daubeny was an active councillor, but he seems to have attended on the King more frequently than his colleagues in the Council.[40] Like any of them who sought to exercise local authority, he had to spend time away from Court, and he must have written letters, as Sir Richard Guildford did, to his 'good neybors', asking them to leave a problem unresolved until 'I shall se therto that hyt shalbe done as reason is at my next comyng downe'.[41] When away, he sought the King's favour with gifts, as many other peers, bishops, and gentlemen did.[42] But when at Court, he waited closely on the King, handing out rewards to those who brought Henry letters or presents, frequently welcoming Henry to his house at Hampton Court, perhaps accompanying him to the hunt in his capacity of Master of the Harthounds, and on occasion touring the royal residences with the King and only a small royal entourage.[43] Such visible proximity to the King caused others to court Daubeny, not least the rulers of the Low Countries and France, who paid him pensions from 1489 and 1492 respectively.[44] Catherine of Aragon estimated his influence with the King highly, and Sir William Capel must have done so too, for it was Daubeny's intercession that moved Henry to reduce Capel's fines for customs offences in 1495 by more than £1000.[45] Daubeny's role as a patronage-broker was significant, and, as one might expect, he operated especially on behalf of the Calais garrison and those to whom he was a local magnate: aspirants for the controllership of the Southampton customs, for the priory of Totnes, for a mortmain licence for land in the West Country, and for the wardship of 'a maiden called an idiot being in th'and[es] of Momp[e]son of Wilt[es]' all used him as an intermediary with the King.[46]

Henry certainly did not grant Daubeny's every wish. He kept a check on the Lord Chamberlain as he did on all his servants, and there were notes among his memoranda to make sure that Daubeny handed over a royal ward who was living in his household, and accounted properly for his offices at Windsor.[47] When Daubeny sought the marriage with a West Country heiress for his son, promising 'largely to diserve it', Henry turned to Sir Reynold Bray, who undertook to 'make it worth v^c m[a]rc to the king'.[48] It was Bray again who negotiated with Daubeny over the size of the benevolence with which the Lord Chamberlain demonstrated his loyalty to Henry in 1499.[49] The financial element in all Henry's relationships made him an unusual king to serve, and in 1506 Daubeny even received a sharp rap on the knuckles for peculation at Calais, agreeing to repay the King £2000 and make over his French pension to the Crown.[50] He may have felt that this was rather a harsh response to his loyal service, as he hinted in his will 18 months later, in prefacing the arrangements for his payments to the King with the observation that 'it pleased the king[es] hignesse whose true serv[a]nt I have ben thise xxvi yeres and above to charge me by recognisaunce unto his grace in the sum[m]e of m^{1}m^{1}li'.[51] Yet in proclaiming his loyalty to the end – Bernard André attributed to him the edifying deathbed declaration that 'it is sufficient for me to leave this life faithful to Jesus my Saviour and to my king' – Daubeny played the courtier to perfection, and through a splendid funeral and burial at Westminster 'where my said sov[er]aigne lorde entendeth his bodye to be entiered', like Hastings in the previous generation and Brandon in the next, he won the honour which crowned his very solid worldly gains from royal service.[52]

Daubeny's deputy and successor as Chamberlain, Sir Charles Somerset, was still more frequent in his attendance at Court, just as Hastings's deputy Sir Roger Ray was the only Knight of the Body on permanent duty under the rota of 1471.[53] The Chamber accounts show Somerset busy about the King from the early 1490s, and as Captain of the Guard from 1486 he must have spent much of the reign at Court, though his increasing importance as an ambassador led to some long absences, and he was away on occasion looking to his own interests in Wales.[54] There Henry steadily built up Somerset's power with leases, stewardships, and constableships to complement the inheritance of Elizabeth Herbert, whom Somerset married in 1492, doubtless with the King's help.[55] Henry's characteristic caution in rewarding his servants made Somerset's progress a slow one, but in 1504 he was first styled Lord Herbert; by that time he was a very regular attender at Council meetings, and in the Court ceremonial of 1506 and 1508 he played a prominent part.[56] Somerset oversaw important ceremonies away from Court, such as Prince Henry's installation as a Knight of the Garter; he also acted as the King's spokesman in delicate matters at home as well as abroad, as, for example, when he and Guildford were sent by Henry to comfort the Queen's household servants on her death.[57] Like Daubeny and Lord Steward Willoughby de Broke, he became a patron at Court for those who valued his help with the King.[58]

Daubeny and Somerset were courtiers of a type familiar to most late medieval and early modern monarchies, but the idiosyncrasies of Henry's kingship bred other courtiers of a more unusual stamp. Foremost among them was William Smith. He was a royal servant, probably a Page of the Chamber, by July 1486, and by May 1488 he had entered the wardrobe of robes as a page: this brought him into regular contact with the King, whose clothes he brought to the attendants who helped Henry dress.[59] Smith soon became one of the King's closest servants, handling his petty cash and making a wide range of small purchases for his personal needs.[60] The King gave him occasional rewards in cash – £5 in November 1498, for instance – but Smith exploited his intimacy with Henry to more impressive ends, collecting leases on Crown lands and local offices in Staffordshire, Cheshire, and Lancashire.[61] In 1498 he became escheator of Lancashire, in 1502 searcher in the ports of Chester and Beaumaris, and in 1504 bailiff of Gresley hundred, bailiff of the Duchy of Lancaster's new liberty in Derbyshire, Master Forester of Needwood Forest and sheriff of Staffordshire, a post he held for three years out of the next four.[62] In 1506 he added the rangership of Cannock Forest to these offices and to his Crown farms and receiverships, which included estates forfeited by Sir William Stanley, Lord Audley, Roger Wodehouse, and Sir Robert Curson, lands given to the King by the Abbot of Tewkesbury, and the wood sales of Sutton Chase.[63] Smith capitalized further on his position at Court to buy at least one wardship, to help the Abbot of Trentham make fine with the King for his temporalities, and to marry one of the co-heiresses of John, Marquis Montagu.[64]

So far his career was not dissimilar from that of the better-known royal attendants and local empire-builders of the next reign, such as William Compton or William Brereton.[65] But with the opportunism of the true courtier Smith saw his chance to reinforce his position in the King's service and in local society by associating himself with the work of the Council Learned in the law, using its authority against his local opponents as early as 1501.[66] From 1505 to 1508 he was active both in the duchy chamber at Westminster and in Staffordshire, Lancashire, and even further afield, taking bonds for appearances before the Council Learned, possibly selling wardships, and generally acting as the council's enforcement officer for the north-west Midlands, rather as Hobart did in East Anglia and others elsewhere.[67] This doubtless kept him away from Court – in August 1505 and February 1506 Henry sent letters to him somewhere in the north-west – but it must have brought him power and profit, and his ability to combine the roles of intimate courtier and junior legal minister made him increasingly the King's man in his region.[68] In 1502 it was Smith who paid out 20s. to a man who rode the King's errands into Cheshire, and in February 1509, as the dying King groped for salvation, it was Smith who saw to it that three gold pieces were offered for his soul before the rood of Chester.[69]

Not even Smith, favoured though he must have been, escaped the King's oversight when it came to accounting. In 1503 the Abbot of Tewkesbury and six others stood surety for his payment of debts of at least £328 14s. 9d., and by February 1505 all but £79 10s. had duly been paid.[70] But outside the King's Chamber Smith had a freer hand. By 1508 Sir Thomas Ashton was trying to traverse the findings of an inquisition held by Smith as escheator in Lancashire, and the King's death opened the way to accusations of perversion of justice and intimidation against him, as against Empson and Dudley.[71] Smith was arrested, replaced in all his offices, and arraigned at the Guildhall as a 'promoter' of malicious prosecutions, but eventually released to retire to Staffordshire and die in 1525.[72] Like the courtier he was, he had fallen from power with none to save him at the death of the master he served, leaving a London chronicler to note drily that 'this Smyth beffore dayes was ... in good ffavour wyth owir soverayn lordis ffadyr Kyng Henry the VIIth'.[73]

Courts were always an arena in which comparatively humble men like Smith could rise to power, and often fall from it again. In late-fifteenth-century Europe they also served as honey pots for the nobility, drawing them into closer association with, and service to, the Crown. Henry liked to have the great peers around him at important occasions of state, just as he valued their increasing military commitment to his regime and their advice in the Great Council.[74] The needs of their estates and affinities, and the benefits to the King of the presence of trusted great men in the localities, made most peers occasional courtiers at best, though this did not make such magnates as the thirteenth Earl of Oxford or the first Earl of Derby any less influential with the King when they did happen to be at Court.[75] Henry may have made conscious efforts to divert the energies and expenditure of younger peers such as Buckingham and Northumberland into courtly service rather than the cultivation of independent political power bases: but their tendency to make splendid appearances at great occasions, yet still find themselves entrusted with no serious responsibilities and financially harassed by the King, may represent rather personal failures on their part in the art of courtly politics than any machiavellian scheme of Henry's.[76]

Other noblemen of their generation fared better. George Talbot, Earl of Shrewsbury, won the King's confidence sufficiently to be appointed Lord Steward of the household in succession to Robert, Lord Willoughby de Broke.[77] Like Broke he did not attend Court as frequently as Daubeny or Somerset, but he played an important part in the great events of the last few years of the reign, and was well placed to benefit from the accession of Henry VIII.[78] Less elevated than Shrewsbury, but more involved in Court life, was Henry, Earl of Essex, who was at Court frequently from the later 1480s and danced and jousted his way through the reign in a career which won him a knighthood of the Garter and at least three grants of land from the King, and included the rare feat of owing Henry VII £160 for 12 years without being unduly pressed for repayment.[79] Essex's companions in jousting and revelling included two young peers who must have been almost permanently at court.[80] Thomas, Lord Harington, who succeeded his father as Marquis of Dorset in 1501, was placed in the King's service at his father's cost under an agreement of 1495, while Lord William Courtenay, the eldest son of the Earl of Devon, was about at Court from at least 1499 and was paid an annuity of 50 marks from March 1501 for his daily and diligent attendance on the King.[81] Courtenay's presence kept him in the King's mind where matters of patronage were concerned, for the Treasurer of the Chamber John Heron, presumably at Henry's dictation, appended the words 'M[emorandum] the L[ord] Willi[a]m' to the note of a bid by Lord Broke for an office in the West.[82] Henry welcomed other young noblemen into his entourage, and Walter, Lord Ferrers, for example, served as a page for the King's cups between the ages of 13 and 18½, in the last five years of the reign.[83] Such men would not be expected to be full-time courtiers once they came of age, but in their formative years they would have seen the King's majesty at first hand, and established a relationship with the monarch and his leading ministers which would make for smooth dealings later in life, or so it must have been hoped.

The life of the courtier was a more permanent career for younger sons of the peerage. Harington's brother, Lord John Grey, was taken on as the King's servant with a £20 annuity, but his career and those of his brothers

did not really flourish until the next reign.[84] Buckingham's brother, Lord
Henry Stafford, made his way at Court faster. He was another member of
the jousting set, and dominated the tournaments of January and March
1508; like his fellow-jousters Essex, Dorset, Kent, and Suffolk he was elected to the Order of the Garter, and by 1506 he had entered the inner ring of
peers and courtiers who gave New Year's gifts to the King.[85] Stafford seems
to have been especially close to Dorset, whose widowed mother he married
in 1505 under a papal dispensation secured partly by a letter from the young
Marquis explaining how the match would increase the amity between the
houses of Stafford and Grey.[86] If it failed to do so, that was because it caused
Lord Henry to fall out with his brother, the Duke of Buckingham, who tried
to withdraw the estate in tail male with which he had endowed Lord Henry
and his bride.[87] Stafford was escaping from the tutelage of his brother, and
using the Court to do so. Not only was the courtly round of tournaments
and processions more congenial than the administrative role in the Welsh
Marches which Buckingham tried to foist on Lord Henry, but the £1 000 life
estate in the Bonvile inheritance which his wife made over to him equipped
him for an independent career, and enabled him to pursue the aim he realized in 1510, the re-creation of the earldom of Wiltshire in the junior
Stafford line.[88] For Stafford, as for everyone else, the King's favour had
financial strings attached. He paid £100 for royal assistance in obtaining the
papal dispensation, and a further £1 000 from his wife's income for the
King's licence to marry; he gave a bond in £1 000 for his loyalty to the King,
and paid £400 for royal favour in the lawsuit over his brother's attempts to
cancel his endowment from the Stafford estates.[89] Yet Lord Henry was considerably richer and more honoured in 1509 than he had been in 1500; and
what he had achieved, he had achieved as a courtier.

Henry's noble courtiers rubbed shoulders with what we might call clerical
courtiers. His deans of the chapel were mostly lawyers chosen for their apti-
tude to chair the council attendant and its judicial manifestation, the nascent
court of requests, but they could also be found attending on the King and paying out rewards to visitors to the Court.[90] The royal secretaries were closer
to the King, and both Oliver King and Thomas Ruthal seem to have forwarded requests to Henry from suitors for favour.[91] For such men, as for the
heirs to peerages, service at Court was merely one stage in a career, a phase
which might end in appointment to a major see and consequent departure
from the Court. The same was true of the young noblewomen who served as
ladies-in-waiting to Queen Elizabeth or her daughters, as part of a preparation for marriage and adult life. There were ladies who stayed at Court
beyond their adolescence, but they usually did so because their husbands'
careers necessitated close attendance on the King. The Queen's household
thus formed a mirror image of her husband's: Ladies Guildford, Bray, and
Lovell were among her courtiers, Mrs Marzen, Mrs Denis, and Mrs Weston
among her servants or those of Princess Mary after her death.[92] Their friend-

ship with the Queen must have helped their spouses' relationship with the King, but there is no sign that they were regarded as important figures in their own right, nor that any woman could do much to forge her own career at Court. Those to whom the Court meant most were lay male courtiers with no family resources on which to fall back. They were the men to whom the King's favour was most important, and they seem to have been the men with whom he spent much of his time.

A number of them were foreigners, and presumably came to England with Henry from Brittany or France. One, Roland de Veleville, may even have been the King's bastard son, but if so he was not treated with excessive indulgence: Henry had to advance him money in 1492 because he could not afford to equip himself to accompany the King's invasion of France.[93] His income consisted largely of the £46 13s. 4d. in royal annuities granted to him in 1493 and 1496, and the decisiveness with which he took up residence at Beaumaris after his appointment as constable there in 1509 suggests that he had no home but the Court.[94] Payments in the Chamber accounts show him to have been closely involved with the King's falconry, and presumably he accompanied Henry when he went hunting and hawking.[95] Perhaps it was to enable him to ride out with the royal party that the King gave him a valuable horse in July 1508.[96] Guillaume de la Ryvers had a similar career. He was Master of the King's Hawks, and as such attended Henry wearing a livery chain worth £1 000 at Prince Arthur's wedding; he also seems to have been charged with the care of foreign visitors to the Court.[97] He received occasional rewards from the King, but his main livelihood must have been his £40 annuity.[98] We cannot tell if he or Veleville used their proximity to the King to speak for others' interests, but they certainly knew how to use it to maintain their own, obtaining frequent orders to the Exchequer for prompt payment of their fees.[99]

Veleville and Ryvers had English and Welsh colleagues. Matthew Baker had been in exile with Henry, guided him on his escape from Brittany to France, and was among the esquires close to the King clothed by the great wardrobe in the early months of the reign.[100] At the same time as he won his place at Court – consolidated with the 50 mark fee of an esquire for the body in 1487 – he established himself with a place in the country at Kenilworth, obtaining grants in September 1485 of a corrody in the abbey there, the constableship of the castle, the keepership of the park, and a lease of the herbage.[101] At the end of the reign he was still active at Court, entertaining visiting ambassadors in his home, taking them and their messages to and from the King, overseeing the construction of nets for the royal hunt, and hunting with Henry at Stratford in July 1508.[102] At his death in 1513 the circle of his friendship lay almost entirely within the Royal Household, and he left gowns, coats, and doublets to a serjeant-at-arms, a yeoman of the guard, a godson in the Queen's wardrobe, one member of the staff of the King's buttery, and five of the royal cellar. He was then living in

Bermondsey Abbey, but retained his interests at Kenilworth, making bequests to the abbey, and the parker and 'waterman of the pondes' there, and leaving a paternal £20 and two feather beds to 'Johane dwellyng at Kyllyngworth [Kenilworth] and to the childe she goth with all'.[103]

If there was something static about the career of Matthew Baker, the same could not be said of Hugh Vaughan, one of a number of Welshmen among the staff of the Chamber, who was distinctly upwardly mobile. He was a Gentleman Usher of the King's Chamber by 1490, but when he tried to joust at Court in 1492 those involved wanted to stop him on the grounds that he was of insufficiently respectable descent.[104] Lady Anne Hungerford, daughter of the third Earl of Northumberland, may have been less choosy than the jousters, or perhaps the King's insistence on Vaughan's merits overcame her resistance as it overcame theirs. She and Vaughan were married by December 1493, when he was assured of an income of £168 a year from her estates while she lived, and £40 a year after her death.[105] He remained active at Court as an esquire of the body.[106] Between 1500 and 1504 he was knighted and entrusted with the custody of royal prisoners in the Tower, and in this capacity Henry called on him to kidnap the Earl of Arran in 1508.[107] Vaughan received grants of office from the King in places as far apart as Jersey and Caernarvonshire, but his career was always centred on the Court and on Westminster, where he rented a house from the abbey which was the residence attributed to him in legal documents. There he held the bailiffship of the abbey's liberty, and both he and his wife were buried in St Michael's Chapel.[108] He foreshadowed the tendency of the next century for courtiers to congregate increasingly in and around London.

That trend coincided with a growing hostility to courtiers as idle leeches on the body politic, hostility redolent of that directed against the courtiers of Henry VI.[109] The King's maintenance of a court and of courtiers could be justified, not least in the monarch's own eyes, only if they served some useful purpose. The courtiers of Henry VII did. At the simplest level they provided for the King's personal needs: after a reform in the 1490s which separated the Privy or Secret Chamber from the Chamber, this was the job of a small group of grooms and pages headed by Piers Barbour, the King's barber, and Hugh Denis, the Groom of the King's Close Stool.[110] By the end of the reign, Denis controlled a growing Privy Purse account, funded directly by the Surveyor of the King's Prerogative, and most of the King's petty cash was handled by him and his colleagues, who bought Henry books, musical instruments, tennis balls, crossbows, and anything else he needed.[111] They carried important messages for the King, and one of their number, Francis Marzen, a Breton, made repeated trips to Calais to collect the pension paid to Henry by the King of France; while there in December 1502, he also took into custody silver plate worth £573 3s. 5d. to pay off the debts to the King of the deceased treasurer of the town.[112] In such activity there were already signs of the authority that accrued to the King's body servants by virtue of their contact with the monarch, authority which would find fuller expression in the next reign.[113]

Courtiers sought to meet the King's emotional needs as well as his physical needs. At the Court jousts of 1494, Henry Winslow, the Gentleman Usher, appeared on a horse wearing a paper trapper, 'ther apon peynted ij men pleyng at dyse and certain othes writtyn nott wrothey her to be rehearsed'. He did so, he told the herald who chronicled the tournament, 'to cause the kyng to laugh'.[114] Winslow's need to explain his action may suggest that the King was not visibly amused, but the joke cannot have misfired too badly, as he kept his job, and a little over two years later Henry stood godfather to his son.[115] More successful was the quip made by an unnamed courtier in 1498, when the King heard unexpectedly that ambassador de Puebla was about to arrive at Court, and wondered out loud why he might be coming. 'To eat', said one wag, playing on the Spaniard's reputation for cadging free meals, and Henry duly laughed.[116] The intensive participation of Henry's esquires of the body and gentlemen ushers in tournaments suggests that this was another way to entertain the King, who sponsored, watched, and judged such exercises with enthusiasm, even though he did not participate in them. Matthew Baker and Guillaume de la Ryvers were frequent jousters, and Roland de Veleville almost obsessive: he probably took part in more tournaments than anyone else at Court, and one May Day he issued a challenge to tilt at Kennington single-handed against all comers.[117] Many more courtiers were involved in the organization of pageantry and the control of building works at royal residences and elsewhere, helping to create for Henry the splendid monarchy he desired.[118]

Henry's desires were not all so conventional: his courtiers had also to adapt themselves to the King's quest to expose and mulct all those who infringed the law, and anyone else who might be construed to be at the royal mercy. Daubeny did so successfully, informing the King of a gentleman in Windsor Forest who had killed one of the King's harts, and undertaking to sue the King's cases against five counterfeiters and thieves in return for a third of the proceeds, a deal on which he apparently made £8 10s.[119] Sir Richard Pudsey, a former serjeant of the cellar and esquire of the body, much involved in organizing Court revels early in the reign and well rewarded by the King, made some recompense by pointing out that clerical tax collectors in the sees of Exeter and Bath and Wells were withholding large sums due to the Crown.[120] Even the pathetic Richard, Lord Grey of Ruthin (the future wastrel Earl of Kent), joined in, earning the slightly derisory reward of £3 6s. 8d. from the King 'for shewyng of usury don unto him by S[ir] Willi[am] Capell'.[121]

Henry deployed his courtiers for tasks that demanded more skill than informing on usurers and poachers. Many of them undertook important diplomatic missions, often paired with a legally trained cleric who could make set-piece orations and check the details of treaties. Early in the reign

Sir Richard Edgecombe, Controller of the Household, Sir John Risley, Sir Richard Nanfan, Sir Charles Somerset, and others carried out such missions, and in the last decade they were supplemented by more junior courtiers such as Sir Thomas Brandon, the Master of the Horse, Matthew Baker, and Francis Marzen.[122] When paired with a clergyman, the lay courtier was nearly always paid larger expenses, presumably in recognition of his need to spend on making an impression at the Court he was to visit.[123] But courtiers were not just sent abroad to look good. Especially towards the end of the reign they fulfilled highly sensitive missions alone, and, in an age when diplomacy was increasingly developing into an exchange of courtiers, they could deal very effectively with the princes they visited. At Grenoble in June 1502 Matthew Baker, who had been on at least three previous missions to France since 1499, apologized to Louis XII for his poor expression of Henry VII's messages, excusing himself with the avowal: 'Your grace knows well that I am no clerk, but a man more familiar with war.' Louis's minister, Cardinal Georges d'Amboise, commented approvingly that neither Baker nor Louis was 'one of those Italian orators', and Louis reassured Baker with a hearty 'I like this better, for we understand each other well.'[124] Since Baker's mission was to turn down as politely as possible a French marriage for Prince Henry, while still urging Louis to use his influence in Germany to enable Henry to buy the fugitive Earl of Suffolk and bring him back to England, any rapport he could strike up with the king was of the greatest value. He went to France at least twice more before the end of the reign.[125]

Diplomacy could be exacting and costly: Sir Charles Somerset spent over a year in the Netherlands in 1501–2 and had to borrow £160 from the King to meet his expenses in France in 1505.[126] But it had its compensations. Sir Richard Nanfan returned from Castile and Portugal in 1489 with accumulated presents of a war horse, two jennets (one worth £200 with its silver-gilt trappings), two mules, 10 yards of silk cloth, 40 marks of silver, and a gold cup worth some 40 marks filled with perhaps 220 marks' worth of coins.[127] Matthew Baker was given a golden collar worth about £90 by Louis XII in 1507, and in 1499 he had been paid £40 in reward by Henry, probably in connection with an embassy to France.[128] When Francis Marzen and James Braybroke, Grooms of the Privy Chamber, went to Spain in 1505 to analyse both the unstable politics of the peninsula and the potential wifely virtues of the dowager Queen Joan of Naples – they reported that she suffered neither from halitosis nor from excessive facial hair, but that her revenues were alarmingly small – Marzen came back as a knight and went on to serve as Henry's agent in his attempts to arbitrate between France, Guelders, and the Netherlands in the following year, while Braybroke returned to continue collecting the wardships and local offices with which the King regularly rewarded him.[129]

Henry's courtiers represented him at his own Court as well as abroad. This was especially the case in dealing with foreign ambassadors, who usually met Sir Thomas Brandon, Matthew Baker, or another courtier sent to welcome them before they reached the King.[130] Once installed in England, they were summoned to the royal presence or informed of important news by the same men or by more minor royal attendants, while Brandon, Somerset, and others entertained them to banquets.[131] Henry's more valued subjects received similar treatment, and the mayor and aldermen of London found themselves 'welcomyd & cherid' by the Lord Steward, the Lord Chamberlain, and the Controller of the Household when they were invited to Court for dinner on Twelfth Night, 1495.[132] The courtiers also formed the core of the broader royal affinity constituted by the King's household. Henry continued the tendency of the Yorkist kings to inflate the number of royal chamber servants to the point where the nominal membership of the household was virtually coterminous with the King's affinity. Where Edward IV had between 30 and 40 esquires of the body by 1483, and Richard III had at least 48 in the course of his reign, Henry VII had 93 or more by 1509, and the expansion was to continue under Wolsey.[133] The difference between men nominally of the household and the King's daily courtiers enabled Henry to use household appointments as a means to reassure many former Ricardian partisans without exposing himself to undue danger from plotters; but he did call on his household men to serve an important military role and to occupy shrievalties and other offices at times of crisis, and he found the prestige and access to royal patronage which accompanied a position as knight of the body well able to draw off the loyalty of some of the leading followers of powerful peers.[134]

It is unlikely that members of the wider royal affinity cultivated a distinctive courtly style together with those more often at Court, though they may have shared a resemblance to Skelton's character Riot, who 'had no pleasure but in harlotrye'.[135] Many of Henry's courtiers produced bastards, and one might wonder what Sir Richard Pudsey thought Sir Thomas Darcy was doing in the West Country in the company of the Dean of St Paul's when he assured Darcy, after a conversation with Lady Darcy, that 'Master Deane shall have noo litill thanke for the supposed good rewle that I have tolde her he hath cawsed yow kepe'.[136] Matthew Baker was accused of running a brothel in the Palace of Westminster. On the other hand, the Court maintained a strict piety with regard to fasting which even Catherine of Aragon found rather oppressive.[137] The level of cultural achievement and interest among some lay courtiers was high, though the message of Henry's taste for magnificence may have been to choose the costly rather than the cultivated. Between them the earls of Essex and Kent and the Marquis of Dorset ran up unpaid bills of over £1000 with one London mercer alone; and when Thomas Savage, the long-serving Dean of the Chapel, headed north to the archbishopric of York, he took his peacocks and hounds, over £1100-worth of plate and over £230-worth of arras and counterfeit arras, though his library was worth only £14 6s. 9d.[138]

The overriding theme in the courtier mentality was loyalty to the prince.[139] Henry's courtiers thought of themselves as 'hys true knyghtes', and displayed their loyalty to the King's person and commands in sometimes self-conscious ways.[140] The only portrait in Sir Thomas Lovell's house at Enfield when he died in 1524 was 'a goodly tablet payntid w[ith] the ymage of King Henry the VIIth'.[141] Thomas Savage insisted that he would 'obs[er]ve ... the kyng[es] comaundment ... letting for no ma[n]' when warning Lord Darcy that he was about to be prosecuted for retaining, an ironic protestation given Savage's consistent abuse of his position to benefit his own family and friends.[142] Vigour and ruthlessness were the qualities the courtier aimed to display in carrying out Henry's orders. Sir Robert Clifford, on embassy to Brittany in 1490, forced the crew of his ship to leave Weymouth in unsuitable weather, forbade them to waste time fighting two French ships off Guernsey, and pestered the Breton officials to find him horses in a hurry so that he could reach Vannes on the same day he landed, all 'for the love of the great charge we have in our embassy'.[143] It was said that, on a ship off Guines in 1502, Lovell cold-bloodedly threatened to throw Sir James Tyrrell into the sea if Tyrrell's son did not surrender the castle.[144]

Such behaviour accorded well with the military tone of Henry's Court. Apart from the almost universal service of 1487, 1489, and 1497 in the suppression of rebellion, and of 1492 in the invasion of France, Roland de Veleville, Hugh Vaughan, and Guillaume de la Ryvers all served in Brittany in 1489, while Thomas Brandon commanded a naval flotilla two years earlier.[145] Their bravado could not be contained by outward war, and courtiers' retinues brawled on the streets of London and elsewhere.[146] A number of Henry's inner circle – Baker, Vaughan, and Veleville – gained appalling reputations for violent and high-handed behaviour when sent to govern such outposts as Jersey and Beaumaris, and in this they resembled the clique of Elizabethan courtiers led by the Earl of Essex, whose stress on the military virtues went with a domineering contempt for those who were not of their kind.[147]

Henry's courtiers manifested these traits in pursuit of their own interests as well as those of the King. When Sir John Hussey thought that one of his servants had stolen money from a casket in his house, he took him into the privy, ostensibly to look for the missing cash. Once there, Hussey produced his dagger and said: 'Thou hast my money. Gyffe it me ageyn and tell trouth or I shall slee the.'[148] The servant confessed, for Sir John was not a man to trifle with. The comparatively poor pickings available at Henry's Court made vigorous self-advancement all the more vital to the ambitious courtier, and in the prosecution of local quarrels a number of the King's servants proved themselves brutal and overbearing.[149] Henry's professed aim was to use his patronage with deliberation and as a reward for conspicuous service, and petitioners certainly did not find the King a soft touch: the story of his alteration of a grant of office to Empson from life tenure to tenure during pleasure is well known, but there are other signs that Henry kept to his line.[150]

Occasionally he may have been taken in by a plausible tale, as when Thomas Nevile, the King's sewer, 'reapported unto' him that, if his annuity due at Easter were paid early, Nevile might 'the better apparaille hym to s[er]ve us at the same fest as it app[er]teyneth'.[151] But Henry was rarely caught off guard, and the courtier had to make the best of what the King gave him. That was not always easy, for attempts to realize the power and profit which a signed bill promised could meet many obstructions, from corrupt Chancery officials who would not provide letters patent, to local rivals who might expel one's deputy from an office 'with force and mighty hand'.[152]

None the less, courtiers prospered. As a rule, the King handed out only small rewards in cash, though the £26 13s. 4d. given to Robert Knolles, the Gentleman Usher, in 1497 was a respectable sum.[153] On the other hand, repeated small rewards could mount up, and most of the Grooms and Gentlemen Ushers of the Chamber could count on £1 or £2 from the treasurer of the chamber each year, a share in the £100 from the Exchequer spread among them each Christmas, and a part of the £40–£100 annually distributed under the aegis of the Treasurer and Controller of the Household: Hugh Denis, Francis Marzen, and William Smith figured frequently on the lists of such payments.[154] Other courtiers borrowed cash or plate from the King; and many more, from Sir Roland de Veleville down to the humblest royal servant, were rewarded in the second half of the reign with grants of the sums forfeited by those who had allowed prisoners to escape or who had given sureties for the appearance in court of absconding malefactors, those who had defaulted on jury service, and so on.[155] Henry's preparedness to feed his ravening courtiers with the fruit of his law-and-order policy left considerable scope for self-help, as the King granted out sums forfeited 'as we be credibly infourmed' at sessions in the counties where his servants had their local interests.[156] These grants multiplied as the reign drew to its close. In all, over £3700 of potential Crown income was alienated in this way between August 1501 and the King's death, whereas less than £700 had been distributed in the same manner in the six years preceding 1501.

Henry was less generous with grants of land, though many courtiers picked up the occasional manor even in the last years of the reign.[157] Purchase was the more effective way to build up an estate, as Empson, Bray and others showed, and Hugh Denis invested over £1500 of his profits from the Court in land in five counties between November 1502 and January 1507.[158] Courtiers clustered around those who were forced to sell their estates, and within four years of succeeding his father as Earl of Kent in 1503, Richard Grey – the most spectacular failure at Henry's Court, who gambled away his livelihood and even managed to break his arm teaching Prince Henry to joust – had sold land to Daubeny, Denis, Herbert, and Hussey among others.[159] Land could be brought under temporary but profitable control through wardships, and courtiers competed successfully for these.[160] Marriages were more valuable still, and the King's tightening assertion of rights over the widows of his tenants-in-chief enabled him to reward many of his servants, from Francis Marzen, who married in 1501 a minor heiress in Hertfordshire, to Sir Thomas Brandon, who married first the dowager Marchioness of Berkeley and then the dowager Lady Fitzwarin.[161] Permission for the last marriage may have cost Brandon and his cousin Sir Thomas Lovell £100, but it was a very small price to pay.[162]

Some payment might also be demanded for grants of office, though Henry may have seen this less as selling offices than as a tax on their occupants.[163] Certainly he did not always grant favours to the highest bidder. Hugh Denis '& his felowes' offered £40 for the keepership of the Palace of Westminster, a post worth over £20 a year to the holder, but Henry granted it to Matthew Baker in 1502, apparently without charge.[164] Whatever the exact financial terms of their grants, most of Henry's courtiers collected a range of offices on the Crown estates, in the forest administration and in the customs service, often in a fairly compact group like the park keeperships, riding forestership and three stewardships in Berkshire and Buckinghamshire assembled by Richard Weston, Groom of the Privy Chamber, between 1504 and 1508.[165] The keeperships of royal houses were especially useful, as those who could not afford country residences near the capital like Daubeny's Hampton Court or Denis's houses at Greenwich and Richmond could set up their homes in them.[166] Marzen did so at Standon, Weston at Sunninghill, while Denis kept up an additional establishment at Wanstead.[167]

Henry's courtiers exchanged offices, arranged to succeed one another in them, and even sold them, with the King's permission.[168] In that they were no different from the courtiers of Henry VI, or those of the later Tudors.[169] Like them they combined their efforts to sue for particular grants for themselves or their clients: Braybroke worked with Smith, Daubeny worked with Braybroke, Denis worked with John Heron and others.[170] The state of the evidence makes it impossible to recover much of the petitioning system at court, but it seems that Denis, Marzen, and Weston were recognized as men who could move the King, even if they took second place in the patronage system as a whole to great councillors such as Bray, Fox, and Lovell, just as their successors in Henry VIII's Privy Chamber took second place to Wolsey, Norfolk, and Cromwell.[171] Certainly Sir Robert Plumpton was pleased to get Richard Weston on his side in his dispute with Empson.[172] Behind the patent rolls lies a world of manoeuvre rarely illuminated by scraps of correspondence, such as Sir Richard Croft's letter to Sir Gilbert Talbot advising him to come to Court because the King seemed well disposed to give him some reward, even though he had failed to obtain the grant that he expected, or the letters of Bishop Fox and Sir Richard Pudsey to Sir Thomas Darcy in 1500, advising him not to pursue a certain suit because (in Fox's words) 'neither my selve ne noone oder frende of yours here thinke that yt it can be eny matier fittynge or convenyente for you'.[173]

Did such cooperation by courtiers and councillors in the pursuit of patronage generate a system of Court politics? The idea would have been abhorrent to Bacon, himself the victim of Court politics, who stressed that Henry 'never put down, or discomposed counsellor, or near servant, save only Stanley the lord chamberlain'.[174] Yet we might add to Sir William Stanley's fall in 1495, as possible crises of political conflict, the destruction of Lord Fitzwalter in 1495–6; the conciliar interrogation and heavy fine of Thomas Rotherham, Archbishop of York, in 1495; the arrest of Lord William Courtenay in 1502; the disgrace and resignation of Sir Richard Guildford in 1505–6; the arrest of Thomas, Marquis of Dorset, and the sudden resignation of Sir James Hobart, the Attorney-General, after a brush with the bishops over *praemunire*, in 1507; and perhaps Daubeny's humiliation in the previous year.[175] Accusations of corruption in the cases of Guildford and Daubeny may well have masked political rivalries, as they did in the reigns of Edward VI and James I (indeed, in Bacon's own fall from power), while the Yorkist sympathies for which the others suffered were perhaps more imagined than real.[176] The evidence against Stanley was little more convincing than that produced against Thomas Cromwell 45 years later, though he was tarred with the brush of militant sacramentarian heresy rather than Yorkist loyalism.[177] Of course there were real Yorkist plotters, but advocacy of the current pretender was too convenient a charge to pin on one's enemies for us to take it at face value in every instance.[178] Henry was known to be hard to convince where accusations of treason were concerned, but equally his servants were conversant with the idea that such accusations might be malicious.[179] When they touched the noblemen in closest attendance on the King, Courtenay and Dorset (and briefly, in 1509, their colleague at Court, Lord Henry Stafford), then the 'Court-centred politics' of the decades to come were very close indeed.[180]

This should not surprise us. Small-scale political groupings with their roots in family connections, shared local interest, and personal friendship could be found at Henry's Court as at those of his successors, and contemporaries recognized that at least on specific issues they might be opposed to each other: Sir Robert Plumpton, backed by Fox, Lovell, Guildford, and Weston against Empson, was warned to ask the King not to appoint Sir Reynold Bray, Sir John Mordaunt, or anyone else linked with Bray to arbitrate his case.[181] The links between central and local politics were also close, and the fall of Guildford and subsequent humbling of his local rival Lord Burgavenny might be linked to the struggle for power in Kent, just as were the plots against Archbishop Cranmer in 1543.[182] Much of the political history of Henry VII's Court will inevitably remain obscure, but the recognition that such a political history may have existed at least marks an advance on Bacon. If Henry's Court was the sort of place where Skelton's Deceit, Dissimulation, Suspicion, and Disdain were at home, then its politics may not have been as straightforward as Bacon liked to imagine.

Those politics came into their own as Henry lay dying. While he discussed with his 'secret servauntes' the changes that would come over his kingship 'yf it pleased god to sende hym lyfe', those same servants were preparing to keep his death secret long enough to be able to spring a coup against Empson, Dudley, and Smith apparently orchestrated by their fellow-councillors.[183] Richard Weston's last service to his master was to smile as he came out of the Privy Chamber to fetch Archbishop Warham in to see the royal corpse, so that no one would guess that the King was finally dead.[184] A new reign had begun, in which the Court and its courtiers would loom large; but both were part of the Tudors' inheritance from Henry VII. Henry's style of kingship may have made his courtiers less influential or even less significant than those of some other monarchs; yet he could no more dispense with courtiers than could Louis XI, a ruler who accounted courtly splendour so unimportant that he allegedly dismissed one of his esquires for wearing a velvet doublet, but who nevertheless ennobled his barber.[185] Henry won his kingdom and kept it at the head of an army, governed it with the authority of a Council, and exploited it with the efficiency of a Chamber; but he lived and died at the heart of a Court. Unless we hold these elements in balance, we shall never strip away Bacon's fictions to see more clearly the King and the reign beneath.

Notes

1 C. D. Bowen, *Francis Bacon* (London, 1963), pp. 54–63.
2 R. Lockyer, *Buckingham: The Life and Political Career of George Villiers, First Duke of Buckingham, 1592–1628* (London, 1981), pp. 29–32, 44–7, 97–100; J. L. Marwil, *The Trials of Counsel: Francis Bacon in 1621* (Detroit, 1976), pp. 15–62.
3 *Bacon's History of the Reign of King Henry VII*, ed. J. R. Lumby (2nd edn, Cambridge, 1892), pp. 215, 217.
4 *Memorials of King Henry the Seventh*, ed. J. Gairdner (Rolls Ser. 10; London 1858), p. xvi.
5 S. Anglo, *Spectacle, Pageantry, and Early Tudor Policy* (Oxford, 1969), pp. 8–108; G. Kipling, *The Triumph of Honour: Burgundian Origins of the Elizabethan Renaissance* (Leiden, 1977), pp. 1–136.
6 *The Paston Letters, 1422–1509*, ed. J. Gairdner (3 vols, London, 1872–5), III, p. 404.
7 K. B. McFarlane, *The Nobility of Later Medieval England* (Oxford, 1973), pp. 43–4; S. B. Chrimes, *Henry VII* (London, 1972), pl. 8.
8 *Original Letters Illustrative of English History*, ed. H. Ellis (1st ser., 3 vols, 2nd edn, London, 1825), I, p. 46 (dated by M. K. Jones, 'Henry VII, Lady Margaret Beaufort and the Orléans Ransom', in R. A. Griffiths (ed.), *Kings and Nobles in the Later Middles Ages* (Gloucester, 1986), p. 267); PRO E 101/413/2/3.
9 PRO E 101/414/16, fos. 250–60; E 101/415/3, fos. 275–99; *Calendar of State Papers, Spanish*, I, ed. G. Bergenroth (London, 1862), no. 210.
10 *Bacon's History*, p. 218; I. Arthurson, 'The King's Voyage into Scotland: The War That Never Was', in D. T. Williams (ed.), *England in the Fifteenth Century*, (Woodbridge, 1987), p. 12.
11 *Calendar of State Papers, Spanish*, I, p. 202.
12 *Calendar of State Papers, Spanish*, I, p. 401: *Calendar of State Papers, Milan (1385–1618)*, ed. A. B. Hinds (London, 1912), no. 618; R. L. Storey, *The Reign of Henry VII* (London, 1968), pp. 62–5, is rightly dismissive of 'flights of Bacon's fancy'.

13 *Calendar of State Papers, Spanish*, I, p. 552; PRO E 36/214, fo. 85ᵛ.

14 PRO E 101/414/6, fo. 25ᵛ; R. Somerville, *History of the Duchy of Lancaster*, I, 1265–1603 (London, 1953), p. 269.

15 PRO E 101/414/16, fos. 10–51.

16 S. Anglo, 'The Court Festivals of Henry VII: A Study Based on the Account Books of John Heron, Treasurer of the Chamber', *Bulletin of the John Rylands Library*, 43 (1960–1), p. 14; *The History of the King's Works*, vol. III, ed. H. M. Colvin (London, 1975), p. 258; Essex Record Office, D/DPr 139.

17 *The Antiquarian Repertory*, ed. F. Grose and T. Astle (4 vols, London, 1807–9), II, p. 316.

18 PRO E 101/415/3, fo. 58ʳ; *A Relation, or Rather a True Account, of the Island of England*, ed. C. A. Sneyd (Camden Soc. vol. 37; London, 1847), pp. 46–7.

19 Anglo, 'Court Festivals', p. 29; J. R. Lander, 'Bonds, Coercion and Fear: Henry VII and the Peerage', in his *Crown and Nobility, 1450–1509* (London, 1976), pp. 286–8.

20 R. Horrox, *Richard III: A Study of Service* (Cambridge, 1989), pp. 250–1.

21 PRO E 404/86/3/33; E 404/86/1/28.

22 PRO E 404/86/3/17.

23 *Original Letters*, I, p. 40; A. Cameron, 'A Nottinghamshire Quarrel in the Reign of Henry VII', *Bulletin of the Institute of Historical Research*, 45 (1972), pp. 35–6; Cameron, 'Complaint and Reform in Henry VII's Reign: The Origins of the Statute of 3 Henry VII c. 2?', *Bulletin of the Institute of Historical Research*, 51 (1978), pp. 83–9; Chrimes, *Henry VII*, pp. 208–16.

24 *Plumpton Correspondence*, ed. T. Stapleton (Camden Soc. 4; London, 1839), pp. cii–cxix; M. R. Horowitz, 'Richard Empson, Minister of Henry VII', *Bulletin of the Institute of Historical Research*, 55 (1982), pp. 41–9; C. J. Harrison, 'The Petition of Edmund Dudley', *English Historical Review*, 87 (1972), p. 85; S. J. Gunn, *Charles Brandon, Duke of Suffolk, c. 1484–1545* (Oxford, 1988), pp. 217–19.

25 Condon, Chapter 11; C. Ross, *Richard III* (London, 1981), pp. 105–12; J. C. Wedgwood, *History of Parliament: Biographies of the Members of the Commons House, 1439–1509* (London, 1936), pp. 237–8, 398–9, 433–4, 477–8, 613–14, 740–1, 884, 889–90, 894, 933–4; W. E. Hampton, 'Sir Thomas Montgomery, K. G.', in J. Petre (ed.), *Richard III, Crown and People* (Gloucester, 1985), pp. 149–55.

26 D. A. L. Morgan, 'The House of Policy: The Political Role of the Late Plantagenet Household, 1422–1485', in D. R. Starkey (ed.), *The English Court from the Wars of the Roses to the Civil War* (London, 1987), pp. 55–70.

27 *Paston Letters and Papers of the Fifteenth Century*, ed. N. Davis (2 vols, Oxford, 1971–6), I, p. 668; E. W. Ives, *The Common Lawyers of Pre-Reformation England: Thomas Kebell: A Case Study* (Cambridge, 1983), pp. 375–6; S. T. Bindoff, History of Parliament: *The House of Commons, 1509–1558* (3 vols, London, 1982), I., pp. 568–70.

28 PRO LC 2/1, fo. 4ʳ; J. Skelton, *The Complete English Poems*, ed. J. Scattergood (Harmondsworth, 1983), pp. 46–61; G. Walker, *John Skelton and the Politics of the 1520s* (Cambridge, 1988), pp. 10–13; A. R. Heiserman, *Skelton and Satire* (Chicago, 1961), pp. 14–65.

29 Condon, Chapter 11.

30 *CPR 1485–94* (London, 1914), p. 23; *A Collection of Ordinances and Regulations for the Government of the Royal Household* (Society of Antiquaries; London, 1790), pp. 109–16, 118; S. J. Gunn, 'Chivalry and the Politics of the Early Tudor Court', in S. Anglo (ed.), *Chivalry in the Renaissance* (Woodbridge, 1990), p. 119. See also S. J. Gunn, 'Sir Thomas Lovell: A New Man in a New Monarchy?', in J. L. Watts (ed.), *The End of the Middle Ages?* (Stroud, forthcoming).

31 Chrimes, Henry VII, p. 111; PRO E 101/415/3.

32 Condon, Chapter 11; R. Virgoe, 'Sir John Risley (1443–1512), Courtier and Councillor', *Norfolk Archaeology*, 38 (1982), pp. 140–8; M. M. Condon, 'An Anachronism with Intent? Henry VII's Council Ordinance of 1491/2', in Griffiths (ed.), *Kings and Nobles*, p. 231.

33 Condon, Chapter 11; Horowitz, 'Richard Empson', pp. 42–3.

34 PRO E 36/214, fos. 114ᵛ, 137ᵛ, 150ʳ.

35 *The Reign of Henry VII from Contemporary Sources*, ed. A. F. Pollard (3 vols, London, 1913–14), I, 152–3.
36 Condon, Chapter 11; P. R. Gaussin, *Louis XI, un roi entre deux mondes* (Paris, 1976), pp. 143–4, 408; W. Paravicini, *Guy de Brimeu. Der burgundische Staat und seine adlige Führungsschicht unter Karl dem Kühnen* (Bonn, 1975); D. A. L. Morgan, 'The King's Affinity in the Polity of Yorkist England', *Transactions of the Royal Historical Society*, 5th ser., 23 (1973), pp. 19–21: Horrox, *Richard III*, pp. 220–2; Gunn, *Charles Brandon*; D. Willen, *John Russell, First Earl of Bedford* (London, 1981).
37 *A Collection of Ordinances*, pp. 109–33; A. R. Myers, *The Household of Edward IV: The Black Book and the Ordinance of 1478* (Manchester, 1959), pp. 104–6; *Letters and Papers Illustrative of the Reigns of Richard III and Henry VII*, ed. J. Gairdner (2 vols, Rolls Ser. 24; London, 1861–3), I, p. 232.
38 *Letters and Papers*, I, p. 232.
39 Wedgwood, *History of Parliament: Biographies*, pp. 259–60; Arthurson, 'The King's Voyage into Scotland', p. 10. See also D. A. Luckett, 'Crown Patronage and Political Morality in Early Tudor England: The Case of Giles, Lord Daubeney', *English Historical Review*, 110 (1995), pp. 578–95.
40 *Select Cases in the Council of Henry VII*, ed. C. G. Bayne and W. H. Dunham (Selden Soc. 75; London, 1964), p. xxxv.
41 *Literae cantuarienses*, vol. III, ed. J. B. Sheppard (Rolls Ser. 85; London, 1889), p. 336.
42 PRO E 101/415/3, fos. 25ᵛ, 43ʳ, 83ᵛ; E 36/214, fos. 9ᵛ, 59ᵛ, 111ᵛ; BL Add. MS 59899, fo. 57ᵛ.
43 PRO E 101/414/16, fo. 49ᵛ; E 101/415/3, fos. 48ʳ, 59ᵛ, 87ʳ, 90ʳ, 97ʳ; E 36/214, fos. 8ʳ, 56ʳ, 102ʳ⁻ᵛ, 113ʳ; *Memorials*, pp. 115–16; E. Law, *The History of Hampton Court Palace in Tudor Times* (London, 1885), p. 16; *CPR 1485–94*, p. 124.
44 HMC, *Various Collections*, vol. II (HMC, 55; London, 1903), p. 334; *Calendar of State Papers, Milan*, no. 550.
45 *Calendar of State Papers, Spanish, Supplement*, ed. G. A. Bergenroth (London, 1868), p. 131; *The Great Chronicle of London*, ed. A. H. Thomas and I. D. Thornley (London, 1938), p. 258.
46 HMC, *Various Collections*, II, p. 327; PRO E 101/414/16, fos. 253ᵛ, 258ᵛ; E101/415/3, fos. 283ʳ, 285ʳ.
47 PRO E 101/414/16, fo. 253ʳ.
48 PRO E 101/415/3, fo. 282ᵛ.
49 PRO E 101/414/16, fos. 225ᵛ, 240ʳ.
50 Condon, Chapter 11.
51 PRO PROB 11/16/16.
52 *Memorials*, pp. 117–19; PRO PROB 11/16/16; J. Stow, *A Survey of London*, ed. C. L. Kingsford (2 vols, Oxford, 1908), II, p. 110; W. H. Dunham, *Lord Hastings' Indentured Retainers, 1461–1483* (Transactions of the Connecticut Academy of Arts and Sciences, 39; 1955), p. 18; Gunn, *Charles Brandon*, p. 222.
53 Myers, *Household of Edward IV*, p. 199.
54 BL Add. MS 7099, fos. 5ʳ, 9ʳ, 19ʳ, 24ʳ, 26ʳ; PRO E 101/414/6, fos. 5ʳ, 10ʳ, 28ʳ; E 101/414/16, fos. 10ᵛ, 17ᵛ, 28ᵛ, 31ᵛ, 53ᵛ; E 101/415/3, fos. 44ʳ, 67ᵛ, 104ʳ; BL Add. MS 59899, fos. 4ʳ, 23ᵛ, 45ᵛ, 49ᵛ; Add. MS 21480, fos. 16ʳ, 23ʳ; PRO E 36/214, fos. 24ʳ, 63ᵛ, 95ʳ, 100ᵛ, 140ʳ; *Materials for a History of the Reign of Henry VII*, ed.W. Campbell (2 vols, Rolls Ser. 60; London, 1873–7), I, p. 327.
55 W. R. B. Robinson, 'Early Tudor Policy towards Wales: The Acquisition of Lands and Offices in Wales by Charles Somerset, Earl of Worcester', *Bulletin of the Board of Celtic Studies*, 20 (1964), pp. 421–7.
56 *Select Cases in the Council of Henry VII*, pp. 33–46; *Memorials*, pp. 107, 288, 292, 295.
57 BL Add. MS 7099, fo. 26ʳ; *Antiquarian Repertory*, IV, p. 655.
58 PRO E 101/413/2/3, fo. 37ᵛ; E 101/415/3, fo. 285ʳ; BL Add. MS 21480, fo. 155ᵛ (Willoughby).

59 *CPR 1485–94*, pp. 129, 228; PRO E 101/412/19, fo. 30[r]; *Materials*, II, p. 179; D. R. Starkey, 'The King's Privy Chamber, 1485–1547' (Cambridge Univ. Ph.D. thesis, 1973), pp. 55–7.
60 BL Add. MS 7099, fo. 21[r]; PRO E 101/414/6, fos. 16[v], 17[r], 21[r]; E 101/415/3, fos. 76[r], 83[r]; E 36/214, fos. 136[r], 152[r].
61 PRO E 101/414/16, fo. 46[r].
62 Somerville, *History of the Duchy of Lancaster*, pp. 466, 546, 549, 560; *Thirty-Seventh Report of the Deputy Keeper of the Public Records* (London, 1876), p. 660; *List of Sheriffs* (PRO Lists and Indexes, vol. IX; London, 1898), p. 128; *CPR 1494–1509* (London, 1916), p. 552.
63 *CPR 1494–1509*, p. 496; BL Add. MS 21480, fos. 32[v], 35[v], 39[v], 96[r]; PRO E 101/413/2/3, fos. 28[v], 102[r]; E 101/414/16, fo. 237[v]; E 101/415/3, fo. 147[v].
64 PRO E 101/414/16, fo. 224[v]; E 101/415/3, fos. 195[r], 212[v]; *Calendar of Institutions by the Chapter of Canterbury Sede Vacante*, ed. C. E. Woodruff and I. J. Churchill (Kent Archaeological Soc., Records Branch, 8; 1924), p. 62.
65 G. W. Bernard, 'The Rise of Sir William Compton, Early Tudor Courtier', *English Historical Review*, 96 (1981), pp. 754–77; E. W. Ives, 'Court and County Palatine in the Reign of Henry VIII: The Case of William Brereton of Malpas', *Transactions of the Historic Society of Lancashire and Cheshire*, 123 (1972), pp. 1–38.
66 PRO, DL 5/2, fo. 27[r]; *CCR 1500–9* (London, 1963), no. 24.
67 PRO DL 5/2, fos. 107[v], 127[v]; DL 5/4, fos. 29[r], 31[v], 37[v], 146[r], 146[v], 149[v]; E 101/415/3, fo. 263[v]; Condon, Chapter 11.
68 PRO E 36/214, fos. 17[r], 161[v].
69 BL Add. MS 59899, fo. 97[r]; PRO E 101/415/3, fo. 80[r].
70 BL Add. MS 21480, fo. 96[r]; PRO E 101/413/2/3, fo. 22[r]; cf. E 101/414/16, fo. 237[v].
71 PRO DL 5/2, fo. 127[v]; C 1/325/4.
72 *Great Chronicle*, pp. 337, 365; E. W. Ives, 'Patronage at the Court of Henry VII: The Case of Sir Ralph Egerton of Ridley', *Bulletin of the John Rylands Library*, 52 (1969–70), p. 350.
73 *Great Chronicle*, p. 365.
74 Condon, Chapter 11; I. Arthurson, 'A Question of Loyalty', *The Ricardian*, 7 (1987), p. 402; P. Holmes, 'The Great Council in the Reign of Henry VII', *English Historical Review*, 101 (1986), pp. 840–62.
75 Condon, Chapter 11; *Memorials*, p. 125; *Letters and Papers*, I, p. 371; HMC, *Various Collections*, II, pp. 34, 38, 40, 49–50; *Plumpton Correspondence*, p. 95.
76 B. J. Harris, *Edward Stafford, Third Duke of Buckingham, 1478–1521* (Stanford, Calif., 1986), pp. 41–3, 155–60.
77 He was Lord Steward by February 1505 at the latest: Lincolnshire Archives Office, Bishops' Register 23, fo. 252[v]. Broke died in Aug. 1502.
78 *Memorials*, pp. 115, 303; Anglo, 'Court Festivals', pp. 40–1; *Letters and Papers*, I, p. 370; 'The Spouselles of the Princess Mary', ed. J. Gairdner, in *The Camden Miscellany*, vol. IX (Camden Soc. new ser. 53; London, 1895), pp. 7–8; Somerville, *History of the Duchy of Lancaster*, pp. 541, 546, 549.
79 *Joannis Lelandi Collectanea*, ed. T. Hearne (6 vols, Oxford, 1774), IV, pp. 238–55; S. J. Gunn, 'Henry Bourchier, Earl of Essex', in G. W. Bernard (ed.), *The Tudor Nobility* (Manchester, 1992), pp. 135–7.
80 Anglo, 'Court Festivals', pp. 30, 36.
81 Lander, 'Bonds, Coercion and Fear', p. 288; PRO E 101/414/16, fo. 53[v]; E 101/415/3, fo. 11[v]; *CPR 1494–1509*, p. 223.
82 PRO E 101/415/3, fo. 291[v].
83 PRO C 24/29, Suffolk v. Powes, deposition of Walter, Viscount Hereford.
84 PRO E 404/85/2/86.
85 *Memorials*, pp. 106, 111; Gunn, 'Chivalry and the Politics of the Early Tudor Court', p. 111; PRO E 36/214, fo. 9[v].
86 Lincolnshire Archives Office, Bishops' Register 24, fos. 254[r]–258[v].
87 Harris, *Edward Stafford*, pp. 53–4.
88 Harris, *Edward Stafford*, pp. 52–3; G. E. Cockayne, *The Complete Peerage*, ed. V. Gibbs *et al.* (13 vols, London, 1910–59), XII, ii, pp. 734–9.

89 BL Add. MS 21480, fos. 114r, 126r; Harris, *Edward Stafford*, pp. 53–4.
90 Condon, Chapter 11; PRO E 101/414/16, fos. 52r, 58r; E 101/415/3, fo. 41v.
91 Chrimes, *Henry VII*, p. 117; PRO E 101/413/2/2, fos. 19v, 22v, 23r, 24r, 25v, 27v, 29r, 39r; E 101/415/3, fo. 295r.
92 *Privy Purse Expenses of Queen Elizabeth of York*, ed. N. H. Nicolas (London, 1830), *passim* I, i, 20. See *infra* for Francis Marzen, Hugh Denis, and Richard Weston.
93 S. B. Chrimes, 'Sir Roland de Veleville', *Welsh History Review*, 3 (1967), pp. 287–9 (I am grateful to Mr W. R. B. Robinson for allowing me to read before publication his paper 'Sir Roland de Veleville and the Tudor Dynasty: A Reassessment', *Welsh History Review*, 15 (1991), pp. 351–67); PRO E 404/86/3, unnumbered.
94 PRO E 404/85/1/31; PROB 11/25/26; *CPR, 1494–1509*, p. 47; PRO E 101/415/3, fo. 17r, shows him not at Court, but somewhere in the south-east.
95 PRO E 101/414/6, fos. 56r, 56v, 58r; E 101/414/16, fos. 9r, 13r, 33r, 39v; E 36/214, fo. 14r; BL Add. MS 21480, fo. 39r.
96 PRO E 36/214, fo. 137v.
97 *Great Chronicle*, p. 311; PRO E 101/414/16, fos. 21v, 49v, 66r. On his continuing involvement with Brittany, see J. M. Currin, 'Pierre le Pennec, Henry VII of England, and the Breton Plot of 1492: A Case Study in "Diplomatic Pathology"', *Albion*, 23 (1991), pp. 4, 16.
98 BL Add. MS 59899, fo. 43v; *CPR, 1485–94*, pp. 238, 451, 464.
99 PRO E 404/85/1/31, 2/24, 2/97; E 404/86/2/20, 3/17, 3/33.
100 *CPR 1485–94*, p. 80; *Materials*, I, pp. 179–83; D. Hay, *Polydore Vergil: Renaissance Historian and Man of Letters* (Oxford, 1952), p. 198.
101 *CPR, 1485–94*, p. 192; *Materials*, I, p. 77; Somerville, *History of the Duchy of Lancaster*, p. 560.
102 *Memorials*, pp. 102–7, 112, 126; PRO E 36/214, fos. 105v, 116r, 125r, 130v.
103 PRO PROB 11/17/18.
104 *CPR, 1485–94*, p. 316; A. R. Wagner, *Heralds and Heraldry in the Middle Ages* (2nd edn, Oxford, 1956), p. 80.
105 *CCR 1485–1500* (London, 1953), nos. 731, 733; *Complete Peerage*, VI, pp. 621–2.
106 PRO E 101/414/6, fo. 58r.
107 *Letters and Papers*, II, p. 89; BL Add. MS 59899, fo. 77v; *Memorials*, pp. 105, 123.
108 PRO C67/93, m. 1; PROB 11/25/40; *CCR 1500–09*, no. 291; B. Harvey, *Westminster Abbey and its Estates in the Middle Ages* (Oxford, 1977), p. 385.
109 Morgan, 'The House of Policy', pp. 43–7.
110 Starkey, 'King's Privy Chamber', pp. 17–55; Starkey, 'Intimacy and Innovation: The Rise of the Privy Chamber, 1485–1547', in Starkey (ed.), *The English Court*, pp. 72–7. The latter suggests 1495 as the date for the change, but this might perhaps be doubted, as the Household ordinance of 1493 already mentioned a Privy Chamber, and the financial role of the Grooms of the Privy Chamber had commenced by the earlier 1490s: *A Collection of Ordinances*, p. 109; PRO E 101/413/2/2, fos. 52v, 56v, 57v, 63v.
111 Starkey, 'King's Privy Chamber', pp. 358–62; Anglo, 'Court Festivals', p. 32; BL Add. MS 59899, fo. 70v.
112 Starkey, 'King's Privy Chamber', pp. 37, 47, 52–3; *Calendar of State Papers, Milan*, no. 550 (cf. PRO E 101/414/16, fo. 8v): BL Add. MS 59899, fo. 77v; PRO E 101/414/16, fos. 4r, 7r, 21r, 28r-v, 34r, 52r; T. Rymer and R. Sanderson (eds), *Foedera, conventiones, literae et cujuscunque generis acta publica* (20 vols, London, 1704–35), XII, pp. 698–9, 732–4, 749–50, 767–9; XIII, pp. 28–9; PRO SC 1/58/52.
113 D. R. Starkey, 'Representation through Intimacy', in I. Lewis (ed.), *Symbols and Sentiments: Cross-Cultural Studies in Symbolism* (London, 1977), pp. 187–224.
114 *Letters and Papers*, I, p. 399.
115 *Letters and Papers*, II, p. 89; PRO E 101/414/6, fo. 58r.
116 *Calendar of State Papers, Spanish*, I, p. 204.
117 Gunn, 'Chivalry and the Politics of the Early Tudor Court', p. 123; F. H. Cripps-Day, *The History of the Tournament in England and in France* (London, 1918), pp. xlvi–lv;

The Great Tournament Roll of Westminster, ed. S. Anglo (2 vols, Oxford, 1968), I, 20, 36 n., 46 n., 95; Anglo, 'Court Festivals', pp. 36, 40; *Calendar of State Papers, Spanish*, I, p. 278; *Great Chronicle*, p. 313; *Letters and Papers*, I, pp. 394–402.

118 Kipling, *Triumph of Honour*, pp. 72–3; Anglo, *Spectacle, Pageantry, and Early Tudor Policy*, pp. 92–4; *History of the King's Works*, III, pp. 207, 312, 314; IV (London, 1982), pp. 78–9, 286, 344, 349; *Letters and Papers*, I, pp. 405–6, 413, 416; Anglo, 'Court Festivals', p. 37.

119 PRO E 101/414/16, fo. 259ᵛ; E 101/415/3, fos. 279ᵛ, 293ᵛ.

120 *Materials*, I, pp. 165, 233, 327, 337, 441; II, pp. 83, 85, 297, 437; BL Add. MS 7099, fos. 16ʳ, 21ʳ; Add. MS 21480, fo. 171ᵛ; *CPR 1494–1509*, pp. 85, 201.

121 BL Add. MS 21480, fo. 181ʳ. On Grey, see *infra*.

122 Rymer and Sanderson, *Foedera*, XII, pp. 329, 348, 351, 352, 353, 403, 417, 511, 682, 695; XIII, pp. 35–6; *Memorials*, p. 125.

123 BL Add. MS 59899, fo. 3ʳ; PRO E 101/414/16, fos. 31ᵛ, 77ʳ; E 101/415/3, fo. 67ᵛ; *Original Letters*, ed. Ellis (2nd ser., 4 vols, London, 1827), I, pp. 167–8.

124 PRO E 101/414/6, fo. 62ʳ; E 101/415/3, fos. 7ʳ, 56ᵛ, 96ᵛ; *Letters and Papers*, II, pp. 340–62.

125 BL Add. MS 59899, fos. 61ʳ, 64ᵛ, 71ʳ, 76ᵛ, 77ᵛ; PRO E 36/214, fos. 88ᵛ, 95ʳ, 98ʳ, 102ʳ, 116ʳ.

126 PRO E 101/415/3, fo. 67ᵛ; BL Add. MS 59899, fo. 4ʳ; Add. MS 21480, fos. 23ʳ, 129ᵛ.

127 *Memorials*, pp. 184, 194–5.

128 *Memorials*, p. 101; PRO E 101/414/6, fos. 77ʳ, 78ʳ.

129 *Memorials*, pp. 101, 223–81; *Letters and Papers*, I, pp. 293–300; *Calendar of State Papers, Spanish*, I, pp. 479–99; R. Wellens, 'Un épisode des relations entre l'Angleterre et les Pays-Bas au début du xvi siècle: Le projet de mariage entre Marguerite d'Autriche et Henri VII', *Revue d'histoire moderne et contemporaine*, 29 (1982), pp. 281, 283; PRO E 36/214, fos. 42ʳ, 50ʳ; PROB 11/16/12; *CPR 1485–94*, pp. 332, 378, 386, 469; *CPR 1494–1509*, pp. 38, 83, 142, 267, 501, 525.

130 *Memorials*, pp. 102, 122–3, 282–303; 'The Spouselles of the Princess Mary', p. 6; J. Anstis, *The Register of the Most Noble Order of the Garter* (2 vols, London, 1724), I, p. 257.

131 *Calendar of State Papers, Spanish*, I, pp. 198, 203; *Correspondencia de Gutierre Gomez de Fuensalida*, ed. Duque de Berwick y de Alba (Madrid, 1907), p. 419; *Memorials*, p. 112; *Calendar of State Papers, Milan*, no. 614.

132 *Great Chronicle*, p. 251.

133 Morgan, 'King's Affinity', p. 13; Horrox, *Richard III*, pp. 227–33; *LP* I, i, 20: J. A. Guy, 'Wolsey and the Tudor Polity', in S. J. Gunn and P. G. Lindley (eds), *Cardinal Wolsey: Church, State and Art* (Cambridge, 1991), pp. 66–70.

134 K. Dockray, 'The Political Legacy of Richard III in Northern England', in Griffiths, *Kings and Nobles*, pp. 205–14; Condon, Chapter 11; M. E. James, 'A Tudor Magnate and the Tudor State: Henry, Fifth Earl of Northumberland', in his *Society, Politics and Culture: Studies in Early Modern England* (Cambridge, 1987), pp. 66–7.

135 Skelton, *Complete English Poems*, p. 56.

136 PRO SC 1/52/46.

137 PRO KB 9/437/69; *Calendar of State Papers, Spanish, Supplement*, p. 22.

138 P. W. Fleming, 'The Hautes and their "Circle": Culture and the English Gentry', in D. T. Williams (ed.), *England in the Fifteenth Century: Proceedings of the 1986 Harlaxton Symposium* (Woodbridge, 1987), pp. 85–102; PRO E 36/214, fo. 136ʳ; STAC 2/7/214; *Testamenta Eboracensia*, vol. IV, ed. J. Raine (Surtees Soc. 53; London, 1869), pp. 311–14.

139 Gunn, 'Chivalry and the Politics of the Early Tudor Court', pp. 120–1.

140 *Letters and Papers*, I, p. 235.

141 PRO PROB 2/199, m. 5.

142 PRO SC 1/60/88; E. W. Ives, 'Crime, Sanctuary and Royal Authority under Henry VIII: The Exemplary Sufferings of the Savage Family', in M. S. Arnold *et al.* (eds), *On the Laws and Customs of England: Essays in Honour of Samuel E. Thorne* (Chapel Hill, 1981), pp. 304–11.

143 *Memorials*, pp. 200–3.
144 *Letters and Papers*, I, p. 181.
145 BL Stowe MS 440, fo. 79ʳ; *Materials*, II, pp. 104, 128.
146 *Select Cases in the Council of Henry VII*, pp. 31, 37; *CCR 1500–9*, nos 304, 559.
147 A. J. Eagleston, *The Channel Islands under Tudor Government, 1485–1642* (Cambridge, 1949), pp. 7–9, 16–32; S. J. Gunn, 'The Regime of Charles, Duke of Suffolk, in North Wales and the Reform of Welsh Government, 1509–25', *Welsh History Review*, 12 (1985), pp. 467–9; M. E. James, 'At a Crossroads of the Political Culture: The Essex Revolt, 1601', in his *Society, Politics and Culture*, pp. 424–32.
148 PRO SC 1/51/179.
149 I am grateful to Dr Christine Carpenter for this point.
150 *Plumpton Correspondence*, p. xcviii; Condon, Chapter 11; Horowitz, 'Richard Empson', p. 44: *Letters and Papers*, II, p. 86.
151 PRO E 404/86/3/14.
152 PRO C 1/286/85; *Pleadings and Depositions in the Duchy Court of Lancaster, Time of Henry VII and Henry VIII*, ed. H. Fishwick (Record Soc. of Lancashire and Cheshire, 32; 1896), p. 36.
153 PRO E 101/414/6, fo. 62ʳ.
154 PRO E 404/85/1/92; E 101/412/19, fos. 29ᵛ–30ʳ; E 101/413/9, fo. 31ʳ⁻ᵛ; E 101/415/4, fo. 32ʳ⁻ᵛ.
155 BL Add. MS 21480, fos. 94ʳ, 164ʳ; PRO E 404/82–86, *passim*; E 404/85/1/79, for £22 to Veleville.
156 PRO E 404/85/2/78; E 404/84/2, unnumbered, 3, unnumbered; E 404/85/2/111, to Christopher Garneys, mostly in his native Suffolk.
157 M. Hicks, 'Attainder, Resumption and Coercion, 1461–1529', *Parliamentary History*, 3 (1984), p. 21; BL Lansdowne MS 127, fo. 34ʳ⁻ᵛ; PRO SC 12/18/58.
158 Horowitz, 'Richard Empson', p. 39; M. M. Condon, 'From Caitiff and Villain to Pater Patriae: Reynold Bray and the Profits of Office', in M. A. Hicks (ed.), *Profit, Piety and the Professions in Later Medieval England* (Gloucester, 1990), pp. 137–68 (I am grateful to Miss Condon for a pre-publication copy of this paper); *CCR 1500–9*, nos 273, 282, 567, 616, 726, 732, 759, 842.
159 G. W. Bernard, 'The Fortunes of the Greys, Earls of Kent, in the Early Sixteenth Century', *Historical Journal*, 25 (1982), pp. 672–8; *Memorials*, p. 122.
160 A. Cameron, 'Sir Henry Willoughby of Wollaton', *Transactions of the Thoroton Society*, 74 (1970), p. 11.
161 *Victoria County History, Hertfordshire*, vol. III (1912), p. 356; Starkey, 'King's Privy Chamber', p. 44; *Complete Peerage*, II, p. 135, V, p. 510.
162 BL Add. MS 21480, fos. 178ʳ, 184ʳ.
163 Ives, *Common Lawyers*, pp. 85–6.
164 BL Add. MS 21480, fos. 173ʳ, 180ʳ; *CPR 1494–1509*, p. 314.
165 *CPR 1494–1509*, pp. 343, 412, 416, 525, 585.
166 PRO E 211/29; cf. M. Howard, *The Early Tudor Country House: Architecture and Politics, 1490–1550* (London, 1987), p. 30.
167 *CPR 1494–1509*, pp. 343, 356; BL Add. MS 59899, fo. 67ᵛ; PRO E36/214, fo. 42ʳ; E 211/291.
168 *CPR 1494–1509*, pp. 416, 446, 500; Wedgwood, *History of Parliament: Biographies*, pp. 167–8, 680–1; PRO SC 1/52/44.
169 R. L. Storey, 'England: Ämterhandel im 15. und 16. Jahrhundert', in I. Mieck (ed.), *Ämterhandel im Spätmittelalter und im 16. Jahrhundert* (Historische Kommission zu Berlin, 45, 1984), pp. 202–4.
170 *CPR 1494–1509*, pp. 142, 591; BL Add. MS 21480, fo. 60ʳ.
171 PRO E 101/414/16, fo. 257ʳ; BL Add. MS 21480, fos. 180ᵛ, 189ʳ, 190ʳ.
172 *Plumpton Correspondence*, p. cxiii.
173 HMC, *Various Collections*, II, p. 317; *Letters and Papers*, II, p. 57; PRO SC 1/52/46.
174 *Bacon's History*, pp. 217–18.
175 Storey, *Reign of Henry VII*, p. 83; A. B. Emden, *A Biographical Register of the University of Oxford to* AD *1500* (3 vols, Oxford, 1959), III, p. 1594; PRO E

101/43/2/2, fo. 83^r; E 101/414/16, fo. 208^r; E 101/413/2/3, fo. 44^r; *Reign of Henry VII from Contemporary Sources*, ed. Pollard, I, pp. 222–3; J. Gairdner and I. S. Leadam, 'A Supposed Conspiracy against Henry VII', *Transactions of the Royal Historical Society*, new ser. 18 (1904), pp. 179–80; *Memorials*, p. 100; Lincolnshire Archives Office, Bishops' Register 23, fo. 211^v; M. J. Kelly, 'Canterbury Jurisdiction and Influence during the Episcopate of William Warham, 1503–32' (Cambridge Univ. Ph.D. thesis, 1963), pp. 105–9; *The Reports of Sir John Spelman*, ed. J. H. Baker (2 vols, Selden Soc., 93–94; London, 1977–8), II, p. 391; Condon, Chapter 11.

176 S. R. Gammon, *Statesman and Schemer: William, First Lord Paget – Tudor Minister* (Newton Abbot, 1973), pp. 180–3; Lockyer, *Buckingham*, pp. 36–7; C. S. R. Russell, *Parliaments and English Politics, 1621–1629* (Oxford, 1979), pp. 107–13, 199–202. Courtenay and Dorset were friends of Suffolk: *Letters and Papers*, I, p. 226.

177 W. A. J. Archbold, 'Sir William Stanley and Perkin Warbeck', *English Historical Review*, 14 (1899), pp. 529–34; G. R. Elton, 'Thomas Cromwell's Decline and Fall', in his *Studies in Tudor and Stuart Politics and Government* (3 vols, Cambridge, 1974–83), I, pp. 222–3. For a reassessment of Cromwell's fall, see G. Redworth, *In Defence of the Church Catholic: The Life of Stephen Gardiner* (Oxford, 1990), pp. 105–29.

178 Arthurson, 'A Question of Loyalty', *passim*; PRO DL 5/4, fo. 138^v; Gunn, *Charles Brandon*, p. 40, for apparent cases of malicious denunciation.

179 *Letters and Papers*, I, pp. 234–5; *Great Chronicle*, pp. 344, 347.

180 E. Hall, *Hall's Chronicle* (London, 1809), p. 505; D. R. Starkey, *The Reign of Henry VIII: Personalities and Politics* (London, 1985), p. 35.

181 Cameron, 'Sir Henry Willoughby', pp. 16–17; Wedgwood, *History of Parliament: Biographies*, pp. 565–6; PRO PROB 11/16/16; 'The Last Testament and Inventory of John de Veer, Thirteenth Earl of Oxford', ed. W. H. StJ. Hope, *Archaeologia*, 66 (1915), p. 313; Gunn, *Charles Brandon*, pp. 3–5, 22; *Plumpton Correspondence*, pp. 177–8.

182 P. Clark, *English Provincial Society from the Reformation to the Revolution: Religion, Politics and Society in Kent, 1500–1640* (Hassocks, 1977), pp. 14–16, 61–6; A. Cameron, 'The Giving of Livery and Retaining in Henry VII's Reign', *Renaissance and Modern Studies*, 18 (1974), pp. 31–4; *Select Cases in the Council of Henry VII*, pp. xxix–xxx.

183 *The English Works of John Fisher*, ed. J. E. B. Mayor (Early English Text Soc., extra ser. 27; London, 1876), pp. 271–2.

184 S. J. Gunn, 'The Accession of Henry VIII', *Historical Research*, 64 (1991), pp. 278–88.

185 Gaussin, *Louis XI*, pp. 125–47, 408–11.

7

Court and government

DAVID STARKEY

On 20 October 1529, 'in a certain inner chamber next to the king's closet' at Windsor, Henry VIII applied the great seal to a few documents with his own hands. Among the witnesses were not only the officials of Chancery, who normally handled the business of the great seal, but also 'Henry Norris, Thomas Heneage and others of the Privy Chamber of the said Lord King'.[1]

The sealing, carefully recorded on the close roll, was a calculated drama. It put to rest the claims of the fallen Wolsey to hold the chancellorship and the great seal for life. And it reaffirmed the absolute dependence of the great seal, the most formal and public instrument of government, on the mere will of the personal sovereign, Henry VIII. The King applied the seal in person, in a secret chamber of the palace and in the presence of his private servants.

But as well as providing an epilogue to Wolsey's ministry, the scene at Windsor in 1529 is also a set-piece illustration of Professor Elton's view of medieval government as 'household' government, in which the driving force was the king and his immediate entourage. In the next ten years, however, Professor Elton claimed in *The Tudor Revolution in Government*, there was fundamental change: 'in every sphere of the central government, "household" methods and instruments were replaced by national bureaucratic methods and instruments'. At the same time the household itself, 'driven from the work of administration', became 'a department of state concerned with specialized tasks about the king's person'; in short, it changed from 'medieval household to modern court'.[2] Subsequently Professor Elton has conceded on specific issues. But he has given no ground on the broad principles. Here, therefore, I shall consider the thesis as a whole, but with one important change of approach. In *The Tudor Revolution* Professor Elton tackled the household last, almost as an afterthought. In contrast, I begin with the history of the household; only once that is established do I examine the fate of 'household' government.

The household: from chamber to privy chamber

The servants of the Privy Chamber who attended on the King at the sealing of 1529 were a novelty. The office held by Norris and Heneage was only 10 years old; the department itself no more than 30. Yet in these few decades the Privy Chamber had become the 'principally and most highly to be regarded' department of the household.[3] So our story is not recessional, as the corpse of the medieval household is embalmed into the early modern Court, but a progression, as a household of two departments – Household and Chamber – is replaced by a household of three departments – Household, Chamber, and Privy Chamber.

The initial impetus for change was architectural. The two departments of the medieval household had corresponded to the two main areas of the royal house (or rather houses, for there were at least a dozen). 'Downstairs' was the Hall, where the king's servants ate, and where the service quarters of kitchens, buttery, and the rest, were situated; 'Upstairs' was the king's private apartment or Chamber. The 'Downstairs' servants formed one department, the Household, under the Lord Steward; the 'Upstairs' servants the other, the Chamber, under the Lord Chamberlain. This two-department household assumed its characteristic form under Edward II and Edward III; 100 years later the *Black Book* of Edward IV, which perpetually harks back to 'the statutes of noble Edward III', gave it final polish and systematization.[4]

The apogee was short-lived, however, for the layout of the palace, the rationale of the two-department household, was changing. The King's original apartment, the Chamber, had been – as its name implies – just one room. It was handsomely proportioned, but it was still a bedsit, in which a whole range of often conflicting functions took place. The solution was to add on separate specialized chambers and by the mid-fifteenth century the greater palaces, at least, contained a suite of three rooms. The first two were more or less public reception rooms, but the third, the Secret or Privy Chamber, was the king's own private room, to which in time a whole complex 'privy lodging' – of bedroom, library, study, and so on – was added.[5] The effect of this was to create a division within the Chamber itself as important as the original distinction between Hall and Chamber: on one side of the door of the Privy Chamber lay public ceremonial; on the other, private life. For some time organization lagged behind the changed layout; then Henry VII took the first steps to bring things into line. He restricted the Lord Chamberlain's direct authority to the outer chambers and their routine ceremonies; and he turned the Privy Chamber into a largely autonomous sub-department of the Chamber, with its own staff.[6]

Henry VII, we are told on all sides, 'was not an original mind; he was no great innovator'.[7] Yet in the history of the household the setting-up of the Privy Chamber is arguably the greatest innovation of all. Its full implications, however, lay in the future. At the time it was small beer, a minor adjustment in the inner recesses of the Court that was unknown to most and unremarked by all. It left correspondingly little trace in the record. The personnel of the new department are listed in the accounts of the Wardrobe, which supplied them with clothing; while their activities can be traced through payments to them by the Treasurer of the Chamber. The only coherent account of the department, however, is given in the household Ordinances of about 1495. Of these, no contemporary copy survives, but their text can be recovered thanks to their reissue in 1526, complete with, by then, quite anachronistic clauses, which in turn establish the original date of publication.[8] Round the clauses of the Ordinances the other fragments of information arrange themselves into a reasonably full picture.

The new sub-department was small and modestly staffed. At its head was the Groom of the Stool, whose original and continuing task was to wait on the King when he used the close-stool (the contemporary form of lavatory). Under the Groom were about half a dozen other grooms and a handful of pages, almost all of whom, in so far as they are traceable, were from modest gentry families. This staff, which was a far cry from the pompous establishment of knights and esquires which the Chamber had supplied (at least in theory) to dance attendance on the royal person, carried out the whole range of the King's private service: they dressed and undressed him; waited on him at table; watched over him at night, and kept him supplied with everyday necessaries.

This modest kind of Privy Chamber was adequate for a king like Henry VII. Indeed, it might very well have been the result of deliberate choice. Its servants could exercise none of the direct political pressure of the Court aristocracy; nor was their service surrounded by the time-consuming cere- monial necessarily entailed by the attendance of the high-born. Instead Henry was free to rule and work as he desired.[9] But his son, Henry VIII, though he was determined to rule, was far less eager to work. A different king needed a different sort of Privy Chamber.

So to architecture we must add the royal personality as a force for change. It is important, however, to be clear about both the pace and the nature of what now happened. And the more so since the Privy Chamber of Henry VIII, in contrast to his father's, is almost too richly documented, with two major sets of household regulations: Wolsey's Eltham Ordinances of 1526,[10] and the Cromwellian Ordinances of 1539–40.[11] The natural temp- tation, abetted by the fact that the text of the Eltham Ordinances has been available in print since 1790, is to see the Ordinances as instituting the changes. This fits well both with our modern attitude to legislation and with our general assumption that it was the ministers, Wolsey and Cromwell, who were the fount of all policy. But the evidence tells another story.

The first decade of the reign saw little structural change in the Privy Chamber. On the other hand, there was a revolution in the style of the Court, as Henry VIII's openness and fondness for sport led to the reappear- ance of a creature missing since Edward IV's reign at least, the Court favourite. Only one of the favourites, however, Sir William Compton, was put into the Privy Chamber as Groom of the Stool. For the rest the depart- ment remained much as before.[12] Then in 1518 things began to change. At home, the King's attention had shifted to a new and markedly younger group of favourites, known as the 'minions'; while abroad, a *renversement d'al- liances* brought England into friendship with France. In France there had been parallel developments at Court which had gone further and resulted in actual institutional change. The foreign and the domestic came together with the grand *entrée* of the French embassy into London on 23 September. To give the English minions parity of status with their French colleagues they too needed office. So the French office of 'Gentleman' was added to the Privy Chamber's establishment and conferred on the minions in a body.[13]

Up to this point there is no trace of Wolsey. The changes arose in the long term from the altered demands of Henry VIII's personality and life style; they were triggered by foreign relations and given shape by the King's tendency to imitate slavishly French fashions. But the creation of the office of Gentleman of the Privy Chamber altered the rules of the game. Until then, with the exception of Compton, the officers of the Privy Chamber were men of no consequence; now the department included the minions. They were high-spirited and high-born and intervened as of right in politics (to support France) and patronage (to challenge Wolsey).[14] The minister, who had been used to no rival in influence, now had one. The following May he struck back and procured the exile from Court of the leading minions. To replace them, 'men of greater age, and perhaps of greater repute, but creatures of Cardinal Wolsey' were brought in.[15] This presented something of a problem. Hitherto, office in the Privy Chamber had carried no separate salary, since formally the Privy Chamber remained a mere sub-department of the Chamber, with most of its staff on secondment from the senior department. However, the new appointees were successful careerists, who reasonably expected cash as well as a title. And their claims were reinforced by personal circumstances. Sir William Kingston had received no substantial appointment hitherto, and was clearly in line for something (Wolsey had already thought of him as standard-bearer in 1517[16]); Sir Richard Jerningham had just lost his major existing post with the return of Tournai (where he had been governor) to France in February 1519;[17] while most pressing was the case of Sir Richard Wingfield, who had resigned the governorship of Calais to take up his Privy Chamber office.[18] So first Wingfield, the elder statesman among the new recruits, was feed (on the very day he surrendered his Calais office);[19] then came fees for his three fellow appointees;[20] and finally all the rest of the department were put on wages at amounts carefully graduated according to rank.[21]

The changes of 1518–19 were merely *ad hoc*. There is no evidence whatever of planning before the event, and not much of coordination after it (even Wolsey had struck first for political motives and only wakened up to the problem of fees later). Yet, however piecemeal the reforms were, their effect was to transform the Privy Chamber from a shadowy sub-department into the fully-fledged third department of the Royal Household: much smaller and newer than the Chamber and Household; yet outranking both in prestige, the distinction of its staff, and the level of their remuneration. A Cinderella had become a *corps d'élite*. After all that, there was not much left for the Ordinances of 1526 and 1539–40 to do with the structure of the Royal Household. They conferred the retrospective sanction of legislative respectability on what had already taken place and they dotted i's and crossed t's. Which is not to deny that they had a wider significance. But their importance is fiscal and political, not institutional. Moreover, 1526 and 1540 do not stand in a tradition, with Cromwell delivering what Wolsey had merely promised; rather, they are mirror images. In 1526, in the aftermath of war, Wolsey was struggling for retrenchment and economical reform;[22] in 1539–40, however, the royal coffers were stuffed with the spoils of the monasteries, and Cromwell and his master could afford to be bountiful. Not only was a new royal bodyguard, the band of gentleman pensioners, set up (which Elton himself characterizes as 'useless and spendthrift' and blames on the King[23]), but also supernumeraries were absorbed into the regular establishment and feed; while wages themselves, for the first and last time in the sixteenth century, were brought into line with inflation, with a one-third increase all round.[24]

Politics presents a similar contrast. The Eltham Ordinances were Wolsey's cover for a renewed attempt to purge and neutralize the Privy Chamber. In 1539–40, on the other hand, Cromwell, far from neutralizing the Court, completed its politicization. He had already packed the Privy Chamber with his own supporters and made himself its honorific head as chief nobleman-in-waiting; now, it seems, he intended to consolidate his grip on the whole upper household, Chamber as well as Privy Chamber, by Frenchifying its structure and assuming the ancient office of Lord Great Chamberlain. The powers of this position had usually slumbered in the hands of its more or less hereditary occupants, the de Veres, earls of Oxford. Held by Cromwell, however, its dormant authority would have wakened into an absolute grip on the Court.[25] In 1526 Wolsey's control of the Court was just as absolute. But he had exercised it remotely and quasi-judicially by giving himself as 'the Lord Cardinal and Chancellor of England' powers to conduct a quarterly inquisition into the observance of the Eltham Ordinances.[26] The contrast with Cromwell's direct assumption of high Court office could not be plainer.

Thus neither the substance of household reform, nor its chronology, nor the reasons for it fit with Professor Elton's arguments. The main theme of the household history of these years is the formation of the Privy Chamber. This begins in the 1490s and is complete in essentials by 1519 – long before Wolsey, let alone Cromwell, gave any systematic attention to the household. And the reasons for change are just as unyielding. An astonishing diversity was involved: fashion in building and life style; the royal personality; international affairs; political self-interest; and fiscal necessity. These do not, of course, exclude broader strategic considerations (though they do not leave a great deal of room for them either). And, indeed, some more or less coherent attitudes can be discerned behind ministerial policy. But they are the opposite of what Professor Elton would lead us to expect. It is Wolsey who displays systematic hostility to the Privy Chamber, and Cromwell who packs it with his supporters, assumes its headship in person, and crowns his career with the great chamberlainship.[27] It remains to be seen whether the attitudes of the two ministers to 'household' government follow the same pattern.

Household government

'Household' government was the king's government *par excellence*, and the King naturally chose its agents from the men closest to him. And this, at the beginning of our period, meant that he chose from the Chamber. The

Household had more skilled accountants and administrators, but the Chamber's proximity far outweighed mere professionalism. So when first Edward IV and then, after some hesitations, Henry VII decided on the slap of firm government, many, though not all of the instruments, were officers of the Chamber. In finance the Treasurer of the Chamber quickly became dominant; in the secretariat the King's Secretary, who was also a member of the Chamber, acquired a more erratic importance. The contrasting fates of these two officers have become test cases for our understanding of administrative development. For Professor Elton the decline of the Treasurer and the rise of the Secretary were the surest testimonies of the administrative revolution. But his account of 'household' government left out the history of the household itself, in particular the formation of the Privy Chamber. When that is put back, a very different picture emerges.

From Chamber to Privy Purse

The years 1465 to 1509 were the golden age of the Treasurer of the Chamber. By the end of Henry VII's reign he had reduced the Exchequer, the ancient national treasury, into a satellite. The Exchequer handled only a fifth as much revenue as the Chamber and handed over its surplus to the Treasurer at the year's end. The Treasurer had gained this pre-eminence largely because he had been made receiver-general of the Crown lands. These lands had been massively expanded in the 'land revenue experiment', begun by Edward IV and accomplished by Henry VII, which had turned the crown estates into the chief anchor of national finance.[28] But the Treasurer's importance went further. The move from Exchequer to Chamber meant the replacement of decentralized debit finance with a highly centralized, wholly cash-based fiscal system. This system, the great achievement of the Chamber, survived (as I argue in my Conclusion) the decline of the Chamber in the years after 1529. Here, though, it is the decline itself which must be anatomized. The attack on the Chamber came from two different directions: from without, by the agencies of 'national' finance, and from within, by the Royal Household. The Exchequer launched its first counter-attack in 1509; this narrowly failed,[29] but in the 1530s the Chamber fell before the assault of Cromwell's own personal treasury, on the one hand, and the series of formal revenue courts he set up, on the other. Finally, in 1554, the new courts of the 1530s in turn were absorbed into an expanded Exchequer, which thus reasserted its supremacy over the whole field of finance (save for the surviving outposts of the Duchy of Lancaster and Court of Wards and Liveries).

This external attack provides both the thread of Professor Elton's narrative and the key to his explanation of financial change. But at the same time there was another, insidious undermining of the Chamber from within, or rather from behind. Originally the Treasurer's household department, the Chamber, had provided the King's most private service. But in the 1490s, as we have seen, it lost this task to the Privy Chamber. The consequences for financial administration were immediate. Long before I found an actual reference to the fact, I guessed that one Hugh Denys must have been Groom of the Stool and head of Henry VII's Privy Chamber. This was because of a unique series of entries in the Chamber books of payments. These entries, numbering hundreds, show Denys handling almost the whole financial side of the King's everyday life: he paid out the King's alms, rewards, and gambling debts, and bought minor items of clothing and domestic utensils. At first he was reimbursed item by item; later he tended to present a consolidated bill three or four times a month. The sums involved were insignificant, averaging only about £220 a year. (The Chamber was handling over £100 000 p.a.) But they have an importance out of all proportion to their size. The Treasurer of the Chamber's original function – and the foundation of all his subsequent importance – was the handling of just this class of expenditure. But now another official, the Groom, had interposed himself between the King and the Treasurer.[30]

This was inevitable. The Chamber itself had become relatively distant from the King; at the same time the Treasurer's national responsibilities kept him at Westminster, in his office in the sanctuary,[31] rather than at Court, which might be anywhere. Nor at first was the Treasurer's control really compromised. Not only was the Groom's account small scale; it was also a mere sub-treasury, drawing all its funds from the Chamber. But towards the end of the reign that changed. In September 1508 Sir Edward Belknap was appointed Surveyor of the King's Prerogative, with the task of exploiting to the utmost the King's financial rights as head of the feudal and judicial systems.[32] In the course of the following six months he raised about £450, all of which he paid over (more or less as the money came into his hands) 'to Hugh Denys by the commandment of our said Sovereign Lord'.[33] At the same time Denys's receipts from the Chamber fell sharply, and after January 1509 he was paid nothing at all.[34] In other words, Denys had ceased to be a mere sub-treasurer; and instead of being funded through the Chamber he was now drawing his receipts directly from Belknap.

The independence of the Groom's account, sketched out in the last years of Henry VII, was powerfully advanced in the first years of Henry VIII, with a new king and a new groom, the favourite William Compton. Four-figure sums were paid from the Hanaper (which dealt with the fees collected by Chancery) 'to the use of the King for the time being Henry VIII, in his Chamber that is to say to the hands of William Compton';[35] together with similar amounts from the land revenues administered by the general surveyors.[36] At the same time Chamber payments fell to £27 000 in 1510–11, which was the lowest total since 1495–6, and whole classes of expenditure, such as building and jewels, almost vanished.[37] Compton clearly was going far beyond Denys. He was tapping revenue sources which had gone in their entirety to the Chamber for the previous 20 years; while his payments (it has to be guessed in the absence of accounts) expanded to take in the types of conspicuous expenditure that disappeared from the Chamber.

But this sudden development was equally suddenly checked – probably by Wolsey's rise to power. He feared Compton's influence and could not let him become a major national treasurer. So from 1513 the revenues which the Groom had poached were restored to the Chamber, and the Groom once more drew his funds from the Treasurer. But, despite Wolsey's pruning, the groom's account clearly remained on a much larger scale than it had been under Henry VII. Between 1514, when payments from the Chamber resumed, and 1519 Compton's receipts varied between £18 000 and £20 000 a year.[38] These amounts were too large and too fluctuating for comfort. So Wolsey decided on a more systematic treatment, and put the Groom's account at the head of the programme of government reform he drew up in 1519. First, a ceiling was imposed on Compton's account: he was to receive £10 000 a year from the Chamber, payable in quarterly blocks of £2 500. Second, a line of demarcation between the Chamber and Privy Chamber accounts was laid down: in future, ambassadorial expenses and building costs (many of which had been diverted to Compton) were to be paid only by the Chamber. Finally, provision was made for proper accounting: Compton was to keep duplicate account books, which were to be audited monthly in the King's presence.[39] In one aspect, the 1519 reform programme was merely a cover for Wolsey's expulsion of the minions from the Privy Chamber in May of that year. But there was substance as well. Even Palsgrave, one of Wolsey's bitterest enemies, admitted of the ministerial reforms that 'every of these enterprises was great, and the least of them to our commonwealth much expedient'.[40] Too many of them were dropped once the political pressure was over, but the scheme for the Privy Chamber account was carried out to the letter: the quarterly block payments were handed over on time and the account books, though they do not survive, were certainly kept.[41]

But in a sense Wolsey's victory in 1519 had the opposite effect from what he intended. The measures limiting the Groom's account also conferred official recognition on it. The result was that, when Compton resigned in Wolsey's second purge of the Privy Chamber in 1526, he handed over to his successor, Henry Norris, not only the groomship but also the quasi-office of 'our purse bearer [and] keeper of our everyday moneys'.[42] The actual name of Privy Purse had not quite appeared (and seems not to have done so until the later sixteenth century); otherwise all the essentials of the post of Keeper of the King's Privy Purse were present and fully formed.

Norris's keepership of the Privy Purse (as we can call it by anticipation) began uneventfully, with the Privy Purse remaining pretty much within the guidelines laid down in 1519. Norris's own early account books have disappeared, but two of the running accounts kept by the clerk who actually did the work survive and show that in the last nine months of 1528 Norris handled £3 000. This was £4 500 less than Wolsey had allowed for such a period; on the other hand, the Groom was once more picking up building bills and even starting to make wage payments.[43] Then in 1529 came dramatic change, followed by the most important three years in the history of the Privy Purse. These years coincide with the only surviving Privy Purse account book for Henry VIII's reign.[44] As it happens, the title-page of the book – and hence the name of the accountant – is missing. But fortunately payments noted in the book appear as receipts in other accounts, where they are unambiguously identified as being 'paid and delivered by the hands of Mr Henry Norris Esquire'.[45]

Norris's book covers three years and two months. During this period £53 488 were spent. Three main classes of expenditure can be distinguished: £33 000 went on the King's personal needs (including £5 000 on building, £3 000 on gambling, and no less than £11 000 on jewels); £5 000 on wages for the private household of falconers, fools and the like; and £16 000 on expenditure of state. The incompleteness of the Treasurer of the Chamber's accounts and the method of calendaring them in *Letters and Papers* makes an exact comparison with the Privy Purse almost impossible and certainly impossibly difficult. But we can produce a useful approximation. In the 18 months between 1 October 1529 and 30 April 1531 the Treasurer accounted for an expenditure of £83 500.[46] So in terms of volume the Chamber was still three times the size of the Privy Purse. But its expenditure was made up very differently. Much the largest sum, £35 000 or no less than 42 per cent of the whole, went on wages. The running costs of defence – for the Marches, Calais, and the navy – took up another £11 000. Other items, however – ambassadors (£11 000), goldsmiths (£2 900), and transfer payments (£13 000) – seem only to duplicate the Privy Purse. But the appearance is deceptive. The Chamber met all usual ambassadorial expenses; the Privy Purse paid for Benet's embassy to Rome, which was Henry's last-ditch attempt at a papal solution for the divorce.[47] The Chamber paid goldsmiths for ambassadorial plate, cramp rings, and the King's stereotyped New Year gifts of plate; but the Privy Purse bore the cost of choice silver for Henry's own table. And nothing in the Chamber parallels the Privy Purse's expenditure on secret matters of state, such as the cost of Wolsey's arrest.[48]

Clearly the old Chamber account of Henry VII's reign had been split into two between the Chamber and the Privy Purse. The Chamber was still larger, but its expenditure was overwhelmingly routine. The Privy Purse, in contrast, dealt with the King's wildly fluctuating private expenses, as well as the cost of high policy. Something of this division had long been apparent. But it seems clear that the date when the Privy Purse book begins, November 1529, is of more than accidental significance. In the year 1528–9 the treasurer had disbursed £3 600 on building works; in the 18 months after

November 1529 he spent only £900. In the year before November 1529 he advanced £23 500 to the cofferer of the household; in the 18 months after, only £13 000.[49] The axis date – autumn 1529 – is of course the time of Wolsey's fall. The King, we know, resolved to take the reins of government into his own hands. It now seems as though he took over finance as well, turning for a brief moment the Privy Purse accounts into a pale imitation of his father's Chamber books. (He even managed to bring himself to sign them, if not like his father on every page, at least by the main monthly totals.) So the 'marked and persistent decline in the scope and competence' of the Chamber, which Elton identified, began in 1529 and not 'with Cromwell's ministry'.[50] Moreover, the decline owed everything to long-term developments within the household, on the one hand, and short-term political considerations, on the other. It owed nothing to any structural changes in the theory or practice of government.

Nevertheless, Cromwell has an important part to play in the story. From January 1531 he started to act as an informal royal treasurer, and from 1532 to 1536 he effectively paid for the expenses of his government of England from the funds under his control.[51] Professor Elton saw the minister carving out his position at the expense of the Chamber. In fact the real victim was the Privy Purse. The minister had taken over the funding of high policy – one of the key elements of expenditure in the expanded Privy Purse between 1529 and 1532 – and to pay for it he made deep inroads into the Groom's revenues as well. These, like the Privy Purse itself, underwent major change in 1529. Ever since the temporary emancipation of the first years of Henry VIII's reign, the Privy Purse had been funded by large block payments from the Chamber. These payments cease in June 1529; thereafter the relationship reversed and the Privy Purse replenished the Chamber to the tune of £6 143.[52] Thus, into the place of the Chamber steps another royal treasury, the Privy Coffers.

The Privy Coffers was the collective name for a series of jealously guarded palace treasuries in which cash reserves were kept. The whole subject of the reserves and their administration is deeply obscure. But there are occasional shafts of light. In 1523, for example, the Privy Coffers at Greenwich could pay out £49 000; while the Coffers at Windsor contained at least £3 000 when they appear to have been cleared out in 1530.[53] At first there is no sign of any relationship between these treasuries and the Privy Purse. But, once again with the fall of Wolsey, a new pattern emerged. At the 'fall of the late lord Cardinal', Thomas Alvard, keeper of his palace of Whitehall, was reappointed by the King. As such, he was in charge both of the reconstruction of the palace as Henry's principal residence and, also, of a new deposit treasury. The Whitehall treasury soon eclipsed the rest. Between November 1529 and April 1531 Alvard accounted for £34 000, of which £8 000 was spent on the rebuilding, and £18 000 paid out 'as well to our said sovereign lord's own hands and to others by his Grace's assignment'.[54] Norris received at least £1 000 (and probably much more) of this, as well as the contents of the defunct treasury at Windsor. At the same time, however, Norris paid Alvard £2 000. This sequence of payments and repayments will be familiar to anyone with a bank account. When the current account (Norris) was flush with cash, money was transferred to the deposit account (Alvard); conversely, when Norris was short, he was topped up by Alvard.[55]

So 1529 saw the appearance of an integrated system of direct royal finance, fashioned from two hitherto disparate household agencies, the Privy Purse and the Privy Coffers. Clearly the Privy Coffers must have contained very substantial reserves (between 1527 and 1529, for example, Henry VIII was able to pay Francis I of France £50 000 cash from the King's Coffers).[56] But the Coffers were no widow's cruse of oil. Luckily they were topped up by two sources. Wolsey had contributed to both. Alvard's original funds were no doubt the Cardinal's own confiscated treasures (like the mountains of gold and silver plate catalogued by Cavendish).[57] And thereafter both Alvard and Norris benefited from what the Cardinal, in the last uncertain throw of his diplomacy, had been able to rescue from the wreck of Cambrai. By the treaty signed in August 1529 Francis I undertook to pay both the arrears of the pension originally granted to Edward IV at Picquigny, as well as to redeem Charles V's huge debts to Henry VIII.[58] The need for French support at Rome in the divorce negotiations led Henry to remit large sums; nevertheless, between 1530 and 1532 he was receiving between £20 000 and £50 000 per year clear from France, paid on the nail every six months at Calais in golden crowns of the sun.[59] Much of this certainly circulated through the private financial machine of the Coffers and the Privy Purse: Norris gave orders for the bringing-over of the money from Calais in 1531 and actually received it in 1530;[60] while both he and Alvard frequently dealt in the actual French coins rather than sterling.[61]

The pension was the foundation of royal finance in these years. But it was a foundation built on the shifting sands of chaotic international politics. Here at last Cromwell comes in. The original purpose of his treasurership was, I suspect, to find a more reliable source of revenue by exploiting the king's prerogatives over the Church.[62] And like the first surveyor of the king's (secular) prerogative, Belknap under Henry VII, Cromwell paid much of the early fruits of his labours to the Privy Purse.[63] But Cromwell soon began to spend what he raised, and more, on his own ministerial expenses. The shortfall was made up from the only available source: the Privy Coffers. On 5 October 1532 £20 000 was transferred from the Privy Coffers at Greenwich to a great chest in the Tower, in the charge (principally) of Thomas Audley, the new Keeper of the Great Seal.[64] In the course of the following year Audley paid out all but £1 000 to Cromwell. The minister also received £3 000 from Alvard and, rather circuitously, £2 000 from Norris. That made up £24 000 of the minister's total receipts of £33 000 for the year 1532–3.[65]

In other words, the interlocking system of deposit and current accounts established in 1529 survived, but with a change of personnel. Cromwell substituted his own account for Norris and the Privy Purse, while Audley and the Tower treasury largely replaced the King as dispenser from the Privy Coffers. At first sight this looks like the 'Tudor Revolution' with a vengeance, as minister and bureaucrat displace courtier and king. But there is a more straightforward politico-fiscal explanation. In 1532–3 money was tight, and Cromwell could run government effectively only if his own hand controlled the flow of cash. But the success of his ministry (which can be seen as a dramatic fulfilment of his first brief as what we might call surveyor of the ecclesiastical prerogative) transformed the financial situation from penny-pinching to affluence. With affluence Cromwell's hostility to the household evaporated. The Privy Purse never resumed its role in national finance (it was in any case only the crisis of 1529 which had propelled it onto the public stage). But the Privy Coffers grew ever larger. From 1536 the Coffers took £178 000 from Augmentations, £96 000 from parliamentary taxation, £28 000 from the jewel house, and £60 000 from First Fruits and Tenths. This totals £362 000 and is by no means exhaustive. The proportions are as impressive as the gross figures: between 1536 and 1539 half the yield of Augmentations; in 1540–1 half of the subsidy, and in 1542–3 no less than 80 per cent of it.[66] Most of these sums finished up in the charge of Sir Anthony Denny, Chief Gentleman of the Privy Chamber and Alvard's successor as the keeper of Whitehall and its deposit treasury. Denny's book of receipts has survived.[67] It shows that between 1542 and 1547 the Whitehall treasury received £240 000 and became (to judge from our imperfect knowledge of its disbursements[68]) the largest war chest hitherto accumulated by an English king. The treasury was also, since Henry handled much of the money himself and kept it, if not under the bed, at least at the back of his bedchamber in the secret jewel house, a dramatic reassertion of the vitality of household administration.

From signet to sign manual

The rise of the Secretary is normally presented as a smooth ascent from fifteenth-century obscurity to sixteenth-century eminence. The record speaks differently. The foundation of the Secretary's office was his custody of the smallest royal seal, the signet. By the later fifteenth century the signet had become the *primum mobile* of government. It validated the king's letters to foreign powers and his own subjects; gave orders to other household departments; and set in motion the formal machine of the privy and great seals which alone could authorize the payment of money from the Exchequer or make grants of patronage. In short, by the reign of Richard III royal action meant an act under the signet: Richard's Secretary John Kendal was one of his principal agents and Kendal's register or docket book is the prime record of Richard's government.[69] But this marked the high noon of the signet and its keeper. Then there is a gap of 65 years before the next surviving docket book, which was kept by Ralph Sadler, Secretary to Henry VIII.[70] In the interval lie archival chaos and obscurity from which a new secretaryship arises. The new secretaryship was based, not on the signet like the old (though it still retained control of the seal), but on the sign manual. The story is untold in essentials and badly needs telling.[71] But it is too big to be tackled here in full. So I shall deal with only a part of it: the rise of the sign manual and its relationship with the Privy Chamber.

The sign manual, as the royal signature was formally known, had developed concurrently with the signet.[72] It could be used in three ways. It could serve as a warrant or instruction to the signet; it could be used in conjunction with the signet, as a reinforcement of the seal; or it could be employed on its own, bypassing the seal altogether.[73] Under Henry VI there were still doubts about the validity of the sign manual (reinforced quite clearly by doubts about the signer).[74] But as the century wore on these doubts disappeared and the sign manual was used ever more frequently and confidently. For instance, under Henry VI it was exceptional for the sign manual to appear on a signet warrant; under Edward IV, however, 'perhaps half or rather more' signet warrants carry the sign manual;[75] and by Henry VII's reign the practice had become universal.[76] The ever-increasing demand for the royal signature even produced a change in Henry VII's sign manual itself. On 28 August 1492 he replaced the spiky gridiron monogram, awkwardly made with several strokes, which he had used since the beginning of the reign, with a cursive 'HR', formed with one long, flowing movement of the pen.[77]

But, despite its close connection with the signet, the sign manual was an 'altogether different method of authentication'[78] – and, it might be added, a rival one. Only the Secretary could apply the signet; anybody could and did get the sign manual. The more important, then, that the sign manual became, the less was left of the Secretary's original position. Personal and other considerations, of course, could override this logic. That is what happened under Richard III. He had the highest regard for Secretary Kendal; he also found the signet office useful as a general coordinator of the governmental machine.[79] But under Henry VII these considerations ceased to apply. He coordinated government himself; and though his first Secretary, Fox, was one of the King's closest advisers, he quickly moved on to better things, leaving the post to the obscure and often absentee.[80] The difference quickly showed in the number of direct warrants to the Chancery. These warrants – usually in fact suitors' petitions or 'bills' signed by the king – were the most sensitive use of the sign manual. Under Henry VI they had been the instruments of the King's prodigal patronage, and in 1444 the Council had tried to get rid of them. No longer were 'signed bills' to go direct to the Chancellor; instead they were to be passed to the Secretary. He would then issue a signet warrant to the Lord Privy Seal, who in turn would draw up a privy seal warrant to the Chancellor.[81] Richard III largely kept to this arrangement. Not, of course, because of pressure from his Council, but because he found that records of the signet office kept a valuable tally on his use of patronage.[82] Bound by this self-denying ordinance he issued very few direct warrants, of which even fewer survive (only 48 for the whole reign[83]). At first Henry VII followed his predecessor's practice, and in his first patent roll only 27 grants are warranted 'By the king' (which in practice means by a signed bill)[84] as against 299 'By privy seal' (which means that the full course of the seals had been gone through).[85] But in the early 1490s, coinciding roughly with the adoption of the new sign manual, the number of signed bills rises rapidly until in the two last patent rolls of the reign the two kinds of warranty are almost evenly balanced: in 23 Henry VII (1507–8) 103 patents are warranted 'By the king' as against 100 'By privy seal'; while in 24 Henry VII the respective figures (perhaps reflecting the King's failing powers) are 60 and 95.[86] 'The sign manual [was] coming into the administrative stream above the signet.'[87]

The change emerged fully into the light of day under Henry VIII. 'The next time that his Grace sign'[88] was the moment on which hung the plans of councillors and the hopes of suitors; while the sign manual, now manifestly the prime motor of government, was given the protection long afforded to the great seal. An Act of 1536 declared anyone who should 'falsely forge and counterfeit the king's sign manual' a traitor,[89] and on 23 December that year a priest was duly hanged, drawn, and quartered for infringing the statute.[90] But there were more dangers than forgery in the new dispensation. The informality of the sign manual made no odds under a king as organized and disciplined as Henry VII. Under Henry VIII, who was spasmodically generous and frequently inattentive, it was a different story. At first the problem was headed off. The young King's Council, conservative and deeply wedded to proper form as we have seen in finance, moved quickly to reintroduce the full course of the seals. There followed a striking change in the Chancery's files of warrants. In April 1509, the first month of the reign, nine signed bills and no privy seals survive;[91] in May the respective figures are 23 and 62;[92] and in June, 14 and 94.[93] Moreover, most of the June signed bills are easily explained: two deal with the marriage settlement for Catherine of Aragon;[94] two concern the Master of the Rolls;[95] and four made arrangements for the coronation.[96] So only three were the usual sort of signed petition,[97] and one of these testifies to the new hurdles which such grants had now to leap, for, accompanying a signed bill granting a sinecure to Anthony Leigh, the chief clerk of the kitchen, is a further warrant, also under the sign manual, specifically instructing the Chancellor to pass Leigh's grant.[98] These formalized procedures broke down in the first French war;[99] and thereafter the floodgates were opened. Signing more or less whatever was put in front of him, the King found himself granting office or lands twice over to different suitors. An attempt to tackle the resulting problems was made by an Act of Parliament of 1515.[100] Whether it achieved much may be doubted.

But a longer-term solution was in the offing. Underlying this confusion, and at first abetting it, then later taming it, was the development of a new secretarial routine in the hands of the Privy Chamber. Some such development (on the lines of the displacement of the Chamber by the Privy Purse in finance) was predictable. But the Privy Chamber's role was made more pronounced by a well-known trait in Henry VIII's character: his detestation of the actual business of writing – even of writing his signature. Any excuse was good enough to put off the signing of documents: a cold, a headache, or the lateness of the hour.[101] He would sign only when the mood took him – and who better to spot the time than the Privy Chamber, perpetually in attendance and deeply versed in the royal foibles?[102]

Quite soon we see State Papers accumulating in the hands of the Groom of the Stool, Compton or Norris, who submitted them for signature at a propitious moment after supper or during mass.[103] These were papers prepared by Wolsey's own secretariat. But the Privy Chamber also took a less passive role. There survives a 12-page letter book for the latter part of 1517.[104] Its contents are very mixed. Some letters are on state business, like the workings of the enclosure commission, but most deal with the personal interests of Henry's intimate attendants. Similarly, letters from the King are blended indiscriminately with letters from his servants. The book, written in a clear secretary's hand, ends 'fynys quod Sygyr'.[105] If 'Sygyr' is the name of the clerk who compiled the book, he is unidentifiable; but the prominence of 'our well-beloved servant ... and in our singular favour', Nicholas Carew, in the matters dealt with suggests that 'Sygyr' may well have been his clerk.[106] Since Carew was the dominant figure in the Privy Chamber in 1517, 'Sygyr' was effectively the clerk of the Privy Chamber, and the book the record of his activities. As such it is a vivid insight into the informality and casualness of a government, in which decisions were taken and implemented in the Privy Chamber. What happened, it seems, was this. The King agreed to make a grant. 'Sygyr' was then summoned into the Privy Chamber and took down in hasty dictation a letter from the King. Standing around were probably the interested parties and their backers, and when the King had completed his business they came in with letters of their own: explaining the royal decision, rounding up support, or heading off opposition.[107]

But all this is very fragmentary. The 'Sygyr' book itself contains only 14 letters, while there are only a couple of references for the whole of the Wolsey's ministry to the Groom's procuring the King's signature. At first sight, it is hard to explain why the Privy Chamber's secretarial role should have been so slow to take off. Certainly there was no good administrative reason, but there was, as the 'Sygyr' book shows, a compelling political one. Four of the letters deal with the suit of William Coffin of the Privy Chamber to marry the wealthy widow, Mrs Vernon of Haddon Hall in Derbyshire.[108] Opposing Coffin was Wolsey himself, who wanted the widow for one of his own servants.[109] But Coffin, backed to the hilt by Carew, was able to procure the King's own letters, and so inflicted public defeat on the minister, 'whereat', as Compton smugly reported, 'my lord cardinal is not content with all'.[110] So the Privy Chamber's access to the sign manual was a valuable weapon in the armoury that turned the newly appointed Gentlemen into some of Wolsey's most feared rivals. He could never allow the sign manual to be formalized in their hands.

Ironically, similar political considerations limited the effectiveness of Wolsey's own counter-measures. Periodically he would single out some-one at Court to handle the mass of his secretarial business conducted with Henry: that is, to cope with the stream of letters between king and minis-ter and to get documents signed. At various times the quasi-secretary was Richard Pace (the *real* Secretary), Thomas More, a councillor attendant, or William Fitzwilliam, the Treasurer of the Household.[111] Always the result was the same. Wolsey became jealous of the chosen intermediary, fearing that he would exploit his favourable position to undermine the minister's own, and the arrangement was abandoned. Only at the end of his ministry was Wolsey forced to take his Court agents more seriously. In response to the rise of the Boleyn faction at Court, the cardinal had put a powerful group of his own supporters in the Privy Chamber. These included Thomas Heneage, who had been head of Wolsey's own Privy Chamber, and Sir John Russell, whom Wolsey had written into the new Privy Chamber list of January 1526 with his own hand.[112] In the summer of 1528 Heneage handled most of the ministerial correspondence at Court;[113] then, as the old problem of distrust reappeared, Russell and Dr Bell, the royal almoner and another creature of the cardinal's, took over. By autumn their role was sufficiently well established for Robert Crawley, the Court agent of an Irish faction, to recommend to Wolsey that he 'send to Sir John Russell, Dr. Bell, and such others as promote bills or letters to the King's sign, that they pass no matters of Ireland till your Grace be made privy to the same'.[114]

So, under threat politically, Wolsey had at last done the obvious and made the poachers of the Privy Chamber into ministerial gamekeepers. But the arrangement was only rudimentary, and it was swept away by the new minister, Cromwell. He excluded the Privy Chamber absolutely from the 'promotion' of documents to the sign manual, and instead entrusted all min-isterial business at Court to servants of his own, in particular to Ralph Sadler.[115] All this was on the most informal footing. Sadler held no official post, while the Privy Chamber were kept out merely by the threat of Cromwell's displeasure. But more radical measures were taken. The first was to restore the ancient course of the seals established in 1444. This did not, of course, touch the sign manual directly; but at least it meant that signed bills would normally have to pass through the hands of the Secretary (that is, Cromwell) rather than, as so frequently happened, going straight to Chancery. As we have seen, both Richard III and the Council of the young

Henry VIII had already revived the course of the seals for their own purposes; now Cromwell would do the same, but on the basis of statute.

The Act was passed in 1536.[116] For Elton it was a major advance in the
bureaucratic revolution. In fact it was an old and increasingly old-fashioned
solution to the perennial problem of the vagaries of royal patronage. More
important still, it was a solution that was not put into effect. Almost before
it received the royal assent, it was overtaken by the great political crisis of
the early summer of 1536. The outcome of this crisis proved to be
Cromwell's double triumph over both his old allies, the Boleyns, and his
recent partners the Aragonese. He now had absolute control over the Privy
Chamber, of which the first fruit was the appointment of Thomas Heneage,
once Wolsey's client and now his, as Groom of the Stool.[117] With the
Groom in his pocket, Cromwell's attitude to the Privy Chamber and the sign
manual reversed. Instead of deflecting business from the Groom, the pro-
motion of papers to the sign manual was now concentrated in his hands.
And instead of relying on the remote and inefficient longstop of the signet,
Cromwell now regulated the application of the sign manual directly.

Quickly a recognizable procedure developed. The minister's office sent a
batch of papers to the chief gentleman at Court, who in turn got them signed
and returned them to the minister, usually at Austin Friars. As well as ministerial papers, documents from other government departments, in particular
Augmentations, and the bills of private suitors, were sent to the Groom for
signing. When Heneage went off duty, any unsigned papers were handed
over to his colleague, Sir Francis Bryan; and by the end of the 1530s there
even seem to have been semi-formal sessions, known in advance to well-
informed suitors, when 'next ... his Grace [shall] sign'.[118] Nevertheless, and
this is the important thing, every stage of the process was controlled by
Cromwell. The chief gentleman reported to him on the progress of State
Papers across the royal desk; Rich, the Chancellor of Augmentations, told
Cromwell when he had sent in papers, and once begged him to 'be a suitor
... for the expedition of the signature'.[119] Private clients would solicit a ministerial letter to the chief gentleman to convey Cromwell's formal consent
that 'he shall proceed and get my bill signed';[120] and – the ultimate sanction
– it looks as though Cromwell himself was present at Court for the later
mass-signing sessions.[121] The minister even took back his control a stage further, to the negotiations that preceded the signing of a bill. This was done by
'Mr. Heneage's Book of Remembrance for the king'.[122] Cromwell had projected the setting-up of the king's book (as it was usually known) in his own
memoranda for May 1537.[123] The note fully describes its purpose: 'a book
[to] be made of the names of such persons to whom the King's Majesty will
give any lands, fees or offices'. The book played, and no doubt was intended
to play, an important part in policing the scramble for preferment that followed the Dissolution, since an entry in it took precedence over any other
commitment (even a promise from the Chancellor of Augmentations).[124] But

Cromwell also had less altruistic motives. For once again, despite the book's name and its custodian, Cromwell seems to have been the true recording angel: if one wanted to put a name in the book, ensure that an entry materialized into a grant, or overturn an entry, one wrote to Cromwell.[125] Cromwell, in short, had done what Wolsey never fully could or would and controlled the sign manual. No longer could suitors 'run in at the window the next way, making immediate pursuits to the King's Highness'. The window was barred and locked.[126]

Here then is a Cromwell both familiar and strange. The familiar Cromwell fulfils what Wolsey promised and shows an unstoppable urge to translate power into regular procedures and record-keeping. The unfamiliar Cromwell puts both the procedures and the records in the hands of the Royal Household. Once again, there is no principled distinction between different types of administration; only a sensible political discrimination between men you can trust and command and those you cannot.

Principal among those whom Cromwell could trust was Ralph Sadler, his general Court agent in the first part of his ministry. Sadler was put into the Privy Chamber as a Groom in July 1536, a month or so after Cromwell's other client Heneage had been made Groom of the Stool. Thereafter the two largely divided any ministerial business about the King between themselves. While the signing of documents was handled by Heneage, Sadler was the main channel of communication between king and minister: expounding Cromwell's minutes to the King and writing the royal replies. Sadler's role was institutionalized in April 1540 when Cromwell divested himself of the secretaryship and divided it between his two clients, Thomas Wriothesley and Ralph Sadler. Wriothesley continued as head of Cromwell's private office; Sadler as go-between in the Privy Chamber.[127]

So the result of the second half of Cromwell's ministry was to recreate the fifteenth-century secretaryship, but in the Privy Chamber and corporately, between Heneage and Sadler. Their fate, and that of their several tasks, varied widely. Sadler was dismissed from the secretaryship in 1543 and none of his successors was a member of the Privy Chamber. So the department lost the role of go-between. The revived secretaryship (no longer held by men who were too small – like the pre-Cromwellian secretaries – nor too big – like Cromwell himself) also began to reclaim a large part of the business of signing documents from the Groom. But then chance dealt the Groom a trump-all. As Henry became inflamed by illness and old age, his reluctance to sign became an aversion. Eventually he freed himself by setting up the machinery of the 'dry stamp'.[128]

This was done in September 1545, although it was only formally authorized nearly a year later in August 1546.[129] There had long been a 'wet stamp', used to rubber (or rather, wooden) stamp circulars. The dry stamp was quite different. It left an uninked impression on the paper which was gone over in pen-and-ink by an expert clerk. The result was a near perfect facsimile, that was used henceforward to authenticate all documents to which the sign manual would ordinarily have been applied. And the dry stamp was firmly in the hands of the Privy Chamber. In overall control was Sir Anthony Denny, the second chief gentleman; while the office routine was dealt with by William Clerk, the 'king's clerk'. He both applied the stamp and kept the monthly registers of documents stamped, which were then submitted to the King for clearance by his real signature. Even the stamp itself, originally held by the King, was entrusted in February 1546 to John Gates, Gentleman of the Privy Chamber and Denny's brother-in-law and factotum.[130] Henry had thus alienated the sign manual to Denny as completely as a seal to its keeper.

Conclusions

In the last years of the reign, then, the Privy Chamber's governmental activities flourished. They were unpruned by any ministerial hand; and they were fertilized by war (which always brought the king to the forefront of government) and Henry's final physical decline (which put unwonted power in the hands of his immediate attendants). The key figure in this was Sir Anthony Denny, second chief gentleman from the beginning of 1539, and Groom of the Stool from October 1546. He controlled the dry stamp; he was also custodian of the hugely expanded Privy Coffers. He had a general personal secretariat run by his brother-in-law Gates; Clerk handled the secretarial duties of the dry stamp; whilst Nicholas Bristowe, clerk of the Wardrobe of the Robes, was chief bookkeeper and accountant of the Privy Coffers (and the Privy Purse as well, though that did not come within Denny's province till he had taken over from Heneage as Groom of the Stool). Round Denny, therefore, was a true inner-household administration – answerable to Denny as first acting and finally formal head of the Privy Chamber – which was actually based in the multitude of strong rooms and closets honeycombing off the privy lodging at Whitehall.[131]

There is a certain rhythm in all this, as the Privy Chamber usurps one by one the functions of the Chamber. First it takes over the task of intimate personal attendance on the monarch; then it displaces the administrators of the Chamber, the Treasurer and the Secretary, from their original household tasks (the keeping of the Privy Purse and the authentication of documents); finally it trespasses on their national responsibilities as well. But the rhythm was not new or progressive. We are not seeing, as Professor Elton thought, a linear movement from medieval to modern. Rather, government was dancing to an ancient roundelay: the cycle of 'going out of Court'. A household department is given national responsibilities; it abandons the Court and settles down in Westminster. In the mean time its neglected tasks about the king are taken over by another household department, which then begins to encroach on the national activities of its predecessor. And so on. The cycle begins under the Anglo-Normans; it is still turning, we now know, under the Tudors. At last! There is a Tudor revolution after all. But it is in their sense of the word, not ours. And the Tudor cycle of 'going out of Court' is never completed. The Privy Purse, well on the way to displacing the Chamber as the principal national treasury in the early 1530s, was, with Cromwell and an altered politics, cut short. The dry stamp became a fully-fledged fourth 'seal' between 1545 and 1547, wholly depriving the signet of original force, but it did so only as a result of the circumstances of the King's failing health, and its dominance died with Henry. Thereafter the sign manual was recaptured by the Secretary, while the members of the Privy Chamber were reduced (as under Elizabeth) to mere barometers of the royal mood to be tapped by the Secretary before he submitted documents for signature.[132] Thus not only is the cycle of going out of Court incomplete; it is not autonomous either. It is subject to pressures of circumstance. But so were the most formal parts of the governmental machine, including the Council. And, like everything else, the cycle is subject to ministerial pressures.

We have already sampled these in our brief account of the rise of the Privy Chamber as a household department. Wolsey was its inveterate enemy; Cromwell its eventual friend. Much the same, it is now clear, would go for their response to 'household' – in effect, Privy Chamber – government as a whole. This is not to try to stand *The Tudor Revolution in Government* on its head and show Cromwell as a backslider from Wolsey's advanced position. (Though it is worth remembering that the original thesis of the withdrawal of the household from national administration was formulated by A. P. Newton, not Elton, and had Wolsey, not Cromwell, as the prime architect of change.[133]) Rather than invert *The Tudor Revolution* (or even perhaps stand it the right way up), I would wish to deny the relevance of its categories altogether. Neither Wolsey nor Cromwell had any theoretical conception of separate models of government, the 'household' or the national/bureaucratic. Both instead were practical politicians, concerned with the realities of power. And power alone shaped their attitudes to the Privy Chamber. Wolsey's power base lay outside the Court; so he viewed the rise of a new constellation within the Court – the Privy Chamber and its agencies – always with unease and usually with outright hostility. Cromwell, on the other hand, began his career where Wolsey finished his, as a leader of a Court faction. And it was as a jealous faction leader that he reacted. Until he controlled the Privy Chamber, his opposition to its activities in government (or anything else) was implacable – as Norris and the Privy Purse discovered. Once the *coup* of May 1536 gave him that control, however, all was sweetness and light: he did not merely tolerate the Privy Chamber, but, as Heneage and the sign manual show, he vigorously developed its activities as agents of his own power.

None of this of course is intended to suggest that the ministers' only concern was the household. They had many other things to think of (though in 1525 Wolsey put the ordinary business of government on the back burner for several months whilst he purged the Privy Chamber). Nor am I suggesting that the household was the government. It was not, and its governmental activities usually took a back seat to other agencies, above all the Council. Yet it was always important, and in the right circumstances, decisive – as the last weeks of the reign bore out. Then it was the dry stamp alone which authenticated both the attainder of the Duke of Norfolk and the King's will. The former removed the only possible challenge to Edward Seymour's takeover of power under the future Edward VI; the latter provided the constitutional machinery to set up the Seymour regime. In 1529, before Cromwell, 'household' government had unmade a minister; in 1547, after Cromwell, 'household' government made both a Protector and a Reformation.[134]

Notes

1 T. Rymer and R. Sanderson (eds), *Foedera, conventiones, litterae et cujuscunque generis acta publica* (20 vols, London, 1704–35), XIV, p. 349.
2 G. R. Elton, *The Tudor Revolution in Government* (Cambridge, 1953), pp. 414–15.
3 Bodl. Laudian MS Misc. 597, fo. 24 (printed from an inferior MS in *A Collection of Ordinances and Regulations for the Government of the Royal Household* (Society of Antiquaries; London, 1790), p. 154.
4 Mark Girouard, *Life in the English Country House* (New Haven and London, 1978), 30 ff.; H. M. Colvin (ed.), *The History of the King's Works* (6 vols, London, 1951–82), IV, 2, pp. 1–40; H. M. Baillie, 'Etiquette and the Planning of the State Apartments in Baroque Palaces', *Archaeologia*, 101 (1967); A. R. Myers, *The Household of Edward IV* (Manchester, 1959), pp. 19, 128, 298–9.
5 Colvin, *History*, IV, 2, pp. 1–40.
6 David Starkey, 'The King's Privy Chamber, 1485–1547', unpublished Cambridge Ph.D. thesis (1973), pp. 17 ff.
7 S. B. Chrimes, *Henry VII* (London, 1972), p. 319.
8 College of Arms, Arundel MS XVII², printed from a later MS copy in *The Antiquarian Repertory*, ed. E. Jeffrey (4 vols, London, 1807–9), II, pp. 184–208; Starkey, 'The King's Privy Chamber', 17 ff.
9 See the rather fuller speculation in David Starkey, 'From Feud to Faction: English Politics c.1450–1550', *History Today*, 32 (Nov. 1982), pp. 16–22.
10 See n. 3 above.
11 BL Add. MS 45 716 A, of which extracts were printed in *The Genealogist*, new ser., 29–30 (1913–14).
12 Starkey, 'Privy Chamber', pp. 64 ff.
13 Starkey, 'The King's Privy Chamber' pp. 80 ff; Edward Hall, *The Union of the Two Noble and Illustrious Families of Lancaster and York* (London, 1809), pp. 593–4.
14 Starkey, 'The King's Privy Chamber', pp. 112 ff. and nn. 103–14 below.
15 R. L. Brown (trans. and ed.), *Four Years at the Court of Henry VIII* (2 vols, London, 1854) II, pp. 269 ff.
16 PRO SP 1/232, fo. 41 (*LP* Addenda I, I, 196).
17 C. A. Cruickshank, *The English Occupation of Tournai, 1513–19* (Oxford, 1971), p. 264.
18 *LP* III, i, 229.

19 PRO C 66/633, m. 9 (*LP* III, i, 231).
20 PRO C 66/633, mm. 11, 12, 15 (*LP* III, i, 247–9).
21 Starkey, 'The King's Privy Chamber', pp. 115 ff.
22 A. P. Newton, 'Tudor Reforms in the Royal Household', in R. W. Seton Watson (ed.), *Tudor Studies* (London, 1929), pp. 238 ff.
23 Elton, *Tudor Revolution*, p. 388.
24 Starkey, 'The King's Privy Chamber', pp. 212 ff.
25 This account of the great chamberlainship is more 'political' than the treatment in my dissertation (Starkey, 'The King's Privy Chamber', pp. 281 ff). I hope to discuss more fully the whole question of great offices of state shortly.
26 Bodl. Laudian MS Misc. 597, fo. 33ᵛ (*Household Ordinances*, 161).
27 As well as the exhaustive account of the institutional history of the Privy Chamber in my dissertation, two shorter and more accessible studies may prove useful: David Starkey, 'Representation through Intimacy' in Ioan Lewis, (ed.), *Symbols and Sentiments* (London, New York, and San Francisco, 1977), pp. 187–224; and David Starkey, 'Intimacy and Innovation: the Rise of the Privy Chamber' in David Starkey, (ed.), *The English Court from the Wars of the Roses to the Civil War* (London, 1987), pp. 71–118.
28 B. P. Wolffe, *The Crown Lands* (London, 1970).
29 Here I differ from Dr Alsop. He is right to argue that there was no fundamental difference in administrative method between Exchequer and Chamber. But there was a difference none the less: a legal one. The Exchequer's activities were grounded in common law; the Chamber's were not. It was on these grounds that the Chamber was attacked and was vulnerable to attack. Cf. Wolffe, *Crown Lands*, pp. 76 ff.
30 Starkey, 'The King's Privy Chamber', pp. 357 ff.
31 Chrimes, *Henry VII*, p. 128.
32 The exact date (8 Sept.) when 'the said Edward received his patent for surveying divers prerogatives' (*CPR 1494–1509* (London, 1916), p. 591) is established by his accounts (PRO E 101/517/15, fo. 2).
33 PRO E 101/517/15, fo. 5.
34 PRO E 36/214, fo. 157ᵛ.
35 PRO E 101/220/1 (*LP* I, i, 579/1).
36 PRO E 101/517/16 (*LP* I, ii, 2766).
37 F. C. Dietz, *English Public Finance, 1485–1641* (2 vols, London, 1964), I, pp. 85, 88, 90.
38 Starkey, 'The King's Privy Chamber', pp. 370 ff.
39 BL Cott. MS Titus B. 1, fos. 188 ff.
40 *LP* IV, iii, 5750.
41 Starkey, 'The King's Privy Chamber', pp. 373 ff.
42 PRO C 66/646, mm. 41–2.
43 Starkey, 'The King's Privy Chamber', pp. 377 ff.
44 BL Add. MS 20,030, printed *in extenso* by N. H. Nicolas (ed.), *The Privy Purse Expenses of King Henry VIII* (London, 1827).
45 PRO E 101/465/20 (*LP* VII, 250).
46 This and the following figures are based on my analysis of the calendared abstracts in *LP* V, 315–25. It is reassuring to note that my figure for wage payments tallies very closely with the Treasurer's own estimate of 'almost £40 000' in 1537 (see Elton, *Tudor Revolution*, p. 152).
47 Nicolas, *Privy Purse*, p. 186.
48 Nicolas, *Privy Purse*, p. 115.
49 *LP* V, 303 ff. (my calculations again).
50 Elton, *Tudor Revolution*, p. 170.
51 Elton, *Tudor Revolution*, pp. 139 ff.
52 Starkey, 'The King's Privy Chamber', p. 388; *LP* V, 312; Nicholas, *Privy Purse*, pp. 19, 22, 24.
53 Starkey, 'The King's Privy Chamber', pp. 397, 400; PRO E 36/221, fo. 9ᵛ; Nicolas, *Privy Purse*, p.22.
54 Starkey, 'The King's Privy Chamber', p. 399; PRO SP1/69, fos. 265–6.

55 Starkey, 'The King's Privy Chamber', p. 400.
56 *LP* IV, iii, 5515.
57 R. S. Sylvester and D. P. Harding (eds), *Two Early Tudor Lives* (New Haven and London), pp. 102–3.
58 J. D. Mackie, *The Earlier Tudors* (Oxford, 1952), p. 319.
59 *LP* IV, iii, 5515, 6040, 6710; V, 222, 1065, 1504–5.
60 PRO SP 1/68, fo. 28 (*LP* V, 487); Nicolas, *Privy Purse*, p. 34.
61 PRO SP 1/53, fo. 273.
62 See particularly the list of his receipts in PRO SP 2 N, fos. 114–17 (*LP* VI, 228).
63 Esp. *LP* V, 1285/ix.
64 BL Royal MS 7 C. xvi, fo. 75. Professor Elton did not turn up this document, which plays a crucial part in unravelling Cromwell's treasurership.
65 Starkey, 'The King's Privy Chamber', pp. 402–3.
66 The calculations are set out in detail in Starkey, 'The King's Privy Chamber', pp. 406 ff.
67 PRO E315/160, fos. 264 ff.
68 Starkey, 'The King's Privy Chamber', p. 409.
69 *British Library Harleian Manuscript 433 (Harl. MS 433)*, ed. Rosemary Horrox and P. W. Hammond (4 vols, Upminster and London, 1979–83).
70 BL Add. MS 33,818 and A. J. Slavin, *Politics and Profit: A Study of Sir Ralph Sadler, 1507–1547* (Cambridge, 1966), pp. 55 ff.
71 Cf. Elton's account in *Tudor Revolution*, pp. 261 ff. Only Tout seems to have understood the way things were going: see T. F. Tout, *Chapters in the Administrative History of Medieval England* (6 vols, Manchester, 1920–33), V, pp. 226–30.
72 J. Otway-Ruthven, *The King's Secretary and the Signet Office in the Fifteenth Century* (Cambridge, 1939), pp. 24–5.
73 Otway-Ruthven, *King's Secretary*, pp. 25–6, 39; *Harl. MS 433*, vol. I, pp. xvii ff.
74 Otway-Ruthven, *King's Secretary*, p. 25.
75 Otway-Ruthven, *King's Secretary*, p. 26.
76 See, for example, the files of warrants to the Great Wardrobe, PRO E 101/413/11, 414/8, 415/7, 416/7, etc.
77 R. L. Storey, *The Reign of Henry VII* (London, 1968), p. 102 and pl. 9.
78 Otway-Ruthven, *King's Secretary*, p. 24.
79 *Harl. MS 433*, vol. I, pp. xiii, xviii–xix.
80 Chrimes, *Henry VII*, pp. 116–18.
81 Otway-Ruthven, *King's Secretary*, pp. 35 ff.
82 *Harl. MS 433*, vol. I, p. xiii.
83 *Harl. MS 433*, vol. I, p. xiii n. 52.
84 *Harl. MS 433*, vol. I, pp. xvii–xviii.
85 *CPR 1485–94* (London, 1914), pp. 1–40.
86 *CPR 1494–1509*, pp. 548–93, 594–626.
87 K. W. M. Pickthorn, *Early Tudor Government* (2 vols, Cambridge, 1934), I, p. 141 n. 1.
88 Starkey, 'The King's Privy Chamber', pp. 324–30; PRO SP 3/4, art. 76 (*LP* XV, 291).
89 G. R. Elton, *The Tudor Constitution: Documents and Commentary* (1st edn, Cambridge, 1960), p. 63.
90 W. D. Hamilton (ed.), *A Chronicle of England*, by Charles Wriothesley (Camden Society, new ser. 11; 2 vols, London, 1875–7), I, p. 60.
91 *LP* I, i, 11.
92 *LP* I, i, 54.
93 *LP* I, i, 94.
94 *LP* I, i, 94/36, 41.
95 *LP* I, i, 94/44, 99.
96 *LP* I, i, 94/43, 87–9.
97 *LP* I, i, 94/60, 71, 110.
98 *LP* I, i, 94/60.
99 *LP* I, ii, 1948.

100 *Statutes of the Realm*, ed. A. Luders, Sir T. E. Tomlins, J. F. France, W. E. Taunton, J. Raithby, J. Caley, and W. Elliot (11 vols, London, 1810–28), III, p. 134.
101 *LP* III, ii, 1399, 1429.
102 See the sequence of events in *LP* XIV, ii, 149, 153, 163.
103 *LP* I, ii, 1960; IV, ii, 4409.
104 Bodl., Ashmole MS 1148, sec. xi.
105 Bodl., Ashmole MS 1148, sec. xi, p. 12.
106 Bodl., Ashmole MS 1148, sec. xi, p. 8.
107 Bodl., Ashmole MS 1148, sec. xi, pp. 7, 9, 11.
108 Bodl., Ashmole MS 1148, sec. xi, pp. 7, 9, 11.
109 Edmund Lodge, *Illustrations of British History* (3 vols, London, 1791), I, pp. 28 ff.
110 Lodge, *Illustrations of British History*, I, pp. 28 ff.
111 Elton, *Tudor Revolution*, pp. 56–9.
112 PRO SP 1/37, fo. 65 (*LP* IV, i, 1939/4); *LP* IV, ii, 3964; *LP* III, ii, 2132; *LP* IV, i, 338/3, etc.
113 *LP* IV, ii, 4005, 4144, 4299, etc.
114 *State Papers during the Reign of Henry the Eighth* (Record Commissioners; 11 vols, London, 1830–52), II, pp. 140–2.
115 Starkey, 'The King's Privy Chamber', pp. 321–2.
116 Elton, *Tudor Revolution*, pp. 270 ff.
117 G. R. Elton, *Reform and Reformation* (London, 1977), pp. 253–4; Starkey, 'The King's Privy Chamber', pp. 239 ff.
118 Starkey, 'The King's Privy Chamber', pp. 324–30; PRO SP 3/4, art. 76 (*LP* XV, 291).
119 PRO SP 1/158, fos. 54–5 (*LP* XV, 347).
120 PRO SP 1/125, fo. 19 (*LP* XII, ii, 739).
121 Starkey, 'The King's Privy Chamber', pp. 330.
122 *LP* XI, 227.
123 BL Cotton MS Titus B.I, fo. 457 (*LP* XII, i, 1315).
124 PRO SP 1/153, fos. 30–1 (*LP* XIV, ii, 47).
125 PRO SP 1/124, fos. 159–60 (*LP* XII, ii, 629); SP 1/125, fo. 101 (*LP* XII, ii, 810); SP 1/105, fos. 240–1 (*LP* XI, 227 misdated).
126 *State Papers during the Reign of Henry the Eighth*, II, pp. 140–2.
127 Starkey, 'The King's Privy Chamber', p. 333.
128 Starkey, 'The King's Privy Chamber', p. 342 ff.
129 *LP* XX, ii, 706; Rymer, *Foedera*, XV, p. 100.
130 PRO E 315/160, fos. 266ᵛ, 267.
131 Cf. Starkey, 'The King's Privy Chamber', p. 417.
132 Conyers Read, *Mr Secretary Walsingham and the Policy of Queen Elizabeth* (3 vols, Oxford, 1925), I, p. 437.
133 Newton, 'Tudor Reforms'.
134 Elton, *Reform and Reformation*, pp. 331 ff.

8

Thomas Cromwell and the intellectual origins of the Henrician revolution

JOHN GUY

The field of English Reformation studies is at present more active than ever before. New books and articles roll off the presses at a formidable pace. Yet among the familiar scholarship and revisionist new learning one topic remains relatively underexplored: the intellectual origins of the 'Henrician' or 'political' revolution itself.[1] The view is too often uncritically repeated that one man, Thomas Cromwell, 'made' or 'was the architect of' these events. 'Wherever one touches Thomas Cromwell, one finds originality and the unconventional,' writes Professor G. R. Elton.[2] Regarding the Act of Appeals (1533) we are told:

> The critical term is 'empire'. Kings of England had before this claimed to be emperors – the title occurs in Anglo-Saxon times and was taken by Edward I, Richard II, and Henry V – but the meaning here is different. Those earlier 'emperors' had so called themselves because they ruled, or claimed to rule, more than one kingdom, as Edward I claimed Scotland and Henry V France. In the act of appeals, on the other hand, England by herself is described as an empire, and it is clear both from the passage cited and from what follows that the word here denoted a political unit, a self-governing state free from (as they put it) 'the authority of any foreign potentates'. We call this sort of thing a sovereign national state.[3]

I wish to look more closely at the Henrician concept of 'empire' – to examine its meaning and native intellectual origins. In doing this, the ideas that underpin the Act of Appeals must be considered, and an attempt made to locate in contemporary debate the definition attributed to 'empire' by Henricians themselves. It then becomes possible to make a case for tracing the origins of the Tudor political revolution back to 1485, and to put forward the necessary arguments to reinforce that position as the basis of an alternative framework of interpretation.

The political creed of Thomas Cromwell, it is said, was most fully declared and expounded in the preamble to the Act in Restraint of Appeals to Rome, passed in April 1533.

> Where by divers sundry old authentic histories and chronicles it is manifestly declared and expressed that this realm of England is an empire, and so hath been accepted in the world, governed by one supreme head and king having the dignity and royal estate of the imperial crown of the same, unto whom a body politic, compact of all sorts and degrees of people divided in terms and by names of spiritualty and temporalty, be bounden and owe to bear next to God a natural and humble obedience; he [the king] being also institute and furnished by the goodness and sufferance of Almighty God with plenary, whole and entire power, preeminence, authority, prerogative and jurisdiction to render and yield justice and final determination to all manner of folk resiants or subjects within this realm, in all causes, matters, debates and contentions happening to occur, insurge or begin within the limits thereof, without restraint or provocation to any foreign princes or potentates of the world ...[4]

Cromwell, it is said, here announced a novel theory of empire. He proclaimed the radical notion that the territorial realm of England was a sovereign national state, because all aspects of law and legislation, both temporal and spiritual, were henceforward within the exclusive competence of England's properly constituted courts which, in turn, derived their authority from the king. Since the highest court of England was that of Parliament, an explicit feature of the Cromwellian revolution was also that the human positive law of the realm as enacted by king, lords spiritual and temporal, and Commons in Parliament assembled, now enjoyed an omnicompetent supremacy over the amalgam of diverse central and local jurisdictions, both ecclesiastical and lay, which formed the Tudor constitution.

The questions to ask are, how accurate is this concept of England's imperial status, and to what extent was it an original exercise in statecraft inspired by Thomas Cromwell? To approach the answers, it is necessary to look at two letters. Writing to Cromwell in 1535, John Stokesley, Bishop of London, explained how some points he had made in an *extempore* sermon were those set out in the 'king's book' made before 'my going over the seas in embassy'.[5] Stokesley had left England in October 1529 as an ambassador to France and Italy, and did not return until October 1530. He described how the 'king's book' had been written by Edward Foxe, Nicholas de Burgo, and himself, being translated afterwards into English with changes and additions by Thomas Cranmer. The 'king's book' was thought by Professors H. A. Kelly and Edward Surtz to be the tract *Gravissimae ... censurae*, a work dated April 1530 in the printer's colophon, but demonstrably not printed until the spring of 1531. Dr Virginia Murphy has now established conclusively, however, that the 'king's book' was an earlier tract, one that lay behind the *Gravissimae ... censurae* (so that Stokesley's comment is explicable), but that was itself a version of the King's own *libellus* submitted to Wolsey's and Campeggio's legatine court at Blackfriars in 1529. The earlier tract was called 'Henricus Octavus', and Dr Murphy has found the authoritative text of it in a binding from the shop known as 'King Henry's binder'.[6]

Stokesley's letter was written in 1535; it perhaps needs some corroboration. And there is, in fact, a second letter. Sir Thomas More, writing to Cromwell in 1534, reported in some detail how, shortly after he became Lord Chancellor, Henry VIII referred him to a team which was working out details of the royal divorce strategy. The team consisted of Thomas Cranmer, Edward Foxe, Edward Lee, and Nicholas de Burgo – the very same persons mentioned by Stokesley save Stokesley himself, who was, of course, away in Europe at the time. More was required to 'confer with' these scholars and to inform his conscience: he was unconvinced by their materials.

> Whereupon the king's highness being further advertised both by them and myself of my poor opinion in the matter ... his highness

graciously taking in gre my good mind in that behalf, used ... in the prosecuting of his great matter only those ... whose conscience his grace perceived well and fully persuaded upon that part.[7]

More was excused on the issue, though Henry's 'great matter' became More's 'matter' too in 1534, when the King decided to test allegiance to his proceedings by means of oaths.

It is thus established that an identifiable team of royal scholars was engaged on the divorce issue in 1529 and 1530; Cranmer, Foxe, Lee, de Burgo, and Stokesley (to whom Dr Murphy would add Stephen Gardiner, because some early drafts of 'Henricus Octavus' are in his handwriting) were busily raiding the libraries of London and Europe and preparing papers on current policies with the characteristic enthusiasm of intellectuals eager to display the relevance of learning to government in the interests of self-advancement. The petulant King had been dismayed by the decision of the legatine court of Cardinals Wolsey and Campeggio to adjourn his case in June and July 1529 and was angry at the greater humiliation of the advocation of his suit to Rome by Pope Clement VII. He had decided to turn for support to other authorities, especially to the universities of the Continent. He continued to rely on his coterie of scholars, who prepared for the printing press the 'king's book'.[8] The pages of the main body of this work were probably ready for printing in October 1529, when Stokesley went abroad. Printing was delayed, however, until the opinions of seven leading French and Italian universities, those of Orléans, Paris, Angers, Bourges, Toulouse, Bologna, and Padua, could be included by way of a preface to the whole work. The *Gravissimae ... censurae* was finally issued in Latin in April 1531, and an English translation by Cranmer was printed the following November under the title *The determinations of the moste famous and mooste excellent vniuersities of Italy and Fraunce, that it is so vnlefull for a man to marie his brothers wyfe, that the pope hath no power to dispence therwith.*[9]

Henry's literary enterprises in 1529 and 1530 introduced him to important sources of knowledge: the councils of the Church, the Fathers Greek and Latin, the writings of the popes, the schoolmen, and so on. The *Censurae* and *Determinations* make plain the purpose to which such learning was applied by the King. The Levitical Law that forbade a man to marry his brother's wife was divine, not human. Such incestuous relationships were also forbidden by the law of nature. If Pope Julius II had granted a dispensation to Henry VII contrary to divine and natural law, upon the strength of which Henry VIII had married Catherine of Aragon, widow of Prince Arthur, Henry VIII's elder brother, that dispensation was invalid and the pope was no better than another human legislator who had exceeded his authority. Indeed, should the pope grant a dispensation against the divine and natural law, any Christian might lawfully resist and condemn him – for this the authorities were no less than St Augustine and St Ambrose. If the pope erred, he was to be corrected or resisted.[10]

The *Censurae* and *Determinations* encapsulated ideas of 1529 and early 1530, not those preparatory to the Act of Appeals. Yet it was out of the endeavours of Henry's research team in 1530 that remarkable ideas evolved. Henry VIII probably sat back while the *Gravissimae ... censurae* and *Determinations* were in the press, though his interest in the finished product of the *Determinations* has been questioned, but not formally proposed, on the basis of some marginal notes in the British Library copy.[11] His scholars, however, continued to work while the King reclined. In particular, they explored anew the sources used for the *libellus* of 1529 and the *Censurae* of 1531, and turned them gradually about to serve a new and revolutionary purpose. Under the direction, perhaps, of Edward Foxe, the author of the *De vera differentia* of 1534, and a member of the royal team since at least 1529, the King's scholars addressed an issue bigger even than that of the divorce – the 'true difference' between regal and ecclesiastical power.[12] It is possible that the Boleyn faction provided the momentum whereby Henry's scholars changed the direction of their research; if so, Thomas Cromwell may have played some part in the shift, though his involvement in Henrician policy-making at any level above that of parliamentary draftsman between 1531 and 1533 remains speculative. Cranmer is a better candidate than Cromwell as agent of the research team's new direction: already part of the team with whom More was obliged to 'confer', firmly attached to the Boleyn interest, and, with Foxe, one of the compilers of the *Collectanea satis copiosa*. We may suspect some truth lies behind the traditions that tell of Henry VIII's meeting with his future archbishop at Waltham.[13]

It was the inquiry into regal and ecclesiastical power that paved the way for the Act of Appeals and the break with Rome. During and after 1530, Henry's scholars compiled a new source collection inspired by but distinct from that upon which 'Henricus Octavus' and *Gravissimae ... censurae* were based. The new compilation was the *Collectanea satis copiosa* which, by September 1530, was indeed literally 'satis copiosa': it was adequate both in quality and quantity to be shown to the King, possibly by Edward Foxe. The document exists only in manuscript in the British Library, but the text there is an original, from which it is clear that Henry VIII himself studied the work closely. Thus Henry's own hand is to be found in 46 places on the manuscript, variously signifying his notes and queries, agreements or disagreements, pleasure or perplexity.[14] The *Collectanea* was discovered and identified by Dr Graham Nicholson, who demonstrated, too, the document's links with the Act of Appeals, the *Glasse of the truthe*, and Foxe's *De vera differentia*.[15]

In fact, Henry applauded the work of his scholars, because Foxe and the others, beginning from the scriptural premises previously invoked to prove the case for Henry's annulment of his marriage, had now validated the king's regal power in such circumstances – not from the viewpoint of immediate need but from general theological and historical perception. Many of the sources used in the *Collectanea* were the same as in *Gravissimae ... censurae* but slanted differently: the Old and New Testaments, the Fathers, Church councils, learned 'authors', and English texts and chronicles. However, councils, Matthew Paris, William of Malmesbury, Bede, Geoffrey of Monmouth, and Anglo-Saxon laws were prominent in the *Collectanea*. The reason was the changed emphasis. Not only did the royal scholars aim to verify the right of the English bishops to pronounce Henry's divorce unilaterally in England and without reference, if possible, to Rome (the policy advocated in the *Glasse of the truthe* in 1531 or 1532);[16] but they had also conceived a revolutionary theory of English regal power, showing how kings in general, and the kings of England in particular, had exercised that power historically in handling the clergy. In short, the *Collectanea* imbued Henry with an 'imperial' sovereignty, part of which had been 'lent' to the priesthood by previous English monarchs. It was this thinking that underpinned the Act of Appeals.[17]

For instance, the authors of the *Collectanea* used the ancient *Leges anglorum* to show that King Lucius I had in AD 187 become the first Christian ruler of Britain. In reality, the *Leges anglorum* was a source less authoritative than it seemed, being a thirteenth-century interpolation of the so-called *Leges Edwardi confessoris*. But it was a most pregnant source. It showed that the mythical Lucius had endowed the British Church with all its liberties and possessions and had then written to Pope Eleutherius asking him to transmit the Roman laws. However, the Pope's reply explained that Lucius did not need any Roman law, because he already had scripture from which he might legislate as King of Britain for both *regnum* and *sacerdotium*. The papal letter is twice quoted in full in the *Collectanea*, the second time immediately beneath the heading 'Institutio officium et potestas Regum Anglie':

> For you are vicar of God in your kingdom ... A king is named by virtue of ruling not for having a realm. You shall be king while you rule well, but if you do otherwise the name of king shall not remain upon you, and you will lose it. The omnipotent God grant you so to rule the kingdom of Britain that you may reign with him eternally, whose vicar you are in the said realm.[18]

In other words, Cranmer and Foxe were not merely justifying Henry VIII's divorce in *Collectanea satis copiosa*; they were simultaneously announcing doctrines of royal supremacy and empire. The result was that Henry, as he read the *Collectanea*, became more convinced than ever before of the rights of his position. But not only should his suit for annulment of his marriage be dealt with promptly and in England, as he had thought previously. He must now reassert, too, the imperial status of which English kings had been deprived by the machinations of popes. For England was an empire; it had been one in the ancient British past, and English imperial jurisdiction was a theological truth which no pope could conscionably disregard.

What exactly was meant by 'empire' in this context? Despite undoubted complexity, it is clear that the authors of the *Collectanea* were seeking to establish three basic principles of English regal power: secular *imperium*, spiritual supremacy, and the right of the English Church to provincial self-determination, i.e. national independence from Rome and the Papacy. Therefore, the *Collectanea* cited the passage of Bracton that makes the king the true sovereign because he has neither equal nor superior and is vicar of God. A phrase was, however, slanted to increase royal power.[19] Next, extracts were made from chronicles in defence of Edward I's claim to suzerainty over Scotland and Wales. Their purpose was to show that the authority of the English Crown extended over other realms, and that the sum of the king's feudal rights amounted to a right of empire. On the question of spiritual supremacy, Cranmer and Foxe relied on the spurious letter of Pope Eleutherius already quoted, describing King Lucius as 'vicarius dei', a position strengthened by the fact that Lucius, it was alleged, had single-handedly endowed the English Church, with the result that the clergy's jurisdiction and standing were vindicated solely by a royal grant of lands and liberties. The implication, as with the theory of Edward I's *imperium*, was that what had been granted remained inalienably in the king's possession, and might be resumed at will by Henry VIII.[20] By way of confirmation, Henry VIII, himself no mean scholar, invoked Justinian in 1531, perceiving a distinct spiritual estate comprising an emperor and his clergy, which took decisions on spiritual matters in Church councils and promulgated them by the emperor's authority alone.[21] The Donation of Constantine, revealed to be a forgery in 1440, was also (perversely) used in *Collectanea satis copiosa* to show, after Marsiglio of Padua, that, if the Emperor Constantine had granted the Roman Church its pre-eminent jurisdiction and temporal powers, such powers plainly could not have been granted by God and the Papacy could not be a divinely ordained institution.

The third and most radical principle of English power, provincial self-determination, necessarily earned the most learned treatment at the hands of Cranmer and Foxe. By provincial self-determination was meant the right of the English Church to settle its affairs unilaterally in national synods and without reference to Rome. If this right could be satisfactorily asserted, the annulment of Henry VIII's marriage might be pronounced by the Archbishop of Canterbury or the English Church in Convocation, declared nationally by letters placard or parliamentary statute, and enforced by new treason laws drawn (plausibly enough) to prevent malcontents dividing the realm over Henry VIII's private life.[22] Needless to say, the authors of the *Collectanea* discovered England's right to ecclesiastical independence in the sixth canon of the Council of Nicaea (AD 325), when the precedence due to metropolitan churches was recognized. Likewise they drew Henry VIII's attention to the Council of Toledo (589), where the bishops assembled at the command of Wambar, King of the Visigoths. Cranmer and Foxe headlined such canons as that of the sixth Council of Carthage (419), which enacted that no bishop, not even the *Romanus Pontifex*, shall be called 'universal bishop'. On the same theme, *Collectanea satis copiosa* included predictable but invaluable material from Gallican sources, Anglo-Saxon pseudo-history, and conciliar theory, notably the view expressed at the Council of Constance (1414–18) that a future pope should reform the 'abuses' of appeals to Rome.

No wonder that Bishop John Fisher and Thomas More found the work of the King's scholars unpersuasive. Yet that is aside from the present analysis. No recorded role in the making of the divorce tracts or *Collectanea* can be assigned to Thomas Cromwell; he was not a member of Henry's coterie of scholars, although he had established himself as a man of business at Court by the spring of 1530, and was a member of the Council by the end of that year. By the middle of 1531 and in early 1532, Cromwell and his assistant Thomas Audley had established themselves as Henry VIII's parliamentary draftsmen working at the King's immediate behest.[23] Indeed, in early 1533 it was Cromwell who was chiefly responsible for drafting the Act of Appeals, the principal legislative instrument of the break with Rome.[24] But the draftsman of a legal document need not be the true author or architect of its content. In short, if Thomas Cranmer and Edward Foxe had attributed secular *imperium*, spiritual supremacy, and provincial self-determination to Henry VIII and England in and after 1530, is this not perhaps the allegedly Cromwellian 'national sovereignty' of the Act of Appeals itself?

It thus becomes a possibility that the concept of Henry VIII's sovereignty erected by Cranmer and Foxe in 1530 is in fact the source of that 'revolutionary' theory of the unitary state attributed to Thomas Cromwell in 1533. Perhaps the key that unlocks the secret is actually buried in the Act of Appeals itself, not in the text as passed, but in its preparatory drafts. In draft form, the opening passage of the Act with which this discussion commenced contained an additional section:

> *In confirmation whereof divers* of the king's most royal progenitors, kings of this said realm and empire, by the epistles from the See of Rome have been named, called and reputed the vicars of God within the same, and in their times have made and devised ordinances, rules and statutes consonant unto the laws of God by their princely power, authority and prerogative royal, as well for the due observing and executing of things spiritual as temporal within the limits of the imperial crown of this realm. So that no worldly laws, ordinances, jurisdictions or authority of any person at the beginning of the catholic faith, nor long after, was practised, experimented or put in execution within this realm, but only such as was ordained, made, derived and depended of the imperial crown of the same, for when any cause of the law divine

happened to come in question or of learning then was it declared, interpret and showed by that part of the said body politic called the spiritualty, now being usually called the English Church, which always hath been reputed and also found of that sort that both for knowledge, integrity and sufficiency of number it hath been always thought, and is also at this hour sufficient and meet of itself without the intermeddling of any *exterior* person or persons, to declare and determine all such doubts, and to administer all such offices and duties as to their room doth appertain, for the due administration whereof and to keep them from corruption and sinister affection, the king's most noble progenitors and ancestors of the nobles of this realm hath sufficiently endowed the said church both with honour and possessions ...

The words in italics were added in one draft by Henry VIII himself, who also wrote that any foreign jurisdiction over English affairs in the past was 'but wonly by necligence or usurpation as we take it and estime'.[25]

It seems that the language of this draft is inherently that of secular *imperium*, spiritual supremacy, and provincial self-determination, and that the basic historical manual referred to, with oblique allusion to the laws of the Anglo-Saxon kings, is quite specifically the passage on King Lucius and Pope Eleutherius from the *Leges anglorum* as expounded in *Collectanea satis copiosa*. No wonder, then, that the early drafts were hastily abandoned in favour of the more arresting respectability of the preamble to the Act of Appeals as passed. To have left King Lucius unexpurgated would have been to proclaim to the world the poverty of the Henrician political alphabet – a schism which rested on pro-baronial propaganda cooked in the reign of King John. It was a sign of weakness and of Henry VIII's desperation that the Act of Appeals as passed defined the king's sovereignty in terms of 'divers sundry old authentic histories and chronicles' alone. Henry VIII became *rex imperator*; England became an empire. But a theological and political revolution was made through necessity – Anne Boleyn's pregnancy – to rest on an assumption that could not be made good by an agreed definition of an imperial constitution.[26]

Yet was the theory of 'empire' in the Act of Appeals in any sense novel? Was it more than the sum of the parts of secular *imperium*, spiritual supremacy, and provincial self-determination? Was it tantamount to national sovereignty and the idea of statutory omnicompetence? Or have such modernist concepts been merely attributed to the mid-1530s by later historians and legal commentators? Certainly the issue of statutory competence aroused perceptible agony in the 1530s. Thomas More knew well enough the efforts made by the draftsmen of the Act of Supremacy (1534) to avoid stating that Parliament had made Henry VIII Supreme Head of the Church of England, but that, rather, the king had always been Supreme Head and that Parliament was simply declaring an historic truth. Naturally More knew also that these efforts were futile, a point he proved definitively by being executed, not for denying the supremacy *per se*, but for refusing to be convinced that Parliament could do what Christendom said it could not. We have the record of More's own words on the subject, spoken to Richard Riche in the Tower on 12 June 1535:

> A king may be made by Parliament and a king deprived by Parliament, to which act any [of his] subjects being of the Parliament may give his consent ... but to the case [in question] a subject cannot be bound because he cannot give his consent ... [in] Parliament, saying further that although the king were accepted [as Supreme Head] in England, yet most Utter [i.e., foreign] parts do not affirm the same'. Whereunto the said Riche said, 'Well Sir, God comfort you, for I see your mind will not change, which I fear will be very dangerous to you ...'[27]

Of course, Henry VIII did not regard the break with Rome as a revolution: that was the ultimate measure of the genius, ingenuity, and ingenuousness of the authors of the *Collectanea satis copiosa*. Indeed, the Dispensations Act of 1534 positively affirmed England's commitment to the Catholic faith.[28] For England's political theory until 1536, when the last vestiges of the pope's authority as pastor, teacher, and interpreter of Scripture were cast off,[29] was less that of statutory omnicompetence, than that which assumed that conflicts between ecclesiastical and secular jurisdiction should properly be resolved in favour of the State and imperial Crown, save in cases where the enabling legislation was directly contrary to divine law.

The fascinating thing is that this last idea was older even than *Collectanea satis copiosa* and the Act of Appeals. Professor John Baker's researches into Tudor law have demonstrated that a belief in the supremacy of common and statute law over canon law and local custom was a shared attitude or cultural assumption among many common lawyers after 1485.[30] For example, Chief Justice Hussey asserted in 1485 that the King of England was answerable directly to God and was therefore superior to the pope within his realm. Thomas Kebell, an Inner Temple barrister, said in the same year that 'if all the prelates should make a provincial constitution, it would be void, because they cannot change the law of the land'. He meant that provincial constitutions were invalid if they contradicted prevailing English law, and the jurisdiction of the Church courts in cases of debt and contract had already been attacked by writs of prohibition awarded by the king's bench. John Hales, another barrister, in a Gray's Inn reading of 1514, expounded his objections to the problems of dual authority caused by parallel jurisdictions exercised by Church and State. He thought it inconvenient that similar questions should be decided differently in different courts, an argument that became the hallmark of the royal cause in the 1530s.[31] In 1512 a law and order statute removed the privilege of benefit of clergy from persons not ordained in the three higher orders of clergy in cases of murder and of robbery in churches, on highways, or in dwelling houses.[32] This act was the beginning of the abolition of clerical immunity from the effects of secular law in cases of felony, the privilege won posthumously by Thomas Becket by the Compromise of Avranches, confirmed by the *Concessimus deo* clause of Magna Carta and many times since. That statute of 1512 was, in turn, contradicted by Pope Leo X's pronouncement during the Fifth Lateran Council (May 1514) that laymen had no jurisdiction over criminous clerks, and was denounced in a sermon preached at Paul's Cross in February 1515 by Richard Kidderminster, Abbot of Winchcombe. Kidderminster said that the statute was against the law of God and the liberties of the Church; that it was void and sinful to put into effect; and that those who had made it, spiritual as well as lay (and including Henry VIII), were subject to ecclesiastical censure, and thus excommunication, if they remained obdurate.[33] This sermon caused a furore: as Hughes aptly remarks, Wolsey 'began his career as a cardinal as he was to end it, kneeling before the king and begging his mercy from the pains and penalties of praemunire'.[34] Henry VIII himself joined the debates in the wake of Kidderminster's sermon. Ending the affair in November 1515 at Baynard's Castle, he declared:

> By the ordinance and sufferance of God we are king of England, and the kings of England in time past have never had any superior but God alone. Wherefore know you well that we shall maintain the right of our crown and of our temporal jurisdiction as well in this point as in all others.[35]

Henry in 1515 had already studied the maxim that a king who does not recognize a superior is free from outside jurisdiction. Furthermore, he spoke in the context of a judge's opinion that the writ of *praemunire facias* ran against all members of convocation who appealed to Roman canon law not demonstrably based on divine law or approved in advance by the king. In other words, Henry, 15 years before *Collectanea satis copiosa*, defined his regal power in terms of his right to monitor the reception of canon law, in which case his 'superiority' was already deemed to embrace denial of the pope's right to infringe his territorial sovereignty on the basis of the Petrine commission.[36]

Another clash occurred in 1519-20 over the ecclesiastical privilege of sanctuary. Matters had come to a head in the wake of a local feud in 1516 when John Pauncefote, a Gloucester justice, was shot and mutilated on his way to the sessions at Cirencester. The murderers and their supporters caused a public outcry by taking sanctuary. Once again the matter was argued in the King's Council and before the judges, and ended by a pronouncement from Henry VIII himself:

> I do not suppose that St. Edward, King Edgar, and the other kings and holy fathers who made the sanctuary ever intended the sanctuary to serve for voluntary murder and larceny done outside the sanctuary in hope of returning, and such like, and I believe the sanctuary was not

so used in the beginning. And so I will have that reformed which is encroached by abuse, and have the matter reduced to the true intent of the making thereof in the beginning.[37]

Chief Justice Fyneux welcomed this statement, and made it the basis of a judgment in Hilary Term 1520 reversing accepted law upon ecclesiastical sanctuary: the notion of permanent sanctuary, he declared, 'is a thing so derogatory to Justice and contrary to the common good of the realm that it is not sufferable by the law' unless usage time out of mind, that is, before 1189, had been recognized at a general eyre. Nor should this allowance be regarded as meaning much, since Fyneux observed that no one had ever found such a recognition in the records of the eyres. This amounted to saying that the only possibility of watertight sanctuary after 1520 was when the privilege had stemmed from a royal grant with papal confirmation and use before legal memory, supported by royal confirmation and use since. Mere papal grants were in breach of the statute of *praemunire*, even if the statute annulled them retrospectively; furthermore, subsequent royal confirmations did not mend the defect.[38]

No doubt all this sounds technical, legal, and dense. But it may point towards an intellectual shift in attitudes to Rome and canon law in the 45 years between 1485 and 1530. When John Colet preached his Convocation sermon in 1512, he appealed to the leaders of the English Church not only to reform the Church, but to defend it against lay encroachments.[39] The same line was epitomized by the career of Sir Thomas More, whose ultimate defences of historic attitudes are best read in his *Apology* and *Debellation of Salem and Bizance*, rather than in the records of his trial and execution.[40] The *Apology* and *Debellation* were More's replies to books by the learned\ Middle Temple lawyer, Christopher St German, author of *Doctor and Student* (1528, 1530), *New Additions* (1531), *A Treatise concerning the Division between the Spiritualty and Temporalty* (1532), *Salem and Bizance* (1533), and numerous other works.[41] In these books, St German made quite categorical statements on the supremacy of English common and statute law over canon and papal law. For instance, he held that the law of the State, not the Church, governed all matters touching property, which, taken to its logical conclusion, meant that the Church retained jurisdiction only over its sacramental life and ceremonies. Discussing the anticlerical legislation passed in the 1529 session of Parliament, which Bishops Fisher, West, and Clerk had asked the pope to condemn as invalid on the grounds that it touched clerical immunity,[42] St German said that this legislation was made

by the assent of the king, and of all the lords spiritual and temporal of the realm, and of all the commons: and I hold it best not to reason or to make arguments whether they had authority to do that they did or not. For I suppose that no man would think that they would do anything that they had not power to do.[43]

Yet St German went further. In his *New Additions*, he observed that the king-in-Parliament was 'the high sovereign over the people, which hath not only charge on the bodies, but also on the souls of his subjects'.[44] A revolutionary proposition – or was it? In fact, St German's intellectual mentors turn out to be Sir John Fortescue, Jean Gerson, the Parisian conciliarist, and Marsiglio of Padua.[45] He had read and digested their writings before producing his own books. His 'revolutionary statement' may therefore really mean that he wanted the king to share with Parliament the *regimen animarum* – the tutorial 'care' or 'charge' of souls already entrusted to princes. Although St German was the first writer to emphasize Parliament as the legislative (and consultative) instrument for achieving the victory of the common over the canon law, it is, however, questionable how far statutory omnicompetence in the modern sense is what he had in mind when he spoke of the king-in-Parliament as 'high sovereign over the people'. We are left wondering where medieval concepts end and modern thought begins – if indeed the transition was ever clear cut, which seems highly unlikely.

If, however, this reading is correct, Cromwell becomes the man who, if he did not 'invent' St German's theory, nevertheless translated it into action between 1534 and his fall, since he succeeded in neutralizing the essentially absolutist characteristics of Henry VIII's 'imperial' kingship.[46]

Yet if 'assimilation' rather than 'revolution' was the keynote of juristic thought in the 1520s and 1530s, the work of St German, notably the twin dialogues of his *Doctor and Student*, testifies to a change since the time of Sir John Fortescue – a shift of either mentality or modes of expression. If a change of mentality occurred, it was inspired, I think, by juristic ideas at the Inns of Court. Thomas Cromwell would have been influenced, with others, but such a change of mentality would have been partial, or partisan, since Thomas More was a common lawyer too. If a shift in modes of expression lies at the heart of changed emphasis, it was signalled by St German's desire to circulate *Doctor and Student* in printed form, particularly by his decision to write and print in Latin and English rather than Law French, for this reveals his conscious wish to appeal to a constituency much broader than that of the Inns of Court.[47]

Another scholar, one directly concerned with the gestation of official Henrician ideology and the concept of 'empire', wrote a Latin treatise for the press. Edward Foxe's *De vera differentia* (1534) must be regarded as an acid test of the extent to which Henrician dogma might be revealed to a learned international audience during the year of the Act of Supremacy. (Foxe's book was in 1548 translated into English and printed in black letter, the preferred typeface of the literate people.)[48]

Foxe had four self-conscious aims in the *De vera*: (1) to establish that ecclesiastical jurisdiction had no foundation in divine law save in respect of the sacramental life of the Church, and that provinces of the universal church were largely self-governing; (2) that the contents of canon law had validity only as 'informations', 'rules', or 'traditions' for the guidance of Christian men, but not as laws that commanded obedience; (3) that holy bishops and Church councils repudiated the dominion of one man, favouring limited episcopal authority in the Church, and that holy bishops had sometimes rightfully resisted papal encroachments when guided by 'conscience' or 'private law' as written in their hearts by the Holy Spirit; (4) that the power of kings in general, and kings of England in particular, vouchsafed them undisputed rights of ecclesiastical government over both their churches and clergy. Both scripture (mainly the Old Testament) and the law of nature validated royal power – it was for kings to govern and judge. Kings were superior to bishops and bishops subject to kings. The clergy were only to administer the sacraments and to guide Christians by the holiness of their examples. Romans 13 was the key New Testament text, as expounded by Fathers and learned 'authors': the text gave authority to kings over bishops and clergy as much as over lay people. The thesis here may be summarized thus: all power was of God and must be so obeyed; the distinction was between lawful power entrusted to kings, and ecclesiastical tyranny permitted by God in order that men might be scourged for their transgressions.

The emperors Constantine and Justinian, together with the Anglo-Saxon kings, and William I and Edward I, were the historical models erected by Foxe. Yet the concept of 'empire' as announced in the Act of Appeals, at any rate in relation to the specific issue of ecclesiastical appeals, is almost overlooked in *De vera differentia*. The issue of appeals is mentioned, but briefly. Following a passage on Justinian, who enacted laws *De episcopis et clericis*, many 'laws' of England were cited to establish that kings there had maintained their historic authority over the Church. The matter of appeals is tucked away in this section between Justinian's laws and the regalian rights of Henry I's reign. Foxe quotes chapter 8 of the Constitutions of Clarendon, which had also appeared in the *Collectanea satis copiosa* in a version taken from William of Malmesbury.[49] The Constitutions of Clarendon were, however, a weak authority for the King's oversight of appeals: it is plain that an attempt is being made to give the legislation of 1533 spurious historical force. Otherwise the Anglo-Saxon kings predominate: the 'laws' of Cnut, Edgar, Aethelstan, Ine, Ethelred, and others are listed. King Lucius turns up again, as ever the joker in the pack. Likewise King Edgar's speech to his clergy, the Acts of the Bishops of Durham, the Battle Abbey charter, William I's letter to the pope, and Edward I's claim to overlordship of Scotland appear. The last issue is represented by long documentary quotation: Edward's royal dignity and customary law demand papal recognition of his right and title to Scotland, which the king must assert as an inalienable function of the English Crown, one that could not be granted away even if an individual English king were willing to do so. The argument is familiar, but Foxe's *De vera* adds nothing to the episode. One senses, above all, no awareness in the work that England's 'imperial' status was perceived as anything beyond what was actually maintained by the Lincoln Parliament in the political context of 1301. If national sovereignty and statutory omnicompetence in the modern sense were at stake in 1533 and 1534, Edward Foxe, one of the minds behind 'Henricus Octavus', *Gravissimae ... censurae*, the *Collectanea*, *Glasse of the truthe*, and the rest, prefers not to say so.

Before we abandon the vexed question of statutory omnicompetence, it does seem bizarre that the supposedly cohesive policy which manufactured the Act of Appeals under the guiding hand of Thomas Cromwell contained so dramatic an internal contradiction as between the notion of the supremacy of statute and that of the caesaropapist supreme head, Henry VIII. If Henry VIII was henceforward to manage the English Church and clergy directly after the manner of a late-Roman emperor, it would appear that Parliament was no more sovereign than it had been when the English Church owed allegiance to Rome and the papacy. The reason for this contradiction was perhaps that the Act of Appeals was itself a compromise document, partly between Henry VIII and Cromwell, partly between Henry VIII and the clergy. It is plain that the King could achieve the declaration of the English Reformation by parliamentary statute only with the cooperation of the lords spiritual in the House of Lords, who, if not in the majority there, were nevertheless in a substantial minority, namely 50 or so as against 57 temporal peers. Since there were conservative lords temporal as well as spiritual, everything depended on politics and parliamentary management. Of course, Henry coerced some of his clerical opponents into submission by threats, *praemunire*, and punitive taxation, but some bishops actually supported the King, and a vital truth lies behind this capitulation. It is beginning to look as if Henry VIII had decided from the beginning of his reign that he meant to control and manage the English Church; for 14 years he ran the Church and clergy through Wolsey, and the clergy connived, because it was better to be ruled by a churchman, however abrasive, than more directly by the king – and Wolsey certainly protected the clergy from the full force of Tudor policy between 1515 and 1529. Then Wolsey was destroyed by *praemunire*; the anticlerical laity and common lawyers were given their heads as an integral aspect of the King's divorce policy; by 1532 it looked as if the Tudor supremacy would be a parliamentary one, not a purely royal instrument of control. The King, who disliked representative assemblies out of 'imperialism' and emulation of the French, wished to cut back Parliament's contribution to the mechanical but still revolutionary task of enacting the requisite legislation. He found among the clergy some unexpected allies, because it was plain to all but the most ultramontane papalists in the years 1532 to 1536 that a parliamentary supremacy would have exposed the clergy directly to the pent-up fury, and hatred, of the anticlerical laity and common lawyers. Thus to politically alert bishops, royal supremacy was the better of two evils: the clergy would not have to counter the approaching anticlerical backlash without the necessary filter of royal mediation.

I have already hinted that the intellectual origins of the Henrician revolution might profitably be traced back before the Act of Appeals to 1485 or before, and that the principles of equality before the law, laicization, and rationalization as espoused by some English common lawyers reflected perhaps some sort of union of the juristic specifics of the English situation with the citizen-centred philosophy of the Renaissance that developed without direct regard to England or the Tudors. Of course, we must recognize the obvious: the 1530s saw dramatic changes; the break with Rome was in this sense a revolution. The triumph by 1580 of Protestantism and the established Church was an even greater revolution. Yet we should return, finally, to my suggestion that a case might be made for 1485 as a date of some significance. In addition to the arguments of the judges and common lawyers in the courts, in their inns, and as members of the King's Council – all of which had a cumulative effect, though they had been fundamental to the English scene for hundreds of years – we must face some harsh political realities. It was the first of the Tudors, Henry VII, who transformed the relationship between civil and Church authorities. The Tudors could not tolerate vested interests incompatible with their secular aims: thus franchises were attacked, liberties suppressed, actions of *praemunire* and *quo warranto* begun in the royal courts against Church and churchmen; appeals to Rome were monitored and suffered decline; requests for secular aid against excommunicates dropped to the lowest level since 1250.[50] All this was happening between 1485 and 1509, and every available method was used: an Act of Parliament of 1489 curtailed benefit of clergy; Archbishop Morton, Henry VII's Lord Chancellor, secured bulls from Rome modifying the privileges of sanctuaries which had become refuges for criminals, and to conduct visitations of religious houses hitherto exempt from royal jurisdiction.[51] We have seen that such policies were continued by Henry VIII.[52] Furthermore, Henry VII changed the character of the bench of bishops to the extent that Professor Knecht has suggested that, in the long term, secularization of the bench may have enervated its religious leadership.[53] First, Henry VII's appointments to bishoprics favoured lawyers at the expense of theologians; the King's first consideration was always that of service to the Crown, thus, of 27 preferments during his reign, 16 were of lawyers, and only six of theologians. Most of his theologians, too, were administrators.[54] Second, service to the State to the detriment of the Church was exacted as a conscious act of policy under Henry VII: thus William Smith petitioned in vain to be allowed to leave the Marches of Wales in order to pay attention to his neglected see, and Richard Redman had to compound with the king for permission to reside in his diocese.[55] The status of bishops in the King's Council declined, and Henry showed a ruthlessness to them typical of his treatment of other peers. Even Richard Fox paid £2 000 for a pardon, while all were subject to fiscal feudalism and the quest for revenue.

Under Henry VIII, though, the clergy were subjected to the harshest and most extensive taxation in previous English history. In addition to normal contributions in other years when general taxation was exacted, in 1523 and 1531 the English provinces were obliged to offer £118 000, the first time as the triumph of Wolsey's legatine ingenuity, and the second in exchange for the ominous Pardon of 1531.[56] Each of these donations was equivalent in value to the yield of a parliamentary lay subsidy of 2s. 8d. in the pound; thus the clergy were paying above traditionally accepted proportions of general taxation as between them and the laity. In short, a systematic attack on ecclesiastical revenues had begun. Henry VIII's attacks on benefit of clergy and sanctuary have already been mentioned; so too has his study in 1515 of the maxim that a king who does not recognize a superior is free from out-side jurisdiction. Yet surely such study was not undertaken in isolation. Henry's imperial ambitions, though they came to new and ripe fruition with *Collectanea satis copiosa* and the Act of Appeals, had more obvious origins even than the pronouncements of 1515. Henry had briefly sought the imper-ial crown of Germany in 1519. He hoped, too, to conquer the throne of France and alongside that ambition, first given military expression in 1512, went the propaganda war in which the French and English monarchs vied with each other for primacy in sacerdotal sovereignty. For instance, the French in 1515 republished the fifteenth-century dialogue known as the *Debate of the Heralds*. The French herald in that exchange praises the inde-pendence of his king from all overlordship, whereas, he jibes, the English king holds from the see of Rome. Moreover, the Frenchman boasts that his king can outshow the English in symbolic emblems of regal pre-eminence.[57] In reply, the English exhumed and embellished the ideology of the Hundred Years War. The exchange ended with an English vernacular edition of the *Debate*, printed in 1550, in which the English herald answered that his king was emperor within his own realm and 'holdeth of no man', that he is supreme head of the churches of England and Ireland, wears an imperial diadem, holds in his left hand an orb representing his empire, and in his right hand carries a sword to minister and defend justice.[58]

The *Debate of the Heralds* has recently been addressed by Professor McKenna; it would be interesting to discover more concerning the transfer of any similar English materials from manuscript to print between 1513 and 1550.[59] Yet such enquiry should be widely extended. Henry VIII, we know, had placed the arched or imperial crown as a decorative motif on his gold and purple pavilion at the tournament of 1511;[60] in 1513 the arched crown was struck on a special issue of coinage during the English occupation of Tournai, that emblem having first appeared on the coinage in 1489, when Henry VII minted his new gold sovereign.[61] When in 1517 Henry VIII was musing on the idea of aspiring to succeed the Emperor Maximilian, who had purported to be willing to resign in favour of Henry in order to gain a sub-sidy, Cuthbert Tunstall informed him:

> One of the chief points in the election of the emperor is that he which shall be elected must be of Germany, subject to [the] Empire; whereas

your grace is not, nor never since the Christian faith the kings of England were subject to the Empire. But the crown of England is an Empire of itself, much better than now the Empire of Rome: for which cause your Grace weareth a closed Crown. And therefore if ye were chosen, since your Grace is not of the Empire the election were void. And if your Grace should accept the said Election, thereby ye must confess your realm to be under subjection of the Empire to the perpetual prejudice of your successor ...[62]

All these matters require further research. Yet one thing is perhaps apparent. Politics, ideology and the divorce issue provided an explosive mixture in the wake of the fall of Wolsey. But the ensuing fusion was of formidable complexity. The opportunities that the political situation created were considerable, but policy could be ambiguous and was not fully coordinated. Many minds were at work; decisions had to be taken under pressure in response to royal requirements and immediate needs. There was no overall blueprint. Furthermore, unexpected traps beset the unwary. One awaited Edward Foxe, whose exposition of 'private law' or 'conscience' in *De vera differentia* justified Thomas More's defensive stand against Henry VIII far better than Robert Grosseteste's against Innocent IV. Finally, the cultural and mental background since 1485 may be significant: we need to know more about the inns of court, who was active there, whether readings and moots reflect discernible patterns of opinion, how widespread were St German's attitudes, how far juristic thought mirrored royal policy or vice versa, and so on.

The search for the intellectual origins of Henrician 'imperial' kingship will thus extend far beyond the achievements, and lifetime, of Thomas Cromwell. It will reach beyond England and the sixteenth century, too, since the theme of imperial *renovatio* was European: Charles V, Francis I, and Henry VIII stood in a tradition that sprang from Augustus, Marcus Aurelius, and Charlemagne. The theme of 'imperialism' in the Renaissance had been articulated by Ariosto in the *Orlando furioso* and was consummated for England by Spenser in *The Faerie Queene*. It is unlikely that Henry VII and Henry VIII were much influenced by this universal outlook, but it is equally clear that the question 'Who was the architect of the Henrician "political" revolution?' is *mal posée*, if Henry VIII and Thomas Cromwell are to be our only candidates. Whatever takes its place, the 'King or Minister' debate is dead. Yet, as Professor Elton had all along emphasized, Thomas Cromwell was not King Utopus.[63]

Notes

1 For the literature on this question, the following works are essential: G. R. Elton, *The Tudor Revolution in Government* (Cambridge, 1953); Elton, *The Tudor Constitution:*

Documents and Commentary (1st edn, Cambridge, 1960; 2nd edn, 1982); Elton, *England under the Tudors* (London, 1955; 2nd edn, 1974); Elton, *Reform and Reformation: England, 1509–1558* (London, 1977); Elton, *Policy and Police* (Cambridge, 1972); Elton, *Studies in Tudor and Stuart Politics and Government* (4 vols, Cambridge, 1974–92), I, pp. 173–88; II, pp. 82–154, 215–58; P. Williams and G. L. Harriss, 'A Revolution in Tudor History', *Past and Present*, 25 (1963), pp. 3–58, 31 (1965), pp. 87–96; C. Coleman and D. R. Starkey (eds), *Revolution Reassessed: Revisions in the History of Tudor Government and Administration* (Oxford, 1986).

2 Elton, *Reform and Reformation*, p. 169. See also Elton, *Reform and Renewal* (Cambridge, 1973); Elton, 'Thomas Cromwell Redivivus', in *Archiv für Reformationsgeschichte*, 68 (1977), pp. 192–208; Elton, *Studies in Tudor and Stuart Politics and Government*, I, pp. 173–88.

3 Elton, *England under the Tudors*, p. 161.

4 Elton, *The Tudor Constitution*, pp. 353–8.

5 *LP* VIII, no. 1054.

6 The 'Henricus Octavus' is named after its incipit, which was the salutation from Henry VIII to the cardinal legates at Blackfriars. See Virginia Murphy, 'The Debate over Henry VIII's First Divorce: An Analysis of the Contemporary Treatises' unpublished Cambridge Ph.D. dissertation (1984), pp. 66–80. Her findings on the 'Henricus Octavus', the *Gravissimae censurae*, and *Determinations* supersede those of H. A. Kelly, *The Matrimonial Trials of Henry VIII* (Stanford, 1976), pp. 180–1.

7 *The Correspondence of Sir Thomas More*, ed. E. F. Rogers (Princeton, 1947), no. 199 (p. 496).

8 Murphy, 'The Debate over Henry VIII's First Divorce', pp. 164–218.

9 The printed tracts are *Gravissimae atque exactissimae illustrissimarum totius Italiae et Galliae Academiarum censurae* .... (London, *c.*1531), and *The determinations of the moste famous and mooste excellent vniuersities of Italy and Fraunce, that it is so vnlefull for a man to marie his brothers wyfe, that the pope hath no power to dispence therwith* (London, 1531). *STC²*, nos. 14286, 14287. See E. Surtz and Virginia Murphy (eds), *The Divorce Tracts of Henry VIII* (Angers, 1988).

10 Cf. *A Glasse of the truthe* (London, 1532?), ready in 1531 or 1532, which is more emphatic. *STC*, nos. 11918–19. A modern edition is by Nicholas Pocock (ed.), *Records of the Reformation: The Divorce, 1527–1533* (2 vols; Oxford, 1870), II, pp. 385–421.

11 Elton, *Policy and Police*, p. 177 n. 2.

12 J. A. Guy, *The Public Career of Sir Thomas More* (Brighton and New Haren, 1980), pp. 131–51. The authoritative account is by G. D. Nicholson, 'The Nature and Function of Historical Argument in the Henrician Reformation', unpublished Cambridge Ph.D. dissertation (1977), pp. 74–156.

13 D. MacCulloch, *Thomas Cranmer* (London and New Haven, 1996), pp. 41–78.

14 Nicholson, 'Nature and Function of Historical Argument', pp. 111–13. The *Collectanea* is BL Cotton MS, Cleopatra E.vi, fos. 16–135.

15 Nicholson, 'Nature and Function of Historical Argument', pp. 74–214.

16 BL Cotton MS, Cleopatra E.vi, fos. 16–42, 64, 76, 84, 92ᵛ, 94–119, 134–5. Cf. Pocock, *Records of the Reformation*, II, pp. 385–421.

17 Nicholson, 'Nature and Function of Historical Argument', pp. 179–214; W. Ullmann, '"This Realm of England is an Empire"', *Journal of Ecclesiastical History*, 30 (1979), pp. 175–203.

18 BL Cotton MS, Cleopatra E.vi, fos. 27, 35. The letter is dated AD 169 in the *Collectanea*.

19 '[Rex debet esse] sub Deo et sub lege, quia lex facit regem', appears as 'sub Deo. Non sub lege, quia Rex legem facit'! (BL Cotton MS, Cleopatra E.vi, fo. 28ᵛ). Were Cranmer and Foxe using a royalist text or were they vetting Bracton?

20 W. Ullmann, *Principles of Government and Politics in the Middle Ages* (2nd edn,) (London, 1966), pp. 178–81, 204.

21 D. Wilkins (ed.), *Concilia Magnae Britanniae et Hiberniae* (4 vols, London, 1737), III, pp. 762–5.

22 Guy, *Public Career*, pp. 181–3.
23 Guy, *Public Career*, pp. 176–99. Much of the paperwork, however, is filed in Cromwell's archive.
24 Elton, *Studies in Tudor and Stuart Politics and Government*, II, pp. 82–106.
25 BL Cotton MS, Cleopatra E.vi, fos. 180–4.
26 Cf. R. Koebner, 'The Imperial Crown of this Realm', *Bulletin of the Institute of Historical Research*, 26 (1953), p. 30; Nicholson, 'Nature and Function of Historical Argument', pp. 182–91.
27 E. E. Reynolds, *The Life and Death of St Thomas More* (London, 1968), pp. 385–6. I have checked Riche's manuscript (PRO SP 2/R, fos. 24–5) under ultra–violet light, and am satisfied that the reading 'consent' (Reynolds, p. 368, line 11) is correct. It is a pity that the document is so badly mutilated.
28 25 Henry VIII, c.21.
29 By 28 Henry VIII, c.10.
30 *The Reports of Sir John Spelman*, ed. J. H. Baker (2 vols, Selden Soc.; London, 1977–8), II, intro. pp. 64–70.
31 *Reports of Sir John Spelman*, ed. Baker, II, intro. p. 65.
32 4 Henry VIII, c.2.
33 J. Duncan M. Derrett, 'The Affairs of Richard Hunne and Friar Standish', in John Guy, Ralph Keen, Clarence H. Miller, and R. McGugan (eds), *The Complete Works of St Thomas More*, IX, The Apology (New Haven, 1987 [1988]), p. 226.
34 P. Hughes, *The Reformation in England* (3 vols, London, 1950–4), I, p. 153.
35 John Guy, 'Henry VIII and the Praemunire Manoeuvres of 1530–1531', *English Historical Review*, 97 (1982), p. 497.
36 Guy, 'Henry VIII and the Praemunire Manoeuvres', p. 497.
37 *Reports of Sir John Spelman*, ed. Baker, II, intro., pp. 342–3.
38 E. W. Ives, 'Crime, Sanctuary, and Royal Authority under Henry VIII: The Exemplary Sufferings of the Savage Family', in M. S. Arnold, T. A. Green, S. A. Scully, and S. D. White (eds), *Of the Laws and Customs of England* (Chapel Hill, NC, 1981), pp. 298–9.
39 J. H. Lupton, *A Life of John Colet, D. D.* (London, 1909), pp. 293–304. For the date, see J. B. Trapp, 'John Colet and the Hierarchies of the Ps–Dionysius', *Studies in Church History*, 17 (1981), pp. 130–3.
40 More, *Complete Works*, IX, pp. 1–172; the *Debellation* is *Complete Works*, vol. X (*STC²*, no. 18081).
41 Alistair Fox and John Guy, *Reassessing the Henrician Age: Humanism, Politics and Reform 1500–1550* (Oxford, 1986), pp. 95–120.
42 21 Henry VIII, c.6; Guy, *Public Career*, p. 139.
43 *St German's Doctor and Student*, ed. T. F. T. Plucknett and J. L. Barton (Publications of the Selden Society, 91: London, 1974), p. 317.
44 *St German's Doctor and Student*, ed. Plucknett and Barton, p. 327.
45 John Guy, *Christopher St German on Chancery and Statute* (Selden Society, Supplementary Series, 6, London, 1985), pp. 35–6, 40, 43–4, 51, 72–3, 87.
46 Elton, *Reform and Reformation*, pp. 197–200.
47 *St German's Doctor and Student*, ed. Plucknett and Barton, pp. lxix–lxxvi, 176–7.
48 *Opus eximium. De vera differentia regiae potestatis et ecclesiasticae, et quae sit ipsa veritas ac virtus utriusque* (London, 1534); *STC*, no. 11218. The translation by Henry, Lord Stafford, *The true dyffere[nce]s betwen yᵉ regall power and the ecclesiasticall power*, is competent but marred by misprints and Protestant influences; *STC*, no. 11220. BL Cotton MS, Cleopatra E.vi, fos. 1–15, is a manuscript of the latter part of the Latin text of *De vera differentia* headed 'De potestate regia'.
49 *De vera differentia*, sigs. M3ᵛ–4; BL Cotton MS, Cleopatra E.vi, fo. 40 (annotated 'de appellationibus' by Henry VIII); W. Stubbs, *Select Charters*, ed. H. W. C. Davis (9th edn, Oxford, repr. 1962) p. 165; Nicholson, 'Nature and Function of Historical Argument', p. 194.
50 R. L. Storey, *Diocesan Administration in Fifteenth-Century England* (Borthwick Papers, 16; 2nd edn, York, 1972), pp. 29–33; *Reports of Sir John Spelman*, ed. Baker, II, intro., pp. 66–8; Henry E. Huntington Library, San Marino, California, Ellesmere MS 2652, fo. 6.

51 Storey, *Diocesan Administration*, pp. 29–30; *Reports of Sir John Spelman*, ed. Baker, II, intro., pp. 332–40.
52 *Reports of Sir John Spelman*, ed. Baker, II, intro., pp. 64–70, 326–46.
53 R. J. Knecht, 'The Episcopate and the Wars of the Roses', *University of Birmingham Historical Journal*, 6 (1957–8), pp. 108–31.
54 M. M. Condon, Chapter 11.
55 Condon, Chapter 11.
56 Guy, 'Henry VIII and the Praemunire Manoeuvres', pp. 481–503.
57 *Le debat des heraulx darmes de Fra[n]ce et de A[n]gleterre* (Rouen, [1515]), BL C.32.g.4; L. Pannier (ed.), *Le Débat des Hérauts d'Armes de France et d'Angleterre* (Paris, 1877). See J. W. McKenna, 'How God became an Englishman', in D. J. Guth and J. W. McKenna (eds), *Tudor Rule and Revolution: Essays for G. R. Elton from his American Friends* (Cambridge, 1982), p. 29.
58 *The Debate betwene the heraldes of Englande and Fraunce, compyled by Jhon Coke, clarke of the kynges recognysaunce, or vulgerly, called clarke of the Statutes of the staple of Westmynster, and fynyshed the yere of our Lorde. M.D.L.*; STC, no. 5530.
59 Cf. McKenna, 'How God Became an Englishman', pp. 27–31, 35–43.
60 C. Whibley (ed.), *Henry VIII* [an edition of Edward Hall's *Chronicle*], (2 vols, London, 1904), I, p. 24.
61 C. E. Challis, *The Tudor Coinage* (Manchester, 1978), pp. 49–51, 65–6.
62 H. Ellis (ed.), *Original Letters Illustrative of English History*, 1st ser. (3 vols, 2nd edn, London, 1825), I, p. 136 (*LP* II, no. 2911). For further evidence of the intellectual origins of Henry VIII's 'imperial' sovereignty, see Walter Ullmann, ' "This Realm of England is an Empire" ', *Journal of Ecclesiastical History*, 30 (1979), pp. 175–203; D. B. Quinn, 'Henry VIII and Ireland', *Irish Historical Studies*, 12 (1960–1), pp. 325–6; D. Hoak, 'The Iconography of the Crown Imperial', in D. Hoak (ed.), *Tudor Political Culture* (Cambridge, 1995), pp. 54–103; T. F. Mayer, 'On the Road to 1534: The Occupation of Tournai and Henry VIII's Theory of Sovereignty', in Hoak (ed.), *Tudor Political Culture*, pp. 11–30.
63 G. R. Elton, 'King or Minister? The Man behind the Henrician Reformation', in *Studies in Tudor and Stuart Politics and Government*, I, pp. 173–88.

9

Reassessing William Cecil in the 1560s[*]

STEPHEN ALFORD

William Cecil's early Elizabethan reputation rests mainly on the work of his most recent biographer, Conyers Read.[1] *Mr Secretary Cecil* was one of Read's last projects and it developed ideas which had guided his interpretation of Elizabethan politics since 1911: the importance of Elizabeth, the central role

[*] I would like to thank a number of institutions and owners of collections for permission to quote from their papers: the Marquess of Salisbury for the Cecil manuscripts; the Earl of Westmorland and the Fitzwilliam (Milton) Estates for the Westmorland (Apethorpe) and Fitzwilliam (Milton) Political papers; the Syndics of Cambridge University Library; the Controller of Her Majesty's Stationery Office for unpublished material in the Public Record Office; and the House of Lords Record Office. I am extremely grateful to Professor John Guy, James Hampson, and John Cramsie for reading and commenting on earlier drafts of this chapter.

of men such as Sir Francis Walsingham and Cecil, and the reality of faction in Court and Council.[2] But Read offered facts and dates without any sense of the mental world of Elizabethan politics, and the preoccupations – and pre-conceptions – of the early twentieth century are considerably different from those of modern Tudor historians. This essay tries to reassess and rehabilitate William Cecil, who has often been dismissed as an Elizabethan bureaucrat: loyal, solid, and dependable, perhaps, but eminently dull and two-dimensional. Equally, the first decade of Elizabeth I's reign was far more disturbing for her subjects than most historians have admitted. From the beginning, Elizabeth refused to marry. But was this a limited issue of family, heredity, and dynasty or a wider political problem? And what part did Cecil, as principal Secretary to the Queen and the administrative workhorse of her Privy Council, play in Elizabethan politics? How did the political system work, and how did education and the intellectual and religious bias of men like Cecil influence or affect their relationship with a queen who refused to marry and settle the English succession? What was the connection between Cecil and the principal issues – succession, religion, and the hostility of Catholic Europe – in the 1560s? These are some of the questions which ought to be asked by Tudor historians. The answers are more difficult to find, but they lie in a new appraisal of Cecil in the early Elizabethan polity.

I

The focus of Tudor political history has changed since 1985 or so. Moving away from the institutional studies inspired by Sir Geoffrey Elton, early modern British historians are starting to write about a politics 'with the ideas put back'. 'Straight' Tudor political and constitutional history has always been popular, and even the debate on Elton's institutional *Tudor Revolution in Government* was still an issue in the 1980s; but there is a very definite exciting emphasis on developing political ideas in sixteenth-century England, the importance of counsel and advice in practical political life, iconography, ritual, the Court, and new ideas of how the monarchy worked.[3] The direction of Tudor, and especially Elizabethan, studies is clear: there is a new sense of the significance of language, monarchy, the state, political ideas, and educational training.

First of all, it will be useful to pin down the chronology of the decade and describe the basic institutions of early Elizabethan government. Mary Tudor died on 17 November 1558, and Elizabeth acceded to the English throne on the same day. Her Privy Council – a compact group of about 14 men, all bound by an oath to the Queen, able to discuss matters of high policy and deal with day-to-day politics and administration – sat for the first time on 20 November.[4] It was a solid core of men who had been in important positions under the Protestant Edward VI and his guardians. It also included some key (and generally solidly Protestant) members of the nobility and a few trustworthy 'civil servants' from the reigns of Henry VIII and Mary Tudor. Most of these men knew each other from the reign of Edward VI, and many of them had been contemporaries at the University of Cambridge in the 1530s and early 1540s.[5] Privy councillors invariably sat in Parliament. There was one Parliament in the 1560s, which gathered in 1563 and, after a long prorogation, in 1566. The relationship between the Queen, Privy Council, and Parliament is a massive historiographical battlefield, but it is one which must be entered because it reflects the significant issues of the decade and has far more to say about the state of Elizabethan government than most modern commentators have conceded.

Europe was a dangerous place for England in the late 1550s and 1560s. Mary Tudor's war against France, according to one contemporary, Armigail Waad, had 'consumed our captains, men, money, victuals, and lost Calais'.[6] Calais was an important issue: England lost its final Continental foothold in April 1559 at the negotiated peace of Cateau-Cambrésis.[7] This was a massive psychological blow, 'the beginning of the same great plague, for it hath introduced the French king within the threshold of our house'.[8] This was the conspiratorial key to the decade. By the middle years of the 1560s, Protestant Elizabethans were absolutely convinced that there was a wide and European Catholic conspiracy against their kingdom, involving the pope, Philip II of Spain, the French Guise family, Italian princes, and Mary Stuart. This was made all the more real by the Queen of Scots' French connection: she was a niece of the Guise, brought up in France, and determined to play Elizabeth for all she was worth. Mary was the great-granddaughter of Henry VII, so her claim to Elizabeth's throne reinforced the ideological and political differences between the two women. The loss of Calais was one piece of supporting evidence in the wider theory, and so, too, was the presence of French military forces in Scotland. England intervened in Scotland to remove the French and support sympathetic Protestant nobles in 1559, and Cecil was the campaign's main sponsor and organizer. In fact, one of the chief justifications for English intervention was Mary's use of the arms and title of Queen of England. In May 1559 Cecil listed Calais and the presence of 'obstinate, traitorous papists' in the kingdom as two matters to be explored,[9] and they were very closely connected in the English Protestant mind: domestic subversion supported by the Continental powers, the support of France for Catholic Mary Stuart, and a rival claim to the throne turned this into a British issue with solid European dimensions.

The dangers and difficulties of Elizabeth's first decade seem to stand awkwardly with her historical reputation, but the Tudor propagandists used the perceived hostility of Europe to its best advantage. They certainly did a good job of stereotyping the Queen as Deborah, a Protestant saviour, and Astraea, the Just Virgin of the Golden Age.[10] In a general introduction to government and politics in the reigns of Elizabeth and James VI and I, Elton maintained as a general principle that the Queen 'alone conducted policy with an eye solely to her success as a monarch and a symbol of national unity'.[11] Wallace MacCaffrey, who has devoted his professional career to chronicling the development of Elizabeth and her government, argued that she 'had an intensely political personality and loved the business of politics'.[12] Sir John Neale, the Queen's biographer in the 1930s and, until the work of Elton, the central authority on Elizabethan Parliaments, provided an index listing for his *Queen Elizabeth* which reads like a compilation of virtues for a model heroine, describing her affability and charm, boldness, caution, clemency, courage, dignity, discipline, eloquence, foresight, graciousness, humanity, and so on.[13] It is, in fact, extremely difficult to move away from these accepted truths. Revisionist studies have struggled to break free from the methodology of this sort of debate. In the 1980s Simon Adams questioned the idea of factionalism at the Elizabethan Court,[14] and Elton challenged Neale's view of the 'government' (Elizabeth and her Privy Council) acting against a 'choir' of radical puritans in the Parliaments.[15] But even this new work challenged old interpretations on their own terms; certainly on some of the 'safe' and standard themes of Elizabethan government – Court faction, patronage, and overt conflict in Parliament – there is a rather disturbing sense of fighting old battles on ancient soil.[16]

To make the problem more complicated than it already is, the real Cecil, in his own time and context, is actually quite hard to pin down. In the 1630s Sir Robert Naunton based his account of Elizabeth's Court on 'factions' and 'favourites',[17] and this approach stuck; similarly, Thomas Babington Macaulay's 1832 review of Edward Nares' *Memoirs of the Life and Administration of the Right Honourable William Cecil, Lord Burghley* established the idea of Cecil as an unimaginative bureaucrat,[18] and this filtered its way straight into Conyers Read's biography. Perhaps more significant is the sense of cultural and intellectual lifelessness in Read's *Mr Secretary Cecil.* Cecil was a centrally important political man, but from what perspective did he approach problems? Read argued that Cecil 'took no interest in the unfolding glories of Elizabethan literature',[19] but did this really matter? In 1566 he asked his old friend and teacher, Sir Thomas Smith, to keep an eye out for books in Paris, and if any 'books be newly set out of Genealogies or of armouries remember me';[20] a few years earlier, he had asked Smith to remind John Somers, Elizabeth's special ambassador in France, 'to buy me some such like French books, as he knoweth I fantasy of Cosmography or Genealogies'.[21] In fact, a whole Cecil manuscript library catalogue survives from 1568, which lists a large collection of Greek, Latin, and Italian texts, from Aristotle, Plato, Xenophon, and Cicero through to Machiavelli and a copy of a collection of letters from his old teacher at Cambridge, Roger Ascham, to Jacob Sturm, an important European humanist.[22] The evidence of this sort of collection, reinforced by the work of historians such as Lisa Jardine and Anthony Grafton, who have demonstrated the way in which

Elizabethans read their books, closely and always with an eye to political parallels and examples,[23] has opened up a new way of looking at men like Cecil, and has made important connections between education, background, intellectual life, and practical high politics.

II

With some work and imagination, it is possible to explore the 'mental world' of Cecil. There are at least three strands in his work in the 1560s: the idea of Britain (and especially its history, written for political reasons), education and training for practical governorship, and religious providence. The last – a strong sense of God's intervention in politics – reinforced Cecil's historical sense of what Britain was and the part it played in Europe in the late sixteenth century. For contemporaries, Protestant England faced the power of Continental Catholicism. In 1569 Cecil prepared a declaration for Elizabeth which stated that England was different from other European countries in its 'ecclesiastical external policy'.[24] This was certainly an understatement, but the chronicle histories read by Elizabethans reinforced and explained the fact. Henry VIII justified the break from Rome and his 'imperial' monarchy by appealing to 'divers sundry old authentic histories and chronicles'.[25] This sort of historical evidence – however suspect it may appear to us – was taken seriously and used by Cecil to explore policy in the 1560s. Richard Grafton dedicated his 1569 edition of *A chronicle at large* to Cecil, and he explained in the preface how Britain had been ruled by Brutus the Trojan and later divided into England, Scotland, and Wales by his three sons, Locrine, Albanact, and Camber.[26] But the reader met this fact on the title page, which merged biblical figures of power and wisdom – Solomon, David, Saul, and Moses – with Brutus and his sons, William the Conqueror, Henry VIII, and Elizabeth. Ordained by God and by history, Elizabethans had a very strong sense of what England and Britain were.

But there were times when England had to defend its position, especially when it was under political and military pressure from the European powers. At least twice in his career, Cecil explained and justified English policy on historical and British grounds. As Lord Burghley, he began to write an *apologia* for the kingdom and its queen called 'England Triumphant', in which the voice of England defended itself in a declaration to 'all monarchs, kings and princes absolute of all regions christened'.[27] Although sixteenth-century histories were usually fairly standard, the narrative of 'England Triumphant' may well have come directly from Grafton: all the details were accurately recorded by Cecil and so, too, were the important points for writers and governors – for example, the original unity of Britain and the imperial power of the English monarch. Cecil rehearsed the reign of Lucius, during which (Grafton pointed out) the pope Eleutherius gave the king the power of

'God's Vicar' in his kingdom.[28] The same was true for the Roman emperor Constantine, who combined the Crown of Britain and 'the Crown Imperial'. This was the 'closed' European crown and it was iconographically central to the later Tudors' perception of themselves as 'imperial' monarchs. Grafton noted that 'close crowns came from Constantine the Emperor', and Cecil, sensitive to the implication, had England declare that 'all my kings successively in all ages have had the honour to wear a Crown close as no other king doth'.[29] Cecil argued that, as an imperial monarch, Constantine had introduced the Bible to Britain, 'granted liberty generally to the Church of Christ', and called a Church council (on his own imperial authority and not on that of the pope) at Nicaea in AD 325.[30]

This was not, for Cecil, an academic exercise but the use of history for a political purpose. 'England Triumphant' was part of a propaganda campaign in 1584 or 1585 to defend Elizabeth from what Elizabethans thought was a violent and organized campaign against their queen.[31] But Cecil had used the same sort of imperial ideas 25 years earlier. In 1559 he prepared some arguments *pro* and *contra* military aid for the Protestant lords of the congregation in Scotland. Some of Elizabeth's privy councillors were convinced that the French were going to fight a war on two fronts against England – south from France and north through Scotland – but the way Cecil justified intervention is perhaps more important than the strategy that lay behind it. Intellectually, it was a complicated business. On the one hand, Cecil supported the lords' Protestant religious stand and sent messages of solidarity and encouragement; on the other, there had to be a way for the English to justify their support for subjects against their rightful prince. This was a sensitive issue for Elizabeth: she had been on the English throne barely a year and was, at least in the eyes of the European powers, a bastard. One of Cecil's arguments fitted the situation perfectly. He maintained that England had a right to 'superiority over Scotland', which was proved by 'good ancient and abundant stories'.[32] These included medieval homages made by Scottish kings to their English counterparts and the idea of the ecclesiastical jurisdiction exercised over Scotland by the Archbishop of York. This argument was deployed for a very definite political purpose in the late 1550s (and once again during the 'first trial' of Mary, Queen of Scots in 1568 and 1569) and it was based on the evidence of chronicle history.

Cecil wanted to demonstrate that Elizabeth, as the senior monarch in Britain, had the right to supervise Scotland and intervene in the kingdom's affairs. He did this by working from many of the sources collected by the Tudors to justify their political and religious claims. Edward I told Pope Boniface in 1301 that English kings had 'prerogatives of right and dominion' over the Scots.[33] In December 1548 John Mason (one of Cecil's Privy Council colleagues in the 1560s) had access to Edward's letter from 'the book of notes gathered out of the King's Majesty's records for the justification of his highness' propriety and superiority to the realm of Scotland'.[34]

This may well have been part of the *Collectanea satis copiosa*, compiled for Henry VIII at the beginning of the 1530s, which reproduced Edward I's evidence for his overlordship of Scotland.[35] Mason's text is in Cecil's archive at Hatfield House in Hertfordshire. The arguments and the sources were repeated and developed by Tudor propagandists in the 1540s, during England's military campaigns against the Scots.[36] Cecil was a member of the English invasion force in Scotland in 1548, and helped William Patten to gather sources for his account of *The expedition into Scotland*.[37] He was part of an English imperial culture and tradition which could be pressed into use for very specific policy reasons.

One of Cecil's intellectual strengths was the ability to stand back and be able to subject policy to a sophisticated and complicated pattern of proof and analysis. He demonstrated this in his 'imperial' notes on Scotland in August 1559. There are two versions of the same discussion, both of them structured in the same way. The two notes begin with a question – in the second draft, 'Whether it be meet that England should help the nobility and protestants of Scotland to expel the French or no'?[38] – and argue reasons 'That no' and 'That yea', followed (in the first version) with 'A conclusion'.[39] The important point to realize is that Cecil's position cannot be gauged from the arguments *pro* and *contra*. The first reason against intervention was that 'It is against God's law to aid subjects against their Natural Prince or their ministers'; this was just as valid as the second, that it was 'agreeable both to the law of God and nature, that every Prince and Public state should defend itself' from present and future dangers.[40] Cecil accepted the accuracy of both arguments: he simply used one to defend a policy option and the other to support a more interventionist line.

This looks like a fairly natural way of looking at policy decisions and, to a degree, it was. But it was primarily based on the sort of rhetorical training Cecil would have received at St John's College, Cambridge, in the late 1530s and Gray's Inn in the 1540s. Two of his near contemporaries make the connection a little clearer: Richard Rainolde, who began his studies at St John's in 1546, the year after Cecil had left Cambridge; and Thomas Wilson, who was a student at King's College. Wilson, in particular, was connected to the circle of Cecil's friends at Cambridge and, later, in government.[41] He was a pupil of John Cheke, who was Cecil's brother-in-law. Cecil himself had been taught by Cheke and men like Thomas Smith, Roger Ascham, and Walter Haddon. All of them were distinguished academics and old friends; they eventually held government posts in the 1550s and 1560s. Rainolde published *A book called the foundation of rhetoric* in 1563, which was an English version of a fourth-century Greek text on rhetoric, but a Latin translation of Aphthonius' original was certainly known to students at Cambridge in the early 1540s.[42] Thomas Wilson's *The art of rhetoric* was published in 1554.[43] Both men explained the theory and the method of the rhetorical form of argument so often used by Cecil to explore policy issues.

Wilson distinguished between two sorts of 'question', definite and indefinite: indefinite questions were more abstract and suited to the abstruser musings of logicians, but definite questions 'set forth a matter, with the appointment, and naming of place, time and person'.[44] Rainolde described the nature and structure of a 'thesis', which he defined as 'a reasoning by question, upon a matter uncertain'. Of these, there were two sorts, civil and contemplative. Cecil's 'questions', according to this model, were civil, dealing with 'the state of a commonwealth: and are daily practised in the commonwealth'. Using Aphthonius' original structure as a template, Rainolde suggested an introduction, a narration, sections broken down into whether the question was lawful, profitable, and possible, and a final conclusion.[45] So Cecil's political pieces in the 1560s were, in rhetorical terms he would have been familiar with at Cambridge, definite questions or civil theses.

Cecil's political notes were based on rhetorical methods of composition, designed to explore difficult issues and questions; this meant that he could approach policy in the 1560s from at least two angles. His memoranda were often extremely complicated, breaking down issues into individual points which were dealt with in their own time and finally synthesized into a narrative account. This approach had two results: first, it forced Cecil to consider options and arguments on both sides of a definite question or civil thesis; and, second, once he had made the connection, Cecil could use individual pieces of evidence, intelligence sources, and basic arguments to form a comprehensive and heavily detailed picture of European and British affairs. One of the best examples of this was written at some point in 1569; the surviving manuscript seems to have been taken from an even larger project called 'the book of the state of the realm'.[46] In papers like this, the rhetorical method of composition reflected Cecil's mental world. They helped Cecil to plan or explore policy, and to develop and explain the personalities and issues in European and British politics in the 1560s.

This was, perhaps typically for sixteenth-century governors, heavily providential, and it was a component part of an apocalyptic vision in which two religious absolutes fought for victory in Europe. Some aspects of Cecil's 'anti-Catholicism' have been worked on,[47] but there is often a more subtle sense of providential action in his personal notes and in the minutes he sometimes made during sensitive Privy Council meetings. Cecil wanted a secure ecclesiastical settlement for England. In a 'Memorial of things to be reported to her Majesty' in summer 1559, he pointed to the seditious and dangerous activities of Jesuits and seminary priests but emphasized the moral failings of the clergy, 'covetousness, looseness of life and with many other defaults importing their discredit as they are rather neglected than reverenced'.[48] An assessment of the kingdom's justices of the peace in late 1564 and early 1565 forced the regime to reconsider the state of the religious settlement, and Cecil expressed his concerns in a Privy Council minute on 4 June 1565.[49] This was, in one sense, a very practical issue: contemporaries made a connection between domestic subversion and the danger of foreign invasion by the Catholic powers. But there was also a spiritual edge to the problem. Cecil corrected at least two prayers in the 1560s, linking the punishment of the kingdom to the Queen's sickness and the sins of her subjects.[50] In 'A necessary consideration of the perilous state of this tyme', which Cecil wrote in June 1569, he argued that God would use the French King as an instrument of invasion because of 'the sins of his people both here and elsewhere that do abuse the name of his Gospel'.[51]

Cecil's constant concern for religious and ecclesiastical order was not only an issue of obedience – and, like any other social conservatives, Elizabethans of Cecil's rank and position would have agreed with the accepted truth that 'Almighty God hath created and appointed all things in heaven, the earth and waters in a most excellent and perfect order'[52] – but a mark of success in practical policy and a reminder that all affairs were carried out under the eye of an arbitrator even more powerful than their Queen. Elizabeth's preachers constantly discussed the themes of their own authority from God and the Queen's obligations to the Church.[53] In 1563 Alexander Nowell, the dean of St Paul's, preached a sermon before the opening of Parliament in which he warned the Queen to accept advice to act on her marriage and settle the kingdom's succession for her subjects' good.[54] Nowell had been one of Cecil's student contemporaries at Cambridge, and this connection was important. In 1551 other old Cambridge students and future Elizabethan Churchmen – John Cheke, Edmund Grindal, Robert Horne, and David Whitehead – met at Cecil's house to debate transubstantiation. These discussions prepared the way for the 1552 Book of Common Prayer, which was promoted in Parliament by Cecil in 1559. Although he was opposed by the House of Lords during the parliamentary sessions, Cecil introduced bills for a Protestant settlement and, in the end, he succeeded.[55] Cecil's Edwardian and Elizabethan careers managed to blend his commitment to Protestantism and a belief in government acted out under the watchful eye of providence.

III

These themes – a British vision, the methods and skills of rhetorical education, and a keen sense of Protestant providence – are some of the keys to Cecil's work in the 1560s. They are part of a new methodology for Elizabethan history which, through an awareness of the importance of political thought and the benefits of archival research, should help to highlight the virtues of these complementary approaches. The Eltonian method of solid empirical work and the 'new' political history of ideas and language can help historians explore the mental world of Cecil, his sense of urgency and mission, of a political life – in Privy Council debates and Parliament, at

Court and with the Queen – constantly judged by God. Cecil's sources are extremely good. He obsessively kept more documents than could be worked through in a professional historian's career. The Elizabethan Domestic State Paper collection at the Public Record Office almost stands as a purely Cecil archive, littered with his notes, memoranda, and endorsements. This complements the British Library's Lansdowne and Cotton Caligula collections and the archive at one of Cecil's houses, Hatfield in Hertfordshire. Taken together, these collections form a defined and basically comprehensive personal and political archive.

An Elizabethan historian needs these archives to reconstruct policy, debates, and political decisions in the 1560s. The sources for the Privy Council are a good example of how manuscripts – rather than volumes printed by Victorian editors – can help to work out what was going on at the highest level of Elizabethan politics. Because the subjects of these meetings were extremely sensitive, the Council's clerks were sent out of the chamber. So most of the critical issues debated by the council in the first decade – intervention in Scotland in 1559, the proposed meeting between Mary Stuart and Elizabeth in 1562, Mary's marriage to Henry, Lord Darnley in 1565, and the 'first trial' of the Queen of Scots in England in 1568 – are preserved in Cecil's own minutes. Only very occasionally did the senior clerk of the Privy Council, Bernard Hampton, copy some of Cecil's notes. The printed *Acts of the Privy Council* record routine day-to-day business but the clerks did not deal with sensitive 'high political' issues. What is more, Cecil's minutes considered Anglo-Scottish relations in their broadest context: Elizabethan privy councillors believed that Mary Stuart was part of a European Catholic conspiracy, helped by her subversive co-religionists in England. Cecil's record of these debates is an invaluable source for Elizabethan councillors' perceptions of the situation in Europe and the state of religion in Elizabeth's kingdom.

At a second level of investigation, Cecil's drafting process reveals something that printed texts cannot hope to show, unless they reproduce every crossing out, insertion, correction, and amendment – in effect, the *way* documents were written and altered and, with some critical guidelines, *why*. When some of these texts were presented to the Queen, especially on sensitive matters of policy or calls for Elizabeth to marry, even slight alterations could apply a definite moral force to the monarch. There are clear examples of this sort of editorial control. In June 1565 the Council debated the threatened marriage of Mary Stuart to Henry, Lord Darnley. Darnley was young, vain, and annoying – an appropriate father to the later Stuart line – but he had a decent succession claim to the English throne through his exiled parents, the Lennoxes, back to Henry VII. Elizabeth and her Council certainly knew that Mary and Darnley were a dangerous dynastic combination, but Anglo-Scottish diplomacy had failed to keep them apart. In this situation, the Privy Council presented its advice to the Queen and Cecil had complete editorial control over the document. The Privy Council's main argument was simple: the Queen's marriage – and with it an heir and a sure succession – was the only way of turning the Mary–Darnley union into an irrelevance. Cecil experimented with the different versions of the text, and there is a clear sense in which he was trying to put linguistic pressure on the Queen by making the petition more urgent and immediate. His first holograph draft read that Elizabeth's marriage 'was consented by all persons, as a thing of most moment and efficacy to remedy all these perils'. After editing, the new and revised version (still in Cecil's hand) had the proposal '*thought necessary* by all persons, as *the only* thing of most moment and efficacy to remedy all these perills *and many others*',[56] and this more immediate text was copied by Bernard Hampton.[57]

Close textual work is central to a reading of Elizabethan political culture in the 1560s. Different drafts, with different emphases, can help to turn two-dimensional historical narrative into a three-dimensional view of the priorities of Cecil and his colleagues and the way they operated. This was certainly the case in June 1565, when the Privy Council was desperate for Elizabeth to marry and settle the problem once and for all. It was also important in 1566, when Parliament tried to press the Queen on her marriage and the kingdom's succession. Here, the sort of activity in which Cecil was engaged during the session raises important questions about the Privy Council's relationship with Elizabeth, the Elizabethan sense of the part Parliament played in its polity, the problems of sworn servants to the Queen tackling issues she did not want them to deal with, and the issue of duty to the person of the monarch balanced against a commitment to the safety of the kingdom. But this is something that even the most recent printed collection of Parliament material cannot touch.[58] The real significance of this Parliament, and Cecil's part in it, lies in an almost hidden world of drafts and draftsmen.

The basic chronology of the 1566 session of Parliament is crucial to this war of words between Elizabeth and her MPs, both principal gentlemen of the counties gathered in the Commons and privy councillors. The Parliament sat from late September 1566 until January 1567, and the questions of Elizabeth's marriage and the succession to the Crown were raised very early on in the session.[59] Almost immediately, the privy councillors in the Commons, as Elizabeth's sworn representatives, told the MPs that the Queen was 'by God's special providence moved to marriage and that she mindeth for the wealth of her commons to prosecute the same'.[60] This was all very well in theory, but there was a massive gap between Elizabeth's meaning and the MPs' interpretation of her message. She tried to make this clear on 5 November, when 60 Lords and Commons gathered to hear Elizabeth's position. In her own short rough draft she wondered 'whether it was fit that so great a cause as this should have had his beginning in suche a public place'.[61] From one copy of the speech, Elizabeth's stand was absolutely clear: she would never break the word of a prince in a public place, but it was not convenient to act. Her main point was less subtle. 'I am your anointed queen. I will never be by violence constrained to do anything.'[62] And that was the problem: Parliament, on the one hand, pushing – as a right and a duty – for action on the succession; and Elizabeth, on the other, a sovereign monarch, arguing that this was a matter to be dealt with at her own convenience.

It was, in a fundamental way, a question of competence. In his work on the later Elizabethan Parliaments, David Harris Sacks has made a distinction between matters of state – which included marriage, succession, religion, war, and royal prerogative – and 'commonwealth' issues – reform of law, economic regulation, and legislation for public well-being.[63] Sir Thomas Smith's *De republica anglorum*, written in the early 1560s, discussed the same areas of activity but it did not make the same distinction. Smith mixed Parliament's authority to alter weights and measures with its concerns for succession and the form of religion; and yet, in *De republica anglorum*, the prince is still 'head, life and governor of this common wealth'.[64] MPs thought that they had a part to play in what Christopher St German had described in 1531 as 'the king in his parliament' as 'high sovereign over the people'.[65] This was Cecil's position: he accepted that Parliament as the 'three estates of the realm' – a term which he used to describe the Lords and Commons[66] – complemented Elizabeth's power as queen and could and should contribute to the important political issues of the 1560s. This put Cecil in an extremely awkward position, and it led him to disobey the Queen in 1566. By tackling what was, for Elizabeth, the prerogative issue of succession, Cecil involved himself in a subject which stretched beyond the traditional limit of his duty to Elizabeth as her privy councillor. There is a hint of this in the main printed source for the Parliament, but the full scale of Cecil's work is only clear in the archives.

A few days after Elizabeth's clear warning to Parliament, Cecil began work on a text thanking the Queen for her decision to assent to marriage, in the name of the 30 commoners who had heard the speech.[67] He worked on two more drafts, but the document was not presented to Elizabeth.[68] These texts demonstrate two things: first, *what* Cecil was thinking; and, second, that he was quite prepared to play word games – determined, in other words, to press the moral and political responsibility of Elizabeth to act on her marriage and the succession. This is where T. E. Hartley's transcript falls down, because his *Proceedings in the Parliaments of Elizabeth I* prints only the third and final draft; unfortunately, this has distanced readers from some very subtle and important alterations in political language.[69] There is a hint in the different titles Cecil gave to the drafts: the document began as a 'thanks', became a 'suit', and ended up as the 'form of a petition', so there was a clear campaigning intention. Cecil noted, rather controversially, that the Commons had been 'deprived or at the least sequestred much to our dis-

comfort and infamy from an ancient laudable custom always from the beginning necessarily annexed to our assembly', which was to 'treat and devise of
matters honourable for your Majesty and profitable for your realm'[70] – a
pretty forceful statement of Parliament's duty and right to counsel in matters of national importance. Other sentences were edited away, but this
principle survived all three drafts. Cecil did exactly the same sort of thing
later on in the session, when he tried to put moral pressure on Elizabeth by
linking action on the succession to her promises as queen. But even in the
Commons' petition in November, Elizabeth's 'manifest and assured declaration' to act became (after Cecil's alterations) a declaration *'publicly to a
select number of your three estates* [i.e. Parliament] *in very* princely words
expressed'.[71] Elizabeth heavily resented 'such audacity',[72] but her own principal secretary was clearly drafting for, and coordinating, the campaign.
Why was this happening?

The short answer is that Elizabeth, clearly and persistently, did not want
to deal with the succession. Early Elizabethans expected their queen to
marry quickly and to marry easily, and it came as quite a shock to their
political system when she did not find a husband. If Elizabeth's claim to the
throne had been universally and enthusiastically accepted, the situation
might have been different; but the presence of Mary Stuart in the wider
equation, apparently backed by the Catholic powers of Europe, has persuaded Patrick Collinson to call the attempts to deal with her an 'exclusion
crisis', and he labelled MPs' and privy councillors' action on the succession
as a sort of independent 'monarchical republicanism'.[73] Even more important than this, perhaps, is the increasingly clear sense of a change in ideas of
duty to the Crown, from purely personal service to ideas of public interest.
Elizabethan sworn servants had to cope with the profoundly difficult problem of expressing private opinions in a system which was not even designed
for a separate political opposition.

IV

As a privy councillor, Cecil had sworn an oath in November 1558 to 'bear
true faith and allegiance to our soveraign lady the Queen's Majesty', to the
safety of Elizabeth and 'to the Commonweal of this realm'.[74] As principal
Secretary he had also promised to be 'faithful to the state'.[75] In a letter to Sir
Thomas Smith, Cecil admitted that, as principal Secretary, he was 'an artifi-
cer of practises and counsels',[76] but in 1559 he told (or meant to tell,
because the letter is in draft) Elizabeth that 'I will never be a minister in any
your Majesty's service, whereunto your own mind shall not be agreable, for
thereunto I am sworn, to be a minister of your Majesty's determinations and
not of my own'.[77] This challenged the notion of 'ministerial' work for the
Crown and how far it could be taken. The issue also highlights the fact that

honest advice from councillors could mean that they were forced to disagree with – or perhaps even disobey – the Queen. These were not academic issues but fundamental problems of royal service. Cecil's brother-in-law and Lord Keeper of the Great Seal, Sir Nicholas Bacon, had a similar problem in 1560 when he had to go before the English justices of the peace to defend a policy which he had vigorously challenged in the Council chamber.[78] On a basic level, working for Elizabeth had its frustrations. Cecil complained in 1561 that, because the Queen did not appreciate his efforts, 'I do only keep on a course for show, but inwardly I meddle not, leaving things to run in a course as the clock is left whan the barrel is wound up.'[79] But intelligent, political men under pressure had to be able to justify their reasons for action.

In part, this was a crisis of counsel. One MP in 1566 described Parliament as a council bound by duty to offer advice to the queen. In other words, the body should be able to influence the head; Elizabeth turned the metaphor upside down and emphasized the right of the head to 'command the feet not to stray'.[80] Parliament did not challenge the authority of the queen but it did sit awkwardly with Elizabeth's own interpretation of it. There is a sense, perhaps, in which the sixteenth century was starting to make a real connection between sentiment and action in politics; in effect, to turn sententious and standard language into an effective justification for the preservation of a kingdom.

This can be taken a stage further. The politics of the 1560s can, in part, be read back to the education of the magistrates and governors of the kingdom. The men who 'resisted', or disobeyed, Elizabeth's commands to Parliament were not religious extremists – the puritan 'choir' of Neale's interpretation – but they were dedicated counsellors (and privy councillors) in the humanist tradition. They understood and accepted models for good government and political change. Sir Nicholas Bacon covered the long gallery of his house at Gorhambury with thoughts and sayings from Seneca, Cicero, and Aristotle; the themes were moderation, ambition, friendship, fortune, and the greatest good.[81] At Cambridge, Cecil would have read the *Nicomachean Ethics* of Aristotle, which – in its 1547 English translation – highlighted the virtues of temperance, fortitude, charity, and liberality.[82] Cicero and Quintilian praised the active civil man who could plead in the courts for justice and take part in councils and assemblies.[83] These classical models were the foundation of Sir Thomas Elyot's programme of education for the future magistrates and councillors of the kingdom, *The Book Named the Governor*. Even Cecil and his friend and colleague Sir Walter Mildmay wrote advice for their sons on the virtues of a gentleman.[84] In a 1556 translation of Cicero's *On Duties*, a sixteenth-century reader would have found that 'if question, or comparison be made, to whom the greatest duty ought to be yielded: our country, and parents be the chief, by whose benefits we are most bound'. Ten years later, one MP opened a speech on Parliament's duty to advise the Queen on marriage and succession with the same text.[85]

It is increasingly apparent that real political change in the 1560s came from *within* the Privy Council and Parliament: these men were redefining their relationship with a monarch who would not play by the rules of monarchy and select a successor. Because Elizabeth effectively refused to settle the important issues of her marriage and the kingdom's succession – she promised to consider her position in 1559, 1563, and 1566 but her words were not backed by any real will to act – some of her most important subjects developed what was, to all intents and purposes, a conservative form of republicanism.

Frustration and a concern for effective government, rather than political ideology, lay at the root of Parliament's and the Privy Council's attempts to counsel Elizabeth on marriage and succession in the 1560s. In 1563 a Lords' petition pointed out to the Queen that day-to-day government rested on the life of the prince as *lex animata*, the 'living law', and 'therefore upon the death of the prince, the law dies'.[86] Cecil used this principle as a justification for 'a clause to have been inserted in an act meant for the succession'. His clause maintained that, in the event of the Queen's death without an heir or a declared successor (and Elizabeth had been seriously ill a couple of months earlier), the Privy Council should sit as a 'council of estate' to 'govern, command, and direct the public affairs of the realm, in like manner, as they have usually done in the lives of the kings or queens of the realm' until Parliament could declare a successor to Elizabeth. In effect, the Privy Council would be able to assume and use the imperial power of the English Crown. This was anathema to Elizabeth. Rejected or not – and the bill on the succession in 1563 was probably stifled by the Queen – the important point is that in the 'clause' Cecil considered a radical option to deal with the future of English government.[87]

Markku Peltonen has argued that 'republicanism' in early modern England was not a 'constitutional goal' – in the sense that in the eighteenth century revolutionary France and America pursued a form of government different from the monarchical one – but 'a theory of citizenship, public virtue and true nobility based essentially on the classical humanist and republican traditions'.[88] Cecil and his colleagues on the Privy Council and in Parliament wanted to be able to preserve their commonwealth, and if this meant putting pressure on Elizabeth they were prepared – perhaps not happy and certainly not comfortable – to do it. The Speaker of the Commons in the 1563 session of Parliament, Thomas Williams, addressed the Queen on the dangers of her death, 'which God forbid to fall upon your subjects to the utter subversion of the whole realm, whereof you have charge under God, if good provision shall not be had in this behalf'. Williams cast her in the role of the emperor Marcus Aurelius, a model of philosophical wisdom. In *The Golden Book of Marcus Aurelius*, Elizabethans could read how Marcus 'desired the wealth of his people, and the people his wealth'.[89] But Williams also reminded his queen of Alexander the Great, who had not made a good provision for his succession, and 'leaving that order and having no regard to his living was destroyed'.[90] Worries over the succession seemed to hone the Elizabethan governor's sense of duty to something more permanent than the reign of a single monarch. 'So citizens', in Patrick Collinson's memorable phrase, 'were concealed within subjects'.[91]

In a short book review, George Orwell described how he once cut a wasp in half while it was eating jam from his plate; only when it tried to fly away, he noticed, did the wasp realize what had been done to it, and Orwell compared it to how two centuries of writers had chipped away at accepted belief without any real sense of the moral and social confusion it would cause.[92] It was the same for Elizabethans: they were cutting links with the past, challenging established relationships in government, and with massive consequences. This was a period when the political creed of Cecil began to silhouette itself against Elizabeth's more imperial sense of her own power. Cecil accepted and promoted Tudor imperialism, but his notes and drafts help to establish two things: first, that he believed that Parliament had an important part to play in the operation of the Elizabethan polity; and, second, that there was almost a quality of *imperium* which existed in its own right, separate from the person of the monarch. In early 1570, after the rising in the north, Cecil made sure that his draft of a defence of the regime had the Elizabethan ecclesiastical settlement 'more clearly recognized by all the estates of the Realm'. In a second version, he altered it to 'more clearly recognized *to the Imperial Crown of this realm* by all the estates', not only of the 'Realm', which he deleted, but 'of the *same in parliaments* as the like hath been in our time'.[93]

In part, the whole problem rested on a fine line between counsel and compulsion, advised by a classical notion of the governor's duty to his kingdom or republic and keenly informed in the 1560s by a providential sense of the need for action before God's punishment. Counsel was based on the honest presentation of advice by councillors, and the free use of it by the monarch. But there were problems. Elizabeth used the mechanism of counsel to disarm opposition – by listening to advice, rejecting it, and issuing a royal command to stop debate or discussion. Also, her subjects were turning counsel into a call for definite action. So Elizabeth, who was free to reject advice but had to hear it, was being given counsel to be followed and accepted as policy, which, as Charles I said in 1642, would damage England's 'regulated' monarchy and turn the King into the doge of Venice.[94] In 1569 Sir Francis Knollys, one of Elizabeth's privy councillors, advised the Queen that 'it is not possible for your Majesty's most faithful councillors to govern your state well, unless you shall resolutely follow their opinions in weighty affairs'.[95] In a period so conscious of the rhetorical and persuasive potential of language, '*shall* Resolutely follow' has a definite ring of compulsion. Elizabeth's sex played a large part in her councillors' perceptions of their place in political life. As a woman, Elizabeth sat below men in the hierarchy of human society.[96] The Privy Council was used to governing England on a day-to-day basis, sending out letters and instructions to the counties. In 1559 John Aylmer, the future Bishop of London, argued that English rulers 'have their council at their elbow' to advise on the choice of the 'executors' of the law, the judges. He used this to counter John Knox's thesis that women were not fit to govern kingdoms. Aylmer suggested, in effect, that a female monarch in England was advised by Council and by Parliament.[97] So when the Queen did not marry or did not seem concerned to settle the succession, this mix of the commitment of Elizabeth's subjects to the preservation of their kingdom and a fiercely independent queen created a rather powerful cocktail. There was far more going on in the 1560s, certainly as far as Cecil is concerned, than most historians have seemed to suggest.

Cecil was not a revolutionary constitutional innovator: the suggestion, and even the implication, would have offended him as a man bound into the natural hierarchy and as a social conservative. But the first Elizabethan decade does demonstrate that early Elizabethan government was not a balanced instrument in the hands of a talented Astraea, but a group of governors operating in an immensely difficult political environment, struggling to cope with the stubborn refusal of the Queen to settle the future of the kingdom and prepared to consider alternatives. Practical government was made more complicated by the dynastic confusion of Mary Stuart's claim to the English throne and the sense of apocalyptic conflict between Protestant Britain and Catholic Europe. The early Elizabethans were more imaginative than historians have generally given them credit for, and some of the old views of Cecil as the 'partner' of the Queen, moderate and conventional, ought to be replaced by a better sense of his political creed. Cecil and his colleagues did their best to adapt to the new politics, using the skills their educational and cultural background gave to them, and they were just about able to pick up the pieces. Things were happening in the English polity, and Cecil, on occasions, was in as awkward a position as Orwell's wasp. Still, this is probably a better historiographical fate than being cast as an unimaginative, dull, and intellectually empty bureaucrat.

Notes

1 Conyers Read, *Mr Secretary Cecil and Queen Elizabeth* (London, 1955).
2 Norton Downs (ed.), *Essays in Honor of Conyers Read* (Chicago, 1953), pp. xvii–xxii; Conyers Read, 'Walsingham and Burghley in Queen Elizabeth's Privy Council', *English Historical Review*, 28 (1913), pp. 34–58.
3 For example, see G. R. Elton, *The Tudor Revolution in Government* (Cambridge, 1953); Patrick Collinson, *Elizabethan Essays* (London and Rio Grande, 1994); John Guy (ed.), *The Reign of Elizabeth I: Court and Culture in the Last Decade* (Cambridge, 1995); Dale Hoak (ed.), *Tudor Political Culture* (Cambridge, 1995); Markku Peltonen, *Classical Humanism and Republicanism in English Political Thought 1570–1640* (Cambridge, 1995); J. G. A. Pocock (ed.), *The Varieties of British Political Thought, 1500–1800* (Cambridge, 1993); Quentin Skinner, *Reason and*

Rhetoric in the Philosophy of Hobbes (Cambridge, 1996); David Starkey (ed.), *The English Court: From the Wars of the Roses to the Civil War* (London, 1987); on Scotland, see Roger A. Mason (ed.), *Scots and Britons: Scottish Political Thought and the Union of 1603* (Cambridge, 1994).

4 PRO PC 2/8, fo. 194; *Acts of the Privy Council of England*, ed. John Roche Dasent *et al.* (NS 46 vols, London, 1890–1964), VII, p. 3; BL Harley MS 169, fo. 1ʳ.

5 Winthrop S. Hudson, *The Cambridge Connection and the Elizabethan Settlement of 1559* (Durham, NC, 1980), pp. 18–24.

6 PRO, SP 12/1, fo. 151ʳ.

7 M. J. Rodríguez-Salgado, *The Changing Face of Empire: Charles V, Philip II and Habsburg Authority, 1551–1559* (Cambridge, 1990 edn), pp. 315–27.

8 PRO SP 12/1, fo. 151ʳ.

9 Hatfield House Library, Hertfordshire, Cecil MS 152, fo. 34ʳ.

10 Helen Hackett, *Virgin Mother, Maiden Queen: Elizabeth I and the Cult of the Virgin Mary* (Basingstoke and London, 1995), pp. 38–93; Joel Hurstfield, 'Queen and State: The Emergence of an Elizabethan Myth', in J. S. Bromley and E. H. Kossman (eds), *Britain and the Netherlands, V. Some Political Mythologies* (The Hague, 1975), pp. 58–77.

11 G.R. Elton, 'The State: Government and Politics under Elizabeth and James', in his *Studies in Tudor and Stuart Politics and Government* (4 vols, Cambridge, 1974–92), IV, p. 35.

12 Wallace MacCaffrey, *The Shaping of the Elizabethan Regime* (London, 1969), p. 299.

13 J. E. Neale, *Queen Elizabeth* (London, 1934), pp. 394–5.

14 Simon Adams, 'Faction, Clientage and Party: English Politics, 1550–1603', *History Today*, 32 (1982), pp. 33–9; Adams, 'Eliza Enthroned? The Court and its Politics', in Christopher Haigh (ed.), *The Reign of Elizabeth I* (London, 1984), pp. 55–77; for a more recent contribution to the debate, see Simon Adams, Chapter 10.

15 G. R. Elton, *The Parliament of England 1559–1581* (Cambridge, 1986); also Elton, 'Parliament', in Haigh (ed.), *The Reign of Elizabeth I*, pp. 79–100.

16 For two interesting examples, see Penry Williams, 'Court and Polity under Elizabeth I', *Bulletin of the John Rylands University Library of Manchester*, 65 (1982–3), pp. 260, 264, and Wallace MacCaffrey, 'Patronage and Politics under the Tudors', in Linda Levy Peck (ed.), *The Mental World of the Jacobean Court* (Cambridge, 1991), pp. 27–9.

17 Sir Robert Naunton, *Fragmenta regalia*, ed. Edward Arber (London, 1870), pp. 16–17.

18 *Edinburgh Review*, 55 (1832), pp. 271–96; Edward Nares, *Memoirs of the Life and Administration of the Right Honourable William Cecil, Lord Burghley* (3 vols, London, 1828–31).

19 Read, *Cecil*, p. 11.

20 BL Harley MS 6990, fo. 72ʳ, Cecil to Smith, 11 Apr. 1566.

21 BL Lansdowne MS 102 fo. 16ʳ, Cecil to Smith, 14 Jan. 1563.

22 Hatfield House Library, Hertfordshire, Library catalogue (1568).

23 Lisa Jardine and Anthony Grafton, ' "Studied for Action": How Gabriel Harvey Read his Livy', *Past and Present*, 129 (1990), pp. 30–78; on Harvey's notes, see G. C. Moore Smith, *Gabriel Harvey's Marginalia* (Stratford-upon-Avon, 1913), and Virginia F. Stern, *Gabriel Harvey: His Life, Marginalia and Library* (Oxford, 1979); William H. Sherman, *John Dee: The Politics of Reading and Writing in the English Renaissance* (Amherst, Mass., 1995), pp. 53–78.

24 PRO SP 12/66, fo. 150ʳ.

25 G.R. Elton (ed.), *The Tudor Constitution* (Cambridge, 1982), p. 353.

26 Richard Grafton, *A chronicle at large and mere history of the affairs of England and kings of the same* (London, 1569).

27 There are two versions, both of which are incomplete. For the first draft, in Cecil's holograph, see PRO SP 12/75, fos. 124ʳ–132ᵛ, which continues (after a missing section) in BL Cotton MS, Caligula B.iv, fos. 236ʳ–237ᵛ; PRO SP 12/75, fos. 134ʳ–145ᵛ,

for a clerk's fair copy with Cecil's corrections; dated by Robert Lemon, *Calendar of State Papers, Domestic Series, Edward VI, Mary, Elizabeth, 1547–1580* (London, 1856), p. 402, *c.*1570, but more likely (from diplomatic and internal evidence) *c.*1584.

28 PRO SP 12/75, fo. 131[r–v]; Grafton, *Chronicle*, pp. 82–3; G.D. Nicholson, 'The Nature and Function of Historical Argument in the Henrician Reformation', unpublished Cambridge Ph.D. dissertation (1977), pp. 182–4; Nicholson, 'The Act of Appeals and the English Reformation', in Claire Cross, David Loades, and J. J. Scarisbrick (eds), *Law and Government under the Tudors* (Cambridge, 1988), pp. 22–3.

29 PRO SP 12/75, fo. 142[r]; Dale Hoak, 'The Iconography of the Crown Imperial', in Hoak (ed.), Tudor Political Culture, pp. 77–86; Grafton, *Chronicle*, p. 89.

30 PRO SP 12/75, fo. 142[v]; cf. Grafton, *Chronicle*, p. 89; Walter Ullmann, ' "This Realm of England is an Empire" ', *Journal of Ecclesiastical History*, 30 (1979), p. 181; J. A. Guy, *Christopher St German on Chancery and Statute* (Selden Society, Supplementary Series, 6; London, 1985), p. 51.

31 PRO SP 12/75, fo. 126[r]; David Cressy, 'Binding the Nation: The Bonds of Association, 1584 and 1696', in DeLloyd J. Guth and John W. McKenna (eds), *Tudor Rule and Revolution: Essays for G. R. Elton from his American Friends* (Cambridge, 1982), pp. 217–22.

32 BL Cotton MS, Caligula B.x, fo. 33[v], Aug. 1559; also BL Cotton MS, Caligula B.x, fo. 86[v].

33 E. L. G. Stones (ed.), *Anglo-Scottish Relations 1174–1328* (London, 1965), p. 97.

34 Hatfield House Library, Hertfordshire, Cecil MS 234, no. 1.

35 Nicholson, 'The Nature and Function of Historical Argument,' p. 177; BL Cotton MS, Cleopatra E.vi, fo. 41[v]; Nicholson, 'Act of Appeals', pp. 20–1.

36 Thomas Berthelet, *A declaration, containing the just causes and considerations of this present war with the Scots* (London, 1542), sig. C1[r]; John Hooper, *A declaration of Christ and of his office* (London, 1547), sig. A3[r–v]; Richard Grafton, *An epitome of the title that the king's majesty of England hath to the sovereignty of Scotland* (London, 1548), sig. A5[v].

37 William Patten, *The expedition into Scotland of the most worthily fortunate prince Edward, duke of Somerset, uncle to our most noble sovereign lord the king's majesty Edward the VI* (London, 1548).

38 BL Cotton MS, Caligula B.x, fo. 33[r].

39 BL Cotton MS, Caligula B.x, fos. 86[r]–88[v], for the first draft; BL Cotton MS, Caligula B.x, fos. 33[r]–37[v], for the second.

40 BL Cotton MS, Caligula B.x, fo. 33[r–v].

41 *Alumni Cantabrigienses: A Biographical List of All Known Students, Graduates and Holders of Office at the University of Cambridge, from the Earliest Times to 1900*, ed. John Venn and J. A. Venn (2 parts, 10 vols; Cambridge, 1922–54), part I, iii, 445 (Rainolde); part I, iv, 432 (Wilson); Skinner, *Reason and Rhetoric*, p. 52.

42 Richard Rainolde, *A book called the foundation of rhetoric, because all other parts of rhetoric are grounded thereupon* (London, 1563); *Aphthonii*, ed. Gentian Hervet (London, *c.*1520); E. S. Leedham Green (ed.), *Books in Cambridge Inventories: Book-Lists from Vice-Chancellor's Court Probate Inventories in the Tudor and Stuart Periods* (2 vols, Cambridge, 1986), I, pp. 36–7, 39–42, 61–70, 70–5; II, p. 29; Skinner, *Reason and Rhetoric*, pp. 29–30.

43 Thomas Wilson, *The art of rhetoric, for the use of all such as are studious of eloquence* (n.p., 1554).

44 Wilson, *The art of rhetoric*, fo. 1[r].

45 Rainolde, *A book called the foundation of rhetoric*, fo. 54[r–v].

46 Hatfield House Library, Hertfordshire, Cecil MS 157, fos. 2[r]–8[v], printed in Samuel Haynes (ed.), *Collection of State Papers ... Left by William Cecil, Lord Burghley* (London, 1740), pp. 579–88.

47 Malcolm R. Thorp, 'Catholic Conspiracy in Early Elizabethan Foreign Policy', *Sixteenth Century Journal*, 15 (1984), pp. 431–48; 'William Cecil and the Antichrist:

A Study in Anti-Catholic Ideology', in Malcolm R. Thorp and Arthur J. Slavin (eds), *Politics, Religion, and Diplomacy in Early Modern Europe* (Sixteenth Century Essays and Studies, 27; Kirksville, Miss., 1994), pp. 289–304.

48 PRO SP 12/4, fo. 135^r.
49 PRO SP 52/10, fo. 149^r; BL Cotton MS, Caligula B.x, fo. 303^r.
50 BL Lansdowne MS 116, fo. 73^r, n.d. but *c*.1563; BL Lansdowne MS 116, fo. 75^r (1568).
51 PRO SP 12/51, fo. 10^v.
52 'An exhortation concerning good order and obedience to rulers and magistrates', in Ronald B. Bond (ed.), *Certain Sermons or Homilies (1547) and a Homily against Disobedience and Wilful Rebellion (1570). A Critical Edition* (Toronto, Buffalo, and London, 1987), p. 161.
53 Margaret Christian, 'Elizabeth's Preachers and the Government of Women: Defining and Correcting a Queen', *Sixteenth Century Journal*, 24 (1993), pp. 561–76.
54 Alexander Nowell, *A Catechism Written in Latin*, ed. G. E. Corrie (Parker Society; Cambridge, 1853), pp. 223–9.
55 John Strype, *The life of the learned Sir John Cheke, kt. first instructor, afterwards secretary of state, to king Edward VI* (Oxford, 1821), pp. 69–86; John Guy, *Tudor England* (Oxford, 1988), pp. 260–3.
56 PRO SP 52/10, fo. 149^v.
57 BL Cotton MS, Caligula B.x, fos. 303^v–304^r.
58 T. E. Hartley (ed.), *Proceedings in the Parliaments of Elizabeth I, I, 1558–1581* (Leicester, 1981), pp. 53–175.
59 House of Lords Record Office, MS Journals, House of Commons 1, fo. 229^v (*Journals of the House of Commons*, I, p. 74), 18 Oct. 1566.
60 House of Lords Record Office, MS Journals, House of Commons 1, fo. 260^r (*Journals of the House of Commons*, I, p. 75), 19 Oct. 1566.
61 PRO SP 12/41, fo. 8^r; Hartley (ed.), *Proceedings*, p. 145.
62 Cambridge University Library, MS Gg.iii.34, fos. 211–211(b); Hartley (ed.), *Proceedings*, pp. 147–8.
63 David Harris Sacks, 'Private Profit and Public Good: The Problem of the State in Elizabethan Theory and Practice', in Gordon J. Schochet (ed.), *Law, Literature, and the Settlement of Regimes* (Folger Institute Center for the History of British Political Thought Proceedings, 2; Washington, 1990), pp. 126–7.
64 Sir Thomas Smith, *De republica anglorum*, ed. Mary Dewar (Cambridge, 1982), pp. 78–9, 88.
65 *St German's Doctor and Student*, ed. T. F. T. Plucknett and J. L. Barton (Publications of the Selden Society, 91; London, 1974), p. 327; Guy, *Tudor England*, pp. 374–5.
66 For example, Hatfield House, Hertfordshire, Cecil MS 153, fo. 34^r, Cecil and Dr Nicholas Wotton to Elizabeth, 6 July 1560; BL Lansdowne MS. 102, fo. 22^r, Cecil to Sir Thomas Smith, 18 Feb. 1563.
67 PRO SP 12/41, fos. 38^r–40^v.
68 PRO SP 12/41, fos. 41^r–44^v; PRO SP 12/41, fos. 45^r–48^v.
69 Hartley (ed.), *Proceedings*, pp. 155–7.
70 PRO SP 12/41, fo. 46^v.
71 PRO SP 12/41, fos. 88^{r-v}.
72 BL Lansdowne MS 1236, fo. 42^{r-v}.
73 Patrick Collinson, 'The Monarchical Republic of Queen Elizabeth I', in his *Elizabethan Essays*, pp. 31–57.
74 PRO SP 12/1, fo. 3^v.
75 PRO SP 12/1, fo. 12^r.
76 BL Lansdowne MS 102, fo. 56^r, 11 Jan. 1564.
77 BL Lansdowne MS 102, fo. 1^r.
78 Folger Shakespeare Library, Washington, MS V.a.143, fos. 40–4.
79 BL Add. MS. 25830, fo. 228^v.
80 PRO SP 46/166, fo. 3^v; BL Cotton MS, Charter IV. 38(2); Hartley (ed.), *Proceedings*, pp. 129–30, 174.

81 Patrick Collinson, 'Sir Nicholas Bacon and the Elizabethan *via media*', *Historical Journal*, 23 (1980), p. 260.
82 *The Ethics of Aristotle* (London, 1547), sig. B3ʳ–D8ʳ.
83 Skinner, *Reason and Rhetoric*, pp. 67–72.
84 Thomas Elyot, *The Book Named the Governor*, ed. S. E. Lehmberg (London and New York, 1962); William Cecil, *Certain Precepts, or Directions* (London, 1617); Northamptonshire Record Office, Westmorland (Apethorpe) Miscellaneous MS 35, fos. 15ᵛ–20ʳ; Northamptonshire Record Office, Westmorland (Apethorpe) Miscellaneous MS 28, fos. 313–22.
85 *Marcus Tullius Cicero's Three Books of Duties*, ed. Gerald O'Gorman (Renaissance English Text Society, Sixth Series, 12; Washington, London, and Toronto, 1990), p. 73; PRO SP 46/166, fo. 3ʳ, printed in Hartley (ed.), *Proceedings*, p. 129.
86 PRO SP 12/27, fo. 136ᵛ, printed in Hartley (ed.), *Proceedings*, p. 60.
87 PRO SP 12/28, fos. 68ʳ–69ᵛ, in Cecil's holograph.
88 Peltonen, *Classical Humanism and Republicanism*, p. 12.
89 Antonio de Guevara, *The Golden Book of Marcus Aurelius, Emperor and Eloquent Orator*, trans. J. Bourchier (London, 1535), sig. Z2ʳ.
90 PRO SP 12/27, fo. 139v, printed in Hartley (ed.), *Proceedings*, p. 91; BL Cotton MS Titus F.i, fo. 72ʳ.
91 Patrick Collinson, 'De republica Anglorum: or, History with the Politics put Back', in his *Elizabethan Essays*, p. 19.
92 George Orwell, 'Notes on the Way', in Sonia Orwell and Ian Angus (eds), *The Collected Essays, Journalism and Letters of George Orwell* (4 vols, London, 1968), II, p. 15.
93 Hatfield House Library, Hertfordshire, Cecil MS 157, fo. 11ʳ; PRO SP 12/66, fo. 150ʳ.
94 John Guy, 'The Rhetoric of Counsel in Early Modern England', in Hoak (ed.), *Tudor Political Culture*, pp. 308–9; J. P. Kenyon (ed.), *The Stuart Constitution 1603–1688* (Cambridge, 1986), p. 19.
95 PRO SP 12/49, fo. 57ᵛ, Knollys to Elizabeth, 17 Jan. 1569.
96 Constance Jordan, 'Woman's Rule in Sixteenth-Century British Political Thought', *Renaissance Quarterly*, 40 (1987), p. 421.
97 John Aylmer, *A harbour for faithful and true subjects* (London, 1559), sig. H3v; for extracts, see Elton (ed.), *Tudor Constitution*, p. 16.

10

Favourites and factions at the Elizabethan Court

SIMON ADAMS

As the household of a virgin queen regnant, the Court of Elizabeth I was all but unique for the sixteenth century. The limited exceptions of her sister's essentially female Privy Chamber and the Court of Mary Stuart in Scotland between 1561 and 1565 prove, as it were, the rule. In institutional terms, Elizabeth's Court was simply a restricted version of its predecessors. The Privy Chamber, central to the Courts of Henry VII and Henry VIII, was reduced to a feminine inner sanctum similar to that of Mary Tudor.[1] As if in compensation, however, the reign produced a controversial novelty: the male favourite, whose leading characteristic was his physical and personal attraction for the Queen. Unlike the 'favourites' of Henry VIII (or, for that matter, those of Francis I), these men were neither a large nor a transient series of companions. Rather, they were individuals who both occupied the central positions at the Court, and enjoyed an apparently unequalled degree of intimacy with and indulgence by the Queen.

By the end of Elizabeth's reign there was general agreement that there had been four favourites of this rank: Robert Dudley, Earl of Leicester, Robert Devereux, Earl of Essex, Sir Christopher Hatton, and Sir Walter Raleigh. But 1603 did not bring the era of favourites to an end. The homosexual affections of James I led to the rise of two men, Robert Kerr, Earl of Somerset, and George Villiers, Duke of Buckingham, whose influence and position were as great if not greater than those of their Elizabethan predecessors.[2] By the date of the assassination of Buckingham (1628) there had been nearly 60 years of favourites; by then also their role had become both the subject of major controversy and a political issue in its own right.[3] This debate has in turn had a major influence on all later comment on the Court of Elizabeth I.

In a perceptive survey of the present state of Tudor studies, Ralph Houlbrooke has drawn attention to a recent revisionist emphasis on 'harmony' in Elizabethan politics. He refers in particular to the work of Sir Geoffrey Elton and Norman Jones on Parliament, which has disputed the presence of 'a powerful puritan opposition', and to an earlier essay of mine on the Court, which 'denies the existence of destabilising factional rivalries at any time before the 1590s'. The latter, he feels, might have gone 'too far in playing down the volatility of court politics'. The comment is a fair one, for the classic image of the Elizabethan Court, as established in such works as Sir John Neale's essay 'The Elizabethan Political Scene', is one of intense rivalry and factionalism.[4] Indeed, it has been considered one of Elizabeth's strengths that she was able in the main to 'manage' this factionalism to her own advantage. What has not been sufficiently appreciated, however, is the way in which this image of the Court was a product of the contemporary debate on favourites. Even less understood is the way in which the Stuart context of the later stages of the debate came to influence the portrayal of Elizabeth's reign.[5] The result has been a confused tapestry in which myth and reality have been deeply interwoven.

About one point there is no real controversy. During the 1590s the Court was nearly torn apart by a factional struggle of major proportions that culminated in an attempted *coup d'état*. The antagonism between the Earl of Essex and Sir Robert Cecil spread into the country at large, and left scars on the English body politic for at least a generation. Less clear, however, is the relationship between the politics of this decade and the three that preceded it. Was the difference one of degree or of kind? If the former, was there a 'controlled' factionalism in the earlier period that degenerated in the latter?

If the latter, did the Essex–Cecil rivalry initiate a new political world quite unlike the earlier years?

Any study of the Elizabethan Court prior to the 1590s must focus on the Earl of Leicester, who, as the leading favourite, was at its centre. Moreover, it was Leicester rather than Essex who inspired the controversy over the favourite. Essentially there were two extreme arguments. Was Leicester an all-powerful, hegemonic, or monopolistic force or was he but one of a number of personalities or factions competing in a more fluid environment? The manner in which these questions were phrased is best revealed if the debate is set in its immediate context, and the ways in which the issues it raised were exploited for later political and polemical ends are examined. Although the debate was primarily concerned with the structure of power at the Elizabethan Court, its implications were much wider. At its heart lay the impact of the Reformation on the English political system.

I

The central document in the controversy is the most notorious of Elizabethan political libels: *The Copy of a Letter written by a Master of Arts of Cambridge* of 1584, better known as 'Leicester's Commonwealth'.[6] It was not, however, *sui generis*. Rather, it formed part of a particular strand of Elizabethan Catholic polemic that included two other important tracts: *A Treatise of Treasons against Q. Elizabeth* of 1572, and *A Declaration of the True Causes of the Great Troubles presupposed to be intended against England* of 1592.[7] Like 'Leicester's Commonwealth', these were celebrated enough to receive familiar titles, 'The Papists' Commonwealth' and 'Burghley's Commonwealth'. In all three cases the putative author or authors are still disputed.[8]

These tracts are distinguished from the main body of Elizabethan Catholic literature by their concern with the structure of politics. They share an initial premiss common to many other sixteenth-century Catholic interpretations of the Reformation: the argument that heresy had been introduced by new men, whose intentions were political revolution. These men were 'machiavellian' in the sense made explicit in *A Treatise of Treasons*: 'it is that I call a Machiavellian state and regiment: where religion is put behind in second and last place, where civil policie, I meane, is preferred before it.' Thus 'to set up a lawless faction of Machiavellian Libertines ... a new religion was pretended'.[9]

The argument was itself a variant on the old theme of evil councillors. Its significance lies in the identification of the supporters of the Reformation as new men, and the attribution of machiavellian motives to them. In this way the cause of the Catholic Church was linked to that of the 'ancient nobility', an association that had first been made in the 1530s. The attacks on

Thomas Cromwell by the rebels of the Pilgrimage of Grace of 1536 and then by Cardinal Pole in 1539 had made explicit both the threat to the ancient nobility and the machiavellianism of the new men.[10] The charge was revived during the rebellion of the northern earls in 1569. In the Darlington proclamation of 16 November the earls of Northumberland and Westmorland identified their enemies as

> diverse newe set up nobles about the Quenes Majestie, [who] have and do dailie, not only go about to overthrow and put down the ancient nobilitie of this realme, but also have misused the Queens Majesties owne personne, and also have ... mayntayned an new found religion and heresie ...[11]

This argument was taken up more extensively in *A Treatise of Treasons*, which was published on the eve of the trial of the fourth Duke of Norfolk for his involvement in the Ridolphi plot of 1571. Its immediate purpose was to defend Norfolk and Mary, Queen of Scots, from the charges against them. To do so it associated Mary's cause with that of the Catholic Church and the ancient nobility. The link was forged by a common threat: the attempt to eliminate Mary from the succession 'under the title of a third family' by 'two Catalines'.[12] The two are not named, but there are sufficient personal allusions to identify them clearly as Lord Burghley and Sir Nicholas Bacon, the Lord Keeper. Their aim was said to be 'a new crew and the setting up of a partie Protestant', by means of a puppet monarchy first under Elizabeth, who had been kept unmarried deliberately, and then under the children of the Earl of Hertford and Lady Catherine Grey. Their control of the Court provided them with the means to do so, for Elizabeth had been isolated and 'al accesse of those that would intimate it unto her is by one crafte or other restrained and prohibited from her'.[13]

A number of subsidiary accusations were also made – financial malversation and corruption, the encouragement of foreign immigration that drove Englishmen out of work, and a major change in foreign policy, which involved the alienation of old allies, the stirring-up of panics of foreign invasions, and the encouragement of rebellion abroad – though little evidence was advanced to support the charges. However, the tract does contain a detailed account of the complex events of 1569.[14] This is of major importance, for the events described were the one apparent example of a major power struggle in Elizabeth's Court. The *Treatise* distinguishes between two separate intrigues. One was the proposed marriage of Norfolk and the Queen of Scots, which it claims was agreed to by all the Privy Council except Bacon. The earls of Arundel, Pembroke, and Leicester, and Cecil himself are specifically mentioned. The second was the attempt to overthrow Cecil, organized by Norfolk 'and the other nobility'. In the belief that the Queen was 'but Queen in name', it was 'at length decided and resolved by a general consent of many both of the council and other nobility ... in removing from her by some good mean, twoo or three persons of meane birth and condition'.[15] Having discovered this conspiracy, Cecil and Bacon then turned Elizabeth against Norfolk. His subsequent imprisonment led the northern earls to fear a wider attack on the nobility, and thus forced them into rebellion – not against the Queen but against her evil councillors.

It does not perhaps need to be emphasized how important the events of 1569 are to any study of Elizabethan Court politics. The significance of this interpretation lies in the theme of the supplanting of the ancient nobility by the new men. The key figures are Cecil and Bacon; Leicester plays hardly any role at all. He is mentioned as a supporter of the Norfolk marriage, but is not included by name among those who sought to overthrow Cecil. In 'Leicester's Commonwealth' the emphasis is reversed, and Leicester rather than Cecil becomes the villain of the piece. The events of 1569 are overtaken by a number of new issues that emerged in the 12 years that separated the two tracts – the execution of Norfolk in 1572, the failure of the Queen's possible marriage to the Duke of Anjou in 1578–81, the spread of puritanism, and the passing of more severe legislation against papal allegiance – yet many of the basic arguments remain. The threat to the Crown is the central political issue. Leicester is said to be seeking a puppet monarchy for his brother-in-law, the Earl of Huntingdon. To that end, the Queen has been kept unmarried (his own efforts in that direction having failed), and the Stuart succession blocked. Leicester is also the enemy of the old nobility and the betrayer of Norfolk. He was less obviously a baseborn new man (despite an attempt to blacken the Dudley ancestry in passing), but his notorious father and grandfather provided a more effective line of attack.[16] In seeking to usurp the Crown Leicester was simply trying to realize his father's earlier ambition. Leicester's influence on the new foreign policy is not so obvious, although he too is accused of exploiting fears of nonexistent foreign threats.[17]

It is, however, for reasons other than its defence of the Stuart succession that 'Leicester's Commonwealth' obtained its notoriety. The intensity of the personal vilification is noteworthy even by contemporary standards. A few themes – notably cowardice and duplicity – are found in the earlier attack on Cecil, but others, Leicester's spectacular sexual appetites and his skill as a poisoner, are unique. More significant, however, is the description of Leicester's dominance of the Court. His 'reign is so absolute in this place (as also in all other parts of the Court) as nothing can pass but by his admission'.[18] The charge is supported by details of a number of incidents of tyranny and corruption, which reveal a considerable knowledge of events at Court between 1575 and 1584. His position had been equalled only by the notorious fourteenth-century favourites, Piers Gaveston, Hugh Despencer, and Robert de Vere. A few councillors, Burghley, Bacon, and Thomas Radcliffe, Earl of Sussex, had been able to remain independent, but they were powerless to halt him. Sussex (who was not mentioned in *A Treatise of*

Treasons) is here portrayed as the surviving representative of the ancient nobility at Court.[19]

Yet Leicester was more than simply a Court figure, for he had been able to create a faction that dominated the realm as well. This was the 'puritan faction', which serves an important polemical purpose in 'Leicester's Commonwealth' and was to some extent its creation. In a novel variant of the machiavellian argument, 'Leicester's Commonwealth' makes an unusual plea for toleration for Catholics, on the ground that they were less of a danger to the Crown than Leicester and his followers. Burghley (it is implied) was open to argument; the real advocate of persecution was Leicester, acting as patron of the puritans.[20] Puritanism thus drives a wedge between Leicester, on the one hand, and Burghley and Bacon, the earlier 'Catalines' of Protestantism, on the other. (There is scarcely any reference to Sir Francis Walsingham, it might be noted.) It also provides the vital cement that holds Leicester's faction together, for without it Leicester was too odious to retain any man's allegiance. As befits the machiavellian emphasis, his purpose in patronizing puritanism was to exploit religion to advance his own political ends. It is revealing that the tract has little otherwise to say about Leicester's involvement in the Church, apart from the claim that the University of Oxford had been ruined by his chancellorship.[21]

'Leicester's Commonwealth' therefore replaces the Protestant faction of *A Treatise of Treasons* with a hegemonical favourite exploiting internal Protestant divisions. 'Burghley's Commonwealth' combined the monopolist of the former with the themes of the latter. The emphasis is very much on foreign policy. Burghley had led England into a series of military adventures and a disastrous war with Spain. Seeking to make himself *dictator perpetuus*, he had overthrown the nobility and ruled all. Recent events confirm his hegemony: 'for better contriving of the whole domination to himself he hath lately brought in his second son to be of the Queen's council and keeper of her privy seal'. Leicester and Walsingham, both dead by 1592, appear only peripherally, and then as tools of Burghley's: his 'chiefest actors'.[22]

Whatever their differences, the three tracts advance the central proposition that the Elizabethan Court had been dominated by a monopolistic figure who had treated the Queen as a puppet. This, Francis Bacon noted in his observations on 'Burghley's Commonwealth', was an old tactic, 'for this hath some appearance to cover undutiful invectives, when it is used against favourites or upstarts and sudden risen councillors'. Moreover, the employment of the charge against more than one of Elizabeth's councillors had weakened the force of the argument: 'When the match was in treating with the duke of Anjou ... all the gall was uttered against the Earl of Leicester'. Lastly, it was an inaccurate description of the relationship between the Queen and her ministers:

> it is well known that ... there was never counsellor of his lordship's [i.e. Burghley's] long continuance that was so applicable to her

majesty's princely resolutions; endeavouring always, after faithful propositions and remonstrances ... to rest upon such conclusions as her majesty in her own wisdom determineth ...[23]

The prominence of Raleigh and Essex in the 1590s and the open factionalism of the decade weakened the argument for the hegemony of the favourite. There were now several favourites whose relationship both to each other and to the Cecils needed to be explained. John Clapham, in his unpublished 'Observations' written immediately after the accession of James I, took the extreme position of playing down the importance of the favourites as a group. A former servant of Burghley's, he saw no shame in the *regnum Cecilianum*. Burghley had ordered 'the affairs of the realm in such manner, as he was respected by his enemies, who reputed him the most famous councillor of Christendom in his time; the English government being then commonly termed by strangers Cecil's Commonwealth'. Clapham refers to a mysterious (though undated) plot to overthrow Cecil by 'diverse councillors of noble birth, pretending that he went about by suppressing them to establish his own greatness', but also relates that Cecil surmounted this and other intrigues 'by advised patience'. The prominence of the four favourites he attributes to the weakness of the Queen, who, he claims, was too susceptible to flattery. Leicester and Hatton were primarily self-interested courtiers; Raleigh and Essex, on the other hand, were at least men of ability and heroic ambition.[24]

The contrast between Leicester's 'domestical greatness' and Essex's martial actions had the paradoxical effect of strengthening the growing legend of Leicester the master courtier.[25] By the end of the reign he was being seen more and more as an intriguer of unrivalled skill.[26] A Welsh author considered 'how wise and politike was the late Earl of Leicester in all the course of his actions' one of the major questions of the day, but refrained from comment on the ground

> it concerneth an honourable personage, the greatest subject of late days in England and now dead. And I do take that it is rather my part and duty being but a poor gentlemen to honour his memory in the grave than to discourse of his life and actions ....[27]

In 1599 a Court observer wrote of Leicester's influence as a model for others: 'I am credibly made beleve ... that at this Instant the Lord Admirall is able to doe with the Queen as much as my Lord Lester was ...'[28]

Simultaneously, a second aspect to the legend emerged as the machiavellian patron of puritanism of 'Leicester's Commonwealth' was taken up by Anglican apologists and employed for their own purposes. During the 1570s and 1580s the standard charge against clerical puritanism and presbyterianism had been that of political subversion.[29] In the 1590s a new theme can be detected. Puritanism was now depicted as a front for lay attempts to complete the expropriation of the wealth of the Church; the motive for lay patronage of puritan clergy was the hope that, in the confusion created by attacks on the government of the Church, the remaining ecclesiastical estates would fall into their hands. Leicester had been simply seeking to continue his father's expropriations of 1552–3. The threat to the Church was made explicit by Archbishop Whitgift in 1585.[30] An early example of the use of the machiavellian portrait of 'Leicester's Commonwealth' to explain the danger to the Church can be found in William Harrison's manuscript 'Chronologie', written between Leicester's death in 1588 and Harrison's own in 1593. Leicester was

> the man of grettest powre (being but a subject) which in this land, or that ever had bene exalted under any prince sithens the times of Peers Gavestone & Robert Vere ... Nothing almost was done, wherein he had not, either a stroke or a commoditie; which together with his scraping from churche and commons ... procured him soche inward envie & hatred.[31]

In 1602 even one of Leicester's former clerical protégés, the Archbishop of York, Matthew Hutton, could write of his designs on ecclesiastical estates.[32] The very range of Leicester's ecclesiastical patronage, of which Hutton himself had been a beneficiary, strengthened the depth of his machiavellianism. Sir John Harington, who was himself no admirer of Leicester, observed at the beginning of James I's reign that, if Leicester 'made no great conscience to spoyle the church lyvings no more than did his father, yet for his recreation [he] would have some choyse and excellent men for his chaplayns'.[33]

II

The growing confusion surrounding Leicester and the Elizabethan Court was not clarified by the Stuart commentary, least of all by William Camden's *Annals*.[34] It has been claimed that Camden 'went out of his way to paint the blackest possible picture' of Leicester.[35] This may be an exaggeration, but it is also clear that Camden's much-praised objectivity did not apply in his case. The reasons have been less obvious, owing in part to the controversy that still surrounds the composition of the *Annals*. It is now accepted that the first three books were not rewritten by James I or Henry Howard, Earl of Northampton, but what can be attributed to the influence of Burghley, who first commissioned the work, is still to be decided.[36] The consistency of Camden's emphasis on Leicester's malignant influence makes its source a question of no small importance.

Camden's observation that 'evill speakers tooke occasion to tugge and tear at him continually, during the best of his fortune, by defamatory libels, which contained some slight untruths', reveals both a knowledge of, and a certain distancing from, 'Leicester's Commonwealth'.[37] The latter is revealed in his handling of two important episodes. The death of Amy Robsart is passed over very rapidly. More striking is the long passage devoted to refuting the charge that Leicester poisoned Walter Devereux, Earl of Essex, in 1576, which 'Leicester's Commonwealth' made much of as evidence for Leicester's plot to destroy the nobility.[38] Yet a number of incidents from 'Leicester's Commonwealth' are found in very similar form in the *Annals*: the disgrace and death of Sir Nicholas Throckmorton, the suspension of Archbishop Grindal in 1577, the fall of Sir John Throckmorton, the Somerville affair, and the attempted assassination of the Duke of Anjou's agent Jehan Simier. There are also a number of further malign intrigues. Several, like Leicester's ambition to become ruler of the Low Countries in 1586–7, or his advice that Mary, Queen of Scots, be poisoned instead of being executed in 1587, occurred after 'Leicester's Commonwealth' was published. Others, however, did not: Leicester's plot against Sir Nicholas Bacon for encouraging the Grey succession tracts in 1564, his involvement in the release of Lord Darnley in 1565, and his sabotaging of the Austrian marriage negotiations in 1565–7.

The accuracy or inaccuracy of Camden's version of these incidents cannot be discussed here.[39] What can be suggested, however, is that they serve a very important purpose. By establishing Leicester as the evil genius of the Court, a number of awkward episodes in the reign can be explained away. This is particularly the case with regard to the two major concerns that Camden shares with 'Leicester's Commonwealth': the cause of Mary, Queen of Scots, and the cause of the ancient nobility. Elizabeth's treatment of Mary provided him with his most difficult problem, and the disproportionate amount of space devoted to her in the *Annals* has been commented on.[40] Thus by emphasizing Leicester's role in the release of Darnley, or his poisoning proposal, for example, Camden is able to defend the Queen's innocence and moderation, and transfer the blame elsewhere.

Camden's loyalty to the ancient nobility comes into play in his account of the tension between Leicester and Sussex in 1565: 'Sussex inuriously despised him as an upstart, and, to detract him, would say, that hee could cite onely to of his pedigree, that is to wit his Father and Grand-father, both being enemies to their Countrey.'[41] From this perspective his account of the events of 1569 is of particular interest. His source (as was probably also the case for Clapham) for the attempted *coup* against Cecil appears to have been *A Treatise of Treasons*, for 'Leicester's Commonwealth' has little to say on the subject.[42] But Camden also provides a much more detailed account of the marriage negotiations between Norfolk and Mary, clearly derived from the text of Norfolk's later confession.[43] It is also heavily edited to convict Leicester of betraying Norfolk. Leicester's revelation of the marriage scheme to the Queen at Titchfield in the summer of 1569 was caused by fear, 'beholding his blood and vitall senses to shrink in himselfe'. Sir Nicholas Throckmorton's involvement in these intrigues is attributed to his being

Cecil's 'ambitious emulator'. His disgrace and sudden death, 'eating salads' at Leicester's house, are portrayed as the consequence of allying with the favourite.[44]

Similarly, the attribution of the fall of Archbishop Grindal, 'because hee condemned as unlawfull the marriage of Iulius an Italian Physician, with another man's wife, which much distasted the Earle of Leicester', to a Court intrigue rather than the dispute over prophesyings serves to obscure an otherwise awkward moment in the Queen's government of the Church.[45] Camden's hostility to puritanism leads him to give the machiavellian theory the full weight of authority. Archbishop Whitgift's attempts to restore unity in the Church in 1583 were hindered by 'certaine Noblemen; who by placing men unfit in the Church encreased their estate, or else had hopes upon the goods of the Church'.[46] The puritan Court faction was thus established, as can be seen in a more elaborate form in Peter Heylyn's later history of the presbyterians. Heylyn explained the growth of puritanism in the 1560s and 1570s by

> the secret favour of some great men in the Court who greedily gaped after the Remainder of the Churches patrimony. It cannot be denied but that this faction received much encouragement underhand from some great persons near the Queen; from no man more than from the Earl of Leicester, the Lord North, Knollys, Walsingham; who knew how mightily some numbers of the Scots, both lords and gentlemen, had in short time improved their fortune, by humouring the Knoxian Brethren in their Reformation; and could not but expect the like in their own particulars, by a compliance with those men, who aimed apparently at the ruine of the bishops and Cathedral Churches.[47]

The faction nearly enjoyed a revival in the 1620s. Both Heylyn in his biography of Archbishop Laud, and John Hacket in his life of Laud's rival John Williams, give their respective heroes the credit for dissuading the Duke of Buckingham from a similar plot to expropriate Church lands in 1624–5.[48]

Camden also strengthened Clapham's distinction between Leicester the courtier and Essex the hero. In phrases echoed by several Stuart commentators, Camden doubted whether Essex was a courtier at all: 'indeed he seemed not a man made for the Court, being not easily induced to any unhandsome Actions ... No man was more ambitious of glory by vertuous and noble deeds, no man more careless of everything else.'[49] Leicester by contrast 'was reputed a compleat Courtier', who 'was wont to put up all his passions in his pocket'.[50] Yet by posing this contrast Camden did create other problems. However unsuccessful Leicester's intrigues may have been, the malignant favourite still raised doubts about Elizabeth's wisdom and judgement. Camden evaded the problem in part by employing the standard trope of the Court as the seat of underhanded behaviour, and thus the natural environment for Leicester.[51] But he is also quick to deny that Elizabeth was a puppet Queen; her favour was a product of her 'rare and royal clemency'. Thereafter he disappears into astrology:

> whether this might proceed from some secret instinct of those vertues apparant in him, or out of common respect, they both being prisoners under Queene Marie, or from their first procreation, by a secret coniunction of the Planets at the houre of their birth combining their hearts in one, no man can easily conceive.[52]

His conclusion 'it is most certain, that onely Destinie causeth Princes to affect some, and reiect others', may legitimately be termed evasive.[53] Camden's primary concern with *res gestae* absolved him from the need to draw any explicit wider political deductions from his history. Nevertheless he was clearly unhappy with a Leicesterian monopoly of the Court and moved tentatively towards a more open environment. Leicester's attempt to obtain a 'general lieutenancy under the Queen' in 1588 was halted by Burghley and Hatton, and the Queen 'betimes prevented the danger which might have ensued in giving too much power to one man'.[54] Similarly, Elizabeth herself attempted to extinguish the Leicester–Sussex quarrel of 1565, 'For she condemned dissension among Peeres, and that old proverbe used by many, *Divide et Impera* ...'.[55]

The publication of the *Annals* had a major influence on the Stuart debate over favourites. The comparisons drawn between Essex and Buckingham in the late 1620s were based in the main on Camden's portrait of Essex.[56] Despite his ultimate obscurity on the relationship between factions and favourites, his portrait of the Elizabethan Court provided evidence for the argument for a 'balanced' Court. In the final version of his essay on 'Faction', Bacon revealed the contemporary concern. Princes should not govern their estates 'according to the respect of factions'; yet the instability of factions enables monarchs to control them.[57] It was, however, Sir Robert Naunton's *Fragmenta regalia* that delivered the most open attack on the tradition of 'Leicester's Commonwealth', and painted the most radical portrait of Elizabeth's Court.

Naunton was nothing if not explicit about his position; Elizabeth was puppet-mistress, never a puppet.

> The principal note of her reign will be that she ruled much by faction and parties, which she herself both made, upheld and weakened as her own great judgement advised, for I disassent from the common and received opinion that my lord of Leicester was absolute and alone in her grace and favour.

The hegemonical favourite had never existed.

> Her ministers and instruments of state ... were favourites and not minions, such as acted more by her own princely rules and judgement than by their own will and appetites; which she observed to the last, for we

find no Gaveston, Vere or Spencer to have swayed alone during forty-four years.[58]

Given the probable date of completion of the *Fragmenta* (1633), and the comparison between Elizabethan and Caroline Parliaments, the implicit contrast between the Elizabethan and the Stuart Court (of which Naunton himself had first-hand experience) is clear. By making this comparison, Naunton's work played a role in the creation of the Elizabethan legend second only to the *Annals*. Yet Naunton also described the Elizabethan Court in terms unlike anything encountered previously.[59] The 22 portraits of the leading men of the reign are divided into two categories, *togati* and *de Militia*, which owe more to classical parallels than historical reality. The portraits include extensive borrowings from Camden, both directly, and indirectly through Wotton's *Parallel* between Essex and Buckingham, but Naunton's most dramatic and frequently quoted anecdotes have no prior source. These include the famous 'I will have here but one mistress and no master' speech (employed to put Leicester in his place), Sussex's deathbed denunciation of the gypsy, Leicester's claim that the Queen's relations were of 'the tribe of Dan', and the Marquess of Winchester's excuse 'ortus sum ex salice non ex quercu'. It may be going too far to dismiss them completely as artistic inventions, but they can be regarded as no more than Elizabethan apocrypha.

Naunton's defence of Elizabeth from the charge of taking into her favour 'a mere new man or a mechanic' on the ground that 'it was part of her natural propensity to grace and support ancient nobility' also reflects the earlier debate.[60] Yet the attempt to restore the nobility to the Court is equally suspect. Nor can the importance he assigns to his characters be accepted outright. His personal animus against Sir Christopher Hatton and defence of Sir John Perrot are well known. Why the relatively obscure Sir John Packington was included, when a number of leading Court figures (like Sir Thomas Heneage) were omitted, remains a mystery.[61] The Knollys–Norris feud to which he gives such prominence is also difficult to trace elsewhere. These biographical details would not in themselves deserve much attention were it not for the profound effect Naunton's picture of a volatile and faction-ridden Court that the Queen manipulated to her advantage has had on so many later accounts of the reign.

III

By the middle of the seventeenth century Naunton's Queen Elizabeth had become the model of political wisdom. As the republican Francis Osborne, who regarded favourites as an 'Epidemical mischief', put it, Elizabeth's inconstancy of favour was a virtue, for it created 'the double and contrary

interests of a divided party, no vertue was excluded or vice admitted'.[62] This
was not, however, the view of nineteenth-century scholarship. J. A. Froude's
portrait of the Queen as an overly indulgent woman was deeply influenced
by his discovery of the Spanish ambassadorial reports of the matrimonial
intrigues of the 1560s. These led him to view Elizabeth as 'dashed with a
taint which she inherited with her mother's blood'. The successes of the
reign were to be attributed to the 'policy' of Burghley and the 'skill' of
Walsingham. Leicester, consumed by his ambition to marry the Queen, was
an ornamental, if malignant, figure:

> he combined in himself the worst qualities of both sexes. Without
> courage, without talent, without virtue, he was the handsome, soft,
> polished, and attentive minion of the Court. The queen ... selected her
> own friends; and in the smooth surface of Dudley's flattery she saw
> reflected an image of her own creation ... [63]

Froude had little to say about faction as an aspect of Elizabethan politics; this
was the discovery (or rediscovery) of Conyers Read. Read's research into the
conduct of foreign policy in the later 1570s and early 1580s led him to query
Froude's description of the relationship between Burghley and Walsingham.[64]
Instead of a single 'policy' there were now distinct rival policies. More profound, however, was his positing of an 'inveterate antagonism [between]
Burghley and Leicester' that decisively shaped the politics of the reign. 'It is
certain that each one continually tried to displace the other from his position
of influence. The contest between them began at the very beginning of
Elizabeth's reign and ended only with Leicester's death.'[65] Arising from these
tensions was a central factional division in the Court. Burghley 'the Erastian'
led a conservative coalition with Sussex, who 'hated Leicester with all the fer-
vour of a passionate nature' as his deputy. Leicester was the patron of what
was a more sophisticated version of the puritan faction of 'Leicester's
Commonwealth', 'not because of his abilities, which were mediocre at best,
but because his commanding position beside the Queen gave them an advocate and won for their ideas a consideration which they could hardly otherwise
have got'. Walsingham 'supplied the brains and framed the policy while
Leicester furnished the court influence of the faction'.[66]

Read's factional division was essentially one over policy. A more radical
approach to the role of faction was taken by Sir John Neale. Not only was
it of the essence of Court life – 'competition at the court was ceaseless' –
but it was less concerned with policy than patronage. 'The place of party
was taken by faction, and the rivalry of the factions was centred on what
mattered supremely to everyone: ... control of patronage.'[67] Neale's
Elizabeth, who 'played the factions one against the other', is openly
Naunton's (an 'astute' observer, who is accepted uncritically), garnished
with examples drawn mainly from the 1590s.[68] Between them Read and
Neale established factionalism as the central phenomenon of Elizabethan

Court politics, yet the bases for their factions – policy or patronage – were fundamentally different. The difficulties thus posed can be seen in Wallace MacCaffrey's two volumes. MacCaffrey also posits an antagonism between Burghley and Leicester, but one more active in the 1560s when it was provoked by Leicester's efforts to marry the Queen. However, once Leicester abandoned this ambition in the early 1570s, factionalism diminished.[69] Patronage does not appear to play much of a role one way or the other, except in the Church. MacCaffrey sees the growing division over puritanism in the 1580s leading to the increased prominence of Hatton, to whom he assigns more importance than his predecessors have done, as the patron of the more conservative clergy.[70]

MacCaffrey's account of Court politics has, if nothing else, raised major doubts about Read's conception of factionalism over policy. There have been similar problems with the role of patronage. In his later work Read was frequently forced to admit that the evidence for the antagonism between Burghley and Leicester was not as clear-cut as he would have liked.[71] Sir Geoffrey Elton, though prepared on balance to accept the existence of factions, has injected an important note of scepticism in the observation that 'we have grown so familiar with the notion of faction ... that we forget how little the structure of those groupings has been studied'.[72] The difficulty of explaining the dynamics of Court politics in conventional terms is revealed in essays published since 1979. Eric Ives comments, 'Burghley and Leicester – Elizabeth's closest confidant and her most intimate courtier – were recognised rivals, but there was never a complete breakdown of relations.'[73] Pam Wright rephrases it slightly:

> [after 1572] the principal contenders for power seem to have decided that while competition was healthy, full-blown factional disputes were a destructive and time-consuming diversion ... This *modus vivendi* among the leaders chimed nicely with the instinct of everyone else to run with the hare and hunt with the hound.[74]

In other words, hard evidence for the central argument that factionalism and patronage were the central constituents of Court politics has so far been lacking. In some cases factions have been created out of thin air – the 'too blatant a vendetta' that William, Lord Cobham, is said to have conducted against Leicester, for example.[75] Equally dubious has been the attempt to build the authors of 'Leicester's Commonwealth' into a 'catholic Court faction'.[76] Patronage struggles within the Court between Burghley and Leicester have been noteworthy by their absence. In fact the opposite is the case. In a number of cases – for example, those of Walsingham himself, Henry Killigrew, Robert Beale, William Herle – clear lines of allegiance have been very difficult to draw. Central to the argument for a struggle between Burghley and Leicester has been Leicester's putative involvement in the attempted overthrow in 1569. Yet the evidence for this incident is very thin. Apart from the tradition of *A Treatise of Treasons*, discussed in this essay, which does not mention Leicester, the only other source is the notorious Roberto Ridolphi, who is scarcely reliable.[77] This does not mean that Cecil looked upon a marriage between Leicester and the Queen with enthusiasm, that they did not disagree over foreign policy, or adopt different approaches to ecclesiastical policy, but these instances must be weighed against the major areas of agreement.

Once the Burghley–Leicester hostility is queried, then the role of the favourite becomes clearer. The favourites, like the other central figures of the Court, were there ultimately at the Queen's choice. Unlike the favourites at the Court of Henry III of France, for example, their rise was neither overtly political nor factional.[78] Yet, unlike Hatton and Raleigh (or the Stuart favourites), Leicester did not come from a minor gentry family, but from the leading family of the Edwardian Court, however notorious it may have become after 1553. Thus, although Elizabeth's attraction to him may have been purely personal, he was a choice of a major political consequence. Much of his relationship to Burghley can be explained by this, for, however much Burghley may have disliked and feared the revival of old enmities that Leicester's rise might threaten, they were at the end of the day men from a similar political milieu, with a similar range of friends and associations. In this respect the Leicesterian monopoly of the Elizabethan Court was a mirage, for it reflected the hegemony of a broader political élite of which both Burghley and Leicester were part. The older Catholic polemic was to this extent correct, for there had occurred in the decades that preceded the accession of Elizabeth a major reshaping of the English political élite in which religious allegiances clearly played a part. This in turn created the social and political basis of the Elizabethan Court. The central figures were all recipients of the Queen's favour, and, however they may have disagreed, they had too much in common for permanent antagonisms to be established. The terms favourite and faction obscure as much of the reality of the Elizabethan Court as they explain.

Bibliographical postscript

The first version of this essay was a paper delivered to the conference on 'The Court at the Beginning of the Modern Age', organized by the German Historical Institute, London, and held at Madingley Hall, Cambridge, in 1987. It was published in the collected papers from that conference in 1991. I have resisted the temptation to make major revisions, and therefore the text and notes are unchanged, with the exception of the correction of some of the punctuation, two typographical errors, and a few of the more egregious solecisms. However, in the five years since it was published there have been a number of important additions to the literature on the subject, and therefore the following brief survey has been added for the benefit of the reader who may wish to pursue points made here further.

As I hope the text has made clear, this essay was intended as a historiographical sequel to my earlier essay on the Court in Christopher Haigh's collection *The Reign of Elizabeth I*. One theme I wished particularly to address was the failure of the existing literature to distinguish between factional disputes over policy and those over patronage. I have since discussed the political role of patronage more fully in an essay published in 1995.[79] Since 1989 substantial sections of my research on the Earl of Leicester have also appeared, which both modify and expand upon points made here. Excluding lighter pieces, these comprise the reconstruction of his surviving papers[80] and the editing of his household accounts[81], three studies of his clientele – one on its Edwardian origins,[82] one on its activities in the House of Commons,[83] and a third on its major regional aspect[84] – and a brief survey of his role in ecclesiastical politics.[85]

A number of lesser points made here can also be expanded upon. A fuller discussion of the contemporary disparagement of Leicester's ancestry can be found in ' "Because I am of that Countrye" '.[86] The reappraisal of the circumstances of the writing of Camden's *Annals* that Dr McGurk initiated has been further developed by D. R. Woolfe in a most exciting way.[87] In discussing Naunton's indebtedness to Camden I overlooked an important piece of evidence: Camden's *Remains* is the source for Winchester's famous description of himself as a willow[88]. It is also clear that my brief comments on the importance of the Elizabethan 'puritan faction' to seventeenth-century Anglican historiography only scratched the surface of a fascinating subject. The theme can be found in numerous works ranging from Sir John Harington's tract on the succession to Isaac Walton's *Life of Mr Richard Hooker*.[89] No less interesting is the role 'Leicester's Commonwealth' continued to play in political debate. An unfortunately anonymous letter of Queen Anne's reign claimed that the recent publication of a new edition of the tract was part of a Tory attack on the Duke of Marlborough as a 'single minister'.[90] This in turn reopens the question of whether the reprinting of 'Leicester's Commonwealth' in 1641 was an example of contemporary anti-puritan polemic.

The wider debate on the role of factions in Tudor Court politics as a whole shows no signs of diminishing. To date the 1530s remain the most hotly disputed subject, particularly the fall of Anne Boleyn, where the earlier theories that a factional struggle was responsible for her demise and the outbreak of the Pilgrimage of Grace (advanced by Eric Ives, Sir Geoffrey Elton, and David Starkey) have been challenged by George Bernard.[91] Even if the question of Anne's 'guilt' remains unproven, Dr Bernard has effectively queried much of the evidence on which the factional argument rests.[92] The Elizabethan debate has been less dramatic, but, as Steven Gunn has perceptively suggested, what provides a continuity between the reigns is the issue of monarchical independence: were decisions made by the monarch for his or her own reasons or under factional pressure?[93]

The issue in Elizabethan politics that has attracted most attention recently has been the distinction drawn between the collegiality of the years to 1590 and the factionalism of the final decade. Susan Doran has continued to argue the case for the importance of factional politics in the earlier period, particularly over the Queen's marriage, though, by simultaneously arguing that the Queen took her decisions independently, she has muddied the waters somewhat.[94] The 1590s have been examined in detail in the contributions to the volume, published in 1995, that John Guy has edited. Paul Hammer argues that policies rather than patronage were the key to the struggles between Essex and the Cecils.[95] Natalie Mears advances a similar case: that the Cecil–Essex struggle was a dispute between martial and civilian codes rather than an attack on a *regnum Cecilianum* by those excluded.[96] An underlying theme in both these essays (and much of the rest of the volume from which they come) is that of a growing loss of control by Elizabeth, a subject to which Dr Hammer has returned in an interesting paper on the rise of Raleigh and Essex in the later 1580s delivered to the conference 'The World of the Favourite' that Sir John Elliott held at Magdalen College, Oxford, in March 1996.[97]

Two further subjects are also relevant. One is the rise of Archbishop Whitgift and the effects of the new tone of ecclesiastical government in the 1590s. In this respect it could be argued that Whitgift's appointment as Archbishop of Canterbury in 1583 was a more important turning point in Elizabethan politics than 1588–90.[98] The other is growing interest in the intermediate level of Elizabethan government and the question of a united political élite, which underpins the case for collegiality. This interest has manifested itself both in the arguments for the continuity of a Protestant élite from the reign of Edward VI[99] and in the debate surrounding the role of the 'men-of-business'.[100] These are important topics to be addressed in any further study of the politics of the Court.

Notes

1 On the structure of the court, see S. L. Adams, 'Eliza Enthroned? The Court and its Politics', in C. Haigh (ed.), *The Reign of Elizabeth I* (London, 1984), pp. 55–77, and P. Wright, 'A Change of Direction: The Ramifications of a Female Household, 1558–1603', in D. Starkey (ed.), *The English Court from the Wars of the Roses to the Civil War* (London, 1987), pp. 147–72.

2 N. Cuddy, 'The Revival of the Entourage: The Bedchamber of James I, 1603–1625', in Starkey (ed.), *The English Court*, pp. 173–225. R. Lockyer, *Buckingham: The Life and Political Career of George Villiers, First Duke of Buckingham, 1592–1628* (London, 1981), pp. 17, 21–2, makes the sexual connection explicit.

3 R. P. Shepheard, 'Royal Favorites in the Political Discourse of Tudor and Stuart England', Ph.D. thesis, Claremount (1985), surveys the literature but draws different conclusions from those advanced here.

4 R. Houlbrooke, 'Politics and Religion in Tudor England', *Historian*, 17 (1987–8), pp. 10–11. See J. E. Neale, 'The Elizabethan Political Scene', in his *Essays in Elizabethan History* (London, 1958), pp. 59–84.

5 See, however, Haigh's comments in the introduction to *The Reign of Elizabeth I*, pp. 1–25, at pp. 6–11.

6 The excellent recent edition by D. C. Peck, *Leicester's Commonwealth: The Copy of a Letter written by a Master of Art of Cambridge (1584) and Related Documents* (Athens, Oh., 1985), supersedes all earlier ones.

7 STC nos. 7601 and 10005. Neither title has been published in a modern edition.

8 For the debate over the authorship of 'Leicester's Commonwealth', see Peck (ed.), *Leicester's Commonwealth*, pp. 25–32. *A Treatise of Treasons* is generally attributed to John Leslie, Bishop of Ross, the agent of Mary, Queen of Scots; *A Declaration of the True Causes* to Richard Verstegan. The tracts are briefly discussed in P. J. Holmes, *Resistance and Compromise: The Political Thought of the Elizabethan Catholics* (Cambridge, 1982), pp. 25–6, 138, 141.

9 *Treatise*, sigs. [a5], a4.

10 See art. 4 of the York Articles and art. 8 of the Pontefract articles, and the advice of Sir Thomas Tempest, printed in A. Fletcher, *Tudor Rebellions* (3rd edn, London, 1983), pp. 105, 109, 111. Cf. W. G. Zeeveld, *The Foundations of Tudor Policy* (Cambridge, Mass., 1948), pp. 196–200, and G. R. Elton, 'The Political Creed of Thomas Cromwell', in his *Studies in Tudor and Stuart Politics and Government* (4 vols, Cambridge, 1974–92), pp. 216–20.

11 C. Sharp, *The Rising in the North: The 1569 Rebellion*, ed. R. Wood (Shotton, 1975), p. 42. The extent to which the rebellions of 1536 and 1569 were revolts of a self–conscious 'old nobility' cannot be adequately discussed here. Certainly the Earl of Westmorland came close to seeing his actions in 1569 in this light. The general point is touched on in passing in M. R. James, *English Politics and the Concept of Honour, 1485–1642, Past and Present*, supp. 3 (1978), pp. 32–43, repr. in James, *Politics and Culture: Essays in Early Modern England* (Cambridge, 1986), pp. 308–415. The long-running debate over the causes of both rebellions has revealed the difficulty of isolating a single issue.

12 *Treatise*, sig. a3ᵛ, fo. 84.

13 *Treatise* sig. [a6ᵛ].

14 The familiarity with the 1569 intrigues supports the case for the authorship of the Bishop of Ross, whose involvement in them was considerable.

15 *Treatise*, fos. 11ᵛ–12ᵛ, 29ᵛ–30ᵛ.

16 Peck (ed.), *Leicester's Commonwealth*, pp. 172–4, 193. Cf. p. 111.

17 Peck (ed.), *Leicester's Commonwealth*, p. 186.

18 Peck (ed.), *Leicester's Commonwealth*, p. 95, cf. pp. 93, 98–9.

19 Peck (ed.), *Leicester's Commonwealth*, pp. 103, 92.

20 Peck (ed.), *Leicester's Commonwealth*, p. 73, cf. pp. 67–9, 104–5.

21 Peck (ed.), *Leicester's Commonwealth*, pp. 115–17.

22 *A Declaration of the True Causes*, pp. 10, 52–3, 70.

23 'Certain Observations made upon a Libel Published this Present Year 1592', in *The Letters and Life of Francis Bacon*, ed. J. Spedding *et al.* (7 vols, London, 1861–74), I, pp. 197–8.

24 E. P. Read and C. Read (eds), *Certain Observations Concerning the Life and Reign of Queen Elizabeth by John Clapham* (Philadelphia, 1951), pp. 75–7, 90–4.

25 The phrase used in a letter of 1 July 1591, PRO SP 12/239/70.

26 See, for example, Sir Walter Raleigh, *Works* (8 vols, Oxford, 1825), VIII, pp. 758–9, 769–70, Lord Henry Howard to Sir R. Cecil, *c.*1602

27 Huntington Library, Ellesmere MS 1598, Treatise by R. Griffith, *c.*1598–1600, fo. 17ᵛ. I should like to thank the Huntington Library for permission to cite this manuscript.

28 A. Collins (ed.), *Letters and Memorials of State in the Reigns of Queen Mary ... from the Originals at Penshurst* (2 vols, London, 1746), II, p. 122, R. Whyte to Sir R. Sidney, 12 Sept. 1599.

29 See, for example, the two anti-puritan tracts of Richard Bancroft, *Daungerous Positions and Practices* and *Survay of the Pretended Holy Discipline* (both London, 1593).

30 BL Lansdowne MS xlv, fo. 98, Whitgift to Burghley. The question of the truth of the charges demands more space than can be devoted to it here. In 1588 Leicester

received a grant of episcopal estates in recompense for his expenditure in the Netherlands. This was supported by both Walsingham and Burghley, see BL Cotton MS, Titus B. vii, fo. 32, and Lansdowne MS xxxi, fo. 103 (misdated to 1580). Leicester's secretary, Arthur Atye, later commented on the 'novelty of it', Longleat House, Dudley MS ii, fo. 261, to Leicester, 27 Aug. 1588. The Welsh separatist John Penry proposed to Essex in 1593 that the Queen should abolish the bishops and 'employ their livings for the benefit of hir crown and the support of hir subjects' (A. Peel (ed.), *The Notebook of John Penry 1593* (Camden Society, 3rd ser., 67; London, 1944), p. 89).

31 F. J. Furnivall (ed.), *Harrison's Description of England* (New Shakespeare Society, 6th ser., I; London, 1877), pp. lviii–ix; cf. pp. lix–lx for Harrison's fears of attacks on Church lands in the Parliament of 1589 and 1593.

32 HMC, *Calendar of the Manuscripts of the ... Marquess of Salisbury*, XII (1910), p. 113, to Sir R. Cecil, 17 Apr. 1602.

33 Sir John Harington, *Nugae Antiguae* (2 vols, London, 1804), II, p. 268.

34 The editions employed here are the Abraham Darcie translation of 1625 (*Annales, The True and Royal History of Elizabeth, Queene of England*) for the first three books (1558–88) and the 1688 translation (*The History of the Most Renowned and Victorious Princess Elizabeth*) for bk IV (1589–1603). Although the Darcie translation is clumsier, it is less influenced by later commentary.

35 W. Camden, *The History of the Most Renowned and Victorious Princess Elizabeth*, ed. W. T. MacCaffrey (Chicago, 1970), p. xxxviii.

36 Camden, *History*, ed. MacCaffrey, pp. xxxv–xxxvi, cf. p. xxvii. H. R. Trevor-Roper, 'Queen Elizabeth's First Historian: William Camden', in his *Renaissance Essays* (London, 1985), pp. 121–48, at pp. 134–5. The only sources Camden specifically mentions are Sir John Fortescue and Essex's secretary Henry Cuffe. See bk IV, pp. 438, 624.

37 Camden, *History*, ed. MacCaffrey, bk III, p. 288.

38 Camden, *History*, ed. MacCaffrey, bks I–II, pp. 100, 366–7. Cf. Peck (ed.), *Leicester's Commonwealth*, pp. 82–4.

39 I have examined one of them in 'The Release of Lord Darnley and the Failure of the Amity', in M. Lynch (ed.), *Mary Stewart: Queen in Three Kingdoms* (Oxford, 1988), pp. 123–53.

40 J. McGurk, 'William Camden: Civil Historian or Gloriana's Propagandist?', *History Today*, 38 (Apr. 1988), pp. 47–53, at p. 52.

41 Camden, *Annales*, bk I, p. 121.

42 See Peck (ed.), *Leicester's Commonwealth*, pp. 172–3.

43 Printed in W. K. Boyd (ed.), *Calendar of State Papers Relating to Scotland and Mary, Queen of Scots*, IV (Edinburgh and Glasgow, 1905), pp. 32–40. Cf. Camden, *Annales*, bk I, pp. 208–13.

44 Camden, *Annales*, bk I, p. 199; bk II, p. 256. Cf. Peck (ed.), *Leicester's Commonwealth*, pp. 84–5. The reference to salads may reflect a well-known taste of Leicester's. See his attempt to hire a French cook to make salads in the winter of 1584–5: Huntington Library, MS HM 21714, to J. Hotman, 2 Nov. 1584, and Paris, Archives du Ministère des Relations Extérieures, Correspondence Politique, Hollande, II, fo. 215, to Hotman, 4 Jan. 1585.

45 Camden, *Annales*, bk III, p. 45. Cf. P. Collinson, *Archbishop Grindal 1519–1583* (London, 1979), pp. 253–6.

46 Camden, *Annales*, bk III, p. 46.

47 *Aerius Redivivus; or the History of the Presbyterians* (London, 1670), p. 258.

48 P. Heylyn, *Cyprianus Anglicanus or, The History of the life and Death ... of William ... Lord Archbishop of Canterbury* (London, 1668), p. 123; J. Hacket, *Scrinia Reservata: A Memorial offer'd to ... John Williams* (London, 1693), pp. 204–6.

49 Camden, *History*, bk IV, p. 624. Cf. Sir H. Wotton, 'The Parallel of R. Devereux, earl of Essex and George Villiers, duke of Buckingham', and [E. Hyde], 'The Difference and Disparity between ... George Villiers, duke of Buckingham and Robert, earl of Essex', *Reliquiae Wottonianae* (London, 1685), pp. 175, 186–7.

50 Camden, *Annales*, bk III, p. 288; Wotton, 'Parallel', p. 175.

51 See, for example, Camden, *History*, bk IV, pp. 509–43.

52 Camden, *Annales*, bk I, p. 57; cf. bk III, p. 288.

53 Camden, *Annales*, bk I, p. 57.

54 Camden, *Annales*, bk III, p. 288.
55 Camden, *Annales*, bk I, p. 121.
56 See the Wotton and Hyde essays cited in n. 49 above.
57 *The Works of Francis Bacon*, ed. J. Spedding *et al.* (7 vols, London, 1857-9), VI, pp. 498-50.
58 Sir R. Naunton, *Fragmenta regalia; or Observations on Queen Elizabeth her Times and Favourites*, ed. J. S. Cerovski (Washington, 1985), pp. 40-1.
59 Shepheard, 'Royal Favorites', p. 134, describes Naunton's portrait of the Court as 'idiosyncratic'; cf. p. 139.
60 Naunton, *Fragmenta regalia*, pp. 69, 72.
61 There is a seventeenth-century life of Packington which portrays him as a defender of the lands of the Church against Leicester: Cambridge University Library, MS MM.i.39, see fo. 224^v
62 *The Works of Francis Osborne ... in four several parts* (10th edn, London, 1701), pp. 562, 559.
63 J. A. Froude, *The Reign of Elizabeth* (Everyman edn., 5 vols, n.d.), I, p. 60.
64 Conyers Read, 'Faction in the English Privy Council under Elizabeth', *Annual Bulletin of the American Historical Association* (1911), pp. 111-19.
65 Read, 'Faction', p. 113.
66 Read, 'Faction', p. 116; Read, 'Walsingham and Burghley in Queen Elizabeth's Privy Council', *English Historical Review*, 28 (1913), pp. 34-58, at pp. 39-41.
67 Neale, 'Elizabethan Political Scene', p. 70. The argument is also developed in W. T. MacCaffrey, 'Place and Patronage in Elizabethan Politics', in S. T. Bindoff, J. Hurstfield, and C. H. Williams (eds), *Elizabethan Government and Society: Essays presented to Sir John Neale* (London, 1961), pp. 95-126.
68 Neale, 'Elizabethan Political Scene', p. 79 and *passim*.
69 W. T. MacCaffrey, *Queen Elizabeth and the Making of Policy, 1572-1588* (Princeton, NJ, 1981), pp. 458-9.
70 MacCaffrey, *Queen Elizabeth and the Making of Policy*, pp. 452-4. However, cf. P. Collinson, *The Elizabethan Puritan Movement* (London, 1967), pp. 313-14.
71 See, for example, Conyers Read, *Lord Burghley and Queen Elizabeth* (New York, 1960), p. 375.
72 G. R. Elton, 'Tudor Government: The Points of Contact: III. The Court', *Transactions of the Royal Historical Society*, 5th ser., 26 (1976), pp. 211-28, at p. 224.
73 Eric Ives, *Faction in Tudor England* (Historical Association, Appreciations in History, 6; 1979), p. 22.
74 Wright, 'A Change of Direction', p. 170.
75 P. Clark, *English Provincial Society from the Reformation to the Revolution: Religion, Society and Politics in Kent, 1500-1640* (Hassocks, 1977), p. 129. This is based on a misreading of D. B. McKeen, ' "A Memory of Honour": A Study of the House of Cobham of Kent in the Reign of Elizabeth I', Ph.D. thesis, Birmingham (1964), pp. 202, 253. Cf. p. 496.
76 Peck (ed.), *Leicester's Commonwealth*, pp. 13-25. P. Roberts, 'Elizabeth and her Dazzling Court', in R. Smith (ed.), *Royal Armada, Guide to the 400th Anniversary of the Sailing of the Armada* (London, 1988), pp. 70-88, at p. 76.
77 See the correspondence printed in J. M. B. C. Kervijn de Lettenhove (ed.), *Relations politiques des Pays-Bas et de l'Angleterre sous le règne de Philippe II* (11 vols, Brussels, 1882-1900), V, p. 307.
78 For Henry III, see J. Boucher, *Société mentalités autour de Henri III* (4 vols, Lille, 1981), I, pp. 199, 208-9.
79 S. L. Adams, 'The Patronage of the Crown in Elizabethan Politics: The 1590s in Perspective', in John Guy (ed.), *The Reign of Elizabeth I: Court and Culture in the Last Decade* (Cambridge, 1995), pp. 20-45.
80 S. L. Adams, 'The Papers of Robert Dudley, Earl of Leicester I-III', *Archives*, 20 (1992), pp. 63-85; 20 (1993), pp. 131-44; 21 (1996), pp. 1-26. Part IV is in preparation.
81 *Household Accounts and Disbursement Books of Robert Dudley, Earl of Leicester, 1558-1561, 1584-1586*, ed. S. L. Adams (Camden Society, 5th ser., 6; London, 1995).

82 S. L. Adams, 'The Dudley Clientele, 1553–1563', in G. W. Bernard, *The Tudor Nobility* (Manchester, 1992), pp. 241–65.

83 S. L. Adams, 'The Dudley Clientele and the House of Commons, 1559–1586', *Parliamentary History*, 8 (1989), pp. 216–39.

84 S. L. Adams, ' "Because I am of that Countrye & Mynde to Plant Myself There": Robert Dudley, Earl of Leicester and the West Midlands', *Midland History*, 20 (1995), pp. 21–74.

85 S. L. Adams, 'A Godly Peer? Leicester and the Puritans', *History Today*, 40 (Jan. 1990), pp. 14–19.

86 Adams, ' "Because I am of that Countrye" ', pp. 24–6.

87 D. R. Woolfe, *The Idea of History in Early Stuart England* (Toronto, 1990), see pp. 215–19.

88 William Camden, *Remains Concerning Britain* (1870 edn), p. 313 (under 'Wise Speeches').

89 Harington, for example, comments, 'Those we call Puritans seemed to adhere to the Earl of Huntingdon's title ... This faction died with my lo. of Leicester' (*Sir John Harington. A Tract on the Succession to the Crown (A. D. 1602)*, ed. C. R. Markham (Roxburgh Club, 1880), p. 41). I hope to explore the whole subject more fully when occasion serves.

90 Lambeth Palace Library, MS 933, art. 93, 'A letter concerning the memoirs of Robert Dudley, Earl of Leicester, now published by Dr Drake'. This was James Drake's edition, entitled *The Secret Memoirs of Robert Dudley*, and published in 1706 and 1708. The letter, which from internal evidence was written before Godolphin's dismissal in 1710, is an informed commentary on both the contemporary context and its background.

91 The best guide to the now extensive literature on this subject is Steven Gunn, 'The Structures of Politics in Early Tudor England', *Transactions of the Royal Historical Society* 6th ser., 5, (1995), p. 59 n. 1. I discuss Sir Geoffrey Elton's contribution to the debate in my paper on 'Politics', which was delivered to the Royal Historical Society conference 'The Eltonian Legacy' in March 1996, and will be published in the *Transactions* in 1997.

92 See his comments in G. Bernard, 'The Fall of Anne Boleyn', *English Historical Review*, 106 (1991), pp. 591–5.

93 Gunn, 'Structures of Politics', pp. 59–60.

94 Susan Doran, 'Religion and Politics at the Court of Elizabeth I: The Habsburg Marriage Negotiations of 1559–1567', *English Historical Review*, 104 (1989), pp. 908–26, and more generally in Doran, *Monarchy and Matrimony: The Courtships of Elizabeth I* (London, 1996).

95 Paul Hammer, 'Patronage at Court, Faction and the Earl of Essex', in Guy (ed.), *The Reign of Elizabeth I*, pp. 65–86.

96 Natalie Mears, '*Regnum Cecilianum*? A Cecilian perspective of the Court', in Guy (ed.), *The Reign of Elizabeth I*, pp. 46–64.

97 Paul Hammer, ' "Absolute and Sovereign Mistress of her Grace"? Queen Elizabeth I and her Favourites, 1581–1592', to be published in Laurence Brockless and J. H. Elliott (eds), *The Age of the Favourite, c.1550–c.1675* (Yale University Press, forthcoming). Although the conference itself was chiefly concerned with the seventeenth century, many of the wider issues raised at it are relevant here.

98 See Guy, 'The Elizabethan Establishment and the Ecclesiastical Polity', in Guy (ed.), *The Reign of Elizabeth I*, pp. 126–149, and the literature cited there.

99 The case for intellectual and religious continuity was made in W. S. Hudson, *The Cambridge Connection and the Elizabethan Settlement of 1559* (Durham, NC, 1980), and N. L. Jones, *Faith by Statute: Parliament and the Settlement of Religion 1559* (London, 1982). In my essay on the 'Dudley Clientele, 1553–1563' (see n.82 above) I sought to add a further dimension. David Loades has challenged the case for the continuity between Northumberland's and Leicester's clienteles made there in the epilogue to his recently published biography of Northumberland (*John Dudley, Duke of Northumberland, 1504–1553* (Oxford, 1996)), but he overlooks much of the evidence.

100 See, in general, Michael A. R. Graves, *Thomas Norton: The Parliament Man* (Oxford, 1994), and Patrick Collinson, 'Puritans, Men of Business and Elizabethan Parliaments', in his *Elizabethan Essays* (London, 1994), pp. 59–86.

SECTION

III

POLITY AND GOVERNMENT

Introduction

This final section groups together five articles that consider some of the wider processes of Tudor statecraft, especially those relating to the exercise of power and authority in the localities. Historians have often discussed Tudor government exclusively from the viewpoint of central structures and institutions. But the structures of public power were local and regional as well as central and national. Court and Country were interdependent, and England's social leaders at whatever level had to cooperate and provide mutual support if order and stability were to be preserved. Fifteenth-century historians have always understood this, partly because their sources often relate to the landed estates of the nobility and gentry, and partly because Court politics and patronage played a lesser role in securing the allegiance of the nation in the fifteenth than in the sixteenth century.

In *The Tudor Regime* (Oxford, 1979), Dr Penry Williams corrected the traditional imbalance by constructing a socially based interpretation. His emphasis was on the ways in which Tudor government actually worked, on the people who ran it, on the impact that it made upon the local communities, and on the reasons for its survival. This, rightly, has been an influential book. Yet, latterly, a new generation has emerged of historians who might argue that even this work – which considered Wales, but omitted Ireland and said extremely little about Northumberland and Westmorland – was too narrow! And it is certainly true that Tudor political history has invariably been practised in ways that are narrowly or unthinkingly 'English', i.e. 'southern' and 'lowland' English. If the debate about 'centre' and 'locality' has often been conducted in terms of 'centre' and 'periphery', the tables can be turned if one considers the 'centre' to be, in fact, Newcastle upon Tyne, York, or Dublin, rather than London or Canterbury. As Professor Steven Ellis has argued in *Tudor Frontiers and Noble Power* (Oxford, 1995) and elsewhere, studies focusing on lowland England as 'the normal context of government' have considerably exaggerated the regime's success by marginalizing the borderlands. Again, the influence of traditional nationalist historiographies has served to conceal the recurring tensions between the constituent parts of the early modern state and of its modern successor: i.e. between England, Wales, Ireland, and (after 1603) Scotland. Tudor bureaucrats (and William Shakespeare in *Richard II*) conceptualized England as a 'scept'red' island or 'other Eden', rather than as simply that part of the British Isles colonized by the English before 1066, but this does not mean that historians must follow suit.

In her essay 'Ruling Elites in the Reign of Henry VII' (see below, Chapter 11), Margaret Condon debates the idea that Henry VII's reign witnessed a significant modification of the prevailing social structures of the later Middle Ages. It is a fascinating article, which casts a spotlight on the inner workings of Henry VII's regime and on the norms of those who were dominant at the centre of power or who governed the localities. The reign became a power nexus dominated by the King personally. This may have contributed to the relatively low intensity of faction during the reign. Henry VII's emphasis on money transactions has been criticized by Dr Christine Carpenter, who notes that a ruler could not hope to win over landowners whom he had alienated 'by trampling over their deepest convictions about the sanctity of landed property' (*Locality and Polity* (Cambridge, 1992), p. 632). Miss Condon does not dissent. As she concludes: everything points to the personal rule of Henry VII, which, in turn, suggests 'a certain superficiality of achievement'; 'a fragility caused in part by the tensions that Henry VII himself created in binding and dividing the ruling élites himself'.

Whether early Tudor government was 'medieval' or 'modern' was a question which troubled examination candidates in the 1970s. In 'Wolsey and the Tudor Polity' (see below, Chapter 12), John Guy offers a *tour d'horizon*. If Court and Council were the hub of national politics, relations between Court and Country were the key to political stability. What is remarkable is the extent to which the Crown retained and refashioned medieval techniques. In particular, 'bastard feudalism' was colonized, for Wolsey (and even Cromwell) bridged the gap between Court and Country by constructing a provincial affinity. Of Edward IV, it had been said that the names and circumstances of almost all men, scattered over the counties of the kingdom, were known to him just as if they were daily within his sight, and that he had only to look at a map in order to recall the names of his 'servants' in the shires. Neither Wolsey nor Cromwell needed a map, because both kept registers of the royal affinity organized by counties. All 38 English shires were represented, along with south Wales, north Wales, Calais, Ireland, and Jersey. The key was 'service' at Court. Recruits were named to posts as carvers, cupbearers, knights, esquires, sewers, and gentlemen-ushers of the King's Chamber. As many as 600 were on the roll, the majority unsalaried.

The purpose of these networks was threefold. Henry VIII sought personal connections among the local 'men of worship' upon whose acquiescence his government depended. Second, he wished to increase his 'following' in county government, especially among the justices of the peace and local officials. Lastly, he needed soldiers for his army. He aimed to recruit to his affinity territorial leaders whose own servants and dependants could be transformed into the nucleus of a battle army.

Such attempts to ensure the interpenetration of central and local power make it easier to understand how stability was maintained in Henry VIII's reign, despite the revival of war and taxation, the Pilgrimage of Grace, and price rises and currency debasements. It becomes possible to explain why opposition to the regime was so limited, when the nobles were transmuted into a nobility of 'service' and a significant proportion of the members of the House of Commons were the King's sworn 'servants' or enjoyed Crown patronage or offices of profit under the Crown. The significant change occurred after Henry VIII's death, when the Crown's networks were usurped by rival courtiers led by the Seymours and Dudleys. The succession to the throne of a minor followed by that of two women seriously weakened the royal affinity. Elizabeth was forced to rely on her family connections and on the clienteles consolidated by her nobles and privy councillors.

As a point of contact between Court and Country, Parliament itself occupied an important place in the thinking of both rulers and ruled in the sixteenth century, though less in relation to debates on affairs of state than in respect of legislation and taxation. As Sir Geoffrey Elton remarks (see below, Chapter 14), even rebels took this view. The leaders of the Pilgrimage of Grace, for example, complained that Henry VIII was surrounded by 'flatterers' and 'heretics' who should be overthrown, yet in these circumstances it was instinctive that they should urge the King to summon a Parliament at Nottingham or York to enact legislation for the reform of the commonwealth. In relation to the social exercise of power, the key contribution of Elton's article is his emphasis on the importance of private Act legislation to Tudor government, a stabilizing dimension lacking, for instance, in Scotland and Ireland. The Crown itself demonstrated how Parliament could be exploited for private business, in particular to reorganize its landed estates. And private and regional interests followed suit. The average number of private Acts per parliamentary session in Henry VII's reign was 18.7 (an untypical figure inflated by restitutions in blood and resumptions of lands confiscated by attainder); in Henry VIII's reign 8.3; under Edward VI 9.2; under Mary 4.3; and under Elizabeth 13.4. And these were only the bills that passed; as the century progressed, abortive bills considerably outnumbered successful ones.

Neither were these supposedly 'private' parliamentary initiatives restricted to personal or local concerns. Urban corporations attempted to promote legislation affecting national as well as regional interests, and so did the justices of the peace. In fact, the technical division of Acts into 'public' and 'private' categories is misleading, since classification was not determined by scope and content; the test was whether fees were paid to the clerks during the passage of a bill and whether the Crown decided to print the Act in full in the 'public' section of the sessional print or simply listed its title in the table of private Acts. Of some 283 private bills introduced during the first seven sessions of the Elizabethan Parliaments, 22 became public Acts, 98 private Acts, and 163 bills failed. In total some 885 bills were introduced during this period, 146 of which resulted in public Acts and 106 in private. Eight per cent of 'private' bills became 'public' Acts, as against 24 per cent of 'public' bills. Elton's figures show that 'public' measures could very definitely be promoted by 'private' members. Furthermore, while, from the Crown's perspective, Parliament largely meant taxation, to ordinary members it meant legislation for the commonwealth. In this respect, Parliament afforded opportunities for 'bottom-up' policy-making that complemented the 'top-down' model centred on the Court and Privy Council. And it is likely that this picture could be filled out by a detailed study of the parliamentary exploitation of Court connections by local interests throughout the sixteenth century.

In view of the centrality of the Court to any discussion of the processes of government, it is surprising how little is known about its organization under Elizabeth I. In his article (see below, Chapter 15) Dr Penry Williams concentrates on the bilateral links between Court and localities. These were achieved in two ways: by the premium set locally on the Court's influence in resolving or defusing tensions and disputes; and by its role in providing access to royal power and influence for men of standing in the shires. Some intractable questions are addressed. How many courtiers, nobles, and others had access to the monarch? How many of the élite were 'usually in Court', and how many were 'usually in their counties'? Generally answers are elusive, despite the Henrician lists of the King's 'sworn' servants, and the records of Tudor Court ceremonies. However, a unique archival discovery enables Dr Williams to debate these questions for the closing years of Elizabeth's reign.

As to the frontiers and borderlands, the article by Steven Ellis shifts the focus away from the centre and south to the north and west (see below, Chapter 13). It is hard to refute Professor Ellis's case that the traditional concentration of historians on 'lowland' England has distorted our vision in favour of the region which was easiest for the regime to govern and control. His argument is undeniable that the real test of the regime's effectiveness was how it tackled the problems of the outlying regions: Wales, Ireland, and the far north of England.

Again, Tudor historians may have been too confident of the apparent benefits of 'centralization' as the motor of change and improvement. Historians of France do not take this view. Professor John Russell Major has argued that Renaissance France was a 'decentralized' monarchy. Francis I was a successful ruler of a country where problems of scale and distance were paramount, because his emphasis was on the *delegation* of power to trusted office-holders and provincial governors, a policy yoked to his independent efforts to construct a 'service' nobility and to reform the structure of the King's Council. There may be alternative ways of looking at the problem of incorporating 'outlying' regions as 'parcels' or 'members' of the metropolis and 'civilizing' their inhabitants.

Nevertheless, Henry VIII adopted a policy of centralization. A wide-ranging review of provincial government was initiated in 1534, which continued throughout the remainder of the reign. The objective was to consolidate control and bring administrative structures for the 'peripheries' or borderlands into line with existing arrangements for the government of lowland England, the 'core' region of the polity. At the time of the planned confiscation of the lesser monasteries, Cromwell scribbled in his memoranda: 'For the dissolution of all franchises and liberties throughout this realm ...'. The result was the Act for Recontinuing of Certain Liberties and Franchises (1536), which drastically curtailed local jurisdictional anomalies. No longer could feudal or ecclesiastical officials prevent the assize judges, sheriffs, or justices of the peace from performing their legal duties within their jurisdictions.

It was possible to subsume Wales administratively within the realm of England because the Union cemented long-standing social and economic changes, and because the Crown's jurisdiction over the principality was well established. It was in the north and Ireland that matters were more complex. When the Council of the North was remodelled in 1537, the aim was to create a supervisory jurisdiction over northern administration comparable to that undertaken for lowland England by the Privy Council and Star Chamber. Councillors had responsibility for the commissions of the peace, musters, and the regulation of trade and food supplies. But the society of the north differed from its heavily manorialized southern counterpart. The region was predominantly upland and pastoral, with a sparser, more turbulent lineage society, and a powerful territorial nobility with compact lordships and a tenantry prone to violence. As the Pilgrimage of Grace revealed, Tudor policy put an intolerable strain on relations between the Crown and the northern communities. Henry VIII may have ousted William, fourth Lord Dacre from the wardenship of the West Marches, but in the process the capacity of royal government was arguably diminished and Dacre was quietly reappointed warden after Henry's death.

More disruptive still were tactics in Ireland, where the traditional technique of aristocratic delegation was subverted by Henry VIII's inconsistent efforts to impose his regal authority over Gaelic Ireland. At counterproductive cost, Kildare's rebellion created a *tabula rasa*. If, however, Henry expanded his territorial power, obstacles were also thrown up. His decision in 1541 to alter the royal style from 'Lord' to 'King' of Ireland committed England to a possible full-scale conquest should the chiefs rebel, or should the Irish Reformation fail. Underpinned by a desire to implement a settlement of Gaelic Ireland by a process of 'surrender and regrant' – the policy associated with Sir Anthony St Leger – the notion of a separate Crown of Ireland was highly dubious. It subverted the process whereby Ireland might have been incorporated into the English polity on the same terms as the other borderlands. And by 1556 the gulf between English and Irish aspirations was becoming almost impossible to bridge.

Following the Northern Rising (1569), the Council of the North was reconstructed in its final form and a comprehensive redistribution of northern patronage undertaken. Lands and offices forfeited by attainted nobles and rebels were to be given only to members of the Elizabethan (Protestant) establishment. Despite the apparent resilience of this continued policy of centralization, it may be illusory to suppose that, at the level of the northern grass roots, the 'state' had triumphed by 1603. Localism and particularism remained endemic, as Dr John Morrill and others have shown for the seventeenth century. In Lancashire the chief magnates were the Stanleys, Earls of Derby, who maintained an armed retinue of household servants and tenants late into the sixteenth century. Apart from the Stanleys, some 10 powerful families ruled in Lancashire as sheriffs, knights of the shire, justices of the peace, and commissioners for musters. Again, in Cheshire the ruling élite were drawn from a dozen local families on whose cooperation the Crown and Privy Council relied to enforce their will in the county.

Elizabeth sought to govern her territory at minimum cost. Innovations were rare. Ireland is the test case. Although St Leger's recall marked the prelude to the 'programmatic' style of government associated with Sir Henry Sidney and his successors, the breakdown between Crown and community did not occur because successive viceroys pursued rigid political programmes. It occurred because the preference for the quick, cheap fix generated chronic instability. Elizabethan Ireland was increasingly subject less to direct English rule than to Thatcherite-style privatization. Any prospective candidate for service could present his own analysis of the Irish problem and propose a solution. The tender least expensive for the Crown was accepted, whereupon the successful bidder invariably fell victim to the fiscal inadequacy of his proposal, to contingent events in Ireland, or to politics at Whitehall or Dublin.

The price of centralization and uniformity was therefore heavy, and the extension of English rule throughout Ireland became wholly problematic. Wales and the far north of England presented fewer problems, since they were more easily dominated from London. But, by Elizabeth's reign, Gaelic Ireland 'had been thoroughly disturbed'. The gradual exclusion of the Old English from real political influence and the consolidation of New English power through the purchase or acquisition of ex-monastic and Gaelic land also created a new and less responsible governing élite in Ireland. Lastly, the greatly increased English expenditure on Ireland had created an influential lobby of adventurers with a strong vested interest in military conquest.

11
Ruling élites in the reign of Henry VII*

MARGARET CONDON

This paper offers a discussion of the idea that Henry VII's reign witnessed a significant modification of the prevailing social structures of the later Middle Ages. Detailed further study is still required at the county and local level in order to understand properly all aspects of the interaction between governors and governed, and, thereby, the full complexities of this difficult and still largely obscure reign, but some suggestions can be advanced meanwhile.

Before the twentieth century, England was dominated by ruling élites, to a large extent divisible under the headings of Court, Country, and Church. Their personnel varied for political reasons and beyond the needs of natural renewal. Even more fundamentally, there was a response to changes within society itself and to relationships within the élites. In this respect, Henry VII's reign was not unique, but neither can it be satisfactorily explained in terms of earlier models or merely as a continuation of the Yorkist polity. After the initial two or three years of the reign, there was a remarkable stability within the ruling groups, with little of the faction characteristic of the reign of Edward IV, and, still more, of Henry VI's. The King's power was increasingly felt in the country generally, partly through the action of men dominant at the centre of power and acting under the King's direction. It became a power structure dominated, to a remarkable degree, by the King himself. This fact may have contributed to an absence of faction in the reign, except between those who belonged to the élites and those who did not, and except for the perpetual struggle for influence at local level which could still occasionally assume a national importance, especially when concerned with the north of England.

The first problem is one of definition. An élite may be described as an exclusive body to which admission is desirable. Although not necessarily static in composition nor in the scope of its powers, it should be capable of regeneration, whether by election, imposition from without, or co-option. In a heavily structured society, élites existed at every level. In this paper they are seen through the King's eyes and are those with which the King himself was most concerned. This perspective results in two most important omissions from our study. The towns lie outside the trilogy of Court, Country, and Church and are ignored. Nor is more than passing consideration given

* For encouragement generously given and criticism offered during the writing of this paper I am particularly indebted to the editor, Professor C. D. Ross; to Dr M. A. Hicks, Dr C. Rawcliffe, Miss E. A. Danbury, and Mr N. E. Evans.

to the power and status of the nobility at the local level, which, in turn, contributed to its standing in the body politic as a whole.

The third element in our trilogy is of least importance and easiest to define. Henry VII's bishops were not, in general, outstanding men. Baronial influence on episcopal appointments under Henry VI gave way to royal initiative under the Yorkist and first Tudor kings.[1] Lawyers became more typical than theologians upon the bench of bishops, and a seat thereon became more regularly a reward for administrative service.[2] Dr Knecht's discussion of this change, through an analysis of the composition of the bench at the beginning and end of each reign, is misleading in suggesting a static situation. Henry VII did not merely imitate the practice of Edward IV. There is a real shift in royal policy. This becomes apparent on analysing, not the appointments as they occurred at some arbitrary point in time, but the bishops themselves. Edward IV's preferments show, at least in his later years, a change from the policy of Henry VI, but the appointments of Henry VII show a more extreme change, whether by comparison with those of Edward IV or as compared with the wider trends of the later Middle Ages.[3] Of the 16 bishops first appointed to English sees by Edward IV,[4] eight (50 per cent) were doctors learned in the law, and six (38 per cent) were theologians. Of 27 similar appointments made by Henry VII, 16 were lawyers, mostly learned in the civil law (57 per cent), and only six (21 per cent) were theologians. These latter were appointed only to minor and less wealthy sees, although some who became prominent in the work of the Council could hope for translation at some later date. Most of Henry's theologians were, nevertheless, administrators, even if his policy was not wholly consistent. That Henry's transformation of the bench of bishops into a body predominantly curial in aspect and legal in training was a conscious act of policy is revealed by developments elsewhere.

A similar pattern is traceable in the Royal Household. Here again a greater degree of secularization occurs under Henry VII. The office of dean was often a route to a bishopric. Two of Edward's deans, both theologians, died in office before they could hope for episcopal preferment. In Henry VII's reign, Geoffrey Simeon died in office in 1508, but he had been prominent in the Council's work as a court of equity, especially in the court of requests, where he sat as a president. William Atwater may have been a product of the occasional piety of Henry's later years, but he too continued in a conciliar role. The legal training of Henry's four other deans, in addition to their constant proximity to the King, may explain their conciliar role in attendance on the King's own person. Three of Henry's four almoners were theologians,[5] but their status outside the household depended primarily on their abilities rather than on their office. It may not be altogether a coincidence that, in place of the able but abrasive Fox, two comparative nonentities (Henry Deane and William Warham) became archbishops of Canterbury in succession to Cardinal John Morton.[6]

Dr Knecht suggests that in the long term this secularization of the bench may have enervated its religious leadership. Throughout Henry VII's reign, service to the state even to the detriment of the Church was exacted as a conscious act of policy. William Smith, for example, petitioned in vain to be allowed to leave the Marches of Wales in order to pay some attention to his neglected see,[7] and Richard Redman, Bishop of Exeter, had to compound with the King for permission to reside in his diocese.[8] The appointment of Italians to the sees of Worcester and Bath in return for services at the papal curia was a logical extension of such an attitude.[9] The Church, of course, was not unused to rule by delegation. Many of its lesser dignitaries also were habitually non-resident.[10] Although the bishops, in the wider social context, remained part of the ruling élite of Henry VII's England, their office was a subordinate part of their national role. They shared influence with their junior colleagues, doctors, and prebendaries of the Church, active in the Council of the King. Moreover, Henry VII showed towards the bishops as temporal lords that same ruthlessness as he displayed towards their secular counterparts. Even Fox paid £2000 for a pardon.[11] Most bishops paid heavily for the restitution of their temporalities, even if a large element in the payment was a composition for the profits of the vacancy.[12] Many suffered for the laxity of their prison keeping.[13] All were subject after their deaths to Henry's revival of the practice of taking multures, following searches by the Council amongst 'old presidentes' in the exchequer.[14] Several bishops, as lords of a separate judicial system no less than other lords in their franchises, experienced royal interference in their courts and suffered charges of *praemunire*.[15]

Of all the ruling élites, the bench of bishops was perhaps the most malleable in terms of direct royal intervention. Mortality enabled Henry rapidly to stamp the mark of his own personality and personal choice upon its members. This, however, is not true of the second great élite dominating the medieval scene. Fortescue was not alone in underscoring the traditional claim of the nobility to dominance within the body politic when he gave them pre-eminence even over the King's great officers.[16] The same point was made, for example, by the rebels led by Warbeck who complained of the lowly birth of the men who influenced the King and ruled the country to the exclusion of its traditional leadership.[17] Admission to the nobility passed primarily by inheritance, over which Henry could exert little direct control. There might be occasional exceptions: for instance, the confirmation of the title of Welles to his uncle and of Devon to Edward Courtenay. Nevertheless, two of the most notable features regarding membership of this élite under Henry VII are the absence of men of the King's own blood and the fact that Henry created so few peers. Henry was himself an only son. Thus, unlike the situation under Edward IV, there was no centre within the King's kindred for rival political tensions and no obvious focus for political discontent. For much of the reign he had no adult heir and Arthur died before he could achieve a recognizable political identity. The second son,

Henry, was kept close about the household of his father.[18] Of the King's uncles, Jasper, Duke of Bedford, had a long record of loyalty to the Lancastrian cause. But his rewards, though great, removed him from the centre of the political stage, with commissions in Ireland and Wales. As Bedford left no heir of his own body, his lands and offices reverted to the Crown and some of his servants, including his secretary, Thomas Lucas, King's Solicitor from 1497, passed into the royal service. John, Lord Welles, was always a minor if loyal figure; though he sat frequently both in Council and on commissions in his native Lincolnshire.

Through his mother's third marriage, and more immediately through the circumstances of his own accession, Henry VII was linked with the Stanleys. Thomas Stanley became Earl of Derby; William, his brother, became Chamberlain of the King's Household. Both eventually were confirmed in part of their Ricardian gains and were generously compensated for the loss of the remainder,[19] though William's possessions returned to the Crown through his forfeiture for treason in 1495. Thomas sat with some regularity in Council, though he was as frequently away from Court, preserving a powerful local influence. He was not included amongst the King's feoffees of 1499, when provision was made for the performance of the King's will.[20] Henry's sense of obligation to the Stanleys, in so far as he felt any, did not outlast the Earl's lifetime. Moreover, once the Stanleys' considerable local power was abused to the King's disparagement, Henry's reaction was swift, and the whole Stanley family was bound in recognizances for future good bearing.[21] Both James, Warden of Manchester and later Bishop of Ely, and Edward were indicted for illegal retaining. The indictment against Edward Stanley is annotated in the King's own hand, an indication of his personal interest.[22] The sole debt to the Stanleys acknowledged by Henry was undoubtedly their political service. Ultimately their place in the body politic was determined by their status in Council.

The Queen's kin could not even claim the obligation of political service. The dowager Queen herself was either stripped of or relinquished her lands in 1487; they were then granted to the Queen.[23] Cecily, Duchess of York, the Queen's grandmother, was no longer a political force, though to some extent she bought her security by her cultivation of the King's household and Council by grants of offices on her estates.[24] Thomas, Marquis of Dorset, paid the penalty for his vacillation in 1483–85. Although admitted of Council, he never recovered his standing, even in terms of membership of commissions of the peace. In 1492 he was bound in a series of obligations and feoffments which, if put into effect, could ultimately have brought about his disinheritance.[25] The one person whose influence was paramount was the King's own mother, Margaret Beaufort. She was granted extensive estates by her son and her standing within the locality was sufficient to attract litigation to her courts.[26] From her household a constant stream of people emerged to find employment in Henry's household, Council, and service. In addition, she had the oversight of several important wards, including Edward, Duke of Buckingham. This absence of the King's kindred from the nobility removed an element which had been a constant force, sometimes cohesive and often disruptive, in political life throughout the fifteenth century.

The small number of peerage creations is equally important. Despite an actual decline in the numbers of the peerage, including the continuance in the Crown of the titles of York and Gloucester and the failure of the male line of no less than 18 peerage families during the course of his reign,[27] Henry VII created very few peers. As a deliberate act of policy this was in part a product of the relative strength of the King's position. Even Henry VIII felt compelled to add substantially to the peerage at a time of crisis in the 1530s. It was also a product of a shift in the balance of power amongst the élites, from the use of the traditional noble councillors of the King, to councillors who held positions about the King only by the King's concurrence and whose authority was the delegated authority of the Crown and not derived from land or title. This was paralleled by a shift in the power balance at local level towards men in the second stratum of society, supported by interference from those of the King's councillors on the spot and active intervention by the central government. The weakness of this arrangement was that it ignored the many bonds which tied the nobility and gentry one to the other, through lordship, intermarriage, and community of interest, although these in turn might be disrupted by royal intervention or regulation, especially at times of crisis, and certainly were curtailed as an act of conscious policy by Henry, particularly in his later years. Such curtailment was achieved by the use of enquiries, informations, prosecutions, bonds, and forced enfeoffments. The same process of regulation, with a shift towards direct reliance on the gentry, is visible in Henry's policy towards retaining. If prosecutions themselves were erratic – exemplary rather than sustained, and only partially effective – Henry also attempted a system of control in the Crown's interest through licensed retaining. This was to be closely regulated by the Council, to which detailed returns were to be made,[28] though the combination of penal legislation and royal licence seems to have caused some confusion in the shires at large,[29] and may be more significant in theory than in practice. Also, as Edward had done at the beginning of *his* reign, Henry could and did build up the power of men whom he trusted in areas of unrest. But the estates and franchises so granted were limited in extent. In only two cases, those of Robert Willoughby and Giles Daubeney, were they accompanied by titles of nobility.

Henry's policy is perhaps seen most clearly – though in no case carried to its logical conclusion, for circumstances and tradition proved too strong – in his treatment of the peripheral areas of his realm; in Ireland, where he was least successful,[30] Wales, and the north. In all three areas Henry's handling of power groupings shows some uncertainty, punctuated by a more aggressive policy. In Wales the sole attempt at a radical interference with traditional élites was abortive. Reginald Bray, who briefly succeeded Arthur's lieutenant, Jasper, Duke of Bedford, on the latter's death in 1495, was far too heavily committed at the centre of government to be spared for the governance of the principality. Moreover Bray, unlike Bedford, neither held land in the area himself nor was he given any such power base by the King.[31] The final settlement was a compromise, which has its parallels in the Yorkist and Henrician settlements, and was successful enough for Henry VII's lifetime. Even after Arthur's death a King's council under William Smith, Bishop of Lincoln, continued to be active in the more vital area of the Marches, leaving Wales itself in the hands of a local leadership, albeit one loosely tied to the Crown through the household and Council. The functions of the Council in the Marches were primarily judicial.[32] Its membership consisted largely, though not entirely, of local gentry, many of whom were councillors also of the King.[33] These were supplemented by professional lawyers and administrators, who also assisted a London-based council in the administration of the Prince's lands.[34] A quarter of a century of dislocation had already disturbed traditional loyalties and structures and perhaps assisted an extension of royal control that was given formal expression in the indentures of the Marches.[35]

Although the north had been similarly disturbed, the dislocation may have been less fundamental, permitting a return to traditional policies promulgated from a position of relative strength. From the early years of the reign, when first rebellion and then the threat of a new Scottish war, precipitated by a border quarrel, alike demanded the King's personal and immediate intervention, the north was an urgent problem.[36] Henry's first solution was the traditional one of harnessing the loyalty and influence of the most prominent local magnates. In the north-east this involved the restoration of a chastened Earl of Northumberland.[37] Although the continuing need to maintain a military presence in the north may have helped to bolster traditional ruling structures, the Earl's unexpected death in 1489 forced a change of policy. The fifth earl was a minor who would never enjoy the influence held by his father. This fact he would bitterly resent, the more so in that Henry, recognizing his potential capacity for mischief, tried to undermine the foundations of a power already eroded by minority and political miscalculation. Under the nominal authority of his second son, Henry now gave power to the Earl of Surrey. Although Surrey's standing and ability commanded influence, he had no territorial power base in the north. His only mandate was the King's authority, continually renewed but never assured, whilst his own wings were clipped by piecemeal restoration of his estates, making him dependent upon the King's continuing favour.[38] It is unlikely that Surrey was the head of a King's council. More probably he governed with the assistance of his own servants and those of the King's council normally resident in the north. Within this partial power vacuum the King's authority was yet more directly asserted from 1494 by Richard Fox, Keeper of the Privy Seal, and Bishop of Durham. In these years Fox was prominent in negotiations with Scotland, a diplomatic activity which itself directly affected the balance of local forces. From 1499 a new element entered the picture – William Sever received a commission as Surveyor of the King's Prerogative, an office potentially prejudicial to the noble interest because of the sharp eye kept by Sever for the King's feudal and fiscal advantage.[39] In addition, a more determined effort was made to exploit the King's own position as a northern magnate by means of reforms in the duchy honours, though Henry's policy proved unrealistic save in purely administrative terms.[40]

By 1500 the achievement of a lasting truce with Scotland and, if less important, the majority of the Earl of Northumberland made possible, and perhaps required, a change of approach. The Earl of Surrey returned south to become, in 1501, Treasurer of the Exchequer. In the last decade of the reign Henry's policy definitely moved towards a rejection, or at least a modification, of the authority of the traditional élites exercising power in the north. Although this change of policy did not survive either its author or his chosen instrument, it was the forerunner of Henry VIII's Council in the North. Thomas Savage, who became Archbishop of York in 1501, had been Dean of the Chapel of the Household and President of the Council attendant on the King, in which his considerable authority was exercised in a mainly judicial capacity. He was now given a commission as President of the Council in the North, with councillors named and appointed by the King. Significantly these did not at first include the Earl of Northumberland,[41] though he had been sworn of the King's Council since 1498.[42]

The establishment of an autonomous King's Council in the North did not mean the total supplanting of the authority so exercised by a traditional élite. The Council itself seems to have included some of the minor barons.[43] Savage, too, was a member of a prominent northern family, though its estates were in Lancashire rather than Yorkshire, and he was quite capable of advancing his own interests as well as the King's. It was a quarrel over rival jurisdictions, combined with Savage's dual exercise of authority in his own and the King's name, which brought both the Earl of Northumberland and the archbishop before the King's Council at Westminster under heavy obligations to keep the peace: a situation which in itself suggests both the aggression in, and the limitations of, Henry's conciliar policy.[44]

The same may also be said of his policy in the West March. Again the military significance of the March suggested a reliance on the local nobility. Henry's policy rested on the exploitation of traditional rivalries and relied upon minor baronial power rather than the major peerage. Although his power cannot be compared with that of the Percies, the Earl of Westmorland was again eclipsed. The third earl was a shadowy figure and not a councillor, whilst the long minority of his heir led to an exploitation still more brutal than that of the Earl of Northumberland.[45] Whereas in the East March Henry continually divided authority amongst a number of nobles and gentry, in the West March he relied principally on Lord Dacre, although Dacre's tenure of office was insecure and he, too, suffered fiscal and feudal harassment.[46] In the long term, the constant renewal of the King's commission encouraged greater baronial influence and independence. This, however, seems not to have become apparent before Henry's death. The effectiveness of the King's Council in London, combined with the ability and loyalty of Dacre himself, did at least promote royal authority in that area. But although unruly local gentry might be bound under heavy recognizances for their allegiance and good bearing, and might also occasionally be brought before the King himself, the very frequency with which such action was forced on the Crown, particularly on charges of retaining and riot, hints at an almost inevitable superficiality in any changes in the structure of power at a local level in the more remote areas of the realm.

In his policy towards the north, Henry attempted a redistribution in the balance of power, partly in favour of the lesser northern families, but also, and more fundamentally, by overlaying the traditional structure of power with the newer élite of the King's Council. This he combined with a more direct application of the royal authority. In using local forces, Henry pursued a policy of fragmentation of interest, whether by dividing authority or by avoiding the continuous, if uncertain, tenure of office by one man.[47] The same process of dislocation in the Crown's interest underlay the *quo warranto* proceedings against several northern lords concerning their franchises,[48] and also the assertion of more direct royal control over the office of warden of the March itself.[49] This is further illustrated by the occasional difficulty which the Earl of Northumberland experienced in exercising his good lordship, and by the way in which he, like many other lords, was unable fully to realize his mesne lordship in matters of feudal tenure. A charge of ravishment of ward involving the daughter of Sir John Hastings brought him into the Exchequer and Common Pleas, and he was finally to compound with the Council Learned for a fine which effectively clipped his wings for the rest of the reign.[50]

The process of recognizance, and the consequent disturbance of the feudal order, was the most effective, and certainly the most interesting, of the ways in which Henry attempted to contain the independence of his nobility, although its political advantages were finite and eventually produced a dangerous reaction which was itself a measure of short-term success. Likewise, the example made of nobles who practised retaining and riot or, in exceptional cases, the feoffments made in the King's interest on noble lands might tend to contain the use to which a noble might put his still vital authority. Ultimately this centralizing royal influence would disrupt the relationship between élites, for it meant influence of the Crown in the locality in channels other than the dominant lord. In the short term there do seem to be changes in the position of the nobility under Henry VII even as against the reigns of Edward IV and Henry VIII. The absence of King's kin and Henry's parsimony in conferring titles of nobility meant that he would not be surrounded by nobles of his own choosing. This, combined with other factors (such as the strength of his position, his unconventional upbringing, and his intensely personal rule), necessarily affected their position. In addition, there were long minorities in several peerage families, especially important in the crucial formative years of the reign; whilst second-generation nobles rarely received the authority enjoyed by their fathers. Mention has already been made of the Stanleys and of the Earl of Northumberland, who, though sworn a councillor in 1498, was not even given the immediate entry to the Council in the North which he considered his natural right.[51] The contrast between the active political career of John, Lord Audley, Richard III's treasurer, and the relative obscurity of his son, James, may be one reason behind the latter's rebellion in 1497. Robert, Lord Broke, son of Henry's Steward of the Household, was not a councillor, even if, following a petition to Bray and a fine with the King, he succeeded to his father's Cornish offices. Like other nobles of his generation, he, too, was bound to the King for livery of his lands and his father's pardon.[52] If George, third Lord Abergavenny, was employed far more extensively in the King's service than his father had been, and was sworn a councillor in 1498, he also the more nearly experienced the King's displeasure.[53] The Duke of Suffolk's heir succeeded only as an earl, and with a diminished inheritance.[54] Successive earls of Kent saw their influence curtailed, Earl Richard's lands were carved up amongst Henry and his councillors, and he himself was placed in ignominious tutelage.[55] The Duke of Buckingham had serious grievances which could not find utterance until the next reign.[56] One measure of this shifting balance of power lies in noble representation on commissions of the peace. The Duke of Buckingham, for example, was not appointed to the Staffordshire commission until 1503, though he was on the Surrey commission from 1499, the year of his majority. Edward IV had been still more severe, excluding Buckingham's father from both counties. In this both Edward IV and Henry VII showed awareness of the importance of local rule. Richard III's more widespread commissions to Buckingham were no less a political act.[57] Nevertheless, there was a difference between the policies of the two kings. Under Henry VII the peers enjoyed a less extensive mandate. Only Bedford was appointed to commissions throughout England.[58] But even this situation contains its own paradox, indicating how far the influence of the nobility was still necessary to Henry for the maintenance of peace at local level. Perhaps partly as compensation for a relative eclipse at the centre of government, peers are recorded in increasing numbers as participating in the work of the sessions in the latter half of the reign.[59]

Henry did not exclude the nobility from the Council and actively cultivated their presence at Court. Yet few nobles could claim any real influence with him save for Oxford, Bedford, perhaps Derby, and the small household-administrative group.[60] Even these were subjected to the control exercised by Henry over the peerage in general. Thus Daubeney was heavily fined for illegal embezzlement at Calais, in which he was said to have taken pay for the ancient rather than the actual establishment of the town,[61] and was also forced to make over his interest in his French pension to the King.[62] He was bound by obligations for payment of the fine at days, and by his will he assigned certain land to feoffees, the issues to be used for these payments. Yet this punishment even Dudley thought over-severe.[63] The novelty of Henry's policy lies in the extent to which he carried the use of such recognizances, rather than in the instrument itself; of this Professor Lander has made a preliminary study.[64] He suggests the increasing use of such bonds as a means of politically disabling the nobility – though any final analysis must await not only a more detailed investigation of the basis on which the bonds were given but also a study of the level of forfeiture and the Crown's success in enforcing fines and penalties. This last may well have borne most heavily on the nobility. The system itself was self-perpetuating, since the corollary to a forfeit bond was a further recognizance for the payment of a fine by instalments. At the same time, the very authority inherent in nobility might work in the Crown's interest, since, given on behalf of lesser men, it might accord ill with honour to be in breach of the bond's condition.[65] Lander demonstrates, too, the penal severity of Henry's conditions for the reversal of attainder, calculating that in all at least four-fifths of noble families in England were under some form of restraint for at least part of the reign. By virtue of their wide estates, the nobility also suffered, perhaps unduly, from Henry's commissions of concealments. The scale of these was such that for the year 1505–6 alone 93 returns survive showing alienations, minorities, idiocies, and intrusions, including one of nearly 40 years before.[66] Seizure of land into the King's hand could mean loss of feudal incidents; whilst, if a lord acted too precipitately in defence of his rights, it meant process in the King's courts. The Earl of Northumberland was not the only magnate to be prosecuted for ravishment of ward.[67] Henry VII himself had a very clear conception of his aims in pursuing such policies, though they may later have been obscured by the avarice for which chronicle tradition appears to be only too justified. Polydore Vergil echoes the words of a conversation between the King and the Spanish ambassador when he wrote that

> The King wished as he said to keep all Englishmen obedient through fear, and he considered that whenever they gave him offence they were actuated by their great wealth ... All of his subjects who were men of substance when found guilty of whatever fault he harshly fined in order by a penalty which especially deprives of their fortunes not only the men themselves but even their descendants, to make the population less well able to undertake any upheavals and to discourage at the same time all offences.[68]

In this atmosphere the Earl of Kent's alleged comment that 'the Kynges grace undoyth no man' was surely a little disingenuous.[69]

It is difficult to ascertain the place of the nobility in the channels of patronage: that is, in the route to the King's ear by which a petitioner might gain his desires. Evidence so far accumulated tends to point away from the nobility and towards the Council and household. This may have become increasingly true with time, as the Council Learned and delegated committees of councillors assumed responsibility for certain matters of grace: particularly pardons and grants of wardship, which were reduced to a common denominator of a financial composition with the Crown.[70] One symptom of this is surely the way in which councillors and household men amassed annuities and stewardships at the gift of nobles, bishops, and religious houses. If Reginald Bray held annuities of, amongst others, the earls of Northumberland, Devon, and Ormond, Lord Dynham, Lady Hastings, and Lord Audley, it was surely Bray who was the dominant partner.[71] In terms of personal profit, it was the councillor who achieved the greater rewards. Beyond the ready employment in the shire, beyond the enhanced personal status that led Dudley, for example, to use his title of King's councillor as proudly as any peerage,[72] beyond the position of influence and the receipt of offices and casualties in the King's gift that were so accessible to him, the councillor could use his position for personal aggrandizement: most notably in the land market, where he was exceptionally well placed to exploit political and legal disadvantage and economic misfortune.[73] Councillors were cultivated and their support enlisted through their employment as feoffees-to-uses.[74] A similar picture emerges from their employment as executors and supervisors of wills. Receivers' accounts throughout England show the extent to which they were felt to command influence and thus merit annuities in cash or office. The wills of Lord Lisle and his wife, who died after him, epitomize this relationship. Lisle desired Bray to be his 'good and especialle mediator' to Henry VII. To Lisle's wife Bray became 'my most single goode frende in this worlde'.[75]

The nobility and episcopate readily present themselves as élites within society at large, but are clearly no more than a part of the ruling élite within that process of governance with which this study is concerned. Within the shire, the framework of rule was provided by land and wealth, affinity and patronage, authority and office, and by the compromise between self-interest and the maintenance of the King's peace in which royal patronage was but one, though the most dominant, regulating factor. There remain, then, three élites requiring consideration. One is the network of county officials, especially the sheriffs, justices of the peace, and the special commissioners operating within the shire, where overall trends are more important than the ever-changing personnel of authority. The second is the King's household, a group to be reckoned with throughout the medieval period, although its use as a power base was constantly changing. The third élite, wherein the uniqueness of Henry's reign perhaps lies, is the Council.

The first group is the least important in the context of this paper. Tenure of office as JP or sheriff was of limited duration. Such offices were essentially executive rather than gubernatorial, and were subject to dominant local influences as well as being subservient to royal mandate. At the same time, though the development was over a period longer than the reign of Henry VII and not unique to it, the transfer of executive power did assist the encroachment of royal authority upon the rule of all other groups. There were, however, subtleties in this relationship; for lords joined with councillors, household men, local lawyers, and their own retainers to form the upper stratum of county society.[76] Justices of the peace, sheriffs, and the lesser figure of the escheator form a homogenous group, and a significant proportion of sheriffs and MPs were drawn in each county from members of the bench.[77] This means that a relatively small, if expanding, section of county society dominated all the rest – the more so as in most counties the burden of the shire's work was borne by a portion only of the current members of the bench, of whom the gentry element was the most prominent.[78] Local gentry were being added to the bench in increasing numbers, accounting almost entirely for the expansion in the actual numbers of men appointed to commissions of the peace during the reign.[79] Despite this, and in contrast to the situation at the end of the century, there is little to indicate manipulation of the lists.[80] Nor was there any need to afforce a commission which always contained a number of lords, bishops, and lawyers who were members of the King's Council. The gentry element included also a number of household men and councillors who might exercise an influence disproportionate to their numbers. This can be seen in indictments returned for Suffolk, where James Hobart sat more than any other JP and where the returns include an unusually large number of matters affecting the King's rights. Similarly, in Hereford sessions tended to approximate to a meeting of the Prince's Council, differing from it only in the manner and matter of its jurisdiction; whilst in Surrey offenders could even be bound over specifically to await the next sitting of Bray and Dynham at quarter sessions.[81] Moreover, the commission could always be overridden by a special commission of *oyer and terminer*, or strengthened by the unwonted presence of an unusually large number of peers and councillors already members of it. The growing importance of this élite is suggested by the increasing responsibilities devolved on it by statute. As the same men were frequently included in special commissions to assess subsidies and other taxes, they were exceptionally placed to affect the lives and prosperity of their fellows within the shire. A greater degree of interference is apparent in the office of sheriff. At times of crisis, responsibility passed to the King's Council and household. No less than five councillors were appointed as sheriffs in 1485, besides others later to become councillors, and a high proportion of household men.[82] In 1497, in the aftermath of the Cornish Rebellion, the sheriffs originally chosen were replaced by household men in seven counties, comprising four shrievalties.[83] There was similar interference in at least five other years, despite the fact that a man was often named for sheriff for several years before finally being picked.[84] The position of the sheriff within the shire is well enough known. Not only was he the direct representative of the King's authority. He was also open to influence within the shire, at elections, in empanelling jurors, or in due process of law. As a figure crucial to a King to whom litigation by common-law process was a principal instrument of authority, the sheriff was subjected to tight control. For many the burden of shrieval office carried heavy consequences in later years when their recognizances were deemed to be forfeit for transgressions real or alleged.[85] Others were the subject of specific prosecutions on penal statutes, whether for taking bribes, allowing prisoners to escape, or otherwise failing in their duties.[86]

The second group, the household, is more readily recognizable as an élite. Again, Henry VII's use of his household was not startlingly new. Even Henry VI had employed his household extensively in the process of government: though in his case in particular it must remain an open question how far the household governed the King and how far men desiring positions of influence could insinuate themselves about the King's person. In examining the household one of the problems is to ascertain how far men were absorbed into it as a way of harnessing their influence within the shire and how far they were delegated office and authority within the shire because of their position within the household. Of this duality of perspective the Crown itself was not unaware.[87] In 1485 at least the choice was very much a military one, influenced by the proven loyalty of Henry's companions in exile, of those who had participated in Buckingham's rebellion, and of those who had supported Henry at Bosworth: together with a strong admixture of Stafford retainers and servants, the adherents of the King's mother.

In a paper to the Royal Historical Society, Dr Morgan has elaborated on the use made by Edward IV of his household.[88] The reign of Henry VII is not dissimilar. The comments of the Croyland chronicler[89] could be applied with equal justice to Henry VII, who, for example, like Edward IV, granted such offices as the constables of castles generally, though not exclusively, to his household knights and esquires. Military expeditions were conducted largely by and through the household. But there are differences between the two reigns. The most noticeable is Henry's treatment of major household offices. These were left vacant for long periods at a time: a pattern from which only the chamberlainship was exempt and in which the coffererership grew immeasurably in stature.[90] Another, more vital, difference is Henry's great extension of Chamber finance, important because of the disturbing influence which it enabled the King to exert upon all ruling groups. Chamber finance meant more than an agency for the amassment of revenue. It was the hub of an administrative system. The concentration of cash and administration in the King's own hands removed a whole dimension from the political scene. It gave the King financial and, in consequence, political independence. As a tool of personal government, using books constantly perused by the King himself and including memoranda pertaining to political matters dictated by Henry and constantly brought to his attention, it provided the King with the means to supervise his policy closely and with which to execute it. Thus the offence of the Earl of Northumberland was noted several months before action was begun in the courts; the possibility of raising an aid for the marriage of the King's daughter was considered two years before the Parliament which compounded for it was summoned.[91] Chamber finance, in conjunction with conciliar control, radically changed the channels of patronage for certain matters of grace, as the whole transaction was reduced to a financial one. This is not to suggest that the King's grace had ever been free. But the rational and extensive application of conciliar control in the King's interest did tend to curtail the special pleading associated with such petitions. The need to pay and outbid became a pressing necessity. John Shaa, for example, promised 500 marks that Thomas Frowyk should be appointed chief justice of the common pleas 'as largely as he that last was gaff therefor'.[92] Equally revealing is a cancelled entry relating to the speakership of the Parliament of 1497. Lord Daubeney bid the fee of the Speaker that Sir Robert Sheffield should have the office. This is cancelled and above there is an interlineation of a bid by Bray for Thomas Englefield, who was indeed appointed, Thomas Lovell himself heading the delegation that preceded his 'election'.[93] Even prominent councillors felt the full impact of a system so closely controlled by the King. If Bray remained immune during his lifetime, his executors paid 5000 marks for a pardon, suffered prosecution for alleged customs offences, and even saw the provisions of Bray's will disturbed partly through the King's ruthless legalism in pursuit of his prerogative rights.[94]

Finally, the Council. How can this be considered an élite at all? Was it not merely an organ of government, albeit a policy-making one? Omnipotent under the King, its relationship with Henry, its membership, and its functions were the keystone of Henry VII's government. Few men had any real influence with him. He was a strong King who could manipulate, though never entirely supplant, even had he wished so to do, the authority of traditional élites in society, and in this he was master of his own policy. There is a remarkable unanimity amongst contemporary observers and chroniclers, including the hostile comments of rebels against his rule, in emphasizing the King's independence and naming those few men who could command influence. Morton, Fox, Bray, Lovell, Daubeney, and, latterly, Dudley were the most frequently mentioned. Others added Savage and the various King's secretaries, notably King and Ruthal, whilst one astute observer noted the influence of Margaret Beaufort on her son.[95] Not all of these are encompassed within the élites already mentioned. The one factor common to them all was their membership of the King's Council, and this indeed proves to be the basis of their power, both inside and outside government. It is true that they might be recategorized into their social classes, but this would illustrate rather the wide base from which Henry drew his Council than say anything positive about them. Still less does it explain their importance within the state. But what then are we to make of the comments of Ayala that by 1498 Henry had shaken off the influence of some part of the Council and would have liked to reduce it still further.[96] Does this not flatly contradict the present argument or else render valueless the ambassador's testimony and political judgement on this and other occasions? In fact there is a grain of truth in such comments if they are set within a fundamentally different interpretation. Henry's relations with his Council did undergo a real change. Power was a dynamic, not a static, force. Throughout the reign, Henry retained ultimate control, whether in matters as major as foreign policy, or as minor as the grant of an office. Even Empson did not escape this minute surveillance. His petition for the grant of a stewardship was amended in Henry VII's own hand from a grant for life to a grant during pleasure.[97] But power within the Council did become concentrated in the hands of fewer men, mostly lawyers, underlining the peripheral status of those who sat only occasionally *in consiliarios* and diminishing also the influence of the nobility as a group, though lip-service continued to be paid to their pre-eminence and their presence was required on all occasions of importance. Even the less prominent councillors were, however, part of a vital chain of command and information binding the King and Council to the country at large. For this statutory provision was both made and realized, if in breach as well as in observance, as in bringing riots and other misdemeanours to the attention of King and Council,[98] in which the Council itself maintained an active interest. Although conclusions are at present tentative, there are some pointers to support Cameron's suggested modification of accepted views of the Council's jurisdiction in criminal and allied actions, though it was with the Council Learned rather than the Council in Star Chamber that the initiative lay. The Council did use common-law process, which had the incidental advantage of making the matter of record and allowing common-law process to run against those accessories in whom the Crown was less interested. But the Council itself might draw up or amend indictments, issue the commission by which they were found, and even on occasion attend at sessions. Process might subsequently follow both before the Council and at common law, and, if the final end was a composition with the Council for the discharge of both processes, composition and the pardon procedure were almost the only available sanctions.[99]

The basic composition of Henry VII's Council was much the same as in the Yorkist period, with which there was some continuity of personnel.[100] No less than 35 of Henry's councillors had been councillors also of Edward IV, continuity being equally apparent in all strata of the Council. But there were also subtle changes in the composition of the Council over the course of the reign, as the *iuris periti* became increasingly prominent. Even if total figures from the reign of Henry VII and Edward IV are compared, the numerical importance of both the peerage and the ecclesiastical groups shows a decline as against the rise of the legal element. This included not only the serjeants at law, who became increasingly important, but also such men as Thomas Lovell, Edmund Dudley, who by his own choice preferred conciliar employment to a legal career, and Richard Empson, Attorney General of the Duchy and Recorder of Coventry.[101]

The fall in the number of secular lords was to some extent outside Henry's control. During the 1490s a number of peers achieved both their majority and a place on the Council, before death had removed some of the older generation. But this decade was also the period when Henry's rule approximated most nearly to that of his Yorkist predecessors. The traumatic events of 1497 and what can only be described as his own increasing avarice, however motivated, turned his mind more sharply to repression, affecting both the use which he made of his Council and the membership of it, and also his attitude to the most 'able' group in society, the peers. At all periods their presence was necessary at moments of solemnity, as meetings of 1499 and 1504 illustrate.[102] But there was a rationalization of the conciliar body, underlining the importance of those few peers prominent in the councils of the King; primarily the household and administrative group, to the exclusion of those merely the King's 'natural' councillors. Yet even the evidence of the presence lists surviving as the *Liber intrationum*, showing a proportional attendance of the peers which varies from 25 per cent to 36 per cent, rising on occasion to 57 per cent, may be misleading. Caesar's lists, however, suggest what was surely the normal situation. On the working Council rather than the plenary session the balance was weighted far more heavily towards the legal element and such assiduous councillors as Sir John Risely.[103] And until the face of the Council was radically changed in the last decade it is again the group who combined household office with a place on the Council who were the most prominent – a group which included Guildford, Lovell, Poynings, Daubeney, and Bray himself.

The importance of the Council lies in its intimate association with the King in the business of government, and the King himself was usually present at its meetings. But its business was not restricted to the range of matters which preface the late-sixteenth-century extracts of its *acta*, comprehensive though this summary seems in its inclusion of much judicial and executive action touching all social classes.[104] From the mid-1490s certain councillors, of whom the chief was Reginald Bray, acted in the presence of the King as a court of audit for both lands and revenue. This committee of council was later to become a conciliar court of audit under Robert Southwell and Roger Laybourne. A second court, no less the King's Council though it generally sat, from 1500 at least, without the King's great officers and met under the presidency of the Dean of the Chapel of the Household, developed (as the Court of Requests) a jurisdiction in equity parallel to that of the Star Chamber. There were similar conciliar committees leasing lands and granting offices in Exchequer patronage, or collecting fines of distraint of knighthood, or organizing the collection of arrears of the benevolence and thus investigating local prosperity and influence. Most significant of all was the Council Learned in the Law, again acting with the full authority of the King's Council though meeting in the duchy chamber under the presidency of the Chancellor of the Duchy and comprised almost entirely of lawyers. It provided a third conciliar court of equity and, more particularly, supervised matters connected with the King's prerogative, whether the grant of wardships, the compounding for intrusions or the finding of them, the punishment of abuse or negligence by the King's officers, compounding with offenders for pardons, investigating treasons and perjuries and other abuses with an energy which made its presence widely felt and its members feared and hated.[105]

Henry VII turned naturally to a conciliar solution for every administrative problem. This resulted in a conciliar omnicompetence which, with the growing importance of only a small part of the Council, meant that councillors formed the only élite which could dominate all the rest. This could have some unique manifestations, whether in terms of the rewards to councillors themselves, their prominence in the land market, or in the system of informers and promoters who bypassed the usual channels and exerted an influence beyond their status, bringing defaulting officers, nobles, clergy, gentry, merchants, and poor men to book before the King's Council or subjecting them to a combination of prosecution in the king's bench or common pleas and appearance before the Council for the more rapid determination of process. Even the rapid expansion of conciliar justice during the course of the reign enhanced its influence, though it was an expansion due as much to pressure from litigants as to a conscious act of policy. Star Chamber cases themselves are almost entirely pleadings between party and party, in which questions of title predominate, rather than criminal actions.[106] Even so, the King might on occasion intervene, stopping the action between Lord Fitzwalter and John Doget, for example, and taking the case into his own hands.[107] This expansion of litigation had several side effects. One was through the Council's use of arbitration, which thus involved in its processes those same classes who provided the JPs and sheriffs, though the Council often retained the ultimate decision in its own hands. A second was the further extension of the system of recognizances, which were usually taken not only for appearance but also for good behaviour, and often for allegiance from parties suing or brought before it.[108] These were not necessarily cancelled, and could be forfeit for breach of the condition. Even some recognizances given for appearance were later deemed to be forfeit, and suit followed in common pleas as on a plea of debt.[109] Such actions may, however, have had on occasion a political motive, for defendants include men of the stature of the lords Clifford and Dacre.[110] The Council itself was of sufficient status and authority to try and condemn the powerful offender, whether in disputes between party and party or for matters involving breach of the King's peace. Thus, for example, the Duke of

Suffolk was ordered to stay process at common law and not meddle in lands in dispute;[111] the lords Dudley and Grey of Powis, having been warned concerning the misdemeanours of their servants, were subsequently committed to the Fleet for an affray;[112] Lord Hastings was heavily bound for his appearance and to keep the peace.[113] But against the determined offender even the Council might have little effective sanction.[114]

The final link in this chain is the Council Learned, which achieved a separate institutional existence by at least 1499, and perhaps by 1498. In the context of this present study it is less important for its membership – though this was small and included some of the King's most powerful councillors, who, by their membership of it, commanded still greater influence in society at large – than for its activities on the King's behalf. These have already been summarized. The Council's preoccupation was with the King's causes, fiscal and feudal, and the prerogative rights of his kingship, in the broadest sense of the word. The Council Learned interested itself also in the maintenance of law and order, and enjoyed a jurisdiction in contempt committed in other conciliar courts, besides by-passing, interfering with, and anticipating action in the common law courts. Through its pre-emptive interception of returned inquisitions, too, it could assert a manipulative influence in the King's interest significant in a society in which authority was so often grounded on personal ties and landed estate. It became increasingly prominent in the administration and enforcement of that system of recognizances which are a hallmark of Henry VII's policy of control. These, the various special commissions, and, to take a crude but easily calculated measure, the great increase in the number of pardons granted 'of special grace',[115] are all yardsticks to measure a general policy which affected an increasing number of the King's subjects. Moreover, the Council, or specified members of it, were given absolute discretion over the issue of certain special commissions and other matters passing under the great seal. This delegation, unusual in Henry, was possible only because of the very close association of the Council Learned with the King. It was a hegemony which, combined with its use of legal process and recognizance, fed by a system of information and enquiry, and governed by astute and searching legal minds and a steady tenacity of purpose, enabled it so to dominate the whole domestic scene in the last decade of the reign. It was the King himself, and his manifestation in the corporate body of conciliar justice, who was the prime dislocating factor in the relationship between élites.

All this draws together under one head, the very personal rule of Henry VII as king. This itself is the key to the relationship of élites one to another and to society at large. Bacon has a story of how, to the great rejoicing of the whole Court, Henry's pet monkey tore up the notebook in which the King had recorded the characters and demeanours of those about him.[116] This trivial incident, whether or not it actually occurred, encapsulates both the essence and the fragility of Henry's rule. It perhaps suggests, too, a certain superficiality of achievement despite all the auguries of change: an impermanence, a fragility caused in part by the tensions which Henry VII himself created in binding and dividing the ruling élites themselves.

Notes

1 R. J. Knecht, 'The Episcopate and the Wars of the Roses', *University of Birmingham Historical Journal*, 6 (1957–8), pp. 108–31.
2 The curial cleric was not, of course, an unfamiliar figure on the medieval stage. But set within the bounds of an exceptional reign, that of Henry VI, and an exceptional period of change, the Reformation, and in a context in which the balance between lay and clerical involvement in government and administration had tipped overwhelmingly in favour of the former, this marked secularization of the clergy becomes worth recording.
3 On the latter point, see T. H. Aston, 'Oxford's Medieval Alumni', *Past and Present*, 74 (1977), pp. 3–40, esp. pp. 27–30. Henry VII's choice of bishops has in itself helped to weight Aston's figures.
4 Welsh sees have been omitted here because many Welsh bishops were too obscure to be included in Emden's register of graduates. Initial appointments only are considered, because Henry VII made unprecedented use of the device of translation – Fox, for example, held no less than four different sees in succession.
5 These figures are based on A. B. Emden, *A Biographical Register of the University of Oxford to A.D. 1500* (3 vols, Oxford, 1957–9); Emden, *A Biographical Register of the University of Cambridge* (Cambridge, 1963).
6 Deane and Warham were both experienced curialists, but neither was of the stature of either Morton or Fox. For an excellent unpublished study of Warham, see M. Kelly, 'Canterbury Jurisdiction and Influence during the Episcopate of William Warham, 1502–32', Cambridge Ph. D. thesis (1963).
7 WAM 16038; noticed by M. Bowker, *The Secular Clergy of the Diocese of Lincoln* (Cambridge, 1968), p. 17.
8 PRO E 101/415/3, fo. 287: a licence for three-quarters of a year paying £100 yearly.
9 Knecht, 'The Episcopate', p. 130; B. Behrens, 'The Origins of the English Resident Ambassador in Rome', *English Historical Review*, 49 (1934), pp. 640–56.
10 Cf. the correspondence and licences for absence recorded in the Act Books of the Dean and Chapter of Wells: HMC, *Report on the MSS of the Dean and Chapter of Wells* (2 vols, London HMSO, 1907–14), II, esp. pp. 150–2.
11 PRO, E 36/214, p. 447; pardon enrolled *CPR 1494–1509* (London, 1916), p. 366. Likewise Audley (1000 marks); Dudley included this in his list of the King's more excessive demands: BL Lansdowne MS 127, fo. 60; 'The Petition of Edmund Dudley', ed. C. J. Harrison, *English Historical Review*, 87 (1972), pp. 88, 93.
12 That the fine for restitution was a composition is clear from the frequency with which prospective bishops had previously been given custody of the temporalities, or, after preferment, were granted the issues of the vacancy: *CPR 1485–94* (London, 1914); *CPR 1494–1509, passim*; cf. PRO E 159/273, *Brevia baronibus*, Hil. rot. 7–7d., a pardon of account save for any escapes of clerks. Yet if Redman paid merely a full assessed rate of £2000 p.a. after a vacancy lasting almost a year, James Stanley was assessed at nearly twice as much after a vacancy of 15 months: PRO E 101/415/3, fo. 291; BL Lansdowne MS 127, fo. 31; *CPR 1494–1509*, pp. 265, 514.
13 This was a genuine problem in which Henry maintained a sustained, though not necessarily disinterested concern. Both lay and clerical custodians came under heavy pressure. The penalties, initiated and enforced by the Council but 'made sure in the lawe' and thus found by common-law process, were duly exacted (cf. PRO Req 2/12/151, a case of embezzlement of the fine by the messenger to whom it was entrusted). The fines themselves are too numerous to list, but are noted in both the king's bench and in the Chamber books. See also R. B. Pugh, *Imprisonment in Medieval England* (Cambridge, 1970), pp. 218–54, esp. pp. 236–40.

14 PRO E 101/415/3, fo. 283; also E 101/415/3, fos. 285, 288. The first recorded mention was in 1497: E 101/414/16, fo. 259.

15 See now *Spelman's Reports*, ed. J. H. Baker (2 vols, Selden Soc., 93–4; London, 1977–8), II, pp. 64–8; M. Kelly, 'Canterbury Jurisdiction', discusses the implications of certain actions. If prosecution was at the initiative of private parties, and if some were no more than cross suits in an accepted tradition of vexatious litigation, the penalties on the Bishop and his officials were real enough, and those against the bishop of Norwich had the active encouragement of the King's attorney, a member of the commission of the peace; cf. PRO KB 9/438/48-54; KB 9/442/111; KB 9/445/26; DL 5/4, fos. 105ᵛ, 111ᵛ.

16 J. Fortescue, *The Governance of England*, ed. C. Plummer (Oxford, 1855), pp. 150–1; noticed by J. R. Lander, *Crown and Nobility 1450–1509* (London, 1976), p. 13.

17 *The Reign of Henry VII*, ed. A. F. Pollard (3 vols, London, 1913–14), I, pp. 150–5.

18 *Calendar of State Papers, Spanish* (13 vols in 20 parts; London, 1862–1954), I *1485–1509* (London, 1862), p. 329; BL Add. MS 28623, fos. 11–12.

19 For an assessment of the Stanleys' gains under Henry VII, see the unpublished study of B. Coward, 'The Stanley Family *c.*1385–1651', Sheffield Ph.D. (1968), pt iii, though he greatly overstates the extent of Henry's confirmation, cf. *CPR 1485–94*, pp. 230–1.

20 *Rotuli Parliamentorum* (6 vols. London, 1832), VI, pp. 444–6.

21 Coward, 'The Stanley Family', pp. 163–186, discusses both the effects of the indictments for retaining and an incident involving the interruption by Stanley retainers of the reading of a royal proclamation. Cf. Dudley's assertion that the second earl was 'often tymes hardly intreated and to sore', (C. J. Hernison, 'The Petition of Edmund Dudley', *English Historical Review*, 87 (1972), pp. 88, 93, 26 n.; BL Add. MS 21480, fo. 191).

22 PRO KB 9/434/30; BL Add. MS 59899, fo. 211ᵛ.

23 See S. B. Chrimes, *Henry VII* (London, 1972), p. 76. Perhaps the sole point to be made is her total absence of political influence.

24 *CPR 1485–94*, p. 189; *CPR 1494–1509*, pp. 56–7; WAM 12179 – though Daubeney, for example, held such office even before 1485.

25 J. R. Lander, 'Bonds, Coercion and Fear', in his *Crown and Nobility*, pp. 286–8. PRO C 255/8/5/3 graphically illustrates the extent to which others were potentially involved in Dorset's fate, being a record of the process of manucaption, not mentioned by Lander.

26 *Calendar of State Papers, Spanish*, I, p. 178. One suit concerning title was even specifically delegated by the King's Council to that of the Lady Margaret, though she was not the immediate lord: PRO Req 2/4/246.

27 Calculated from *Complete Peerage*; 19 if Lincoln is included.

28 PRO E 34/3: service to the King was to be exclusive. The long list of men retained with Thomas Lovell may be one such list, its size explained by his prominent conciliar status and its composition by his access to the Roos tenantry through his wardship of Lord Roos; HMC, *Report on the MSS of the Duke of Rutland* (4 vols, HMSO, London, 1888–1905), IV, pp. 559–66.

29 Cf. the indictments against several members of the King's household, though the retainers wore the King's badge of the red rose; or the indictments brought against the King's own mother which resulted in the enrolment of her licence in King's bench: PRO KB 9/436/7, 13, 16; KB 27/926, Trin. 20 Hen. VII, Rex rot. 3.

30 A. Conway, *Henry VII's Relations with Scotland and Ireland, 1485–98* (Cambridge, 1932); *Select Cases in the Council of Henry VII*, ed. C. G. Bayne and W. H. Dunham (Selden Soc., 75; London, 1958), pp. 46–7.

31 Bray was Chamberlain of Chester, 1495–1500 (PRO Ches. 1/2/57) and steward of Monmouth and the duchy lands in Herefordshire (R. Somerville, *The Duchy of Lancaster* (London, 1953), pp. 636–7, 648). There is little evidence of Bray's active interest. In south Wales the vacuum was filled to a limited extent by Charles Somerset (W. R. B. Robinson, 'Early Tudor Policy towards Wales: The Acquisition of Lands and Offices in Wales by Charles Somerset, Earl of Worcester', *Bulletin Board of Celtic Studies*, 21 (1964), pp. 422–6).

32 T. B Pugh, 'The Magnates, Knights and Gentry', p. 115, and R.A. Griffiths, 'Wales and the Marches', pp. 163–5, both in S. B Chrimes, C. D. Ross, and R. A. Griffiths (eds), *Fifteenth-Century England, 1399–1509* (Manchester, 1972).

33 The initial composition of the Council may be deduced from the various *oyer and terminer* commissions: *CPR 1485–94*, pp. 434, 441, 488; PRO Ches. 1/2 offers evidence of its changing composition.

34 Cf. J. A. Guy, 'A Conciliar Court of Audit at Work in the Last Months of Reign of Henry VII', *Bulletin of the Institute of Historical Research*, 49 (1976), pp. 289–95; PRO E 315/263, where most, and perhaps all, of the entries relate to the Prince's lands; E 163/11/27.

35 T. B. Pugh, 'The Indenture for the Marches between Henry VII and Edward Stafford, Duke of Buckingham', *English Historical Review*, 71 (1956), pp. 436–41. This had been preceded by an indenture with Rhys ap Thomas in 1490, and Charles Somerset was similarly bound concerning south Wales in 1496; PRO, E 175/5/18; C 255/8/5/88; *CCR 1485–1500* (London, 1955), p. 894.

36 Chrimes, *Henry VII*, p. 71; J. A. Guy, *The Cardinal's Court* (Hassocks, 1977), p. 19.

37 M. A. Hicks, 'Dynastic Change and Northern Society: The Career of the Fourth Earl of Northumberland', *Northern History*, 14 (1978), esp. pp. 89–103.

38 J. R. Lander, 'Attainder and Forfeiture, 1453–1509' (1961), repr. in his *Crown and Nobility*, pp. 146–7; PRO E 40/14646. R. Virgoe, 'The Recovery of the Howards in East Anglia, 1485–1529', in E. W. Ives, R. J. Knecht, and J. J. Scarisbrick (eds), *Wealth and Power in Tudor England* (London, 1978), pp. 12–15, presents a more optimistic assessment.

39 WAM 12247, 16028, 16073. Although entries in the Chamber books can rarely be dated precisely, Sever's appointment seems to have been made in the spring of 1499: PRO E 101/414/16, fo. 288ᵛ.

40 Somerville, *Duchy of Lancaster*, pp. 265–74, 524, 541.

41 PRO E 163/9/27. The Council's authority seems to have been restricted to Yorkshire, although Savage's position as archbishop may have blurred this limitation, and in 1504 he could term himself 'the Kings lieutenant and high commissionar withynne these the North parties of his realme' (PRO Req 2/3/347; Req 2/10/72; *York Civic Records*, ed. A. Raine (Yorkshire Archaeological Society, Record Ser., 1939–53), III, p. 5).

42 *Select Cases*, p. 30.

43 An inference drawn in part from the composition of the peace commissions, and also from indictment and plea roll evidence of justices participating at sessions. (Commissions, *CPR 1494–1509*, pp. 666–9.)

44 *Select Cases*, pp. 41–4.

45 Cf., for example, the conciliar discussion of the inquisitions made after the death of the third earl: BL Lansdowne MS 639, fos 33–4ᵛ.

46 Instances were listed by Dacre himself: PRO SP 1/1, fos. 71ᵛ–72; *CCR 1500–9*, p. 543, records a recognizance without condition which was to hang at the king's pleasure.

47 *Materials for a History of the Reign of Henry VII from Original Documents Preserved in the Public Record Office*, ed. W. Campbell (2 vols, Rolls Ser., London, 1873–7), I, pp. 242–3; II, p. 533; *Calendar of Documents Relating to Scotland, 1357–1509* ed. J. Bain, (London, 1888), pp. 311, 314–15, 332–5, 337, 349–51; *CPR 1485–94*, pp. 40, 213, 314; *CPR 1494–1509*, pp. 200–2, 213, 379, 442.

48 PRO KB 27/975, Pasch. 20 Henry VII, Rex rot. 11 (Dacre); KB 27/980, Trin. 21. Hen. VII, Rex rot. 6; BL Lansdowne MS 127, fo. 22ᵛ (Clifford).

49 Cf. the convoluted terms of the bill for the Lord Conyers's patent for the wardenship of the East March, which terms him warden-general 'videlicet in partibus de la Est March' and on which Dudley has noted 'this bill is made for the lord Conyers for the Est marche oonly and not as deputie to my lord prince but Immediatly by the Kinges grace as the lord Darcy was' (PRO C 82/325, 16 Mar.).

50 Initially recorded in the Chamber books and subsequently annotated by Henry VII with a reference to Dudley, process followed before the Council, in common pleas and the Exchequer, members of the Council being present in court when judgment was given. The process ended with an appearance before the Council Learned and a

composition with King and Council for a pardon and the fine, secured by a feoffment on the Earl's lands. A later reference suggests that the fine itself may have been augmented by a composition for offences involving retaining. PRO DL 5/4, fos. 20v, 32v, 83; CP 40/974, Mich. 21 Hen. VII, rot. 419; E 159/284, *Brevia Baronibus*, pasch. 2d; E 36/214, fos. 479, 530; BL Add. MS 59899, fo. 213.

51. See *Letters of Richard Fox, 1486–1527*, ed. P. S. Allen and H. M. Allen (Oxford, 1928), pp. 43–4.

52 WAM 16047, 9222/11; PRO E 101/415/3, fo. 298; BL Add. MS 21480, fos. 88ᵛ, 89.

53 *Select Cases*, pp. xxix–xxx, 30; Lander, 'Bonds, Coercion and Fear', pp. 289–90. Lists of New Year gifts recorded in the Chamber books tend to confirm his frequent presence about Court. Yet he was also several times indicted of illegal retaining, accused of treasonable words, briefly imprisoned in the Tower, and eventually pardoned but heavily fined; see also PRO KB 9/430/49–59; KB 9/443/2–3; KB 9/441/6; C 237/58/6/1.

54 Lander, 'Bonds, Coercion and Fear', p. 275; PRO E 101/414/6, fo. 210ᵛ.

55 Lander, 'Bonds, Coercion and Fear', pp. 290–1; CCR 1500–9, *passim*; PRO SC 12/18/53.

56 Buckingham petitioned the Council. Moreover, if his brother was allowed to make an advantageous marriage to the widowed Cicely, Marchioness of Dorset, the King's extreme interest in his financial profit from the transaction is suggested by his retention in his own hands of Stafford's obligation (BL Add. MS 59899, fo. 178ᵛ).

57 CPR 1494–1509, pp. 658, 661; CPR 1476–85, pp. 553–580.

58 CPR 1485–94, pp. 481–508; CPR 1494–1509, pp. 629–69.

59 PRO KB 9/368–450, *passim*.

60 Surrey, Daubeney, and, less emphatically, Broke, Ormond, Shrewsbury, and Herbert. Three of these were peers of Henry's own creation, and perhaps only Daubeney and Surrey were really significant.

61 PRO E 101/640; BL Lansdowne MS 127, fo. 32ᵛ; CCR 1500–9 p. 686.

62 BL Lansdowne MS 127, fo. 34.

63 PRO, C142/25/22, 128, 138; PROB 11/16/16; Harrison, 'The petition of Edmund Dudley', pp. 88, 93–4.

64 Lander, 'Bonds, Coercion and Fear', pp. 267–300. The defective calendaring of the early close rolls, and the fact that not all bonds were enrolled, has decreased the count for the first part of the reign, although it remains true that the years after 1497 show an escalation in the number of recognizances taken. The penal use of bonds by Edward IV has been discussed by P. M. Barnes, 'The Chancery Corpus Cum Causa File, 10–11 Edward IV', in R. F. Hunnisett and J. B. Post (eds), *Medieval Legal Records* (HMSO, London, 1978), pp. 438–40.

65 WAM 16020; HMC, *Rutland MSS*, I, p. 19.

66 *Calendar of Inquisitions Post Mortem, Second Series, III, Henry VII, years 20–24* (London, 1956), pp. 10–107. Subsequent legal proceedings in Chancery, king's bench, and the Exchequer yield evidence which would increase this count; e.g. PRO C 43/1/31, 34.

67 PRO CP 40/985, Trin. 23 Hen. VII, rot. 345d (Oxford); PRO SP 1/1, fo. 72; DL 5/4, fo. 89; BL Lansdowne MS 127, fo. 44d, 48 (Mabel, Lady Dacre).

68 Polydore Vergil, *The Anglica Historia of Polydore Vergil, AD 1485–1537*, ed. and trans. Denys Hay (Camden Soc., 3rd ser., 74; London, 1954), pp. 127–9; *Calendar of State Papers, Spanish*, I, pp. 177–8.

69 PRO KB 9/961/52.

70 This remains true even if the nobleman still had an important part to play at an earlier stage in the chain of patronage.

71 Hicks, 'Dynastic Change and Northern Society', p. 93; Exeter Record Office, Court Rolls 540; PRO C 146/3273; *Calendar of Inquisitions Post Mortem, Second Series, II, Henry VII, years 13–20* (London, 1915), p. 434; WAM 16066; PRO SC 11/828: this list is clearly not exhaustive. Other lords, including Bedford, and the Countess of Warwick, made grants of office: PRO KB 9/377/17; SC 6/Hen. VII/1373.

72 PRO E 326/8898; CP 40/979, Hil. 22 Hen. VII, *Rot. Chart.* 3.

73 For example, Bray's landed estate, almost all acquired after 1485, suggests the extent to which that advantage could be carried. It was sufficient to endow two peerages in the reign of Henry VIII, and Dugdale estimated a value of over 1000 marks for the purchases of 1497–1503 alone: W. Dugdale, *The Baronage of England* (2 vols, London, 1675–6), II, p. 303. The familiar case of the Plumptons, involving charges of maintenance, corruption, and a feigned inquisition, was extreme rather than unique, and forms of pressure applied beyond mere investment might include intercession with the King for a pardon, exploitation of unquiet titles, or financial difficulties arising from recognizances due to the King.

74 This may be traced both through wills and through feet of fines, although a number of such transactions conceal a use in favour of Henry VII himself: for example, the related enfeoffments on the lands of the heirs of Thomas Green: PRO, CP 40/982, Mich. 23 Hen. VII, rot. 301–301d, 309–309d, 614–8, 706; BL Lansdowne MS 127, fos. 45d, 50.

75 PRO PROB 11/9/13; PRO PROB 11/12/10.

76 The comments which follow are based primarily on a study, using patent roll, pipe roll, and indictment evidence, of a group of counties falling alphabetically between Salop and Sussex. Since this essay was written, several important studies have appeared, including those of Professor Baker and Dr Virgoe already cited, and M. L. Zell, 'Early Tudor JPs at Work', *Archaeologia Cantlana*, 93 (1977), pp. 125–43. Dr Zell's detailed study of Kent JPs parallels much that could be said about the present sample.

77 An average of 30–40 per cent of the JPs were, or became, MPs either within the county studied or an adjacent county; likewise at least 50 per cent of the sheriffs were, or became, JPs and the proportion rises to 92 per cent in the joint shrievalty of Surrey and Sussex.

78 Although there are considerable variations between counties, perhaps only 50–60 per cent of the 'gentry' members of the commission were active at sessions, although it was on them, rather than on the bishops, lords, and lawyers, that the main burden lay.

79 In four of the counties studied the commission increased between 60 per cent and 100 per cent in size, though in Salop and Southampton the rise is less marked.

80 On the later sixteenth century, see A. Hassell-Smith, *County and Court: Government and Politics in Norfolk, 1558–1603* (Oxford, 1974). This rich evidence does not exist for Henry VII's reign, and Virgoe's study would suggest rather the multiplicity of connections which might be involved: Virgoe, 'The Recovery of the Howards', pp. 10–14.

81 PRO C 255/8/5/94; C 244/146/2.

82 CFR, XXII, *Henry VII, 1485–1509* (London, 1963), 95–6; 97–8; cf. CFR, XXI, *Edward IV – Richard III, 1471–1485* (London, 1961), 861–2; PRO C 82/14 shows that, not surprisingly, the September commission was not a pricked list in the normal sense.

83 PRO C 82/180. These were the four counties most affected, Devon, Somerset, Dorset, Berkshire (and thus Oxfordshire), and also Norfolk and Suffolk. A change seems to have been contemplated in Surrey and Sussex, but in the event Richard Sackville was confirmed as sheriff. The appointment of Eggecombe to Devon was ordered by the King himself before he left Exeter: PRO C 82/331, 2 Nov. (13) Hen. VII.

84 PRO C 82/56; C 82/329; C 82/330; C 82/332. Again, though the theory must often have failed in practice, the mere suspicion of retainer with a lord other than the King could bar appointment: PRO C 82/332, 16 Nov. (16) Hen. VII.

85 In 1506 prosecution was made the responsibility of the Under-Treasurer, John Cutte, and Edmund Dudley, *vice* Bray's executors. The terms of their commission emphasize the likelihood of forfeiture, past and future, and allowed a fixed rate of composition: PRO E 404/85, 16 Apr. 21 Hen. VII.

86 *Select Cases*, pp. cxxviii–ix, lists those cases brought by Henry Toft in *qui tam* actions: these ended in the inevitable pardon and composition with the Crown for

the King's interest: PRO E 36/214, p. 461. For other royal actions against sheriffs, see PRO SC 1/51/179; E 101/415/3, fo. 291 (John Hussey); PRO C 142/19/4; KB 9/440/1; KB 29/135, Pasch. 21 Hen. VII, rot. 28–9; DL 5/4, fos. 95ᵛ, 98, 111ᵛ, 113ᵛ (several Northumberland sheriffs); PRO CP 40/479, Mich. 22 Hen. VII, rot. 102–3d; CP 40/982, Mich. 23 Hen. VII, rot. 405; CP 40/983, Hil. 23 Hen. VII, rot. 495; CP 40/985, Trin. 23 Hen. VII, rot. 349; DL 5/4, fos. 107ᵛ, 151ᵛ–152ᵛ.

87 For example, PRO E 36/130, a county-wise list of household officers, *temp.* Henry VIII.

88 D. A. L. Morgan, 'The King's Affinity in the Polity of Yorkist England', *Transactions of the Royal Historical Society*, 5th ser., 23 (1973), pp. 1–25.

89 *Rerum Anglicarum Scriptorem Veterum*, vol. I, ed. W. Fulman (Oxford, 1684), p. 652.

90 Published lists obscure this point, though it is symptomatic of Henry's attitude to rule within society at large. There was thus, for example, no treasurer 1488–*c.* 1502 and no controller 1505–7, nor for the years following the deaths of Eggecombe in 1489 and of Tocotes in 1492.

91 Much of what follows on both Chamber and Council is based on detailed research on which it is hoped to enlarge at a later date. Footnotes have therefore been here curtailed, pending a fuller discussion. BL Add. MS 59899, fo. 213; PRO E 101/415/3, fo. 296.

92 PRO E 101/415/3, fo. 299; annotated with receipt of 200 marks and an obligation for £200, BL Add. MS 21480, fo. 185.

93 PRO E 101/414/6, fo. 128. The interlineation is in Henry's own hand. For the election and presentation of the speaker, PRO E 101/414/6, fo. 232; *Rotuli Parliamentorum*, VI, p. 510.

94 BL Add. MS 59899, fo. 182; BL Landowne MS 127, fo. 11ᵛ; PRO E 159/283, *Recorda*, Trin., rot. 5–6; E 36/214, pp. 441, 475, 635; E 101/413/2, p. 63; C 82/245, 28 June; Kent AO, U 455/T138. The record of the prosecution for customs offences suggests an offence against the letter, rather than the spirit of the law, for the duties were paid, though not in Bray's name. Cf. also Dudley's comment on Henry's treatment of the executors, or the more general remarks of Vergil: Harrison, 'The Petition of Edmund Dudley', pp. 88, 94; *Anglica Historia*, p. 129.

95 *Calendar of State Papers, Spanish*, I, pp. 168, 178; *Calender of State Papers, Spanish and Manuscripts Existing in the Archives Collection of Milan*, I, ed. A. B. Hinds (London, 1913), pp. 299, 335, 351; *Calendar of State Papers and Manuscripts Relating to English Affairs. Existing in the Archives and Collections of Venice, and in Other Libraries of Northern Italy*, ed. R. Brown, I. *1201–1509* (London, 1864), p. 285; *The Reign of Henry VII*, ed. Pollard, I, 150, 152–3.

96 *Calendar of State Papers, Spanish* I, p. 178.

97 PRO C 82/305/13 Sept. 23 Hen. VII; likewise PRO DL 12/1/2/6.

98 For example, *Letters and Papers Illustrative of the Reign of Richard III and Henry VII*, ed. J. Gairdner (2 vols, Rolls Ser., London, 1861–3), II, pp. 75–84: the same offences (with others) were still being presented in 1509: PRO KB 9/953/229–61; PRO E 101/415/3, fo. 297ᵛ; PRO KB 9/427/80; KB 9/430/49; WAM 16057, 16020; BL Add. MS 59899, fo. 153ᵛ; likewise, the watching brief given Darcy after riots at Knaresborough: PRO KB 9/445/29; SC 1/58/53. The sheriff's oath, too, enjoined that he, if he could not himself maintain the King's rights, should 'certifye the Kyng or summe of his counsell therof, such as ye hold for certayn will say it unto Kyng', *Registrum Thome Myllyng, Episcopi Herefordensis*, A.D. *1474–92*, ed. A.T. Bannister (Canterbury and York Society, 26; Canterbury, 1921), p. 133.

99 A. Cameron, 'A Nottinghamshire Quarrel in the Reign of Henry VII', *Bulletin of the Institute of Historical Research*, 45 (1972), pp. 35–7; cf. Harrison, 'The Petition of Edmund Dudley', p. 93 n. 25; see above, n. 86; PRO KB 9/445/1–11; KB 9/435/45; KB 9/427/83–4; E 101/415/3, fo. 297ᵛ.; E 36/214, p. 475; DL 5/4, fo. 157ᵛ; C 82/294, 28 Dec. Even in 1511 action before the Council and imprisonment in the Tower could follow indictment in common law: PRO KB 9/456/5; Huntington Library, Ellesmere MS 2652, fo. 8ᵛ. I am indebted to Dr J. A. Guy for a copy of this latter MS.

100 For the Yorkist Council, see J. R. Lander, 'Council, Administration and Councillors' (1959), repr. in his *Crown and Nobility*, pp. 309–20. For Henry VII, the author's own research has been used.
101 Although a detailed chronological breakdown makes this still more apparent, for a thoughtful development of the general thesis see E. W. Ives, 'The Common Lawyers in Pre-Reformation England', *Transactions of the Royal Historical Society*, 5th. ser., 18 (1968), pp. 154–6.
102 *Select Cases*, pp. 30–44; cf. Guy, *The Cardinal's Court*, p. 12.
103 *Select Cases*, pp. 53–8.
104 *Select Cases*, pp. 6–7; cf. also the thematic arrangement of Ellesmere MS 2652.
105 The standard account, now in need of a revision which it is hoped eventually to provide, is the seminal article of R. Somerville, 'Henry VII's Council Learned in the Law', *English Historical Review*, 54 (1939), pp. 427–42.
106 *Select Cases*, pp. cxxxix, clv–viii; Guy, *The Cardinal's Court*, pp. 15–18, 53–57.
107 Guy, *The Cardinal's Court*, pp. 16–17.
108 Ellesmere MS 2652, fo. lv; confirmed not only by the evidence of the *corpus cum causa* files, but also by Henry VII himself: PRO C 244/138–157, *passim*; DL 42/21, fo. 21.
109 For example, PRO CP 40/983, Hil. 23 Hen. VII, rot. 348d, 353, 353d; E 101/414/6, fo. 232ᵛ, 226ᵛ; BL Add. MS 59899, fo. 153ᵛ. More generally, in 1505 a large number of obligations, including many for appearance or good behaviour, were delivered to Edmund Dudley to sue for the King's profit – though not all would in practice have been forfeit, whilst the mercers sued as a body for their discharge: PRO E 101/517/11.
110 PRO CP 40/983, Hil. 23 Hen. VII, rot. 406 (obligation of 1486); CP 40/985, Trin. 23 Hen. VII, rot. 374 (obligation of 1488); cf. SP 1/1, fos. 71ᵛ–72; Harrison, 'The Petition of Edmund Dudley', pp. 90, 98.
111 *Select Cases*, p. 19.
112 Ellesmere MS 2652, fo. 6ᵛ; cf. PRO C 244/139/93.
113 PRO C 244/146/26. Instances might be multiplied: see also above, n. 99.
114 If the most obvious instance lies in the proclamation of rebellion in a final attempt to secure appearance, neither the Council of Richard III nor that of Henry VII was, for example, able permanently to enjoin good behaviour on Thomas Cornwall, Richard Corbet, and Richard Croft: *Select Cases*, pp. cxxiii–iv; 9, 14, 19, 50–1, 78–87; PRO C 244/136/111, C 244/139/101, 156, 174; C 244/140/80; C 244/143/25; C 244/147/135; C 255/8/5/7, 8; E 404/82/ 3 Dec. 12 Hen. VII; CP 40/983, Hil. 23 Hen. VII, rot. 364d.
115 The detailed particulars of the hanaper accounts, which do not, however, survive for the last two and a half years of the reign, show a rise in the number of such pardons from an average of 20–30 p.a. in the 1490s to 50–100 p.a. in the years before 1507. The artificially inflated account for 18–19 Hen. VII has been discounted. PRO E 101/217/14, 15; E 101/218/3–6, 8, 10, 12; E 101/219/2, 4, 6–8.
116 Francis Bacon, *The History of the Reign of Henry VII*, ed. R. Lockyer (Folio Soc.; London, 1971), p. 233.

12

Wolsey and the Tudor polity

JOHN GUY

> . . . in the Chamber of Stars
> All matters there he mars,
> Clapping his rod on the board.
> No man dare speak a word,
> For he hath all the saying
> Without any renaying.
> He rolleth in his records,
> He saith, 'How say ye, my lords?
> Is not my reason good?'
>
> (Skelton, *Why Come Ye Nat to Courte?*)[1]

For centuries the wit and wisdom of John Skelton underpinned debate upon
the achievements of Cardinal Wolsey even though his criticisms were calumnies. This fact was acknowledged by Richard Fiddes as early as 1724.[2]
George Cavendish, Wolsey's gentleman usher, himself made the essential
point when he completed his *Life and Death of Cardinal Wolsey* in the summer of 1558. He protested: 'And since his [Wolsey's] death I have heard
divers sundry surmises and imagined tales made of his proceedings and
doings, which I myself have perfectly known to be most untrue.'[3]

Historians have been wary of Skelton since the early 1980s, and in a major
new study his satires have been systematically debunked.[4] It is certainly
insufficient to identify them as calumnies if they are still allowed to dictate
the historical agenda.[5] Whatever emerges from the current process of revi-
sionism, Tudor propaganda should be recognized for what it was: opinion
of Wolsey was moulded by his opponents. The ballads of the London citizens mirrored Skelton's satires in the early 1520s.[6] When Wolsey silenced
Skelton with a promise of lucrative patronage, John Palsgrave continued
where the poet had left off, overstepping the mark by April 1528, when he
was hauled before the Council for writing his thundering 'remembrances'.[7]
When Wolsey's fall was imminent in the summer of 1529, Lord Darcy
experimented with draft accusations which have survived.[8] When the
Cardinal's dismissal looked irrevocable, articles of attainder were formulated by members of the Reformation Parliament.[9] Although unashamedly
manufactured to condemn Wolsey, the 44 articles were signed by Thomas
More, which enhanced their credibility. It is true that Richard Moryson paid
a gracious tribute to Wolsey in his *Remedy for Sedition*, published in 1536.[10]
His compliment is usually dismissed as a piece of special pleading by a client

on behalf of his former patron. Yet the same conventions permit indiscrim-
inate citation of Edward Hall's chronicle, a work blatantly hostile to Wolsey
by an anticlerical lawyer who in May 1539 supervised the destruction of St
Thomas Becket's window in Gray's Inn chapel.[11] Lastly, the smear spread by
Catholics and Protestants alike in the sixteenth century that Wolsey was the
instigator of Henry VIII's first divorce proved highly tenacious.[12]

Historians have scrutinized the primary sources rigorously since the late
1960s: Wolsey's correspondence and the records of Chancery, Star Chamber,
and the Exchequer.[13] More accurate impressions have been obtained, but the
verdict is mixed. On the one hand, writers applaud Wolsey's zeal for better
law enforcement, justice for the poor, the restraint of illegal enclosures, and
efficient taxation. On the other, they acknowledge that he overreached himself, notably in the Parliament of 1523, and especially two years later over the
Amicable Grant, when he attempted to levy taxation without parliamentary
consent and sparked a regional revolt. In this chapter I shall revisit and
reassess Wolsey's contribution to the two most central aspects of Tudor political life: the King's Council and local government. What emerges is less the
'case for the defence' than a perspective on Wolsey's career which is more
sharply focused and yet more favourable than previous synoptic assessments.

I

Despite the controversy that currently rages over the reconstruction of the
Privy Council in the 1530s, no one would dispute that the Council was the
matrix of Tudor government.[14] Under Henry VII it met regularly in Star
Chamber, but these assemblies were large and unwieldy and the King rarely
attended them in the second half of his reign. Moreover, fiscal and enforce-
ment decisions were at first taken by Henry VII and his Council attendant at
Court; then, after the deaths of Archbishop Morton and Sir Reynold Bray,
they were vested in the hands of the King and the members of the Council
Learned in the law. Under Wolsey the main forum of activity was Star
Chamber, but this position was reversed immediately upon his fall, when
Henry VIII's 'political' councillors raced to serve the King at Court.[15] By 1540
the Privy Council had been reconstructed as an executive board acting corporately under the Crown. Policy-making at the highest level was subsumed
within the Court, and it remained so throughout Elizabeth's long reign.[16]

The creative vigour of Wolsey's management of Star Chamber is unchallenged. His first policy was his law-enforcement plan, unveiled in Henry
VIII's presence on 2 May 1516 and reiterated in May 1517 and October
1519. This was a two-tiered strategy emphasizing law enforcement and the
impartial administration of justice irrespective of social status. Wolsey's second policy was to publicize the merits of the justice of Star Chamber and
Chancery for private parties. I have discussed these keynote policies

elsewhere, and will not repeat myself here.[17] I want instead to look at the dynamics of the Council, which are more difficult to reconstruct.[18] The best place to begin is Cavendish's *Life*, which paints its canvas with bold brush strokes. Cavendish reports that Wolsey rode in state each weekday morning during the four legal terms from York Place to Westminster Hall. When he had arrived and exchanged words with the judges, he went into the court of Chancery, where he sat until 11 o'clock hearing suits. 'And from thence he would divers times go into the Star Chamber, as occasion did serve, where he spared neither high nor low, but judged every estate according to their merits and deserts.'[19]

Wolsey sat in Star Chamber between three and five days a week.[20] He was therefore absent from Henry VIII's Court, which settled itself during term at Greenwich or Windsor, or sometimes Eltham, Richmond, or Bridewell.[21] Westminster had been abandoned as a royal residence in 1512 after a disastrous fire, and it was not until Wolsey's own York Place became Henry's property upon the Cardinal's conviction for *praemunire* in 1529 that the King acquired a suitable replacement.[22] So a problem of communications arose. Wolsey wrote regularly to Henry VIII, and on Sundays during term he travelled to Court to clear the week's business in person with the King. This Cavendish confirms, and he adds the information that on Sundays the Court was much better attended than during the week, since others followed Wolsey there. 'And after dinner among the lords, having some consultation with the King or with the council,' Wolsey returned home. This arrangement, Cavendish says, his master 'used continually as opportunity did serve'.[23]

Henry and Wolsey might therefore consult members of the Council on Sundays. Nor is this the only instance of counselling outside Star Chamber, since urgent business could arise in vacation. At Whitsuntide 1523, to take just one example, Henry and Wolsey were immersed in two highly important debates. The first concerned a proposal that the Anglo-Habsburg 'Great Enterprise' against France should be abandoned in favour of an invasion of Scotland.[24] By 2 or 3 June the Earl of Surrey, the King's lieutenant in the north, had been summoned to Court. Surrey replied that he hoped to be with Henry and Wolsey on the 9th, and thereafter Wolsey wrote to Lord Dacre of the north, whom Surrey had appointed his deputy, informing him why Surrey had been summoned and what had subsequently passed in the Council.[25]

The scheme for the invasion of Scotland was dropped when Charles, Duke of Bourbon, Constable of France, agreed to commit treason, a prospect which made the 'Great Enterprise' suddenly seem feasible. This was the second great issue over Whitsuntide: the earliest hints that Bourbon might prove a realistic ally reached Wolsey's ears at the end of May. So Wolsey provisionally agreed with Charles V's ambassador that the English would invade France with an army of 15 000 foot under the Duke of Suffolk in the summer. And throughout he involved the Council. The Duke of

Suffolk, the Earl of Shrewsbury, Sir Robert Wingfield, and three bishops were among those consulted. Moreover, these consultations were begun and completed during the vacation.[26]

It is often remarked that Henry VIII felt himself ill-attended by his Council.[27] His actual words were that he lacked 'some personages about him, as well to receive strangers that shall chance to come, as also that the same strangers shall not find him so bare without some noble and wise sage personages about him'.[28] Earlier he had complained that he had 'but few to give attendance'.[29] Neither statement supports the view that Henry was uncounselled; he seems to have been demanding that Wolsey supply him with some noble attendants. The conventional picture of an uncounselled king sulking at Court while Wolsey ruled the roost in Star Chamber is heavily overdrawn. True, the King's 'continual' Council was virtually extinguished: councillors attending Henry VIII daily at Court were reduced by the spring of 1518 to Thomas More, John Clerk, and Richard Pace, who were joined at Easter by the dukes of Buckingham and Suffolk, Sir Thomas Lovell, and Sir Henry Marney.[30] Nor, on at least this occasion, were these councillors kept properly informed. Wolsey was secretly negotiating a *rapprochement* with France in a tense atmosphere, and Henry VIII told Clerk 'that in no wise he should make mention of London matters before his lords'.[31] But the Council attendant still functioned when necessary. In 1521 More was authorized on appointment as Under-Treasurer of the Exchequer to reimburse the costs of the diets of the lords of the Council for their meetings in Star Chamber and at 'other places'. These meetings debated 'matters concerning as well the common weal and politic rule and order of this our Realm ... as also our own particular matters and causes'.[32] Although the phrase 'other places' is elliptical, it suggests that the Council had held some meetings at Court, or at the very least somewhere outside Star Chamber.

If Henry VIII believed that he was ill-served, he was probably thinking of weekdays during term, or more likely of the lengthy vacations between the legal terms when Wolsey retired to The More, Hampton Court, or Tyttenhanger instead of following the royal progress. By withdrawing to his own houses in vacations Wolsey was taking a risk. Richard Fox, his former mentor and patron, had warned him in April 1516, 'And, good my lord, when the term is done, keep the council with the King's grace wheresoever he be.'[33] Wolsey sometimes celebrated the great religious festivals at Court, but mostly spent the festivals of the 1520s at his own houses. His lengthy absences from Court exposed him to a series of whispering campaigns and attacks which explain his various swoops on the Privy Chamber and efforts to manipulate the King's secretaries.[34] Yet the bonds of Wolsey's personal friendship with Henry VIII were so secure until the summer of 1527 that he could *afford* to risk long separations from the King. It cannot seriously be maintained that Henry would have tolerated Wolsey's frustration of his consistently expressed wishes on such a vital matter as political counselling over a period of a decade had the King *really* sought a genuine Council attendant meeting daily at Court before 1525.

It is well known that from the beginning it was Henry VIII's special relationship with Wolsey which underpinned the latter's ascendancy: the overriding issue was Wolsey's ministerial status.[35] This is not to deny that he consulted the Council, but rather to acknowledge that the inner circle of Henry VIII's advisers during his chancellorship was reduced to one. Whereas Henry VII, and Elizabeth before the Cecil–Essex feud, opened the inner circle to five or six leading councillors and courtiers, who thrashed out policies at Court before presenting them for wider discussion in the Council, Henry VIII and Wolsey first decided policy between themselves, and only then consulted the Council. Cavendish describes the process when discussing the decision of 1523 to treat with Bourbon. He says that Wolsey first 'move[d] the King in this matter', whereupon Henry 'dreamed' of it more and more, 'until at the last it came in question among the council in consultation'.[36] Moreover, Wolsey in 1524 clarified that this was indeed the way things worked when overruling the suggestions of Pace, Henry's ambassador with Bourbon during the siege of Marseilles. He wrote: 'All which matters by the King's Highness and me first apart, and after with the most sad and discreet Lords of his most honourable Council, substantially digested, and profoundly debated, it hath been finally, by good deliberation determined ...'.[37]

Wolsey's ministerial status marked a dramatic turnabout from earlier practice under Henry VIII. Between 1509 and 1513 the Council had worked as a corporate board. Councillors who counter-signed documents included Archbishop Warham (Lord Chancellor), Bishop Fox (Lord Privy Seal), the earls of Shrewsbury and Surrey, Sir Edward Howard (Lord Admiral), Lord Herbert, Thomas Ruthal (Bishop of Durham), Sir Henry Marney, and Sir Thomas Lovell. They exercised control over policy as well as patronage, and generally ran the country while the young king found his feet.[38] Of course, the Council liked this arrangement and tried to protract it. Henry VIII disliked it and turned to Wolsey, who liberated him by combining the roles of councillor and courtier at once.[39] As Cavendish explains, he was

> most earnest and readiest among all the council to advance the King's only will and pleasure without any respect to the case. The King therefore perceived him to be a meet instrument for the accomplishment of his devised will and pleasure.[40]

Wolsey started to break the mould in May 1511, when he delivered in person a signed bill to Warham in Chancery, and told him by the king's command to seal the letters patent without countersignature.[41] It took two more years finally to overthrow the embargo on signed bills, but Henry and Wolsey had their way over this as over everything else.[42] By February 1514 the corporate board was a dead letter, and by the end of 1515 Wolsey was unchallenged as the King's minister.[43] Wolsey was in his element, for Henry esteemed him so highly 'that his estimation and favour put all other ancient councillors out of their accustomed favour'.[44] When Wolsey subverted the Council's standing as a corporate board, he acted unilaterally and this was his offence. It was why he rarely got any credit later for his attempts to consult the Council: he was seen to be ministerial, even when his efforts to involve the Council were sincere. It was why he was said to have arrogated power to himself, depriving the King of attendant councillors at Court.

In particular, it was why he was charged with saying and writing, 'The King and I would ye should do thus: the King and I do give unto you our hearty thanks'.[45] For 14 years Henry and Wolsey worked as a partnership.[46] The King needed a minister to accomplish his 'will and pleasure' and in general Wolsey succeeded. True, there were tensions in their relationship, especially in the field of ecclesiastical politics.[47] Only rarely did Henry and Wolsey disagree, however, as in the summer of 1521, when Wolsey was at Calais and unable to ride to Court, or in the spring of 1522, when he urged a combined attack on the French navy at anchor in various ports, but Henry thought the plan too dangerous.[48]

Although Wolsey became notorious for his pomp and circumstance as papal legate, he seems genuinely to have tried not to flaunt his relationship with the King. Only once does he seem to have been observed strolling arm in arm with Henry.[49] On the contrary, Wolsey consistently maintained the posture of the King's loyal executive, which was not simply a matter of tact or presentation; it was strictly true.[50] By definition Henry was the senior partner in any relationship with a subject, and he occasionally fumed that he 'would ... be obeyed, whosoever spake to the contrary'.[51] But, although he alone was in charge of *overall* policy, only in the broadest sense was he taking independent decisions whilst Wolsey's career was at its height. Until the summer of 1527 it was Wolsey who almost invariably calculated the available options and ranked them for royal consideration; who established the parameters of each successive debate; who controlled the flow of official information; who edited correspondence from Europe by summarizing it in his own letters to Henry; who selected the King's secretaries; and who promulgated decisions he himself had largely shaped, if not strictly taken. In foreign affairs, although Henry's overall responsibility for policy is not in doubt, more than mere details were left to Wolsey. To ambassadors Henry seemed largely consistent: he was bent on conquering new territory in France, an objective which in principle Wolsey shared, but about which in practice he reserved judgement. Wolsey always saw ambassadors first, replying to them extempore, and what he said was normally repeated unchanged by Henry at a later interview.[52]

Did the Council in these circumstances steadily abdicate its executive role to Wolsey and concentrate instead on the mass of judicial business that his keynote policies created? A mass of evidence has survived to show that judicial business was increasingly important, justifying the frequency of Council meetings in Star Chamber as well as spawning new conciliar sub-committees or 'under-courts'.[53] But I have always stressed that Wolsey's Council remained a real governing institution. It supervised the swearing-in of sheriffs and JPs, made arrangements for the redistribution of grain stocks following bad harvests, fixed and enforced the prices of many basic com-modities, attacked racketeering in essential foodstuffs, debated projected legislation, attempted to relieve poverty in London and its suburbs, and enforced the statutes against vagrancy and unlawful games. The Council was especially active in the socio-economic sphere in the latter half of the 1520s, and was engaged in debates throughout Wolsey's chancellorship that were far removed from the set-piece formalities satirized by Skelton.[54] Moreover, the Council was consulted about strategic foreign-policy options, even if Henry and Wolsey had already discussed or settled in principle the policies they proposed to adopt.

The name of the game was politics. As Henry's partner, Wolsey enjoyed the King's special trust and confidence, but the Council was far from eclipsed. The minister had continually to earn his place and keep ahead of the field: this is the context of his Eltham Ordinances, published in January 1526. The débâcle of the Amicable Grant in the spring of 1525 was fol-lowed by the Anglo-French peace in the summer. The French alliance was a diplomatic volte-face and therefore controversial; within two years it had become the mainspring of a foreign-policy crisis and of a public breach between Wolsey and the Duke of Norfolk, who criticized it continually in the King's presence.[55] In addition, the peace brought about the return of the magnates to domestic routine at a time when Wolsey was weakened by the uproar over the East Anglian revolt.[56] Writing to Wolsey in May 1525, the day after receiving the submission of the rebels of Lavenham, the dukes of Norfolk and Suffolk insisted that 'all things well considered ... we think we never saw the time so needful for the king's highness to call his Council unto him to debate and determine what is best to be done'.[57] Whether this appeal should be linked to the gestation of the Eltham Ordinances is unclear. But the final text of that document and Wolsey's preparatory drafts signal his intentions, which were to satisfy Henry VIII's demand by the end of 1525 to have 'an honourable presence of councillors about his Grace', and to reconstruct the Royal Household, and in particular the Privy Chamber, in such a way as to limit the access to the King enjoyed by Wolsey's political rivals.[58]

The Eltham Ordinances instructed twenty 'honourable, virtuous, sad, wise, expert, and discreet' councillors to give 'their attendance upon [the King's] most royal person', and to perform the Council's full range of advis-ory, administrative, and judicial duties. The councillors named included Wolsey, the dukes of Norfolk and Suffolk, the marquises of Dorset and Exeter, the earls of Shrewsbury and Worcester, Bishop Tunstall, Lord

Sandys, Sir William Fitzwilliam, Sir Henry Guildford, Sir Henry Wyatt, and Thomas More. They were the leading office-holders of Court and state; had the proposed Council come into effect and acted as a corporate board, it would have been in size, function, and place of meeting the close equivalent of the Privy Council of 19 which declared its hand in August 1540.[59] It would have been a powerful counterbalance to the ministerial status of Wolsey, who was obliged by his official duties as Lord Chancellor to keep the legal terms in Chancery and Star Chamber at Westminster. Moreover, the Eltham Ordinances would be implemented when signed by the King's hand and published.[60] The Earl of Worcester even felt obliged to obtain a licence, signed by the King, excusing his daily attendance in the Council as specified by the Ordinances on account of age and ill-health, and providing that Lord Sandys should undertake his duties in his absence, but without assuming his style of Lord Chamberlain.[61]

If the Eltham Ordinances were implemented, however, the plan for the Council of 20 was not. Wolsey immediately devised that 'by reason of their attendance at the [legal] terms for administration of justice' and other duties, the lords of the Council 'shall many seasons fortune to be absent from the king's court, and specially in the term times'.[62] This was written into the Ordinances themselves, whereupon Wolsey reduced the 20 councillors to a committee of 10 and then to a sub-committee of four, it being finally provided that two councillors from among those resident at Court should always be present to advise the King and dispatch matters of justice unless Henry otherwise gave them leave. The councillors 'so appointed for continual attendance' were to meet at 10 a.m. and 2 p.m. daily in the King's dining chamber 'or in such other place as shall fortune to be appointed for the Council chamber'. 'Which direction well observed,' concluded Wolsey in a final ironic flourish, 'the king's highness shall always be well furnished of an honourable presence of councillors.'[63]

What Wolsey did in 1526, then, was to offer his fellow-councillors on paper the corporate political role he had denied them since February 1514, but in reality to thwart exactly that. The conciliar chapters of the Eltham Ordinances were designed to reinforce Wolsey's ministerial status. For 18 months, moreover, the ploy worked. Until the summer of 1527, when the twin crises of the king's divorce and foreign policy interacted to sap the minister's power, the councillors daily attendant at Court were still only the royal secretaries. True, the Marquis of Exeter, nominated to the titular headship of the Privy Chamber by the Eltham Ordinances, probably became more active.[64] He was on Wolsey's list of 20 councillors, and as Henry VIII's kinsman had long been close to the King. His exact role in 1526 is, however, hard to interpret, for he was barely active as a councillor and was probably chosen for that reason.[65] Certainly the Gentlemen of the Privy Chamber appointed by the Ordinances were selected expressly because they were not councillors.[66] Even then they were warned not to approach the

King unless summoned, and Wolsey's working papers reveal his nagging concern that Privy Chamber staff should not follow the King into 'secret places' to play politics.[67]

Many historians, myself among them, have at various times criticized Wolsey for failing to disentangle and reconstruct the Council's executive and judicial components in the 1520s. Wolsey's system in Star Chamber almost collapsed under the bulk of litigation that his keynote policies created. He was forced to remit the vast majority of suits either to the regional councils or *ad hoc* commissioners, or else to abandon them to the common law.[68] Of course, Wolsey was hamstrung politically. Had he reconstructed the Council in the interests of bureaucratic efficiency, the end result would most likely have been a council of lords at Court and a council of lawyers in Star Chamber.[69] Indeed, when Wolsey experimented with drafts to streamline the Council in February 1525, this was precisely the impasse he reached. 'An order taken for the division of such matters as shall be treated by the King's Council' projected reform by differentiation of function, and was intended to relieve leading office-holders of routine judicial work.[70] Twenty-eight lesser councillors, the judges, king's serjeants, and the attorney-general were deputed to deal with 'matter in law'. Inevitably the plan was dropped. It released the lords of the Council from the very tasks for which the Eltham Ordinances would demand their presence. In the face of Henry VIII's increasingly insistent demands for 'an honourable presence of councillors about his Grace' by the end of 1525, it would have enabled the lords themselves to reconstruct the Council attendant at Court – the threat Wolsey always sought to avert.

Within two years the Council attendant was in any case in process of reconstruction. Wolsey could not maintain his supremacy when confronted by a European situation that forced him to develop the French alliance at ever-increasing cost in order to obtain progress on the divorce. The dukes of Norfolk and Suffolk and Viscount Rochford, Anne Boleyn's father, were prominent among the unusually large group of lords resident at Court in the summer of 1527 and dining with Henry in the Privy Chamber.[71] Already the King had started to show Wolsey's letters to Norfolk and Rochford, and by the following Easter Norfolk and Rochford were being directly consulted on matters of policy without reference to Wolsey.[72] By March 1529 Henry was showing all his European correspondence to Suffolk as well as Norfolk and Rochford.[73] For Wolsey it was the beginning of the end. When Henry began openly to criticize his minister and the nobles returned to Court to attend the King daily, Wolsey had to work by different rules from those he had previously sustained. The lesson was not lost on Thomas Cromwell, who avoided the office of Lord Chancellor with its heavy legal responsibilities at Westminster. Moreover, in January 1537, when his own career was on the line, Cromwell resolved to 'keep the Court ordinarily'.[74] That was the option Wolsey had denied himself, and he paid the price.

II

If, however, Court and Council were the hub of national politics, relations between Court and Country were the key to political stability. Central government was effective only when it enjoyed the support of local magistrates. Henry VIII 'was far from omnipotent, and the real measure of his power was his ability to have his decisions executed at the level of the county and village'.[75] Judged in these terms, his reign was successful. The ability to tax efficiently is a valid measure of the strength of an early modern European state, and Roger Schofield has argued that Henry VIII created such strong bonds of political cohesion between the leaders of provincial society and the Crown that 'the former displayed an unparalleled willingness to operate a system of taxation, which ... was several centuries ahead of its time'.[76] Certainly Henry's government was stable despite war and taxation, the break with Rome, the Pilgrimage of Grace, the steep rise in population after 1520, and social distress caused by inflation and unemployment.

Henry and Wolsey built bridges between Court and Country by constructing an affinity in the provinces. This was a long-established Crown policy. Beginning with Richard II during his last years, the Crown had attempted to split entrenched noble and gentry affinities and to create networks of royal power instead. Some 300 to 400 knights and esquires were invited to Court for reasons which were local rather than military, conciliar, or diplomatic. They were not given salaried Court appointments, but they often received annuities and robes. Richard II realized that he needed to cultivate local landowners in order to widen his power base and win the support of their own retainers and followers.[77] Political security was the key to his plan, which failed because he was vindictive to persons he suspected, and because he moved too quickly and ended up by dividing the counties. But the essential step was taken: the value to the Crown of a governing élite more broadly based than in the past was recognized.[78]

Henry IV followed Richard's example. In 1400 his Council advised him

> that in each county of the kingdom a certain number of the more sufficient men of good fame should be retained ... and charged also carefully and diligently to save the estate of the king and his people in their localities.[79]

Again, Edward IV managed his household appointments so as to create an interlocking system of territorial lordship centred on the Court and the Yorkist dynasty. It was said that 'the names and circumstances of almost all men, scattered over the counties of the kingdom, were known to him just as if they were daily within his sight'.[80] The ultimate weapons of political discipline were acts of attainder and penal bonds or recognisances, but strategic deployment of Crown patronage was essential. Between 1461 and 1515 grants of lands, salaried offices, and annuities, on the one hand, and parliamentary acts of resumption, on the other, were wielded in a judicious combination of carrot and stick.[81]

The Crown's resources were, however, limited before the dissolution of the religious houses. Only a small minority of local magnates or JPs could receive a grant; a wider mechanism for Court–Country cohesion was needed. That mechanism under Henry VIII was furnished via the Chamber, the main ceremonial department of the royal household where the King sat under a canopied throne on days of estate and received ambassadors, etc. Between April 1509 and the fall of Wolsey at least 400 Chamber officials were appointed at Court, including 45 knights of the body, 54 esquires of the body, 41 sewers, 59 gentlemen ushers, 47 yeomen ushers, 36 pages, 30 yeomen, and 59 grooms.[82] Some of these posts were salaried, but most were supernumerary. The exact ratio of salaried to supernumerary appointments is impossible to compute owing to imperfect sources, but of the 41 sewers appointed only six were paid, of the 59 gentlemen ushers only 12 were paid, and of the 36 pages only eight were paid. Although the knights and esquires of the body had already surrendered their duties as intimate royal body servants to the Gentlemen of the Privy Chamber, their posts were not abolished, and several incumbents were later advanced to the Privy Chamber or the Council.

Despite the rise of the Privy Chamber by 1518, Henry and Wolsey continued to recruit supernumeraries from the counties. In 1519 Wolsey made a 'privy remembrance' for Henry 'to put himself in strength with his most trusty servants in every shire for the surety of his royal person and succession' – Edward IV's policy by another name.[83] Soon a special book recorded the names 'of the king's servants in all the shires of England sworn to the king', listing knights, esquires, carvers, cupbearers, sewers, and gentlemen ushers in order of their counties.[84] All 38 English counties were represented, as were south Wales, north Wales, Calais, Ireland, and Jersey. Although the book is severely damaged by water, the names of 184 knights, 148 esquires, 5 carvers, 13 cupbearers, 107 sewers, and 138 gentlemen ushers can still be read.[85] This was the roll-call of Henry's local men in the 1520s, and, like Edward IV, he must have known their names 'as if they were daily within his sight'. Some 200 county landowners or their sons were listed as unsalaried supernumeraries at Court by 1525.[86] What proportion of these 'king's servants' ever set foot in a royal palace is a question for which evidence is lacking, but the opportunity to do so when they had business at Court must have added to the attraction of their appointments. An obvious fiction was in play; supernumeraries did not receive 'bouge of Court',[87] therefore their attendance was likely to have been occasional. Yet their loyalty was assured once they were 'sworn' and their names entered in the register. What happened to a 'king's servant' who did not abide by the rules is amply demonstrated by the misfortunes of Sir William Bulmer, whom Wolsey hauled into Star Chamber in a show trial for wearing the Duke of Buckingham's livery in the King's presence.[88]

This approach to local government was consistently bilateral. Not only were county landowners or their sons sworn as the 'king's servants' and given supernumerary positions at Court. In addition, a direct if admittedly fluctuating relationship existed in many counties between the king's affinity and the commissions of the peace. By 1500 the expanded role of JPs as the Crown's unsalaried agents in the provinces had been cemented. Their judicial and administrative duties had been defined by innumerable statutes and proclamations as well as by the commissions themselves. It was axiomatic that the roll-call of the 'king's servants' should be consulted when appointments to the commissions were pending. It was equally important that the Crown augment its influence by recruiting to its affinity established 'men of worship' or their dependants in the localities. With hindsight it might be supposed that the membership of the king's affinity and the commissions should ideally have coincided. One might even expect a majority of JPs to be listed on the roll-call of the affinity, but this is vastly to overestimate the Crown's regional power. The exact relationship between the affinity and the commissions was complex, and varied considerably in individual counties.

Some preliminary conclusions emerge if the composition of the affinity by the early 1520s is compared with that of the commissions. I shall here attempt this exercise for a sample of 14 counties: Buckinghamshire, Cumberland, Devon, Kent, Norfolk, Northumberland, Oxfordshire, Shropshire, Somerset, Suffolk, Surrey, Sussex, Warwickshire, and Yorkshire.[89] It is immediately clear that the greatest correspondence between the membership of the affinity and the commissions was at the highest social level. A majority of peers and knights of the affinity also served as JPs in their counties. Generally, however, the degree of correspondence is lower. Only in Suffolk, Surrey, Kent, and Norfolk were more than one third of the affinity named as JPs in their counties. In Suffolk 12 out of 25 members of the affinity were JPs; in Surrey 6 out of 13; in Kent 10 out of 23; and in Norfolk 9 out of 24. Counties where one fifth or fewer of the affinity were named JPs included Somerset, Buckinghamshire, and Oxfordshire. Moreover, in the north the correspondence between the affinity and commissions was almost negligible. In Yorkshire (all Ridings) only eight out of 52 sworn 'King's servants' were appointed JPs; in Northumberland the figure was three out of 10; and in Cumberland none.

If, however, membership of the King's affinity seems to have complemented rather than duplicated that of the commissions of the peace, the direction of flow between the two is fairly clear where correlation of membership exists. Henry and Wolsey almost invariably augmented the affinity from the ranks of established 'men of worship' in the shires, and not vice versa. Counties where at least half the JPs among the affinity were existing members of the commissions who were thereafter sworn the 'king's servants' included all those sampled except Cumberland, Shropshire, Somerset, and Yorkshire. Only in Kent, Norfolk, and Suffolk is there additional evidence to suggest that new JPs were selected from the roll-call of the affinity, and even then the numbers involved are very small.

On the other hand, the king's or Wolsey's own servants seem to have numbered consistently among those JPs placed as 'outsiders' on the commissions of the peace for other counties. Wolsey is known to have made several attempts to reconstruct certain county benches, for instance those of Kent and Gloucestershire, where the proportion as well as the number of resident JPs was reduced.[90] He deployed his power most obviously in the north, appointing JPs who were prepared to implement Crown policy at the expense of local vested interests. In Yorkshire the number of local gentry in the commissions was significantly reduced during the 1520s, and the number of 'outsiders' correspondingly increased. Six clerical JPs with close ties to Wolsey (of whom five were appointed to the Duke of Richmond's Council in the North) were placed on the commissions for Cumberland, Westmorland, Northumberland, and Yorkshire.[91] In the West Riding of Yorkshire the reconstruction of the bench was undeniably systematic. Although some former JPs had died, the exclusion of so many leading local gentry from the commissions can only have been the result of deliberate planning.[92]

Wolsey's household was noted as a training-ground for agents in central and local government. He named his dependants to offices and commissions, and some two dozen were placed on the county benches.[93] They included Sir William Gascoigne of Cardington, Bedfordshire (treasurer of Wolsey's household 1523–9), Richard Page, Thomas Heneage, Ralph Pexsall (clerk of the Crown in Chancery from 1522), and Sir Thomas Tempest (controller of the Duke of Richmond's household). Gascoigne was appointed as an 'outsider' in Berkshire, Buckinghamshire, Hertfordshire, Oxfordshire, Surrey, and Yorkshire.[94] Page was named in Surrey, Cumberland, Westmorland, Northumberland, and Yorkshire.[95] Heneage and Pexsall between them covered Surrey, Berkshire, and Devon.[96] Lastly, Sir Thomas Tempest was appointed in Cumberland, Westmorland, Northumberland, and Yorkshire.[97]

Wolsey turned his attention to local government as soon as his law-enforcement policy was promulgated. Between 1516 and 1519 he orchestrated a series of exemplary cases in Star Chamber and king's bench for 'negligence', corruption, or maladministration in local government. Those accused of aiding and abetting homicide in their counties included Sir John Savage, Sir John Hussey, Sir Robert Sheffield, and Sir William Brereton. Savage, whose family had increasingly monopolized Crown appointments in Worcestershire and Gloucestershire after 1488, was imprisoned in the Tower, indicted in king's bench, and dismissed in favour of Sir William Compton.[98] Hussey, a courtier and king's councillor as well as a JP in Lincolnshire and Huntingdonshire, was bound over to avoid treason, felony, robbery, murder, or other acts of violence following a private complaint.[99] The proceedings against him collapsed and he was discharged, unlike Sheffield, a former councillor, Speaker of the House of Commons, and JP in

Lincolnshire and Nottinghamshire, whom Wolsey convicted in a Star Chamber show trial before sending him to the Tower, where he died.[100] Lastly, Brereton, who became increasingly involved in power struggles in the palatinate of Chester, was subjected to a rigorous public examination and compelled to attend daily in Star Chamber for almost a year while the allegations against him were pursued by Wolsey's own local commissioners.[101]

Wolsey ordered the assize judges to file reports about the 'misdemeanours' they encountered on their circuits: 'that is to say, who be retainers or oppressors, or maintainers of wrongful causes, or otherwise misbehaved persons'.[102] These enquiries increasingly extended to the localities, and the JPs of Norfolk and Suffolk were among those compelled to appear in Star Chamber to answer complaints about their conduct.[103] Wolsey also tackled the endemic factionalism among the JPs of Surrey which had led to violence, corruption, and perversion of justice in the shire. Lord Edmund Howard, Sir John Legh, and Sir Matthew Browne were prosecuted in the summer of 1519 for 'maintenance, embracery and bearing'. At least eight Surrey JPs were examined, and Wolsey obtained from Sir William Fitzwilliam a long list of 'misdemeanours contrary to the king's laws and statutes' committed in the shire since Henry VIII's coronation.[104]

Later the same year Wolsey issued revised instructions for use at the annual swearing-in of sheriffs, which explained more precisely than before how sheriffs were to exercise their offices. They were to prevent their subordinates from embezzling royal writs and perverting the Crown's directions. Juries were to be composed of honest and impartial residents of the county 'most near to the place where the matter or cause is alleged'. Sheriffs were not to accept money or favours for naming a corrupt jury or otherwise obstructing the course of justice, and they were to demand the highest standards of conduct from their undersheriffs and clerks, who were to be sworn. Lastly, the oath sworn by sheriffs in Star Chamber upon their admission into office was tightened and printed alongside the new instructions.[105]

At the same time Wolsey insisted that as many JPs as possible should attend Star Chamber to be 'new sworn' immediately before the swearing-in of sheriffs.[106] This enabled him to deliver a homily driving home the duties of JPs and stressing the links between central and local government. Such occasions could also be used to collect information. As many JPs and other commissioners as could conveniently be crammed into Star Chamber were assembled in July 1526 to hear a speech from Wolsey, whereupon 110 JPs were required to supply written answers to a 21-section questionnaire concerning the state of the realm.[107] Although a majority of JPs plainly could not be expected to attend personally in Star Chamber to be sworn, absentees were subsequently sworn in their localities by commissioners led by the assize judges.[108]

Wolsey also taught some two dozen delinquent sheriffs and JPs the 'new law of the Star Chamber'. Most offenders were dealt with summarily by the Council or appeared in Star Chamber as defendants in private suits, but Wolsey seized the initiative by urging litigants frustrated by corruption or malfeasance in their counties to travel to Star Chamber 'where the complainants shall not dread to show the truth of their grief'.[109] Moreover, his policy was sustained for a decade, especially in the north. Thus the bailiffs of Beverley were threatened for failing to report riots and unlawful assemblies to the nearest JPs; the mayor of York was deposed for offences against justice; and Wolsey kept a list in Star Chamber of 'misdemeanours, enormities, injuries and wrongs' committed in Yorkshire which remained 'unreformed'.[110] In the summer of 1524 he appointed special commissioners to enquire into the administration of justice and to reform 'enormities' in Yorkshire and Northumberland.[111] The Duke of Norfolk, sent to the region for the second time in two years, sat at York and Newcastle upon Tyne and duly reported to Wolsey, who promptly summoned Lord Dacre of the north into Star Chamber to answer corruption charges. Dacre compounded in the sum of 5 000 marks to reappear in Star Chamber at any time upon 20 days' notice. He was also required to compensate those he had injured, but died within two months following a riding accident.[112]

Of course, Wolsey's impact on local government should not be exaggerated. If he aimed at centralized administration and a Crown-controlled magistracy, the balance of power in the counties still remained with local landowners. A plethora of local networks bisected central ones, and the limited extent to which Wolsey or (later) Cromwell might purge the commissions of the peace exemplified this fact. In 1524 the numbers appointed to the commissions began to swell in almost every county. True, the Crown needed active JPs to implement its policies, but the root cause of the expansion was that new appointments could not be offset by the removal of unworthy JPs. Almost all those dropped from the Kent commission in 1521 had crept back within three years. Again, the 'outsiders' Wolsey appointed in Surrey had only a marginal impact. Local power remained in the hands of the resident gentry, and it was difficult to purge even serious offenders from the commissions. Lord Edmund Howard, Sir John Legh, and Sir Matthew Browne remained on the Surrey commissions, despite Wolsey's Star Chamber proceedings. All that resulted from his disciplinary action was that gentry feuding in Surrey went underground.[113] Cromwell encountered identical problems during the break with Rome, when only active opponents of the regime were purged from the benches. Passive opponents were ignored, and critics of the divorce continued to be recruited as supernumeraries at Court. It was therefore recognized that good relations between Court and Country depended on the willingness of each to respect the other's interests.

III

'We have put about the King and Queen such as we listed.' 'We have wearied and put away, both out of the King's council and out of his house, all such officers and councillors as would do or say anything freely, and retained such as would never contrary us.' 'We have begun to make learned men sheriffs of the shire.'[114] These accusations, levelled by Palsgrave, are as superficial and distorted as Skelton's satires. The partnership between Henry VIII and Wolsey was acrimoniously dissolved in October 1529, but it proved a resounding political success until the summer of 1527. True, Wolsey's status was ministerial, but the issue of 'ministerial' versus 'conciliar' methods of government was not finally resolved until 1558–9. It is especially misleading to claim that Wolsey did not involve the Council. He usually settled policy first with Henry in outline, and then consulted councillors. The Amicable Grant may prove to be the crucial exception, but the facts there as yet remain uncertain.[115] At the level of central government Wolsey worked on a broad front; his sweep was wider than I have had space to describe. In particular, his achievements should not be measured against the criteria laid down by his opponents. Palsgrave was himself equivocal, supporting in principle many of Wolsey's ideas. He wrote: 'Every of these enterprises were great, and the least of them to our commonwealth much expedient ... but that they have been begun, and brought to no good end.'[116]

In local government Wolsey was less dominant than at the centre, but he still played a significant role. Taken together, his efforts to cement the king's affinity in the provinces, to appoint the king's servants or his own to key positions in local administration, and to place 'outsiders' in the commissions of the peace in particular shires contributed to the stability of Henry VIII's regime. True, it was difficult to make more than marginal inroads on county government. Nor were Henry's and Wolsey's techniques intrinsically new. Only in the fourteenth and early fifteenth centuries had the Crown limited itself when selecting JPs to landowners resident in the shire. Edward IV and Henry VII had each nominated 'outsiders'. They had also recognized the need to appoint JPs who would serve regularly in quarter sessions at a time when perhaps less than half the bench of justices in any shire was normally active at sessions. It is possible that Wolsey was the first administrator to appreciate the potential of assigning JPs to the task of policing the parishes, but this is among several questions that require further research.

When reaching historical assessments, the context is decisive. Too often historians have brought prejudiced or anachronistic assumptions to their evaluations of Wolsey's career, for which Palsgrave bears as much of the blame as Skelton. His laconic litany 'We have begun ...' has led generations of students to believe that Wolsey rushed out a superfluity of ill-considered reforms which he inevitably dropped or failed to sustain. Wolsey was far from perfect, and he certainly began some ambitious projects which he was unable to finish.[117] Particularly damaging is that his concern to defend his own ministerial status prevented him from completing the organization of the 'Court of Star Chamber', the one institution that his policy had almost single-handedly created.[118] Yet to launch initiatives that subsequently collapse is not uncommon among politicians; a more realistic standard of assessment is required. From the standpoint of 1558, Cavendish wrote: 'I never saw this realm in better order, quietness, and obedience than it was in the time of his [Wolsey's] authority and rule; ne justice better [ad]ministered with indifferency.'[119] His words were exactly what Wolsey had always liked to hear, but his judgement is still one that historians ought to consider.

Notes

1 *John Skelton: The Complete English Poems*, ed. J. Scattergood (London, 1983), p. 283 (spelling modernized).
2 R. Fiddes, *The Life of Cardinal Wolsey* (London, 1724).
3 R. S. Sylvester and D. P Harding (eds), *Two Early Tudor Lives*, (New Haven and London, 1962), p. 4.
4 G. Walker, *John Skelton and the Politics of the 1520s* (Cambridge, 1988).
5 In some respects the satires do still dictate the agenda. The offending work here is A. F. Pollard, *Wolsey* (London, 1929; repr. in the Fontana Library with a critical introduction by Sir Geoffrey Elton, 1965).
6 A. G. Fox, *Early Tudor Literature: Politics and the Literary Imagination* (Oxford, 1989).
7 PRO SP 1/54, fos. 244–52; *LP* IV, iii, no. 5750; PRO C 54/396, m. 31.
8 SP 1/54, fos. 234–43 (*LP*, IV, iii, no. 5749).
9 Fiddes, *Life of Wolsey*, collections no. 101 (pp. 215–23).
10 The passage concerns Wolsey's brief diocesan career. It begins 'Who was less beloved in the North than my lord cardinal (God have his soul) before he was amongst them? Who better beloved after he had been there a while?' It is reprinted in D. S. Berkowitz, *Humanist Scholarship and Public Order* (Folger Books; Washington, 1984), pp. 134–5.
11 *The union of the two noble and illustrate famelies of Lancastre and Yorke* (London, 1548); *STC²* 12721; *The House of Commons, 1509–1558*, ed. S. T. Bindoff (3 vols, London, 1982), II, pp. 279–82; *The Pension Book of Gray's Inn*, ed. R. J. Fletcher (2 vols, London, 1901–10), I, p. 496.
12 That Wolsey first proposed the idea of Catherine of Aragon's divorce to Henry VIII was variously asserted by Polydore Vergil, Edward Hall, William Tyndale, Nicholas Sander, and Nicholas Harpsfield.
13 G. R. Elton, *The Tudor Constitution* (Cambridge, 1960; 2nd edn, 1982); J. J. Scarisbrick, *Henry VIII* (London, 1968); Scarisbrick, 'Cardinal Wolsey and the Common Weal', in E. W. Ives, R. J. Knecht, and Scarisbrick (eds), *Wealth and Power in Tudor England* (London, 1978), pp. 45–67; F. Metzger, 'Das Englische Kanzleigericht unter Kardinal Wolsey, 1515–1529', unpublished Erlangen Ph.D dissertation (1976); J. A. Guy, *The Cardinal's Court: The Impact of Thomas Wolsey in Star Chamber* (Hassocks, 1977); Guy, 'Thomas More as Successor to Wolsey', *Thought: Fordham University Quarterly*, 52 (1977), pp. 275–92; Guy, 'Wolsey and the Parliament of 1523', in C. Cross, D. Loades, and J. J. Scarisbrick (eds), *Law and Government under the Tudors* (Cambridge, 1988), pp. 1–18; R. S. Schofield, 'Taxation and the Political Limits of the Tudor State', in Cross, Loades, and Scarisbrick (eds), *Law and Government*, pp. 227–55; P. J. Gwyn, 'Wolsey's Foreign Policy: The Conferences at Calais and Bruges reconsidered', *Historical Journal*, 23 (1980), pp. 755–72; G. W. Bernard, *War, Taxation, and Rebellion in Early Tudor England: Henry VIII, Wolsey, and the Amicable Grant of 1525* (Brighton, 1986); Walker, *Skelton and the Politics of the 1520s*; S. J. Gunn, *Charles Brandon, Duke of Suffolk, c. 1484–1545* (Oxford, 1988). P. Gwyn, *The King's Cardinal: The Rise and Fall of Thomas Wolsey* (London, 1990). See also H. Miller, *Henry VIII and the English Nobility* (Oxford, 1986); B. J. Harris, *Edward Stafford, Third Duke of Buckingham, 1478–1521* (Stanford, Calif., 1986).

14 *Select Cases in the Council of Henry VII*, ed. C. G. Bayne and W. H. Dunham (Selden Soc. 75; London, 1958); M. M. Condon, Chapter 11; Guy, *Cardinal's Court*, pp. 9–21; G. R. Elton, *The Tudor Revolution in Government: Administrative Changes in the Reign of Henry VIII* (Cambridge, 1953); Elton, 'Tudor Government', *Historical Journal*, 31 (1988), pp. 425–34; D. R. Starkey (ed.), *The English Court from the Wars of the Roses to the Civil War* (London, 1987); D. R. Starkey, 'Tudor Government: The Facts?', *Historical Journal*, 31 (1988), pp. 921–31; Starkey, 'Court, Council and Nobility in Tudor England', in R. G. Asch and A. M. Birke (eds), *Princes, Patronage and the Nobility* (Oxford, 1991), pp. 175–203; Starkey, 'The Lords of the Council: Aristocracy, Ideology, and the Formation of the Tudor Privy Council', paper read to the 101st Annual Meeting of the American Historical Association, 27–30 Dec. 1986; S. L. Adams, 'Eliza Enthroned? The Court and its Politics', in C. Haigh (ed.), *The Reign of Elizabeth I* (London, 1984), pp. 55–77; J. A. Guy, *Tudor England* (Oxford, 1988).
15 J. A. Guy, 'The Privy Council: Revolution or Evolution', in C. Coleman and D. R. Starkey (eds), *Revolution Reassessed: Revisions in the History of Tudor Government and Administration* (Oxford, 1986), pp. 68–74.
16 Adams, 'Eliza Enthroned?'; M. B. Pulman, *The Elizabethan Privy Council in the Fifteen-Seventies* (Berkeley, Calif., 1971); Guy, *Tudor England*, pp. 266, 309–19.
17 Guy, *Cardinal's Court*, pp. 23–78, 119–31; Guy, 'Thomas More as Successor to Wolsey'.
18 The problem is the huge gaps in the sources; see J. A. Guy, *The Court of Star Chamber and its Records to the Reign of Elizabeth I* (London, 1985).
19 Sylvester and Harding (eds), *Two Early Tudor Lives*, p. 25.
20 See esp. PRO STAC 10/4, pt 2 (bundle of unlisted papers including notes, drafts, and minutes of the clerk of the Council); Henry E. Huntington Library, San Marino, California, Ellesmere MSS 2652, 2654, 2655.
21 PRO OBS 1419 (Henry VIII's itinerary).
22 *The History of the King's Works*, IV, ed. H. M. Colvin *et al.* (London, 1982), pp. 286–8; Starkey (ed.), *The English Court*, p. 18.
23 Sylvester and Harding (eds), *Two Early Tudor Lives*, p. 26; Starkey, 'Court, Council and Nobility'.
24 Guy, 'Wolsey and the Parliament of 1523', p. 15.
25 *LP* III, ii, nos. 3071–2, 3114–15.
26 *LP* III, ii, no. 3064; *Further Supplement to Letters, Despatches and State Papers ... Preserved in the Archives at Vienna and Elsewhere*, ed. G. Mattingly (London, 1940), pp. 233–6; Bernard, *War, Taxation and Rebellion*, p. 12. For the approximate dates of the legal terms, see *Appendix to the Twenty-Eighth Report of the Deputy Keeper of the Public Records* (London, 1867), no. 12; C. R. Cheney (ed.), *Handbook of Dates for Students of English History* (Royal Historical Society; London, repr. 1970), pp. 65–8. The Scottish debate is likely to have taken place at Court: Surrey was told to attend on Henry VIII, and the King spent the entire month of June at Greenwich. By contrast, the consultations leading to the agreement with Louis de Praet were probably held at York Place: Sylvester and Harding (eds), *Two Early Tudor Lives*, p. 39.
27 Cf. Elton, *Tudor Revolution in Government*, p. 64.
28 *LP* III, ii, no. 2317; Starkey, 'Court, Council and Nobility'; Guy, *Cardinal's Court*, pp. 23–50.
29 *LP* II, ii, no. 4355.
30 *LP* II, ii, nos 3885, 4025, 4055, 4124–5.
31 *LP* II, ii, no. 4124; Gunn, *Charles Brandon*, p. 58.
32 PRO E 404/93 (privy seal dated 23 July 1521). I am grateful to Margaret Condon for this reference. For the difficulties faced by attendant councillors in obtaining their subsistence allowances, see *LP* II, ii, no. 4055.
33 *LP* II, i, no. 1814; Starkey, 'Court, Council and Nobility'.
34 Starkey (ed.), *The English Court*, pp. 101–8; Starkey, 'Court, Council and Nobility'; J. A. Guy, *The Public Career of Sir Thomas More* (Brighton, 1980), pp. 15–18; J. J. Scarisbrick, 'Thomas More: The King's Good Servant', *Thought: Fordham University Quarterly*, 52 (1977), pp. 251–6.

35 Pollard, *Wolsey*, pp. 99–164; G. R. Elton, *Reform and Reformation: England 1509–1558* (London, 1977), pp. 42–114; Scarisbrick, *Henry VIII*, pp. 41–162; Guy, *Cardinal's Court, passim*; Starkey, 'Court, Council and Nobility'.

36 Sylvester and Harding (eds), *Two Early Tudor Lives*, p. 39.

37 *State Papers during the reign of Henry VIII* (11 vols, Record Commission: London, 1830–52), VI, p. 334.

38 PRO C 82/335, 338, 341, 355, 364, 365, 374; Elton, *Tudor Revolution in Government*, pp. 62–5; Starkey, 'Court, Council and Nobility'; Guy, *Cardinal's Court*, pp. 23–4. Henry VIII was only 17 years and 10 months old when he succeeded to the throne, and therefore technically not of age as king until he was 18. I argued that the Council at this point was functioning almost as a council of regency in 'The Privy Council: Revolution or Evolution', p. 63. The significance of the contrast between 'conciliarist' and 'ministerial' approaches to Tudor government was first discussed by Dr Starkey. See also T. F. Mayer, 'Thomas Starkey: An Unknown Conciliarist at the Court of Henry VIII', *Journal of the History of Ideas*, 49 (1988), pp. 207–27; Guy, *Tudor England*, pp. 159–64, 189.

39 Starkey, 'Court, Council and Nobility'.

40 Sylvester and Harding (eds), *Two Early Tudor Lives*, p. 12; Starkey, 'Court, Council and Nobility'.

41 *LP* I, i, no. 784 (44); Starkey, 'Court, Council and Nobility'.

42 Starkey, 'Court, Council and Nobility'.

43 Elton, *Tudor Revolution in Government*, p. 63.

44 Sylvester and Harding (eds), *Two Early Tudor Lives*, p. 12.

45 *LP* IV, iii, no. 5750; Fiddes, *Life of Wolsey*, collections no. 101 (p. 216).

46 Scarisbrick, *Henry VIII*, pp. 43–6; Bernard, *War, Taxation and Rebellion*, pp. 3–45.

47 Wolsey's request at Baynard's Castle in 1515 that Convocation might refer the matter of clerical immunities to Rome for a 'solution' following the Hunne and Standish debates was refused by Henry VIII: J. D. M. Derrett, 'The Affairs of Richard Hunne and Friar Standish', in *The Complete Works of St Thomas More*, IX, *The Apology*, ed. J. B. Trapp (New Haven and London, 1979), pp. 215–37.

48 Scarisbrick, *Henry VIII*, pp. 90–2; *Further Supplement to Letters, Despatches and State Papers ... Preserved in the Archives at Vienna*, ed. Mattingly, p. xvi.

49 Sylvester and Harding (eds), *Two Early Tudor Lives*, p. 208.

50 Walker, *Skelton and the Politics of the 1520s*, pp. 154–87.

51 *State Papers during the Reign of Henry VIII*, I, p. 79.

52 *State Papers during the Reign of Henry VIII*, I, p. 165; *Further Supplement to Letters, Despatches and State Papers ... Preserved in the Archives at Vienna*, ed. Mattingly, pp. xv–xvi; Bernard, *War, Taxation and Rebellion*, pp. 60–3; Guy, *Cardinal's Court*.

53 Guy, *Cardinal's Court*, pp. 29–50.

54 Henry E. Huntington Library, San Marino, California, Ellesmere MSS 2652, 2654, 2655; Guy, *Cardinal's Court*, pp. 23–35, 119–24.

55 *LP* IV, ii, 3105 (pp. 1410–11), 3663.

56 Starkey (ed.), *The English Court*, pp. 105–7.

57 PRO SP 1/34, fo. 196 (*LP* IV, i, no. 1329); Starkey, 'Court, Council and Nobility'; Bernard, *War, Taxation and Rebellion*, p. 85.

58 Bodl. Oxford, MS Laud Misc. 597; PRO SP 1/37, fos. 65–103; BL Cotton MS, Vespasian C.XIV, fos. 287–94ᵛ; *A Collection of Ordinances and Regulations for the Government of the Royal Household* (Society of Antiquaries; London, 1790), pp. 159–60; Starkey, 'Court, Council and Nobility'; Starkey (ed.), *The English Court*, pp. 105–7; Guy, *Cardinal's Court*, pp. 45–6.

59 MS Laud Misc. 597, fos. 30–1.

60 PRO LC 5/178 is the later copy used for official reference in the Royal Household, and it refers to a lost 'Liber Vetus'. See also *LP* IV, iii, App. 65; *LP* XIV, ii, no. 3.

61 BL Cotton MS, Vespasian C.XIV, fos. 295–7. Elton, *Tudor Constitution*, pp. 94–5 creates confusion by muddling Worcester's office with that of the Earl of Oxford, and glossing Sandys as Chamberlain. Worcester was Lord Chamberlain of the Household; Oxford was Lord Great Chamberlain; Sandys was not appointed Lord Chamberlain of the Household until April 1526.

62 MS Laud Misc. 597, fo. 31.

63 MS Laud Misc. 597, fo. 31.
64 MS Laud Misc. 597, fo. 24.
65 He did not attend a single documented meeting in Star Chamber under Wolsey. He also opposed the French alliance. For Henry's insistence on retaining Exeter in the Privy Chamber and Wolsey's counterbalancing action, see Starkey (ed.), *The English Court*, p. 107.
66 MS Laud Misc. 597, fos. 24–9; Starkey, 'Court, Council and Nobility'.
67 BL Cotton MS., Vespasian C.XIV, fo. 290ᵛ; Starkey, 'Court, Council and Nobility'.
68 Guy, *Cardinal's Court*, pp. 46–50.
69 This was especially so at a time when the King did not reside at Westminster and did not attend Star Chamber.
70 PRO SP 1/59, fo. 77 (*LP* IV, iii, pp. 67); SP 1/235 (pt 1), fo. 37 (*LP Add.* 481). The documents are dated 5 February. The year is established from internal evidence, in particular from the fact that Fyneux CJKB died in November 1525. I owe the date of Fyneux's death and therefore that of these documents to Dr Amanda Bevan and Dr John Baker.
71 *LP* IV, ii, no. 3318; Gunn, *Charles Brandon*, p. 102.
72 *LP* IV, ii, nos. 3360, 3992–3; *State Papers during the Reign of Henry VIII*, I, p. 261.
73 *State Papers during the Reign of Henry VIII*, I, p. 332; Gunn, *Charles Brandon*, pp. 106–14.
74 *The Lisle Letters*, ed. M. St Clare Byrne (6 vols, Chicago and London, 1981), IV, p. 242. I am grateful to Dr Starkey for this reference.
75 R. B. Smith, *Land and Politics in the England of Henry VIII: The West Riding of Yorkshire, 1530–46* (Oxford, 1970), p. 123; P. Williams, *The Tudor Regime* (Oxford, 1979).
76 Schofield, 'Taxation and the Political Limits of the Tudor State', p. 255.
77 Cf. *The Governance of England*, ed. C. Plummer (2nd edn, Oxford, 1926), p. 129.
78 C. Given-Wilson, *The Royal Household and the King's Affinity: Service, Politics and Finance in England, 1360–1413* (New Haven and London, 1986), pp. 203–57.
79 Cited in Given-Wilson, *The Royal Household*, p. 219.
80 D. A. L. Morgan, 'The House of Policy: The Political Role of the Late Plantagenet Household, 1422–1485', in Starkey (ed.), *The English Court*, pp. 64–7.
81 B. P. Wolffe, *The Crown Lands, 1461–1536* (London, 1970); Wolffe, *The Royal Demesne in English History* (London, 1971); S. J. Gunn, 'The Act of Resumption of 1515', in D. Williams (ed.), *Early Tudor England* (Woodbridge, 1989).
82 Compiled from *LP*. These figures are provisional, and derive from my current research.
83 BL Cotton MS, Titus B.I, fo. 192 (formerly fo. 184) (*LP* III, i, no. 576 [3]).
84 PRO E 36/130, fos. 165–231 (*LP* III, i, no. 578). This document can be read only under ultra-violet light.
85 The book concludes with a consolidated list of 74 grooms. My figures exclude chaplains and a handful of foreigners on the lists.
86 *LP* IV, i, no. 1939 (8).
87 i.e. free food and accommodation.
88 Guy, *Cardinal's Court*, pp. 32, 74.
89 I am here comparing the roll-call of the 'king's servants' in E 36/130 with the commissions in force during Wolsey's chancellorship. All material concerning the composition of the commissions is taken from my computerized database of JPs appointed in the reign of Henry VIII. This database draws on commissions recorded on the patent rolls and in Crown Office books (as calendared in *LP*), supplemented by unpublished commissions enrolled on the Originalia Rolls of the Exchequer at the PRO. The lists in E 36/130 were compiled over several years, and the exact date of this document is unknown. Some entries must have been made before 1523 while others were made after 1522, but internal evidence suggests it is safest to think in terms of *c.*1520–5.
90 M. L. Zell, 'Early Tudor JPs at Work', *Archaeologia cantiana*, 93 (1977), pp. 126–7.
91 The dispositions were as follows. Thomas Dalby (Archdeacon of Richmond), JP Westm 1525; JP Northumb 1525; JP Yorks East Riding 1525; JP Yorks North Riding 1525; JP Yorks West Riding 1525. William Franklin (Chancellor of

Durham), JP Cumb 1525; JP Westm 1525; JP Northumb 1525; JP Yorks East Riding 1525, 1529; JP Yorks North Riding 1525, 1528; JP Yorks West Riding 1525, 1528. Brian Higdon (Archdeacon and Dean of York), JP Cumb 1525; JP Westm 1525; JP Northumb 1525; JP Yorks East Riding 1525, 1529; JP Yorks North Riding 1525, 1528; JP Yorks West Riding 1525, 1528. William Holgill (Wolsey's steward as Archbishop of York), JP Yorks East Riding 1525, 1529; JP Yorks North Riding 1525, 1528; JP Yorks West Riding 1525, 1528. Thomas Magnus (Archdeacon of East Riding, Wolsey's secretary as Archbishop of York), JP Yorks North Riding 1528; JP Yorks West Riding 1528; JP Yorks East Riding 1529. William Tate (almoner to the Duke of Richmond), JP Cumb 1525; JP Westm 1525; JP Northumb 1525; JP Yorks East Riding 1525, 1529; JP Yorks North Riding 1525, 1528; JP Yorks West Riding 1525, 1528. All except Holgill were members of the Council of the North appointed in 1525. R. R. Reid, *The King's Council in the North* (London, 1921; repr. 1975), pp. 103–4.

92 Smith, *Land and Politics*, pp. 153–5, and table 15.

93 They were Sir Edward Aston, Sir John Aston, Thomas Audley, Sir Christopher Conyers (Lord Conyers), Sir Thomas Denys, William Drury, Sir William Gascoigne of Cardington, John Hales, Anthony Hansard, Thomas Heneage, Richard Lee, Thomas Lisle, Walter Luke, John More, Richard Page, Ralph Pexsall, John St Clere, Henry Saville, John Skewes, Thomas Stanley, Thomas Straunge, Sir Thomas Tempest, Henry Torrell, and Edmund Wyndham. Names of members of Wolsey's household were obtained from the Subsidy Rolls, PRO, E 179/69/8–10. The extent to which Wolsey's dependants were active JPs is a subject for further research.

94 Sir William Gascoigne of Cardington, Bedfordshire, JP Beds 1510, 1512, 1514, 1515, 1521, 1524, 1525, 1529; JP Northants 1512, 1514, 1515, 1523, 1524, 1526, 1528; JP Hunts 1510, 1513, 1514, 1524, 1525, 1528; JP Berks 1525, 1526; JP Bucks 1525; JP Herts 1525, 1526, 1528; JP Middx 1524, 1526, 1528; JP Oxon 1525, 1526; JP Surrey 1525, 1526, 1528; JP Yorks North Riding 1525, 1528; JP Yorks West Riding 1525, 1528; JP Yorks East Riding 1525, 1529.

95 Richard Page of Flamstead, Hertfordshire, JP Cumb 1525; JP Westm 1525; JP Northumb 1525; JP Surrey 1522, 1524, 1525, 1526, 1528; JP Middx 1524, 1526; JP Yorks East Riding 1525; JP Yorks North Riding 1525; JP Yorks West Riding 1525.

96 Thomas Heneage of Lincolnshire, JP Lincs Lindsey 1520, 1522, 1524, 1526, 1528; JP Middx 1523, 1524, 1526, 1528; JP Berks 1526; JP Surrey 1525, 1526, 1528. Ralph Pexsall of Hampshire, JP Hants 1513, 1514, 1515, 1518, 1523, 1524, 1525, 1526, 1529; JP Surrey 1514, 1528; JP Devon 1522, 1524, 1526; JP Middx 1528.

97 Sir Thomas Tempest of Holmside, co. Durham, JP Yorks North Riding 1511, 1512, 1514, 1528; JP Cumb 1525; JP Westm 1525; JP Northumb 1525; JP Yorks East Riding 1525, 1529; JP Yorks West Riding 1525, 1528.

98 Henry E. Huntington Library, Ellesmere MS 2652, fo. 3; PRO KB 29/148, *roti* 37d–38d, 44, 50–5; R. Keilwey, *Relationes quorundam casuum selectorum ex libris Roberti Keilwey* (London, 1602), fos. 188–96; E. W. Ives, 'Crime, Sanctuary and Royal Authority under Henry VIII: The Exemplary Sufferings of the Savage Family', in M. S. Arnold, T. A. Green, S. A. Scully, and S. D. White (eds) *Of the Laws and Customs of England* (Chapel Hill, 1981), pp. 296–320.

99 PRO STAC 10/18 (recognisance dated 20 Oct. 1516 among bundle of unlisted documents from Exchequer KR, Miscellanea B/2); STAC 2/30/23.

100 PRO STAC 10/4, pt. 2 (unlisted bundle), fos. [127–32]; SP 1/16, fos. 141–3ᵛ (LP II, ii, 3951); STAC 2/17/227; C 54/386; E 36/216, fo. 176; Guy, *Cardinal's Court*, pp. 76–8.

101 PRO STAC 2/3/311; 2/17/185, 227; 2/18/162, 2/19/81, 2/20/175; 2/22/113, 2/24/434; 2/26/370. For further references to Brereton, see Guy, *Cardinal's Court*, p. 116; E. W. Ives (ed.), *Letters and Accounts of William Brereton of Malpas* (Lancashire and Cheshire Record Society, 116; 1976), pp. 6, 31, 33, 55. In addition, Lord Ogle was punished in Star Chamber in July 1519 after admitting to the 'supportation' of a murderer: Henry E. Huntington Library, Ellesmere MS 2652, fo. 6ᵛ.

102 Henry E. Huntington Library, Ellesmere MS 2655, fo. 13.

103 PRO STAC 2/26/395; STAC 2/17/347; STAC 2/32/fragment (bundles of unlisted papers and fragments); Henry E. Huntington Library, Ellesmere MS. 2655, fo. 15ᵛ.
104 PRO STAC 2/2/163, 178–82, 194–7; 2/6/183–4; 2/18/246; 2/22/50; 2/26/252, 355; STAC 10/4, pt 5 (unlisted bundle); Guy, *Cardinal's Court*, pp. 72–4; W. B. Robison, 'The Justices of the Peace of Surrey in National and County Politics, 1483–1570', unpublished Louisiana State University Ph.D dissertation (1983), pp. 100–43.
105 PRO SP 1/14, fos. 108–13 (LP, II, i, no. 2579ᵛ); the date is established by Henry E. Huntington Library, Ellesmere MS 2652, fo. 7. See also Ellesmere MS 2655, fo. 15ᵛ.
106 Henry E. Huntington Library, Ellesmere MS 2655, fo. 15ᵛ.
107 Ellesmere MS 2652, fo. 12; *Tudor Royal Proclamations*, ed. P. L. Hughes and J. F. Larkin (3 vols, New Haven and London, 1964–9), I, pp. 153–4.
108 PRO C 254/161/25–6.
109 *State Papers during the Reign of Henry VIII*, IV, p. 155. A full summary of Wolsey's law-enforcement policy in Star Chamber may be found in Guy, *Cardinal's Court*, pp. 30–5, 72–8, 119–131.
110 PRO SP 1/51, fos. 288–92 (LP IV, ii, no. 5107); LP IV, i, no. 1218; Pollard, *Wolsey*, p. 319; PRO STAC 2/24/79. The manuscript 'correction' inserted into the Kraus reprint of the official PRO list which re-dates this last document to the reign of Henry VII is itself incorrect. Several of the offences in the document pertained to the activities of the fifth Earl of Northumberland, whom Wolsey had humbled in Star Chamber in 1516.
111 *Tudor Royal Proclamations*, I, pp. 143–4.
112 Henry E. Huntington Library, Ellesmere MS 2652, fo. 6; BL Lansdowne MS 1, fo. 105; PRO C 244/168/15A; LP IV, ii, no. 3022; Guy, *Cardinal's Court*, pp. 122–3.
113 Robison, 'The Justices of the Peace of Surrey', pp. 143–53; Zell, 'Early Tudor JPs at Work', p. 127.
114 LP IV, iii, no. 5750 (pp. 2557, 2560).
115 Cf. Bernard, *War, Taxation, and Rebellion*, p. 155. I largely accept Bernard's argument that councillors did their best to implement Wolsey's policy in difficult circumstances, but I doubt that the proposal for the Amicable Grant was backed in Council on 10 March 1525. The document cited by Dr Bernard is not a minute of a Council meeting, but a diplomatic report to Margaret of Savoy by her London representatives. They called on Wolsey after dinner (probably at York Place) and 'were introduced into the council chamber' where, in the presence of some councillors, Wolsey 'asked them their advice'. But it was the envoys and Wolsey alone who then spoke. So, even supposing this was a formal meeting of the King's Council rather than a rendezvous of diplomats, it is unlikely that the English councillors could have aired their true opinions. See *Calendar of State Papers, Spanish* (13 vols in 20 parts; London, 1862–1954), III, i, no. 39 (p. 86).
116 LP IV, iii, no. 5750 (p. 2562).
117 For instance, the military reorganization that should have followed from the surveys of 1522; the crackdown on crime, prostitution, and vagrancy in London and its suburbs; the prosecution of graziers and butchers reported for racketeering in the meat trade; and the attack on fraudulent recoveries. See J. J. Goring, 'The General Proscription of 1522', *English Historical Review*, 86 (1971), pp. 681–705; Guy, *Tudor England*, pp. 94–5; Guy, 'Wolsey and the Parliament of 1523', pp. 7–10.
118 Guy, *Cardinal's Court*, pp. 119–39.
119 Sylvester and Harding (eds), *Two Early Tudor Lives*, p. 4.

13

A crisis of the aristocracy?
Frontiers and noble power in the early
Tudor state

STEVEN ELLIS

In May 1534 Henry VIII began a major overhaul of Tudor provincial government which lasted throughout the 1530s. He replaced the key officials in charge of the more remote provinces by other, more trusted men, and he later reorganized the provincial councils and other administrative structures for these regions. In Ireland the Earl of Kildare was dismissed as governor and replaced by a military captain, Sir William Skeffington; in the north, Lord Dacre was removed from the wardenship of the West Marches towards Scotland and replaced by the Earl of Cumberland; and in Wales Bishop Rowland Lee replaced Bishop Vesey of Exeter as president – all in the same month. Dacre and Kildare indeed found themselves charged with treason, allegedly because of their contacts with the King's Scottish and Irish enemies.

The overall thrust of the changes was to centralize control and to bring administrative structures for the 'peripheries' more into line with the arrangements for the government of lowland England, the 'core' region of the Tudor state. From the perspectives of the Tudor Court and the 'central government' based in London, it no doubt made considerable sense to extend the effective and highly centralized system of government devised for lowland England to outlying parts. And historians of differing sympathies have generally approved these reforms as bringing about a greater degree of uniformity and integration in the Tudor state.

Yet the debate about the effectiveness of Tudor government and the changing role of the Tudor nobility has not so far taken much account of the impact of change as seen in the borderlands or Marches. How heavy was the price paid there for centralization and uniformity? The attempted assimilation of its government to that in lowland England, where conditions were quite exceptional and uniquely favourable to royal authority, was certainly not the unqualified blessing it seemed in London – hence the major rebellions in Ireland in 1534–5 and in the north in 1536–7. The problem was not uniformity and centralization *per se*, but the assumptions which came with it. Tudor officials sometimes seemed to think, for instance, that England was an island – Shakespeare's 'scept'red isle' – so that no special arrangements were needed for the defence of the long landed frontiers which formed the northern and western boundaries of the Tudor state. The Crown had no standing army, but the Marches had hitherto protected lowland England from the mere Irish and Welsh to the west and Scots enemies to the north. The Tudors aimed at a greater diffusion of power in the provinces, curbing overmighty subjects, replacing the feudal liberties and marcher lordships of the borderlands with English-style shires governed through substantial county gentry, and intervening to support the merchant oligarchies of the towns against outside interference.

Marcher society, however, was quite unlike the heavily manorialized English lowlands. The borderlands were predominantly upland, pastoral regions far from London, with a sparser, more turbulent, lineage society, and a powerful territorial nobility, with compact lordships and a warlike tenantry. Distance and geography hindered central control; quarter sessions were not always held because there were few substantial gentry to put on the peace commissions; and there existed few major towns to act as a counterweight to magnate power. Thus the overall thrust of early Tudor policy – greatly accelerated by the changes of the 1530s – placed great strains on relations between the Crown and the border communities. In particular, it created considerable difficulties for the traditional leaders of these communities the nobility, as they tried to respond to the conflicting demands of the Crown and the reality of marcher conditions.

Historians have long agreed that the Tudors were not averse to noble power as such. They continued to rely on the nobility to supervise local government as the natural leaders of local society. Yet the kind of noble power which most effectively addressed border conditions as shaped by early Tudor policy – strong marcher lordship geared to defence – increasingly conflicted with the sort of aristocratic values which the Tudors wished to promote. Basically, the Tudors wanted what historians have called a 'service nobility' – a subservient, loyalist nobility, which was dependent on the Crown for fees and office, and which divided its time between great state occasions at Court or in Parliament and the local supervision and enforcement of royal policy from its country houses in the provinces.

Unfortunately for the Tudors, however, a service nobility of the kind which developed in the more peaceful conditions of lowland England lacked the power to maintain good rule in the Marches. And the territorial magnates who alone possessed the *manraed* (the men a lord could call on in wartime) to discharge effectively the key border offices were increasingly distrusted by the Tudors because of their ability to use their power and influence in other, less acceptable ways. Some nobles, such as the seventh Earl of Ormond (1477–1515) or the fourth Earl of Shrewsbury (1473–1538), tried to respond positively to the new Tudor demands. But in Ormond's absence at Court, his estates in Tipperary and Kilkenny were destroyed by Gaelic raids, and Shrewsbury's lordship of Wexford was so persistently neglected that the King eventually confiscated it. At the other end of the spectrum, Robert, fifth Lord Ogle (1530/2–1545), simply ignored the Court: he never attended Parliament, but served the King all his life on the borders, and in 1545 died of wounds sustained in battle. Thus the 1530s witnessed something of a crisis of marcher lordship as ruling magnates such as Dacre and Kildare found it impossible to reconcile their position to these conflicting sets of demands.

Traditional 'Westminster-centred' scholarship has by and large ignored the plight of Tudor marcher lords, though the work of Mervyn James offers some valuable insights. There has been some discussion of differences between the new Tudor service nobility and traditional territorial magnates, but it reflects too easily contemporary Tudor assumptions that the 'normalization' of border rule and the reduction in the powers of the marcher lords should lead automatically to the growth of a more ordered 'civil' society there. The fact is, however, that marcher society was a function of the survival until 1603 of the English state's long landed frontiers; and the kind of marcher lordship which aroused Tudor suspicions of 'overmighty subjects' reflected the sort of society in which the nobility was obliged to operate.

This point can be established from a consideration of the careers of the two magnates whose fall in 1534 epitomized the crisis facing the nobility. The careers of the eighth and ninth Earls of Kildare (1478–1513; 1513–34), who dominated the governorship of Ireland from 1478 to 1534, have hardly been considered by Tudor historians, presumably because like most of the peers of Ireland they lacked an English title. And exclusion of the Irish peerage – almost all of them marcher lords – allows a major figure like Thomas, third Lord Dacre of the North (1485–1525), warden of the West Marches for 40 years and usually warden-general for the last 14, to be dismissed as a feudal anachronism whose fall in 1525 'marked the end of the age of the medieval robber baron' and 'a major triumph for [Cardinal] Wolsey's policy of [law] enforcement' through Star Chamber. The reality, however, was that before 1461 the Dacres and Fitzgeralds had both been minor peerage families, of purely local significance, who were deliberately built up by the Crown as ruling magnates.

The Dacre patrimony consisted chiefly of border manors in two north Cumberland baronies (Burgh and Gilsland) which were regularly wasted by war with the Scots. For the income tax of 1436, Dacre had been rated as among the poorest of the baronage, worth a mere £320 per annum; but after the death in 1487 of another northern peer, Lord Greystoke, Lord Thomas was gradually allowed to secure the whole Greystoke inheritance by an advantageous marriage to Elizabeth Greystoke. When Dacre died in 1525 his landed possessions were worth over £1500 net per annum, and as warden-general he had enjoyed an annual salary of £433 6s. 8d. The rise of the Leinster Fitzgeralds was equally spectacular. When Thomas Fitzgerald was recognized as seventh Earl in 1454, his wasted inheritance was worth no more than £250 a year, mainly from lands in Co. Kildare, with a secondary cluster of manors in Co. Limerick. Earl Thomas increased this significantly by recovering family lands which had been reconquered by the Gaelic Irish, but the financial basis of Kildare power was a succession of grants to the Fitzgeralds of royal manors and lordships, the result in part of astute marriages by the eighth and ninth Earls into the royal family. The Irish grants alone were worth IR£350 a year, with a further IR£100 worth of lands in Warwickshire, Gloucestershire, and Norfolk. By 1534 Gerald, ninth Earl of Kildare's landed possessions were worth around IR £1586 a year, and his income comfortably exceeded IR£2000 (2000 marks sterling) a year.

Historians sometimes draw up tables which appear to indicate the relative importance of individual nobles on the basis of their income. These tables relegate most of the northern peers to the second division, and exclude almost all the Irish peers on the grounds that they held insufficient property on the mainland. If, however, a combined table of the Tudor nobility were drawn up, instead of dividing them along nationalist lines, both Dacre and Kildare would reach the Tudor top ten under Henry VIII. But landed income is a very crude guide to the relative power of Tudor nobles and the extent of their landed possessions. Rents per acre in the pastoral uplands were generally far less than in lowland England, and even where the land was suitable for tillage, the more turbulent border conditions were a severe disincentive because, unlike cattle and sheep, crops could not be driven from the path of impending raids. The estate-management policies of marcher lords such as Dacre and Kildare were thus geared chiefly towards military considerations rather than the maximization of profits.

Undefended marchlands were worthless: they needed castles and tenants to protect them. This meant that border lords and gentry continued to live in castles and peles rather than the country houses now favoured by southerners. Thomas, Lord Dacre, spent much of his income on building small castles at Drumburgh, Rockcliffe, and Askerton to protect his estates and on strengthening those at Naworth and Kirkoswald, all in Cumberland. He normally resided in the Marches, at Naworth, Kirkoswald, or Carlisle, although as warden-general after 1511 he lived at Harbottle or Morpeth in the Middle Marches, and left his son, William, or his brother, Sir Christopher, as his deputy in the west. He was also a member of the King's Council, but rarely attended council meetings or Parliament. Traditionally, individual members of the northern nobility were excused attendance at Parliament in wartime so that they could be available for border defence.

Kildare's initial response to a summons to Court was often also that he could not be spared, since his presence was necessary for Ireland's defence – as the King's Council there or the lords of Parliament would certify. When not on campaign, Kildare usually resided at his chief castle of Maynooth, from where he could ride to Dublin for Council meetings. Among his more substantial building projects were the castles of Powerscourt, Clonmore, Castledermot, and Lea, which, together with Maynooth, ringed his chief possessions in Co. Kildare. Similarly, both lords attracted tenants to settle on wastelands by offering holdings at low rents in return for military service. Dacre instructed his estate officials in 1536 to let any vacant holdings to good archers, even if this meant a lower entry fine; and his tenants were generally bound by their tenures to maintain horse and harness and to take part in raids against the Scots.

In Ireland, Kildare's tenants were also bound to accompany their lord on hostings against the Irish, and many holdings were let rent-free in return for defending particular marches. In both regions the lords attracted to their estates large numbers of Scots and Irish respectively who were 'sworn English' and given tenements in more exposed districts such as Bewcastledale or Offaly where Englishmen were afraid to live for fear of the wild Irish or Scots enemies nearby. Reputedly, Lord Dacre 'may at all tymes with little charge have 4 or 5,000 men off his owne' to resist invasion, and at the siege of Dublin in 1534 the rebel army raised by Kildare was 15 000 strong.

The military character of marcher lordship reflected the political instability of the English borderlands, but it was greatly accentuated by early Tudor policy. During the Wars of the Roses, the private armies built up by Richard, Duke of York, as lieutenant of Ireland and Richard Neville, Earl of Salisbury, as warden of the West Marches from the inflated stipends they received enabled them to challenge the Crown. The Crown's response after 1471 was to ensure that these offices presented no threat to the dynasty. They were entrusted to less powerful lords and the salaries attached to them were reduced sharply, to around an eighth of the previous levels. This greatly reduced the threat to the dynasty from pretenders such as Lambert Simnel and Perkin Warbeck.

In Ireland, moreover, fortunes of war had removed from the political stage the great houses which had dominated the viceroyalty under the Lancastrians – Richard of York, the Talbots and, until 1515, the Butlers. In the north, the Percies and the senior branch of the Nevilles remained available, but until the mid-1520s they were deliberately excluded from office by a suspicious king. Yet as the threat to the dynasty declined, so also did the rule and defence of the Marches. The King's officers were forced to develop an alternative means of defence, since they now lacked the funds to maintain retinues and fee the leading gentry as formerly. Indeed, in the far north, where the Scots proved a much more formidable adversary than Irish chiefs, the Marches were greatly weakened and local government virtually collapsed, to be replaced by feuds and compositions for murder.

One reason why the Dacres and Fitzgeralds had such a monopoly of these border offices was that very few nobles could afford to discharge them and defend the Marches with the reduced resources now available. Dacre and Kildare both established new systems of defence in their respective Marches by exploiting the extensive military powers inherent in their offices to build up the military preparedness of their own estates. The link between 'public' and 'private' was most obvious in the clause in successive commissions to Kildare as governor granting him any Crown lands he could recover from the Gaelic Irish. But both lords were given control of actual Crown lands in the areas of their jurisdiction and the leading of the King's tenants during their tenure of office, and they integrated them into the one defensive system.

In the Marches, a major weakness of the 'normal' English system of government was the juridical division between lordship of land and lordship of men. Territorial magnates had compact holdings of land, but seigneurial authority over tenants was (in theory at least) heavily circumscribed by royal authority over subjects. When real peace was a rarity and frequent war followed uneasy truces, absentee lordship was a major liability, and the Crown was the worst offender. The key to the defence of the English West March was the most northerly, royal barony of Liddel, with its castle known as Liddel Strength built on a cliff commanding the river crossing 160 feet below. The barony had once been worth £295 per annum, but after 1296 it became a war zone, nominally in Crown hands. The burden of defence fell on the lords of the small barony of Levington immediately to the south, and on the Dacre baronies of Burgh and Gilsland. But Levington was in turn partitioned between six co-heiresses and passed to absentee lords who lacked the resources to defend it. Thus border defence was thoroughly undermined. By 1485 much of the region, including large parts of Gilsland, had long been uninhabited wasteland. The abeyance in the earldom of Kildare after 1432 had an equally disastrous impact on the English Pale in Ireland.

Lord Dacre's extended tenure of the wardenship enabled him gradually to patch up this hole in border defence, even though he could not afford a garrison to plug the gap. He gradually bought up freeholds in the strategically important border manors north of Carlisle. These wastelands could be purchased cheaply, but once they were tenanted and defended Dacre's purchases in north Cumberland yielded over £130 a year in rent, even though their main value was strategic and the military service owed by tenants. Commenting on the sale of his lands there to Dacre, Sir John Stapleton observed that 'he dwelt at London so farre from his land & that his tenauntes could have no socoure of hym'.

The kind of overlapping, official and personal responsibilities inherent in this situation are well illustrated by arrangements in the Crown outpost of Bewcastle. Bewcastle had a separate royal keeper, based in the castle there, who was responsible to the warden; but quite bizarrely, its feudal overlordship pertained to the Dacre barony of Burgh, even though it was geographically separate and lay between Gilsland and the border. For almost forty years (1493–1530) the keeper was Sir John Musgrave, knight for the King's body, and his son Thomas, but, since the Musgraves were Dacre followers, the conflicting demands of the situation were amicably resolved by having all the inhabitants (including Dacre's tenants) do suit at

Dacre's court of Askerton in Gilsland, and by giving Dacre the rule of the Bewcastlemen under their keeper.

Dacre also worked in other ways to build up his control of the Marches. Actual war with Scotland was not the only cause of disorder. To the east of Gilsland, in the Northumberland highlands, lived the quasi-independent border surnames or clans of Tynedale and Redesdale. Like the Scottish surnames, they got their living largely by thieving and robbery among the wealthier and 'more civil' lowland communities – 'the king's true subjects'. The same was true in Ireland, where Kildare had to control the English marcher lineages of Wicklow and Westmeath, and also in the Welsh Marches. As wardens, the Percies had traditionally solved this problem by retaining the leading gentry, both those of the highlands who maintained the thieves, and the lowland gentry who suffered at their hands. In 1489 the fourth Earl of Northumberland was spending 42 per cent of his income on maintaining a large following of county gentry.

Dacre, by contrast, spent very little on feeing the leading gentry, even after 1511 when he reluctantly assumed responsibility for the East and Middle Marches. There were indeed relatively few substantial gentry families in Cumberland, and, since their lands were mostly in the west and south, they would have been little help to him in controlling the surnames. Instead, and especially as warden-general, he built up a following among the humbler border squires who kept thieves, and even among the thieves themselves. Indeed, 'bearinge of theaves' was a principal reason for his disgrace in 1525. Like Gaelic chiefs, the surname captains and headsmen were sometimes forced to surrender leading clansmen as pledges for good conduct – in effect, they were told to direct their activities northwards. Yet Tynedale and Redesdale could each raise around 500 men for military exploits, so Dacre had a considerable force available at virtually no cost to harass the Scots – so long as the Marches remained disturbed and worthwhile preys presented themselves in Scotland.

The other main way of defending the Marches without a garrison was by building up cross-border ties. In 1534 William, fourth Lord Dacre (1525–63) was tried for treason on a charge of holding secret meetings with Scots enemies in wartime and making 'a wicked and treacherous agreement' with Lords Maxwell and Buccleuch and the Scots of Liddesdale for mutual immunity from raids and invasions for the lands and tenants of either party. Dacre was extremely fortunate to escape when his peers decided that the charges were malicious, since it was no defence to say that the meetings and agreements had served the English interest. In fact, the charges broadly correspond with Dacre's known cross-border contacts before the war. Nor is this surprising, because after 1452 none of the Scottish border lords had the power and possessions of a Percy or a Dacre, and lacking the support of their central government they were anxious for some private understanding to safeguard their estates. By early Tudor times, moreover, attempts to conquer Scotland were a distant memory, and Henry VIII could generally rely on the support of one or two of the Scottish nobility in each of his wars with Scotland.

Cross-border ties were facilitated by the region's common culture and the similarity of administrative institutions on both sides of a border line which, despite many disputes about debatable lands and outposts like Berwick, was increasingly seen as fixed. In Ireland, however, the gulf between English civility and Irish savagery proved harder to bridge. There was a remarkable coincidence of geographical, cultural, and political boundaries between the English-speaking arable lowlands of the Pale and the Gaelic pastoral uplands and boglands of the Irishry. Yet in Ireland, where power was more decentralized and the Marches more fluid, cross-border ties were more thoroughgoing. Intermarriage between the English and Gaelic aristocracies was a very common means of stabilizing the Marches – in the Anglo-Scottish Marches it was restricted to the lower orders – and even English magnates like Kildare married their daughters to prominent Gaelic chiefs. Yet the corollary was that successive earls of Kildare were able to bring unprecedented pressure to bear on the weak and divided Gaelic chieftaincies, so that the English Pale expanded significantly during the Kildare ascendancy. As with Lord Dacre, however, Henry VIII grew increasingly suspicious of the Earl's links with Gaelic Ireland and the frequent complaints that his deputy was maintaining English rebels and Irish enemies against the King's true subjects. Thus in both borderlands the new system of defences, though much cheaper, had considerable shortcomings in terms of order and good government.

In the short term, however, Henry VII's overriding concern was that the arrangements for the borderlands should present no threat to the Crown. Once he was assured of this and had sorted out his initially difficult relations with Kildare, he showed more interest in restoring the Crown's finances than in promoting good rule in the Marches. Thus from 1496 the English Exchequer was absolved from all responsibility for Ireland's defence; while in the north the King even resorted to farming the shrievalties. He also accepted Dacre's offer to assume responsibility for Carlisle, thus saving the cost of a garrison.

In the 1520s, however, as Henry VIII's attention shifted from war against France to the need for internal reconstruction, he began to take more interest in border rule. But the demands he made of his officers there were a good deal less realistic. The King was no more willing to pay for an effective system of administration and defences than his father had been, but Dacre and Kildare were none the less charged with failing to maintain good rule and dismissed. Their successors, however, immediately ran into the problem of how to deploy, respectively, the Dacre and Fitzgerald *manraed*, still essential for border defence, when neither lord now had any incentive to cooperate. And by then both nobles had exploited their extended occupation of key border offices to build up their local connection and influence, so that they were less dependent on royal support.

For his part, the King apparently assumed that individual magnates were expendable, and that these border offices could be exercised equally well by other nobles simply by issuing them with the King's commission. Thus when, after a reconnaissance in force by the Earl of Surrey, Henry appointed Piers Butler, Earl of Ormond, as deputy of Ireland in 1522 on the same terms Kildare had enjoyed, Ormond quickly discovered that he lacked a sufficient following in the Pale for its defence, and the resultant feud between Butler and Fitzgerald retainers led to violent disorders throughout the lordship. The same happened in the West Marches in 1525, when Henry, Lord Clifford, was promoted Earl of Cumberland – a very provocative title considering he had little land in the county – and appointed warden in place of Dacre. Serious disputes arose concerning the custody of Carlisle Castle, farms of Crown land which were traditionally associated with the wardenry, and arrangements for Bewcastle's defence; and the Marches were disturbed by feuds between Clifford and Dacre followers.

Cumberland proved no more capable of ruling the West Marches from Skipton Castle than Ormond could the Pale from Kilkenny Castle. In both cases, the King was forced to back down within two years, and the old order was temporarily restored. The basis of trust between king and magnate, and between the respective lords and their retainers, was not so soon restored, however, although the system's effective operation depended on this. And both Cumberland and Ormond found themselves pressed into service again – with even less happy results – after the traditional ruling magnates had been restored, and again found wanting.

The increasingly strained relations between king and magnate and the charged atmosphere at Court during the Reformation crisis led to the events of May 1534. Henry suspected that disaffected nobles were actually plotting against him, and he lashed out against the two magnates he suspected might be his most dangerous opponents. In Kildare's case, the Earl's mishandling sparked off a major rebellion which took 14 months and cost £40 000 to suppress. Dacre was found not guilty at his trial, but none the less paid an enormous fine of £10 000, and his disgrace meant that he too was unusable as warden for the rest of the reign.

In the 1490s 'riottes and insurrections' provoked by disagreements between Lord Dacre and Sir Christopher Moresby forced the King's Council to intervene, because 'the kinges strength in the counte of Cumberland dependith in effect oonly betwixt thaym too, and also remembryng the great unstabilnes of the peax' with Scotland. Similarly, the King's Council in Ireland observed in 1523 that 'the quietie and restfullnes' of the King's subjects there 'standith in the unitie and concord of the noblis', particularly the Earls of Kildare and Ormond. Thus the King's decision in the 1530s to appoint 'mean men' to rule the borders – Skeffington in Ireland, Sir Thomas

Wharton in the north-west – was really an admission of failure. By curbing magnate power, Henry VIII was in effect reducing the capacity of royal government there. Unable to rely on the defensive system built up by Kildare and Dacre respectively, or to deploy their *manraed* effectively, the new order proved both more costly and less effective in defending the borders.

After Henry's death, the fourth Lord Dacre was quietly reappointed warden of the West Marches. The problem of the north was eventually solved, not by a policy of centralization and uniformity, but by improved Anglo-Scottish relations and then the dynastic union of 1603, which eliminated the need for a defensive frontier. The year 1603 also saw the dismantling of the state's western frontier, with the completion of the Tudor conquest. In the interim, however, Tudor policies for the reduction of Ireland had proved so disastrous that their legacy continues to sour Anglo-Irish relations to the present day.

The disgrace of the two magnates does not, of itself, amount to a crisis of the aristocracy. Yet Henry VIII's relations with other long-established territorial magnates – the Percies, Staffords and Courtenays – were also problematic. The fall of Dacre and Kildare was thus more than an isolated incident. In discharging these key provincial offices, the nobility was increasingly caught between the changing demands of service to the local community and the revised expectations of Crown and Court, although all marcher lords faced these choices to a greater or lesser degree. They could not afford to spend long periods at Court without neglecting the defence of their estates, but the King seemed increasingly distrustful of nobles who reflected most effectively traditional aristocratic values of strong resident lordship and extended military and political service to the Crown.

The price of centralization and uniformity was thus heavy: the demise of the marcher lords was closely linked to complaints about 'the decay of the borders' and the marked decline in English military preparedness which characterized the mid-Tudor period. And the Marches were not a marginal addition to the Tudor state; in 1534 they covered half its geographical area and constituted a central aspect of its defences. Thus, while the growing influence of the Tudor Court and of the politics of faction may provide a key to developments in lowland England, their impact elsewhere was less decisive and less fortunate. Lowland England was no more then the Tudor state than is modern England now the British state.

Bibliographical note

This essay first appeared under the title 'Frontiers and Power in the Early Tudor State', *History Today*, 45/4 (Apr. 1995), pp. 35–42. Its aim was to reopen the debate about the nature and role of the early Tudor nobility and to respond to recent work written from a nationalist perspective, notably the misleadingly titled *The Tudor Nobility* (ed. George Bernard (Manchester, 1992)). Unfortunately, this purpose became less apparent when the original, more provocative title had to be replaced by a shorter one in order to suit the format of *History Today*. In preparing this re-issue of the article, I have therefore taken the opportunity to restore the title I had originally intended, as well as to make some minor, editorial changes in the text. Full references for the arguments deployed will be found in my recent monograph, *Tudor Frontiers and Noble Power: The Making of the British State* (Oxford, 1995). Also relevant are S. G. Ellis and S. Barber (eds), *Conquest and Union: Fashioning a British State, 1485–1725* (London, 1995); R. Bartlett and A. MacKay (eds), *Medieval Frontier Societies* (Oxford, 1989); Mervyn James, *Society, Politics and Culture: Studies in Early Modern England* (Cambridge, 1986); S. G. Ellis, *Tudor Ireland; Crown, Community and the Conflict of Cultures, 1470–1603* (London, 1985).

14

Tudor government: The points of contact: Parliament

G. R. ELTON

It is one of the functions of government to preserve in contentment and balance that society which it rules. Some of the tasks involved in that general purpose are familiar enough. Government exists to maintain peace in the nation – to prevent disturbance, punish crime, and generally ensure that people can lead their lives without threats from others. Government must therefore provide the means for resolving disputes peacefully: it must administer justice and be seen to do so. In addition, since no society can ever stand absolutely still, government is charged with the task of reviewing existing relationships – relationships of rights, duties, burdens, and privileges – with an eye to supplying reform, that is, changes designed to keep the general balance and contentment from deteriorating. Most discussions of problems of government revolve around these points. Analysis has concerned itself with the machinery available for discharging these tasks, and assessment has concentrated on establishing the degree of success obtained.

However, there is more to it than this. It has long been realized that the so-called realities of government involve further the social structure of the body governed. Government, we know, cannot work unless it obtains obedience and (preferably) consent from the governed and that recognition has led to a good deal of work on the power structure among the governed and its integration into the exercise of power relinquished to the ruler. With respect to the Tudor century, for instance, we have learned something about the way in which power and rule devolved outwards from a monarchy which, however hard it tried to centralize management, still depended greatly on the cooperation of the so-called rulers of the countryside, and we have increasingly come to understand the degree to which the necessary tasks of government continued to be discharged at decentralized points – in local courts and through the often spontaneous action of lesser organs of rule. The vital role of magnates, gentry, and municipal oligarchies has been much emphasized since 1970, to a point where mistakenly low assessments of the power of the centre have unhappily become current. Arising out of this, questions have been asked about the means which help to tie peripheral authority to central; some of the lines of communication among rival interests have been traced; some patronage systems have been analysed. True, we have had rather more calls for this kind of study than performances, and such examples of revealing importance as have appeared have tended to restrict themselves territorially, to concentrate on the land market, and to go easy on the politics; but then, in the conditions set by sixteenth-century evidence, such things as political attitudes (thought, feeling, and programmes), or the role and significance of patronage (the pool of favours and advantages, on the one hand, the search for them, on the other) are more readily apprehended in general terms than documented in working detail.[1] At any rate, we now know that Tudor government depended not only on the activities of rulers both central and local, and on the management of the machinery available, but also on the organization and rivalries of patronage systems constructed around local, familial, and political focuses which everywhere penetrated the visible politics of the day.

One matter, however, it seems to me, has received little attention: or rather, one particular type of question has not been asked; and since I think that that question (and if possible the answers to it) may bring us a little nearer to understanding why Tudor government remained pretty stable through a difficult century, while instability and collapse attended upon the government of the early Stuarts, it is a question I should like to look at here. Stability is the product of moderate contentment: it is preserved if the operations of government are thought to conduce to order and justice, and if they succeed in taking account of the claims to power entertained by inferior authorities. This last point has, as I have said, been largely seen in terms of local rule and ties of patronage; one element in the system is missing. We know what people wanted and can trace the contacts that put them in the way of getting it, but we have not asked whether the machinery existed to transform ambition and favour into achievement. To be stable, any system needs to include organized means – public structures – to provide for the ambitions at the centre of affairs of such persons as can, if those ambitions remain unsatisfied, upset that stability. The question I want to ask is really very simple: did Tudor government contain within its formal structure conventional means for the satisfaction of such people? Did it provide known and accessible instruments which enabled positive interests, demands, and ambitions on the part of the politically powerful to achieve their ends? Alternatively, did the politically powerful discover in the machinery of government such means of self-satisfaction? The question is simple, but the answers, to be reasonably complete, would be very complex indeed, involving, for instance, a full study of all office-holders. All I can hope to do is to draw attention to unstudied problems, or perhaps to a new way of looking at problems studied often enough before, and to offer some preliminary suggestions. I also hope that others may feel encouraged to pursue these issues further.

When we think about the social organization of the sixteenth century from this point of view – when we ask ourselves whether the system of government provided obvious organization points at which the purposes of rulers and ruled (Crown and 'political nation') came into the sort of contact which could prove fruitful to the ambitions of those not yet part of the central government – we are first, and obviously, driven to look at Parliament. Parliament, after all, was thought of as the image of the nation in common political action, where, to quote Thomas Smith's familiar words once again, in the making of law the whole realm participates because 'every Englishman is intended to be there present, either in person or by procuration and attorney'.[2] The political reality of this concept needs no further discussion – or should I say that it ought to need none, though there are still some respected scholars who have their doubts about it. And yet the evidence has been accumulating, and continues to accumulate, that the sixteenth century had a clear understanding of the notion of legislative sovereignty – of the supreme power to make laws in all respects that touch the body politic; that it unquestioningly vested that power in the mixed entity called Parliament – king, Lords, and Commons jointly; and that it was right to treat the operations of that mixed body as politically genuine rather than prejudged, constrained, or merely formal. It seems to me that memories of royal claims in the fourteenth and fifteenth centuries, or of the more explicit monarchic doctrines which appeared in the seventeenth, combine with misleading interpretations of the high executive authority vested in Tudor monarchs to call in doubt the reality of what Smith, and many others, regarded as the fundamental commonplace of the English constitution. One man who attended upon that constitution for half a century was quite clear on the point, and, since Lord Burghley's opinion has not been often cited, it may be worth producing here. He held

> that their Lordships of the Upper House ... are one member of the Parliament; and also that the Knights, Citizens and Burgesses of this House representing the whole Commons of this Realm are also another Member of the same Parliament; and her Majesty the Head; and that of these three Estates doth consist the whole Body of the Parliament able to make laws.[3]

In addition, he was quoted later as not knowing what the English Parliament could not do in the way of law-making. Full legislative supremacy vested in the image of the nation and politically active there: that was the basis of Tudor government. True, the full doctrine was of recent standing; in the Reformation Parliament, members of both Houses were still troubled to know whether the legislative authority of Parliament extended to the government and order of the Church, a severe limitation.[4] The years of that assembly, however, settled the matter and completed the institutional and doctrinal claims of Parliament. I repeat all this only because we are still told at intervals that institutionally Tudor Parliaments were nothing new and politically they marked a decline. The evidence will not support this double scepticism: it points to a novel recognition of the doctrine and an increased political vigour.

As the sovereign maker of laws, Parliament thus stood ideologically central to the problem of political stability; it was potentially at least useful to all who had purposes to serve, whether those purposes were national, sectional, or personal, so long as they required innovation and change. On Parliament converged of necessity all ambitions to maintain or to reform the system: it was the chief organ for absorbing and satisfying the demands made upon stability in government. Even rebels regarded it in this light: the Pilgrims of Grace, for instance, while they might denounce alleged recent practices of packing and influencing, nevertheless called for a Parliament after the old and uncorrupted sort to bring peace in the realm.[5] Yet surely to anyone raised in the traditions of English parliamentary scholarship there is something odd about the notion that the institution should be treated as an instrument of stability. Our historians have traditionally concentrated on conflict and have studied all meetings of Parliament with an eye to dispute and opposition. Sir John Neale, to take a very relevant case, found the main theme of his history of *Elizabeth I and her Parliaments* in the accumulation of unremitting political differences.[6] The impression he leaves is that meetings of the Elizabethan Parliament were notable mainly because they set the stage for collisions between rulers and ruled and gave dissent an opportunity to disrupt the secret ways of government and policy. If James I came to think of Parliaments as like to cats that grow cursed with age or complained that his predecessors had saddled him with this tiresome burr under the tail of the body politic, it was certainly not because he distrusted stability and saw in Parliament a means for creating such political stability as might grow from participation in affairs or from the satisfaction of ambitions. It could be argued that parliamentary conflict only demonstrated the existence of disagreements which the airing they got there might even help to resolve. Parliaments might be regarded as useful safety valves in the engine of government. However, this is a sophistical rather than a sophisticated point: months of quarrelsome debate, so far from removing the poison of disagreement, tend to increase enmity and 'polarization'. There is really no sign that in the sixteenth century disputes in either House helped to allay conflict, and from the 1590s the history of Parliament is one of increasing criticism, increasing exasperation, increasing failure to restore stability. In any case, even if Parliaments had helped to release troublesome vapours, they would still not have been serving as means for satisfying legitimate aspirations on the part of the governing nation, the role for which I am trying to cast them. So long as historians of Parliament devote themselves to the description of political disputes and rival assertions of authority, they are bound to see in Parliament not a means towards stability but an instrument of real or potential opposition.

Is this preoccupation justified – a preoccupation which (as Neale did) skates over things done by agreement, or even comes to believe that agreement could only be the result of pressure from above, subservience from below?[6] Did people at the time share this view? It is necessary to enquire what those concerned wanted from Parliament and why they wanted it at all. In Parliament the nation (according to contemporary experts) met to deal with its affairs. This does suggest that in the first place harmony rather than dispute was intended, and that a prevalence of opposition and conflict should be treated as a sign that the necessary stability was in danger. The monarch's purposes are reasonably clear. Mostly they called Parliament to get money: Elizabeth was the first ruler of England who let not a single session pass except that of 1572 without obtaining supply.[7] They also wanted laws, especially in the revolutionary years between 1532 and 1559 when every session witnessed a full-scale government programme of legislation. Arguably, the Crown had less of an interest thereafter in parliamentary assemblies because, anxious now to hold a line rather than promote reform, it felt less need for continuous further legislation. As is well known, meetings grew much rarer in the second half of the century, though government legislation certainly did not come to an end in 1559. The demands of the struggle with Catholicism saw to that, and even reform, though less intense, did not terminate; not even Elizabeth could make time stand still. However, these practical needs of cash and laws do not fully explain the attitude of Tudor governments to Parliament, at least not after 1529, when all possibility ceased of ruling without the meetings of the estates. Parliaments were wanted because there the great affairs of the nation could be considered, debated, and advertised: Parliament was a part of the machinery of government available to active rulers.

In its earlier days, the idea of the image of the body politic called into existence to produce the active cooperation of all its members was the property of the Crown, even if a century later it became the weapon of an opposition. The conviction behind the royal summons was, for instance, expressed in the circular which instructed sheriffs about their duties in the elections of May 1536. Evidently it was thought desirable to offer some explanation why, only a few weeks after the long Reformation Parliament had at last gone home, it should be necessary to burden the country again with a Parliament.

> Such matters [the king was made to say] of most high importance have chanced as for the preservation of our honour, the establishment of our succession in the Crown of this our realm ... have been to us and to all the lords of our Council thought necessary to be discussed and determined in our high court of Parliament to be assembled for that purpose.[8]

These delicate phrases hide the miserable business of the palace revolution which destroyed the Boleyns, and thus far the calling of Parliament seemed necessitated only by the 1534 Act of Succession, now out of date and in need of replacement. But the letter went on to explain that the business was urgent and involved both the public weal and the personal security of the monarch; a matter of high policy, very personal to the King, was described as truly the concern of the nation assembled in Parliament. As practice proved, this was more than rhetoric: Henry VIII, at least, and Thomas Cromwell treated Parliament as though they believed in this stabilizing function. We need to remember the positive note struck – the ringing assertion that public affairs of real import were the business of Parliament and justified the calling of an unexpectedly sudden one.

Henrician Parliaments unquestionably concerned themselves with affairs of state, and not necessarily only at the Crown's behest; they were freely given information on diplomatic negotiations, like those with France in 1532 which pleased both Houses;[9] in the Cromwell era, as also in the difficult years of Edward VI and Mary, no one attempted to deny (as Elizabeth was to do on occasion) that Parliaments, and indeed the House of Commons, had an active part to play in the high politics of the nation. And even Elizabeth readily conceded a political function to her Parliaments, provided she was allowed to turn the tap off when it suited her. Compelled to use Parliament for the imposition of taxes and the making of laws, Tudor monarchs also thought it necessary and desirable to involve the potentially powerful and potentially difficult in the affairs of the realm by offering the occasions of debate, discussion, and support which Parliament represented. For most of the century, so far as we can judge, government certainly saw in Parliament a means of preserving stability and adjusting balances. And, despite the occasions of 'conflict' (often no more than a proper exchange of views and arguments), the outcome usually produced consensus and contentment, thus justifying the theory behind the practice.

What, then, of those who came when called? We know at present far too little about the Lords, though work is in progress.[10] That people sought election to the Commons in the reign of Elizabeth has been sufficiently proved by Neale: I need only point to his evidence of new boroughs created by the demand for seats, or of contested elections as demonstrating the desire of

rival local individuals and factions to get to the place of power and influence.[11] But similar things evidently happened in the reign of Henry VIII,
too. Some of the newly enfranchised boroughs may well have anticipated
the sort of purposes well vouched for in the daughter's reign, though most
of the new seats were certainly added by Crown policy. Tournai, Calais,
Wales, and Chester owed the bestowal of the franchise to the King's desire
to centralize the realm and demonstrate its unity in the visible image of the
body politic. However, there are sufficient signs that individuals strove
actively, and against other individuals, to get elected: the 'secret labours'
made in 1534 when a by-election fell due in Warwickshire, the riotous disputes accompanying the shire election for Shropshire in 1536, the uncalled-
for ambitions in Norfolk in 1539 of Sir Edmund Knyvet, who managed to
affront both Cromwell and the Duke of Norfolk, the troublesome intervention in 1542 of one Richard Devereux at the first ever election for
Carmarthenshire.[12] The beginnings of a systematic use of influence on elections which marked the Parliaments of 1536 and 1539 themselves testify to
ambitions to enter the Commons, and the familiar story of the clumsy interference in Kent by Edward's Privy Council in 1547 brings out the real
involvement in parliamentary affairs of both gentry and freeholders.[13] There
is no reason to doubt that throughout the century the theoretical attachment
to the representative institution was matched by a widespread desire to
share in its operations. And it would be very rash to suppose that behind this
desire was only some mildly pompous wish to enhance one's standing in the
eyes of one's fellows. The people who sought election may well be pre-
sumed to have wanted to use their place for identifiable ends.

What, then, did people want from Parliament? We may assume, without
question, that they were not seeking taxation, though it needs to be pointed out that, from 1534 onwards, Parliaments came to terms with the fact
that peacetime taxation had come to stay.[14] I am not suggesting that the
Tudor Commons embraced taxes with the self-sacrificing masochism displayed by twentieth-century Parliaments; but I would suggest that they did
not either automatically regard all taxation with the bigoted irresponsibility
too readily ascribed to them by some historians. They knew as well as we do
that government needed to be financed, and, when persuaded that the purposes of government were sound, they proved far less difficult about granting money than one might suppose. The only Parliament of the century
which made really serious trouble about supply was that of 1523, a
Parliament which deliberately expressed its grave disquiet about Wolsey's
policies. Nor was taxation seen as a bargaining counter: apart from the session of 1566, when fears for the succession produced a real conflict, no
Parliament seems ever to have attempted to use supply for the extraction of
political concessions, and on that occasion no one doubted that the money
grant itself was justified. Tudor Parliaments voted supply soberly and
responsibly, and it should be recognized once again that the principle and

practice of taxation by consent made a very real contribution to the political stability of the system. We know what happened in the next generation, as soon as serious attempts were made to tax without consent.

Still, it was not the prospect of taking money out of constituents' pockets that lured men into service in the House. Some, of course, did want to pursue political ends. Some men, well aware of the platform which Parliament provided, wished to use it to promote policies or hinder those they thought were likely to be promoted by others. This is as true of the group supporting Catherine of Aragon who organized opposition in the Reformation Parliament,[15] as it is of the 'puritan choir' of 1563 or the brothers Wentworth. But these men, seeking legitimate conflict, clearly formed a small minority of the members of the House. The main part of those who looked beyond the personal gratification and local repute which election to Parliament might bring with it seem to have had one of two ends in view: the obtaining of legislation for themselves or for groups or individuals with whom they were connected, and personal advancement. In other words, to them Parliament offered just that opportunity of fulfilling particular ambitions which are required in an instrument of political stability.

If so far I may well have seemed to be digging over well-tilled ground, I have now to confess that for the rest of this paper I can do little more than suggest lines of enquiry. That all sorts of people – individuals, interests, institutions, companies – wished to use Parliament in order to get their programmes and necessities embodied in legislation is, of course, a familiar point. Very little, however, has been done to see what sort of success they had in this. We need to study Acts passed and failed bills, assign them to this or that initiative, and explore local and private records systematically in order to discover who attempted what and who managed to achieve what. The problems of legislative initiative are many and in the past have too often been solved by despair – by simply assuming that all reasonably general Acts owed their origin to the Crown or 'the government', while those touching particular interests may safely be ascribed to those interests. This rule of thumb offers an unsafe guide. I have before this attempted to penetrate some of the jungle for the 1530s (and have disconcertingly discovered that even then we cannot be sure that king and minister worked always in mutually informed harmony),[16] while the Parliaments of 1547–57 and of 1589–1610 are being studied with such questions in mind.[17] Professor Helen Miller's revealing study of the manner in which the city of London used Parliament needs to be followed up after 1547.[18] There are other well-organized towns to consider, as well as bodies of gentlemen in the shires. How important was it for a burgess, especially if he was what Neale has termed a carpet-bagger, or even for a knight, to serve the purposes and respond to the demands of his constituents? Can we discover anything touching the relations between electors and the man they sent to Westminster? Did re-election have to do with the successful promotion of bills? How many men in the Commons were in fact active about bills? How serious were constituencies about bills they had in the House, and can we find out anything about the cost of obtaining an Act of Parliament? There are no answers at present – or only the most tenuous ones – to these and similar questions; and yet we must have answers if we are to understand what went on in Parliament and what men wanted from it. The question is the more obviously important because the existence of private Act legislation is peculiar to the English Parliament, distinguishing it, for instance, from those of Scotland and Ireland. We are well advised to seek at least part of the explanation for the political differences between these assemblies in this simple fact.[19]

I cannot on this occasion attempt to fill the gap, but I can offer a few examples from the reign of Henry VIII to show how very real and active this involvement of private interests in the work of the session was. To many men, even the Reformation Parliament signified less a time of revolution in State and Church than an opportunity to advance their own business. The sheriffs and escheators of Northumberland who for years had been paying over the profits in their charge to the Chamber, in 1536 found themselves troubled with process out of the Exchequer for some 70 years' arrears; they petitioned the King for a bill of indemnity back to Edward IV, a move which yielded no result.[20] One of the King's chirurgeons did better in 1545 by getting royal approval for a bill to create a profitable monopoly in the appraising of dead men's goods; but despite the stamped royal signature the bill got nowhere, unlike four others for the settlement of various estates which were similarly approved.[21] The Abbot of Conway hoped to introduce a proviso into the Dissolution bill of 1536 with which to save his house but without success.[22] In 1539, a priest trying to help a couple who had married before learning that the lady's first husband was probably still alive, advised a private Act of Parliament to resolve the embarrassment.[23] No act resulted, and it may be doubted whether Parliament would ever have entertained an indemnity bill for bigamy, however inadvertent. In the middle of the 1540 session Thomas Wyat, the poet, could not find time for social courtesies because he was in the thick of preparing his two bills for Parliament,[24] both, incidentally, passed. The best documented seeker after useful bills in Parliament was Lord Lisle, deputy at Calais – best documented because his correspondence was confiscated and survives, but also because absence from England made statute his best hope for protecting his interests. By 1539, when he was advised that his plan to buy some woods from the Earl of Bridgewater could most readily be realized by private bill legislation,[25] he had considerable experience of watching the vagaries of affairs in Parliament. With Sir Richard Whethill, a personal enemy in Calais, he had been at the receiving end: Whethill tried for legislation in 1534 to confirm a patent for a spear's place for his son which he had obtained in the teeth of the deputy's opposition, and two years later he attempted a similar *coup* on his own behalf.[26] On both occasions Lisle's close contacts with Cromwell enabled him to thwart his enemy. In the new Parliament of 1536 he in his turn tried to use statute to do down an opponent. Sir Robert Wingfield held the grant of a marsh in the environs of Calais which the deputy found irksome and wished to see resumed. His agents, talking to Cromwell actually in the Commons' chamber, persuaded the minister that the grant was indeed against the public interest; Cromwell there and then moved the matter in the House, obtained a vote that something be done, and commissioned the drafting of the necessary bill. But, despite his repeated promises, the bill, produced within 24 hours by William Portman of the Middle Temple (later a judge), hung in the House, in which Wingfield's friends had evidently also managed to raise some support. In the end it passed, only to be held up in the Lords, but at this point Wingfield voluntarily surrendered the patent into the King's hands, rather than suffer the indignity of an Act of Parliament against himself.[27] Even the haphazard evidence of the State Papers demonstrates the importance of private bills, and therefore the importance of Parliament to private interests; how much more can we learn from less official archives? They need to be searched.

Though the absence of work done at present prevents a thorough discussion of these important issues, one aspect is more readily accessible and can yield some quite interesting answers even to distinctly preliminary enquiries. The Acts passed which dealt with the affairs of individuals – usually but not always property matters – can safely be ascribed to their beneficiaries' initiative, and, though the Acts themselves are in print only down to 1539, full lists are available in the *Statutes of the Realm*. Though strictly speaking their contents need to be analysed, and though most certainly it would be desirable to consider also failed bills of a like kind, a look at mere numbers of such Acts passed has its uses. Private Act legislation was a well-established practice in the sixteenth century, but the pattern is far from uniform.[28] Much the biggest number of Acts for private persons' concerns was passed in the reign of Henry VII, whose first, third, and fifth Parliaments yielded 50, 25, and 27 respectively. The average for the reign is 18.7 per session, as compared with 8.3 under Henry VIII, 9.2 under Edward VI, a mere 4.3 under Mary, and a significantly increased 13.4 under Elizabeth. However, the high figures for the first Tudor arise simply from the consequences of the civil wars: the bulk of those private Acts dealt with restitutions in blood and resumptions of lands confiscated, being thus necessary products of earlier acts of attainder. This untypical activity apart, private legislation runs around a median of four or five per session down to the last session of the Reformation Parliament. Meanwhile, Acts dealing with the private affairs of the royal family had also come in a steady stream – a total of 24 under the seventh Henry and 81 under the eighth. Strikingly enough, Edward and Mary each used Parliament only once for their private concerns, and Elizabeth not at all.

If one ignores the accident of the post-civil-war settlement, it becomes apparent that it was actually the Crown, under Cromwell's guidance, which first discovered and demonstrated how the machinery of Parliament could be exploited systematically for private business. The reorganization of the royal estates in the 1530s over which Cromwell and Audley presided necessitated 14, 16, and 13 private Acts in the sessions of 27, 28, and 32 Henry VIII. Private interests, possibly somewhat frustrated by the massive public legislation of the Reformation Parliament, immediately picked up the idea, with 18, 16, 13, and 10 Acts in the sessions 27–32 Henry VIII. The unexpected Parliament of 1536, called really to deal with the settlement of the succession, was thus very thoroughly used also for the settlement of property matters both royal and private. Detailed research is needed to discover why the Crown came to abandon the method after 1546 and why private bill legislation altogether declined thereafter until 1558, but even this superficial survey shows that in the reign of Elizabeth the landed classes came increasingly to rely on Parliament. At the same time, though public Acts declined rather in political and social significance, they remained stable in numbers: the total amount of business transacted in every session – remembering that sessions themselves occurred at longer intervals of time – increased in the second half of the century.[29] The real breakthrough for private Acts, whatever reason may have been behind it, came in the reign of James I, whose seven sessions yielded an average of 23.3 private Acts, and that despite the fact that two sessions remained totally blank. The average for the productive sessions is thus over 32: we have entered a new era in the use of Parliament. While the import of failed bills needs to be taken into account, and though the crude figures of Acts passed need to be refined by further classification, it is manifest that in the course of the sixteenth century Parliament came to be a very important instrument in the management of the political nation's private affairs. Neale's remark that, while for the Crown Parliament meant money, to the Commons it meant private Acts,[30] does indeed, as he says, oversimplify; but the epigram displays real insight, and I could wish that its author had not in his narrative history of the Elizabethan Parliaments told us very little about the first and almost nothing about the second. People wanted Parliaments not only to make laws for Church and commonwealth, not only to serve the economic and social needs of particular areas or sectional interests, but also as the major – the most conclusive – means for settling the legal problems involved in their estates policies. Here, then, is a clear way in which the institution acted to promote satisfaction and stability, and the problems caused in James's reign by sessions which failed altogether to serve this purpose need surely to be taken into account when we consider why the consensus and stability expressed in the work of the Tudor Parliaments began to disappear in the following century.

Lastly, I want to take a look at the question whether election to the House of Commons could be important in serving personal ambition and progress in a man's career. Again, this is much too big a problem to tackle thoroughly here. Some hints are scattered in Neale's book: lawyers found membership a useful way to attract the kind of attention which led to office and promotion, and some individuals actively exploited the parliamentary service they could render to patrons.[31] A systematic study must await the publication of the relevant volumes of the *History of Parliament*, which should supply all the information required. Meanwhile, let me look briefly at the tip of this particular iceberg – at the relationship, if one existed, between election to the Commons and membership of the Privy Council. We have long been familiar with the point that Tudor councillors regularly sat in the Commons and that the failure of the Stuarts to provide such a 'Treasury bench' played its part in the collapse of cooperation between Crown and Parliament. Here I am concerned with the reverse of all this: could prominence, or even presence, in the House contribute to a man's rise into the Council? Of one man we know not only that it did but also that he deliberately chose Parliament as a place in which to attract the monarch's attention and work his way into power. When Thomas Cromwell told George Cavendish in November 1529 that by his belated entry into the Reformation Parliament he had 'once adventured to put in his foot, where he trusted shortly to be better regarded',[32] he spoke for more than his personal fortune. He prophesied no less than the characteristic way to eminence which was to dominate English politics certainly from the Restoration onwards. Did anyone else in the sixteenth century employ it?[33]

There are, in fact, interesting hints that in this respect, once again, things changed in the 1530s – that Cromwell initiated a later practice. Information, as usual, is difficult to get for the councillors of Henry VII, a high proportion of whom, being bishops, peers, doctors of law, judges, and serjeants-at-law, do not in any case come within the range of this question. In 1504 a single Council meeting included 11 men who could have sat in Parliament before becoming councillors.[34] Totally deserted by official returns, we have only the patchiest notion of their possible presence in the Commons, but the indications are against a notion that they were parliamentarians before they were councillors. Sir Thomas Lovell was Speaker in 1485 and Sir Robert Drury in 1495, but the latter had already had a full career as king's legal counsel, while the former (in company with Sir Richard Guildford, Sir Edward Poynings, Sir Gilbert Talbot, Sir Walter Hungerford, and Sir Henry Wyat) had been among Henry's supporters before or at Bosworth. None of them needed to sit in the Commons to attract the King's favour, and all of them almost certainly were councillors from the beginning of the reign. Sir Thomas Bourchier probably belongs to the same category; he attended the Council by 1486.[35] Nothing useful can be established about Sir Robert Litton and Sir John Risley. That leaves Edmund Dudley, Speaker in the Parliament of January 1504. It appears that the first payment to him of a councillor's fee is recorded for October that year,[36] but as a member of the Council Learned he

was clearly of the Council before that year. Thus none of Henry VII's councillors can be thought of as using Parliament as a foundation for their careers;
if they did seek election, it was either as established king's men and leaders
of the government, or for private reasons of status and local importance.

Much the same was true of the first half of Henry VIII's reign. The
reduced Council projected in Wolsey's Eltham Ordinances of 1526 included five men of interest in this context.[37] Sir William Fitzwilliam the
Younger, Sir Henry Guildford, and Sir William Kingston are not known to
have sat before 1529; yet the first two are vouched for as councillors by
1522 and 1516 respectively, while the last, though possibly not formally a
councillor before 1533, was a well-established courtier by May 1524 when
he became constable of the Tower.[38] All three, in fact, were courtiers in
terms of a career structure. Sir John Gage (Vice-Chamberlain) had been
prominent at Court for several years; he is not known ever to have sat in
Parliament. As for Sir Thomas More, though he may have sat in the
Parliament of 1504 (and I am very doubtful of this story of Roper's, as of
some others he tells), he certainly owed neither his entry into the Council in
1517 nor his Speakership in 1523 to any species of parliamentary career.[39]

Biographical study of the first properly listed Privy Council in August
1540, on the other hand, yields a quite dramatically changed picture.[40]
Edward Seymour, never apparently elected to a Parliament, was there as the
king's brother-in-law and uncle to the heir apparent. Sir John Russell, Sir
Thomas Cheyney, Sir Anthony Wingfield, Sir Richard Rich, and Sir John
Baker had all sat in 1529 (and probably not before); all of them made it into
the Council between 1531 and 1539. It would be wrong to conclude that
they all owed their advancement to membership of the Commons; Russell
and Cheyney, for instance, were courtiers first. So was Sir Anthony Brown,
a burgess in 1539, the same year that (probably) he became a councillor.
Still, all these men went through the Commons on their way to the Council
table, and Rich and Baker – professional civil servants – do seem to have followed in the footsteps of Cromwell by making their mark in Parliament.
(Cromwell was in effect accompanied by Thomas Audley, Lord Chancellor
by 1540: another veteran of the 1523 Parliament and Speaker in 1529, by
which time as Chancellor of the Duchy he was a member of the unreformed
Council.) Thomas Wriothesley and Ralph Sadler, the principal Secretaries of
1540, owed their promotion to Cromwell, whose private secretaries they
had been, but again he got them into Parliament a year before they made it
into the Privy Council.[41] Naturally, one must be careful not to assume simply
that temporal order (Parliament first, Council after) equals cause and effect,
but it does begin to look as though by the 1530s membership of the House
of Commons was something that men with political ambition could and
would use as a stepping stone in their careers.

And this situation continued and developed. The privy councillors of
November 1551 included seven men who could have done what has here

been postulated: all of them did.[42] Sir Robert Bowes first entered Parliament in 1539 but joined the Council only in 1551. Sir John Gates, William Cecil, and Sir Edward North sat first in 1542: they were of the Privy Council by 1551, 1550, and 1547 respectively. North, incidentally, was the first clerk of the Parliaments ever to sit in the Commons afterwards. Sir John Mason and Sir Philip Hoby sat in Parliament in 1547, but in Council only in 1550 and 1551. As for Sir William Petre, that Cromwellian survival, he had passed through those stages at an earlier date: Parliament 1536, Council 1545. By this time, therefore, all the commoners on the Privy Council (and some since promoted to the peerage, like William Paget) had had a career in the Commons before they achieved membership of the government. And the same remained true for new arrivals in Elizabeth's reign, when appointment to the Council often came a long time after a man had first gone into Parliament and began to attract attention there. Here are some typical examples, with the date of first election followed by the date of appointment to the Council: Sir James Croft, 1542, 1570; Sir Francis Knollys, (?)1533, 1559; Sir Walter Mildmay, 1545, 1566; Sir Thomas Smith, 1547, 1571; Sir Francis Walsingham, 1559, 1563; Sir Christopher Hatton, 1571, 1577; Thomas Wilson, 1563, 1577; Sir Henry Sidney, 1547, 1575; Robert Cecil, 1584, 1591; Sir Thomas Egerton, 1584, 1596; Sir John Fortescue, 1559, 1589; Sir William Knollys, 1571, 1596.

I am not, of course, suggesting that all these men, and others, reached councillor's status simply because they had served a political apprenticeship in Parliament. But they had indeed served such an apprenticeship, and the only new recruit to the Council in the reign who had not was apparently (*quia non potuit*) Archbishop Whitgift. I am not prepared to say that membership of the Commons had become a necessary prerequisite for elevation to the Privy Council, but it looks very much as though it had become a very useful first step. From the 1530s onwards, and not before the time that Thomas Cromwell showed the way, getting elected to Parliament was one way – and a prominent way – to get to the top. Men who wished to reach the Council, men who hoped to help govern the country, needed other means as well and other connections, but increasingly they discovered that they could lay sound foundations by seeking election to Parliament. The Queen may not have consciously chosen her councillors from members of the Commons (though we do not know that she did not, and we may suppose that her advisers, a Cecil or Leicester, kept their eyes and ears open in the Parliament), but in effect she there found the necessary reservoir of talent. Once again, the point was brought out more clearly in the reign of her successor, because then it ceased to be so easy to use this particular staircase to the top. Men such as Sir Edwyn Sandys, Sir John Eliot, Sir Thomas Wentworth, or William Noy knew perfectly well that their talents were superior to those promoted by foolish and incompetent kings dominated by favourites whose advancement had owed nothing to membership of the

House. Men like these, given the opportunity, soon enough proved that their real purposes were to govern, to sit in the Privy Council. Left out in the cold, they could only agitate in a species of opposition, in the hope of attracting attention that way: and Wentworth and Noy achieved the purpose of their disruptive activities.

Thus the ineptitude of early Stuart rule produced a new political sophistication: the ambitious politician who made the life of government so difficult that it seemed best to solve the problem by giving him office. Under Elizabeth, resisters in Parliament were not men who sought high office; those who did found that an active and helpful conformity served the purpose best. So long as trouble in Parliament gathered around natural opposition men like the Wentworth brothers or around men like Norton or Fleetwood who found satisfaction in careers outside the inner rings of government, that trouble was politically insignificant. When men appeared who had hoped to use Parliament for a career leading to the Privy Council and found the road blocked, every sort of warning light went on in Parliament and Council alike. The opposition which mattered was not – then or at any other time – that of irreconcilable principle but that of frustrated political ambition.

Thus Parliament, the premier point of contact between rulers and ruled, between the Crown and the political nation, in the sixteenth century fulfilled its function as a stabilizing mechanism because it was usable and used to satisfy legitimate and potentially powerful aspirations. It mediated in the touchy area of taxation; by producing the required general and particular laws it kept necessary change in decent order; it assisted the rich in the arranging of their affairs; and it helped the ambitious to scale the heights of public power. What more could we ask of the image of the body politic? Only that it should satisfy liberal preconceptions by regularly undoing governments. But that was not a function which sixteenth-century theory ascribed to Parliament, and I can see no reason why it should have done so.

Notes

1 An attempt to analyse attitudes in the north is M. E. James, 'The Concept of Order and the Northern Rising of 1569', *Past and Present* 60 (1973), pp. 49 ff.
2 Thomas Smith, *De republica anglorum*, ed. L. Alston (Cambridge, 1906), pp. 48–9.
3 Quoted in Simonds D'Ewes, *The Journals of all the Parliaments during the Reign of Queen Elizabeth* (London, 1682), p. 350 (said in 1585).
4 G. R. Elton, *Reform and Renewal* (Cambridge, 1973), p. 67; and Elton, *Studies in Tudor and Stuart Politics and Government* (4 vols, Cambridge, 1974–92), II, no. 22.
5 *LP* XI, 1182(2), 1244, 1246.
6 J. E. Neale, *Elizabeth I and her Parliaments* (2 vols, London, 1953–7, repr. 1969).
7 Cf. J. Hurstfield's argument that in the sixteenth century consent only hid constraint: 'Was There a Tudor Despotism after all?', *Transactions of the Royal Historical Society*, 5th ser., 17 (1967), pp. 83–108.
8 BL Harl. MS 283, fo. 256 (*LP* X, 815).
9 *LP* V, 1518.

10 Especially in the hands of Dr Michael Graves.
11 J. E. Neale, *The Elizabethan House of Commons* (London, 1948), esp. chs 2–7.
12 *LP* VII, 1178; X, 1063; XIV, i, 672, 706, 800, 808; XVII, 48.
13 *Acts of the Privy Council of England*, ed. J. R. Dasent, E. G. Atkinson, J. V. Lyle, R. F. Monger, and P. A. Penfold (46 vols, London, 1890–1964), II, pp. 516, 518.
14 G. R. Elton, 'Taxation for War and Peace in Early Tudor England', in *Studies in Tudor and Stuart Politics and Government*, III, no. 37.
15 G. R. Elton, 'Sir Thomas More and the Opposition of Henry VIII', in *Studies in Tudor and Stuart Politics and Government*, I, no. 8.
16 Elton, *Reform and Renewal*, ch. 4.
17 By Professor C. Erikson, Mr A. L. Jenkins, and Miss M. A. Randall.
18 Helen Miller, 'London and Parliament in the Reign of Henry VIII', *Bulletin of the Institute of Historical Research*, 35 (1962), p. 128 ff.; the unsystematic remarks in Neale, *The Elizabethan House of Commons* – e.g. pp. 336–8, 383–7 – are but a beginning.
19 For Ireland, see the remarks by B. Bradshaw in B. Farrell (ed.), *The Irish Parliamentary Tradition* (Dublin, 1973), p. 71.
20 *LP* X, 1260.
21 *LP* XX, ii, 1067, nos. 35, 37, 48–49; XXI, ii, 770, no. 80.
22 *LP* X, 1046.
23 *LP* XIV, i, 896.
24 *LP* XV, 783.
25 *LP* XIV, i, 780, 877.
26 *LP* VII, 1492; X, 580.
27 *LP* XI, 34, 61, 94, 108; *LJ* I (12 July 1536).
28 These calculations are based on the tables of contents in *Statutes of the Realm*, vols II–IV, counting as private Acts those that had not previously been printed or still remained unprinted.
29 From 1529 to 1601, the average of public Acts passed in each session is about 21.
30 Neale, *The Elizabethan House of Commons*, p. 383.
31 e.g. Neale, *The Elizabethan House of Commons*, p. 151.
32 R. S. Sylvester and D. P. Harding (eds), *Two Early Tudor Lives* (New Haven and London, 1962), p. 116.
33 For information I rely in part on such obvious sources as *DNB* and the *Official Return of MPs*, and in part on the biographies in the files of the History of Parliament Trust. I am grateful to the Trust for permission to use their files, and to Dr Alan Davidson for searching them in reply to my questions.
34 *Select Cases in the Council of Henry VII*, ed. C. G. Bayne and W. H. Dunham (Selden Soc. 75; London, 1958), p. 40.
35 *Select Cases*, p. 8.
36 *The Tree of Commonwealth*, ed. D. M. Brodie (Cambridge, 1948), pp. 2–3.
37 G. R. Elton, *The Tudor Constitution: Documents and Commentary* (1st edn, Cambridge, 1960; 2nd edn, 1982), pp. 93–4.
38 *LP* IV, 390 (28).
39 G. R. Elton, 'Thomas More, Councillor', in *Studies in Tudor and Stuart Politics and Government*, I, no. 7.
40 Elton, *Tudor Constitution*, p. 95.
41 Sadler certainly sat in 1539 (A. J. Slavin, *Profit and Power* (Cambridge, 1966), p. 40); the History of Parliament Trust suspects a possible election in 1536.
42 *Acts of the Privy Council*, II, p. 403.

15

Court and polity under Elizabeth I*

PENRY WILLIAMS

By inviting me to deliver this lecture the University of Manchester has done me a sovereign honour and has provided me with the dual opportunity of commemorating the foremost Tudor historian of his generation and of recording a personal debt. Sir John Neale became Professor of History at Manchester in 1925 (the year of my own birth) and in 1927 departed, sadly for Manchester, to the Astor Chair of History at London, a post which he held until 1956. It is therefore appropriate that he should be honoured here, as well as at London; and I am especially gratified to inaugurate this series of lectures, not only because I myself served, much later, at this university, but because I owe much to Sir John personally. When I first plunged into the ocean of historical research I met the not uncommon difficulty of find-ing a subject with adequate sources. I wanted to work upon the interplay of faction and clientage in Elizabethan Wales and its borders, a topic very much inspired by Sir John's own writings. But wherever I looked the docu-ments had been consumed by fire, rodents, or time. At my tutor's suggestion I wrote to Sir John, who generously gave me an afternoon of his time and the excellent advice that I should study the Council in the Marches of Wales. I took the advice, have never regretted it, and am happy now to be able to acknowledge his kindness and wisdom.

Sir John's own books and articles have been distinguished by a rare abil-ity to combine detailed scholarly research with a vivid and lively presenta-tion that has ensured for them a wide and enduring readership. His most substantial work has undoubtedly been on the history of Parliament, espe-cially of the Elizabethan House of Commons, where he displayed his gift for relating institutions to people. His life of Elizabeth I has achieved a deservedly high place among historical biographies. But for this lecture I have chosen to explore a third field in which he worked. His Raleigh Lecture, 'The Elizabethan Political Scene',[1] was a short and brilliant piece, of seminal importance, whose ideas have resounded in the writings of many other historians. And yet some of its most interesting leads have been little followed. There is no history of the Elizabethan Court, although much has

* This article is a slightly revised version of the J. E. Neale Memorial Lecture delivered in the John Rylands University Library of Manchester on 14 May 1982. I am most grateful to the University for inviting me to deliver the inaugural lecture in this series, which has been endowed by the generosity of Sir John Neale's family.

been written on its politics and its ceremonial. Only two writers, I think, have explored systematically the paths opened up by Sir John in that lecture: Professor W. T. MacCaffrey and Professor G. R. Elton.[2] As the latter remarked in his own lecture, much remains to be done, in particular on the working and personnel of the Royal Household and the Chamber. I do not claim that in a single lecture I can supply those needs, and indeed far more research is required than I have yet been able to devote to the matters in hand. I hope on this occasion merely to map out the ground very broadly, suggesting a scheme for analysing the role of the Court in politics and in the polity, taking up certain themes which arise from this analysis, and posing further problems for investigation.

The royal Court played four major roles in the *political* life of the nation – I cannot here discuss its contribution to England's intellectual and cultural world. It was a theatre of display. It provided a clearing house – a sort of royal exchange – for the distribution of patronage. It was the principal arena in which political decisions emerged and in which political rivalries were conducted. Finally, it acted as an all-important link connecting the Crown and the shires, resolving local grievances and preserving by personal contacts the loyalty of county families. Much has been written on the first two of these subjects, ceremonial and patronage, though neither topic has been exhausted. The third – the interplay of faction – needs more than one lecture for any sort of justice to be done to it. And I therefore propose to concentrate upon the fourth, but to say something initially and briefly about each of the other three, because it is part of my theme that the interaction of these roles provides much of the fascination of Court life and accounts for conflicting attitudes towards it. Having discussed these various roles, I shall turn at the end to considering the success of Elizabeth's Court in sustaining her regime and providing political stability.

The Court as a theatre of display, as the gallery in which the monarch's glory was supported and enhanced by the great men of the realm, is indicated by lines from Marlowe's *Edward the Second*, when Young Mortimer rebukes the King for his failure to achieve just this:

> Thy Court is naked, being bereft of those
> That make a King seem glorious in the world,
> I mean the peers, whom thou shouldst dearly love.[3]

Francis Bacon made the same point in 1599 when he warned Elizabeth of the dangers created by her treatment of Essex, then at the head of his army in Ireland:

> If you had my lord of Essex here with a white staff in his hand, as my lord of Leicester had, and continued him so about you, for society to

yourself, and for an honour and ornament to your attendance and
Court, in the eyes of your people, and in the eyes of foreign ambassadors, then were he in his right element.[4]

The cult of Elizabeth – with its elaborate tilts and tournaments, costly progresses, reverential royal portraits, celebrations of her accession day, 17
November – has been lovingly recreated and interpreted for us by Dame
Frances Yates and Dr Roy Strong. Too lovingly and too lengthily for the
patience of one distinguished historian: 'we need no more reveries on accession tilts and symbolism, no more pretty pictures of gallants and galliards,'
protested Professor Elton.[5] I agree with him on the need for 'painful studies'
of the officers of the Court and the workings of its intricate machinery. But I
believe that we should be mistaken if we dismissed the pomp, symbolism, and
display as insignificant. The 'dignified' part of the constitution was – and still
is – essential to the regime and the unity of its subjects. Some men were sceptical about the tilts. Francis Bacon, himself hardly built for the jousting-yard,
was clear in his mind that nobles should be ornaments of the Court rather
than commanders of armies; but he was sceptical about tournaments: 'these
things are but toys to come among serious observations.' But he added that,
'since princes will have such things, it is better they should be graced with eleg-
ancy rather than daubed with cost'.[6] Courtiers saw these occasions as an
opportunity for impressing their qualities upon the monarch. When Robert
Cary was out of favour with Elizabeth for making an unsuitable marriage, he
decided to win his way back by attending the tournament at Windsor. After
spending £400 on 'things necessary for the triumph', he entered the list dis-
guised: 'I was the forsaken Knight that had vowed solitariness, but hearing of
this great triumph thought to honour my mistress with my best service ....' The
ceremony went well, Cary made himself known and was received at Court;
but the Queen was still offended and sent him on a mission to James VI without speaking to him.[7] His story suggests that performance at the ceremonies
was certainly thought at the time to be an important means of advancement,
but may not in practice have been as effective as courtiers believed. Yet the
ceremonies certainly had their effect in the wider role of establishing and celebrating the image of the monarch.

However, the Temple of Astraea, the Virgin Queen, was the haunt of the
money-changers. The golden images of Gloriana and her Knights must be
viewed beside the reality of men and women intensely ambitious for prestige, often greedy for money and lands, with their way to make in the world.
These two aspects of the Court are strikingly preserved in the monument to
Blanche Parry, one of Elizabeth's longest-serving gentlewomen, in the small,
remote Herefordshire church of Bacton.[8] Blanche Parry kneels before an
effigy of Elizabeth, who faces the viewer: here, in the chancel of a parish
church, the monarch, rather than a religious symbol, is venerated.
Underneath the two figures are carved verses, probably by Blanche Parry

herself, in which she describes her training in the princess's household before 1558 and then speaks of herself as

> Prefferrynge still the causys of eache wyghte,
> As farre as I doorste move Her Grace hys eare,
> For to reward decerts by course of ryght ...[9]

Attendance at Court was a means of gratifying and rewarding others – as well as securing gains for oneself, a matter discreetly passed over by Mistress Parry. Professor Elton is surely right to insist that formal ceremony was not the only style of the Court. Blanche Parry and others close to the Queen could approach her in a relaxed, even casual way.[10] But I would go further than stressing the coexistence of strict ceremonial and easy informality. There was a contrast, in many ways a *conflict*, between the ideals of Gloriana's Court and the arena in which men sought the Crown's patronage for offices, leases, licences to trade, monopolies, wardships, gratuities, pensions, titles, and honours. Fortunes could be made and lost at Court as nowhere else. Competition for office was intense and seems to have been growing in the latter part of the reign. 'The Court', wrote Rowland Whyte to his master, Robert Sidney, in 1597, 'is full of who shall have this and that office.'[11] The press of suitors was such that in 1594 special orders were issued to control entrée to the Court: Masters of Requests were given offices outside its gates to scrutinize suitors and issue passes for entry. Courtiers were ordered to provide lists of their servants so that no unauthorized persons might gain admission.[12] One gets the impression that before this 'passport' system was instituted the Court was not so much informal as chaotic; and it may well have continued to be so. However, the problems of access and patronage are closely linked to other aspects of the Court to which I shall turn before coming back to these central matters.

The Court was also the arena in which political factions formed and fought. Their divisions and contests sprang partly from the competition for patronage, partly from disputes about government and policy. Here it is important to remark that the great officers of state in the Privy Council must be counted as part of the Court.[13] Great ministers like Burghley belonged as much to the Court as did the officers of the household; and leading courtiers were mostly – though not all – members of the Council. This identity had not always held true in the sixteenth century. Under Henry VIII the Gentlemen of the Privy Chamber – Sir Anthony Denny and Sir William Herbert especially – controlled access to the monarch and were courted by the conciliar factions. Under Edward VI Lord Darcy, the King's Chamberlain, and Sir John Gates, the Vice-Chamberlain, manipulated the young King on behalf of Northumberland. Under Elizabeth – and probably before that under her sister as well – ministers had no need to place their creatures in the royal bedchamber. Burghley enjoyed closer relations with his Queen than anyone else. That is not to say that royal favourites were unimportant, but that the household officers had no special advantages of contact with the Queen, and that Council, household, and monarch revolved within the same orbit. I have not the space to investigate the problems of Elizabethan faction, on which much remains to be said.[14] Here I would remark only that, while major issues of policy – the Queen's marriage, the succession, foreign policy, military affairs, and religion – did stir heated debate and divide courtiers from one another at times, there was more agreement than dissonance among Elizabethan politicians, at least until the 1590s. The Leicester and Burghley 'factions' – so-called – were loosely constructed and volatile groupings: most men kept a toehold at least in both camps and political argument was as often conducted between the Queen and her ministers as between the 'factions'. After the death of Leicester the political atmosphere and pattern changed. Usually this is explained by the intrusion of the unruly, uncontrollable personality of Essex – and he was certainly a disruptive force. But I think that some of the responsibility lies with the Cecils. Thomas Lake wrote in 1591 to Robert Sidney, warning him against making too many friends apart from Burghley. The ageing Lord Treasurer was angry with Edward Norris for 'nourishing a dependency on others'. 'Old Saturnus', commented Lake, 'is a melancholy and wayward planet, but yet predominant here ...'; if Sidney had a turn to do, it must be done that way.[15] Arguably, Burghley, having survived almost alone from the first generation of Elizabethan politicians, was set on perpetuating his new concentration of power and transmitting it to his son, Robert. Not surprisingly, Essex reacted by adopting a similar posture. He demanded of Lord Grey that he declare himself to be either his – Essex's – man or else the Secretary's and therefore Essex's enemy.[16] In such a climate the Temple of Astraea was uncomfortably ridden with strife.

The fourth role of the Court – linking the central government and the localities – was performed in two ways: by resolving or deciding local disputes and tensions; and by giving access to men of importance in the shires. I intend to examine elsewhere in greater depth and detail the impact of the Court upon local politics and government;[17] and I will now deal only briefly with that part of the subject. But I want to comment upon one feature of Tudor politics which arrested my attention from the moment that I began to work upon it: the continuous, and sometimes impassioned, involvement of major courtiers and politicians in apparently trivial local affairs. Here is one example, which I have treated at greater length elsewhere.[18] When a well-to-do, but not outstandingly rich, Glamorgan landowner named John Gamage died in 1584, there was immediate and intense competition over the marriage of his sole heiress, Barbara. Several Welsh and Marcher landowners had already put their sons into the field, but Herbert Croft, grandson of Sir James Croft, Controller of the Royal Household and a member of the most prominent family in Herefordshire, was thought the favourite – and certainly believed himself to be so. But when young Croft went to visit his 'intended' after her father's death, he was refused admission by her self-appointed guardian, her cousin Sir Edward Stradling. Sir James mobilized backing at Court and a cascade of letters reached Sir Edward: Burghley told him to hand the girl over to a neutral party; Raleigh and Howard of Effingham ordered him to do nothing without their prior consent. Stradling ignored all this and allowed in a new suitor, Robert Sidney, younger brother of Philip, son of the Lord President of the Council in the Marches, and brother-in-law to the Earl of Pembroke, the most powerful magnate in Glamorgan. The Sidneys called upon Pembroke, upon Robert's uncle, the Earl of Leicester, and upon Philip's father-in-law, Sir Francis Walsingham, for protection. What might have been a painful and disruptive local feud was quickly resolved by the intervention of Sidney's friends. Walsingham, who had initially ordered Stradling to send Barbara up to Court, now countermanded this instruction, informing Stradling that, being given to understand that he acted from 'the good will you bear unto the Earl of Pembroke ... I cannot but encourage you therein'. Fifteen days after her father's death Barbara Gamage was married to Robert Sidney, whom she had probably never seen before. The marriage was, incidentally, loving, harmonious, and companionable. Sidney's letters to his wife display a moving affection; and Ben Jonson later praised the virtues of the mistress of Penshurst, the Sidney home:

> These, Penshurst, are thy praise and yet not all,
> Thy lady's noble, fruitful, chaste withall.
> His children thy great lord may call his own,
> A fortune in this age but rarely known.[19]

At a higher level the Court, in particular the Privy Council, resolved or calmed religious feuds in Suffolk. In 1583 Bishop Freke of Norwich, assisted by the assize judges of the circuit, set out to crush puritan reformers in his diocese. Five leading ministers of the shire were imprisoned at the assizes for failure to conform in religion. Ten gentlemen of the county then protested to the Privy Council, which admonished the judges to treat the ministers 'according to their quality, not matching them at bar or in the indictment with rogues, felons or papists'. In the following year Archbishop Whitgift renewed the attack upon the puritans, suspending several; but Robert Beale, clerk to the Privy Council, managed with the aid of Lord Burghley to secure the restoration of most of the deprived ministers. From 1585 the fierce religious bickerings of Elizabethan Suffolk seem to have subsided. For this there were probably many reasons: but one was the role of Court and Council in keeping the quarrel within bounds. Not that Court and Council were harmoniously united: far from it. But, as Dr MacCulloch comments, 'there was more than one road to Westminster', and, since neither faction in the diocese could expect complete success, compromise was achieved and moderation prevailed.[20] Writing of the reign of Charles I and the dominance of

Buckingham, Professor Hirst has shown how much damage could be inflicted upon the political system if all but one road to Westminster were closed.[21] The monopolizing of influence at Court by one great favourite or by a single faction bred grievance and forced the dissatisfied to look elsewhere – probably to Parliament – for help. Such road closures do not seem to have happened under Elizabeth, not even in the days of Cecilian hegemony.

The role of the Court in providing the landowning families with access to the monarch was admirably described, after Elizabeth's death, by John Holles, Earl of Clare:

> For it was the constant custom of the Queen to call out of the counties of the Kingdom the gentlemen of greatest hopes and of the best fortunes and families, and with those to fill the most honourable rooms [= offices] of her household servants; by which she honoured them, obliged their kindred and allegiance, and fortified herself.[22]

Clare presents this harmonious account of Elizabeth's Court in the course of criticizing her successor. Nevertheless it stands as an ideal picture of what the Court should do, and of what one man at least thought that it had done. But how closely did reality approach Clare's retrospective ideal? Was Elizabeth's Court the assembly room for the major families of the land? Was access to it reasonably open to members of good families? These questions are much more easily asked than answered. Appointment to Court office was informally made and not recorded in the patent rolls; lists of their holders are few; and membership of the Court has to be pieced together from scraps of information provided by miscellaneous sources. There is, however, one list, of about 1598, which records 54 'principal gentlemen of value and service that have been and are usually in Court'.[23] It is preceded by a list of 23 noblemen who have served in war or held office, and succeeded by a third and longer list of 272 'principal gentlemen that dwell usually in their counties'. Lancashire and the Welsh counties are excluded from this third list, and if we make allowance for them we can suggest that there were perhaps 300 men in the category of 'principal gentlemen'. Set against this figure, the number of 54 'that have been and are usually in Court' is quite high. There are, however, difficulties in comparing the two lists and in analysing the roll of courtiers. The distinction between the two categories is not absolute, for several men are named both as being 'usually in Court' and as 'gentlemen that dwell usually in their counties'. Second, the list of courtiers is selective – and we are given no hint about the criteria for selection. It omits several men known to have held office in the Court at that date: Edward Darcy and Sir Edward Denny, both Grooms of the Privy Chamber; Dru Drury, Gentleman Usher; and Philip Gawdy, esquire of the body, to name only a few.

Nevertheless some tentative conclusions can be drawn from examining the 50 knights and four esquires named. First, the great majority come from the coastal shires between Norfolk and Cornwall, from London and the Home Counties, and from the East Midlands. Not surprisingly, the distant areas of the north, Wales, and the Welsh Marches were poorly represented; so, less predictably, were the West Midlands. Many, however, come from the south-western counties: the Gorges family from Devon; Sir John Gilbert; Sir Henry Killigrew; Sir George Carew; and, naturally, Sir Walter Raleigh. They balance the south-eastern bias of the majority. Second, the friends of Essex are well represented: Sir Robert Dudley; Sir William Knollys; Sir Oliver Lambert; Sir Robert Sidney; Sir Francis Vere; Sir Conyers Clifford; and, above all, Sir Charles Danvers, who was executed for his prominent part in the Essex rising. Third, many of the courtiers had seen military action in recent campaigns and several were soldiers or sailors above all else. Sir Ferdinand Gorges, for instance, served under Essex in Normandy and then became lieutenant-governor of Brill. Sir Mathew Morgan also fought with Essex in Normandy, being knighted at Rouen, followed him on the Cadiz expedition, and held the rank of colonel in Ireland. Some of them indeed can hardly have been in England long enough to spend a great deal of time at Court. Sir Robert Sidney was Governor of Flushing from 1589 until 1616; for most of that time he conducted his courtly manoeuvres through friends and agents, in particular through Rowland Whyte, who kept him – and us – fully informed about the intrigues of the politicians. But the military men – Bingham, Blount, Chichester, Clifford, Crosse, Danvers, Dockwray, Dudley, Ferdinand Gorges, Harvey, Lambert, Morgan, Henry Norris, Raleigh, Sidney, Uvedall, Vavasor, Vere, to name a selection of them – were obviously important courtiers when they were present. Finally, although there are some prominent stars of the political firmament on this list, many of the old county families are missing. Indeed, this was bound to be so with only 54 names drawn from 40 English and 13 Welsh counties, allowing an average of only one per shire.

Yet how many of these 54 courtiers had effective access to the Queen? And who were they? In an earlier reign one could have answered the second question by pointing to the privy councillors, the most notable favourites, and the gentlemen of the Privy Chamber. But, as one might expect, membership of the Privy Chamber was not the ladder to success which it had been under Henry VIII. Certainly the position was worth having. In 1601 John Chamberlain reported that at Court there 'is much jostling and suing for places in the Privy Chamber'.[24] Most of the gentlemen of the Chamber had grown old and were weary of attendance there; but they were anxious to be succeeded by sons or relatives: Sir William Killigrew by his son; Sir Edward Carey by his son; and Sir Thomas Gorges by his cousin Ned. This suggests that the position did not lead on, as it had under Henry VIII, to major political influence, though at least one member of the Privy Chamber, Christopher Hatton, had attracted the Queen's interest sufficiently to rise very high indeed. But the Privy Chamber was a useful place to which to belong. Apart from gratuities and the prospect of minor offices, to which I shall return shortly, it certainly carried the favour of the Queen. Sir John Stanhope relates a bizarre incident in 1601, when Sir Thomas Gorges of the Privy Chamber was rebuffed by a widow named Dent. The Queen was furious, and told the widow that she need expect no favours from her hands and that she, the Queen, would take any advantage of her that was possible. Exemplary punishment was to be meted out to those of the widow's household who had insulted Gorges, so that they should know how to respect members of the royal chamber.[25]

However, the essence of power and influence at Court was not merely presence there but regular access to the Queen. The Earl of Essex made a critical distinction, writing to Francis Bacon about the latter's disgrace after an incautious parliamentary speech in 1593. Initially Bacon was forbidden the Court entirely; then he was to be allowed 'access' but not, said Essex, 'near access', which was allowed only to those that the Queen 'favours extraordinarily'.[26] At the time of the Lopez conspiracy in 1594 the Queen is said to have allowed only four persons near her, other than 'ladies in near attendance' and councillors. In February of the following year the Court was alleged to be so void of noblemen and councillors that only seven or eight persons of note were there.[27] Bishop Goodman, writing much later, in the reign of James I, commented that Elizabeth was 'ever hard of access and grew to be very covetous in her old days'; towards the end of her life, he alleges, 'the Court was very much neglected, and in effect the people were very generally weary of an old woman's government'.[28] It is hard to know how much to make of all this. But the more one examines lists of courtiers and hints about access, the stronger grows the suspicion that effective access to the monarch was becoming, in the final decade, restricted to a small clique, or perhaps one should say cliques. The inner group was dominated by a few individuals and families: the Cecils; Essex until 1599; the Howards; Raleigh; the Careys; the Sackvilles; the Knollys; and the Stanhopes. But I do not believe that the Cecilians had a monopoly of power. Apart from Essex and his friends, who still had place and favour until his senseless return from Ireland, Buckhurst, Raleigh and Nottingham (previously Lord Howard of Effingham) provided independent strongholds of influence. Only *after* the accession of James was Robert Cecil able to exclude his rivals, destroying Raleigh and Cobham, depriving Fulke Greville of office. Many problems remain about the composition of the Court and about the ease of access to Elizabeth; the suggestions I have made are tentative. But I think we can say that there was some narrowing of access towards the end of the reign, although several independent paths remained open until 1603.

Whether access was easy or difficult, once achieved it certainly provided men of very different status with excellent routes to preferment. Some Court officials secured monopolies. Simon Bowyer, Gentleman Usher in the

Chamber, was licensed to investigate and prosecute offences against statutes regulating the wool trade. Edward Darcy, Groom of the Privy Chamber, held a patent for sealing leather and later a monopoly of the manufacture and import of playing cards. Richard Mompesson, esquire of the royal stables, received a licence to import aniseed and sumach. Other men rose to much greater heights than these. Apart from the earls of Leicester and Essex, sons of noble houses, Christopher Hatton and Walter Raleigh started from relatively modest beginnings to achieve notable success. Hatton, the second son of a Northamptonshire landowner, rose through the ranks of gentleman pensioner, gentleman of the Privy Chamber, Captain of the guard, and Vice-Chamberlain, before being appointed privy councillor and, eventually, Lord Chancellor. Raleigh, too, was a younger son, of an old but unpretentious Devonshire family. He never travelled as far as Hatton, whom he succeeded as Captain of the Guard; but he received generous grants from the Queen of custom-farms, monopolies, and lands, including 40 000 acres in Ireland. The failure and catastrophe of his last years should not make us forget the glittering prizes which he won under Elizabeth. Certain families established themselves as influential groups of kinsmen at Court: the Careys, Gorges's, Greys, and Stanhopes were particularly successful. One striking connection was forged between Sir Thomas Parry and Sir John Fortescue. Parry had joined Elizabeth's household as her cofferer when she was a princess. On her accession he was first made Controller and then Treasurer of the Household, entering the Privy Council and becoming Master of the Court of Wards. His unexpected death abruptly halted this swift ascent. But he had married the mother of John Fortescue, who almost certainly owed to his stepfather his entry to the princess's household in about 1555 and his promotion to be Keeper of the Wardrobe in 1559. From that base Fortescue moved steadily upwards, collecting offices and estates as he went, entering the Privy Council as Chancellor of the Exchequer in 1589. The networks of family connection at the royal Court were certainly extensive and may well have obstructed access for those outside the privileged kinships.

Court office and preferment provided a platform from which a man could build a strong position of influence within a locality. Sir Thomas Heneage and Sir Francis Knollys were outstanding examples. Heneage's father was a Lincolnshire gentleman with a post in the Duchy of Lancaster; his uncle had been a gentleman of the Privy Chamber under Henry VIII. This gave him an entrée to the Court, where he seems to have become established as a gentleman of the Privy Chamber early in the reign of Elizabeth. He became Treasurer of the Chamber in 1570, Vice-Chamberlain and privy councillor in 1587. Gradually he built up estates and influence in Essex, where he had probably had no possessions before Elizabeth's accession. The Queen granted him Copt Hall in 1564, following this with grants of other manors and of local offices in the 1570s. By 1584 he was established firmly enough to be elected senior Knight of the Shire, holding that position in the next three Parliaments.[29] Knollys had begun to establish his position at Court under Henry VIII and became Master of the Horse to Edward VI. From those two monarchs he received considerable grants of land in Oxfordshire, so that he was able to sit as Knight of the Shire in 1563 and in every subsequent Parliament until his death. Elizabeth made him her Vice-Chamberlain and a privy councillor, rewarding him over the years with grants of land in several counties, mostly in Oxfordshire, Buckinghamshire, and Berkshire.[30] While Heneage seems to have made his way largely by personal charm, Knollys had the advantage of being married to a cousin of the Queen, Catherine Carey, Anne Boleyn's niece. Heneage and Knollys provide examples of the reverse of the 'Clare effect', courtiers using their position to establish themselves in a county, rather than county gentlemen being rewarded with Court office. While this may on occasion have caused resentment – as it did when Robert Dudley tried to secure the submission of gentry in Snowdonia – it mostly seems to have provided the Crown with useful means of influencing and controlling the shires: in north Wales, once the initial hostility – anyway limited – had subsided, the Earl of Leicester was able to attract a considerable following.

Of course, some apparently distinguished courtiers were disappointed in their hopes of advancement and probably few got as much as they thought they deserved. Sir Philip Sidney, paragon of courtly virtues, admired for his qualities over most of Europe, obtained relatively little from the royal bounty. Certainly his rewards were small in relation to his great repute. But he was probably exceptional; and he anyway created his own difficulties by openly opposing Elizabeth's marriage with Anjou. Some great noblemen spent their fortunes at Court without much recompense and had to retire to the country in order to recover their fortunes. But probably most of the officers of the Court – as distinct from aristocratic hangers-on – were adequately rewarded. However, it is sometimes suggested that towards the end of the reign the springs of Court patronage were drying up, as the Crown's finances came under the pressures of war. It may be that outright grants of land, pensions, and annuities were fewer in the 1590s than they had been before; but I have seen no evidence to support this view. It is possible, and indeed more likely, that the number of competitors for royal patronage was growing, or that under the stress of lavish expenditure at Court their needs and demands were greater. But there were still plenty of lucrative opportunities open to members of the Court. A list of wardships allocated in 1594–8 shows that ladies and officers of the Court – in some cases quite lowly ones like Stone, the Queen's footman, and Mattingley, the Queen's joiner – were receiving useful grants.[31] Monopolies and licences proliferated during this decade and many of them went, in the first instance, to courtiers. The grant of leases of Crown land in reversion was another means of rewarding men at no direct cost to the monarch. Such reversionary leases were made personally by the Queen rather than through the normal bureaucratic processes of the commissioners appointed for letting out Crown lands. The great advantage of such reversions was that they exempted the beneficiaries from paying entry fines but enabled them to levy such fines on the existing tenants.[32]

The wars and revolts of the last 18 years of Elizabeth's reign undoubtedly strained the government's resources. But they also opened avenues for military employment and command – avenues which seemed highly attractive to many courtiers. I have already remarked on the large number of military officers in the list of 1598. In January of the following year Chamberlain reported that the Queen had forbidden several of her servants from going to Ireland with Essex: he names 11 of them, but writes that there were several more.[33] If an Irish campaign seemed attractive, how much more so would the wars in France and in the Netherlands? War on land and at sea promised opportunities for honour, command, glory, and material rewards. The commanders were certainly appointed and some achieved glory, even if it was sometimes tarnished. But did soldiers get the profitable offices, the wardships, the lands, the ransoms, and the booty for which they had hoped? Many of them complained that they did not and that the hopes engendered by war were unfulfilled. Such complaints are not reliable evidence, but I get the impression that those who stayed at home did better than those who fought. However, such an impression needs testing and I advance it as no more than a possibility.

Discussion of rewards prompts a further question. Were the grants of wardships, monopolies, reversionary leases, and so on the preserve of courtiers rather than gentlemen who served in their counties? Again, the evidence needs much more examination before one can give a firm answer. But many wardships do seem to have gone to the officers and ladies of the Court; and the same seems to be true of reversionary leases. Of 13 monopolists named in the Commons committee on the subject in 1601, seven can quickly and certainly be identified with the Court.[34]

The roles of the Court as a theatre of display and a link between the Crown and the shires were therefore threatened by the competition for patronage, the factious divisions between politicians and the disreputable means used to reward courtiers. In 1589 Mathew Hutton, then Bishop of Durham, wrote to Whitgift that 'there are some men in this north and rude county in opinion that if the Court were reformed all England might easily be reformed'.[35] It would be crudely oversimple to treat Elizabethan politics in terms of Court versus Country. However imperfectly the Court might function, the country magnates and gentry still needed it to further their own causes and to buttress their local influence. But the Court certainly aroused in men, especially in courtiers themselves, strong feelings of attraction and repulsion. Lawrence Stone perceptively remarked, in a different context, that 'the conflict between loyalty to the particularist locality and loyalty to the nation was fought out within the mind of each individual gentleman'.[36] One could well say the same about attitudes to the Court.

Those who hated it and condemned its corruption were often the men who accepted its values and pursued the rewards it had to offer. Attraction and repulsion, love and hatred, were near neighbours in the minds of men.

Edmund Spenser's *Faerie Queene* was designed in part 'to fashion a gentleman or noble person in virtuous and gentle discipline', in part to glorify Elizabeth, for, he wrote, 'In that Faery Queene I mean glory in my general intention, but in my particular I conceive the most excellent and glorious person of our sovereign the Queen ...'.[37] But for Spenser the Court was not always a place of happy resort and he bitterly condemned its ways and its ethos in *Colin Clouts Come Home Again*:

> Forsooth to say it is no sort of life,
> For shepherd fit to lead in that same place,
> When each one seeks with malice and with strife,
> To thrust down other into foul disgrace,
> Himself to raise; and he doth soonest rise
> That best can handle his deceitful wit,
> In subtil shifts, and finest sleights devise,
> Either by sland'ring his well-deemed name,
> Through leasings lewd, and feigned forgery,
> Or else by breeding him some blot of blame,
> By creeping close into his secrecy . . .[38]

The view of Courts as centres of deceit and deception had already been expressed by George Puttenham in his *Arte of English Poesie* (1589) when he described the 'profession of a very courtier' as being 'cunningly to be able to dissemble'.[39] Admittedly Puttenham exempted the English Court from such strictures and insisted that only in his art need the courtly poet dissemble in England. But the exemption is not entirely convincing: for many, deceit, deception, and insincerity had long been and still were the marks of the courtier. The plays of Webster, Ford, and others depict courtly life as a Hobbesian state of nature, a war of all against all. These dramas of ruthless and dark intrigue were, it is true, set abroad, and the most savage of them were written after the accession of James. But Elizabethan history plays hardly present royal Courts as abodes of sweetness and harmony. Elizabeth herself saw the parallel when she commented bitterly to Lambarde, a few months after the Essex revolt: 'I am Richard II. Know ye not that?'[40]

John Donne, who had a successful career at Court under James I, wrote vituperatively of courtiers in his *Satires*, composed in the 1590s. No man, he said, is

> As prone to all ill, and of good as forgetfull,
> As proud, as lustful, and as much in debt,
> As vain, as witless, and as false as they
> Which dwell at Court ...[41]

Why, asks Professor Carey, should Donne, who viewed the Court with such abhorrence, have spent the greater part of his life seeking preferment there?[42] Answering his own question, he observes that it is naïve to ask it: Donne's hatred grew from thwarted ambition. And the same could be said of Spenser. But the vices of the Court were none the less real, and their condemnation by courtiers as well as preachers was no mere pretence, even if vice was more plainly seen by men disappointed in their expectations.

The ambivalence of attitudes to Court and city life is effectively illuminated in *As You Like It*:

> *Enter Duke Senior, Amiens, and two or three Lords dressed like foresters:*
> DUKE. Now my co-mates and brothers in exile,
>   Hath not old custom made this life more sweet
>   Than that of painted pomp? Are not these woods
>   More free from peril than the envious court?
>   Here feel we not the penalty of Adam,
>   The seasons' difference, as the icy fang
>   And churlish chiding of the winter's wind,
>   Which when it bites and blows upon my body
>   Even till I shrink with cold, I smile and say
>   'This is no flattery; these are counsellors
>   That feelingly persuade me what I am'?
>   Sweet are the uses of adversity,
>   Which, like the toad, ugly and venomous,
>   Wears yet a precious jewel in his head;
>   And this our life, exempt from public haunt,
>   Finds tongues in trees, books in the running brooks,
>   Sermons in stones, and good in everything.
>
> AMIENS. I would not change it. Happy is your grace
>   That can translate the stubbornness of fortune
>   Into so quiet and so sweet a style.[43]

Yet, at the end of the play, after all these fine sentiments have been uttered about life in the forest, when the usurping Duke Frederick is rather unconvincingly converted 'Both from his enterprise and from the world. / His crown bequeathing to his banished brother', Duke Senior and his courtiers all, except for the solitary Jacques, troop back to the recently despised life of city and Court.

The use of literary evidence is nowadays looked on suspiciously by historians; and often with good reason.[44] But the writers whom I have quoted had close contacts with the Court. Indeed, the Elizabethan Court was the epicentre of literature and of literary patronage; and dramatists depended utterly upon the protection of noble courtiers. Poets and dramatist provide poor evidence for the average age of marriage; but who can better reveal to us attitudes towards the Court of those who lived within it? And the attitude emerges as one of distaste overcome by ambition and attraction.

However, if the critics of Elizabeth's Court often depict it as the home of deceit and corruption, their hostile comments are rapidly brought into perspective when one contemplates the Court of King James I. A few years after his accession, in 1606, James held a masque to celebrate the visit of his brother-in-law, the King of Denmark. Sir John Harington left a delightfully malicious account of this disastrous performance:

> Now did appear, in rich dress, Hope, Faith and Charity. Hope did essay to speak, but wine rendered her endeavours so feeble that she withdrew. Faith left the Court in a staggering condition, Charity came to the King's feet and in some sort she made obeisance. She then returned to Hope and Faith, who were both sick and spewing in the lower hall. Next came Victory in bright armour and by a strange medlay of versification did endeavour to make suit to the King. After much lamentable utterance she was led away, and laid to sleep in the outer steps of the antechamber.[45]

Gervase Holles and his kinsman, the Earl of Clare (whose commendation of Elizabeth I quoted earlier), were scathing about James's hangers-on. He entered the realm with acclamation, Holles recalled,

> yet he brought along with him a crew of necessitous and hungry Scots, and filled every corner of the Court with these beggarly blue-caps. This was that which first darkened the glory of the English Court, which Queen Elizabeth had ever maintained in so great a lustre.

After a time the best household offices came to be possessed by these 'trotting companions' and 'the better sort of the gentry declined the Court as scorning their fellowship'.[46]

Bishop Geoffrey Goodman, who wrote largely to *defend* James against the scabrous attacks of Antony Weldon, and whose criticism of Elizabeth I have already noticed, describes too the revival of the Queen's reputation:

> But after a few years, when we had experience of the Scottish government, then in disparagement of the Scots, and in hate and detestation of them, the Queen did seem to revive; then was her memory much magnified – such ringing of bells, such public joy, and sermons in commemoration of her, the picture of her tomb painted in many churches, and in effect more solemnity and joy in memory of her coronation than was for the coming in of King James.[47]

Fulke Greville had no pressing reason for gratitude to Elizabeth: she had appointed him Treasurer of the Navy but had neglected his beloved friend,

Philip Sidney. Yet, in his *Life of Sidney*, written about 1610, he praised Elizabeth for the restraint with which she exercised power:

> she did not affect, nor yet would be drawn (like many of her ancient neighbours the French Kings) to have her subjects give away their wealth after a new fashion, viz without return of pardons, ease of grievances or comfort of laws ...

She even, according to Greville, foresaw

> what face her estate was like to carry, if these biassed humours should continue any long reign over us, viz contempt to be cast over the Majesty of the Crown, fear among the people ... the Court itself becoming a farm, manured by drawing up, not the sweat, but even the brows of humble subjects ...

Greville's testimony to Elizabeth was certainly heightened by his dismissal from office under James; he might well not have been so effusive in her lifetime. But weighing one monarch with another he had no doubt where his favour lay.[48]

I have no dramatic new conclusions with which to round off this lecture. Various opinions have been expressed about the Elizabethan Court: Professor Stone considers it to have impoverished and discontented the nobility. Professor Elton believes that it supplied a stabilizing element in politics.[49] My purpose is not to adjudicate between them, for truth lies in both views. I have tried rather to show how the Court operated within the political system, performing roles that were complex, multiple, and conflicting. The contrasting pictures of the Court painted by contemporaries confirm the tensions between its functions. They also suggest that reality lay in a country between the kingdom of Spenser's *Faerie Queene* and the Italian palaces of Webster. But even these extremes tell us something of its potential for good and ill: it is easy to understand how the Court could appear sometimes golden and desirable, sometimes hostile and frustrating. In a personal monarchy government would fall apart unless the Court performed all its contradictory roles, each of them necessary, but immensely difficult to keep in balance. Henry VIII inflicted destruction by his gullible fears and vengeful suspicions, forcing the competition between factions into a matter of life and death. James VI, by closing all roads but one from the shires to the centre, allowed Court rivalries to spill over into Parliament. Elizabeth was never able to ensure perfect harmony: no monarch could. During her early years her flirtations with Dudley threatened and alarmed his rivals: in the final decade factions *seemed* to be getting out of control. But for most of her reign the contradictions within the system were sufficiently resolved for men later to look back upon her reign as a golden age. However, such conclusions are impressionistic and general: both the problems and their solutions need to be brought into a sharper focus. I shall have achieved my purpose if I have indicated some of the ways in which this can be done: by a functional analysis of the role of the Court; by examining its membership and the extent of access to the Queen; and by investigating the distribution of patronage to the various groups in society, within the Court and outside it.

Appendix: the political élite, c.1598

Among the State Papers Domestic, Elizabeth, in the Public Record Office is a list, accompanied by an earlier draft, of noblemen who have served the Queen in war or office, of gentlemen attendant at Court, and of gentlemen normally resident in their counties.[50] The third part also includes the names of the principal civil and common lawyers. Lancashire and the Welsh shires are omitted; so are the names of privy councillors. With those exceptions the document presents the names of the most important men in central and local politics – at least in the view of the unknown compiler. It can be dated to the latter part of 1598, following the death of the first Lord Burghley, whose son is included in the list of barons. The list has been used, as far as I know, only by one other historian, Professor Lawrence Stone.[51] His conclusion, that 60 per cent of the peers and only 20 per cent of the gentlemen attended Court, is not justified from this evidence, since inclusion in the list of peers is not, as the heading makes clear, an indication of such attendance.

I have printed the document, in the original spelling, as it stands in the later version (269/46), adding names which appear only in the first draft and marking them with an asterisk. I have also added Roman numeral headings in brackets to distinguish the three separate lists. At the end, in order to complete the tally of the political élite, I have given the membership of the Privy Council, as it stood in the later months of 1598, after the death of Lord Burghley.

STATE PAPERS DOMESTIC, ELIZABETH, 269/46

[I] NOBLEMEN THAT HAVE SERVED IN HER MAJESTIES WARRS OR BORNE PUBLICK PLACES, NOT BEING NOW OF THE COUNSELL.

Earles

Northumberland	Sussex
Shrewsbury	Southampton
Worcester	Lincolne
Cumberland	Hertford*
Rutland	

Barons

Thomas Howarde	Zouche
Henry Seymor	Willoughby of Ersby
Audley	Cobham

Grey
Scroope
Mountjoye
Sandes
Cromwell
Eure

Sheffield
Burghley
Norreys
Darcy of Chichester*
Chandos*
St John of Bletso*

[II] PRINCIPALL GENTLEMEN OF VALUE AND SERVICE THAT HAVE BEN AND ARE USUALLY IN COURT.

Knights
Henry Lea
William Russell
Walter Raleigh
John Stanhope
Thomas Leighton
Edward Stafford
Edward Dyer
Edward Wootton
Robert Sydney
Thomas Gorges
George Carew
Francis Vere
Henry Killigrew
Anthony Mildmay
Richard Bingham
Thomas Knollis
Charles Blunt
Ferdinand Gorges
Robert Dudley
Henry Norreis
Coniers Clifford
Nicholas Parker
Henry Dockwray
Oliver Lambert
Henry Palmer
Thomas Vavasor
William Harvy
Robert Crosse
Matthew Morgan

Edward Yorke
Samuel Baghenell
Henry Power
Robert Mansfield
Thomas Garrett
Amyas Preston
Richard Leveson
Arthur Gorges
Edmund Uvedall
Arthur Savage
John Barkeley
Arthur Chichester
John Gilbert
Callisthenes Brooke
John Brooke
Charles Danvers
Henry Davers
Alexander Ratcliff
Robert Drewry
William Woodhouse
Richard Warburton
William Knollis*
John Fortescue*

Esquires
Fulk Grevill
John Herbert
Thomas Bodley
Robert Beale
Cap. Price*

[III] PRINCIPALL GENTLEMEN THAT DWELL USUALLY IN THEIR CONTREIS.

Bedfordshire
Sir Edward Ratcliff
Sir Richard Dyer

Buckingh.
Sir Henry Lea
Sir Robert Dormer

Myles Sandes
Henry Butler
John Dive
* Nicholas Luke

Berkshire
Sir Francis Knollis
Sir Thomas Parry
Sir Humfry Forster
Henry Nevill
Samuel Backhouse

Cambridge et Ely
Sir John Cutts
Sir Horatio Palavicino
Sir John Cotton
Sir John Peyton
Thomas Wendy
Antony Cage

Cornwall
Sir Francls Godolphin
Sir William Bevill
Sir Jonathan Trelawny
Christopher Harris
Bernard Grenvile
Reginald Mohun
Richard Carew of Anthony

Cumberland
Nicholas Curwin
Richard Lowther
Francis Lampleigh
Lancelot Salkeld
Henry Leigh

Cheshire
Sir Raphe Brereton
Sir Edward Fytton
Sir William Brereton
Sir Hugh Cholmley
John Savage
John Holcroft

Francis Fortescew
Francis Goodwin
Thomas Tasborough
Alexander Hampden

Devonshire
Sir William Courteney
Sir Thomas Dennys
Sir George Carew of Cocking
Sir John Gilbert
Sir Ferdinand Gorges
Sir William Strowde
Christopher Harris

Dorset
Sir Walter Raleigh
Sir Matthew Arundell
Sir George Trenchard
Sir Raphe Horsey

George Mooreton

Essex
Sir Henry Gray
Sir Thomas Lucas
Sir Thomas Mildmay
Sir John Peeter
Sir Edward Denny
Jerome Weston
Francis Harvy

Eborac' Estr'
Sir William Mallory
Sir Christopher Hilliard
Sir William Bowes
Sir Thomas Fairfax

Westrhyd
Edward Talbot
Francis Clifford
Sir John Savile

Northrhyd
Sir John Carey

Derbyshire
John Manners
Sir Humfrey Ferrers
William Cavendish
William Bassett
Thomas Grisely
William Kniveton
Sir John Hungerford
Sir Edward Winter

Huntingdon
Sir Henry Cromwell
Sir Jarvais Clifton
Sir Edward Wingfield
Oliver Cromwell

Hertford
Sir Ed. Carey
Sir Henry Cock
Sir Philip Butler
Sir Arthur Capell
Sir Tho. Sadler
Rowland Litton
Raphe Coningsby
Rich. Spencer*

Hereford
Sir Jo. Scudamoure
Sir Tho. Coningsby
Sir William Herbert
Roger Bodenham
Herbert Crofts
Thomas Harley

Kent
Sir Rob. Sydney
Sir Edward Wootton
Sir Edward Hobby
Sir Moyle Finche
Sir Thos. Wilford
Sir John Scott
Sir John Leveson
Sir Tho. Walsingham
Sir Tho. Fame

Sir William Belasis

Gloucester
Sir Richard Barclay
Sir Henry Poole
Sir Tho. Throgmorton
Sir John Tracy
William Pelham
Thomas Grantham
Robert Carr*

Leicester
Sir Edward Hastingues
Henry Beaumond
Thomas Cave
Thomas Skevington
William Skipwith

Middlesex
Sir Drew Drury
Sir John Peyton
Sir Rob. Wroth
Sir Arthur Throgmorton
Thomas Knivett
William Fleetwood

Northampton
Sir William Russell
Sir Richard Knightly
Sir Edw. Montague
Sir John Spencer
Sir Geo. Farmer
Valentine Knightley
Sir Anthony Mildmay*

Nottingham
Sir John Biron
William Cecyll
Sir Charles Cavendishe
Sir John Holles
John Stanhope
Henry Peirpoint
William Sutton

Lancaster
[no names]

Lincoln
Sir Edward Dymmock
Sir George St Pole
Sir William Wray
Sir Thomas Munson

Northumb'
Sir William Reade
Thomas Caverly
William Selby
Raphe Grey
Robert Woodrington

Oxon
Sir Michel Blunt
Sir Richard Fines
Sir William Spencer
Sir Anth. Cope
Raphe Warcoppe
John Doyley

Rutland
Sir Jo. Harrington
Sir Andrew Noell
— Dighby

Surrey
Sir William Howarde
Sir William Moore
Sir Francis Carew
Sir George Moore
Richard Drake
Oliver St Johns

Stafford
Sir George Devoreux
Sir John Bowes
Sir Edw. Littleton
Sir Christopher Blunt
Francis Trensham
Walter Bagott

Norfolk
Sir Arthur Henningham
Sir William Paston
Sir Thomas Knivett
Sir Christopher Heydon
Sir John Towensende
Nath. Bacon
Henry Gawdy
Sir John Seymor
Rich. Kingesmill
Edward Moorel
Richard Norton

Suffolk
Sir Philip Parker
Sir Robert Jermin
Sir W. Springe
Sir Nicholas Bacon
Sir John Heigham
Sir W. Walgrave
Sir Anth. Wingfield

Somerset
Sir Francis Hastingues
Sir Henry Barclay
Sir Anthony Pawlett
Sir Hugh Portman
John Thinne
Mr Coles
Sir John Stowell [*inserted in margin*]

Sussex
Robert Sackvile
Sir Walter Couert
Sir Nicholas Parker
Sir John Carrell
Thomas Pelham
Thomas Bushop

Westmerl'
John Bradley
Richard Hutton

Salop
Sir Rich. Leveson
Sir Henry Bromeley
Sir Edward Kynnaston
Sir Robert Nedeham
Francis Newport

South'ton
Sir Thomas West
Sir Walter Sandes
Francis Clare
Jerome Corbet
Edmund Coles

Warwick
Sir Fulke Grevill
Sir John Conway
Sir Edw. Grevill
Sir William Leigh
Richard Verney

Civil Lawyers
D. Binge
D. Dunne
D. Caesar
D. Parkins
D. Rogers

Judges
L. Cheef Justice[52]
L. Anderson
L. Cheef Baron[53]

Wiltshire
Sir James Mervin
Sir William Eyer
Sir Walter Longe
Sir Francis Popham
Carew Raleigh
Edward Penruddock

Worcester
Sir John Packington
Justice Gawdy
Justice Shuttleworth
Justice Owen

Common Lawyers
Serjeant Yelverton
Serjeant Hele
Atturney Generall Coke
Mr Solliciter Fleming
Atturney of the Duchy,
  Brograve
Atturney of Wards,
  Hesketh
Mr Philips
Mr Tanfield
Mr Foster
Mr Houghton
Mr Coventree
Mr Moore
Mr Wilbraham

THE PRIVY COUNCIL IN THE LATTER PART OF 1598

John Whitgift, Archbishop of Canterbury
Earl of Essex, Master of Horse; Earl Marshal
Earl of Nottingham, Lord Admiral
George, Second Lord Hunsdon, Lord Chamberlain
Lord Buckhurst
Roger, Lord North, Treasurer of the Household
Sir John Fortescue, Chancellor of the Exchequer

Sir Robert Cecil, Secretary of State
Sir Thomas Egerton, Lord Keeper of the Great Seal
Sir William Knollys, Controller of the Household

Notes

1 J. E. Neale, 'The Elizabethan Political Scene', *Proceedings of the British Academy*, 29 (1948); separately printed 1948; repr. in Neale, *Essays in Elizabethan History* (London, 1958).
2 W. T. MacCaffrey, 'Place and Patronage in Elizabethan Politics', in S. T. Bindoff, J. Hurstfield, and C. H. Williams (eds), *Elizabethan Government and Society: Essays Presented to Sir John Neale* (London, 1961), pp. 95–126. G. R. Elton, 'Tudor Government: The Points of Contact. III. The Court', *Transactions of the Royal Historical Society*, 5th ser., 26 (1976), pp. 211–28. Since this lecture was delivered much has been published. See, in particular, D. M. Loades, *The Tudor Court* (London, 1986), David Starkey, *The English Court from the Wars of the Roses to the Civil War* (London, 1987), Simon Adams, 'Eliza Enthroned? The Court and its Politics', in C. Haigh (ed.), *The Reign of Elizabeth I* (London, 1984), pp. 55–78; John Guy (ed.), *The Reign of Elizabeth I. Court and Culture in the Last Decade*, (Cambridge, 1995), chs 1–4.
3 Christopher Marlowe, *Edward the Second*, Act II, Sc. ii, lines 175–7. Except in one instance (p. 359) I have modernized the spelling of quotations.
4 Thomas Birch, *Memoirs of the Reign of Queen Elizabeth* (2 vols, London, 1754), II, p. 432.
5 Elton, 'Tudor Government', p. 225.
6 Quoted in Jean Wilson, *Entertainments for Elizabeth I* (Woodbridge, 1980), p. 11.
7 *The Memoirs of Sir Robert Cary, Earl of Monmouth*, ed. H. G. Powell (London, 1905), pp. 32–3.
8 Blanche Parry's tomb itself is in Westminster Abbey.
9 So bizarre is the spelling of the verses on this monument that I have preserved the original.
10 Elton, 'Tudor Government', pp. 218–21. Cf. J. Harington, *Nugae Antiquae* (2 vols, London, 1804), I, p.169.
11 HMC, *De L'Isle and Dudley Manuscripts*, II (1934), pp. 245–6.
12 *Calendar of State Papers Domestic, 1591–1594*, pp. 432–3.
13 Cf. Elton, 'Tudor Government', pp. 215–16.
14 Adams, 'Eliza Enthroned?'
15 Arthur Collins, *Letters and Memorials of State* (2 vols, London, 1746), I, p. 331.
16 HMC, *Salisbury Manuscripts*, VIII (1899), p. 269.
17 Penry Williams, 'The Crown and the Counties', in Haigh (ed.), *The Reign of Elizabeth I*, pp. 125–46.
18 In *Glamorgan County History*, IV, ed. Glanmor Williams (Cardiff, 1974), ch. 3, pp. 183–6; and in P. Williams, *The Council in the Marches of Wales under Elizabeth I* (Cardiff, 1958), pp. 242–6.
19 Ben Jonson, *Penshurst*, lines 89–92.
20 Diarmaid MacCulloch, 'Catholic and Puritan in Elizabethan Suffolk: A Suffolk Community Polarises', *Archiv für Reformationsgeschichte*, 72 (1981), pp. 275–84. I am grateful to Dr MacCulloch for sending me an offprint of this article.
21 Derek Hirst, 'Court, County and Politicians before 1629', in Kevin Sharpe (ed.), *Faction and Parliament* (Oxford, 1978), esp. pp. 111–16.
22 Quoted by Clare's kinsman, Gervase Holles, in his *Memorials of the Holles Family* (Camden Soc., 3rd ser., 45; London, 1937), pp. 94–5.
23 PRO SP 12/269, nos. 46, 47. See Appendix for further details of this document and a full transcript of the names.

24 *The Letters of John Chamberlain*, ed. N. E. McClure (2 vols, Philadelphia, 1939), I, p. 133.
25 HMC, *Salisbury Manuscripts*, VI (1895), pp. 33–4, 37.
26 Birch, *Memoirs*, I, pp. 120–1.
27 Birch, *Memoirs*, I, pp. 151, 155.
28 Godfrey Goodman, *At the Court of King James the First* (2 vols, London, 1839), I, pp. 96–7.
29 See *The House of Commons, 1558–1603*, ed. P. W. Hasler (3 vols, London, 1981), II, pp. 290–3.
30 *The House of Commons, 1558–1603*, ed. Hasker, II, pp. 409–14.
31 J. Hurstfield, *The Queen's Wards* (London, 1958), pp. 125–7.
32 David Thomas, 'Leases in Reversion on Crown Lands, 1558–1603', *Economic History Review*, 30 (1977), pp. 67–72. Simon Adams, 'The Patronage of the Crown in Elizabethan Politics: The 1590s' and Paul E. J. Hammer, 'Patronage at Court, Faction and the Earl of Essex', both in *The Reign of Elizabeth I*, pp. 20–45 and 87–108.
33 *Letters of John Chamberlain*, I, pp. 65–6.
34 Hurstfield, *The Queen's Wards*, pp. 125–7. Thomas, 'Leases in Reversion', pp. 67–72. *Tudor Economic Documents*, ed. R. H. Tawney and Eileen Power (3 vols, London 1924), II, pp. 283–4.
35 Quoted by Peter Lake in 'Mathew Hutton – a Puritan Bishop?', *History*, 64 (1979), p. 203.
36 L. Stone, *The Causes of the English Revolution* (London, 1972), p. 108.
37 Edmund Spenser, *The Faerie Queene*, ed. J. C. Smith (3 vols, Oxford, 1909), II, pp. 485–7: the Letter to Raleigh.
38 Spenser, *Colin Clouts Come Home Again*, II, pp. 688–706. Cf. the better-known passage from Mother Hubbard's Tale, II, pp. 684 ff.
39 G. Puttenham, *Arte of English Poesie*, ed. G. D. Willcock and A. Walker (Cambridge, 1936), p. 299.
40 John Nichols, *The Progresses and Public Processions of Queen Elizabeth* (3 vols, London, 1823), III, p. 552.
41 John Donne, *Satyre* iv.
42 John Carey, *John Donne: Life, Mind and Art* (London, 1981), p. 63.
43 *As You Like It*, Act II, Sc. i.
44 See, for example, Peter Laslett, 'The Wrong Way through the Telescope', *British Journal of Sociology*, 27 (1976), pp. 319–42.
45 Harington, *Nugae Antiquae*, I, p. 348 ff.
46 *Memorials of the Holles Family*, pp. 94–5. See above.
47 Goodman, *At the Court of King James the First*, I, p. 98.
48 Fulke Greville, *The Life of Sir Philip Sidney*, ed. Nowell Smith (Oxford, 1907), pp. 191, 195. On the revival of Elizabeth's reputation, see Anne Barton, 'Harking Back to Elizabeth: Ben Jonson and Caroline Nostalgia', *English Literary History*, 48 (1981), pp. 706–31. I am grateful to Professor Barton both for an offprint of this article and for much enlightening discussion of the topic.
49 L. Stone, *The Crisis of the Aristocracy, 1558–1641* (Oxford, 1965), pp. 476–504. Elton, 'Tudor Government', *passim*, esp. pp. 227–8.
50 PRO. SP 12/269, nos 46, 47. This transcript of Crown-copyright material in the Public Record Office appears by permission of the Controller of HM Stationery Office.
51 Stone, *Crisis of the Aristocracy*, p. 463.

Index